THE PORT OF LEITH

Its History and its People

To
Tom Skinner
who launched the project
and to
John Landels
who guided, supported and encouraged.

The Port of Leith

Its History and its People

SUE MOWAT

FORTH PORTS PLC, LEITH, EDINBURGH
IN ASSOCIATION WITH
JOHN DONALD PUBLISHERS LTD., EDINBURGH

ISBN 0 85976 403 6

The illustrations on the front and back covers are respectively,
A View of the Port of Leith, with Arthur's Seat in the Distance,
and *The Port of Leith with Numerous Figures and Boats*,
both by A. Mitchell, 1880,
reproduced by courtesy of Trinity House, Leith.

A catalogue record for this book is available from the British Library.

Typeset by ROM-Data Corporation Ltd, Falmouth, Cornwall.
Printed in Great Britain by J. W. Arrowsmith Ltd, Bristol

Contents

Acknowledgements

I must begin by acknowledging my indebtedness to the late Professor Gordon Donaldson. Until just a few weeks before his death in the winter of 1993 he was kind enough to read each chapter of the book as it was produced and to take time to discuss it and suggest corrections and improvements. His passion for accuracy was very helpful to one whose knowledge of Scottish history was limited, and his unfailing interest in the progress of the work was a great encouragement. Professor Donaldson's personal interest in Leith and its history was well-known, and I am grateful to have been its beneficiary.

Once the book reached the stage of using original material the Edinburgh City Archive became almost a home from home. The Archivists, Arnot Wilson and Alan Murdoch, and the Search Room staff, Richard Hunter, Margaret Mcbride, Alison Scott, Elaine Anderson and Brenda Connoboy, were unfailingly helpful in finding documents, some of which I had not even asked for! I also appreciated being able to bring my children with me on occasion, during the school holidays.

The other archive chiefly used at this stage was the Scottish Record Office - both Main and West Search Rooms. Both are housed in rather dauntingly impressive buildings, but in both cases the staff could not have been more helpful. Even the cataloguing system lost its terrors after a while, under their patient guidance.

Some documents were found in the Edinburgh Room of the Central Library, where all possible assistance was given.

I am very grateful to Captain Hamilton, Master of Trinity House Leith and Captain Thomson, Assistant Master, who gave me free access to their unique collection of paintings, artifacts and books at the House, while at the same time extending warm hospitality.

At Leith Port Office itself, I was grateful for unlimited access to computer, photocopier and coffee machine. All of this was organised by Maureen Handley the Port Manager's Secretary. She and Margaret Allardice also uncomplainingly fitted in several printouts of the full text in addition to their own workloads. Thanks also to Ian Parker who drew the maps and to Stephen Thomson who took the photographs.

Finally I must thank my family. My mother for looking after the children when necessary. Adrian and Elinor themselves for being so patient and quiet when dragged to the various archives and my husband, Robert, for his support.

Introduction

For some six centuries Leith was Scotland's premier port. When it was founded by David I in the early twelfth century, Berwick upon Tweed dominated Scottish foreign trade, but the loss of the town to the English in the next century opened the way for Leith to become pre-eminent. It is likely though, that even if Berwick had remained in Scottish hands, Leith would have overtaken it simply because it is the port attached to Edinburgh.

Once Scotland gained a reasonably stable monarchy, in the early fifteenth century, Edinburgh's rise to become the Capital City was assured. Its harbour at Leith shared in its rise. So successful was the port that Edinburgh periodically took vigorous measures to ensure that it was not outshone by its satellite. Leith was subject to a series of restrictions on its trade long after the laws on which they were based had become obsolete in the rest of Europe, causing much resentment on the part of its inhabitants towards Edinburgh, an attitude which has not fully disappeared even today.

Histories of the town have been written by men from both sides of the fence, and the feud between the two communities dominates their pages. However, these accounts deal with the town as a whole. In researching this present book, which concentrates on the maritime affairs of the place, it has become evident that the seafaring community had its own methods of circumventing the Edinburgh bye-laws.

The skippers of Leith were a tough and independent breed, not about to be pushed around by a parcel of landlubberly petty dignitaries. Moreover, the local bye-law makers were mainly merchants, who depended on the Leith mariners to carry their trading goods to foreign markets and were often part-owners of their ships. At a very early date the practice arose of allowing the skipper and crew an agreed proportion of their freight charge in the form of goods with which they themselves might freely trade. That proportion was used to the limit and beyond. In the absence of any effective form of policing, 'extra' goods could easily be unloaded under cover of darkness and spirited away into cellars and lofts for surreptitious sale at a later date. The prosperity or otherwise of the average Leith skipper depended far more on the chance of shipwreck or capture by pirates than on the activities of the Edinburgh Council.

By the sixteenth century Leith so dominated the trade of Central Scotland that it became the key to control of the country south of the Forth. Edinburgh might be the main seat of Government, but the money and high-quality armaments which were needed to give that Government teeth in unsettled times were imported through Leith from the Low Countries and England. This strategic importance led to sixteenth-century Leith being twice destroyed, twice fortified, once beseiged and once becoming a centre of Government. During the first half of the seventeenth century, control of the port continued to be a major factor in the political domination of Scotland, and it was twice re-fortified in the face of possible invasion. In the Parliamentary occupation of the mid-century, Leith played a pivotal role in Oliver Cromwell's Scottish strategy.

The eighteenth century saw a rise in trade through the port, but development was always held back by Edinburgh's reluctance to spend money on improving facilities. At last, in the first twenty years of the nineteenth century, two docks were built, but the real expansion of the docks complex only came after control of the operation was finally wrested from Edinburgh in the 1830s. Thereafter the fortunes of Leith fluctuated with the state of trade, but it took two World Wars and the Depression of the 1930s to seriously affect the port.

The main events of Leith's history have been thoroughly chronicled, notably in the two monumental late Victorian volumes of Campbell Irons' *Antiquities of Leith*, and anyone might be forgiven for wondering if there was anything left to say about the port. While researching a pamphlet about the Metters (whose history is traced in this book) it became evident that there was much material available which had not been used by former writers. Until fairly recently, historians were mainly concerned with the Great Men and Important Events of the past. The testaments, deeds, property deals, trading records and other documents of ordinary people did not interest them or, presumably, their readers. The sources they did use, such as charters, court cases, Government records etc, also contain information about these 'ordinary people', but it was not used in their accounts of Leith. Other sources, such as English records, were not as easily available as they are today. There is indeed much more to say about Leith, and the present volume by no means exhausts the subject.

So what does this book set out to do? Its main purpose is to flesh out the earlier histories with more detail about the people of Leith. As far as possible it does not repeat material already used, although the significance of the lives of individuals is largely meaningless without the framework of history; local, national and international. This framework exists in former books about Leith, and they have been used to that extent. However, as far as possible statements made in earlier works have been checked against original documents. For instance, it has been assumed that the first bridge over the Water of Leith was built in 1493, but the bridge is actually mentioned in a charter written over fifty years earlier. Even printed versions of original sources can be misleading. An entry in the published *Extracts From the Council Records of Edinburgh* states that a certain sixteenth century Leither was the skipper of a pirate ship. The original manuscript, however, says that he commanded the ship which captured the pirate - a rather different matter. Again, an eighteenth century history quotes a report on Leith in 1710 as stating that ships of 30 to 40 tons had been repaired there. The original MS, however, reveals that the ships were of 30 to 40 *guns*....

From the late sixteenth century onwards it has been possible to use much unpublished material from personal papers, local court books and the mass of supplementary Edinburgh records which are held in the City Chambers. Earlier primary source material had been published, in the sense that it exists in printed collections, mainly of nineteenth century date, but even here it has been a case of fitting together snippets from diverse sources to form a picture. A complete picture? By no means.

One of the first and most important pieces of advice given to the would-be researcher is to avoid getting sidetracked. How very difficult this is, when so many of the sidetracks could easily become main-line investigations in their own right. There is always the nagging feeling that if they were pursued they might throw more light on the subject, perhaps make the account more accurate or more interesting. However, as there are only 24 hours in any day, the line must be drawn somewhere. One can only hope that it has been drawn in the right place.

Those sidetracks still remain to be explored. There was not time, for instance, to even begin to search old newspapers, which might have shed much light on events of the eighteenth century onwards. The relationship of the Edinburgh merchant community with the port was obviously of great importance, but has remained unexamined for the same reason. Some of the lives of individual seafarers could be further investigated, and the copious Admiralty records of the eighteenth century would yield much information. Other areas may occur to readers as they progress through the book. I hope they will, and that further work will be done. The significance of Leith and its people in the history of Scotland has yet to be fully appreciated.

1

Beginnings

Early morning at Leith, 28 May 1329. The tide is out, and a small ship anchored in the narrow river channel rests on the mud, slightly heeled over. Her cargo of boards from the Baltic lies on the shore and her crew are already on deck, preparing to sail when the tide rises. Out in the Roads, a Flemish ship loaded with fine cloth, wine and spices is waiting for the water to cover the sand bar at the river-mouth so that she can enter the haven.

Smoke is trickling through the thatch of the hamlets of little houses on each side of the river. On both shores fishing cobles are drawn up, and boats which will later row out to take off the cargo of the Flemish ship when she arrives in the Haven. Above the trees which line the river banks can be seen the two peaks of Arthur's Seat and Calton Hill. Edinburgh castle is visible, perched on its crag; and the roofs of one or two of the taller buildings of the Burgh which crowns the eastward-sloping ridge connecting the Castle with the Abbey of Holyrood.

Away to the west, in his castle of Cardross, king Robert the Bruce stirs in his bed. He is dying of leprosy and in less than a fortnight his life will have ended. But a monarch must rule to the last and there is still official business for him to see to. Among the documents which lie ready for him to seal later in the day is a charter granting his harbour, where the Baltic ship now lies, to the burgesses of his Royal Burgh of Edinburgh.

Robert I is generally remembered for the day when the Scottish army stood against the forces of Edward II at Bannockburn. A momentous day indeed for the nation. The painful sealing of a piece of parchment on a May morning was perhaps even more significant for the people of Leith over the next 600 years. It was the first step in the process which brought the town under the domination of Edinburgh.

The Burgh

Much ink has been spilt and much bitterness nursed in many hearts concerning Edinburgh's treatment of Leith, and a fair degree of paranoia developed on both sides. The main bone of contention was the fact that the burgh forbade the people of Leith to trade in the goods which they unloaded into their town, often from their own ships. Looked at from our late twentieth century perspective, it would seem that nothing could be said in Edinburgh's defence. However, in every age people generally work within the system as it exsists - especially if it is to their own advantage. Trade in medieval Europe was very different from what we are used to today. We set up commissions to prevent monopolies.

The Great Seal of Robert the Bruce, 1326.

Medieval trade was founded on them, and the bedrock of the system was the Burgh.

This Anglo-Saxon word originally denoted a defended town, where the local inhabitants might be safe in time of war. From a very early date some of these towns, if they belonged to the Crown or to a powerful nobleman, were granted charters by their overlords, bestowing on them the privilege of holding a weekly market. Buying and selling anywhere other than at the official market was forbidden. The landward (country) people had to bring their produce to the burgh on market day, and pay a toll called petty custom at the gate before they could get in. If they were caught trading outside the burgh they were fined. Royal Burghs belonging to the King, of which Edinburgh was one, also had a monopoly on foreign trade.

The burgh council fixed prices too, usually, it must be said, with the object of keeping them as low as possible. Buying goods outside the market for resale (regrating) was very much frowned upon because regraters often hoarded goods in order to push up prices. The council also appointed inspectors to ensure that the quality of food produced in the burgh, such as ale, bread, and meat was high enough. Producers of inferior goods were fined. Craft incorporations grew up, each headed by a deacon who monitered the quality of the goods made by his members. The top-dogs, however, were the members of the Guild Merchant, the traders and shopkeepers. These were the men who really ran the burgh. They constituted the majority of the council, originally elected yearly by the whole body of burgesses, but later by the council members themselves.

Even within the burgh itself not all inhabitants were eligible to enjoy its privileges. The free burgesses - the merchants and craftsmen who paid an entry fee for their burgesship or inherited it from a parent - were the ones who might sit on the Council, join the Guild and keep shops or booths. They were also liable for any tax the king might decide to levy, and because of this burden paid only half rates of petty custom and other dues. The majority of the population were 'unfreemen' who could only trade in the official marketplace, and paid full dues on all their goods. This class included servants, beggars and most women. A daughter who was the sole heir of a freeman father would inherit his freedom on his death, but usually gave it up to her husband or to a male relative.

Wherever he went to trade in western Europe, a Scottish merchant would find himself in a burgh run on very similar lines to his own home town. There were local variations and bye-laws, but in the basic organisation of its burghs, medieval Scotland was very much a part of Europe.

The Rise of Edinburgh

Until the reign of David I (1124-1153) Edinburgh was not a particularly important town. The Castle had long been a Royal residence, one of a number periodically visited by the king and his court. It is well known that before the advent of effective plumbing, royalty led a peripatetic life, moving on from each residence when the stench from the overburdened gardrobes (draughty lavatory chutes in the thickness of the walls) became unbearable. Early Scottish kings had two other reasons; they were expected to dispense local justice personally, and they had inherited the Celtic system of 'conveth'. This meant that each household in the area surrounding a royal residence paid a rent of food - meat, corn, cheese, butter, poultry etc., which was stored at the residence. The king and his court had to visit in order to eat.

Of course there were favourite residences, and some evidence suggests that Malcolm Canmore, David's father, preferred Dunfermline. His mother, the English Queen Margaret, is traditionally credited with having encouraged foreigners to trade with Scotland, and it is possible that Edinburgh became a Royal Burgh during her lifetime. However, its earliest surviving charter implies that it was David who made the original grant. It seems to have been in his time that Edinburgh began her progress towards pre-eminence among the Scottish burghs.

David spent his early years at the English court, where his sister Matilda married Henry I. In 1114 he himself married a great-niece of William the Conqueror. During his reign he granted Scottish lands to many of his Anglo-Norman friends. (These possibly included one Peter, who held the lands of Restalrig - then called Lestalrik - in which the hamlet of Leith was situated.) Scottish kings who spent time in England, whether willingly or not, always brought back with them a taste for luxury, and there is no reason to believe that David was any exception. When his sophisticated court resided at Edinburgh the demand for French wine, expensive fabrics, spices, silverware and all manner of luxury items must have risen. All these had to be imported, and the fishing harbour at the mouth of the Water of Leith was the obvious place for the ships to put in.

The Early Development of Leith

In 1128, David founded Holyrood Abbey, and endowed it with many of his own lands, including the lands of Inverleith 'nearest to the harbour, with the said harbour, half of the the fishings and teinds of all the fisheries belonging to the church of St Cuthbert'. It is apparent from this charter that fishing was the chief trade in Leith at that time.

The placename 'Inverleith' is a Gaelic one, denoting the mouth of the Water of Leith. From the evidence of later charters, it would seem that the 'lands of Inverleith' comprised a wide band on each side of the river estuary, stretching from the Forth on the north to the boundaries of Broughton and Bonnington on the south.

The 'harbour' which was granted to the Abbey lay at the place where the Water of Leith deviates from its north-south course and runs east-west for a short stretch, (the place now called the Coalhill). This small area was the only part of Leith on the eastern side of the river which ever belonged to the Abbey. It was known for some 500 years as St Leonard's Lands, presumably because it's proceeds were used by the monks to finance the hospital of St Leonard, which they built to the south of Edinburgh. The main part of the Abbey's grant of Inverleith comprised the area on the western side of the river which came to be known as North Leith. St Leonard's Lands, lying due south of the Water of Leith were also known by the monks as South Leith, a name which came to be applied to the whole of the village which later grew up on the eastern bank of the river.

Having granted his harbour to the Abbey, David established another one for himself in the area which has traditionally been regarded as the nucleus of Leith, the short stretch of the Shore between Broad Wynd and Burgess Close. Here a few 'tofts' were laid out - long narrow plots facing onto the Shore, each with a house or warehouse at its head. It was the stretch of river adjacent to this hamlet which was granted to Edinburgh by Robert the Bruce 200 years later.

David's new foundation continued a process of seaward expansion which had begun as early as the Stone Age, when shellfish gatherers formed a 'shell midden' in the area around the present Junction Street Bridge. This development has continued down to the twentieth century, culminating in land-reclamation to the north of the present Docks complex.

At some time between 1140 and 1178, Edward, son of Peter de Lastalrik, granted Newbattle Abbey a toft in Leith. There are records of several early grants of property which lay neither in St Leonard's Lands nor in the King's new settlement. The most likely site for these would be on the south side of the present Tolbooth Wynd which, at the time when the original harbour was founded presumably formed the foreshore, along which a few fishermens'

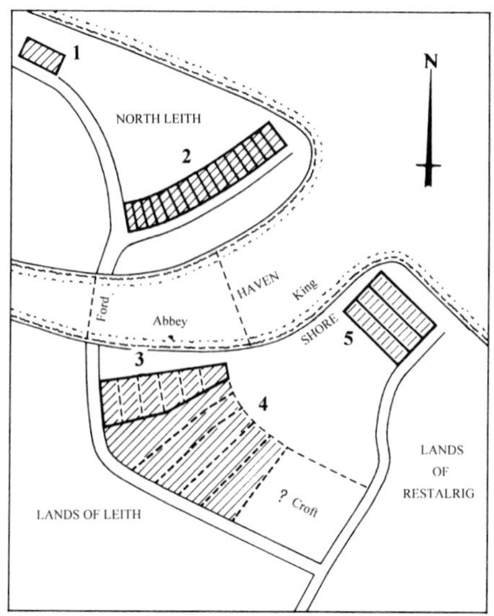

Plan of Leith in the twelth century

1=St Nicholas' Chapel
2=North Leith tofts
3=St Leonard's lands
4=Tofts which seem to be contemporary with St Leonard's lands
5=The King's new harbour

cottages would have been built. The arable land belonging to the tofts lay to the south of this line.

Edward's gift signifies the growing importance of the harbour. Monastic houses made a practice of obtaining properties in ports, which they used as warehouses for their exports and imports. Newbattle was a Cistercian foundation, daughter house to the great abbey of Melrose. Cistercians were instructed by their Rule to derive their income from the labours of their own hands rather than from extensive property holdings. Farming was their speciality. Melrose built up an important export trade in high quality wool through the port of Berwick on Tweed. Newbattle probably used Leith for the same purpose, as did Melrose itself when Berwick was later lost to the English. In about 1220, Thomas de Restalric (probably Edward's son) granted Newbattle a house in Leith 25ft long and 30ft wide, between the lands of John son of Ralph and those of William Meisser. This sounds like a barn or warehouse. Whatever it was, it cost the Abbey all of 2½d (1p) per year in rent.

Thomas was a considerable benefactor to the Church. At around the same time as his gift to Newbattle he granted to Inchcolm Abbey the rents from all the property which Baldwin Comyn held from him in Leith, and a good chunk of arable land beside the road to Edinburgh. Dunfermline Abbey received a toft which seems to have faced onto the Shore, its neighbouring toft, which belonged to Philip de Valognes, being next to the high-water mark (where Broad Wynd now runs).

Philip de Valognes was no less a personage than the Royal Chamberlain to William the Lion (1165-1214), in charge of the administration of the King's revenues. His duties included selling surplus produce from the royal estates, some of which would have been exported, and purchasing goods which could not be supplied by those estates. He would also have been responsible for collecting the king's 'cain of ships', a toll on all imports. (A contemporary list of the commodities involved mentions grain, salt, wine, honey, oil, dried fruit, nuts, spices, dyes, iron, alum and brass pots.) This may be one reason why Philip de Valognes had such a conveniently sited property in Leith. He or his deputies would have to be on the spot when a ship was being unloaded, in order to caclulate how much was due to the King. Like all the other nobility he would have done a significant amount of trading on his own account, in the fish, salt, wool, sheepskins and hides produced on his estates of Benvie and Panmure in Angus.

Baldwin Comyn was also a member of a powerful family, and the other two known Leith property-holders of the time, John son of Ralph and William Meisser, have Norman names, which suggests that they were influential men. It must have been the opportunity for trade that attracted aristocrats as well as merchants to such an obscure little settlement. What were they trading in, and with whom? Wine, spices, fine cloth, and other luxury goods for the King's court and anyone else who could afford them, came from France and the Low Countries. Some timber may have come from the Baltic and Scandinavia, and in times of shortage, grain was imported from England. The earliest records of exports survive only from 1326, but there is no reason to believe that the commodities traded were any different before that date - wool, sheepskins and hides, mostly going to the Low Countries. Dried and salt fish was also exported from early times, much of it to England.

After the Death of Alexander III

Although Leith was held back from full expansion by its non-burghal status, it undoubtably benefited from its proximity to Edinburgh when times were good. However when troubles came Edinburgh, as the chief burgh of the realm, was a prime target for enemy action, and Leith invariably suffered too. Easy access by sea made it as vulnerable as any Border village.

Most of the thirteenth century was a peaceful time for Scotland. The Treaty of York in 1237 defined the border with England, and good relations with Norway were cemented by the marriage of Alexander III's daughter to the Norwegian king. The 'Savage Scots' of the Highlands were always inclined to make trouble and there were the usual power struggles among the nobility, but this was all part of normal life in medieval Scotland. Potentially more dangerous was the relationship between Scotland and England.

Since the time of David I the Scottish crown had held lands in England for which each Scottish king did homage to the English monarch. This precedent caused no real problems until there arose the combination of a rapacious

English king (Edward I) and a weakened Scottish monarchy. Alexander III died one dark night in 1286 when his horse fell over a cliff near Burntisland. He left only a young heiress, his grandaughter, the Maid of Norway. For three years the country was ruled by six Guardians, but in 1289 ambassadors were sent to Edward I with the proposal that the Maid should marry his son. A marriage treaty was drawn up which gave Edward definite rights over Scotland. A ship was sent to fetch the Maid from Norway, but she died on the way. Edward then undertook, as was his legal right, to preside over a court to choose a new king from the thirteen men who laid claim to the Scottish throne (including the grandfather of Robert the Bruce.)

Before we plunge into the trauma of the Wars of Independence we will pause to look more closely at the arrangements for bringing the Maid from Norway, because it illustrates some of the perils of sea travel at the time. A 'great ship' was provisioned at Yarmouth at a cost of, £265 5s 11d, with wine, beer, salt meat, hams, dried fish, beans and peas. As well as these staples of the medieval diet, there were walnuts, sugar, ginger, figs, gingerbread, spices and other delicacies. Flour was provided for over half a ton of the notorious 'ships biscuit'. On board were her master with 40 crew, and the official party, consisting of 4 clerics, 18 horses with their grooms, and a dozen or so other servants. A month after sailing she returned without the Maid. Her father King Eric, had decided to send her in one of his own ships to Orkney and there transfer her to the care of her future subjects. The ship set off again for Wick, but first 11 of the crew had to be replaced, being either sick or dead. She arrived at Orkney only to find that the Maid herself had died soon after her arrival. When the great ship made her home port again, it was found that all her remaining stores, except some wine and corn, were rotten. If these were the conditions on board a ship destined to carry Royalty, what must they have been like on an ordinary merchantman?

The process of choosing the Scottish king began in 1291 and ended in 1292, when Edward decided that John Balliol had the best claim. To us it seems inconceivable that an English king should be allowed such influence over the Scots. In order to understand it we have to try to put ourselves into the skins of the men who held power in Scotland. Perhaps the most important thing to appreciate is that patriotism and nationalism as we understand them hardly existed at that time. In England the main loyalty was to the all-powerful crown, rather than to any concept of 'my country'. In Scotland the king was first among equals as far as the nobility were concerned and the degree of their loyalty depended largely on their degree of kinship to him, and his generosity to individuals and families. This independent outlook made the support of the Scottish nobility for the crown a very equivocal matter, a fact which was to bedevil Scottish history right up to the Union of the Crowns three centuries later. In the main, each man's loyalties lay where he saw his best interests being served.

Coupled with this autonomy was the fact that the majority of the powerful families were recently descended from Norman incomers, and most of them still held land in England, in some cases quite extensive estates, for which they did homage to the English king. Even some native nobility had property in the south and were almost Anglo-Scots. The third main factor was that there was as yet no background of oppression, which would cause Scots to see the English as the traditional enemy. In fact in the run up to delivering his verdict on the succession, Edward I went out of his way to grant concessions to lords, churchmen and burgesses, and each claimant to the throne acknowledged him as overlord in order to further his own claim. It was only after the choice of John Balliol was confirmed that the English king began to make his authority felt.

The Wars of Independence

Balliol reigned until 1296. In this year Edward I was involved in a war in France, and the French were only too happy to make a treaty against him with the Scots, who were by now very aware of the mistake they had made in allowing Edward such a free rein. Edward's reaction to the Franco-Scottish treaty marked the beginning of the Wars of Independence. He marched north and took Berwick upon Tweed, then defeated the Scots army at Dunbar. Fourteen of the Scottish royal castles had already been ceded to him in 1291, now he gained seven more; Dunbar, Roxburgh, Jedburgh, Dumbarton, Stirling, Edinburgh and Perth.

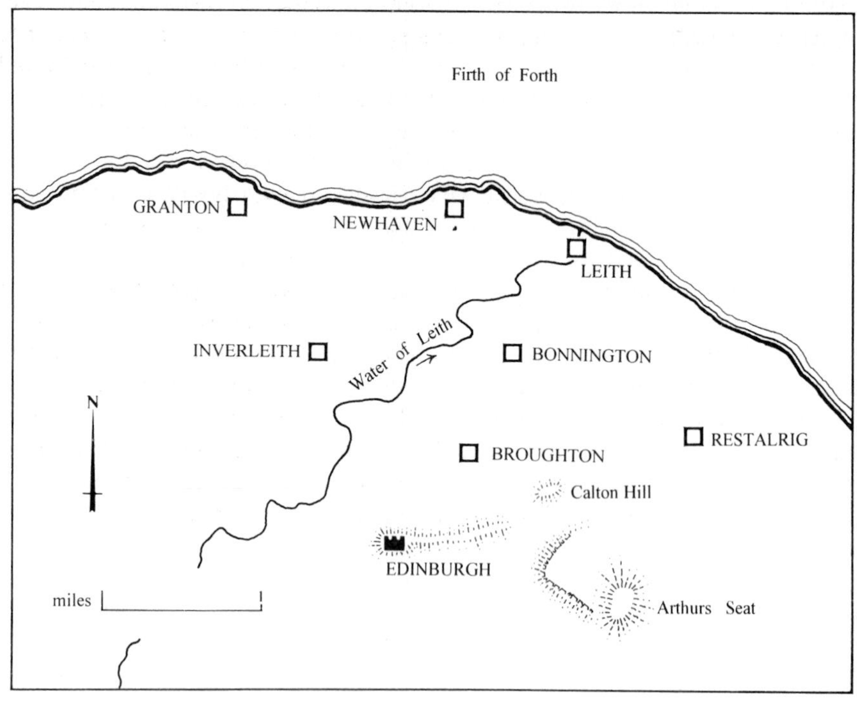

Plan of Leith, Edinburgh and the surrounding district.

Edinburgh withstood a siege of nearly a week before surrendering. One Englishman kept a diary of the campaign in which he recorded that the army arrived at Holyrood on Wednesday June 6th, 'and caused there to be set three engines casting into the castle day and night, and the fifth day they spake of peace'. The English then moved on, and had captured Linlithgow by June 14th. On 17 August they returned to Edinburgh, staying one night on their way back to Berwick. John Balliol was stripped of his kingship, and Edward received the submission of many Scots at Berwick, including Sir John of Restalrig, and the parson of Restalrig. If they had not submitted they would have lost their lands. (When Robert Bruce later set up his resistance Sir John joined him, and his property was indeed escheated to Edward, but by then it was worth the risk, as there was a good chance he would get it back when Robert was successful, as indeed he did.)

Almost immediately after this conquest by Edward I a rebellion was raised by Andrew Moray and William Wallace in an attempt to replace John Balliol on the throne. In 1297 they defeated the English at Stirling Bridge. A month later they wrote from Haddington to the headquarters of the Hanseatic League (a powerful trading confederation of Baltic and Prussian burghs) at Lubeck. The letter thanked the people of Lubeck and Hamburg for help rendered to Scotland in the past, and asked them, 'to make it known among your merchants that they can now have a safe access with their merchandise to all harbours of the Kingdom of Scotland, because the Kingdom of Scotland has, thanks be to God, by war been recovered from the power of the English.' This respite did not last long. The following year, 1298, Wallace was defeated at Falkirk and retreated north of the Forth, but until 1303 only southeast Scotland, which of course included Leith, was under English control.

The Hanseatic League, however, continued to trade with Scotland. What is more its German merchants carried out widespread blockade-running to get Scottish goods in their ships past the patrols on the east coast of England and into the ports of the Low Countries. They even loaded goods destined for Scotland at English ports. (All this was not done entirely out of the goodness of their hearts, shortages must have pushed prices sky-high in Scotland.) In 1303 the Franco-Scottish alliance broke down and Edward once more came north. This time he reached the Moray Firth, and it was not until 1308 that Aberdeen was once again in Scottish hands, after an action in which German merchants fought side by side with Scots. Once a safe headquarters had been established at Aberdeen, the audacity of the Germans merchants increased. In 1309 Edward II wrote to Flanders protesting at the trade in Scottish goods which was being carried on there. The following year he ordered a general arrest of Germans in England.

By now Scottish fortunes were rising again. The movement in support of John Balliol had been much weakened, and in 1306 Robert Bruce had been crowned king of Scotland. His triumph at the Battle of Bannockburn (near Stirling) in 1314 finally brought the whole of Scotland under his control. After Bannockburn, Edward II strengthened his blockade of Scottish ports, giving authority to any English shipowner to act as a patroller. The organiser of the German trade with Scotland, John Witte, was in fact captured by Ralph Ambrose of Winchelsea, who had pursued his ships to Flanders. His company was suspected of selling goods, bought or pirated, to the Scots. John himself was accused of allowing his seal to be used to stamp bales of wool exported from Scotland so that they would pass English inspection. At least 30 Germans were involved in his company. They came mainly from Hamburg, but Lubeck, Dortmund, Cologne, Bremen, Griefswald, Recklinghouse and some Baltic ports were also represented.

An English Supply Port

How had Leith fared during the eighteen years between the capitulation of Edinburgh in 1296 and its recovery into Scottish hands after the Battle of Bannockburn? As was to be the case so often in the future, Leith's fortunes at this time were bound up with those of Edinburgh Castle. Sir Walter de Huntercombe had been appointed keeper of the Castle in 1296, and during the next eighteen years Leith was the channel through which supplies reached the garrison.

The provisions for the garrison of each captured Scottish castle were calculated yearly in London, by a committee headed by the king's Keeper of the Wardrobe and the Steward of the Household. The estimates for Edinburgh in 1300 reveal that the garrison numbered 208 soldiers. There were 64 warhorses, 72 hackneys (smaller horses and ponies) and 8 pack or cart horses, with 128 grooms to look after them. As well as the military contingent, there were 29 clerks and 'valets of office'. These last were probably the individuals enumerated in a later document - a carpenter, a mason, a smith, a chaplain, a baker, a brewer, a miller, and a clerk who kept the wine.

The amount of grain needed by all these mouths was immense, at least 60 tons of wheat per year to make bread, and twice as much malt to brew ale. Each warhorse was given half a bushel of oats a day and other horses one peck (¼ bushel). A carcase of beef fed 80 men. Six salt herring was held to be sufficient for one portion, and there was an allowance of 60 dried white fish a day. Peas and beans were needed to make pottage. It has been calculated that the diet provided a staggering 5,500 calories a day, but there may have been a generous allowance for wastage. The estimate of a few years later is a little less generous, but it also includes 100 tuns of wine, and such luxuries as honey, sugar, garlic, onions, pepper, saffron and cumin; perhaps local supplies were running out. The figures for Berwick in this second estimate included cheese, but Edinburgh supplied this from its own dairy. Other supplies were running low. Linen cord, tanned hides, and iron were all needed, and 300 yards of canvas for making sacks. There was also the matter of some 200 tons of coal. (It seems strange that a castle situated on the edge of an immense coal field should need to import that commodity. Either Lothian coal was not being mined in sufficient quantity at the time, or it was for some reason unavailable to the garrison.)

Once the calculations had been made in London, the goods were requisitioned from different areas of England. In 1309, for instance, wheat, malt, peas and beans came from Norfolk, Suffolk and Lincoln, and wheat and malt from the Vale of York. All the stores for the east coast garrisons were gathered at Berwick on Tweed and divided up for distribution to the different centres. The autumn months saw a steady stream of chartered English vessels sailing into Leith to discharge their cargoes. Private individuals were also allowed to bring 'comforts for the troops'. In 1313, for instance, the *Plenty* of Kings Lynn was carrying lampreys, salt and cloth to the garrison at Perth when she was captured by German merchants and her cargo sold at Aberdeen.

The use of Leith to supply the English garrison is certain. What can only be a matter for conjecture is the extent of other shipping at the port. There were some exports but the volume was extremely small. In 1311-12 just over £25 was collected in Great Custom at Edinburgh, compared with £439 in 1326. (Great Custom, levied on the chief exports and collected by Burgh Customars, had replaced the king's cain on imports at some time between 1275 and 1292, in the reign of Alexander III.) Before 1303 and after 1308, 'Free Scotland' lay just over the Forth, and it is quite probable that a certain amount of smuggling went on in small boats at dead of night, loaded with goods for export via Dundee or Perth.

Once the first shock of conquest was over, life for most people probably settled down to something like normality - always rather uncomfortable for the average medieval man! The market in Edinburgh would have continued to function, with the little boats from the country arriving at Leith as usual. The fishermen of North Leith can hardly have been affected at all, their cobles still putting out to sea. The big exporters of salt and dried fish, staples of the Medieval diet, were the east coast seaports. The fishermen of ports in the Forth would have been more dependant on local markets which continued to function as normal.

In the Time of Robert the Bruce

After 1314 an uneasy peace prevailed between Scotland and England, until 1322, when Edward II invaded again. This time King Robert pursued a 'scorched earth' policy in the Lothians, so that by the time the English army reached Edinburgh it was starving. At Leith on 23 August, 7000 men at arms were paid in money and flour. However they had come to the end of their endurance and had to retreat back to the border. The following year a 13-year truce was ratified.

The truce removed the major threat to security and Robert I was free to concentrate on rebuilding the economy. He was already doing what he could to foster good relations with Flanders whose weavers used most of the wool exported from Scotland. Berwick's near-monopoly of wool exports had been effectively ended during the Wars of Independence, and much of the Borders wool was now shipped at Leith. Some Royal Burghs, including Edinburgh, were now 'set in feu-ferme'. This meant that all the revenues of the burgh which had previously gone to the king, except for the Great Custom, became the property of the community, in return for a fixed yearly sum (ferme) paid to the crown. As important as the financial gain to the burgh was the fact that it also became completely self-governing, with the power to elect its own alderman (provost) and bailies, who had previously been appointed by the Crown.

In 1328, England at last recognised Robert's right to the crown of Scotland. As a further safeguard against any future hostilities, Edward III's sister Joan (aged 7) was married at Berwick to Robert's son and heir, David Earl of Carrick (aged 4).

The earliest Great Custom records for Edinburgh, and thus for Leith, begin in 1326. The number of trading ships visiting the harbour in the early fourteenth century was not all that high. In 1326 itself, 35 ships carried exports from Leith, but the number fluctuated wildly from year to year. There could be fewer than 10, and the average was nearer 20.

Later records show that sailings were seasonal. The bulk of the wool, which was by far the most important export, was shipped in the late summer and early autumn. For a couple of months from the end of July, relays of burdened packhorses would stream into the town, unload into barns and warehouses and return home for further loads. Sheepskins, however, went mainly in the spring and summer, the traditional time for slaughtering lamb. Hides came mostly from the thousands of cattle which were slaughtered around Martinmas (early November) to be salted for use through the winter. As far as possible ships did not sail in December and January, so most hides were exported in spring. The relatively low number that left before Christmas were probably salted rather than tanned. The value of cargoes could be quite considerable. In 1275 the goods of a Leith merchant confiscated at Hull had been valued at £100 sterling.

There were two customars at Edinburgh. In 1327 they were John Bolgy and Robert the chaplain. These men recorded that between 4 March 1327 and 29 January 1328, 39 ships and boats left Leith loaded with Scottish goods. During that time, helped by a weigher (tronar) of wool and a counter of sheepskins and hides, the customars inspected 1093 sacks of wool (each weighing 24st and representing the output of some 270 sheep), 2541 sheepskins and 8324 hides. Each load was stamped with a special seal called a coket, without which it could not be exported. John and Robert collected £439 3d 8½d in custom. Over the next six months they accounted for 212 sacks of wool, 6719 sheepskins and 4000 hides in 11 vessels, realising £95 5s 6d.

As well as collecting the custom they made payments, authorised by the Chamberlain or the King, to a variety of merchants. From their names it would seem that Robert I's policy of encouraging Flemish trade was working: Yuoni Pykard, Beydino Wlpe, Lawrence de Castro, Gerkin, Arnald Buyd, Matthew Gupil (later a prominent name in Edinburgh and Leith), Oliver de Boryngs, John Clauson. Many of them were probably supplying luxuries for the wedding of the Earl of Carrick, the future David II.

The next audit of the customs was on 12 August 1329, and the disbursements included £4 3s 8d refunded to the canon Thomas of Kirkcudbright for 'distributions' on the day of Robert I's funeral. Six other burghs also exported goods through Leith in that year. The country was now being ruled by a guardian while David II was a child, and it may be for this reason that the payments to foreign merchants cease abruptly. Foreigners were still active in Edinburgh, however. From 1331 the accounts separate out the quantities of goods exported by them. Between December 1331 and March 1332 they were responsible for (roughly) 15% of the wool, 10% of the sheepskins and 5% of the hides. In the year which followed only 12 sacks of wool were exported, but other exports were normal, and foreigners dealt with 33% of the skins and hides.

An idea of the kind of goods being imported is given by the accounts of the royal Chamberlain for 1333. He bought; wine, olive oil, vinegar, 144 ells (yards) of linen, 72 ells of twill, 546 ells of canvas, 8 bolts and about 100 ells of other cloth (the length of cloth in a bolt varied according to the kind of fabric), pepper, ginger, saffron, mace, sugar, rice and figs.

Fourteenth Century Leith

We have now arrived back near the point at which we began, the grant of the harbour of Leith to Edinburgh by Robert the Bruce in May 1329. The town of Leith at this date probably still consisted of two separate blocks of buildings. The first was St Leonard's Lands with a line of tofts stretching to the east behind it, and the second the block of tofts to the north which had been founded by David I. (The space between the two had still not been built on 100 years later.) On the eastern side of the lane behind the second block lay the lands of Restalrig. By the next century this lane was known as Rotten Row, which has nothing to do with rubbish or riding. It was a fairly common Medieval street name, and derives from the Old Scots 'rattan', meaning un-dressed timber. It seems that 'log cabin' style barns, stables and sheds had been built at the feet of the tofts and possibly on the eastern side of the lane itself.

What evidence there is, suggests that there was no attempt at this time to improve the haven in any way by building quays or wharves. In fact a late fourteenth century charter makes it clear that at the time it was issued, ships were secured at their berths by having their anchors brought ashore and fixed in the river bank.

Ships and Shipping

The ships which visited the harbour were of two main types, which had evolved from the longships of the Norsemen. Both were clinker built; that is with the planks of the hull overlapping. One was basically a shorter and broader version of the longship, better adapted to carrying cargo. It was propelled by a single square sail. These ships had originally been steered by means of a large oar attached to the starboard ('steerboard') side of the stern, as can be seen on the Bayeux Tapestry. In the twelfth century the fixed rudder was introduced. A

Scottish document of c.1180 mentions that some of the fishing boats coming into Pittenweem and Anstruther at that time had fixed rudders. Vessels visiting Leith during the thirteenth century were of both kinds, with the more up-to-date type predominating as the century wore on. At the same time another innovation was being introduced. In order to make them more efficient in battle, when twelfth century ships were commandeered by the king for war they were fitted with platforms or 'castles' fore and aft. During the thirteenth century these castles became permanent fixtures.

The other type of ship was called a 'cog'. It seems to have developed around the Baltic region and was the kind most used by the Baltic and German merchants of the Hanseatic League, who carried on an important trade with Scotland. The cog had a deeper draught than the vessels we have just been considering, and the ends of the hull were straight rather than curved, so that it could cleave a path through the water more efficiently. The greater depth of hull meant that it could carry more cargo. The early cogs had a castle fore and aft, but from the end of the thirteenth century the aft castle began to disappear and the forecastle became larger. The cog also had only one square sail. Neither kind of ship was very large - between 50 and 100 tons, mostly nearer the former.

Although overseas trade may not have produced much activity, there were plenty of local craft sailing in and out of the Haven, The fishing cobles of North Leith would be busy whenever the weather was suitable. They could not however sail just wherever they pleased. Each fishing community had its own strictly defined stretch of water which was subdivided into areas. These 'fishings' had individual names, and were let out by the year to individuals or partnerships. Each boat had to keep within its own bounds. Poaching on someone else's preserve was a matter for the local law court. Early records still exist for the fishings of Aberdeen and Berwick, but those for Leith have not survived. However, some idea of how they were delineated and operated may be gained from records of disputes over the nineteenth century oyster scalps of the Forth.

The King's business created a considerable traffic of its own. Leith became the collecting point for much of the rent in kind owed to the King from local estates. Cattle, grain, dairy produce, even live poultry, were brought in boats from the Lothian and Fife shores of the Forth. Special provisions such as salt herring and salmon were bought from other parts of the country for the Royal household and transported to Leith by water. If the King's travels brought him to anywhere within hailing distance of the sea, his goods were brought to him by ship. This was very much easier than transport by packhorse and primitive cart over roads which might disappear completely in bad weather. Royal residences were practically unfurnished when not in use. Everything had to be provided to keep the King in the manner to which he was accustomed, from beds and hangings down to kitchen equipment. All this was organised by the Clerks of the Wardrobe and the Kitchen who must have been familiar figures in Leith.

Boats also arrived each week with goods for sale at the market in Edinburgh. The Burgh always jealously guarded its exclusive rights over foreign trade, but the existence of an apparently well-established 'petty custom of Leith' by the mid-fifteenth century, suggests that some goods were allowed to be sold there at quite an early date. Royal purchases of timber, for instance, were always made at Leith, and all the evidence implies that wood was always sold at the Port rather than in Edinburgh. Its comparatively low value made the cost of transporting it to the Burgh for sale uneconomic.

Although no direct evidence for it exists, there can be little doubt that Leith was then, as later, the centre for a great deal of local shipping, especially from the little harbours which still line both sides of the Forth. As we have already noted, water transport was far easier than bulk carriage by land. When the court was at Edinburgh the nobility would need a wide variety of goods brought to them from their estates. Some of the wealthier burgesses would have owned land in the countryside and have had produce brought to town. We must not forget human cargoes. Ferry boats plied from Leith to the other harbours of the Forth from a very early date, carrying passengers and their horses.

The Second English Occupation

In 1332, three years after the death of Robert I, Edward Balliol, the son of John, invaded from England with a band of other Scots who had been dispossessed of their lands for supporting him. He was successful enough to have himself crowned at Scone in 1332 and hold a parliament at Holyrood in 1334. The young King David II and Queen Joan (now aged 10 and 13 respectively) were sent to safety in France. In July 1335 Edward III invaded Scotland from Berwick, while his ally Balliol led a force from the west. By August they had reached Perth. After an interval of 21 years, Edinburgh Castle was once again in English hands.

This second English occupation was much shorter than the first, only 6 years, but it is far better documented. The garrison was headed by 13 knights; five of these were German mercenaries, but the rest were Scots, at least two of whom, William Ramsay and Alexander Cragy, stayed at the castle until the end. Nearly half the 60 men-at-arms were also Scots, some of them with names that later became very prominent in the affairs of Leith and Edinburgh; Dalmahoy, Forster, Brown, Fairly, and Livingstone for example. (The Fairlys were lairds of Inverleith.) The 71 archers and 3 watchmen were all English. Altogether about a third of the garrison were Scots, followers of Edward Balliol, who saw themselves as restoring the true King to Scotland. They either did not realise or could not accept that he was primarily a puppet of the English crown.

John of Stirling was appointed Sheriff of Edinburgh and custodian of the Castle, with power to 'receive to the faith' of Edward III any Scot who made a due submission. He was allocated all the revenues of his sherrifdom to finance repairs to the Castle (which had been all but demolished) and pay his men. They were not sufficient, and in November 1335 Thomas de Burgh, Chancellor of Berwickshire, was ordered to release all the revenues of Lothian for the Martinmas (autumn) term to pay for the repairs, which occupied most of the first year. Among the local workmen employed were John the cooper and two sawyers, all from Leith. For the roofing of the buildings, hundreds of Eastland (Baltic) boards were bought and transported from Leith. Spanish iron, which can only have come from the port, was also used in large quantities.

The initial provisioning of the castle was an ad hoc affair, with John of Stirling buying grain as and when it was needed. Meat and fish were presumably 'requisitioned' from the surrounding district! At the same time that Thomas de Burgh was ordered to finance repairs to the castle, he was instructed to send flour, wheat and wine from his stores to provision the garrison. By February 1336 the familiar supply organisation had swung into operation. Grain was brought to Berwick from Norfolk, Suffolk and Huntingdon and supplied from there to the castles of the east coast.

The customs accounts for 1335-1336 allow us a rare glimpse into the workings of the port of Leith. For once we have the names of the ships and their masters, the cargo of each and the names of the merchants involved. Only three ships were specifically stated to be English; *Blithe* of Lynn, *Purchace* of Doncaster, and *Leonard* of Hull. The rest, *Nicholas, Mariola, Godyear, St Mariship, Trinity, Plenty* and *Godsgrace* could have been Scottish, although the names of their masters sound English. Twentyfive merchants exported during the year, all with English names. The details of goods in the cargoes reveal why the amount of custom was so low, only £26 8s 1½d. The amounts of sheepskins and hides were normal, if on the low side. The quantity of wool, which paid the highest custom, was very small, only 42 sacks, compared with between 880 and 1840 during the period 1326-33. The situation in the following year was even worse - only £13 3s 5d was collected. Just six sacks of wool went from Leith, and no sheepskins at all. Only the number of hides was fairly normal, 3350 altogether.

A good half of the estates in the sheriffdom of Edinburgh were escheated (confiscated) by Edward III because the holders supported David II. One of the escheated estates was that of John of Restalrig, held by Hugh Freygne because John had died and his heirs were minors. When Hugh died on 28 December 1336 the estate passed into the hands of king Edward. At some time between that year and 1351 it came to the Logan family.

The state of Edinburgh itself in the year following the English occupation can be glimpsed in the accounts of the bailies; Walter Curry, Henry Multray and Patrick of Riston. The rents collected from tenement-holders amounted to £7 3s 4d 'and no more'. One house had been commandeered to accomodate some of the garrison. Eleven tenements and annual rents had been escheated; one of the tenements, which had belonged to William Martin, was worth the enormous sum of £7 14s 4d to the town (most paid only a few shillings). Five of the escheated tenements had already been granted to new owners, but the bailies had only been able to raise six months rent from them. Four buildings were said to be in ruins. Including the huge rent of William Martin, the town had lost revenue amounting to £14 7s 10d; two thirds of its income.

In 1337 Edward III brought a great fleet into the Forth and 'maid grete herschipps (destruction) be fire and swerd on all partis theraboute'. The money due from the sherrifdom of Edinburgh could not be raised 'because of the destruction of war', and the Edinburgh baillies could only collect £2 10s. The condition of the town was not helped by a siege of the castle by Scots troops, to flush out the Duke of Gueldres who had taken refuge there after a battle on the Borough Muir.

It seems that some of Edward III's subjects were not wholeheartedly behind him in his warlike activities north of the border. There was a mutiny on one of his warships, and his archers demanded a 50% pay increase to stay in Scotland. In 1337 came the first of an escàlating series of orders from the King forbidding English merchants to trade with the Scots, and a royal letter to the men of Newcastle and Hartlepool complaining that they were neither capturing Scottish ships nor protecting English ships from them.

In 1338 there was 'a miserable dearth in all the bounds of Scotland, to the great mortality of the people, because the land lay waste without any store or corn, for continual wars before past.' In spite of King Edward's orders, food still reached Leith from England. As a result of the dearth in Scotland, English merchants could no doubt command their own prices there, and they were not about to pass up such a golden opportunity. In 1338, the custodian of Perth received a letter from the King warning him that ships coming with supplies for his men were trading in the Forth, and in the same year Edward himself caught the *Falcon* of Ravensere supplying food to the Scots and handed her over to the warden of Edinburgh castle, who presumably kept her at Leith. (Ravensere is one of the lost towns of the East Coast, it was submerged by the sea at the end of the fourteenth century and now lies some two miles off Spurn Head.)

The system for supplying the garrisons did not function at all well. We have already seen that John of Stirling had to do his own provisioning to start with, in fact he complained to the king that he had paid for the transport costs of victual from Berwick out of his own pocket, only to find that the Chamberlain at Berwick would not re-imburse him. A few months after the English took Perth in 1338 the new warden of the town threatened to resign if he did not receive his supplies of grain, wine, salt and building materials immediately. He had also had to fit out a galley and transport his men to Perth at his own expense. In 1338 Thomas Rokeby, who was now custodian of both Edinburgh and Stirling castles organised his own supplies, bypassing Berwick altogether. The following year he even used his own ships, *Eleyne* of Ravensere, and *Lawrence* and *Michael* of Hull.

In February 1340 an attempt was made to improve matters. Four English merchants were contracted to supply about 600 tons of grain, dried peas and beans and 40 tuns of wine to Berwick and about 350 tons and 20 tuns of wine to Edinburgh and Stirling, the ships carrying the latter were to go to the Roads of Leith where their cargo would be transferred to small boats, some to be unloaded at Leith and the rest to go upriver to Stirling. The Admiral of the Fleet was ordered to provide an escort, and the receiver of victual at Berwick was told how much he was to keep and how much was to go on to Leith.

All this proved to be academic. At the end of July Edward III received a complaint that the four merchants who were supposed to bring provisions had only delivered a fraction of the amounts required to Berwick 'so that the granary has been empty for a month'. They were also charging the smaller Scottish measures at English prices, an overcharge of 50% for wheat and malt and 100% for peas and oats. The merchants were ordered to fulfill their contracts and the following month Edinburgh and Stirling at last received 650 tons of supplies, although this did not include wine. (Some at least of these provisions may have come in two ships of Thomas Rokeby which were granted safe conducts that summer.) At the same time two ships and a barge were being fitted out at Berwick to prevent unauthorised English ships taking food to the Scots.

The year 1341 was in many ways a bad one. There was 'such dearth in Scotland and England that the people were constrained to eat horses, dogs and other suchlike forbidden flesh'. But for the Scots it was the year when they finally threw off the English yoke - for the time being at any rate. On 16 April Edinburgh Castle fell to a strategem which is part of Scotland's epic history.

It was in fact the desperate supply situation which led to the recapture of the Castle. A mariner named Walter Curry pretended to the Governer of the Castle that 'he was a merchant and had come from England in the interest of Edward Balliol [currently 'king' of Scotland] and the king of England, to his assistance with supplies of very good wine and corn to see and try, and vowed he would freely give one cask of wine and another of corn for his favour and protection, that no-one should do him violence or wrong. The commandant gratefully accepted them and returned thanks and earnestly besought the said merchant Curry to come at daybreak to the castle gates with the wine and corn'.

Curry, however, had arranged that Sir William Douglas and 200 men would be hidden near the Castle when he arrived with his cart-full of goods at the agreed time. He himself was accompanied by fourteen armed men disguised as mariners. When the Castle gates were opened, Curry stopped the cart in the entrance so that they could not be closed. His men slew the gatekeepers and kept the rest of the garrison at bay until William Douglas and his force arrived.

Some of the English garrison were stationed at Leith and were able to sail to freedom. The Custodian was even able to take his accounts with him, and present them to Edward later in the year. From them we learn that 49 men at arms, 60 archers and 6 watchmen surrendered to William Douglas. Two Scottish knights and eight men at arms of the Edinburgh garrison later became pensioners of Edward III, having lost their lands in Scotland. Rokeby was made Warden of the Marches.

The Reign of David II

On 2 June 1341 David II and Queen Joan returned to Scotland from France, and the seventeen-year-old King set about restoring his devastated realm. The

English now held only the Marches (the area around the Border). One of the decisions made at the King's first parliament after his return was the granting of £100 to Walter Curry and another prominent Edinburgh merchant, William Fairly, for their part in the retaking of Edinburgh castle. William Bartholomew received £40 for the same reason. Walter Curry and William Fairly both served as Customars at divers times. In 1344 the King granted William Bartholomew the escheated Edinburgh property of Thomas Harper ' a rebel in England '.

No sooner had the country begun to recover than she found herself without a king again. In October 1346 David was taken by the English at the battle of Neville's Cross near Durham, and went into a captivity that was to last 11 years. The following year Edward Balliol recovered the sheriffdoms of Berwick, Roxburgh, Peebles and Dumfries and the forests of Jedburgh, Selkirk and Ettrick. It was to take the Scots more than a century to get them back again. Hostilities were halted by the outbreak of the Black Death, which hit England in 1348 and Scotland in 1349 and 1350.

During David II's captivity in England, Scotland was governed by Robert the Steward (later Robert II, the first Stewart king). There is no evidence that he was a very effective governor, but in the absence of war, the country continued to recover and trade began to flourish again. Scottish merchants were no longer having to rely on German and Flemish merchants to carry their goods overseas. In 1347 they established a base or 'staple' at Middleburgh in Zeeland, with its own resident governor or 'conservator of the staple'. This arrangement lasted until well after the Middle Ages, although the staple moved from port to port in response to changes in the political situation between Scotland and the various States of the Low Countries. It was usually at Veere, and sometimes at Bruges.

Scottish ships were still in danger along the east coast from English pirates, although Edward III's official policy towards the Scots was one of encouragement. In 1348 the first English safe-conducts appear, to three Aberdeen merchants. Five years later, Andrew Beet of Edinburgh sailed from Leith to England in the service of William Douglas of Liddesdale, with another merchant and four Edinburgh men who are described as his servants, but appear in later records as merchants in their own right.

In 1357, when a truce was signed and arrangements made for the release of David II, Edward issued a general order that any Scots merchant might trade in England, and the following year the first of a regular stream of Edinburgh traders received their safe-conducts. Over the next eleven years, until 1369, when political events temporarily brought contact with England to an abrupt end, at least 70 Edinburgh merchants loaded their goods onto ships at Leith and sailed down to English ports. Some went only once, others plied a regular trade. An average of 15 went each year, but in the peak year of 1365 this was nearly doubled, to 29.

It was the Scottish custom for several merchants to share a ship, which was cheaper and offered greater protection from pirates, as the ships were armed, but greatly increased the chance of a devastating loss from shipwreck. (Merchants of other countries would distribute their goods among several ships to avoid this disaster.) The ships that sailed to England brought back grain, malt and fine woollen cloth. Many returned via the Low Countries or France, where Scottish merchants had special trading privileges in Normandy. These vessels brought wine, fine linens, silks and velvets and spices - as well as more mundane items like wheelbarrows!

Trade with the Baltic is less well documented, but it expanded considerably during the fourteenth century, especially after the opening of a route through the Öresund in the 1380s. The timber mentioned in various records as having been bought in Leith came from the 'Eastland'. By 1382, the Teutonic Order (originally crusaders but now traders), whose headquarters was at Konigsberg, had a factor in Edinburgh. A list of their Scottish debtors compiled about the end of the century, included the Customars of Edinburgh (£20), and several Edinburgh and Leith names such as Lamb, Tours, Preston and Guppil; William Tours owed the large sum of £82.

The records for the middle of the fourteenth century are rather sparse, but they contain tantalising hints of the growing importance of Leith. The first occurs in three lists of 'contributions' for the ransom of David II after his release in 1357 from captivity in England. The lists in question are of the contributions of the Burghs - and they include Holyrood Abbey's holdings of 'Norleith' and 'Suthleith'. They could not have possibly been included in this list of burghs by accident, so what is the explanation? A possible clue may be found in the fact that in 1342, David II had granted to Holyrood Abbey the right to hold all its possesions ' in Regality ', which meant that it could create its own Burghs. The Canongate was a burgh of the Abbey, and its earliest surviving Court records show that it included North Leith and St Leonard's Lands in its jurisdiction. It may be that their association with the Canongate afforded them some kind of Burgh status, sufficient at any rate for them to be made to 'contribute' along with the rest, which they did in 1366, 1370 and 1373.

The assessments were made on the basis of 12d in the pound (5%) on the value of movable goods, and the Canongate, North Leith and South Leith each paid roughly the same amount: £3 9s, £3 14s and £3 19s respectively in 1370. These amounts were tiny in relation to the £123 13s 5d paid by Edinburgh, but more than Musselburgh (£1 13s) and North Berwick (13s 4d). It is interesting to note that 'Suthleth', which consisted of a row of half a dozen properties at St Leonard's Lands, was worth more than the Canongate. If part at least of Leith now had some sort of burgh status, this would account for the fact that two of the merchants who received safe-conducts from Edward III to trade in England came from the town; Robert Clerk in 1366 and John Cairns in 1368. The unfree inhabitants of a non-burghal settlement would certainly not have been able to set up as merchants trading to another country, especially under the ever-watchful eye of Edinburgh!

The Late Fourteenth Century

The last quarter of the fourteenth century was one of fluctating tension in relationships with England. A number of English merchants were granted licences to take grain to Scotland. Most Scots seem to have landed in England only by accident, although a few safe-conducts were still issued, some to Edinburgh merchants.The average number of ships exporting annually from Leith rose during the century, although the yearly numbers continued to fluctuate widely.

It has been traditionally held that in 1380 the Masters and mariners of Leith were granted by the king (Robert II) the right to levy a duty, called Prime Gilt, of 12d on each tun of goods imported into Leith. The money was used to relieve sick, poor and aged mariners. This implies that the Masters and mariners had formed some kind of Incorporation, one of whose functions was always the support of its own poor. In theory, this should not have happened in an unfree town, but the seafaring population of Leith was always something of a law unto itself. Its relative independence was strengthened by the favour of successive monarchs, who usually recognised the vital contribution of their mariners to the commerce and defence of the realm. For many years the skippers of North Leith levied their Prime Gilt separately from those on the other side of the river.

In 1396 we at last learn the name of a Leith ship. The *Thomas* belonged to Alan Ballon of Edinburgh who sailed her to England with Thomas Ballon and William, John and Peter Forsyth. Two years later Edinburgh extended its influence over part of Leith, when Sir Robert Logan of Restalrig granted the Burgh a wide-ranging charter which gave it a strip of land on the eastern river bank, (the Shore). Logan also renounced his right to keep taverns in Leith for the sale of wine, or shops for merchandise, or to 'grind bread for sale'.

This charter has generally been seen as the beginning of the real subjection of Leith to Edinburgh and the name of Sir Robert Logan has been laid under a number of curses over the years. Edinburgh, of course, paid handsomely for its new rights, and Sir Robert has been denounced as a money-grubbing tyrant, but he may have simply been hard up. Three years before the granting of the charter the laird had been jousting in England and this was a very expensive pastime, even if he confined his subsequent activities to Scotland.

The Logan charter contains details which give some insight into the development of the port. It mentions that there was a wide paved road (Rotton Row) leading from the east side of Leith to the sea, on the east side of which the arable land of Restalrig began, including Sir Robert's rabbit warren. It also hints at the intentions of the burgesses for the improvement of the harbour. They are empowered to ' enlarge, lengthen and construct ' their port. This implies that they wanted to build a pier and wharves. They also had permission to build a bridge, but it was the Abbot of Holyrood who did that, in the next century.

2

The Fifteenth Century

The new century opened for Leith with another visit from the English army, in the year 1400. This time its stay was only a brief one, albeit under rather strange circumstances. The English were in Scotland at the invitation of the Earl of March, who had paid Robert III a large sum of money to secure the betrothal of his daughter to the Duke of Rothesay, the heir to the throne. Archibald the Grim, Earl of Douglas, had subsequently paid even more, and Rothesay had married Marjorie Douglas, the Earl's daughter. Moreover, the King would not refund the Earl of March his money. Henry IV, who had just come to the throne of England, was March's fourth cousin, and it was on the strength of this relationship that the Earl wrote to him, asking for his help. On 21 August Henry and his army arrived at Leith.

A small advance fleet of supply ships from England, under the direction of Richard Clitheroe, had recently arrived in Leith harbour carrying wine and flour. It was made up of barges, balingers and crayers, small craft of about 50 tons or less. The crayers were the smallest vessels; the *Trinity, Marie* and *Lawrence* of Boston (Lincolnshire) and the *Christopher* of Zeeland, each carrying 7 or 8 crew. William Hankey's balinger from Scarborough had a crew of 14, and the *Blithe* of Boston, with 12, was probably another balinger. The largest ship, the *Trinity* of Hull, had a crew of 34 and was probably a barge (needing a large crew in case it was necessary to row), and the 'flagship' of the fleet.

For about a week Henry unsuccessfully besieged the Duke of Rothesay in Edinburgh Castle, but by 3 September he was back in Newcastle. Apart from the normal depredations of an army on foreign soil, very little damage was done to property, although the Edinburgh tron had to be repaired, at a cost of 17s. (The tron was a stout weigh-beam with large pans called 'brods' hung at each end, on which all goods coming into a burgh were weighed.)

This interlude was the only direct interference by England in Scottish affairs for many years, but during the first quarter of the century tension between the two nations caused a renewed upsurge of piracy, the maritime equivalent of border reiving. The problem was compounded by a period of weak government in Scotland. Not long after the incident recounted above, the Duke of Rothesay, who was at the time virtual ruler of Scotland owing to the poor physical and mental state of the king, began to assume powers that went beyond his remit and was imprisoned at Falkland, where he died. Some said he was starved to death by his uncle the Duke of Albany, who had governed during Rothesay's youth. Whatever may by the truth of this, Albany immediately reassumed the mantle of Governor, and held it until his death. Contemporary accounts describe him as an attractive and popular figure, but Albany was also devious, unscrupulous, and unable or unwilling to restrain the nobility from pursuing their own ends, particularly after his brother the king died and he became in effect the sole ruler of Scotland.

A Fifteenth Century Scottish Merchant

We will soon see how the political climate affected the affairs of Leith and Edinburgh, but first let us take a look into the life of a merchant of the time. He was called John Meffon (Methven) and he possessed a little book in which he recorded some of the details of his life, both sacred and profane. He seems to have been a lively character, with a sense of humour, for the book contains a joke letter to his wife written in rhyme, and also the following verse, whose sense may be familiar:

> Whosoever does on me look,
> I am by rights John Meffon's book.
> If I be lost and you me find,
> I pray you heartily be so kind
> To take upon you so much pain
> As for to send me home again.

The essential meaning of this rhyme has more recently been tersely expressed: 'If this book should dare to roam, box its ears and send it home'.

The first part of the little volume contains a selection of prayers in Latin, and it may have been John's intention to fill it in this way, but his business interests were too pressing, and after the prayers come several pages of calculations. These comprise information about the weights and measures of the Low Countries, and tables for reckoning the cost of a single unit from a bulk price. This was a very important exercise for the Medieval merchant, who bought in bulk and sold direct to the consumer. The term for retailing used in Scotland at the time was 'pack and peel', which referred to the splitting of bulk goods into smaller quantities suitable for selling in booth or market.

If some of us have trouble converting into metric weights and measures, we should spare a thought for medieval merchants. In those days each country had its own measures, which could even vary from town to town. John Meffon was naturally sufficiently familiar with Scottish measures not to have to note them down, but Flemish weights were quite different. He was dealing in wool, sheepskins, hides, cloth, iron and wax. Wool was sold by the sack as in Scotland, but the units which went to make up a sack were 'nails' of 6lb Bruges weight, not stones (16lb) as in Scotland. (If he had also been trading in England he would have had to deal with 'sarplers' of wool as well.) Wax was sold by the 'weigh' of 30 nails. Pieces of cloth went by the hundred of 5 score, but skins by the long hundred of 6 score. Iron was sold by the '100' (100lb).

As if this was not complicated enough, the money was a nightmare. Until Philip the Good of Burgundy introduced a standard currency in Flanders in

1434 there was a mixture of local currencies, but the two main systems were 'esterlin' (sterling or 'inglis') and 'gros' or 'grete'. The latter was introduced at the end of the thirteenth century and so called because it was heavier, and worth three times as much as sterling (ie, £1 gros = £3 sterling). Sterling continued to be used especially at Bruges for reckonings to do with wool and cloth, but even this was not straightforward. John Meffon priced his wool in marks sterling (1 mark = 13s 4d) and then converted into Flemish pounds gros for further calculations. Sheepskins were sold by the Flemish noble of 6s gros. Added to all this was the fact that Scottish currency was already falling in value against sterling, and continued to do so until the seventeenth century. John certainly needed his sense of humour! There is no evidence to connect John Meffon with Leith, but his book demonstrates some of the problems that all merchants were facing at the time. They also affected mariners, who did a certain amount of trading on their own account, and were paid their freight money in a variety of currencies.

The Rule of the Duke of Albany

After the death of the Duke of Rothesay, the king became increasingly concerned for the safety of his only surviving son, James. Finally the decision was taken to send him to France, ostensibly for his education. Early in the spring of 1406 he was taken to North Berwick by a trusted counsellor of the king and rowed out to the Bass Rock to await a ship. He waited for a month until he was finally picked up by the *Maryenknight* of Danzig, bound out of Leith for Flanders with a cargo of skins and hides. The delay meant that there was plenty of time for the English to be informed of what was happening, and on 14 March the *Maryenknight* was intercepted off Flamborough Head by Hugh-atte-Fen of Yarmouth. James later described what happened:

> Upon the waves weltering to and fro,
> So unfortunate was us that strange day,
> That in spite, plainly, whether we would or no,
> With strong hand, as by force, shortly to say,
> Of enemies taken led away
> We were all, and brought in their country

He was then aged twelve, and he remained in captivity in England for the next 19 years. When the news was brought to his aged father 'his spirit forthwith left him, the strength waned from his body, his countenance grew pale, and for grief thereafter he took not food'. The king died just over three weeks later.

The Duke of Albany was now ruler of Scotland. His own son Murdach was a prisoner in England, having been captured at the battle of Homildon Hill in 1402, and he made great efforts to get him released, finally succeeding in 1416. James always considered that his uncle was less enthusiastic about his nephew's freedom, which did not come until eight years later. Albany's official title was 'Lord Governor', and he governed with the help of two King's Lieutenants.

North of the Forth, the Lieutenant was his nephew, Alexander Earl of Mar, the eldest of the many illegitimate sons of The Wolf of Badenoch, Albany's late unlamented younger brother. Alexander, though a flamboyant man of action and a notable warrior, was a very different character from his savage father. He had gained his Earldom by an extremely convenient marriage, possibly helped by his uncle, and his rule in the North seems to have been no more corrupt than was normal for the time. Although he did cause some problems for Leith, as we will see, his dependence on Albany's favour to maintain his position kept him loyal and checked any tendencies to excessive corruption.

However, the Lieutenant in the South, the Earl of Douglas, was a very different matter. The Douglases had been a powerful family for over a century. The Earl could call on the traditional support of a numerous following. If a full-blown power struggle had ever developed between himself and Albany it was quite possible that he would have won. Albany seems to have decided to prevent such a situation from arising by allowing the Earl a great deal of licence.

The Edinburgh Customars

The few records of this period tell of a time of increasing lawlessness, but usually without giving details about who was responsible. One source which gives a very graphic picture of what was going on is the accounts of the customars of the Burghs. The customars had to attend a yearly audit (literally 'hearing'). There they read out their accounts, which were then recorded in the rolls of the king's Exchequer. As well as recording the amounts of custom received, the customars had to account for money paid out by them for various royal expenses. These had always included a number of pensions, and remissions of customs duties granted by the king for one reason or another. Under the Governorship of Albany these outgoings multiplied until they swallowed up nearly the whole revenue. The accounts of the Edinburgh customars are especially informative about the activities of the Earl of Douglas.

The customars during the whole period were Sir John Forrester of Corstorphine and Alan of Fairley of Inverleith. They did their best in the face of mounting corruption. In normal times anyone drawing revenues from the customs had to produce a letter or some other mandate from the king. Now just about anyone was helping himself, and the best the auditors could do was make a note to consult the Lord Governor about each unauthorised payment. The exactions seem to have started almost as soon as Robert III was dead. At the audit held in March 1407, the customars reported that James, the brother of the Earl of Douglas, had taken £23 5s 2½d on the authority of letters patent signed by himself! He said it was for his expenses after the burning of Berwick. The next year James commandeered a similar sum, ostensibly for the relief of Aberdour Castle in Aberdeenshire.

In 1408-9 came the first evasions of custom, by five merchants. They included the worst scourge of all, Sir William Crawfurd, who had been appointed warden of Edinburgh Castle. He was in league with the Earl of

Douglas, who took £465 12s 6d 'on his own authority'. Sir William, besides his legitimate expenses for the repair of the Castle, took a total of £318 13s 7d, and his brother Robert had £13 6s 8d on the strength of a letter with William's seal, and a further £5 17s 9d, 'which James of Dundas had paid for wool weighed and sent to sea'. When the customars protested to Sir William he promptly had them imprisoned in the Castle.

An obvious response by the Duke of Albany would have been to replace the customars with a pair of men who would be willing to turn a blind eye. However, these were Royal appointments, held for life. It seems that even the Duke was not so far gone in his disregard for the law as to interfere in this particular sphere. John and Alan served until the return of James I in 1424. The Duke may have even taken some action with regard to James Douglas, as there were no unauthorised seizures in 1409-10.

There was no audit in 1411, possibly because this was the year of the Battle of Harlaw, near Aberdeen. It was fought between the Earl of Mar and Donald, Lord of the Isles, who had brought an army into the Lowlands, ostensibly to claim the Earldom of Ross, which he had acquired through his wife. This 'invasion' was interpreted at the time as an attempt by Donald to seize power over the whole of Scotland north of the Forth, and the battle was long remembered in story and song. In 1412, when the audit was finally held, it was found that the depredations on the Customs were relatively minor; two merchants had not paid, and James Douglas had taken a small sum.

The Pirate Earl

In the meantime, however, the Earl of Mar had made his own contribution to the history of Leith. His first wife had died after a few years, and he had married a Flemish lady, thereby acquiring property in the Low Countries. Perhaps because the lady was said to have a husband still living from whom she was not legally separated, his new tenants would not pay the Earl any rent, in spite of frequent attempts by his agents to collect it. He decided to recoup his losses by 'confiscating' goods from Flemish ships. Accordingly he captured a ship bound for Flanders and took her cargo. He let the captain and mate go, in a boat which later safely made land, but the rest of the crew he took back to Scotland and put them to work carrying stones for the building of a castle, almost certainly Inverness, which he was rebuilding at the time. (Shortly after the date of the Earl's act of piracy, six men were delivered to the warden of Inverness castle. They stayed for about three years and were fed, clothed and paid 1d per day.)

Unfortunately the ship was not Flemish at all, but came from Danzig, and the Hanseatic League, already plagued by Scottish pirates, decided that the time had come to put a stop to their activities. At their next general meeting it was proposed that they place a complete embargo on trade with Scotland. Danzig and Stralsund must have had the most to lose by this proposal, because they managed to delay ratification until 1415, when the measure finally came into force. The effect on Leith was immediate. In that year the number of ships carrying goods from the Port dropped from over 20 to 'several' and the following year to four. In fact the actual volume of exports was unaffected, but the figures suggest the amount of Hanseatic shipping visiting Leith. (Aberdeen, Dundee and Perth were relatively unaffected.)

Just how seriously the loss of imports from the 'Eastland' affected Leith it is not possible to tell. They mainly comprised timber, grain and salt. The last two were obtainable locally and from England and it is probable that the only result of the embargo was a price rise, although this could be serious enough to those on the borderlines of poverty. As we shall see later, it is likely that there was a fairly flourishing shipbuilding industry at Leith, and the shortage of timber may have been more serious in this area. German beer was also very popular with those able to afford it, the local brew being best described as 'more a food than a drink', and the superior beverage would be unobtainable while the embargo lasted. In effect this was not for very long. Although it was officially in force until 1435, by 1416 the number of ships at Leith had picked up again, and the Hanseatic League was forced to issue 'reminders' about the embargo to its members every few years.

The Customs Again

The situation concerning the Edinburgh customs once again deteriorated. In 1413/14 the Earl of Douglas appropriated £1339 7s 8d, all that remained after deducting the fees of the tronar who weighed the wool, the man who counted the skins and hides, and the clerk who stamped goods with the 'coket' seal to show that they had paid custom. The next year he authorised the seizure of a total of £532 16s 2d by a number of individuals:

Walter Haliburton, husband of the Duchess of Rothesay	£320 6s 8d
James Douglas, brother of the Earl	£122 6s 8d
The Earl of Orkney	£42 6s 8d
William of Borthwick	£41 6s 8d
Lord William Douglas of Drumlanrig	£3 5s 8d
John Hart and Robert Barton	£3 2s 0d

> About which the custumars said, [to the auditors] that they neither received nor gave out the said money, but that those abovenamed took the said amounts of money on their own authority, without consent of the custumars.

In 1415/16 the evaders of the Great Custom included the customar of North Berwick and the vicar of Musselburgh! Out of the £759 7s 1d that was left, the Earl of Douglas took £490, 'which he said he had expended at Truce Days and in ridings in time of war on the Marches'. Truce Days were meetings of the English and Scottish Wardens of the Marches, during which serious business may have been discussed. Their main attraction, however, lay in the tourneying and feasting which made up the bulk of the proceedings. The next year the Earl took £378 18s 3d without explanation, and the list of customs evaders had swelled to 21 names, many of them prominent local merchants.

In 1419 no audit was held, the accounts for two years were presented in July 1420. The figure for 1418/19 was £1160 11s 7d, quite normal. For 1419/20 however it was only £503 16s 4d and 'The Lords auditors, considering that much wool and many fells and hides passed through the town of Edinburgh and were loaded into divers ships at the port of Leith, accused the customars, tronar, coket clerk and others of taking the money.' They must have known what was really going on, and were giving the customars the chance to have their story officially recorded.

The customars, tronar and clerk replied that they had been discharged from office by the Lord Governor the previous November, and had not been allowed to weigh any goods since that time. Asked whether they knew the amount of wool weighed since their dismissal, and by whom it had been weighed, they said that Alexander of Liddale had done the weighing, by order of William of Borthwick who was now captain of Edinburgh Castle, and that the wool amounted to 28 lasts of sarplers. The auditors estimated that this was the equivalent of 30 lasts (ie 30x10) of sacks, on which the custom would amount to £400. Robert of Lorn had been deputed by Borthwick to count the fells and hides. He was present at the audit, and stated that he had handled 10,286 fells and 50 lasts (ie 50x20) of hides. 'Asked if he had the books containing the names of those who owned the said skins and hides he replied that as he was getting ready to come to this Exchequer, William of Borthwick sent for him and took his books, nor would he give them back.' Altogether the auditors reckoned that the Earl of Douglas, William Borthwick and their agents had taken £884 16s from the customs, 'about which the Lord Governor is to be consulted.'

By 1421 the Duke of Albany was dead and his son Murdach governed in his place. The depredations of the Douglas continued, but the end was in sight. Murdach totally lacked the abilities and popularity of his father, and his brothers also began to give trouble. The nobility decided that the time had come for the return of the King. Serious negotiations began at last, and on Palm Sunday 1424, accompanied by his recently wedded English wife Joan Beaufort, James I entered Edinburgh

James I

The king was an intelligent and energetic man who had learned a lot about government during his stay in England. He had also become accustomed to a life of considerable luxury compared with the standards prevailing in Scotland at the time. The Duke of Albany, for all his faults, had been a man of moderate tastes, and the other men of power had been more familiar with the tough existence of the warrior. James also needed as much money as he could raise,in order to pay the enormous ransom of 60,000 merks demanded by the English as the price of his release. He began his campaign for better government and increased revenue by eliminating the Albany family and the Earl of Douglas, and confiscating their estates. The Earl of Mar he left alone, but when he died in 1435 his estates were also escheated to the Crown. As the Earl was illegitimate this would have been quite in order, if it had not been for the existence of a legitimate heir, Lord Erskine, to whom the vast Mar inheritance should have reverted.

The elimination of powerful men took time. More immediate results could be had by restoring the revenue from the Customs to the control of the Crown. James replaced one of the Edinburgh customars, Alan of Fairley, with John Turing, a member of a mercantile family to which the king entrusted much of his business. The tron was also thoroughly overhauled to make sure it weighed true. In 1425/6 the Edinburgh customs provided the king with £2616 15s 7d. A new duty was introduced, on exported woollen cloth. Two men were appointed to deal with this in Edinburgh, George Lauder and Thomas Cranston, and in its first year the new impost realised £252 1s 2d.

Within three months of his restoration, James sent two of his ships to Burgundy, presumably for wine and other luxuries, and in October another ship of his also sailed south from Leith. In July 1426 *Marie* of Leith, belonging to David Lindsay and manned by a crew of 16, carried the king's goods to London to be sold. Details of her return cargo are not given, but in 1430 the *John* of London sailed into Leith carrying a wide variety of presumably similar goods, which had been bought in England for the king. As well as 20 tuns of wine, there was cloth of scarlet, ruby, mulberry, black, 'motley' and other colours, red leather, a hackney saddle (ie for a small horse), a lady's saddle and pack saddles, pewter vessels, and arquebuses (guns). Even if James himself had not been interested in maintaining a high standard of living, his English bride was no doubt struck by the way of life of even the wealthy Scots. All contemporary commentators were united in praise of the fighting prowess of the Scot and in condemnation of his notions of domestic comfort.

Financing Harbour Improvements

In 1414 Sir Robert Logan of Restalrig had granted a charter to Edinburgh. It attempted to limit the access of the burgesses in Leith to a strip of land 'from the gate of John Pettindreich to the wall newly built by the Water of Leith'. (John Pettindreich was joint master, with two others, of the *Katherine*. His toft faced onto the shore and stretched back to Rotten Row.) The land mentioned in the charter later became the alley known as Burgess Close, but at the date of the charter it was merely a strip on the northern side of the open space between the two halves of South Leith. Later evidence suggests that this space was used as a market place, which would account for it not yet having been built up. The reference to the new wall suggests that the Burgh had already begun to improve the harbour by building a wharf at the Shore.

Once he had restored law and order and a degree of political stability to the country, James I set about other improvements. Having lived in London, one of the great seaports of the time, he would have been well aware of the shortcomings of the principal port of his kingdom, and he took measures to remedy them. The work which Edinburgh seems to have been carrying out at

Leith in 1414 was presumably complete by the time of the king's restoration, but James knew that in order to keep everything in good repair, money was needed in fairly large quantities. His solution was based on the same principal as road tax - let the user pay. In 1428 he granted Edinburgh a charter empowering her to levy dues on goods and vessels entering the Port ('haven silver').

The list of dues gives a picture of the kinds of commodities being handled at the port at the time and of the ships in which they were carried. Wool, skins and hides we have already encountered, but there was much more: wine, corn, malt, bere (a kind of barley used in brewing ale), meal, salt and herring were the items of food. There was wood in the form of boards, planks and bowstaves; and coal, iron and tar. A notable omission from the list is cloth, but this was covered by the provision for 'all other things, poke pack and barrel, proportionately answering to the serplare (pack of wool) and to the tun'. Tuns and other kinds of barrel were the only waterproof containers available. Silks, linen, spices and small delicate articles were packed into them and further protected by a covering of canvas. Coarser fabrics were made up into canvas covered packs.

The dues varied from 32d on every last (200) of unfreemens' hides, to 1d on a chalder (about 2 tons) of coal. Unfreemen paid double dues on wine, wool, skins, hides, and girnal (granary) goods. This double payment by non-burgesses was standard practice wherever a Burgh held jurisdiction, and continued in force until the nineteenth century in Scotland. The original rationale for it was that burgesses were periodically liable for the payment of taxes, and therefore should be excused a proportion of other exactions.

The ships mentioned in James' grant were of various kinds, the dues they paid giving some idea of their relative sizes:

Item, of hulks and forecastled ships that come in the haven	10s
Of each crayer, busche, barge and balinger	5s
Item of each farcost [usually a fishing boat]	1s
Of each great boat with victual or other goods	6d
Item, of each small boat	2d

The larger ships obviously did not vary sufficiently in size to warrant differing dues. About this time, safeconducts to England begin to mention the tonnage of each Scottish ship, and nothing over 100 tons appears until 1452, This does not mean that larger ships did not exist, but either they were not so common as they later became or else were not much used for voyages to London.

The Preceptory of St Anthony

The new dues were very necessary and the use for which they were intended was praiseworthy, but they meant that a ship might now be liable for three sets of payments; Great Custom to the king if she carried wool, fells or hides for export, Primegilt to the Masters and Mariners, and the new Harbour impost. Two years later, in 1430, the foundation of the Preceptory of St Anthony of

Leith was confirmed by Bishop Wardlaw of St Andrews, and it was not long before the monks were granted a measure of wine from every tun unloaded at Leith. The land for the building of the Preceptory had been given by Sir Robert Logan of Restalrig, but at the time his grant was confirmed by the bishop, he was far away in England. The payment of James I's ransom was supposedly guaranteed by the sending of noble Scottish hostages to England. These men 'served their turn' in rotation, and Sir Robert was away from 1427 until 1432.

The Preceptory at Leith is the only known house of its kind in Scotland, and why Sir Robert chose that comparatively obscure order is something of a mystery. One possible explanation might be that he suffered from erysipelas, known at that time as 'St Anthony's Fire', because prayers at the shrine of the Saint at Viennes were held to be efficacious in gaining healing. Maybe he founded the Preceptory in hope of a cure or in thanksgiving for a restoration to health.

The brothers of the order were well known as 'hell fire' preachers, and specialised in promising absolutions from sin in return for donations to their work. The brothers of Leith employed a 'pardoner', who, as the name indicates, sold pardons for sins, as well as spurious relics of saints. The man who held this post at the end of the fifteenth century was William Grant. He appears in the records of Dunfermline as a burgess of the town in 1496, dying at some time between October 1502 and February 1505.

The seal of the Preceptory of St Anthony at Leith, showing the Saint with a sow behind him, its bell hanging round its neck.

As well as its activities in the sphere of 'pardoning', the order specialised in the keeping of pigs, animals with which St Anthony was particularly associated. These swine roamed the streets with those of the townspeople, but each had a bell hung round its neck to mark it as the property of the friars. When David Leslie wrote the lines of the Pardoner in his 'Satire of the Three Estates', was he thinking of the brothers of Leith and William Grant?

> The gruntle of St Anton's sow
> Which bore his holy bell
> Whoever he be hears this bell clink
> Give me a ducat for to drink.
> He shall never go to hell
> Unless he be of Belial born.
> Masters trow ye, that this scorn.
> Come win this pardon, come.

Until comparatively recently among the fishermen of the north shore of the Forth, the pig was regarded as such an unlucky animal that it was never mentioned in conversation, and if a man were so unfortunate as to catch sight of one on his way to set sail for the fishing, he would postpone his voyage until the following day. It would be interesting to know whether the mariners of Leith shared this superstition.

The King's Wark

Another act of James I which aimed at the improvement of trade, was the setting up of a mint in a room of a house near the Kirk Stile of St Giles. This was financed partly by payments from the customs, and the first moneyer, installed in 1428, was Robert Gray, a burgess of Edinburgh who later took up residence in Leith. He was obviously a man of many talents, because by 1433 he was 'master of the mint and the building of the castles of Edinburgh and Leith'. The 'castle of Leith' was the building which later came to be known as the King's Wark. Archaeological excavation has demonstrated that its first phase, the one overseen by Robert Gray, was constructed on a promontory bounded by the Shore to the north and the sea to the north, and west.

A rather indistinct picture map of 1560, and sketches made in the seventeenth century, show that the 'castle' was a square tower situated at a little distance to the north of Broad Wynd. These 'tower houses' had superseded the magnificent but costly curtain-wall castles of the Norman period in Scotland. They had three or more floors connected by a turnpike stair in one corner, the ground floor being used for storage and the upper stories for living accommodation. There might also be cellars or a dungeon. (There is a fairly complete example not far from Leith, at Cramond, which once belonged to the bishop of Dunkeld.)

The fact that the King's Wark was sometimes referred to as the Palace, may mean that the king had an apartment there, though there is no evidence that he ever stayed in it. The main purpose of the tower was to act as a food store and arsenal. The royal household had previously hired storage accommodation for grain and other food stuffs at Leith, and it was doubtless a convenience to have a place to put it all under one roof, but James seems to have been more interested in his new tower's function as an arsenal.

The king imported ordnance and skilled gunsmiths from the Low Countries, but there is some evidence, if slight, to suggest that Leith already contained a body of specialist weapons manufacturers. John Major, the sixteenth century historian, states that the 'Leith double axe' was used at Bannockburn. It was, he says, 'very much the same as the French halberd, yet it is a little longer, and on the whole a more convenient weapon. The smiths put a piece of iron formed hook-wise at the end of a stout staff - this serves as bill-hook or axe: this most serviceable weapon is in use among the English yeomen.' If the manufacture of this weapon did indeed have such a long history, the smiths of Leith had a wider than average range of skills. At the end of the fifteenth century it was a Leith smith who was James IV's best native gunmaker. St Mary's church, built at that time, contained an altar to St Barbara, the patron saint of gunners.

Shipbuilding at Leith

Unfortunately Robert Gray's first recorded accounts for the King's Wark only go into details about the sources of his income. The details of his disbursements were contained in three books and three lists, which have not survived. If we had them, we would know the names of some of the earliest shipbuilders to work at Leith, because they contained the accounts for the building of a large barge for the king.

James IV is usually cited as the first Scottish king to take an interest in naval affairs, but James I seems to have assembled a small fleet almost a century previously. Two of his ships (one of them called the *Kele*) were repaired at Leith, and provisioned to sail to the North for timber to build the barge. In 1435 she was completed and handed over to her master, Thomas Pulti. In 1436 'a great ship of the king's father' was also repaired, it may have been for this ship that Robert Gray received 45 ells (metres) of canvas to make sails in 1437. The Duke of Albany had used a ship called the *Tay*, which could be the one referred to here. By 1437 the royal fleet consisted of one 'great ship', two or more of normal size (which seems to have been about 100 tons at that time), a barge and the queen's balinger, which she used to trade in the goods produced on her dower lands.

Although the king had at least five ships of his own, it was still necessary to hire a vessel in 1437 to bring lead from Berwick to roof the great chamber in Edinburgh Castle. Probably all the other ships were away on trading voyages, for this was the primary use of the king's fleet. They carried his own wool, skins and hides to be sold in England or the Low Countries, and were hired out to other merchants when not needed for that purpose. In wartime they would form the core of a naval fleet.

Archaeological excavation has shown that the area immediately to the east of the King's new tower at Leith was below the high water mark for several decades after it was built. At that time ships were built on stocks on the foreshore and dragged to the water when they were finished, if necessary by way of a specially dug channel. The spit of land between the tower and the town would have been an ideal place on which to build and repair ships, and launch them on a conveniently high tide. It would also have been suitable for the digging of the primitive docks in which large vessels were built.

A charter of 1439 mentions the earliest known Leith shipbuilding family, the Corntons. John of Cornton was then living in St Leonards Lands in a house which was passed down to his descendants for over a century and a half. He himself was paid £10 in 1455 as part of his fee for work on James II's ships. If he was not wholly employed at the King's Wark, he probably had a yard on the stretch of river to the south of St Leonard's lands, in the area later known as Sherrif Brae.

One problem facing the king may have been a lack of shipwrights with the necessary skills to build anything larger than a fishing boat. When more detailed information about Scottish shipbuilding becomes available, at the end of the century, one of its most striking features is that most of the technical terms used are Dutch in origin. This implies that Scottish shipwrights had learnt much of their trade from their Dutch counterparts. James I is the first Scottish king known to have positively encouraged shipbuilding, and it may be that he imported Dutch wrights to build his own vessels, who improved the skills of native tradesmen. The ships built at Leith later in the century seem still to have been quite small; barges and balingers are mentioned, of about 50 tons or less. Even smaller would be fishing vessels, and the boats which were used for unloading ships anchored in the 'Road', for coastal traffic, and as tugs and ferries.

The Freighting of Ships

One of the earliest surviving Acts of the Burgh Council of Edinburgh was passed in 1437, about the time that the King's Wark and his little fleet were completed. It concerns the freighting of ships at Leith:

> Whatever men freight any ship of Edinburgh, inward or outward, shall specify in the freighting of the ship and in the charter party that there be no good wool nor skins spakit nor shorn, no hides kept to be shorn up, nor (blank). And any master who does or allows the contrary to be done, shall lose the freight of those goods and make up the loss to the merchant in the presence of other merchants: and that no ship be freighted without these conditions being contained in the charter party, both on this side of the sea and beyond. If anyone freights either in this side of the sea or beyond, any ship, and does not specify these conditions in the charter party, he shall pay to the kirk work [St Giles] 5 nobles, without exception. It is [also] statute that anyone freighting a ship outwards shall give a sacks worth of freight [money] to St Ninian's aisle in Bruges, and anyone freighting a ship homewards shall give a tun's worth of freight money to St Giles work.

An eighteenth century drawing of Holyrood Abbey's Bridge, built in the early fifteenth century to link its properties in North and South Leith.

Trade was by now so well established with the Low Countries that a Scottish colony existed in Bruges which had erected an altar to St Ninian in the church there and supported a chaplain to say masses at it for the welfare of souls. The hazards of sea travel put sailors in particular need of this service, and they contributed to it through the toll on freight money. St Giles was being extensively rebuilt in the fifteenth century, and as it housed a plethora of chaplains, all saying mass daily, it was no doubt felt appropriate for seamen to further that work as well. As the parish church of Leith was at Restalrig, it may have caused some resentment among Leith skippers that they were made to contribute to the restoration of a church in Edinburgh.

The Bridge of Leith

In 1439, Alan de Farnley (or Fairly), burgess of Edinburgh, granted to the altar of St Ninian in the church of St Giles, 30s per annum from the rent he was paid by John of Cornton for his house 'at the end of the bridge'. Holyrood Abbey's bridge stood upstream of their harbour, its eastern end being to the south of St Leonard's Lands. This mention of it in 1439 means that it existed long before 1493, the building date previously assigned to it. Robert Logan's 1398 charter to Edinburgh had granted the town the right to build a bridge over the Water of Leith, so it seems that at this time none existed and they were intending to construct one. This would have been built upstream of the Burgh's harbour, preventing ships from coming upriver to the Abbey's harbour at St Leonard's Lands. It might also have deprived the Abbey of a source of income in ferry fares. Possibly these considerations provided a spur to the Abbey to get in first with its own bridge, which was therefore built at some time between 1398 and

1439, the Abbey collecting tolls from its users. It was a handsome edifice of three spans, which stood until it was demolished in the late eighteenth century.

James II

James I was murdered in 1439, when his son, James II was still a child. in 1449 the young king was old enough to marry, and the preparations for the wedding included the repair of a royal carvel at Leith, which was either one of James I's original fleet or had been acquired between 1437 and 1449. The ship was to sail to Flanders to bring the bride, Mary of Gueldres, to Scotland. The King's Chamberlain paid £28 5s to the carpenters who repaired the carvel, for boards, bitumen and other materials, and refunded her captain, John Matheson, £10 which he had paid out of his own pocket. Mary of Gueldres landed at Leith on 18 June 1449. It is not stated that John Matheson came from Leith, but he bore a Leith surname, and the annual pension of 20 merks which the king awarded him for his service was always paid out of the Edinburgh Great Customs. The pension was supposed to be for life, but for some unstated reason it ceased in 1469, although Matheson lived for some years after that date.

In 1458 James II had a long, low extension built onto the southern side of his tower at Leith, under the supervision of Thomas Oliphant, who was also Master of Works of Edinburgh Castle. In this year the customars of Edinburgh paid for the shipment of 10060 tiles from Dundee to the King's Work at Leith. Whether they were intended for roofing or flooring, that number of tiles would cover a large area. The picture map of 1560 shows a long building attached to the tower of the King's Wark, running parallel with the Shore. The new building occupied all the space between the tower and what is now Broad Wynd, and would have severely curtailed any shipbuilding which might be going on there. Although he continued with royal trading activities, James II was more interested in ordnance than in ships, and the new 'Work' was probably an arsenal housing his expanding store of guns of all sizes, and workshops for his smiths. It may have been in his time that the Leith smiths began to specialise in the making of firearms, which would also have been in demand for arming merchant ships.

In 1460 James was accidentally killed when he came too close to a 'bombard' which exploded while it was being fired, and Scotland once again had a child-king, James III. Three years after the death of James II, a small amount of work was done on the new building at the King's Work, and it may have been at this time that the area behind it, which was still below the high water mark, was filled in with cartloads of sand and household rubbish. If shipbuilding was to continue on the site on any scale, it would have been necessary to create a new foreshore, with ready access to the sea.

A Coin Hoard

Archaeological excavation has shown that crude stone buildings were soon constructed on the reclaimed land, presumably workshops and storehouses. In the floor of one of these sheds, at some time during the next 22 years, a local man buried his savings for safekeeping. This hoard of 358 coins, consisted mainly of Scottish pennies (placks) of James II and III. If the man had been a merchant he would have been careful to acquire plenty of foreign currency, which was far more stable and desirable than Scots money. Perhaps he was a wright or a smith, a skilled man who earned enough to be able regularly to add a few pence to his savings.

The usual reason for burying a hoard of coins was the approach of an enemy who might sack or destroy ones home. In 1481, Leith was indeed threatened in this way. Relations with England, which had been good during the first part of James III's reign, deteriorated sharply in 1480, and in the late spring or early summer of 1481, an English fleet appeared in the Forth off Leith, Kinghorn and Pittenweem, and captured eight great ships. A Scottish fleet was hastily assembled from the merchant ships in the Forth at the time. They put up a good fight, as the English only managed to land at Blackness, which they burnt. Perhaps our man took service in one of the Leith ships sent out against the English, and was killed or captured, never returning to retrieve his savings.

The Freighting of Ships

It was during the reign of James III, in 1467, that Parliament passed a statute regulating the freighting of ships. It was stipulated that no ship should be freighted without a charter party, which was to cover the following points:

1 The master should find a competent steersman, timbermen (carpenters) and crew, sufficient for the ship.
2 The master must provide his merchant passengers, at his own expense, with fire, water and salt.
3 Any dispute between master and merchant must be settled under the jurisdiction of the Burgh to which the ship was freighted. (This eliminated the possibility of staving off judgement by refusing to agree on the place where the case should be tried.)
4 If any goods were spoilt by careless stowing, the master was to lose the freight of the goods and pay compensation to the merchant.
5 Any goods stowed on the 'ourlop' (an area of raised decking forward of the mast) were not to pay freight. Goods carried under the 'ourlop' were not to be mixed with those on top in case they were spoilt.
6 Every ship freighted of more than 100 tons was to pay the Scots chaplain at Bruges one sacks worth of freight. Ships under 100 tons were to pay half a sack.
7 No 'drinksilver' (tip/bribe) was to be accepted by the master or his men.

An Edinburgh statute of 1499 describes the way in which the freighting of ships was carried out there. Although this record dates from more than 30 years after the act of Parliament it seems reasonable to assume that its provisions applied in earlier times, and so it is quoted here. It was entered in the Burgh records on the occasion of the appointment of eight freightsmen.

> When any ships are freighted, they all, or at least four of them, with the town clerk, shall sit down with the skipper and no other merchants, and do their best to freight all ships at the lowest and most reasonable prices, to the profit of all merchants. Upon the condition and freighting of each ship, the clerk shall make a charter party under his signature, the merchants having one half and the skipper the other half, containing in it all the points contained in the Act of Parliament. The Water Bailie (one of the three Edinburgh bailies, who was responsible for running the Port) shall allow no ship to sail after she is freighted until the master shows his charter party under the clerk's signature. Merchants are to pay no freight, here or beyond the sea, until the charter party is shown and the day limit observed. No merchants are to sit with the freightsmen, under pain of a fine of 8s.

The Seafaring Community

As the century progresses, and records become more plentiful, it becomes increasingly clear how the sea dominated the life of Leith. There were always two interlinked communities in the town, comprising the essentially land-based trades such as brewing, and those which depended on the sea. The restrictions on trading imposed by Leith's non-burghal status largely prevented the first group from becoming as prosperous as they might otherwise have been (although they did well enough on the whole), but the second group had opportunities that were relatively unaffected by the status of their town.

The shipbuilding Corntons became an influential family in the community, but they were not alone. By the end of the century at least five other shipbuilders appear in the records; Thomas Dais, who had a yard on the foreshore of North Leith roughly where the Old Custom House now stands, Richard Torry, John Loudon, John Brown, and Thomas McKaskey/Balcasky. Ships carpenters and shipbuilders were known as 'timbermen' which could also mean a dealer in timber - many combined both functions, and some shipbuilders were also skippers. They employed wrights, sawyers, sailmakers and general labourers, and kept the smiths of the town busy making thousands of specialised nails of all sizes, as well as all the other iron 'graith' needed on a ship or boat.

One trade that always flourished in seaports was that of the cooper. Thousands of barrels needed to be made or repaired every year to carry just about any commodity apart from wool, woollen cloth, skins and hides. Wine, vinegar, pitch, fat, dyestuffs, soap, salt, fish, grain, apples, onions, spices and oil are all mentioned as passing through Leith in barrels, and every ship needed stores of barrels of water, pickled meat and fish, and 'biscuit'.

Crews on sailing ships were comparatively large, because sufficient were needed to handle the sails, and it was necessary to have at least two 'watches'. Some of the smaller vessels, such as barges and balingers could be rowed as well as sailed. In the second half of the fifteenth century Leith ships varied in size from *Gabrielle* of 200 tons with 30 crew, which sailed to England in 1457, to *Mary* of 50 tons, with 12 crew.

Two other trades which might be forgotten are the very necessary porters and carters, who transported goods to and from the ships, although these were rather lowly occupations at which it was difficult to make more than a bare living.

At the pinnacle of the sea-related occupations were the skippers. They were important men in their own right, but if skilled enough to be employed by the Crown, could become men of wealth and influence. In the middle years of the fifteenth century the Pulti/Powty family seems to have been in such a position. Thomas Pulti was master of James I's barge which was built at Leith in 1434/5. His family must have prospered because Andrew 'Powty' of Leith owned an armed carvel in 1448. James I also granted a yearly pension of £13 6s 8d to James Johnson, who had commanded one of his ships. We have already met John Matheson who commanded the carvel sent to collect Mary of Gueldres in 1449. Like the previous Queen, Mary also had a balinger. In 1461, her master, George Abernethy, was reimbursed 50s which he had paid out for her to be repaired at Leith. The most famous of the Leith skippers in royal service, Andrew Wood and Robert Barton, belong to a later stage in this story.

Ships and Boats

The ships these men commanded were undergoing considerable development throughout the fifteenth century. The cog, which had been the typical trading vessel of the previous century, was gradually superseded by a succession of larger and faster craft. The single square sail which had been the ubiquitous rig, was augmented in the fifteenth century to improve the speed and handling of ships.

Hulks, which are mentioned in the haven silver grant of 1428, were capacious cargo-carriers which began to replace cogs from the late fourteenth century. A hulk's timbers converged fore and aft, giving it a strongly curved shape. This shape, together with the lack of a keel and stern post or transom was typical of the hulk. The method of construction of the cog meant that the size to which it could grow was finite, but hulks could be built very much larger and came to be preferred as merchant ships.

Although hulks are sometimes pictured on coins and seals as having 'castles' they are not, on the whole, typical of these vessels. Lack of 'castles' was also a feature of the early forms of the other type of trading ship which became predominant as the century wore on, the caravel or carvel, which was developed by the Portuguese, reputedly by Prince Henry the Navigator (1394-1430). Portuguese 'caravelas' were mentioned as fishing boats as early as the thirteenth century, and the first carvels were quite small, 25 - 60 tons, although they later became as large as 200 tons. They were carvel-built. i.e. the planks of the hull were laid edge to edge. The technique originated in the Mediterranean, as did the lateen (triangular) sail which typified the carvel's rig.

The earliest known picture of a multi-masted ship is of a Portuguese vessel carrying a large square mainsail, a lateen mizzen (the sail on the after-mast) and a small square foresail, which improved manoeverability. This was the typical rig of the carvel throughout the century, although some lacked the foremast, and some were entirely lateen rigged. By the end of the century some carvels had a topsail on the mainmast. One advantage of these vessels as far as Leith was concerned was their shallow draught, as little as 5ft, which made it a lot easier to get over the 'bar' which was always a problem at the entrance to the harbour. Although primarily a trading vessel, the carvel could be armed with guns, and some acquired a poop deck (a raised half-deck which made it easier to board enemy ships).

Scottish merchants probably first encountered carvels in Flanders and France, where the Portuguese also traded. They would have been attracted by the extra speed produced by the multi-sailed rig. The use of several sails meant the need for a larger crew, thus increasing costs, (the edict of James II that skippers must provide a crew sufficient for the size of the ship suggests that some were apt to cut costs by employing too few men, which could be fatal if the ship got into difficulties). However, greater speed meant that more voyages could be made in a year, and therefore a greater profit.

The first known carvel in Scottish ownership was the aforementioned armed vessel of Andrew Powty of Leith, captained by Alexander Wallace. In 1448, this ship captured Thomas Boton of Hastings, Thomas Shepherd of Winchelsea and 16 of their men, as they were fishing off Yarmouth. The captives were taken to Aberdeen, where they were imprisoned and held to ransom for 90 marks (£60). A year later they were still there, and Henry VI had to write to James II to ask for their release. (This was just one of the acts of piracy that pepper the records of the time.) Although it was in 1448 that the first actual mention of a Scottish carvel occurred, the fact that James II's carvel had to be repaired in 1449 implies that it had already seen some years of service. It might be reasonable to date the arrival of the carvel in Scotland at some time around 1445.

Carvels were not the only large craft plying to Leith, as is shown by a grant of anchorage dues to Edinburgh by James III in 1482:

Of each great ship single or double forcastled	13s 4d	(1 merk)
The secondary	10s 0d	
The middlest	6s 8d	
Caumferis	5s 0d	

The rather mysterious 'caumferis', which are the smallest vessels in the list, could be boat-types originating from Campveer (Veere) in Flanders, the principle Scottish staple port. The people of the Low Countries had developed a number of small craft to navigate their system of inland waterways, such as pinks and schouts, which are both mentioned in Scottish records of the time. A wide variety of small craft were in use in Scotland in the fifteenth century, both native types, developed in response to local conditions, and 'imports' like the kinds mentioned above. Unfortunately almost nothing is known about their individual characteristics, but they were used as fishing boats, ferry boats and coasting vessels.

Port Administration

The rather fragmentary records of the Burgh Council of Edinburgh which have survived from the fifteenth century provide an insight into the way in which the Port was administered. As well as the usual two bailies of Edinburgh, each year the Council also elected from among their number a bailie of Leith, also called the Water Bailie, who held regular courts to govern Leith affairs insofar as they affected the trade of Edinburgh. Leith was also within the jurisdiction of the Logans' barony court of Restalrig, where matters such as 'strublance' (disturbing the peace) would be dealt with. The first Water Bailie named in the Burgh records is Oswald Gilmoreson who held office in 1442, when he was ordered to uplift the toll of 2d on each boat coming into the harbour (instituted by James I in 1428), with Thomas Preston as his assistant. Initially, the Water Bailie held his court in Edinburgh, but at some time about 1490 it was thought necessary to move the venue to Leith:

> It is statute and ordained that from this time forth there be no water court held in the Burgh, but in Leith, until the time that reformation and good rule may be had and brought in upon the enormities, injuries and usurpation made by them in Leith upon the freedom of the Town. And what times and whensoever the council of the town find injuries and usurpation used upon the Town's freedom, that all neighbours (burgesses) and all deacons with their craftsmen be ready daily, when they are charged by the provost and bailies, be ready to pass with them to Leith for the holding of the water court for reforming of injuries done against their freedom, under the pain of an unlaw (fine) of 8s, to be paid and not remitted, and that the common suitors roll [register of men who were obliged to attend the court] be read in Leith and he that is absent without lawful cause to be punished by the said unlaw of 8s for each court [not attended].

Such a large assembly of burgesses was no doubt intended to have the effect of intimidating the wrongdoers of Leith, but it was also necessary to have sufficient freemen present to constitute an 'assise' or jury, without which sentence could not be passed. (Under this system of trial by a partial jury, Leithers brought to court could hardly expect a fair verdict.) 'The time that reformation and good rule may be had' was long in coming, in fact it seems that the above edict set a precedent and that the Water Court was henceforth habitually held in Leith. The merchants and craftsmen of Edinburgh seem to have tired of being continually on call to troop down to Leith in a body, and the council later decided that only sufficient were needed at each Water Court to constitute a legal assise.

Other officials concerned with Leith were the 'tacksmen' of the various dues and customs owed to Edinburgh. A 'tack' was a lease, and in effect the tacksman bought the right to collect the Burgh customs for one year, he keeping the proceeds. All the tacksmen and their officials were supposed to be burgesses of Edinburgh. In fact this was not always the case, and in 1485 the Council ordered that a burgess who collected 'any custom [may not] set them to any man of Leith, nor have any of Leith partner thereof with him, nor yet to have in service thereof under him any person dwelling in Leith'. This act has been quoted as a prohibition against taking Leithers into trading partnerships. Such prohibitions were indeed promulgated later, but this one applies solely to the collecting of the Burgh's dues. As we shall see, from the point of view of Edinburgh there were very good reasons for this statute.

The least profitable of the Leith tacks was that of the water mett, worth only 2 merks (26s 8d) in 1453. 'Mett' was the old word for a measure, the old Scots dry measures being the firlot, boll and chalder (see the table on page). The boll mett of Edinburgh was a straight sided half barrel, measuring 27.5 inches internally, 29 inches externally and 19 inches deep. The water mett was slightly smaller than this, which may be the reason why, when James I attempted to reform and standardise the measures of Scotland in 1424, he left the water mett alone:

> The water mets that now are shall remain and be used through the realm in time to come. And in each place and town where the goods are sold and met by the water, that there be ordained by the alderman and bailies a lele man sworn to measure all goods sellable by the water met, coal as well as other goods, and neither the sellers nor none on their behalf to interfere in the metting of such goods.

To increase the size of the water mett would lead to a loss of profits by merchants. James may also have had his profits from the Great Custom in mind, as he instituted the payment of custom on exported salt, and on goods imported from England, which often included grain, both salt and grain being goods measured by the water mett.

The 'lele man sworn to measure all goods sellable by the water met' was called a 'metter'. His fee at Leith was ½d per boll, he would have to mett 40 chalders (80 tons) of goods in order to earn the two merks which was the value of the tack. The annual figure was almost certainly higher, however, as the tacksman would have to pay the metter and make a profit on his outlay.

More lucrative was the custom on goods coming in by ship to be sold in Edinburgh, and on goods of foreigners and unfreemen exported at Leith. This duty was initially called the 'petty haven silver' but by the end of the century was known as the 'wild adventures', the tacksman being called the 'farmer of the wild adventures'. (Later times knew him as the more prosaic 'collector of shore dues'.) This custom was worth 33 merks in 1458, 420 merks in 1480 and 260 merks in 1493, (mirroring the decline in trade at the end of the century). The Farmer of the Wild Adventures was supposed to carry out his business in the Edinburgh Tolbooth, but it was obviously more convenient to work down at Leith, and in 1496, the Farmer had to be reminded by the Council that the Tolbooth should be the scene of his labours.

The tacksmen of the customs employed their own staff to help them, and like all such officials were kept busy searching out 'undeclared' goods. This was no doubt the reason for the rule of 1485 that no man of Leith might be employed by a tacksman. Leithers, even if they were not actually the offenders themselves, would be more likely to abet than to betray defaulters.

Trade in Leith

Perhaps the most unexpected of all the dues is the 'Petty Custom of Leith', first mentioned in the Council records in 1453. Petty custom was the toll paid on goods coming to a Burgh market. The petty custom of Leith was completely separate from the petty custom of Edinburgh, collected by a different official, and it is quite clear from the records that it comprises the dues paid on goods sold in Leith itself. In 1458 the tack of the Leith petty custom was worth 22 merks (in the same year the petty custom of Edinburgh was worth 62 merks), in 1480 it was 175 merks (Edinburgh 116 merks) and in 1493, 115 merks (Edinburgh also 115 merks). As with the petty haven silver, these figures reflect the late-century decline in trade.

In view of all the stern edicts issued by the Edinburgh council over the years, on the subject of trading in Leith, it comes as something of a surprise to learn that not all goods were carted up to the market in Edinburgh. In fact as the volume of goods passing through the port increased it must have become obvious that to do so was a waste of effort and money. Foreign goods were supposed to be sold only in the market place at Edinburgh, so the market in Leith was officially confined to dealings by Scots. The following list of goods owing petty custom details the commodities involved; and shows that 'unfreemen' might sell their produce in Leith, as was usual in an official burgh market. Imports would be sold by merchant burgesses, but they were not allowed to open shops anywhere but in Edinburgh. In fact it would seem that the market in Leith was regarded as an extension of those in Edinburgh.

On each barrel of tar sold to unfreemen - likewise on all barrel goods.	2d
Each load of onions, apples, corn and other goods that are sold to unfreemen and mett (measured) in Leith.	1d
Each load unmett	1s 2d
Each load of white fish or herring	1d
Each 100 great fish not barrelled - keeling, stockfish, salmon	4d
Each chalder of corn of unfreemen that comes from the North or other parts of the country	8d
Each boat that comes into the haven with coal or lime	1s 2d
Each 100 boards from the northlands	8d
Each load of salt, butter, cheese and similar goods	1d
Each great dormond (joist)	1s 2d
12 joists	4d
100 spars	8d
100[lb] weight of unfreemans iron	8d
Each daker (10) of unfreemens hides from the North	2d

100 woolfells, goatskins, calf, kid or rabbit skins that do not come to the Town (ie Edinburgh) 4d

This list is undated, although there is some evidence that it may have been made in 1468. Notable omissions from it are wine, fabrics and spices; foreign goods which would have been sold in the booths of the merchant burgesses of Edinburgh. One rather surprising inclusion is corn. The sale of staple foods was subject to strict procedures, designed to prevent hoarding and to keep prices reasonable. Thus it had been enacted by Edinburgh Council as early as 1436:

> After the coming in of any ship entered in the tolbooth with wheat, meal, rye, malt, bere or any other victual, the alderman [provost], bailies and council buy this victual at as reasonable a price as they can, and then distribute by two distributors competent to answer for their deeds, to the people of the town. If any take on hand to buy this victual for a higher price than is bid for it in the tolbooth, without consent of the alderman etc, the people shall have it for the same price that was bid for other of similar quality in the tolbooth. The buyers shall pay the higher price to the merchant and lose their freedom for a year.

Loss of 'freedom' did not mean imprisonment, but it was probably an even worse penalty, as it meant the merchant had his burgess privileges withdrawn and could not trade for as long as the punishment lasted. Such a penalty was only imposed for very grave misdemeanours. The 'distributors' mentioned in the statute ensured that no purchaser bought more than was needed for his own household or trade. The statute only applied to victual 'entered in the Tolbooth', ie the goods of foreigners, who were bound to pay their dues to the Farmer of the Wild Adventures. Native Scots could sell directly in Leith and pay Petty Custom there.

A Council statute of 1439 implies that corn was sold in Leith only under strict supervision:

> Whoso brings victual to Leith shall be welcome to sell their victual as they best may, and house it if they wish, but the searcher (a customs official) shall see what goods of victual come into the haven, and whosoever addresses themselves to buy that victual shall swear that they shall not buy more than may suffice to the dispenses of their household, and that thereof they shall not sell again for profit, and searchers shall each day certify the governance of Leith, and one of the three Bailies shall labour hereupon in Leith.

In 1479, perhaps as a result of shortages, the Council enacted that all victual must be sold only in Edinburgh. It would initially be bought by the Provost and Bailies on behalf of the community and only after that could it be resold, at a price fixed by the Council. Any that was to be resold in Leith would be taken down there by a bailie, two of the Council and a clerk. This matter was not mentioned subsequently in the Council records, so it may have been purely an 'emergency measure' passed in a time of shortage. A charter of James II granted three years later, in 1482, confirming the Customs of the harbour of Leith to Edinburgh, mentions corn in its list of goods which might be sold in Leith:

Item, of freemen of other burghs buying any goods in Leith to have away, to pay at the outpassing	4d per tun
Of each tun of goods sold in Leith by freemen to freemen or unfreemen, passing outwards	4d from the buyer
Each barrel of tar, pitch, ash or any other barrel goods sold there (Leith) to unfreemen	2d
Of each load of onions, apples, corn, butter, cheese or other goods met and sold in Leith to unfreemen to be had away	1d
And of each load unmet	1s 2d

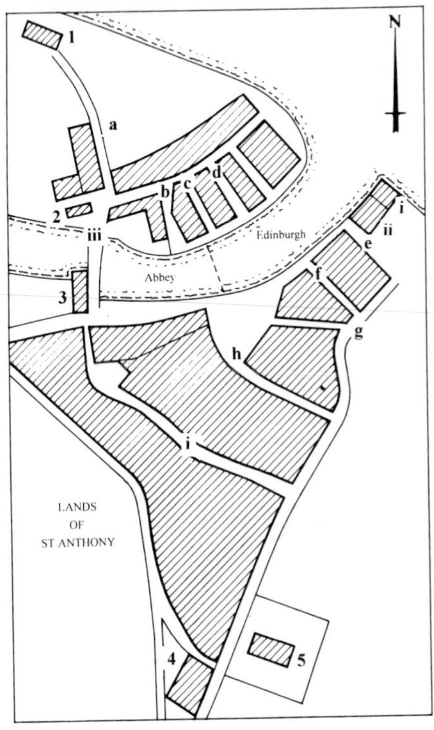

Plan of Leith at the end of the fifteenth century, showing the growth of the town. St Anthony's lands were built over after the Reformation (1560), but the town did not expand much eastward until the mid-seventeenth century.

1 St Nicholas Chapel
2 St Ninian's Chapel 1493
3 House built by Abbey 1493
4 St Anthony's Preceptory 1430
5 St Mary's Church 1483

i First phase of King's Wark 1428
ii Second phase of King's Wark 1458
iii Bridge built by Holyrood Abbey - early 14th cent

a St Nicholas Wynd
b Broad Wynd, North Leith
c Short's Wynd
d Sea Wynd
e Broad Wynd, South Leith
f Burgess Close
g Rotten Row
h High Street
i Dub Row

The marketplace itself was probably the triangular area now bounded by the Shore, the western end of Tolbooth Wynd, and Queen Street. As we have already seen, the market may date from the time when Leith consisted of two distinct blocks of property. The linking row of tofts which grew up along the line of the present Queen Street was set at an angle, to leave a clear space which thus acquired a triangular shape. As far as the surviving records show, it was not until the early sixteenth century that Edinburgh began to forbid the selling of native goods in Leith, and it was presumably at this time that the market began to decline and the open space to be built over. However, when Leith acquired its own Tolbooth in 1565, it was built at the apex of the triangle, and the street in front of it was still used as a Fleshmarket three centuries later. Dairy products were sold at the Bridgend by St Leonard's Lands, which was still on land not owned by Edinburgh.

Foreign Goods

The procedure for declaring imports for payment of the Wild Adventures and harbour dues depended largely on the honesty of the skippers, and might almost have been designed to be evaded. When a ship came into port the skipper was supposed to go straight up to the tolbooth in Edinburgh and enumerate the contents of his cargo to the Town clerk, who entered them in his book. He was then free to unload, while the Town treasurer calculated the dues owing by the merchants who owned the goods or by their factors. The skipper paid the anchorage dues, which he reclaimed from the owners of the ship. The Burgh tolbooth was, of course, the official place for the transaction of business, and in any Burgh which was itself a seaport the official system probably worked well enough, but in the case of Edinburgh, the physical separation of her officials from the cargoes they were supposed to be overseeing was a far from satisfactory situation. It is hard to understand why the Burgh did not establish some kind of Town Clerk's office on the Shore, thus making the collecting of dues infinitely more efficient.

The Great Custom

In 1493, Parliament tried to curb the evasion of Great Custom, specifically mentioning Leith as a trouble spot. The statement of the problem which was recorded in the minutes, shows how easy it was to evade dues of any kind:

> For the defraud done to our Sovereign Lord in his customs, by strangers and aliens of other realms, who come to this realm and take their lodging and inns in the town of Leith and at other ports of the realm, and charge their goods and other merchandise to the sea, not paying their customs and duties to our Sovereign Lord, because they are unentered, nor their merchandise shown to the custumars and clerks of the coket.

The subsequent law stated that aliens must lodge only in the principal town of the port (Edinburgh, in the case of Leith) and that if they left without paying custom the innkeeper would be liable for the debt! There is no evidence that this unworkable statute was ever put into effect.

Ferrymen

Parliament also enacted a series of laws regulating the activities of ferrymen, who seem to have been a fine set of scoundrels. They do not specifically mention the ferrymen of the Forth, but these men effectively controlled the main land routes from the North to Edinburgh, and no doubt used their power to maximise their profits. A weary traveller arriving at Burntisland, for instance, and faced with the choice of paying an exorbitant ferry fare or making a laborious detour via Stirling bridge, was really in no position to argue. At intervals throughout the century, parliament considered allegations that ferry operators were charging as much as four times the official fare. No doubt the debate was carried on with extra vehemence by members from the North who had recently been charged these exorbitant rates in order to cross to Leith and attend the sitting. Acts were passed, but with little obvious effect.

Another aspect of ferry operations concerned the shipment of travellers' horses. On several occasions Parliament ordered ferrymen to provide gang-planks, so that horses could be more safely loaded onto their boats. If this was not done there was a high risk of the animals sustaining injuries as they attempted to scramble aboard. The very idea of an unconfined horse being transported in an open boat is somewhat startling at the present day, but was common practice in the Northern and Western Isles well into living memory.

The End of the Reign of James III

The reign of James III is not remembered as a high spot in the history of Scotland, in fact he was possibly her most unpopular king. Like David II and James IV he took a great interest in the arts, but unlike them, he was not energetic in government and the dispensation of justice. He was also accused of having low-born favourites. Consequently he forfeited the respect of a large number of his nobles. His reign coincided with a general decline in British trade with Europe whose most damaging aspect was the drop in the demand for wool, which had been the bedrock of Scotland's prosperity. James and his Parliament tried to deal with this situation by successive devaluations of the currency, which, necessary though they may have been, did nothing for his popularity. In 1481 things became so bad that he was actually imprisoned for a while in Edinburgh castle, and in 1488 an insurrection arose with his son James, the heir to the throne, as its figurehead. The Prince established his 'court' at Linlithgow, where it was gradually swelled by desertions from Edinburgh, until the King was left virtually alone and surrounded in his Castle. His escape brings into our story one of Leith's most famous sons - Andrew Wood.

Andrew Wood is believed to have been born in Largo around 1460, but as an adult he lived in Leith. He owned a large block of property in the southwest corner of North Leith, comprising houses, barns, a kiln and a garden containing either a plane or a sycamore tree, both being 'exotics' in medieval Scotland. His two ships, *Flower* and *Yellow Carvel* traded to the continent, and he was in the service of James III who granted him land in Largo in 1483 and knighted him a few years later. This reward was a distinct improvement on the annual pensions granted by previous monarchs to the captains of their ships. James III was later heavily criticised by his detractors for favouring 'low born' men. These accusations, when applied to some specific individuals, have been shown to be exaggerated, but perhaps he was the first Scottish monarch to truly appreciate the services of his more humble subjects. In 1488, after the desertion of his court, James escaped on one of Sir Andrew's ships, which lay in Leith ready to sail to Flanders. It took the king, however, to Fife where he raised an army from among his northern subjects, who were more loyal to him. They marched to Blackness, and Sir Andrew shipped them supplies and reinforcements through the harbour there. A period of skirmishes and inconclusive negotiations produced no result except the loss of some supporters. The king withdrew to Edinburgh, while Sir Andrew's ships patrolled the Forth. Once again they helped him to reach Fife, and this time the army he raised there came to a conclusive engagement at Sauchieburn, not far from Stirling and very close to the field of Bannockburn. Prince James displayed the Royal Standard, and by the end of the day had true entitlement to it, for his father was killed as he tried to escape from the field of battle to the safety of one of Sir Andrew's ships.

Thus began the reign of one of Scotland's most remarkable kings; one who always carried with him a reminder of the manner of its beginning. For the rest of his life, it is said, James IV wore an iron belt next to his skin, in penance for his part in the downfall of his father.

3

A Fleet, A Factor and Notary Young

The reign of James IV may be thought of as Scotland's golden age. Like the later Elizabeth I of England, James possessed a personal magnetism which still casts about him and his reign an almost impenetrable aura of glittering triumph. He was one of the few Stewart monarchs who was adult, or nearly (15 years old), at the time of his accession, and also one of the few who could successfully manage a traditionally fractious nobility. It was this skill which helped him to weather the storms of the first couple of years after his accession, during which the faction which deplored the manner of it was brought to accept the status quo.

For most of his reign the king also had the advantage of a peaceful neighbour south of the Border. Henry VII was almost unique among monarchs in seeing no point in wasting good money on warmongering. It was not until his son, Henry VIII came to the throne in 1509 that there was any real threat from England.

James was an energetic and charismatic young man, who threw himself enthusiastically into every enterprise he undertook. These enterprises were legion, as he took an interest in a wide variety of activities. His curiosity about the natural world led him to establish a menagerie at Holyrood, but also, distastefully to us, a collection of human 'specimens' at court. As well as the dwarves and fools which were at that time kept in every noble household, the king had a band of African dancers and a pair of Siamese twins, joined from the waist down. This insensitivity was typical of the age, but with James it did not extend to his own poorer subjects. He gave alms generously and rewarded any poor man or woman who brought him a gift, however small, or performed a service for him. The peasant girls who sang and danced for him as he journeyed through his domains could be sure of largesse.

The king was a great sportsman, shooting with bow and arrow and gun, and holding regular tournaments on Shrove Tuesday each year. The most spectacular tournament ever seen in Scotland was held by James IV, and it was typical of him that the lady in whose honour it was fought was a negress. Dancing was a favourite indoor occupation of his time, and on at least one occasion James rewarded his African drummer for devising a new dance, from which we might infer that he favoured a vigorous style. When forced to sit still he played cards and other games of chance.

By the lights of his own times he was also very pious. We might have reservations about applying such a description to man who planned his pilgrimages to include a visit to his latest mistress, and went to great lengths to obtain the revenues of bishoprics for his (non-ordained) illegitimate sons. However, he was only following the teaching of the church at the time, which held that the way to heaven led via religious exercises such as attendance at Mass, confession and going on pilgrimage. Giving to the poor was important, but the sums expended on charity were far exceeded by donations to chaplains to say masses for ones soul. This was hardly surprising as each mass was thought to shorten the soul's stay in painful Purgatory. Church appointments were seen mainly as a path to enrichment, and were sought by the supposedly celibate clergy for their own sons. The heretical Lollards had already challenged the practices and beliefs of the church but they menaced too many vested interests to be accepted by the establishment, and within a generation, Protestantism would be discouraged by burning its adherents alive.

James gave money to the church and to the poor with great openhandedness, was meticulous about performing his personal devotions, and was an enthusiastic pilgrim. There was a kind of 'league table' of pilgrimages. The apogee was a journey to Rome, or the shrine of St James at Compostella, these counted for many centuries remission of the pains of purgatory, but one could accumulate equivalent benefits by repeated journeys to lesser shrines. James was restricted to the confines of Scotland to fulfill his quota, and his favoured destinations were the church of St Ninian at Whithorn, and the shrine of St Duthac at Tain. He also paid many visits to the Shrine of St Triduana at Restalrig, and made his devotions at the church of any region in which he might be staying.

Considering all the activities he pursued in his personal life, one might be forgiven for wondering if James ever had time to spare for official business. In fact, he was a very successful ruler, fulfilling all the kingly functions that were expected of him with seemingly effortless ease. His frequent journeys around the country were not undertaken purely for pleasure, although he was well entertained on the way by his subjects, both high and lowly. He personally dispensed justice in the regions he visited and was accessible to his subjects of whatever degree. His general popularity helped him financially as well. During his reign, Scotland was more highly taxed than it had ever been. Former kings had tried in vain to get Parliament to agree to taxations which had often been for very good and necessary purposes. James, it seems, had only to ask and the money poured in.

The Beginnings of the Scottish Navy

One of the reasons why he needed money was that England had ceased tearing herself apart in the Wars of the Roses and the defence of his realm was once more a matter of some importance. Although Henry VII was peaceful, there was no knowing when he might be superseded. The Borders had traditionally been well defended, but Scotland was very vulnerable to attack by sea. Increasingly, the wealth of the nation was coming to be concentrated in Edinburgh, which presented a soft target for a seaborne force. However, the first vessel James had built was destined to serve in the West.

At the Parliament of May 1493, the troublesome Lord of the Isles had been forfeited, and his domains annexed to the crown. Later that summer the king paid his first visit to the Western Isles to assess how they might best be brought under his control. As a result, Tarbert, a castle built by Robert the Bruce, was repaired and garrisoned and a new castle erected at what is now Campbeltown.

There was an obvious need for a naval force base in the Clyde, and in the autumn a start was made on assembling a small fleet. Initially the king's ship the *Christopher* was to be repaired and a new barge built, at Dumbarton.

On the advice of the king's Comptroller and Treasurer, and Master Alexander Inglis of Leith, six Leith shipbuilders were hired to undertake the work. George Cornton and Richard Torry were the foremen, each receiving 5s a day. Roger Cornton and John Loudon were each paid 4s, and John Brown and Thomas McCasky (or Balcasky), 3s. They worked a six-day week, and the accounts carefully detail their exact pay:

> The above workmen started building the barge on September 8th (1493) continuing to March 25th (1494), in which time there are 28 weeks. Of which there is to be deducted 2 weeks of the time of Yule (holidays were unpaid) and to be deducted for other holy days in the rest of the time, 9 days. So remains to be paid for 23 weeks and 3 days clear, which comes to £176 8s.

It has been said that it was James IV who initiated shipbuilding at Leith, but the fact that the town could provide six men capable of building a sizeable barge in 1493 confirms that the craft had been pursued in the town for many years before that time. The shipbuilding Cornton family had been settled at the Port from at least 1439, and by the end of the century were the Robbs of their time. It seems that it was James I who initiated shipbuilding in Leith, probably upgrading the skills of exsisting builders of fishing boats. James IV took the process one stage further by introducing Leith shipbuilders to the techniques of building vessels larger than about 50 tons.

The king's Master of Works, sir George Galbraith, took charge at Dumbarton (sir George was the sub-dean of St Andrews - 'sir' being a courtesy title given to clergy who had not taken a Masters degree). Although the skilled shipwrights came from Leith, the rest of the workforce was hired locally. The first task was to 'fell, square and dight (prepare)' timber in the woods around Loch Lomond. One William Clemy spent four weeks at this work, helped by seven other wrights who each worked six days. They were all paid 1s a day. When a batch of timber was ready, five or six wrights would make a boat trip up the river Lieven to fetch it, taking provisions with them. The logs were towed behind the boat, and on two occasions the rope broke and a new one had to be fetched from Dumbarton. Altogether, nine trips of between three and five days were made to the Loch, including one to Inch Caillach. One was made to Sallach for eight trees, and one to Luss for 40 feet of boards.

The barge was being built on stocks in a waterside yard belonging to one Robin Atyen, and once the logs arrived at Dumbarton from Loch Lomond they were dragged onto dry land, where four wrights shaped the 'great timbers' (ribs and keel). Twentyfive pairs of sawyers worked for eight weeks in their sawpits, making the planking. Even after all this, there was not enough timber for the work. A wreck was raised at Dumbarton and its timbers were dismantled, dried off over a fire of heather and bracken and reshaped. In September, 260 boards were bought at Leith and transported to Glasgow in five carts, then presumably being floated over to Dumbarton. The following month, 300 more boards were bought locally. The fact that the frame of 'great timbers' was assembled first suggests that the barge was carvel-built.

By October the work was sufficiently far advanced for waterproofing materials to be needed - two barrels of tar, two of pitch (tar which had been boiled to make it thicker) and one of rosin, with a rubber for applying the tar.

Apart from timber, the other main requirement was for nails and other iron 'graith' (equipment). Most of this was made by the smith John Lamb of Leith, (who was also James' chief Scottish gunsmith). In September, John made 300 nails and seven stone of iron work. Twelve stone more of iron was sent to Dumbarton, and another 12 stone was taken there by a smith of Leith or Edinburgh called Edward. In December John Lamb went to Dumbarton himself, an anvil was bought for him and a smithy set up on site. He worked there until at least 7 February, along with Edward and another smith called Stene. Much of the metal they used was Spanish iron, bought at Glasgow. From it they fashioned a variety of boatbuilding materials; some familiar, such as chains, bolts, rivets and collars, and some most definitely strange, such as single and double buspikers, yong frows and seme nails.

The rest of the gear was bought from various merchants, most of them Leithers. John Logan supplied a great mast, topmast, 'top' (lookout post at the top of the mast, usually made by a cooper), rigging and a pump. Lord Bothwell donated another mast. One small mast was bought from James Wood, and another from James Tait of Ayr 'at the command of the king'. Sails, both for the barge and the *Christopher* were made from 300 ells of canvas bought from James Fairley of Edinburgh. Needles and sail thread cost 12s. The Abbot of Cambuskenneth donated three bonnets (extra pieces added to the bottom of a sail to increase its area in light winds). For the barge and the boats, 68 oars were bought from Sir Andrew Wood, Peter Falconer and William Todrig (there were two William Todrigs at the time, one was a skipper who lived in Leith and the other was a wealthy Edinburgh burgess who married the king's cousin in 1507), and carried to Dumbarton in three carts.

William Forster supplied three anchors, an enormous cleat weighing 84lb, for attaching the main yard to the mast, was bought from Thomas Rugy, and ropes and cables from Henry Rugy, William Forster and Robert Barton. It seems that the labours of three smiths were not sufficient, as 1900 more nails had to be bought; more buspikers of both kinds, dur (door) nails, baulk nails and bodwin nails, along with 4 stone of rivets and seme nails. The number of merchants involved seems high, but this is because individuals did not have sufficient capital to lay in large stocks of merchandise, and a large requirement could only be met by piecemeal purchasing. Most of the Leith merchants mentioned above were ship-owners or skippers who had brought the goods, especially ropes, sail canvas and anchors, from Flanders.

Once the barge was finished her seams were caulked with moss and she was 'tallowed' below the water-line with dripping (tallow usually means mutton fat), melted in a cauldron bought for the purpose and applied with bundles of thrums (short woolen or linen threads left over from weaving, which were probably tied to sticks to make mops). The barge was launched by dragging her to the water down a specially dug channel.

Tallowing, which was part of the routine maintainance of a vessel, acted as a form of anti-fouling, discouraging the buildup of wood-boring organisms on the ship's bottom. A ship which had been in the water would be singed before tallowing, with a fire of heather, to dry her timbers and help remove seaweed and barnacles.

Altogether, the building of two small boats, the barge and the repairing of the *Christopher* employed a workforce of 6 shipbuilders, 12 wrights, 50 sawyers and 3 smiths, not to mention the various carters, porters and boatmen involved in transporting materials. It is not surprising that 17 years later, when James came to build the enormous *Michael*, he had to employ 'all the wrights of Scotland' and many foreigners as well.

This record gives us a unique insight into the way in which shipbuilders of the time went about their work. The main difference between this Royal commission and the building of vessels for private individuals probably lies in the sources of timber. As there is no record of payment for the wood cut in the forests of Loch Leven, these presumably belonged to the king, and royal forests would provide much of the timber for the king's own ships. Great magnates would be able to draw on their own estates in a similar way. Lesser men would largely depend on timber imported from abroad, possibly supplemented by sound wood from dismantled wrecks. There may have been limited commercial sources of native timber, but this could only be transported at a reasonable cost from forests near a large water course. It is possible that shipbuilding and repair at the port contributed to the early buildup of timber imports to Leith from the Baltic and Scandinavia.

The Conservator

In 1493, the same year that the king was beginning to assemble his navy in the west, a man named Andrew Haliburton was also starting a new venture. He was a Scottish merchant living in Campveere in the Low Countries. A man of some substance, he also owned a house in 'Bery' (Bergen op Zoom) which was looked after by a housekeeper called Belkin. In 1493 he began a new Ledger containing copies of his accounts, which ran until 1503. It contains many details of the way in which merchants conducted their business, and gives us valuable information about Leith shipping of the time. In it we can trace the building up of a group of merchants to whom Andrew acted as a 'factor' or agent, receiving the goods they sent from Scotland, selling them in Flanders or Holland, and buying and shipping home to them merchandise for sale in the booths and markets of Edinburgh.

At the core of his clientele was a circle of Edinburgh merchants, most of them connected by a complex web of blood relationships, marriages and partnerships. At the heart of the circle were the Carkettle and Cant families, who had been prominent in Edinburgh since at least the beginning of the fifteenth century, and continued to flourish well into the sixteenth, when some Cants had become influential Leithers. The Carkettles seem to have been particularly prolific, and only one branch of the family was connected with Andrew Haliburton. Altogether it has been possible to find some interconnection for all but two of Andrew's main Edinburgh clients.

To trace Andrew's dealings in detail, fascinating though this would be, is outside the scope of this book, which must mainly concern itself with the light he casts on merchants in general and Leith shipping in particular. However, it is worth outlining the first few years covered by his Ledger, as it illustrates the way in which a factor abroad might build up his circle of clients.

In June 1493 he made a voyage home to Edinburgh in the *Flower*, the king's ship which had been commanded by Sir Andrew Wood. With him he took some money and breviaries (prayerbooks) which Master James Cumyng of Antwerp had entrusted to him. (The title 'Master' denoted the holder of a Masters degree.) Andrew sold the books in Scotland and on his return to the Low Countries in October, he visited James in Antwerp to give him the money. This seems to have marked the beginning of their association, which lasted until 1499. During that time, Andrew acted as banker to James, and they traded jointly in books, bere, sheepskins and wool. The partnership ended, as did several of Andrew's ventures, in an acrimonious dispute, of which the details are unfortunately not given.

During his visit home, Andrew also went into partnership with his sister Helen's second husband, the merchant Lawrence Telfer. They bought jointly, a sack of skins and eight sacks of wool. If earlier Scots merchants had tended to entrust their goods to one well-armed ship, by this time they had learnt the wisdom of distributing their merchandise between several vessels. Andrew and Lawrence put four sacks of wool in *Flower*, two sacks in William Peterson's ship, and the other two sacks and the sack of skins in James Mackeson's. William Peterson may have been from Dundee or Aberdeen, but James Mackeson was a Leith skipper.

In this first year of 'factoring', Andrew also sold three bags of wool and seven steiks of cloth (one of them moth-eaten) for James Turing, one of the customars of Edinburgh, and a dealer in luxury fabrics, furs, embroidery silks and gold thread. Andrew supplied him with some cheap fur and mundane fabrics - which may be the reason why this was the full extent of their dealings.

John Tweedie seems to have been acting as factor for several Scots, including the Archdeacon of St Andrews, when he fell ill at Middleburgh in November 1493. Andrew defrayed his expenses until he died the following May at the Haliburton house in Bergen op Zoom. After this, Andrew acted for his widow in settling his affairs in the Low Countries. It seems that the John Tweedie was a personal friend rather than a client, and it may have been from him that Andrew 'inherited' the business of the Archdeacon.

John Whitehead may also have been a friend. Between 1493 and 1495 Andrew supplied him with a few personal items: velvet, lawn, figs, wine and a 'bag iron'. (This last was a metal frame, sometimes of gold, to which fabric could be sewn to make a bag. It was probably very similar to the articles still sold in craft shops for the same purpose.) Andrew also laid a tun of woad in pledge with a Flemish banker for a sum of £10 which John Whitehead owed the bank.

Andrew's dealings in 1493 would hardly have brought in enough money to maintain two houses. He must have had private business ventures which were recorded in another book, (probably the 'Journal' or daybook mentioned several times in the Ledger). It is possible that he may not even have set out to be a factor in the first place. However, in 1494, an event occured that almost pushed him into his extra career. His cousin, John Carkettle, was married to Janet Paterson, daughter of his uncle John, a wealthy Edinburgh merchant. John Carkettle was acting as factor for his uncle when he died in Bruges in Februaury of that year. Before he died he handed a purse over to Andrew, in the presence of John Cant (son of Thomas Cant, one of John Paterson's partners) and Mr John Bary, who was possibly in attendance to take down the dying man's testament. In the purse was money belonging to John Paterson, illustrating very well the variety of foreign coinage commonly used by Scottish merchants at the time, much of which was in circulation in Scotland. There were:

31 ducats	2 Flemish rydars	1 1/4 Harry nobles
6 Horne postilats	1 Utrecht gulden	1 demy
2 1/2 angels	1 Ongres ducat	2 French crowns
1/2 a testoun	1 rose noble	1 gulden
1 Ghent gulden	2 parts of a salut	50 Byres guldens and Georges

In Flemish money this totalled £23 2s 8d grete, about £77 scots.

John Paterson was a substantial Edinburgh merchant who had supplied the Royal Household with fine fabrics and furs since at least 1474. Andrew's association with him lasted until John's death in 1497. At least four of Andrew's clients were partners of John Paterson - Thomas Cant and George Tours were both major suppliers of the Royal Household; Alexander Lauder, the second husband of Janet Paterson, was Provost of Edinburgh from 1501 until 1513, when he fell at Flodden; Walter Chapman was married to a Carkettle and was a clerk to the king. He is chiefly remembered, however, for being partner to Andrew Myllar in setting up the first printing press in Scotland, in 1507.

Another early client of Andrew's was Robert Rynd. Their association began in 1493 in dramatic circumstances:

The night he left for Calais I sent Rowll (skipper of a merchant ship) after him with a bill to warn of the Lombard that was set to arrest him at Gravelines,

which Rowll cost me	- 5s grete
Paid to the barber's son to convey him by night	- 12d grete
Given for drink silver to let them out at the gates of Bruges after 10 pm	- 6d grete

The rest of their business that year was prosaic enough. Andrew sent Robert six bag irons, and they went shares in two pipes of teazles (used to raise a nap on woollen fabrics) which Andrew sent to Scotland. Andrew continued his factor until 1497.

From the end of 1495 onwards, Andrew Haliburton's Edinburgh clientelle increased in number, peaking in November 1496, when he acted for 11 merchants. One reason for this may be found in events in Scotland at the time, and the origin of these must be sought in happenings south of the Border. The disappearance of the 'Princes in the Tower' has been one of the most debated mysteries in English history, at least for those who do not accept that they were murdered by order of their wicked uncle, Richard III. Henry VII had, of course, himself dealt with Richard at Bosworth Field, married the sister of the Little Princes and settled down to bring a sorely needed peace to England. However, as the bodies of the Princes had not been found, remaining supporters of their house of York tried to erect two pretenders to the English throne during Henry's reign.

One of these was Perkin Warbeck, a native of Tournai, who was 'discovered' when he went to Ireland in the service of a Breton trader in 1491. Whether for some political reason, or just to tease the king of England, James decided to acknowledge him. He received the 'Prince' with honour and in January 1496 married him to his own cousin, Lady Catherine Gordon, at Holyrood. The wedding celebrations were lavish, and included an elaborate tournament. The king and his court ordered a large quantity of new clothes in the latest fashions. The limited resources of the Edinburgh merchants must have been over-stretched that winter, as orders poured in for velvet, damask, satin, taffeta, fine lawn, and embroidery silks and gold thread. They also supplied wine, spices and dried fruit for all the extra private and commercial catering which was needed for visitors to the celebrations.

It was not until the following spring that they were able to set about preparing to replenish their stocks. The traditional time for the Flemish weavers to buy Scottish wool was in early summer, when they made the journey to the Burgh markets of the Low Countries. Scots merchants depended on selling in those markets to raise cash to buy new stock. In May 1496 Andrew began to receive his clients' wool (40 sacks in all) to sell in the markets of the Low Countries They seem to have relied on other factors to buy the goods they needed. Thomas Cant, for instance, had supplied the king with silk fabrics worth £263 3s, including 13 ells of white damask for the wedding gown of the 'Prince'. His son John came to the Low Countries to buy more goods in the summer of 1496, lodging at Andrew's house in Bergen op Zoom.

For the next two years, until it was reduced to a trickle by an outbreak of the Plague, Andrew's Edinburgh business flourished. We can trace from his ledger the movements of a number of Leith ships and skippers. In a typical year each ship made two voyages to the Low Countries port of Middleburgh, and stayed about six weeks to unload and load up again. At least 36 vessels can be distinguished in the Ledger, and of those 19 belong either to the king, an Edinburgh burgess or an inhabitant of Leith, and have Leith as their home port. Many of the rest are mentioned only in the Plague years, when Andrew dealt almost exclusively with Aberdeen/Dundee merchants.

Leith Ships and Skippers

From the Ledger and other contemporary sources we can distinguish eighteen Leith skippers who were operating in the last decade of the fifteenth century.

Robert Barton	Gilbert Edmondston	David White
Andrew Barton	James Mackeson	David Croole
John Barton	John Irwin	William Todrig
Andrew Wood	John Stairhead	John Hopper
James Wood	George Cornton jnr	David Gourlay
William Wood	William Paterson	William Gray

The Woods and the Bartons are well-known, well documented, and much chronicled, but the others all have their story, and some were of equal importance at the time.

Gilbert Edmondston was a close friend of Robert Barton. They and their wives stood godparents to each others' children, and after Gilbert died early in the next century, Robert married his widow. In October 1493, Edinburgh brought a complaint before the Lords of Council against Gilbert and five other Leith skippers; David White, William Wood, George Cornton jnr, John Stairhead and David Croole. They were accused of two-years nonpayment of anchorage, customs and duties of their ships and goods, for which the punishment was the escheating of the uncustomed goods, half to the king and half to Edinburgh. The Provost was given until the following February to produce evidence that the goods had been imported and exported as alleged, and no duty paid on them. No more is heard of the case, so either the evidence could not be brought, or the miscreants paid up.

This is not the only source to indicate that Leith skippers were importing goods on their own account, which, as unfreemen, they should, in theory, have been barred from doing. However, in the course of a much later court case, it emerged that 'from time immemorial' skippers had received part of their freight money from impecunious merchants, in the form of trading goods. They were also allowed to fill up empty spaces in the ship's hold with goods of their own, in order to make a voyage more profitable. This was all the more important to the many skippers who were part-owners of the ships they commanded. Ships' crews also had a share in these 'perks'.

Gilbert Edmondston himself was sufficiently prosperous to become landlord of a property on the south side of Edinburgh High Street (Thomas Carkettle was one of his neighbours). In 1499 he gave 12 merks a year from its rent, for the upkeep of a chaplain to say masses at the altar of St Barbara (patron saint of gunners) in the church of St Mary in Leith. Among the witnesses to this gift of Gilbert Edmondston were two other Leith skippers who are frequently mentioned in Andrew Haliburton's ledger, John Irwin and James Mackeson.

John Irwin was skipper of the king's ship the *Christopher* which we have already encountered being refitted at Dumbarton in 1493. John chartered the ship from the king for £100 a year, which suggests that he expected to make a considerable profit on each voyage. Sometimes, however, he had trouble paying. Once he could only manage £60, and once he had to pay in kind - a bolt of black Rysills (Lille) cloth worth only about £30. In 1496 the *Christopher* was in the Western Isles in the king's service, but she still managed to fit in two voyages to the Low Countries, one in April/May /June and the other in November. She was still in service in 1502, when she formed part of a fleet sent by James to support the Danes against the Swedes. In 1496 John Irwin bought a piece of waste land in Broad Wynd, North Leith . It had still not been built on by 1514, so perhaps he used it to store bulky goods such as wood

Another royal ship was the bark/barque (caravel) *Douglas*. She was leased to James Wood for £45 a voyage, round trip. Like John Irwin, James had to pay in kind on one occasion - two bolts of tawny Rouen cloth. However, this occured in 1498, when the Plague was playing havoc with trade. James himself survived the Plague, but died before the launch of the *Michael*. By the time of his death he owned two ships of his own.

James Mackeson had a ship of 100 tons, but Andrew Haliburton does not give us her name. She was sometimes chartered by the king, notably to bring home from France the keel of the first large ship to be built at Leith. As well as Gilbert Edmondstone's gift, James witnessed a charter for Robert Barton and seems to have been well into the 'inner circle' of Leith skippers. In 1494, along with William Todrig and John Hopper (also mentioned in the Ledger) he was ordered by the Lords of Council to pay dues to the chaplain at Bruges. The paying of dues to this chaplain by skippers had been originally instituted at a time when the Scottish Staple was fixed at Bruges, making it the 'home port' for Scottish ships sailing to the Low Countries. This had not been the case for many years past, so the skippers may perhaps be forgiven for feeling that they no longer owed anything to the chaplain. In his history of the Scottish Reformation, John Knox pinpointed the ports of the land as centres of Protestantism, the doctrine having been imported from the Continent by merchants and seamen. Among other things, the Protestants challenged the traditional authority of the Church, and it may be that non-payment of dues to the Bruges chaplain was an early form of 'silent protest'.

William Todrig seems to have been a troublesome character. In 1495, a year after the incident of the Bruges chaplain, he captured Thomas Weldon, factor to a Newcastle merchant. Thomas held a safe-conduct from James IV, but this made no difference to William, who forced him to hand over the goods he was taking home from Leith for his master - 16 barrels of salted salmon and 300 dried fish. The case was brought before the Lords of Council (the forerunner of the Court of Session), who ordered William to release his captive and restore the fish.

The details of the evidence are not given, but it is quite possible that the Newcastle man had at some time appropriated some goods belonging to William. (This may be why he went to the trouble of procuring a safe-conduct for his servant.) These tit-for-tat actions were the cause of much of the piracy that was so rife at the time. If a large amount of goods or property were involved, and the pursuer could not gain redress in the courts of the offender's country, his own sovereign might issue him with 'letters of marque'. These constituted a licence to seize goods of equivalent value from ships of the offending nation. It was the issuing to the Bartons by James IV of letters of marque against the Portuguese that signalled the beginning of the family's rise to fortune. As was often the case, they took the opportunity to engage in wholesale piracy which, however, did them no disservice in gaining the favour of the king. Lesser mortals merely engaged in private reprisals, which only came to court if they were seen as being blatantly unfair. Most Leith skippers would engage in piracy if the opportunity arose, hence, possibly, their devotion to St Barbara, patron saint of gunners.

Within two years, William Todrig was involved in yet another 'incident'. This time, he and an Edinburgh burgess called Thomas Bard were accused of the wrongful arrest of another Englishman, Thomas Watson. This unfortunate man had agreed to pay ransom for three English prisoners held by the two Scots who, 'took the said Thomas Watson and had him forth of Leith to the town of Edinburgh upon Candlemas Even (1 February) that last was, under silence of night, and led him openly in sight of the common people as if he had been a trespasser and a thief' They took him to the officers and bailies, who ordered Thomas Bard to pay the ransom. In February the case came before the Lords of Council who dismissed it, as the indenture made between the three men fixed the date of payment as Candlemas, and the arrest had been made the night before.

In 1500, William Gray also appeared before the Lords, but as a pursuer. He was then Master of the King's ship the *Barque of Liddale*, but eight years previously his own ship had been captured by an expatriate Scot, John Chapman of Umfleet (Honfleur?). He was given six weeks to prove his allegation, but there is no sequel, so perhaps he was unable to do so.

Christopher and *Douglas* are the only ships mentioned in Halilburton's Ledger whose skippers are known. Several others are mentioned by name, and were probably commanded by some of the men who have already been mentioned. The owner of *Vardur* was Nicholas Bowar, who may be the same Nicholas Bowar who was the King's bowmaker from 1489 to 1495. The *Julian* belonged to Sir Thomas Tod, a wealthy Edinburgh burgess. The *Eagle* was the ship of Lord Seton, from whom James IV bought her for £200 in 1504, when he was beginning to build up his fleet. A ship which Andrew Haliburton calls the *Cowasch* was, surprisingly enough, a Scottish vessel. Her name appears as *Towaich* in the Royal Treasurer's accounts, which could be a rendering of the Gaelic word 'teuchat' meaning 'lapwing'. Alternatively she may have been one of the ships bought by James IV from two Bretons in 1495. She is not mentioned in the Ledger until 1496, and a Breton origin might account for her name, as Breton and Gaelic are both Celtic languages.

Trading

We have already looked at the work of the customars of Edinburgh and their servitors as they weighed hundreds of sacks of wool each year and counted thousands of sheepskins and hides. Andrew Haliburton's ledger gives us details of what happened to some of those goods when they reached their destination. Most of his clients traded in wool, and a good example of a straightforward transaction is contained in an account rendered to Thomas Cant in April 1497.

January 1497

Received out of 'Julian' in Middleburgh	2 sacks of Newbattle wool
	1 sack of middling wool
Received out of 'Christopher' in Middleburgh	2 sacks of Newbattle wool

Sold

2 sacks of Newbattle in Bruges to Francis Amand	£39 16s 5g
2 sacks of Newbattle in Bruges to Peter von Artrick	£39 10s 8g
1 sack of middling to men of Tourcoing	£18 0s 14g
(all prices are in Flemish gros money, multiply by three for the approximate Scottish equivalent.)	
Total costs on these sacks	£10 1s 7g
(costs included freight charges, porters fees, and hire of a 'schout' boat to take the wool to Bruges from Middleburgh.)	
Received from James Cant on behalf of Thomas Cant, 50 French crowns at 5s 6g each	£13 5s gr
For my service on each sack sold; May 1496 to April 1497 - 23 sacks at 16s	£18 8s
Total receipts; May 1496 - April 1497, minus costs and service	£400 15s 2g

Scottish wool came in different grades. The finest was 'Forest', from the Borders grazings of Jedburgh and Ettrick. 'Newbattle' and 'middling' were next in quality. Brown wool fetched the lowest price. On at least one occasion, Andrew received a sack which was affected by rot, and had to pay for it to be sorted, washed and repacked. The Continental market for wool had been declining throughout the fifteenth century, Scottish exports dropping in sympathy. As time went on Andrew Haliburton found it increasingly difficult to sell the wool that was sent to him. Towards the end of the decade he sometimes had to store wool received in May until the autumn, when the big Fairs were held, having been unable to sell it in the local markets as he had previously done. In a letter to a Scottish correspondent in 1502, he says that there is more demand for skins and hides than for wool.

Once the wool had been sold, Andrew would buy and ship items ordered by his clients. This is the other half of his transaction with Thomas Cant:

Packed in Middleburgh and put in Sir Thomas Tod's ship (*Julian*), a pipe (large barrel) containing:

1 steik Ryssils black, new price	£9
1 steik Ryssils brown, old price	£8
1 steik velvet, 36 ells @ 10s	£19
1 steik velvet, 31 ells @ 10s	£15 10s
2 tops raisins @ 5s the top	10s
4 tops figs @ 20g the top	6s 8g
1 roll of canvas (to cover the pipe)	7s 6g
for the pipe	1s 4g
packing, porter and schout	8g
a box for the silk	1s 4g

In the same ship:

1 small barrel containing 7 tops of figs	£1
barrel, packing and schout hire	8g

Bought in Veere and shipped in the same ship:
6000 (lb) iron between Thomas Cant and John Paterson
@ 23 sturs per 100
costs 6½g per 1000

On 26 July 1500, the king appointed Andrew Haliburton Conservator of the Scottish Privileges in 'Flanders, Brabant, Zeeland, Holland and all other domains of the Archduke of Flanders'. The Conservator was responsible for seeing that Scottish trading privileges in the Scottish Staple Port were upheld. The Staple was a Burgh port where Scottish merchants paid low duties and were protected under an agreement negotiated between the Convention of Royal Burghs and the Scottish government. In return for the privileges they enjoyed, Scottish merchants were supposed to use the Staple as their sole port of entry. If relations became difficult, the Staple agreement would be renegotiated with another port. The Conservator had the legal status of a Provost, settling disputes between merchants using the Staple and punishing wrongdoers. At the time of Andrew's appointment, however, the influence of the Conservator seems to have extended far beyond the confines of a single port. He was paid a salary gained by a levy on Scottish goods imported into the area of his jurisdiction, with power to distrain goods if the levy was not paid.

Plague

In common with every other country in Europe, since 1339 when the Plague first appeared, Scotland had been subject to periodic outbreaks of disease. 'Plague' was really a blanket word covering not only the Bubonic disease carried by rats and fleas, but probably also outbreaks of influenza and similar viral infections which have caused epidemics throughout the continent well into the present century. An outbreak seems to have started in Scotland at some time in 1495/6, when the king ordered the Chamberlain of Fife to give 2 chalders of malt to the people infected with Plague at Leith and Inchkeith. By September 1497 the disease had been identified as Grandgore, which had first appeared at the Seige of Naples in 1495. It had spread very quickly to Scotland, perhaps brought back by mercenaries.

The king issued a proclamation that, 'for the eschewing of the great apparent danger of the infection of his lieges from this contagious sickness called the grandgor' all infected persons and their attendants were to gather on the sands at Leith by 10.00 of the morning, 'and there they shall have and find boats ready in the haven ordained to them by the officers of this Burgh (Edinburgh) readily furnished with victuals to have them to the Inch (Inchkeith) and there to remain until God provide for their health.' Any infected person who was not on Inchkeith by sunset the following Monday would be branded on the cheek and banished from the Burgh. This last was a standard punishment for disobeying the bye-laws concerning Plague - during later outbreaks it was 'upgraded' to drowning!

These draconian quarantine measures have been criticised, but it is hard to see what else could have been done. There was no known cure, and isolation of the sick had been found to be the only way of limiting the spread of the disease. The fact that it was relatively ineffective was due more to the reluctance of individuals to be isolated than to any fault in the method itself. Inchkeith was to be used again on more than one occasion for the same purpose, and had probably been used in the past. In fact all the precautions used in 1497 had probably become familiar over the previous one and a half centuries, it is just that the records of those times have not survived.

By the following March, six villages to the west of Edinburgh were affected, and eight months later Grandgore had spread to 'the east parts' and to Glasgow. Further edicts by Edinburgh forbade its inhabitants to have any contact with people from the affected areas without official permision. A Watch rota was set up to ensure that strangers did not enter the town, especially under cover of darkness or by priv^te gates. News had also arrived of an outbreak in England, and English cloth was banned. Taverns, alehouses and schools were closed, and children under 13 years of age ordered to stay at home, as were servants who lived outside the Town.

By June 1499 things were so bad in Leith that the Edinburgh Council forbade all contact with the Port. Any merchant having corn, wine or flour there was to bring it up to the Burgh immediately, as no-one was to be allowed to go to Leith to buy or sell. In October the Council was faced with a new problem. In a normal year, this was the time when the season's wool clip began to be loaded into ships to be taken to the Low Countries. Even as things were, wool was coming to the Tron in Edinburgh, and some safe way had to be found to get it to the ships at Leith. The Council issued instructions:

> anent the furnishing and loading of ships that are loaded; that in time to come no manner of person, from Tuesday next to come, pass with any goods to Leith, or send, because of the danger of sickness that is in Leith, but that they carry their goods with carters of this town to Leith Hill beside the Abbey (Abbey Hill) and discharge their goods there, that the carters of Leith may there receive the same to the Port, to be had to the ships, and this loading to be made in the hastiest manner for to eschew danger.

After the end of October 1499 there were no more edicts concerning the Plague, so it seems it was at least waning by then. It may not have completely died out, as there was another outbreak within five years.

The progress of the disease is mirrored in both Andrew Haliburton's Ledger and the accounts of the Great Customs. Exports from Edinburgh dropped by a third in 1496. The following year, however, they doubled. Perhaps merchants waited to see if the disease would abate before risking contact with the Port, but became so desperate to sell their accumulated goods that they decided to risk the danger. By 1498 the disease had encircled Edinburgh, and in this and the following year, exports were a mere fraction of previous figures. The Ledger shows a similar pattern. In 1498 the amount of wool handled by Andrew was almost halved. The pattern of shipping shown in his ledger also changed in that year. Normally sailings clustered around spring and late autumn 'peaks', with no activity in March and late summer/early autumn. In 1498, March is the only month that shows no activity at all. The number of ships is generally lower, sailings continue throughout the summer, and the autumn 'peak' begins in October rather than November, as it had previously done. In December 1497, Andrew's clients had begun to use the barque of 'Toni the Brabanter'. In 1499, this and the ship of one Peter Halket are the only vessels from Edinburgh that Andrew had dealings with, and the number of his Edinburgh clients dropped to three. In 1500 he dealt only with James Hommil, his sister's third husband, who used Toni's barque and John Barton's ship. During these years, he dealt mainly with ships and merchants of Aberdeen.

For those in Leith who escaped the contagion, the chaos of Plague Years, relatively free from supervision by Edinburgh, possibly provided something of a trading bonanza. After the outbreak we have just considered, the Burgh council had to 'remind' Leith that all ships must be freighted in the Tolbooth in Edinburgh and that the goods of foreigners must not be stored or sold at the Port. After the virulent outbreak of 1505 (in which all but two of the Friars of St Anthony died) the King himself had to intervene, with a statute forbidding 'packing and peeling' in Leith and the Canongate and the selling of foreign goods in Leith. He also reminded skippers that they were not to sail until their cargoes had paid custom.

North Leith

One dodge that skippers could use to evade the jurisdiction of Edinburgh was to live or to store their cargoes in North Leith or St Leonard's Lands, which belonged to Holyrood Abbey. The loss of almost all the Abbey records means that there is little early information about its properties, but for the years 1483 to 1515 there survives a document which gives a picture of North Leith in the late 15th and early 16th centuries.

All legal transactions made at that time had to be recorded by a notary public in a volume called a 'Protocol Book'. James Young was the notary for the Abbey during this period. His Protocol Books (of which twelve volumes survive) cover the Canongate, North Leith, Broughton and other Abbey properties. The bulk of the contents consists of 'instruments of sasine' recording the transfer of property from one individual to another. A typical sasine followed a formula which went something like this:

> The Abbot and convent of Holyrood grant sasine to John Brown, indweller of Leith, and Agnes Black his wife, of the land of Andrew White in North Leith, having the land of Thomas Smith to the east, the land of James Wright to the west, the Green to the north and the King's Gait to the south.

The sasine would be dated, and end with a list of witnesses, which usually included neighbours, friends and relatives. Given enough of these documents, it is possible to gain an idea of the inhabitants of some streets and the positions of their properties in relation to one another. Sometimes other information is given, such as details of the buildings, the price paid, family relationships and occupations.

Using the information from James Young's book, together with later charters and maps, it is possible to build up a plan of North Leith, and even to mark in a few details (see map on p 65). What emerges is a little settlement of typical Anglo-Norman layout. Whoever was responsible for this, whether David I, one of his predecessors, or Holyrood Abbey, they started with a block of tofts laid out at right-angles to a street which ran parallel with the river bank. There were probably sixteen of these original tofts. It was a well established custom in Scotland to divide land into multiples of eight, and by the end of the fifteenth century there were still only seventeen properties in the original block, one of which had been formed by subdivision of a toft. Behind and to the west of this block was an area of common grazing land, 'The Green'. Further to the west, bisected by the road to Bonnington, lay an area of common arable land, 'Hillhousefield', which extended as far as the Bonnington boundary dyke on the south and stretched for some distance westward.

The main street was known as the King's Gait, Common Way, Hie Gait or simply 'the Street' for the next 800 years. It was not until the nineteenth century that it was named Sandport Street. Its curving line suggests that it was originally laid out close to the high water mark. North Leith does not seem to have grown very much northwards, as did South Leith, but southeastwards, considerably narrowing the Water of Leith. This process was helped by a natural drop in the

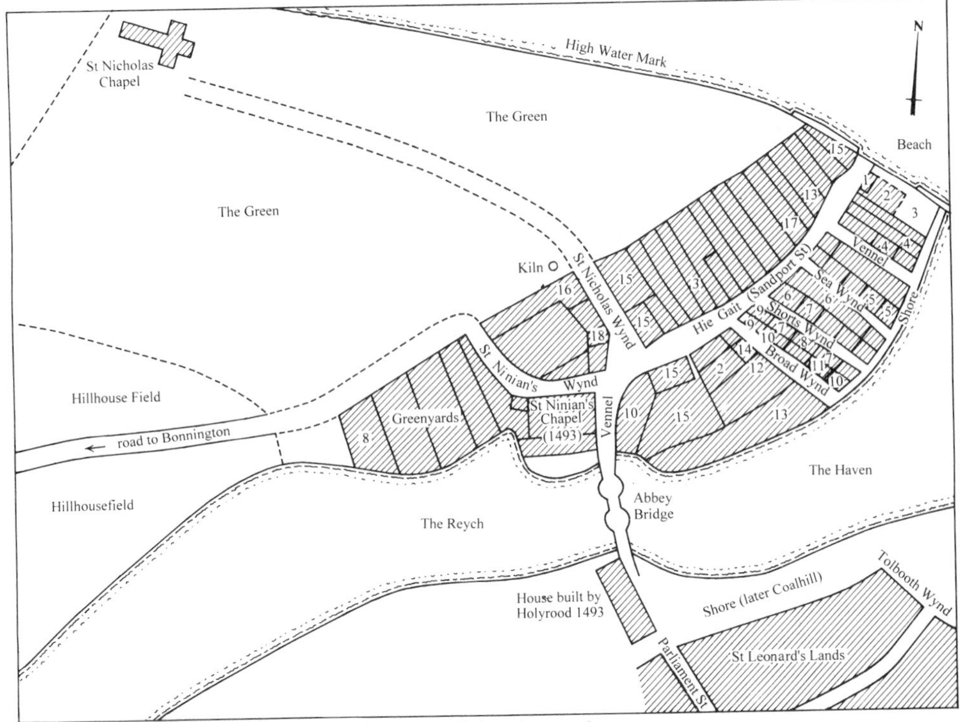

North Leith at the start of the sixteenth century.

1=House of William Merrymonth
2=William Dais (sailor)
3=Thomas Dais (shipwright)
4=John Dawson (skipper)
5=John Balyard (skipper)
6=Chaplain of St Nicholas
7=Isabella Short
8=John Gardener (skipper and shipwright)
9=Crawfurds of Bonnington
10=Late John Bully (sailor)
11=John Irwin (skipper of *Christopher*)
12=William Wood (skipper)
13=Thomas Bannatyne (skipper)
14=Late Thomas Murray (sailor)
15=John Stairhead (skipper)
16=Sir Andrew Wood of Largo
17=John Downie (sailor)
18=John Newton (sailor)

water level of the Forth, but could also have been the result of deliberate land reclamation and\or the building of wharves. St Nicholas' chapel (dedicated to the patron saint of seafarers and in particular pilots) was erected to serve the little community, but it is not at all clear why it should have been built at the furthest boundary of the Green. Perhaps it served as some kind of navigational leading mark, possibly in line with the Castle Rock (it stood due south of the entrance to the river channel). Presumably Hillhousefield was originally farmed as 'run rig'; divided into strips whose owners 'rotated' each year. By the late fifteenth century, although individuals owned blocks of land which were still scattered throughout the open field, rotation had ceased and holdings had become permanently fixed.

Although the people of North Leith grew crops in their fields and grazed animals on the Green, they naturally looked to the sea for at least a part of their sustenance. The fishings of the town paid a teind to Holyrood Abbey. As the waterline receded to the southeast of the Hie Gait, the new land had been claimed for beaching and repairing boats and drying and mending nets. Short wynds were formed at right angles to the main street, giving access to the water. They were given names: Broad Wynd, Shorts Wynd (Isabella Short still held three properties here at the end of the fifteenth century), and Sea Wynd. Part of the Green to the west of the original row of tofts was built over, leaving an access road to the chapel - St Nicholas' Wynd. Further still to the west, the formation of the Greenyards crofts caused the Bonnington road to be diverted into a curved street, which came to be known as St Ninian's Wynd after the chapel of that name was built in 1493.

Altogether, it is possible to distinguish 70 - 80 properties in North Leith at around the year 1500, belonging to about 40 individuals. Of these, 23 definitely and 15 probably lived in the town. The Crawfurds of Bonnington held some land in North Leith, as did Sir Andrew Wood of Largo.

In 1486, two brothers, William and Thomas Dais, bought a plot of land (later known as the Sandport) at the seaward end of the south side of the Street. William was a sailor. Thomas's occupation is not stated, but it is more than likely that he was a shipwright. The plot of land was ideally situated for shipbuilding and repair, right on the highwater mark. Three later Dais men, another Thomas, Adam and Alan were shipwrights who worked on the building of James IV's navy between 1504 and 1513.

Thomas senior (who died in 1497) lived in a house on the north side of the King's Gait. His brother William owned a piece of land at the other end of the town. It lay at the heart of a block of properties which belonged or had belonged to various seamen. The house to the east of it, which stood in Broad Wynd, had belonged to a skipper called Thomas Murray. William was married to Margaret Murray, and in 1489 acted as forespeaker (advocate) for Marion, Thomas Murray's widow. From this we might conclude that Margaret was Thomas Murray's daughter, and that Marion was William's mother-in-law. William does not seem to have owned a house of his own, so they probably all lived in the house in Broad Wynd.

Their neighbour to the south was William Wood, one of the Leith skippers of the day, to the south of him was one of the many properties in the town acquired by John Gardener, a successful skipper and shipwright. South of John Gardener, right beside the Water of Leith was a large yard belonging to another skipper, Thomas Ballantyne, who later commanded one of James IV's ships. This yard was ideally placed for shipbuilding, and it is quite possible that Thomas Ballantyne built ships as well as sailing them - the Cornton family and others also combined both professions.

To the west of Thomas Ballantyne, with access to the Water of Leith, was one of the properties of John Stairhead, who we have already met as a Leith skipper. He retired early in the 1490s and began disposing of his properties. Some he sold, and one (at the extreme end of the north side of the King's Gait) provided a tocher when his daughter married David Wood. He did not, however, dispose of this property beside the Water of Leith, so it probably contained his dwelling house.

St Ninian's Chapel, built by Holyrood Abbey in 1493. The drawing shows the chapel in the early nineteenth century, when it had all but disappeared within an accretion of later buildings such as the manse.

His neighbour to the west, beside the vennel that led to the bridge, had been John Bully, a sailor who died in 1497. Sometimes when a landholder died his property was not immediately sold or granted to his heirs, (in some cases this was not done until his widow died). When this happened the land was said to belong to 'the late ——'. John Bully must hold some kind of record in this respect. He appears in sasines as 'the late John Bully' for nearly a century after his death!

At the head of William Dais' yard beside the sea stood the house of William Merrymonth. On 25 May 1505, the king ordered a payment of 42s 'to the men that jousted in the boats of Leith'. Two days later he told Robert Barton to give 14s to William Merrymonth of Leith, 'King of the Sea'. The royal Treasurer issued the money to Robert Barton and duly noted it in his accounts. It has been assumed from this reference that William Merrymounth was one of James IV's famous skippers. However, it is clear from other sources that he never commanded any craft larger than a boat. A more likely explanation is that a regular boat-jousting contest was held in Leith, possibly as part of the Mayday celebrations, and that 'King of the Sea' was the title given to the victor.

The King's Fleet

By 1500, James possessed at least six ships; *Christopher*, the barque *Douglas*, *The Barque of Liddale*, the barge built in Dumbarton, and two or more vessels bought from the two Bretons, one of which may have been the *Towaich*. As we have seen, it was standard practice for a king to own ships which he could hire out to traders or use in time of war. It is quite possible that initially James had no notion of doing more than this. However, in 1502 his uncle, king Hans of Denmark, under attack from Swedes rebelling against his rule, appealed to him to send ships to his aid. Scotland could never have assembled a fleet to take on a country like England, whose king could call on the ships of scores of ports, and casually order the building of four vessels of 800 tons. However, the appeal from king Hans may have shown James that the possession of a number of ships could make him more desirable as an ally.

The links between Scotland and Scandinavia, both warlike and peaceful, went back for centuries. The marriage of James III to Margaret of Denmark had finally brought Orkney and Shetland into the Scottish kingdom, and in 1494, James IV had ratified an alliance treaty with king Hans. Over the next 20 years growing numbers of Scots settled in Denmark, mainly along the Öresund, the principle route to the Baltic, taking advantage of the considerable mutual trading privileges granted by the treaty.

James received his uncle's appeal for help early in 1502, and by April preparations to send a small fleet to Denmark were under way. *Douglas* was being fitted out at Leith and Robert Herwood the king's gunner went over the water to Kinghorn for weapons. Messengers were sent to Fife, Forfar, Perth, Ayr, Kirkcudbright, Dumfries and Wigtown, 'with warning for the passage to go to Denmark' - both seamen and soldiers were needed. Within three weeks, *Eagle* and *Towaich* were in Leith Roads being refitted.

On May 22, the *Trinity*, which had been in Denmark, came home to Leith with news of how things were going for Hans. At the end of the month James spent four days being rowed about the Forth to visit his fleet. He had dinner on *Eagle*, and even there was pursued by his subjects, eager to bring him gifts - in this case 'podlocks' (sprats) brought by fishermen, who were given 12d for their trouble. James had a wager with John Barton 'upon the forth having of *Eagle*'s boat', and lost 28s. Another ship called the *Jacat* was also in the Forth, and her tabroners (drummers) were given 14s for playing for the king. Soon after the king's visit the fleet sailed and by 6 June were at North Berwick, where James sent them some last minute instructions. Ten weeks later they were back, having failed to prevent the capture of Stockholm by the Swedes.

Building the First Ship

In the meantime the king had made the decision to build up a larger fleet. On 27 June 1502 his Treasurer paid 2s to a boy 'to go and see if the king's writings had gone to France for the wright'. This insignificant little sentence, tucked away among the miscellaneous disbursements of the king's Privy Purse, signals the quiet beginnings of an enterprise that was to dominate the life of Leith and the surrounding area for the next 11 years, culminating in the building of the maritime marvel of the age, the great *Michael.*

'The king's writings' had gone to Dieppe. This was the French port used by Scottish ships at the time, and there was an expatriate community there which included men well able to choose a good shipwright for the king. Scottish wrights were perfectly competent to build small vessels of about 50 tons, but James intended to include much larger ships in his fleet. The man who arrived in Scotland in November 1502 was John Lawrence, 'the French wright who came first for the shipbuilding'. His name suggests that he was one of the expatriate community of Dieppe. He was paid £7 per month, £2 more than the highest paid native shipwright.

The bureaucracy of the king's household assigned shipbuilding to the department of the Master of Works, who was also responsible for the building and repair of the royal castles and palaces. He paid out the money, but the responsibility for the organisation of the actual 'shipwerk' rested with Robert Barton. As well as being a shipowner and a ferocious pirate, Barton was a very capable administrator who later became the royal Comptroller.

Robert Barton's assistant was George Cornton, who had been one of the foremen at the building of the king's barge in 1493. By 1501 he was in the king's employ organising the reception, storage and disposal of the king's goods in Leith, probably based at the Kings Wark. Some dues were still paid to the king in kind, such as the grain and fish that William Merrymounth brought in his boat from Moray to Leith and landed at the Shore by the King's Wark. George gave out malt to the king's brewers. He sent corn to be ground and then gave the flour to the king's bakers. He issued fish to the king's kitchen. Although he is never mentioned as such, he was probably also 'Overseer of the King's Ships', an office which was later held by another Cornton under James V.

Once the building of the fleet began, George organised the work at Leith, and sometimes accompanied Robert Barton on his trips to the Continent to buy materials. The Cornton family of Leith was fairly numerous by this time, and most of them were shipwrights, but another George (junior) was, as we have seen, a successful skipper. He acquired the family property in St Leonards Lands in 1506 and added to it a fair portion of the land of his neighbour, Robert Logan of Coatfield, including that sixteenth century status symbol, a garden. George senior seems to have died in 1509, but for the previous six years he had enjoyed yearly remissions of custom on his exports of cloth, hides, suet, wool and salt herring, a privilege he shared with Robert and Andrew Barton. Those of Leith on whom the king's favour rested could afford to ignore the Burgh laws of Edinburgh!

A few days after the arrival of John Lawrence from France in November 1502, John Barton, one of Robert's brothers, who was also involved with the administration of the 'shipwerks', was given money to hire four wrights; Lawrence Cornton, Thomas Dais, James Gray (all of Leith) and a Dutchman called Jacob. They went with John Lawrence to the woods at Cambusnethan in Liddesdale to cut timber for the first new ship. In January 1503, more wrights were sent to Logan wood in Annerdale for timber. By February enough had been felled at Cambusnethan for the sawyers to begin work. The four wrights there were paid off at the end of March 1503, but John Lawrence was still at Cambusnethan in April, presumably supervising the transporting of the timber to Leith.

In May 1503 a second wright, Jennan Diew (a Breton, probably from Conquet), arrived in Scotland, having been hired in France by Robert Barton. Almost at once he set off to Badenoch for yet more timber. Meanwhile the skipper James Mackeson had arrived home with a keel for the new ship, which Robert Barton had had made in France, and George Cornton was supervising the construction of a dock at Leith in which to build her.

As there is no record of payment for hire of land for the dock, it was almost certainly situated on the foreshore behind the King's Wark. The digging of it took nearly 250 man-days, and it was finished by 14 July. If, as seems most likely, the new ship was the *Margaret*, she was to be over 300 tons, and a dock was needed as she would be too large to be dragged to the water, so an area was constructed which could be flooded when she was ready to be launched. The method used was probably to dig into the slope of the foreshore and close the mouth of the resulting dry pool with a dam which could be breached on a high tide when the time came. The shell of the dam was probably constructed with the 200 trees which were laid 'forth of the dock' early in July. Once built, the shell would be filled with cartloads of earth and this is probably the process referred to as 'filling the dock'.

By the time the dock was ready yet another wright hired by Robert Barton had arrived from France, having overseen the cutting of more timber in the woods near Dieppe, and the making of another keel which was probably intended for the barque that was built at Leith at the same time as the new ship. The new wright was Jacat Terrel, who replaced John Lawrence, and remained in Scotland for the next 10 years. It was Jacat who oversaw the building of the *Michael*.

On 8 August 1503 James IV, now aged 30, was married at Holyrood Abbey to the 13-year old Margaret Tudor, sister of the later Henry VIII. The wedding festivities lasted five days and cost James enormous sums of money - more than £2000 for the wine alone. The new little Queen had made an exciting and exhausting journey overland from London, and soon after the wedding had to say goodbye to most of the familiar courtiers and servants who had accompanied her. She was, understandably, rather upset. In Leith, however, some of her new subjects had cause to be pleased at her presence. Their new queen had magnificent ideas about the amount of luggage needed by travelling royalty, and the carters of Leith had transported 20 cartloads of her gear from Dalkeith to Edinburgh. Moreover, whenever she travelled in future, she took a similar amount with her, providing the carters with a good extra income.

Jennen Diew took over work on the ship at Leith in August 1503, and Jacat Terrel seems to have gone to oversee operations in the West. The following January (1504) the King heard mass twice in St Nicholas' chapel, and visited the dock, where he gave 'drinksilver' to the shipwrights and to the man who kept the dock in repair. In March 1504 more work was done on a dock in Leith. Either the original one was in need of repair after the winter storms, or a new dock was being constructed for the building of a barque which was begun later in the year. Diggers were employed for 56 man-days and carters bringing loads of earth for 30.

The New Haven

The pynours (porters/labourers) seem to have been responsible for the May celebrations in Leith. On 27 April 1504, the King gave 5s to their 'Abbot of Unreason', and two years previously they had been involved in carrying an image of St Michael on May Day. The main reason for James' presence in Leith in April/ May 1504 was to see the start of work on 'The New Haven' which was being constructed on a site to the west of North Leith, which the king had acquired from Holyrood Abbey. There was a greater depth of water at this point, making it more suitable than Leith for the building of large ships. James was rowed to the new site from Leith on 9 May, perhaps for an inaugural blessing of the spot. The sixteenth century historian Pitscottie says that the building of the *Michael* 'wasted all the woods of Fife', but the records suggest that it was the building of the New Haven which was mainly responsible for this destruction. During the two years of its construction, timber came there from Kircaldy, Cambuskenneth, Dysart, Kincardine, Alloa, Irneside and Dalhousie. Inverleith and Clackmannan also contributed. By the time the *Michael* came to be built, the king was looking much further afield for timber.

By the time the New Haven was under way, a barque was being built at Leith under the supervision of Jenen Diew. Another new ship was being built at Dumbarton by Jacat Terrel, the first of several vessels built on the West Coast over the next eight years. James was still keeping a close eye on the Western Isles, and these vessels were no doubt intended for that purpose. In July 1504, Robert Barton made the first of his annual visits to France to buy timber and equipment for the ships. On this occasion, besides timber, his shopping list included, nails, saws, gimlets, augers, two 4-wheeled carts and harness for four horses, a keel for the barque to be built at Leith and a whole ship, the *Columb*, which went to serve on the West Coast under the command of John Merchamstone.

On 3 February 1505, 17 months after she was begun, the first ship of the fleet to be built in Scotland was launched at Leith. Amid much playing of minstrels and general rejoicing, the dam of the dock was breached and she was taken off the stocks, floating off at high tide. She was almost certainly the *Margaret*, named in honour of the Queen. As yet she was only a shell, her completion taking several further months. Almost as important an occasion as the launching was the putting up of her masts. Sailors were always involved in this process, presumably because they were most familiar with the fixing of the rigging. They always received 'drinksilver' from the king if he happened to be present. The *Margaret* had three masts; mainmast, foremast and mizzen, for each of which a streamer was made. Each of the two larger masts had a 'mers cloth' hung from its fighting top, and she flew a blue banner with the St Andrew's cross, and two standards of yellow 'say' (a coarse woolen cloth) each with a red lion rampant appliquéed onto it. *Margaret*'s mainmast was put up in April, and in the same month her tackle came home from Flanders in James Mackeson's ship. (Miles of rope and cable was bought in Flanders over the next eight years, and most of the guns and ammunuition came from the same source.)

The Great Ship

Early in 1506 the New Haven was ready for shipbuilding to begin. The new ship whose keel seems to have been laid there in April was almost certainly the *Michael*, built in response to the current fashion for each nation to possess as large a vessel as possible for its flagship. The *Michael* is said by the historian Pitscottie to have been 240 feet long by 36 feet wide and to have had a crew of 300. Whatever may be the truth of this statement, she was certainly the largest ship ever to have been built in Scotland and was a source of immense pride to the king.

It has sometimes been assumed that Newhaven was the place where the bulk of James's fleet was built, but the surviving records show that the 'shipworks' were divided almost equally between Newhaven, Leith and Dumbarton, with two small craft being built at Ayr and Glasgow. Newhaven seems to have been intended mainly for the building of the *Michael*, and in 1510, when this was well under way, the king granted the Port to Edinburgh. The *James* or the *Gabriel*, which were launched in 1512, may have been built there (although they could equally well have both been built at Leith), and in 1513, on the eve of Flodden, a small galley was under construction, but this seems to have been the full extent of the shipbuilding at the New Haven.

We have already seen that the barque *Columb* was sent to the West almost as soon as she arrived from France in August 1504, and she was still in the Isles the following May. In June 1506, William Brownhill of Leith skippered his own vessel as flagship of the fleet in the Isles, carrying the Earl of Huntly to rendezvous with one of the king's new ships from Dumbarton. Later they were joined at Lewis by *Raven*, which sailed from Leith in September.

During the summer of 1506, George Cornton was in France with Robert Barton, buying timber for the 'great ship' and hiring mariners from along the River Seine. While they were there they ran into some trouble and their purchases were confiscated, but they appealed to the King of France, who intervened on their behalf and the goods arrived safely in Scotland. In August, *Treasurer* arrived from Brittany, skippered by her builder, Martin le Nault who subsequently went to build a ship at Dumbarton.

Airth

In the same month that *Treasurer* arrived from Brittany, we find the first mention of a dock being built higher up the Forth at Airth. This was a large undertaking. Two years later the king paid the curate of Airth two years teind hay of a meadow that his horses had grazed while they were employed in hauling timber for the construction of the dock. The place where it was built was referred to as the Pool or Pow of Airth. Drainage and land reclamation have reduced this waterway to a muddy ditch, but in the sixteenth century it was deep and wide enough to receive ships as large as the 300 ton *Margaret* for repair and refit, the purpose for which the dock was built.

Lying much higher up the Forth than Leith, in the 'Narrow Waters', Airth was less vulnerable to attack by sea and would provide a safer haven for the fleet if it should be needed.

Leith Skippers

In November 1506, William Brownhill returned from Lewis, but his place was taken by a ship belonging to David Logan of Leith, skippered by William Duncan. It would seem that the King had no ships of any size in the West, and had to charter large vessels from Leith to go there.

Another Leith skipper, William Stewart, took Mountjoy Herald of France to Denmark in May 1507 in his ship *Wanton*, and in June, John Dawson of North Leith carried the Ambassador of Gueldres to France. Mountjoy Herald returned to Scotland in September in one of King Hans' ships, which was subsequently loaded with 39 chalders (about 80 tons) of coal from Dysart to take back to the Danish King. *Wanton* returned to Leith in October. *Treasurer*, meanwhile, had sailed to France skippered by John Barton. She carried Alexander Stewart the Archbishop of St Andrews, the teenaged illegitimate son of the king. Alexander was a promising youth, who was going abroad to pursue his education.

At some time in 1507, William Brownhill returned to the Isles. While he was there he encountered a Spaniard, Juan Lopez, who had lost a ship of 200 tons. William gave him a ship of 100 tons and 500 ducats, on condition that the Spaniard would deliver him a new ship of the same burthen at a port in the Spanish-held Low Countries port of Zeeland before Easter 1508. Unfortunately, Ferdinand, the king of Aragon, had placed an embargo on the export of ships from his territories, and James IV had to write to him asking him to make an exception in this case.

During 1508 the Barton brothers were kept busy. John Barton returned from

France with *Treasurer* in January. (On a subsequent voyage from France, *Treasurer* was wrecked off the English coast.) Andrew Barton returned from service in Denmark in March, only to go back almost immediately in command of *Margaret*, which James had agreed to send to help his uncle, who was once more under attack from the Swedes. However the fighting was nearly over by the time *Margaret* arrived. Robert made his usual visit to Dieppe and Martin le Nault also returned to France, having presumably finished the ship he had been building in Dumbarton. In his ship he transported the horses of two French knights who had been taking part in the spectacular Tournament of the Black Knight and the Black Lady, which was held in May of that year.

In 1509 king Hans once more appealed to his nephew for help, and this time James sent both Andrew and Robert Barton. A year later, Robert Barton was back in Scotland for reinforcements, and by the end of 1510 Andrew Barton had set sail with the *Lion*. He also took the *Jenny Pirwin*, which seems to have been a gift to Hans from James.

Tension

The years 1509 and 1510 are missing from the Treasurer's records, which contain most of the information about the growth of the fleet. When they begin again in August 1511, the political situation has changed for the worse. The death of Henry VII in 1509 brought to the English throne his gifted but vainglorious son, Henry VIII. This monarch is popularly remembered for having had six wives, but this came later in his career, after a long marriage to his first queen, Catherine of Aragon. In 1511 he was 20 years of age, athletic, handsome, untried, and out to prove himself as a King. He was quick to take offence, and had none of his father's reluctance to make war.

In 1511, James IV reissued letters of marque against the Portuguese to the Bartons and in the summer Andrew Barton left the Baltic, where he had been harrying the Hanseatic merchants of Lubeck, which had declared war on king Hans. He sailed to the coast of Portugal in order to take advantage of his letters of marque. In the Downs he encountered the English Admiral, Sir Edward Howard. Whether Andrew had been preying on English ships or Sir Edward believed in the pre-emptive strike, on 2 August 1511 the English Admiral was in action against the Scots. Andrew Barton was killed and the *Lion* and the *Jenny Pirwin* were taken. In spite of protests from James IV, Henry VIII refused to arraign his Admiral or return the ships, which he in fact added to his own fleet. (King Hans wrote to Henry asking for the *Jenny Pirwin* but with no success.) In December, James informed the Pope that he assumed this action by Henry nullified the oath both kings had taken at the ratification of a recent Peace Treaty. A step had been taken on the road to Flodden.

James was now ready to co-operate with the French, who wanted to use Scotland as a catspaw in their wars with England. (In many ways the 'Auld Ally' was just as dangerous to sixteenth century Scotland as was the 'Auld Enemy'.) A French Ambassador, de la Motte, was in Scotland at the end of 1511, and it may have been during his visit that it was decided to send a Scottish fleet to help France against English seapower. The 18 months leading up to the departure of the fleet from Leith in July 1513 are well documented. A new generation of Leith skippers was kept busy bringing materials from Flanders and France. They also transported the various Ambassadors in the three-cornered negotiations that were going on between Scotland, France and Denmark. As relations between Scotland and England deteriorated acts of piracy increased, and Henry VIII found it expedient to send Ambassadors to Scotland, who reported back on the state of the Scottish navy.

The Launch of the Michael

In January 1512, de la Motte left for Denmark, in the ship of William Mure of Leith, who was later to command one of the ships of James' fleet. On 7 February a start was made on dismantling the supporting cradle of the *Michael* at Newhaven. (If she was the ship whose keel had been laid there in 1506, she had

An artist's impression of 'the Great Michael' (By courtesy of Trinity House, Leith).

taken six years to build.) The king was naturally present at this great occasion, and he dined that day at the house of William Brownhill.

William was by now a man of some substance. He had sold the king some silver tableware for a parting gift to de la Motte, and the hall of his house in Leith was obviously large enough to accommodate the royal retinue. The dinner was organised by the king's Master Cook, who began the preparations three days in advance, when he took a considerable amount of equipment down to Leith. The upheaval in the Brownhill household may be easily imagined, and on the day of the dinner, the Master Cook was given 20s by the king to distribute between William's maids and menservants as a reward for all their extra work.

The king returned to Newhaven a week later to see the *Michael* freed completely from her cradle. She was towed out into the Forth on 18 February, and four days later James had supper on board her. To rig, fit out, caulk and tallow her occupied the following 18 months.

The Sailing Season of 1512/13

In April 1512 the spring sailing season began, and the ships of Leith set out once more on the king's errands. John Morrison took *Clofars*, ballasted with 42 chalders of Dysart salt, to Danzig for timber, pitch and tar. Thomas Bannatyne of North Leith went to Norway for timber in a small vessel which the king had bought, with a crew of ten men. With him were William Duncan, who later skippered another ship for the king, and the wright, Robert Hawick. They returned in August. John Balyard of North Leith took Lord Ross to France in his little barque. He returned in June with timber he had bought in Dieppe and equipment from Flanders, and two months later set out again for France. William Brownhill and George Paterson were also at sea at this time, in May they returned to Leith with materials from Flanders.

In the spring of 1512 James wrote to Henry declaring himself in favour of peace if the question of his captured ships *Lion* and *Jenny Pirwin* could be settled. Dr West, the Dean of Westminster, and Lord Dacre travelled to Scotland to discuss the matter. It seems that these Ambassadors did not initially make much headway in convincing James that England had been justified in her actions. A few weeks after their arrival, they presented seven 'bills' accusing various Scots skippers of capturing English vessels within the past year. There was no charge against Andrew Barton, but Robert was accused of taking six ships; three off Norfolk the previous May and three more which seem to have been taken somewhere near the entrance to the English Channel (possibly Robert had been with Andrew in his voyage off the Portuguese coast).

The other 'accused' was David Falconer of Leith, who was said to have taken two ships off Yarmouth. David must have been connected with Peter Falconer of Leith, who was sufficiently important to have entertained the king's Danish uncle Gerhart, when he visited Scotland in 1493. Peter also endowed a chaplaincy in South Leith church. David Falconer may have been the brother-in-law of William Brownhill - his wife's name was Elizabeth Brownhill. He was accused by Henry VIII of 'many acts of piracy' and before his death in 1528 he was to commit many more, but in 1512 he became the central figure in another of the incidents which were nailing the coffin of Scots/English relations.

In the second week of July 1512, William Brownhill set sail from Leith to take de la Motte back to France. With him went a convoy consisting of the ships of David Falconer, Robert Barton and two or three others. Rather than take the safer but longer route by the West Coast, they set their course down the North Sea. The English had been alerted to this by Lord Dacre, and their ships intercepted the Scottish convoy. William Brownhill's ship was holed by canon shot and made for Denmark. Robert Barton and the others also escaped, but David Falconer's ship was sunk and he himself was captured. He was imprisoned in London and sentenced to death. In August, Henry VIII wrote to Dacre about some Scottish ships which had been detained at Berwick on Tweed. With the letter he enclosed a reprieve for David Falconer, which Dacre was to use as a bargaining counter. By the beginning of September, Brownhill and Barton were back in Scotland, each blaming the other for leaving David Falconer to his fate.

De la Motte seems to have reached France somehow, and may have picked up David Falconer from England on his return, because Falconer was in command of the French Ambassador's ship when she anchored off Leith in a violent storm on the night of 29 November 1512. They announced their arrival by firing the ship's guns, with the result that panic reigned in Edinburgh for three hours, until the inhabitants realised that the shots had not heralded an English invasion. Meanwhile, the ship had dragged her anchor and was driven up to Blackness, where de la Motte met the king on board the *Michael.* With him he had brought a Spanish 'prize' laden with wine and peppercorns which the king shared with his Lords and the merchants of Edinburgh. James himself bought the ship and almost immediately sent her to Norway under the command of a Danish skipper called Andreas Jensen, who had been unsuccessfully searching in the Highlands for trees to make masts for James' ships. The 'Portingall Bark' subsequently formed part of the Scottish Fleet, skippered by William Mure of Leith.

The Fleet Grows

While all these stirring events were taking place on the high seas, work continued on the ships at Leith, Newhaven and Airth. The fitting out of the *Michael* occupied all that year and much of the next. *Margaret* was at Airth being overhauled for most of the year, being joined by *James* in the autumn. Roger Cornton and his son were at Newhaven working on the *Gabriel*, a two-masted barque. In September the king attended the first mass held aboard the *Gabriel* and a Frenchman called Perynot was appointed her skipper. John Newton of North Leith with his crew of three, were employed in a boat captured from the English to ferry materials and supplies to the *Michael.* This must have been a lucrative occupation, because in 1513 Newton was able to buy a property in St Nicholas Wynd.

It seems that the French also were not averse to a little piracy. According to a list compiled by Dacre in 1512, de la Motte had captured some half a dozen ships on his way to Scotland the previous year and sold them in Leith. One of them, the *Merrybuttocks* was bought by John Balyard and Walter Carr of Leith. They seem to have sold her to the king, for she was sent to Norway in May 1513 under the command of William Duncan. In fact, John and Walter, sometimes in partnership with Andrew Gray, were said to have bought all the prizes brought in by de la Motte, together with another vessel belonging to a woman of Newcastle, valued at £40. The fact that these skippers, who do not seem to have been the wealthiest in Leith, could find the money to buy six or seven ships, even small ones, points to the prosperity of the profession at the time.

On 3 February 1513, *Gabriel* set sail from Leith to take de la Motte back to France. (Two of the shipwrights who sailed in her were John Gardener of North Leith and his son.) With her went de la Motte's own ship, which had arrived at Leith the previous month. Off Flamborough Head they captured a Newcastle crayer (a small undecked vessel) laden with wine and salt. De la Motte put a French crew in her and sent her back to Leith.

In February 1513, Dacre compiled a long report for Henry VIII on James' preparations for war. He wrote that there were 13 great ships of three tops in Leith Haven, together with 10 small craft and a ship of (Kings) Lynn which had been taken by William Brownhill. At the New Haven were two great ships, the *James* and the *Margaret.* A galley was also being built there, of 30 oars a side. James was building a tower on a crag (Inchgarvie) at Queensferry, with a stone 'house' at each side of the Ferry to protect his ships, which he intended to lie above it. (He does not mention that a dock was also being dug at the 'Dublar Land' near South Queensferry.) William Brownhill was about to sail to Flanders in company with two merchant ships of Edinburgh. He intended to go on to France if he could evade the English.

The large number of 'great ships' at Leith was due to the arrival earlier in the month of 14 French ships laden with artillery intended for a Scottish invasion of England. By the time Dr West, the other English Ambassador, was able to engage in a little spying, on April 4 1513, they had left, leaving behind only 'some balingers and crayers, and nine or ten small topmen, only one rigged for war'.

During April 1513, Roger Cornton and Thomas Scot were building boats for the great ships and Lawrence Cornton was working on *Michael.* James Scot was in charge of work on the *Barque of Abbeville* at Leith. In May, *Gabriel* arrived safely at Ayr, accompanied by a French ship named the *Louis.* Henry Cornton, one of her wrights, had been building a galley at Ayr. He may have settled in the area, as he appears later as a witness to a charter from Longcaster in Wigtown.

The sailing of the fleet to France was now less than three months away, and messengers were sent to Fife, the West Coast, Stirlingshire, Liddesdale, East Lothian, the Merse, Teviotdale and far to the North for mariners. During June the fleet assembled in the Forth, and at the beginning of July provisioning began.

For the next three weeks, over thirty men worked day and night six days a week, ferrying provisions and artillery to the ships. The food was sufficient for 40 days (the traditional period of conscript service in medieval Scotland). There was biscuit and 'sour bread', both made from a mixture of wheat and rye flour, which was needed in such quantities that the local bakers could not make sufficient and some had to be brought from Dundee. Wheat bread was provided for the 'higher ranks'. Flour and oatmeal were taken so that more bread could be baked in the clay hearths and ovens which had been built on the ships. Salt and fresh meat, salt and dried fish, cheese, eggs and butter made up the rest of the solid food. To drink there was ale, beer and water.

The Fleet Sails

Between 22 and 25 July 1513, the king's fleet of fifteen ships at last sailed from the Forth. Nine of these were Scottish vessels, mostly commanded by Leith skippers. The rest were probably French. In overall command was the Earl of Arran, with the Lords Ross and Fleming. They sailed via the West Coast, maybe taking in some of the ships from Ayr. The voyage was broken by an attack on the English stronghold at Carrickfergus. This has been represented as a vain-glorious action on the part of the Earl of Arran, and Pitscottie accuses him of dallying for nearly six weeks in Ayr, enjoying the spoils. As the fleet arrived at Brest early in September, this is obviously completely untrue. One of Pitscottie's informants was Sir Andrew Wood of Largo, and it is quite possible that the Earl and the 'old sea dog' had a difference of opinion over the conducting of the expedition, which was later blown up out of all proportion. In all, the voyage took little longer than the 40 days for which the ships had been provisioned, so it is perfectly possible that the attack on Carrickfergus was part of the planned course of action. John Barton may have been wounded in the attack, as it was later reported that he had been put ashore and died at Kirkcudbright.

On 23 September 1513, a week or two after their arrival at Brest, the Scottish ships were sent to Honfleur to be provisioned and equippped to help the French in an assault on the English fleet, which was due to sail home from Picardy at the end of October. In the event, the French fleet was scattered by a storm and the English escaped unscathed.

By now, news had reached the Scots mariners of the disastrous defeat and death of James IV and 10,000 of their countrymen, including most of the nobility, in battle with the English at Flodden, on 9 September. Leaving *Michael*, *Margaret* and *James* behind, the rest of the Fleet made all possible speed for home. On 13 November, Dacre was writing to Henry VIII that they had arrived. *Michael* was bought by the French king in 1514, but was seldom used, eventually being left to rot in harbour. *Margaret* and *James* were back in Scotland by 1515.

Flodden had been an unnecessary battle, fought in the cause of a cynical ally, the French having used the Scots in the hope of diverting Henry VIII from an attack on their territories. It did nothing to deflect Henry from his purposes in

France, and plunged Scotland into decades of convoluted politics, during which first one then another faction siezed power. She was practically helpless in the face of attacks by the English, and the French forces sent to her aid became almost equally hated. Added to this was the civil conflict brought on by the Reformation and a continuing fall in the value of the currency. The Golden Age was followed by a plunge into the Abyss which lasted for over half a century.

4

Falconer, Fogo and Barton

The situation facing Scotland after Flodden was thus summed up by one of her Lords:

> For King James the Fourth brought the realm of Scotland to the best that ever it was, and by his war it was brought to the worst almost that it might be.

These words were spoken with the benefit of hindsight, in 1522. In the time directly after Flodden it was not obvious that Scotland, for reasons both familiar and novel, was entering on more than half a century of conflict. The immediate problem was the accession of yet another under-age king. James V was only 17 months old when his father died. Although he was crowned almost straight away, it was obviously going to be many years before the country would again have a competent monarch.

Margaret Tudor, the Queen Mother, had been named 'tutrix' to James in his father's will, and she headed the Council of Regency that was set up on his behalf. However, within a year she remarried, thereby nullifying her tutrixship, and the infant king's cousin, the Duke of Albany was invited to come to Scotland as Governor of the Realm. Six months after Albany's arrival, the death of the Queen Mother's posthumous second son, made the new Governor heir pre-sumtive to the throne. Albany had been born and brought up in France, and it was during his governorship that Scots began to discover some disadvantages of close contact with the Auld Ally.

Margaret had made just about the worst possible choice of a second husband - Archibald Douglas, Earl of Angus, the head of a selfseeking and unreliable family. He immediately set about encouraging Margaret to challenge the authority of the Council of Regency and tried to intrude one of his relatives, Gavin Douglas, into the vacant Archbishopric of St Andrews. (It very soon became clear to Margaret that her main attraction to Angus was as a stepping-stone to power for himself, and within two years of their marriage they were estranged.) The disruption of the peace by Angus added urgency to the Council's requests to Albany to come to Scotland, and in May 1515 he finally arrived at Dumbarton, having taken the safer Western sea-route. His plans were in fact known to the English. The Duke of Suffolk had been visited in Paris by the pilot who had brought the *Michael* to France. This man knew that Albany would take the western route, and offered his services to the Duke. In Flanders, the Lombard bankers Frescobaldi and Gualterotti, who acted for the Scottish Crown, told Spinnelly, Henry VIII's spy, what Albany's plans were. However, either the English decided not to act on the information, or else they were not successful in intercepting the Duke.

In a later statement of his reasons for coming to Scotland, Albany said;

> A great cause thereof was to bring you to a unity when ye were in division, by reason of which division your realm was likely to have been conquered and destroyed.

He achieved his aim as far as preventing any conquest of Scotland was concerned, but far from 'bringing it to a unity', his presence and that of his French troops during the next decade, did much to foster division. It has to be said, however, that so factious were many of the Scottish nobility, it would have taken a far higher power than Albany to create unity among them.

Broadly speaking, the divide lay between those who favoured supporting France and those who wanted peace with England. Individual reasons for choosing one side or the other changed as the century progressed and political conditions altered, but during the minority of James V they were roughly as follows. The pro-English party included: Margaret, because she was English; Angus and his associates, because Henry VIII supported their disruptive bids for power in Scotland; many merchants, because peace was more conducive to trade; and landowners in areas which were liable to be devastated by English armies in wartime. In later years it included the increasing number of Protestants, who saw the Reformation progressing more quickly in England than in Scotland. The pro-French party is less easy to define, but probably included 'tous les autres', and in particular, the religious conservatives.

Albany was in Scotland from 1515 to 1517, and again from 1521 to 1524. In the intervening period another Council of Regency was in charge, headed by Angus. For four years after Albany's final departure, the Douglases gained control of the country, but in 1528 James V was old enough to oust them and begin his personal rule.

Leith After Flodden

We will see later where Leith stood in all this, but first let us try to visualise the Port in the immediate aftermath of Flodden. No record survives to tell us whether any Leith men were among the 10,000 who fell in the battle. The two customars of Edinburgh certainly did, and their widows took over their duties for a couple of years. One of these women was Janet Paterson, daughter of the John Paterson who had been a client of Andrew Haliburton.

We can say a little more about the skippers and mariners who went with the fleet. Robert Barton returned and ultimately rose to high office, playing a prominent part in Leith affairs. William Brownhill, along with Edward Cockburne of Leith, was summoned to give evidence before the auditors of the royal ship accounts in 1516. John Balyard, who had skippered the *'James'*, was sentenced to death in 1517 for importing false coins into the country from Flanders, but obtained a remission.

Roger and Lawrence Cornton, and Thomas and Adam Dais presumably returned to their boatyards and carried on with whatever private commissions constituted their normal business. The docks behind the King's Wark probably crumbled away from lack of use and repair. Any royal shipworks were carried out on the West Coast, where *James*, *Margaret* and *Gabriel* were based at Ayr from 1515 to 1517, and used in operations in the Isles. The fate of the other vessels of the fleet is unclear. Albany sold two of them besides the *Michael* to the French king. The rest probably continued to be used until they rotted or were wrecked.

The increase in royal interest in the Port during the building of James IV's ships had evidently spurred Edinburgh into improving the facilities in the harbour. Twice at least they had paid for rocks to be removed from it, and by 1504, a pair of 'bekynys' had been provided to light the entrance to the channel at night. This, however, was the sum total of improvements.The burgh had been given the New Haven by the King in 1510, but this harbour the burgesses did not improve at all. Their sole aim was to prevent it rivalling Leith.

The immediate effect of Flodden on the port itself was to severely curtail or even halt the movement of shipping. Between July 1513 and July 1514 only half the normal quantity of goods were customed. In January 1514 the Lords of Council heard a complaint from Edinburgh merchants that some Leith skippers had goods on their ships freighted for Flanders, but had delayed sailing for so long that their cargoes were in danger of rotting. The Lords ordered the skippers to sail by the 25th of the month or else unload the goods. If sailing had been prevented by bad weather everyone would have understood the reason and no action would have been brought against the skippers, so it looks as though they feared interception by the English. The threat must have been quite considerable to daunt these normally fearless men! However, three months after the merchants' complaint, the Queen and council were receiving applications for Leith ships to be licenced to sail to England with cargoes of fish, oil and salt.

The year 1515 seems to have been relatively uneventful for Leith, but in February 1516 something quite unprecedented occured; the town was assessed for £80 in a taxation made to raise money to send ambassadors to France. As an 'unfree' town, Leith was not liable to pay taxes, (one of the few advantages of this low status) and so the bailies informed the king's messenger who came to collect the money on 26 February. The following day the messenger returned with reinforcements, but still the bailies would not pay up. On the 29th the macer and three officers of the Court of the Lords of Council appeared in Leith to apprise the goods and lands of the bailies with a view to poinding for the tax. One of them, William Forrester, 'deforced' the macer and ended up in prison in Edinburgh Castle.

In the end, Sir Robert Logan of Restalrig paid the £80 on behalf of his tenants of Leith, but he appeared before the Lords of Council on 3 March to protest about the imposition. The Lords decided that as the money had been paid William Forrester and his goods could be released, but that Leith should not pay taxes in future. The 'bailies of Leith' who were involved in this dispute were not the Water Bailies, appointed by Edinburgh, but the bailies of the Barony of Restalrig, appointed by the laird. Their existence is a reminder that Edinburgh did not yet have complete control over the town. Several bailies are mentioned by name during the following 50 years, and it is clear from what is known of them that they wielded a fair degree of power in the community.

Robert Barton and David Falconer

Later in 1516, Robert Barton became the king's Comptroller, sharing with his Treasurer the management of royal and national finances, with power to buy directly from foreign ships anything that he needed in his official capacity. He was also made a customar of Edinburgh. It may have been this alarming combination of offices that decided Edinburgh to appoint a 'searcher of ships', whose job it was to make sure that all goods coming into the Port paid customs to the king and to the burgh. (Within a few years they found it necessary to raise the number of searchers to three.) Provision had been made for such an appointment in an Act of Parliament of 1489, but the burgh does not seem to have bothered with a searcher before. However, faced with a 'free spirit' like Robert Barton in such a position of power, the Council seems to have decided to safeguard its rights as far as it could.

As it turned out, their fears were fully justified. At the beginning of July 1517, a ship came into Leith with a cargo of timber. The skipper duly went up to the Edinburgh Tolbooth and 'declared' his cargo to the treasurer and one of the bailies, who accompanied him back to Leith to take possession of it in the name of the burgh. However, they were met on the Shore by Robert Barton 'and with him a multitude of his neighbours and men of Leith, [who] came and masterfully took the said timber from the said treasurer and bailie' Robert's excuse, that the wood was needed for the king's use, was not accepted and he was admonished by the Lords of Council and reminded of the rules.

It is not to be supposed that this scourge of the high seas would be daunted by a mere admonition from the Lords. Just over a year later he was again in court being pursued by Edinburgh on six counts of illegal trading. He was accused of cornering the market in wool south of the Forth and buying hides, cloth, skins, salmon, wine, wax, victual and other staple goods. His defence was that he and others in Leith had always done this. It appears that not only did he buy illegally, he also exported goods without paying custom (which privilege he quite rightly said had been granted him by James IV), and 'regrated' imported goods (which he admitted). He had been buying and salting fish which came into Leith then selling it in England, and had created an 'exorbitant dearth' of tallow by buying it from all parts of Scotland and exporting it. On top of all this, as customar, he would not custom any goods to go to Flanders or France until his own ships had been fully laden (this he denied). In view of his royal protection, all the Lords could do was order him to desist. Neither he nor his associates took much notice of this order. In November 1519, the burgh again passed a prohibition against men of Leith buying foreign goods before they had been 'entered' at the Tolbooth, or selling goods in Leith. The (Water) Bailie of Leith was ordered to assist the searcher in his duties.

In 1520, the question of dues to the chaplain at Bruges arose once more. Alexander Fotheringham, who held the post, complained that masters of Scottish ships had been refusing to pay. A letter was written in the name of James V to the chief towns of the Low Countries, asking them to deal with the matter 'as it would be troublesome to start a suit in Scotland'. The officials in the Low Countries decided that they would find such an action equally 'troublesome', and in 1526, Alexander Fotheringham was back before the Lords of Council, requesting the poinding of the goods of skippers for non-payment of the dues. David Falconer (whom we have already met as one of James IV's men and who later became a Leith bailie) argued for the skippers that as the Staple had moved from Bruges many years before, it was no longer incumbent on them to pay anything to the chaplain. Furthermore, it transpired that not only had there been no divine service at the altar since 1519, but that Alexander had sold all the relics and vestments, together with the chalice and other jewels. He no longer even lived in Bruges. In spite of all this, the Lords did not feel they could give a judgement against Alexander until 1529, when he finally gave them an excuse by acting illegally in a process against a Canon of Aberdeen.

The next concerted attempt by Edinburgh to clip the wings of Leith came in 1523, and concerned the buying of 'prize' ships and cargo. We have already seen that this was one way in which the well-off in Leith made their money. The fact that Edinburgh decided to try and curtail this activity suggests a lack of success in curbing other trading ventures. The Provost and Bailies brought a 'test case' against Robert Barton, David Falconer, Edward Cockburn, John Kerr and John Loch, all of Leith, accusing them of buying English prize goods recently brought into Leith by a French ship. Edinburgh's contention was that prizes were comprehended in the legislation which forbade packing and peeling in Leith. The defence of the Leith skippers that they had always been in the habit of buying prizes was not accepted by the Lords, who ordered them to desist in future. They also ordered them to give the goods in the present case to Edinburgh, in spite of the fact that the skippers had a 'respite' granted the previous year by Albany which rendered them immune from poind and escheat for 19 years. Sir Robert Logan of Restalrig (who was still the feudal superior of Leith) made it clear that in his view the judgement was invalid as the king was a minor, and that he intended to pursue the matter 'when time is'.

As the century progressed, Edinburgh successfully attempted to gain increasing control over Leith. Before too roundly condemning the burgh's actions it should be remembered that this was a time of serious decline in Scottish trade, and that Edinburgh was ever less able to afford a potential rival on her doorstep. Also, in the first half of the century Leith enjoyed extensive royal protection. One of Edinburgh's defences against competition was to attempt to stamp out practices which she had winked at for years past. Leith was paying the price for her increasing prosperity.

It is in 1523 that we come across the first concrete reference to the 'Market' of Leith. In October Albany was preparing an army for a campaign against the English in the Borders. The maltsters of Leith were ordered to have their wives and servants provide 10 chalders (about 20 tons) of malt a day for brewing into ale for the soldiers. There was a great reluctance, or perhaps an inability, to conform with the order. Four searchers were appointed to commandeer all the malt in Leith, if necessary breaking down doors in order to search storehouses. All the inhabitants of the Lothian and Linlithgow were commanded to bring their bere to the 'market of Leith' in order to sell it to the maltsters.

David Falconer, who had represented the skippers in the action against the chaplain of Bruges, was one of the most powerful men in Leith at this time. He was a close associate of Robert Barton, and was drawn with him into the politics of the day. As Comptroller, Robert was in close contact with the Queen, and became a supporter of her and her wing of the pro-English party. The estrangement of the Queen and Angus had brought about a split in the pro-English ranks, and Henry VIII chose to support Angus, who could be the most use to him. His sister, by 1520, was sending him anguished appeals for money. The tenants of her Scottish estates were refusing to pay their rents and if Robert Barton had not lent her £500 of his own money she would have been constrained to live 'like a poor gentlewoman'. As it was, she had been forced to dismiss many of her servants. Robert lent her a further £100, but thereafter refused to give her any more. He had good reason for his refusal. Albany's foreign notions of household expenditure had forced the books well into the red, and Robert had been making up the deficit out of his own pocket. In 1525, he resigned the Comptrollership. His loyalty to the Crown did not extend to bankrupting himself in its service.

Shortly before his resignation he had a meeting with Dr Magnus, the English Ambassador in Edinburgh, who duly reported back to Henry VIII. Magnus had been understandably suspicious of the Comptroller, who had long been known in England as Hob-a-Barton (besides being a diminutive of Robert, 'Hob' was a name given to the Devil). The Ambassador was very surprised to find that the Comptroller was better disposed to England than to France, and that his companion, David Falconer, was ready to fight against Albany. Magnus reported that he had learned many things from Barton, and mentioned the Comptroller's concern over the Royal depredations on his purse.

The Ambassador might have been less surprised at the pro-English stance of Barton and Falconer if he had known that they had both been in contact with the Duke of Norfolk (the English Admiral) at Newcastle in September of the previous year. As far as we know the errands were perfectly innocent: Robert Barton's son carried a request from the Queen for a safeconduct for a ship to go to England for goods for her household, David Falconer's servant came on behalf of the Earl of Cassillis (also pro-English) about payment for some fish bought by men living in Norfolk's Lordship. The servant had also seen Norfolk a month earlier, when he brought the Duke a letter from the current English Ambassador in Edinburgh. This, at least, is all that Norfolk reported to Cardinal

Wolsey. Any other transactions that may have been carried out were not written down and so will never be known.

Even after his resignation of the post of Comptroller, Robert Barton continued to support the Queen, along with David Falconer. By this time the Douglases were firmly in control, with strong support from Edinburgh. This fact in itself may have provided an added reason for the powerful in Leith to champion Margaret.

Leith and The King of Denmark

A sub-plot in the political story was Scotland's continuing connection with Denmark, which was now facing civil strife, on top of her continuing problems with Lubeck. King Hans' son Christian II had come to the throne. As he acquired the soubriquet of, 'The Nero of the North', it is not surprising that some of his subjects felt they would rather be ruled by his nephew Frederick. In 1519, ships were sent from the west coast of Scotland to Copenhagen in support of Christian, but nothing more is heard from Scottish sources until 1524. By then Frederick had gained the Danish throne, and Christian was seeking Scottish help to restore him to his rightful place, through his agent Alexander Kinghorn, who was based at Leith. After Albany's final departure for France in 1524, Kinghorn informed Christian that he was now able to act. If Christian would tell him when he intended to make an attempt to regain his throne, he would find Kinghorn there before him with a force. Robert Barton and David Falconer had promised him ships, and men whom he had formerly hired were willing to serve again. Preparations went ahead - until Angus got wind of them. In May 1525 the government took steps to prevent a Scottish force from going to Denmark:

> As our Sovereign Lord and Lords of Council are reliably informed that certain masters, owners and mariners of ships dwelling in Leith are to depart in warfare....we charge and command all indwellers of Leith; owners, masters, skippers and mariners of ships, that none of them are to make war at sea without a special licence of the King.

As might be expected, Robert Barton took no notice of the directive. Within a month he was writing to Christian assuring him of his co-operation, and informing the king that he was preparing a small fleet to come to his aid. He did, however, make it clear that his support depended on prompt payment of 2,500 gold florins still owing for a ship called the *Lion* which Barton had sold to the king. In October 1525, Kinghorn wrote an encouraging letter to Christian, telling him that Scottish support for him was growing and would become even greater if the king made more efforts to recover his kingdom (a recurrent motif in letters to Christian from his supporters). The following January, Christian wrote to Angus, asking if his ships could use Scottish ports as bases. Permission was granted, but not all the ports were as friendly to Christian as Leith. Late in 1526, his ship the *Peter Hull* was wrecked in Aberdeen harbour, another ship with her sold to the Provost and a third taken by the people of the town.

By February 1527, Angus had undergone a cautious change of heart towards Christian. He wrote promising his assistance, but in July the Government was writing to Frederick I about two Danish ships which had been brought into Leith as a 'prize' assuring him that as there was some doubt about their status they were being carefully looked after until their owners could get to Scotland to recover them. The letter does, however, point out that Scots returning from Denmark had reported that numerous Scottish merchants and vessels had recently been arrested at Copenhagen and elsewhere. From this time on the Scottish policy seems to have been to 'run with the hare and hunt with the hounds' as far as Christian and Frederick were concerned. Robert Barton and David Falconer, however, continued to come down on the side of Christian, and in 1528, Frederick wrote to the king of France, asking him to use his influence to have them restrained.

Another Leith skipper who claimed to support Christian was Robert Fogo. This piratical character enters our story in June 1524, when some Edinburgh men came before the Lords of Council to testify that Fogo had captured a Dutch ship belonging to one Albrecht Wangork, while in command of the *Martin*, which he owned jointly with Robert and Alexander Barton. The captured Dutch ship was now in Leith, but as there was no war with Holland it was doubtful if she was 'just prize' and the complainers asked the Lords to order the owners of *Martin* to keep the Dutch ship and her cargo safe in case she had to be returned. Twelve days later the wives and children of the merchants who had been in the *Martin* appeared before the Court to tell a pitiful tale. Their vessel had been bound for Danzig when the Dutch ship was taken. Fogo had returned to Leith with his prize, leaving a substitute captain in charge of the *Martin*. They put in to Copenhagen and the merchants went ashore. The crew, on hearing that they were liable to be arrested for taking the Dutch ship, hauled up the anchor and sailed away, leaving their passengers stranded and penniless. Now the bereft families implored the Lords to order Fogo to go back and pick up their men-folk. Fogo made the unlikely plea that the merchants had stayed behind on purpose, and was given two weeks to prove it. No more is heard of this side of the story, presumably someone took pity on the unfortunate merchants and brought them home.

However, Albrecht Wangork was not one to give up easily. In October 1524, a letter in the name of James V was sent to king Frederick. It told how the ship and cargo of Edward Crawfurd of Edinburgh had been arrested at Copenhagen on information from the Dutchman. Frederick was asked to return Crawfurd's property and tell Wangork to seek restitution in the Scottish courts. In December, Robert Barton was before the Lords complaining that his ship the *Hoye* with the *Christopher* and the *Nicholas*, also of Leith (*Nicholas* belonged to David Falconer and *Christopher* was possibly the ship of Edward Crawfurd) had been arrested at Copenhagen at Wangork's instance, in revenge for the taking of his ship. The Lords ordered that the owners of the *Martin* should relieve the supplicants. As one of those owners was Barton himself, one wonders exactly how this was arranged.

During the next year Fogo was implicated with Patrick Barcar of Leith in another act of piracy (or maybe the same one, the evidence is confused) and in December 1525 they were both ordered to answer charges in Denmark. They tried sending a proxy in June 1526, but the pursuers did not compear and in December they were once again ordered to go to Denmark. This time they pointed out that as Christian of Denmark was their master they should not be made to appear before Frederick, and although again ordered to attend in Denmark in June 1527, they did not go, and in December were distrained for 9000 golden guldens to compensate the victims of their actions against the Dutch. Perhaps they managed to wriggle out of this as well, but no more is heard of the case.

The King and the Skippers

In September 1528 James V, who was now 17 years old, finally escaped from the semi-captivity in which he had been kept by Angus, and established his personal rule. A hurriedly convened Parliament put Angus and his supporters to the horn and they took refuge in Tantallon Castle, an impregnable stronghold perched on the edge of a sea-cliff not far from Dunbar. The king, who had conceived a bitter hatred of his step-father over the past few years, was determined to flush him out, and ordered a muster for 10 October to raise a besieging force. David Falconer was made Captain of Foot. On the way to Tantallon the king's forces borrowed artillery and gunners from Dunbar castle, where a French garrison was stationed, to augment the cannon they had brought from Edinburgh. Ships were sent round to guard the seaward side of the castle.

According to an account written by Angus a month after the event, the besiegers arrived before Tantallon on 18 October. On 4 November, having been unable to take the castle, the king returned to Edinburgh, leaving a band of foot and a company of cavalry to bring home the artillery. That night Angus issued out against the depleted forces with 160 horse to make his escape, and in the fighting David Falconer was killed: 'their principal captain of foot, their best man-of-war on sea'. According to the historian Pitscottie it was Archibald Douglas, Angus's uncle, who perpetrated the deed, but this was never proved. At the slaughter of David Falconer, 'the king was heavily displeased, and lamented the same greatly'. Although Angus was now out of reach, James returned to the siege in order to obtain the castle and prevent the Earl from using it again. It was finally handed over by the captain whom Angus had left in charge.

James was, as Pitscottie said, extremely upset at the death of David Falconer, probably blaming himself for leaving his Captain with an insufficient force. He treated the killing as murder, and when those who had been with Angus in his sortie later purchased remissions of their death sentences from the king, each contained the proviso that it was only valid so long as the holder was not convicted of the slaughter of Falconer.

In October 1529, David's widow, Elizabeth Brownhill, and her son were granted the escheated goods of two servants of Angus to compensate for the loss of their goods in the *Little Martin*, which had been wrecked near Innerwick in November 1528 and plundered by Angus's men. Three years previously she and her husband had been licenced by the king to buy bere and produce malt. Maltmaking probably now provided her main livelihood, although she owned land and a house at Newhaven, which she sold to some Danzig merchants in 1533 for £100.

The accession of James V put an end to internal political instability. James, determined to rid himself of any reminders of his despised step-father, favoured a French alliance, and his attitude determined the trend of foreign policy during his reign. The Queen Mother no longer counted in political life. She was now married to a third husband, Henry Stewart, Ist Lord Methven. This union was no more personally successful than her previous attempt, but at least Methven was a lightweight figure who had no influence on national affairs.

As far as Leith was concerned, it was James' attitude to Denmark which was the most significant political factor. Shortly after he assumed power he wrote to King Frederick, who had heard that the deposed Christian was to visit Scotland. James assured him that he would not permit such a visit, but made it clear that he intended to adopt a strictly neutral stance towards the warring monarchs. Alexander Kinghorn, writing to Christian in the spring of 1529, felt that there had been a danger that James would make a treaty with Frederick, but that it had been averted by the intervention of Charles V (Emperor of the Holy Roman Empire, which included Spain and the Low Countries). Christian had ordered Kinghorn to issue a stern reminder to Robert Barton about his duty to his employer. Kinghorn felt it best to tone this down somewhat, as Barton was now restored to his old position of power, as Comptroller, Treasurer, Customar and Master of the Mint. James had made Barton hand over to him some property or money of Christian's, but Kinghorn had extracted a promise that it would soon be repaid, with interest. This, however, was probably his last letter to the exiled King, as he died later in the year, ending Leith's political connection with Denmark. The trade connection continued to flourish. As Treasurer and Comptroller, Robert Barton had to contend with the old problem of royal insolvency, and he resigned the posts after a year, by which time the crown owed him 10,000 merks (£6,666).

In 1531 a dispute arose between the shipowners, skippers and mariners of North Leith and the Kirkmasters of St Mary's church in South Leith. St Nicholas' Chapel, which the former frequented, was in need of repair and threatened by coastal erosion. In the past the primegilt paid by men of North Leith had been used for the benefit of St Nicholas (which had a hospital or almshouse attached to it), but was now being appropriated by the Kirkmasters. The skippers had refused to pay and the Kirkmasters had seized their sails and anchors. According to the Kirkmasters, the North Leithers had in the past assigned their primegilt to St Mary's, and they needed the money to repair and extend that church. The outcome of the case is not recorded, but the Lords of Council appear to have been sympathetic to the skippers, and the chapel of St Nicholas was still standing many years later.

Piracy and War

Relations with England had been fairly quiet for a few years, but piracy was a way of life for Leith seamen, and they would not desist for long. A letter written by an Englishman in 1532 gives a vivid picture of the panic which could be caused by the presence of a few Scottish privateers in the Channel. Vessels scattered in all directions for the safety of harbour, and hysteria rose as succeeding ships made it to port, each skipper with his story of witnessing or experiencing the Scottish menace. Our letter writer was called John Chapman, and he had been on his way to Bordeaux when he was chased into Fowey by a Scottish man-of-war. Here he met a merchant who related how on his way home from Bordeaux he had seen four Scottish ships take fourteen English vessels and a Spaniard of 300 tons laden with English goods. A shipowner of Bordeaux was certain that he had only been saved by the fact that his ship was of Breton build. When chased, he had managed to get ashore and find four Bretons, whom he had persuaded to pretend to the pursuing Scots that the ship was theirs. Once the coast was clear he had set sail and crossed the Channel under cover of darkness. Two shipmasters of Loo reported that they had seen nine or ten ships chased into Brest. These intrepid men had made contact with the enemy, having gone on board the Scottish ships to see if they could arrange to ransom the English sailors 'after the old custom of the sea' of 20s for a mariner and 40s for a master. For some reason the Scots would not agree to this, which caused worried headshaking among the assembled company. The Scottish ships were still lying off the coast, 'so that no man dares look out'. All this panic was caused by the presence of just four vessels, one of 160 tons and the rest of 100 tons - and a rumour that more were waiting off Lands End and the Scilly Isles.

There is no direct proof that these particular Scottish pirates were Leith men, but it is very noticeable that whenever names are given, in court cases or correspondence concerning piracy, the offenders are almost invariably from our port. Leith skippers were among the most prosperous Scottish mariners of the day, able to afford both the superior ships which could chase and capture several vessels at a time, and the necessary armaments.

By the start of 1533, Scotland was briefly at war with England in good earnest. In February, Sir George Lawson was sent by Henry VIII to Berwick on Tweed to oversee the provisioning of English troops in the Borders. Over the next four months he sent back reports to Thomas Cromwell, the English Chancellor, which were triumphant concerning operations on land, but despairing when they touched on the subject of grain transport ships. He pleaded in vain for warships to be sent to protect these vessels, and even went so far as to forbid the waiting convoys to leave their ports in the Humber until help arrived.

At least five Scottish ships were lying in wait off Tynemouth, two of them skippered by George Wallace and William Clapperton of Leith and two more possibly by John Kerr and John Barton (son of Andrew). George Wallace was James V's chief skipper, given command of the *Mary Willoughby* which had been captured from the English. By the beginning of April it was clear that no escorts would be sent for the English grain ships and they had to set sail from the Humber unprotected. Inevitably, twelve were captured, reportedly by a single barque, and taken to Leith. Only six got through to Berwick. As it happened, all this danger was endured for nothing. By the middle of May the campaign was over, and Sir George was complaining that he would have to sell off his left-over grain at a loss, as local prices were lower than those he had paid for it. He had not even needed the grain brought by the ships as he had been able to buy good supplies in the local markets.

In London Chapuys, the ambassador of the Holy Roman Emperor, was vainly attempting to prevent Henry VIII from divorcing Charles' aunt, Katherine of Aragon. He wrote enormously long gloomy reports home to his master which usually included information about Scotland, which at that time an was ally of Spain. While Sir George was begging for warships, Chapuys noted that four were in fact being fitted out, but their purpose was to prevent the Scots getting ammunition and supplies from Flanders. They left the Thames on 23 February, and by the middle of March four more were being made ready. 'People here are astonished at the number of ships the Scots have and suspect they receive help elsewhere' (ie France). The English reinforcements did not sail until the end of the month. Chapuys' opinion was that until then they had not dared leave the river, but were forced out by the taking of eight English ships by the Scots. At the end of May he reported that the Scots were still preying on English ships in spite of a truce which had just been agreed, and had taken seven very rich prizes ten days before.

The truce may have been ignored by the more piratical Leith skippers, but it had a positive effect on trade. The traffic in dried and salt fish (Scotland's main export to London) had suffered during the time of tension, but in the year August 1533 to September 1534 exports of fish from Leith doubled, and the duty paid on English goods imported into Leith jumped from £3 2s to £47 9s 6d. While there was a threat of war, the customars had been ordered not to coket fish for England, but in late February 1534, Nicholas Carncours petitioned the Lords of Council for permission to have the order suspended so that he could export nearly 200 barrels of herring 'as the season thereof is fast ganging'. The 'season' was Lent (which in that year extended from 18 February to 5 April) when fish took the place of the meat which was a forbidden food during that time of abstinence.

Leith Heretics

In the spring of 1534, the Council of Edinburgh chartered the *John*, belonging to Henry Cairns of Leith, to carry goods to France. This was probably the last trading voyage Henry ever made from Leith. By the summer he had become a victim of the persecution of Lutherans which broke out in Edinburgh in that year.

According to John Knox, individuals in all the East Coast towns had at an early date embraced the Lutheran doctrine which taught that salvation from the spiritual consequences of sin was to be achieved through faith in Christ. The Church, on the other hand, had evolved a lucrative belief in the efficacy of penance through the buying of pardons, and more importantly, the giving of money - possibly to the poor, but preferably to itself. Doctrinally, another debate centered on the precise sense in which the bread consecrated at the Mass 'became' the body of Christ. Pragmatically, the adoption of Luther's beliefs would cause much of the funding of the Church to dry up. Wealthy bishops and abbots enjoyed a lifestyle as luxurious as that of the king, and many laymen were financially dependent on the revenues of church lands which they had acquired. It was the prospect of losing all this wealth which carried most weight in Scotland at this time.

Lutheran books had been smuggled into Scotland through the ports of the east coast almost as soon as they began to be published in 1517. Eight years later the Scottish Parliament imposed a ban on their importation, but with little effect. By 1527, Denmark was supporting Lutheranism, and Leith's close links with that country may have helped to strengthen the growth of the sect in the port. The resistance by skippers to paying dues to the non-existent altar at Bruges suggests that they were at least questioning the traditions of the Church.

In 1528, Patrick Hamilton, the first Scottish Protestant martyr, was burnt at the stake, and in May 1534 the king wrote to the Lords of Council about the growing 'menace' of Lutheranism:

> We are reliably informed of divers tracts and books translated from Latin into our Scots tongue by heretics, favourers and of the sect of Luther, [which] are sent into this realm to divers parts such as Leith, Edinburgh, Dundee, St Andrews, Montrose, Aberdeen and Kirkcaldy to infect the inward parts of the same, unless hasty remedy is taken.

The Lords were commanded to forbid anyone to communicate wuth Lutherans coming to Scotland or to own heretical books, on pain of arrest of persons, goods and ships. If these measures did not suffice, the Lords were authorised to stamp out the sect in the king's name by any means they saw fit. The result of this permission was a concerted effort to seek out offenders, at the instance of Archbishop Beaton of St Andrews. This in turn led to a major heresy trial in Edinburgh, four months after the king wrote his letter.

At least thirteen people were indicted at this trial of 1534 and five of them came from Leith. William Kirk of Leith was one of the three priests involved. Of his fate nothing is known, but Norman Gourlay (a Fife and Leith name) had picked up the doctrine in the Baltic, almost certainly in Denmark, and had gone so far as to marry when he returned home - he was burned. The third priest was Andrew Johnston, the prebendary of St Andrew's altar in St Giles, who fled abroad, as did an advocate called William Johnston. Skipper Henry Cairns of Leith fled to the Baltic. His goods were escheated to the crown, but five years later James granted them to Henry's seven sons and five daughters.

Adam Dais of North Leith was one of the shipwrights who had worked on the *Michael*. In 1532, he was still holding out against paying primegilt to the Kirkmasters of South Leith, for a cargo of wine from Bordeaux, and only the previous year had been one of the assise that apprised Elizabeth Brownhill's lands in Newhaven before they were sold. He was indicted for heresy and is said to have fled also. However, there was an 'Adam Dais, timberman' in Leith the following year. The family was not numerous, so it may be that this was the same Adam who had, in fact, recanted. (The Dais family seems to have had a tradition of taking religion seriously. In the 1480's, Alexander Dais of Leith had got into difficulties as he returned from a pilgrimage to Rome, and had been convicted of vagrancy in Danzig.) Adam's troubles did not end with his escape from the flames. The following March his ship the *Gabriel* went aground and was plundered off the English coast. He tried unsuccessfully for five years to get restitution, and finally, in 1540, James V had to write to Henry VIII on his behalf.

A Leith woman was convicted at the Edinburgh trial on the evidence of a midwife who reported that she had refused to call on the Virgin Mary for help while in labour, but insisted on praying to Christ. She was persuaded to recant, but escaped confiscation of her goods as she was married (so that all her goods were the property of her husband). A Leith man called John Stewart died in exile.

Persecution did nothing to halt adherence to heretical beliefs in Leith. William Clerk, who had been on the assise with Adam Dais, may have been the man of the same name, heretic and clerk of *The Barge*, whose escheated goods were granted by the king in 1539 at the same time as his grant to Henry Cairns' brood. In 1542 it was reported to Henry VIII that the people of Leith were 'all good Christians', and in 1543, the touring Protestant preacher George Wishart knew that the port was one of the places where he would find a sympathetic congregation.

Tie with Denmark Severed

In 1534, Frederick I of Denmark died and was succeeded by his son, Christian III. Christian soon found himself menaced by the Lubeckers of the Hanseatic League. In 1535 The Danish king sent his envoy Peter Suavenius to Scotland with a letter for James V asking him to send Christian his famous seamen Albert Bartuen and Albert Fagow (Robert Barton and Robert Fogo). To Peter's frustration, although everyone in Scotland behaved very amicably towards him, everyone purported to believe that Denmark was in no danger from Lubeck. He did not even manage to see the king until he had been in Scotland for three months. After the interview he went to Leith and showed his letters to Robert Barton who was equally unhelpful, saying he could do nothing unless Suavenius brought him an order from James.

The fact was that Scotland's special relationship with Denmark was currently in abeyance. James was more interested in strengthening his ties with France than with supporting the small and perpetually troubled kingdom of his remote relation. The skippers of Leith were no longer as independent as in the days of the king's minority. Robert Barton, at least, was not the man he had been - just a year later, he was described as being 'of great age, feeble and weak in person' and the king took all his dependants under the royal protection.

The King in France

Barton was not too old and weak, however, to accompany the King on a long visit to France, at the end of which James returned with a Queen, the consumptive Madeleine, who lived for only six weeks of a Scottish summer. James and his court had set sail for France from Leith in late July 1536 but were forced back into the Forth by a storm. They set out again from Kirkcaldy at the beginning of September. The king was in the *Mary Willoughby*, skippered by George Wallace, and with him went five other ships which, according to an English informant who saw them at Dieppe, were 'in comparison but ballingers' when seen alongside the 280 ton 'flagship'.

The King spent the winter in Paris, where he went on a monumental spending spree. After the booths of Edinburgh High Street, the markets of a major Continental city must have seemed like a consumer's paradise. In March 1537, a fleet of fourteen Scottish ships arrived at Le Havre to escort home their King and his bride, including John Barton's great hulk which was to bring back the horses the King had bought. The French King provided a further eight vessels one of which, the *Salamander*, was a wedding present. James needed a strong escort as he had been warned that twenty English ships were lying in wait for him on his way home. However, the King and Queen arrived safely in Scotland. The English were left to pursue vigorous enquiries into a rumour that when James had landed at Scarborough for fresh water, he been invited to invade the north of England, which was at that time in revolt over Henry VIII's divorce and split with Rome. James is said to have politely declined the invitation.

A New Fleet?

It is after James' return from France in 1537 that we begin to discover more about the royal ships, and it may be that at this time he decided to build up a fleet to rival that of his father. At the time of the king's return home, three ships are mentioned by name. The pride of the fleet was the *Mary Willoughby*, captured from the English and skippered by George Wallace. She had been named, in happier days, after Katherine of Aragon's favourite lady in waiting, Maria de Salinas, who married Lord Willoughby in 1516. Maria remained faithful to her mistress through the dark days of the divorce procedings, and comforted Katherine's dying moments. *Salamander* was, as we have seen, a wedding gift from the king of France. The *Moriset* (skipper Robert Smalum) had been bought in France.

In 1538, two shiploads of timber were brought from Lochaber to Leith 'for the king's galleys', which were being built there and were probably the *Lion* and the *Unicorn* mentioned in the Treasurer's accounts for the following year. Also in 1538 the *Moriset* was repaired at Leith, so the shipbuilders of the port were by no means redundant. By 1540 one Walter Howison had been appointed 'Master Wright of the King's Ships' and based at Leith.

In this year the name 'Falconer' once more enters the records.The King gave Peter Falconer, who was almost certainly David's son, £60 towards the ship he was having repaired at Leith in partnership with Alexander Wallace (son of George?). Three years later, the King gave Barbara Falconer 9 ells of rich black fabric for her wedding gown - he seems to have been keeping a fatherly eye on the children of his old favourite. Another familiar name which reappears is 'Cornton', this time Florence. He seems to have been the last of the line in Leith, but he remained in the royal service in one capacity or another for more than 20 years.

By 1540, the King's naval base at Leith was well established. John Barton had been seeing to the refitting and provisioning of the King's ships since 1538, Walter Howison the Master Shipwright was appointed in November of that year with his two 'servants', and Florence Cornton had been made Overseer of the King's Ships by a letter of the King under the Privy Seal. He looked after the dismantled rigging, masts, anchor and other equipment which was removed whenever the ships were laid up. As well as the *Mary Willoughby* (skipper John Anderson of Leith), the *Salamander* (skipper John Kerr of Leith) and the *Lion* (skipper John Brown of Leith), there were the *Great Unicorn* and the *Little Unicorn*. In 1538 there had been mention of the *Mareval* and the *French Shallop*, but they do not appear again, and there is no further notice of the *Moriset* after that date. Yet another 'New Haven' was being built, this time at Burntisland. Maybe the intention, if the King had lived, was to make this a new base for the royal ships.

A ship belonging to Thomas Richardson of Leith was sometimes used by the King, and it is a measure of the resurgence of royal employees that he, John Kerr and Florence Cornton felt themselves to be in a position to flout the Edinburgh bye-laws. Finally, in 1540, the Council complained to the Lords that as inhabitants of North Leith (in Florence's case, St Leonard's Lands) the three had evaded paying petty custom for some years, on the grounds that they dwelt in the Regality of Holyrood and were answerable only to the Abbot. One would have thought they had a point, but the Lords ruled otherwise. This was such an important precedent that the decree was stowed away safely in the Burgh's Charter Chest. In 1541 the three wrongdoers were again up before the Edinburgh Council, for non-payment of petty custom. Thomas was accused of not paying dues on goods carried by his boat to a ship in the Roads, for which he had stood surety. John and Florence owed petty custom on fish which they had exported from Leith - 60 and 102 barrels respectively. As the market for wool, skins and hides dwindled, the export of fish, much of it from the burghs of the Fife coast, became increasingly important to Leith.

Another commodity that attracted a surprising amount of legislation was tallow, hard mutton fat, used to make malodorous candles. The cost of wax candles put them out of reach of all but the rich, so a shortage of tallow was almost equivalent to a power cut in its effect on everyday life. Parliament was so alarmed at the amount of tallow being exported that in 1538 a law was passed forbidding its removal from the country. The customs duty on it had already been raised to a swingeing £1 per barrel (other goods paid 3s per barrel at the most), but this only created a smuggling boom. In the same year that the law was passed, James Mowbray was rewarded for his 'diligence in tracing the tallow taken furth of the country without any custom being paid'. Just 18 barrels of tallow were customed at Edinburgh that year. In Leith, James Mowbray searched out a further 103!

The End of Robert Fogo

In 1538 James V remarried. His bride was Mary of Guise, the young widow of the Duc de Longueville. Henry VIII had also been interested in making her his third wife, after the execution of Anne Boleyn, but she refused his offer, remarking that her neck was too small! Mary was a remarkable and courageous woman, who was later to play a major part in the story of Leith.

1539 saw the beginning of the end for Robert Fogo. In April, along with five others, he was granted letters of reprisal against the Dutch and the Frieslanders for injuries suffered in 1530. The letters authorised the arrest of Dutch or Friesland ships in Scottish ports until reparation was made. Fogo interpreted this as a licence to seize ships wherever they might be, and on 18 June the

The Armorial Bearings of Mary of Guise, once built into the wall of a house in Leith.

following year he took three Dutch ships which were fishing off Fair Isle and sold them and their cargo in England. When he returned to Scotland in July he was immediately imprisoned by the King, who informed Charles V of his action in reply to a letter of protest. He also took the opportunity to point out that Scots were not infrequently robbed by subjects of the Emperor, and he expected reciprocal action if he was to deal with Robert Fogo. He even sent John Campbell of Lundy to negotiate with Charles.

On 18 December 1540 Fogo was still in prison, not to be released until he made restitution. By December 1541 he was dead. His two sons were put in the care of James Robertson of Stirling, the King paying for their board.

The King's Voyage

On 24 April 1540, one John Heron wrote to Thomas Cromwell in London, that king James had four or five ships at Leith, armed and ready to sail, but John did not know to what destination. This news caused a certain amount of nervousness among the English, and over the next six weeks various informants kept London posted with the latest rumours: There were twelve ships and James was going to France or Flanders: There were sixteen ships and James was going to Honfleur, then to Paris and returning via the Western Isles: The King was going to Ireland to receive the homage of eight Irish Earls who had been at the Scottish court during the winter. In response to this last piece of information, the English fitted out twenty ships to prevent him.

In fact, when James finally left Leith, on 12 June 1540, it was to voyage to Orkney and thence to the Western Isles, in order to remind the Lords there of their allegiance to him. He himself went in the *Salamander* and the rest of the court in the *Mary Willoughby, Lion, Great Unicorn* and *Little Unicorn*. All these vessels were well armed - it had taken six boats six days to ferry all the ordnance aboard. With them went a hulk (possibly belonging to John Barton) to carry the baggage, and several other escort ships, including the vessels of John Anderson and Thomas Richardson of Leith. No doubt the fleet was intended to put up a good show of strength to any Northern or Western Lord who might be thinking of making trouble. James ended his voyage at Whithorn, returning overland to Edinburgh.The fleet returned to Burntisland in August.

The pilot on the voyage had been Alexander Lindsay, who passed on his knowledge of the coasts of Scotland to the French king's cosmographer, Nicholas D'Arville. Nicholas wrote it all down, and it no doubt proved useful to him seven years later when he was in the French galleys that besieged St Andrews.

War Again

The years since James' coming to power had seen just about every possible permutation of alliances and tensions between Scotland, England, France and Spain. In the main, Scotland was a friend to France, although a pro-English faction still existed, and gained ground as the Reformation gathered momentum in England. Even James was willing to listen to the overtures which Henry made to his nephew when it suited him politically. In 1541 he at last agreed to meet Henry at York, but was prevented from going by his Council, and Henry made the journey north for nothing. Incensed at this treatment (and at the frustrating of his secret plan to have James kidnapped) he mobilised an army in the North in the late summer of 1542. Initially the English suffered a defeat, at Haddon Rig in August, but Henry responded by sending even more forces to the borders. The Duke of Norfolk was sent to York to organise the supply of provisions.

Like Sir George Lawson at Berwick in 1533, the Duke was very concerned about the possibility of Scottish ships disrupting his supply fleet. The Captain of Berwick informed him that four ships had been fitted out and were lying at Burntisland. It was his opinion that the Scots were afraid of the five English ships which then lay near Holy Island, but Norfolk thought it more likely they were awaiting the return of twelve merchantmen from Danzig, which might be carrying supplies. He urged that the English ships should leave Holy Island and lie in wait for the Scottish merchantmen, which had been held up at Elsinore by adverse winds. By 7 September the English ships had sailed, and Norfolk was heartened by news from two seamen who had just been released from captivity in Leith. According to them, on hearing that the English ships had come out, the Scots had sent their own ships up beyond Queensferry, to the anchorage guarded by James IV's forts on Inchgarvie and the adjacent shores of the Forth. Four days later the Duke wrote to the Council, 'Pray God the King's captains in the North do their devoir for of liklihood the Scots from Danske came forth this day, the wind being favourable.'

Meanwhile, Henry's Council had been getting information from George Douglas and the Laird of Drumlanrig about the amount of shipping in the Forth, and they wrote anxiously to Norfolk asking whether he had enough ships to deal with them. On 14 September, he replied that 'If all named in the bill (list) were in the Firth, they (the English ships) might lie there as long as they liked ere the Scots ships would meddle with them. All Scotland has but one ship of 260 or 280 tons, one of 200 and one of 160, the rest being small men of 100, 80 and under.'

On 19 September, a letter from York to London bore the frustrating news that the English fleet had waited for reinforcements from the Thames, and had thus missed taking the Scottish ships bound from Danzig. The Commissioners at York must now have been daily expecting word of a Scottish fleet coming out of the Forth, but it never appeared. Norfolk's information about the size of the Scottish ships was accurate, but in the past this had never deterred the Scots from attacking larger vessels. The aim of the Scots, had they appeared, would probably have been to harass the English supply convoys bringing provisions to the army in the North. As it happened, bad weather and bad organisation was rendering any such action on their part superfluous.

By the end of September, Henry was becoming impatient. He had spent a lot of money on a campaign which was getting nowhere, and was looking for ways to wear down the Scots for a quick victory. He had heard that the 'enemy' was being supplied with grain and meat from Orkney and Shetland, and wrote to the Commissioners ordering that the fleet be sent to devastate the Islands. As he had never been any further north than York, he might be forgiven for not appreciating the absurdity of his suspicions. The Commissioners must have smiled as they politely replied that the expedition would be too dangerous and there would be found nothing to destroy. In Orkney, 'the people live by fishing and have nothing to devastate save oats and a few beasts, which are so wild they can only be taken by dogs'. (Milking time must have been quite an experience!)

The Council wrote back that if the enterprise of Orkney and Shetland was not feasible, the Commissioners should try for a landing in the Forth and the burning of the Scottish ships. As the said ships had not menaced the English in any way, it is possible that the Commissioners might have made an excuse not to embark on this unprovoked action. However, before they had time to reply to the Council, Ross Herald arrived at York with letters from James and the news that 16 French ships laden with wine had evaded the English fleet and lately arrived at Leith. The information seems to have been untrue, but Norfolk did not know this, and from his point of view it made the situation much more dangerous. He informed the Council of the new developments, and it was decided to send six or seven warships to Scotland and cause as much damage as possible. Nearly three weeks later the English ships put boats ashore at Coldingham and burnt Eyemouth, then re-embarked and sailed on into the Forth.

In the meantime Norfolk, ill and depressed, begged to be relieved of his post and the Earl of Hertford took his place. It was he who reported on 7 November that Henry's ships were lying above Leith on the north side of the Forth, and had burnt Aberdour. Twelve days later they had returned to Newcastle. Preparations for the retreat of the army were now under way, and the rest of Henry's warships had already left the Humber for London.It may have been in the knowledge of this depletion of the English maritime forces that the Scots began to fit out warships, but their purpose was to escort a merchant convoy to Flanders, rather than to attack English shipping.

They left Leith early in December, but by then the war was over. The Scots army had been defeated on 24 November, at Solway Moss in the West Marches, by a small force left behind by the retreating English army. The King was unhurt, but the disaster had broken his spirit and after spending a week with the heavily pregnant Queen at Linlithgow, he retired to Falkland, where he died on 14 December, a week after the birth of his daughter Mary. Once again Scotland was to suffer the consequences of a royal minority, but the suffering was hardly alleviated when her Queen did finally take the throne. Mary inherited much of her mother's courage, but more of her grandmother's inability to keep her head where men were concerned.

5

The Worst ... That It Might Be

After the death of James V, Scotland was left with the familiar problem of a child monarch, in this case the infant Queen Mary, who was in the care of her mother, Mary of Guise. The Earl of Arran (heir presumptive to the throne) was appointed Governor and head of the ruling council. Cardinal Beaton was Chancellor. The presence of Beaton, the pursuer of heretics, and Arran, a committed Protestant, on the same 'board' could only lead to trouble. Not only were they diametrically opposed on religious issues, but their sectarian differences inevitably placed them on opposite sides of the political fence. Arran supported friendship with England; the Cardinal favoured France. The situation was further complicated in late December 1542, by the return from exile in England, of the Earl of Angus, his brother George Douglas, and Lord Bothwell. On 18 January 1543, Angus and Arran came to an agreement, Cardinal Beaton was placed under house-arrest, and the pro-English faction was, for the time being, firmly in the saddle.

Arran may have been encouraged to embrace the English cause by the letter he had recently received from the English Admiral, Lord Lisle, setting out Henry VIII's expectations of the new Scottish government. Lisle had heard that *Salamander* and *Unicorn* were at Leith, being rigged out for war. He hoped Arran had not ordered this, 'for it would hinder the King's good opinion of your inclination not to suffer anything that might irritate him.' The English took the Scottish threat to their shipping very seriously, and informants in France, the Low Countries and Scotland itself kept the Council and the Admiral up to date with news of Scottish maritime activities.

Lisle's letter to Arran did not prevent *Salamander* and *Unicorn* from sailing from Leith to join *Lion* and *Mary Willoughby* in the English Channel. The squadron was under the command of John Barton, 'Vice-Admiral of Scotland', and John Kerr captained *Mary Willoughby*. There were reportedly several richly laden Scots ships at Campveere; others were sighted by English spies at Dieppe and Le Havre. Although they were merchantmen, they would have been armed, and quite capable of capturing small craft such as fishing boats. The French were said to be about to sell the Scots three ships of between 300 and 150 tons, and to be preparing six more at Dieppe which the Scots would use to intercept Henry's merchantmen, which were currently bringing his wine from Bordeaux.

In response to this threat the English fitted out a fleet to intercept the Scots. Six of the ships were supposed to come from Newcastle, but there was some delay while they were freed from the ice, which lay two fathoms thick by the quayside. On 2 February 1543, Lisle informed the Duke of Suffolk that a spy had just brought word that *Mary Willoughby* and *Salamander* had come home with 19 English prizes (which included some laden with Henry VIII's wine). *Lion* and four other vessels were still out.

While *Mary Willoughby* and *Salamander* had been away Angus, arch-friend of England, had returned home, and John Barton deferred his vessels' triumphal entry into Leith with their English prizes, while he found out how the land lay. However, on contacting Arran, Barton found him so keen to have the ships brought in, that he was able to extract a promise that he and his companions would be allowed to sell their prize cargoes of wine themselves. Barton and Kerr were before the Lords of Council on 9 February, accused of selling the wine 'in small' instead of wholesale. Lord Lisle, who had hoped that the Governor would arrest the wine in order to restore it to the king, could only console himself with the thought that, 'It is ill wine and very dear'.

An English fleet assembled off Holy Island to lie in wait for the other Scottish ships still making for Leith, but it was scattered by a great storm, and most of the vessels so badly damaged as to put them out of action for some time to come. On 9 February Henry VIII granted a four-month 'abstinence from war', and ordered all his ships to cease hostilities. This state of affairs did not last for long. Rumours were still flying about concerning French aid being prepared for the Scots by the Duke of Guise, and on 28 February, Henry appointed one William Woodhouse 'Admiral on the North Seas', in command of four ships from Newcastle, to take all Scots and French ships 'as good prize'. As it happened, Guise never came to Scotland, and neither did the little fleet take any Scottish ships. The incident is, however, a fine example of diplomatic hairsplitting. Scotland might not be attacked as an enemy of England, but her ships could be taken as allies of France.

In March 1543 Arran held his first Parliament. As a supporter of Angus, the Laird of Restalrig provided a bodyguard for the Governor of 500 Leith men; 200 with guns and 300 with pikes. For four days they attended Arran from his lodging to the Edinburgh Tolbooth and back 'with flags and drums'. The pro-English ruling party were obviously nervous; Arran and Angus brought 300 halberdiers of their own, and a further force of 1000 men kept order in the burgh.

The situation was further complicated by the arrival from France of the Earl of Lennox, who stood next to Arran in the succession to the throne. He took the Western route to avoid Henry's warships, landed at Dumbarton early in April 1543 and by the fifth of the month had joined the Queen Mother at Linlithgow. Despite the advent of Lennox, affairs seemed to be going well for the English party. Sir Ralph Sadler, the English Ambassador entered into negotiations with Angus and his friends, during which they were promised English money and men if they could guarantee to keep hold of Edinburgh and Leith, but even at this early stage, there were doubts about the alliegiance of Arran, even though he assured Henry that it was only Angus and the rest who kept him in power.

At the end of April Sadler heard from the Duke of Suffolk, who was alarmed at reports from his spies that a large fleet of warships was about to set out from

Leith and Aberdeen. Sadler assured him that his information was quite wrong, no warships were even in preparation, and even if they had been, Scotland could only muster at the most, fourteen suitable vessels. There were, however, four or five merchantmen preparing to sail from Leith, and eight or ten were on their way home, so Suffolk could warn the Admiral to look out for them. More serious was the growing number of French ships putting in at Scottish ports. At the end of June 1543, 16 French sail were reported to be off the Scottish coast. One of them put in to Leith, where the Frenchmen, 'make merry with John Barton', the rest went to Aberdeen, well out of the orbit of Angus. In July, Suffolk received news that 27 French ships lay off the shore between Leith and St Abbs Head. They must subsequently have come under attack from the English fleet. On 17 July, according to Sadler, eleven Frenchmen were at anchor behind the May, and seven had come in to Leith and Burntisland, 'so beaten that they cannot keep the seas.' Six or seven others had been sunk. The *Sacre* was so badly damaged that she needed all her rigging replaced, and her companions were waiting until she was ready, before leaving Leith.

While the French ships were making all haste with their repairs, Henry was negotiating with George Douglas to keep them in the Forth until he could raise a fleet to come and capture them. The Scots were to provide victual for the English ships when they arrived (Sadler advised Suffolk not to rely on this, as there was not even enough bread available for the local people). By 9 August, the French ships were all afloat and sailing round in the Forth waiting for a suitable wind. Arran delayed them for three further days by pretending he was preparing letters for them to take back to France. By now 10 English ships, 'marvellously well equipped', were on their way. They were too late to prevent the French from leaving the Forth, but on 16 August, the two fleets met off Tynemouth, and at least 10 French ships were taken. During the next ten days, English vessels chased the stragglers around the North Sea and captured four more.

On 25 August 1543, a treaty of marriage between the infant Mary and Henry VIII's son Edward was ratified by Arran, but Henry had already begun the course of action that would bring all to nought. On the pretext that they were supplying his enemies, the French, he had seized Scottish ships in English ports. This action did more than anything to fuel anti-English feeling in Scotland. On 1 September, Sadler wrote to Henry, 'The Governor is so faint-hearted that he will never abide by the extremity, but will rather put himself into the hands of his enemies, to his own confusion.' Four days later Arran had indeed gone over to the Cardinal, who was now at liberty and in open alliance with the Queen Mother.

Some of the ships Henry had seized were from Leith, (belonging to Archibald Pennicuik, Walter Paterson, Archibald Dawson and James Lightman) and some belonged to Edinburgh men. Sadler described the people of Edinburgh as being so enraged by the loss of their property that they had threatened to burn him alive in his house if the ships were not released.

Henry might have been more concerned about this if the situtation in Scotland had not suddenly taken a turn for the better (from his point of view).

Angus returned to Edinburgh and was understood to be strong enough to stand against the Cardinal. By 11 October the Queen and Cardinal had fled to St Andrews and Arran had returned to Angus and his allies. Lennox, whose intended bride, Henry VIII's niece Margaret Douglas (daughter of Margaret Tudor and Angus), was at the English court, had come out in support of Henry and was prepared to give up Dumbarton Castle, together with the stores of money and munitions which had lately arrived in French ships.

At Leith, John Barton was preparing *Mary Willoughby*, *Lion*, and another ship to sail against Portuguese shipping, the Barton letters of marque originally granted to his grandfather having been once more revived. He also had plans to trade in Bordeaux, and as his ships were kept in port for some time by contrary winds, they were joined by others anxious to sail under their protection. By 25 October ten vessels had gathered at Leith, and Sadler wrote to Henry's Council that if the king's ships could prevent them from sailing out, 'it will utterly beggar this town'. He had some reason to feel vengeful towards Edinburgh, as his life was still in danger there, but within a fortnight he was safe at Angus's castle of Tantallon.

A week after the Ambassador's escape, John Barton's ships left Leith, and Sadler had been persuaded that Barton was a man, 'than whom no man in Scotland more desires to further the King's godly purpose.' As a result, Henry granted Barton a safeconduct for his own two ships, and Suffolk in the North and the Admiral Lisle in the Channel gave orders to English ships not to molest them.

The 'Rough Wooing' Begins

The case of the captured Scottish ships dragged on, and at last it became obvious that Henry was not going to restore them. The pro-French party gained ground, and on 11 December 1543 the Scottish Parliament repudiated the treaty of marriage between Mary and Prince Edward and confirmed their alliance with France. Five days later, at Edinburgh, an English herald proclaimed Henry's declaration of war on Scotland. The 'Rough Wooing' of Mary Queen of Scots by Henry VIII on behalf of his son had begun.

The Queen Mother made a pilgrimage on foot and spent 20 days praying for peace between her lords, but their differences were beyond the reach of divine intervention. For a week in January 1544, Leith was given a fortaste of things to come. At the beginning of the month, there was yet another split in the pro-English party. Angus, Lennox, Cassillis, Glencairn and Kilmaurs entered Leith and began to fortify the town against Arran, who was based at Edinburgh. George Douglas joined them with a force of 500 men, despite being opposed at Musselburgh by Bothwell with a band from Edinburgh. Arran was reinforced by the arrival of the Cardinal and Argyll with a 'great host'. On 10 January he hired more soldiers, including 145 gunners. The next day, artillery was brought out of the castle, set up in the High Street and fired at Leith. (Four pieces of shot were returned to Arran by some poor men, who were rewarded with four shillings.) There were skimishes in the fields near Edinburgh, but Angus and the others could not assault the town itself as it was too strongly defended and they were outnumbered in manpower. Arran had more guns set up nearer to Leith, but they were probably never fired, because on 12 January the Lords surrendered and on the following day Angus signed a bond with Arran at Holyrood.

Although forced to accept the rule of Arran, the defeated Lords were still faithful to the English cause. By the end of March Lennox and Angus were entrenched at Glasgow, where they were besieged by Arran during April and forced to surrender. Angus was imprisoned but Lennox went free and sailed from Dumbarton at the end of May.

Meanwhile, Henry had realised that he was never going to achieve his aims in Scotland simply by relying on his allies there. The time had come to put into operation an invasion plan which had been defeated by bad weather the previous September. The basic strategy remained the same; a large army would invade by land, and another force would be transported in ships to Edinburgh. The idea of causing widespread damage around the Forth had been implanted in Henry's mind in 1542. The naval expedition of that year, which had burnt Aberdour, had been something in the nature of a sop to Henry's pride when it seemed that land operations had failed. Now that pride had taken an even harder knock, and the consequences would be proportionately greater.

The Invasion of Scotland

The Duke of Suffolk was at Newcastle overseeing the organisation of the invasion force. At the end of January Henry ordered him to invade in March, when there would still be some stores of food and fodder left in the countryside. Suffolk knew that he would not be able to provide for a fleet and an army in such a short time, but told Henry he would do what he could. One problem was that during winter and early spring it was impossible to use carts for supplies, which would have to go to the Forth by sea. Suffolk intended to use the normal victual fleet which brought supplies to Berwick, with extra escorts. On 14 February he began assembling his fleet, writing to the mayors of East Coast Ports for information about what vessels were available. Lord Lisle began pressing men into service as crews for the escorting warships of the King.

The plan was to send 14000 foot and 4000 horse by land and 15000 men by sea. Suffolk did not see much point in a seaborne force. He argued that its only purpose could be to cause destruction rather than to achieve any permanent conquest. As this was in fact Henry's intention, he ignored the Duke's strictures. Suffolk sent him the estimates he had been asked for, assessing the number of ships and men which would be needed.

Each ship would carry two men per ton, plus one month's victual. Total tonnage needed for one month was 7500, which would be made up as follows:

5 ships of 200 tons	10 ships of 100 tons	10 ships of 80 tons
50 ships of 50 tons	50 ships of 40 ton	10 ships of 20 tons

Total: 135 ships

Half as many again would be needed to carry victual for another month, and 10 more for artillery and horses.

Sum Total: 212 ships

Conduct money to shipowners for 1200 soldiers, both ways.	£4000
Wages to soldiers, 44 days	£4800
Victual for soldiers, 44 days	£4800
Wages to 3000 mariners	£1500
Victual for mariners	£1900
Horses	£ 266 13s 4d
Garrison of horsemen for two months	£6000

Provisions would consist of: biscuit, beer, fish, cheese, salt meat (the last to be served four times a week).

The estimate included a list of the tonnages of ships at East Coast ports from Newcastle to Ipswich. Information about ships available in the Thames was more detailed. There were 12 hulks 'which draw little water', and 10 Portingale (Portuguese) barques, which sailed well to windward and might each be armed with a brass cannon as they had no foremast.

In the first week of March, the Earl of Hertford arrived in Newcastle to replace Suffolk. On 21 March he informed Henry that French ships were arriving daily at Leith with supplies, boasting that they knew where the English ships were, and had eluded them by sailing at night. *Lion* was ready at Leith waiting for a wind to take her to France with the French Ambassador. It was rumoured that the Cardinal and George Douglas would also be aboard, and Hertford strongly advised that the Navy should look out for her.

Four days later, Hertford received the welcome news that 160 ships, victualed for 56 days, were on their way to pick up his soldiers from Newcastle. By 30 March a few ships had made it to harbour, having become separated from the main fleet in fog, but Hertford was increasingly worried about what to do with the troops who were continually arriving and needed paying and feeding. On 4 April he wrote that he had, 'looked for the Lord Admiral and the rest of the fleet at this tide, for the wind has blown so fair these three days, but there is no word of them. I lie here with the army, spending treasure in vain and consuming victual so fast that unless relief come shortly I must send the men far south.'

It was all the more frustrating because he had just received some interesting news from James, son of George Douglas. Angus and several other of his relatives were in Arran's custody and James was afraid they would be sent to France in *Lion*. He urged Hertford to take *Lion* and hurry his army to Scotland.

As Arran was now besieging Lennox at Glasgow, 'the King will never get so good a time again' for an invasion.

Henry's council, however, were of the opinion that the 'capture' of Angus was only a ploy to cover up an actual defection. On 10 April, they informed Hertford that this necessitated a change of plan. It had been the king's intention to fortify Leith, but if the English could no longer rely on Angus, it might subsequently be recovered by the Scots. Therefore Hertford was to sack and burn it, along with Edinburgh, Holyrood, and all the surrounding villages. He was to do the same in Fife, especially at St Andrews, the Cardinal's town.

Hertford raised no objection to the bulk of these orders, but he was horrified at the prospect of burning Leith. As soon as he had read the Council's letter he composed a reply imploring them to think again. His objections were strategic rather than humanitarian. He could not bear to see Henry throw away such a potential asset. 'If Leith is fortified, for which all provision is made and the charges thereof passed, it shall be more honour to the King and annoyance to his enemies for, it being their chief port, the King shall have good entry into Scotland and, by stopping fishing and traffic, force the town of Edinburgh and the countryside round to fall to his devotion, and also keep out their aid from France and elsewhere.' This would also encourage Lennox, 'The King may have Dumbarton from him, and holding it and Leith could in time force all south of the Forth to become his subjects.' After a sleepless night, Hertford sent a second letter after the first, recounting how he had been told by a Scots sailor that if Inchkeith were fortified, no ships could get into Leith, and suggesting that this might be done, as well as fortifying the port.

Four days later, the Council replied that they had considered his suggestions, but had to reject them, on the grounds that arrangements for supplies might prove unreliable. (They had good historical justification for this opinion.) The letter contains a veiled warning, when the Council assure Hertford that they think his proposal, 'proceeds from an earnest mind to serve the King and realm, and so we humbly desire the King to take it'. Henry was now ageing, increasingly irascible and autocratic, and had no qualms about imprisoning (or worse) those who questioned his decisions.

Hertford at Leith

On 21 April 1544 the fleet of transport ships at last arrived at Newcastle, and the embarkation of the English army began. By the 23rd most of the men were on board, and within three days the fleet was at sea. It was formed up into three groups, the vanguard, the main body and the rearguard, each with five 'wafters' (escorting warships). They ran into a storm and had to put into South Shields for a day or two, but after that the wind was fair, and on 4 May, Hertford was writing to the Warden of Berwick 'beside Leith in the field of the west side of the town'.

The Destruction of Leith

The arrival of the fleet had taken the Scots completely by surprise. Either they had not felt it necessary to post spies at Newcastle, or there had been none there during the embarkation of the English army. As long as anyone could remember, the English 'Iceland Fleet' of numerous fishing vessels with attendant 'wafters' had made an annual voyage north. When 200 ships appeared in the Forth one afternoon, it was assumed by many that they were the Iceland fleet, putting in to make a show of strength. Those who said they had come to invade were dismissed as scaremongers. It was not until the following day that it became obvious that they were right, when the fleet weighed anchor and began its progress up the Forth.

The only warships in Leith at the time were *Unicorn* and *Salmander*, and there was no way they could attack the fifteen English escort vessels. The fleet sailed past the Port, to Granton Crags, and there the army disembarked, at nine oclock on a Sunday morning. Once Arran and the Cardinal realised what was happening they moved quickly to raise a force to oppose the English. However, the 6000 Scots who met Hertford's troops at the Water of Leith that day were hopelessly outnumbered and unprepared, and the engagement lasted only half an hour. The English marched on to Leith, which they found 'stoutly defended and fortified with ditches and ordnance'. The ditches must have been made by Angus's forces during his brief occupation of Leith in January 1543. Some of the ordnance probably came from the Kings Wark, and some of the smiths of Leith specialised in making cannon. The wealthier skippers had their own arsenals, which could have been pressed into service in this emergency. Resistance, however brave, could not keep out such a strong force, and the English soon entered the town.

Looting began almost immediately, and the soldiers were surprised at the wealth they found, which was much more than they had expected in a Scottish town. Hertford reported that they had taken a great store of grain, and goods worth £10,000 (£30,000 Scots). Once he was settled in, he brought into the haven those of his ships which carried ordnance and horses, which were unloaded at the Shore. Together with the Admiral, Lord Lisle, he wrote to Henry on 6 May, when they had been at Leith for two days. Probably feeling that no-one could now accuse him of disloyalty, and being backed up by the Admiral, Hertford once more expressed his feelings about his orders; 'to use extremity would be to lose the hearts of all the people of this realm, which might easily be won if this town were fortified and Edinburgh town and castle conquered and garrisoned, by which the King would be sure of all on this side of the Forth and also shortly come by the rest of the realm'. James IV's blockhouse on Inchgarvie had been taken and would be razed, 'which, if the first determination to fortify here had continued, had been worth the keeping'.

Lisle, in a private letter, expressed the same opinion as Hertford. 'This town might be made very strong and has no hill nigh to hurt it, and all the country would be glad to be the King's subjects.' The second half of the sentence may have been somewhat over-optimistic, but there is no doubting the strategic importance of Leith. The presence or otherwise of a hill near the town was important because artillery was always most effective if placed on a eminence. The nearest hill to Leith was the Calton Hill, but only the very largest calibre of 16th century cannon would have been a threat to Leith from such a distance. Lisle obviously did not consider it a significant danger.

Whatever may have been the personal feelings of the commanders, orders are orders, and they set out to fulfill theirs to the letter. Their dispatch of 15 May detailed what they had 'achieved' so far, and declared their intention to burn Leith the following day and then head south with the army, destroying as much as possible on the way home. The Admiral returned with the fleet, which now included *Unicorn* and *Salamander*, ballasted with 80,000 cannon shot which had been found in store in Leith. Some of the fleet were sent towards St Andrews with orders to burn towns and villages on its way, but this seems to have been an effort to comply with the letter rather than the spirit of their instructions.

The picture painted by Hertford and Lisle in their dispatches to Henry and the Council, is of a wasteland surrounding Edinburgh. The country had been devastated to within six miles of Stirling and all stores taken to feed the army on its homeward march. Edinburgh and Holyrood were burnt. On its way south, the army burnt all coastal settlements as far east as Dunbar. Ships and boats had been burnt in harbours on both sides of the Forth. Leith was burnt and its pier destroyed. The best ships in the harbour had been taken and the rest burnt.

Recovery

How, one wonders, does a community go about recovering from such a blow? It was fortunate that the attack came in the spring rather than just before the onset of winter. The Scottish summer may be far from tropical, but at least there was not much risk of people dying from exposure before their houses could be rebuilt. It is by no means certain that every house was in fact completely destroyed. Many were, after all, built of stone. It is even possible that Hertford and Lisle exaggerated their reports to Henry in order to satisfy his thirst for revenge. (Their statement, for instance, that they had destroyed South Leith church, was untrue.) Using the rural method of building low drystone or turf walls and roofing with rough poles covered with heather or turf, shelters could be built, which would serve until there was money available to construct something better.

A much more serious problem would be shortage of food. The coastal strip from Stirling to Dunbar had been devastated, but crops growing inland would be available at harvest time - at a price. However, harvest was some three months away. All that was immediately available would be a share of the meagre stores left on inland farms. There were reports of many people dying of starvation in the months after the disaster.

Some at least of the inhabitants had assets, not least of which were ships. At the time of the English attack, most of the merchant ships of Leith were away in the Low Countries or France. The chief losers would be the fishermen and ferrymen, whose craft were based at Leith. Once the merchant ships returned with their cargoes, who would have had the money to buy the goods? A lot of merchandise must have initially changed hands on credit, but the nobility and some of the wealthier merchants posessed estates that were totally untouched by the invaders. Rents were due at Whitsunday (late May/early June), and once they came in there would be cash to spend. Some money may have been successfully hidden from looters.

Shipowners, however, had a resource which could be exploited for quick and profitable returns, and they were not slow to use it. In September (between trading seasons) *Lion*, *Mary Willoughby*, and *Andrew* (which belonged to Andrew Sands) were marauding off the north-east coast of England in company with three French ships. They took at least two English ships and harried the Yarmouth fishing fleet. They also attacked the Dutch fishing fleet, took 17 great 'corvers' laden with fish and sailed them to Leith and Dundee (possibly the home port of *Andrew*), and then put out to sea once more. On 26 October the bailiff of Scarborough informed the Governor of Hull that three Scottish warships of three, two and one top were at anchor off his town. On 3 November, the Earl of Shrewsbury informed Henry that the Scots had taken the 80-ton *Anthony* of Newcastle and six or seven smaller vessels. 'They are desperate merchants of Leith and Edinburgh, who, having lost almost their whole substance at the army's late being in Scotland, seek adventures either to recover something or lose the rest.' John Barton was said to be about to sail with 10 or 12 other ships. He did not in fact leave Leith until the end of December, in command of a fleet of 20 vessels, including *Lion* and *Mary Willoughby*, on their way to France with the French Ambassador.

The depradations of the Scots privateers continued throughout January and February 1545, with the loss of only two Scottish ships. One of the prizes they took was laden with wool which had been looted from Leith! By the spring some Scots were based in Brittany, preying on ships of the Emperor Charles V. By August the English were fitting out a fleet to keep the Channel clear of Scots and French pirates. Not only merchants and shipowners profited from privateering. Everyone involved in the venture, down to the cabin boy and including the ships' victualers, was entitled by law to a share of the proceeds.

Peaceful trading also continued. An English agent in the Low Countries reported a Scottish merchantman laden with goods which were sold there. Two more were taken by the English on their way back from France, and in March 1545, six Scottish ships called at Le Havre on their way to Bordeaux. An English herald reported from Hamburg that Scottish ships arrived there daily in April. In June an Englishman gave an account of personally seeing *Mary Willoughby* and six other ships coming in to Leith laden with merchandise.

Internal Scottish politics were more settled during 1545. The Queen Mother, Arran and the Cardinal led a council which included members of all political complexions who, for once, managed to co-exist reasonably peacefully. Hertford was again active, devastating the Borders, but this did not affect Leith directly, although some of the poorest men went with the Scottish army that opposed Hertford - their service at least ensured them something to eat. Some were killed, but many more must have died in the violent plague which raged among the weakened populations of Edinburgh and Leith during the summer.

1546 saw the mariners of Leith engaged in the familiar mixture of piracy and merchant shipping. By the beginning of the year, the Port had recovered sufficiently to be once again a threat to the trade of Edinburgh, itself hardly recovered from the late occurances, and the Burgh responded with the familiar series of statutes regarding selling to and by unfreemen. In August, yet another shortlived peace was made with England, and Arran issued a proclamation to mariners of all ports in the Forth and as far north as Aberdeen, forbidding them to make war on English ships. Instead, they turned to preying on Spanish ships sailing to Flanders via the English channel. Even some Englishmen were involved - pretending to be Scots!

On 29 May, Cardinal Beaton was murdered in his bed at St Andrews by a group of Fife lairds, who then occupied the castle. The subsequent siege lasted until 31 July 1547, when the castle surrendered to a fleet of French galleys.

In the same month, the Barton letters of marque made their last appearance. John Barton, now laird of the estate of Craigs, appointed John Cockburn of Leith (captain) and Alexander Herring (master) of the *Michael*, to sail against the Portuguese in his name. At the bottom of the document of appointment is appended John Barton's seal, bearing his coat of arms; 'a shield charged with three bars wavy in chief, at foot an anchor in fesse.'

The Second Destruction of Leith

Henry VIII was now dead and the boy-king Edward VI sat on the English throne. The real ruler, however, was Hertford, now Duke of Somerset and Lord Protector of England. At the beginning of September 1547, Somerset once more invaded Scotland, in the second phase of the 'Rough Wooing'. On 10 September, Black Saturday, the Scots were defeated at the battle of Pinkie. The next day the English set up camp at Leith to tend their wounded, and stayed there for ten days, stabling their horses in the town. They found little of value there as 'the inhabitants overnight had packed away with them.'

On 17 September, Somerset gave orders that the army was to leave the next day, and, according to a member of the English forces;

> Minding before, with recompense according, to reward one Barton [?John] that had played an untrue part, commanded that overnight his house in Leith should be set afire. And as the same night about 5 of the clock was done, many of our soldiers, that were very forward in firing, fired with all haste all the town beside. But so far forth (as I may think) without commission or knowledge of my Lords Grace, as right many horses, both of his Graces and divers others, were in great

danger e'er they could be quitted from the town. Six great ships lying in the haven there, that for age and decay were not so apt for use, were then also set afire, which all the night with great flame did burn very solemnly.'

The English navy captured all the Scottish ships in the Forth, so that no warship remained. They also took Inchcolm and left a garrison on it. As there was little food available locally and winter was coming on, the army retreated south. The navy sailed to the Tay and took the castle of Broughty, leaving a garrison there also. Somerset had at last achieved his aim of occupying strategic strongholds in Scotland.

The destruction wrought in the vicinity probably affected Leith worse than the events of 1544. The English army would certainly have consumed, destroyed or carried off all the recently-harvested grain, but it was the loss of the ships that affected the port most. September did not fall within the regular trading season, so many ships would have been in the harbour at the time of the invasion. Nothing more is heard of *Mary Willoughby* or *Lion*, so they must have gone, along with all the other vessels of any size. Florence Cornton continued to be paid £40 per annum 'for attendance on the King's (sic) ships', but this must have been a purely honorary position until new vessels could be built or bought. When an expedition was mounted in October to recover Inchcolm, a ship called *The Shallop* was commandeered, which was not even necessarily Scottish.

The attack on Inchcolm did not dislodge the commander, Sir John Luttrell, but he was subsequently blockaded by 'two small boats and a pinnace'. Sir John also had a pinnace, the *Double Rose*, but he felt that without a decent-sized ship the most he could do was hold his postion; 'there is such pestilence and famine here, if their river [the Forth] were strongly kept, they cannot hold out long.' He was forced to watch helplessly while ship after ship sailed into Leith laden with merchandise. The most he had been able to accomplish was to drive ashore near St Nicholas' Chapel, a ship of two tops with a cargo of wine for the Governor. He also complained to the council of a lack of ordnance and powder. Cold comfort was his only reply: he was to save his powder and do his best with the *Double Rose*.

If she was like another pinnace described at the same time, it is obvious that, although fast, she was otherwise rather inadequate for her task. The dimensions of the vessel in question were as follows:

Foreship to stern - 39ft
Beam at the mast - 9ft
Depth in hold - 3ft
Keel - 30ft
Draught - 2ft

In November, ships were prepared at Leith to besiege the English in Broughty Castle. An English fleet was sent, under Thomas Wyndham, to relieve the besieged, and on its way it was blown into the Forth by contrary winds. While he was there, Wyndham visited Luttrell on Inchcolm. When he left, he took the *Double Rose* with him. He must have left a more effective ship behind, because at the beginning of January, Luttrell was able to report that around Christmas time he had achieved several 'successes'. The ferry boat of the North (Queens) Ferry had been captured and the town burnt, along with a house in Aberdour. All the boats at Burntisland pier and many new houses there were burnt, and its castle captured. Wyndham, meanwhile, had found the siege of Broughty already raised and the Scots forced to accept the Warden's terms. He took up station in the Tay, and from there in January sent the *Sacre* to Luttrell, which captured a 100 ton hulk bound from Flanders to Leith.

Wyndham stayed in the Tay even after Dundee fell to Angus in January, but thought he could cause more damage if he were to lie in the Forth. As he wrote in February, 'for now is the Scots chief fishing time, and I can do them no hurt here [ie in the Tay]' By March, Dundee had been regained by the English, and Luttrell was put in charge of the new fort there. He thankfully abandoned Inchcolm, taking with him all the stores he could carry, and burning what had to be left behind.

The growing coal trade of Lothian, which exported largely through Leith, was severely hit by the events of 1547. Eighteen months after Pinkie, pitowners were still very short of men to work the seams. This led to 'poaching' of workers from rivals, but there was not sufficient manpower to produce enough coal to satisfy demand, so that a:

> great and exorbitant dearth [has] lately risen upon coals within this burgh [Edinburgh] and other parts hereabout, so that the lieges of this realm resorting to the same and the inhabitants thereof cannot be furnished with fire for baking, brewing, making malt and furnishing of strangers without ruin, and all by occasion of the owners and tacksmen of the coal heuchs hereabout which have raised the price of each load of coals at their pots 14d dearer than they were sold before.

The affected pits were at Pinkie itself (which belonged to Newbattle Abbey) Tranent, Elphinston, Newbattle, Cockpen, Edmondston, the Grange, Dryden, Pettendriech, Niddry and Wallyford. (There is a mid-sixteenth century reference to a road along which coal was carried from the latter to Holyrood and Leith.) Previously the price of coal had been 6d or 7d a horseload, but this had now been increased to anything from 16d to 20d, (from which one might deduce that production had dropped to as little as a third of former levels). The various lairds and grieves who ran the pits were ordered to charge no more than 10d.

It seems recovery was on its way, however. In the year 1550 to 1551, coal exports through Leith were equal to the total for the previous four years, and the next year they were even higher. Salt production, which was largely dependant on supplies of coal, was harder hit. In most years since around 1530, between 150 and 250 chalders of salt had been exported through Leith. In the years 1546 to 1550, there was only total of 37 chalders, and in 1551, none at all. It was to be some time before the 100 chalder mark was reached again.

The French in Leith

In June 1548 there arrived the first of the French troops who were to become so familiar, and eventually hated, in Leith. The English were by this time entrenched at Haddington, and the Frenchman d'Esse came with 8000 troops to help the Scots remove them. The French troops were transported in a fleet of between 120 and 130 ships which arrived at Leith on 16 June. Rather belatedly, at the beginning of August, an English fleet came into the Forth after them, under the command of Lord Clinton. All but 22 of the French ships had left Leith by that time, many of them to act as escorts to the child-queen Mary, who sailed from Dumbarton for the safety of France at the end of July. Clinton found 40 vessels in Leith Roads, which scattered to Inchcolm and Burntisland. He pursued them and burnt 12 grainships at Burntisland, and also burnt Kinghorn, Kirkcaldy and other towns. While in the Forth he heard that Leith was being fortified, and a ditch dug round it by 300 Scottish pioneers (military engineers).

The French overwintered at Leith and almost immediately some disadvantages of their presence made themselves felt. When the Governor wanted goods from the town, he had to send a French speaker to convey his orders to the guards. It also became more convenient for Scottish ships to go to ports on the north side of the Forth. In January, John Barton and William Hume brought prizes in to Burntisland, and in February, James Fogo's prize was arrested at Kirkcaldy. In March, yet other prizes were at Pittenweem, Kinghorn and Inverkeithing. In April there was another at Burntisland. The Edinburgh Council had to forbid the burgh's merchants to load goods at Burntisland.

The designer of the French fortifications was an Italian, Piero de Strozzi. Instead of the medieval wall and tower, he used the latest Italian design, first seen at Verona in 1530. When further work was done at Leith in 1559, features were used which had only been introduced in Italy since 1550. The new style used relatively low earthern ramparts which sloped inwards to deflect cannon shot. Rather than the rounded towers which had provided flanking fire from bow and arrow in earlier times, at the corners and at intervals along the walls the new plan provided angular bastions, each of which formed a platform for heavy guns. (This arrangement produced a characteristic shape which led to the name 'star fort' being applied to these structures.) Nothing like the Leith fortifications was seen in Britain for another ten years, until the fortification of Berwick, where the basic pattern can still be seen. (As at Berwick, the Leith ramparts were faced with stone, but once the defences were no longer needed, much of it was deliberately removed and the rest was quarried for house building.)

The ramparts enclosed the whole inhabited area of North and South Leith in a rhomboid shape with its broad end to the east and two long sides running east-west. The eastern and southern ramparts followed the lines of the present Constitution and Great Junction Streets. The main gate of the fortress lay in the southeast corner, at the head of the Kirkgate. The western earthwork enclosed St Nicholas's chapel and part of the site of the later Citadel. A bastion (Ramsay's fort) which was built just east of the Pier, later became a convenient place for the storage of timber - the Timber Bush. The northeast corner bastion became known as Little London. At the Sandport (known in the 16th century as the Sand Ness), where the Custom House now stands, was a little enclosed basin for ship repairing, protected on the seaward side by a palisade with a gap in it for launching vessels. This was where the timbermen of the Dais family had their yard in the first half of the century.

In June 1549, the English briefly captured Inchkeith, but they were soon removed and a French garrison established on the island. In July, Haddington surrendered. In December the castle of Home was recovered, and Somerset's dream of the subjugation of Scotland was effectively finished. In January 1550, John Barton was gathering a fleet to attack seven English ships which had brought supplies from Berwick to Broughty castle. Leith could no longer produce sufficient mariners for the fleet, and they had to be sought also in Queensferry, Inverkeithing, Dunfermline, Kinghorn, Kirkcaldy, Dysart, Anstruther and Pittenweem. The ships themselves came from Queensferry, Burntisland, Kinghorn and Kirkcaldy.

The French habit of commandeering boats to transport men and munitions became very unpopular around the Forth. In April 1550, boats were needed to carry French ammunition to the siege of Dunglas. It seems the boatmen of Leith had developed the tactic of quietly slipping out of harbour whenever such a task was in the offing. The Governor employed two men to remove the rudders from all the boats in the haven, and a body of pynours (labourers or porters) to carry them to a storehouse where they could be locked away until they were needed. When the time arrived, messages were sent to the harbours north of the Forth, from Kinghorn to Crail, to send all available ships and boats to Leith. It seems they were equally reluctant to be inconvenienced, because on 12 April they were warned that all boats must be at Leith within three hours, on pain of escheat of the vessel and death of the owner. The French became increasingly unpopular with all Scots who came in contact with them, especially after 1554, when Mary of Guise became Regent and began to appoint her fellow countrymen to powerful administrative positions, such as that of Keeper of the Great Seal. In 1555, Parliament had to make it an offence to speak ill of the Queen and of Frenchmen.

Leith Recovers Again

There are signs that 1551 saw the beginnings of recovery in Leith. The Royal Treasurer's Account mention two new royal ships, skippered by William Forester and James Cullan (who improved his house on the Shore by building out a turnpike stair tower). Edinburgh again began to pay attention to the port, in an attempt to counteract the effects of the French occupation. The buying of foreign grain and selling of goods by foreigners of which the Burgh complained at this time, was probably a result of the influx of French troops who bought their provisions locally. This increase in the number of consumers probably contributed greatly to the recovery of Leith from its double destruction. The measuring of the grain which the troops bought, and of salt, was also causing the Burgh problems. In May 1551 the Burgh made its first official appointment of three metters (measurers) of grain and salt at Leith, and arranged for a suitable official to have custody of the measures. In 1553, burgesses were forbidden to use Leith men as their factors in taking goods abroad or bringing them home. The following year the procedure for 'entering' ships at the Tolbooth was tightened up, and four indwellers of North Leith - John Wardlaw, James Litster, James Barton and John Colle - were in trouble for non-payment of customs. Edinburgh's uneasiness could only have been fuelled by the increasing power of the Queen Mother, who bestowed much favour on Leith. The escalation of the Burgh's regulation of the Port, indicates its determination to keep a grip on an increasingly slippery potential rival.

The port's facilities were also improved, probably at the insistence of the French. In April 1553, the westernmost of the beacons at the entrance to the harbour was replaced. Two 'trees' were driven into the seabed and secured by piling stones around them. A 'great joist' was fixed between them to hold the lantern. The work took Adam Purves the wright and two men two days to complete, with six men to do the digging and stone-piling. A month later it was demolished by an English ship! However, the master paid most of the expenses for re-erecting it.

In March 1553, work had begun on what must have been a complete rebuilding of the Shore. The work took three years to complete, working several months in each year. The laird of Carnbe gave permission for stone to be quarried at Granton, and Alexander Reid was installed there as quarrier. The hundreds of tons of stone - hewn stone, rubble wall stone, and flagstones - that he extracted were carried to Leith mainly by Lawrence Tod in his two boats, one large and one small. Sometimes carters were used, especially for the flagstones. David Graham, who was the Burgh's master mason at the time, was in charge of the masons who dressed the stones at the quarry and built the quay. There were usually between four and eight masons with their 'servants' working at any one time, helped by half a dozen barrowmen, whose number was sometimes augmented at low tide by a few casual labourers. At the end of each week, as well as their regular pay, the men were given drinksilver. Lime came from Cousland, Gilmerton and Westhouses, and was stored in a locked 'limehouse'. Sand and clay were available locally, transported in boats and crayers. Tools and other materials were stored in a 'fold' which had a lockable gate.

The stretch of the Shore they were working on extended between the present Tolbooth Wynd and Bernard Street. It seems they began work on the side furthest from the water, as it was not until June that extra workers began to be hired at low tide. On 17 June, Lawrence Tod brought the first consignment of '60 great flags for the ground of the shore'. The work finished for the year on 23 December, by which time it had cost Edinburgh £774 2s 9d. David Graham personally gave Alexander Reid and four of the masons a pair of hose and a fustian (velveteen) doublet each, as a bonus.

Work continued in 1554, from the beginning of April until the end of December, but at less than half the cost: £341 2s 10d. In July, August and September 1555, the final mooring rings were fixed. These were enormous affairs, weighing about 20 pounds, each attached to an iron bolt, which was driven into a hole in a large stone and fixed in place with 14 pounds of lead. Over the next few years, sporadic improvements were made to the Shore, as in September 1558, when a great stone with a mooring ring in it was set up 'at the foot of Andrew Lamb's close'.

Also in 1558, the haven was 'clenged'. For twelve days in August, a dozen men, using ropes, pulled boulders out of the mud. The stones were picked up by four men in a boat and unloaded onto the West Bulwark (North Leith wharf or pier), from where they were barrowed away. One particularly large rock on the west side of the haven could only be removed by the combined efforts of 15 men, using an anchor cable which they borrowed from Andrew Lamb and Andrew Sands.

Once the work on the Shore was substantially completed, Edinburgh turned its attention to the New Haven. It may have seemed prudent at that time to establish a harbour outwith the control of the French. The Council invited contributions, and raised £500 to pay for the work. During 1555 and 1556, several shiploads of timber were bought in Norway and brought to the New Haven to build or rebuild the bulwarks. A map made in 1560 shows two curving structures extending out into the Firth, forming an ovoid harbour with its entrance to the north. A new crane was also provided for the haven.

It was not only Edinburgh that was taking an interest in improving facilities at this time. In 1555, the kirkmasters of Leith acquired a piece of land in the Kirkgate and began building a 'hospital' for aged and infirm seamen, financed by the Primegilt money. The hospital was owned and run by the Fraternity of Masters and Mariners of Leith, and came to be known as the Fraternity House, a name which was later corrupted to 'Ternity House', then to 'Trinity House'.

Leith and Mary of Guise

After Mary the Queen Mother was made Regent in 1554, she followed a wise policy of tolerance towards the growing number of Protestants in Scotland. However, their growing hatred of the French and adherence to Protestantism pushed many Scots into a determination to get rid of her and her fellow countrymen, and establish a Protestant church in Scotland. It did not take Mary long to see which way the wind was blowing, and realising Leith's potential as a refuge at need, she set about gaining the support of the town. The establishment of a Reformed Church was dear to the hearts of many in Leith, but the idea of complete independence from Edinburgh was even more attractive. Mary made it known that she would be willing to buy the superiority of Leith from the laird of Restalrig, with a view to erecting the town into a Royal Burgh. The inhabitants of Leith were so enthusiastic about this idea, that they paid the laird themselves, plus a handsome present to Mary herself. The cost of the superiority was £3000, to be paid in six annual instalments of £500, beginning in 1555. In February 1556, Mary appointed Walter Cant and Florence Cornton bailies of Leith, and in the same year forced Edinburgh to appoint her nominee, John Little, to fill the vacant post of Water Bailie.

From the records of the Admiralty Court for the years 1556 to 1561, we get the feeling that things are really back to normal in Leith a decade after its destruction. The Admiral in question was the Earl Bothwell, the post having been hereditary in the Hepburn family since the beginning of the century. He did not preside at the court hearings, leaving that task to his deputies David Kintore and Richard Trohope. His favoured skippers, the ruffianly Blacaders (one of whom was later executed for complicity in the murder of Lord Darnley), do however figure in some of the cases.

One of the earliest cases in the volume (September 1557) concerns a tremendous row over the shareout of prize goods captured by a Leith ship. It was a complicated case which rumbled on for some years and supplies details of how such matters were regulated. The ship which had taken the prizes (four English fishing vessels) was the *Kate*, which had herself been captured from the English in 1555 by Andrew Sands in his ship *Andrew*. Her owner and captain was William Gibson, the master was John Gibson. Her four quartermasters, each responsible for one quarter of the crew, were John Lightman, William Brown, Gilbert Edmondston and John Smith. The Admiral was suing these six men for auctioning their prizes without his representative being present, and for not handing over the one tenth share to which he was entitled. (One master in a later case tried to wriggle out of this duty to the Admiral by claiming that his prize was taken under letters of marque and not in warfare.) Various members of the crew also had not been paid their shares by their respective quartermasters. There was a wrangle over the captain's right to the best anchor and tackle of the captured ships. The case became so complicated with accusations and counter accusations flying, that at last, in 1557 all parties agreed not to proceed further.

In July 1558, *Kate*, captained by Gilbert Edmondston and in company with *Andrew*, took the *Grace of God* of Scarborough. This time there was no trouble. The captain and master of the English vessel were produced in court and admitted that their ship was 'just prize', having been taken in a time of 'tension' between the two countries. An inventory was given of her contents (various pieces of artillery and 44 prisoners), and all was done legally and aboveboard.

Sometimes, of course, the shoe was on the other foot, and Scots were captured by the English. A case of 1 April 1558 is typical of the complications which could arise as a result. A couple of months previously, William Nicholson, Robert Little, John Luikup, Andrew Cant and John Mackeson (all of Leith) had been captured by some Newcastle men. William Nicholson was left as a hostage for payment of their ransoms, and when he was finally released his captors made him pay them, as was customary, for the expenses of keeping him during his imprisonment. His shipmates were refusing to pay their shares of the expenses, which amounted to 27s each. The court ordered them to pay up.

It would be easy to assume from much of what we have learnt so far about sixteenth century Leith, that its mariners spent most of their time pursuing and capturing foreign ships. There can be little doubt that the skippers of well-armed vessels took full advantage of such opportunities, but the bulk of the business of the port consisted of peaceful trading ventures. If the records of ships' clerks and the ledgers of merchants had survived, we would know much more about this side of the life of the port. As it is, the balance is heavily tipped in favour of the more spectacular exploits, which were recorded in official correspondence and the minutes of law courts. The Admiralty Court, however, dealt with cases arising out of the normal business of the port, and gives us some idea of the day to day life of Leith.

Ownership of vessels inevitably caused problems, especially when they changed hands. Very few belonged to a sole owner. Some had three, with equal shares, but the most popular division was into quarters. The smallest share was a half quarter, but even some of these were jointly owned. On 25 October 1557, for instance, Blais Mowbray of Leith sold to James Ferry and George Fergusson of Restalrig, his half quarter of the *Mary Gallant* for £120, and signed the receipt 'with his hand led at the pen'.

Heirs of shipowners could find themselves in trouble if the deceased had made transactions without proper documentation. On 22 April 1558, Patrick and Andrew, sons of the late Robert Dawson, began a process regarding their father's one-third share in the *Luce*. Robert had died at Dieppe a year previously, but before he died had sold his share to James Sleich for £67 10s, being in urgent need of money to pay a debt. His sons said that the share was worth £120, and denied that their father had sold it. They were suing James Sleich for one-third of the profits of four voyages that he had since made in the *Luce*, viz:

Dieppe to Bordeaux - with red herring	£100
Bordeaux to Dundee - with wine	£100
Dundee to Ree - with merchandise	100 merks
Ree to Dundee -	£100

Eventually, in August, the court found that James Sleich had indeed bought Robert Dawson's share of the *Luce*, which was worth £67 10s. However, he had not paid in full, and there was still £47 10s owing, which James and his father John were ordered to pay to Patrick and Andrew.

Non-payment of freight money was a recurring problem, as in July 1560, when William Kylour, master of the Queen's barque, sued Elizabeth Ker and Thomas Kinkaid her husband for the freight of four tuns of wine from Bordeaux, at £15 10s per tun. Later in the year, a more complicated case involved 21 Edinburgh merchants. Their goods had been loaded into *Angel* to be taken to Campveere, and freight charges of 40s per sack agreed with her skipper, Thomas Nicholson. *Angel* set out for Flanders, but ran into a storm, was chased by an English ship and had to take refuge in Crail 'for lyff and deid'. The ship must have been too badly damaged to continue with her voyage, because the goods were returned to the merchants, and John Watson of Anstruther and John Davidson of Crail became sureties for the payment of half freight, which was due to the skipper in such circumstances. John Watson was now refusing to pay his share. The court ordered him to do so.

A complete list of the ship's cargo is given - 79 barrels of salmon, 27 dakers of hides (540), 11 bags of wool, 1280 skins and 5 bolts of cloth. The computation of freight charges 'per sack' had originally been instituted when wool was Scotland's chief export. Things had changed a lot since then and formulae had been worked out as to what constituted a 'sack' of other goods, eg - 20 hides (one daker), 60 skins, 12 barrels of fish (one last), 25 bolts of cloth.

The court dealt with disputes between skippers and crew. These usually concerned payment of wages, but in July 1561, a case was brought arising from a violent fracas. Francis Loch, a Leith mariner, had taken service in the *Whitehound*, skippered by James Malville of Glasgow, for a voyage to Bordeaux. Francis must have been an officer, perhaps a quartermaster, because he had his own cabin. While they were in harbour in Bordeaux, for some reason the skipper threw Francis off the ship at swordpoint. The dismissed mariner went to Rochelle, where he had to wait three weeks before he could find another ship. He was suing the skipper for the expense he was put to during that time. As well as throwing him off the ship, the skipper had broken into Francis' cabin and removed all his possessions, which he refused to return:

1 mantle gown	2 serviettes	1 Bordeaux flask	100 oranges
1 grey coat	3 nightcaps	2 glasses	2 prs tailors shears
2 pr breeks	1 slack bonnet	1 box with books and writings	1 woven petticoat
2 pr short hose	1 pillow, 2 covers	1 pr boots	1 hood
2 black bonnets	1 pr cloth blankets	2 prs shoes	3-4 pieces of linen cloth
1 bonnet cover	1 palliasse	1 pr mules (slippers)	
5 shirts	a leather bag with a compass and a book		

The skipper was ordered to return the goods, and Francis to bring proof of his expenses.

The Reformation and The Siege of Leith

The period covered by the Admiral's court book was one of major upheaval for Leith and for Scotland, although little hint of what was going on appears in its pages. Opposition to Mary of Guise continued to grow, and in May 1559 came the first open acts of rebellion. On the second of the month John Knox, who had been in Dieppe, landed at Leith. On the eleventh he preached a sermon at Perth which led to rioting and the spoilation of the houses of the Black and Grey friars and the Carthusians. Government forces sent to restore order were unsuccessful and were forced to retreat as far as Dunbar.

By the end of June the rebels had occupied Edinburgh, but their supporters soon began to trickle away, and a month later the Queen's forces were able to re-occupy Leith. They began to strengthen the fortifications of the town, and in the next two months, 1800 more French troops arrived, some with their wives and families. They brought the number of French troops in Scotland to between 3000 and 4000. In those days there was no thought of compensation for individuals who might be inconvenienced by military operations. Andrew Dawson of North Leith lost part of his land to the building of the 'North Fort'. He was a well-to-do skipper, and was able to obtain a grant of remission of Great Custom in recompense. There must have been many lesser men who were seriously affected by the building of the fortifications.

In August 1559 the Congregation (as the rebels were now called) approached England for help. In October the Queen, who was already suffering from her last illness, moved her goods from Holyrood to Leith. Randolph, one of the English commanders, reported that he had seen a map of Leith, and also the place itself from a distance. 'It is very strong both by art and situation and well

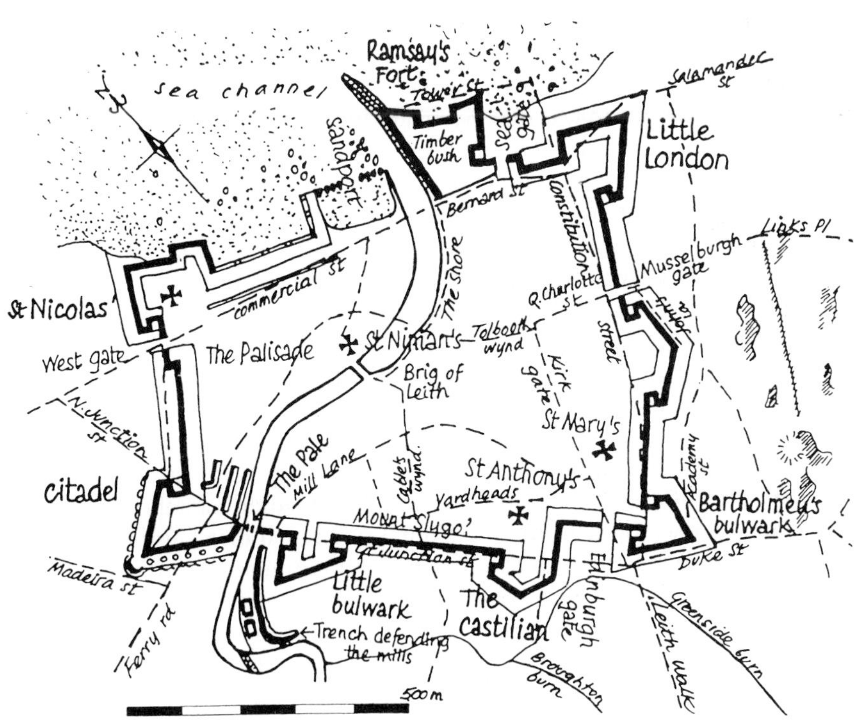

Plan of the French fortifications at the time of the Siege of Leith in 1560, as far as can be ascertained from later evidence (By courtesy of Mr Stuart Harris & The society of Antiquaries of Scotland).

victualled, but slenderly manned for so large a place.' He reckoned it would take 3000 foot and 300 horse a month to recover it.

In November the royalist Lords Seton and Borthwick were in Leith, with a force of 3000 Scots and French. They were said to be so short of food and fuel, that unless they were speedily aided they would have to leave. The news from France was that no Scots ships were being allowed to sail unless they undertook to sail to Leith with supplies for the garrison. By December the French were said to be treating the Scots in Leith so badly that they were leaving the town. Presumably this means that they were keeping all the available supplies to themselves. But help was on its way. In the second week of December a French supply fleet of 16 ships sailed into the Forth.

Meanwhile, in England, Queen Elizabeth's councillors were having trouble persuading her to support the Congregation. It was not until her irreplacable Secretary, the remarkable William Cecil, threatened to resign if she did not intervene, that she finally gave way. Winter, the English Admiral was ordered to follow the French ships into the Forth with a fleet of similar size, but to take no action against them unless provoked. He was to blockade Leith and aid the Congregation.

On 20 December, Arran wrote to Sadler (who was at Berwick) that French ships were still arriving in the Forth, and the English fleet should be hurried up. It had actually left but was so delayed by contrary winds that it did not arrive until 22 January. In the meantime Andrew Sands 'a great Protestant', who had left his home in Leith and was now based at Dundee, had captured two French ships laden with armour, money and horses, in Leith Roads.

On 12 January, Mary began to make arrangements for a French march via Stirling and Fife to St Andrews, where the Lords of the Congregation were assembled. The people of Newbattle, Dalkeith, Musselburgh, Fisherrow and Prestonpans were ordered to bring bread, drink, flesh and fish to Leith. Four days later the boatmen of Musselburgh, Fisherrow and Prestonpans received orders to bring their boats to Leith to take these provisions over to Fife for the French army. The French had reached Elie and their supply vessels - two ships, a hoy and several barques - still lay at Dysart, when the English fleet arrived and captured them. The English Admiral's dispatch to the Duke of Norfolk, who was directing operations from Newcastle, contained the information that there were only 600 troops left in Leith and that it would take the rest four or five days to get back there from Fife. Winter had sailed into Leith Roads after capturing the French supply ships, but had come under fire from Leith and Inchkeith, so his fleet was now lying in Burntisland Roads.

Winter also wrote to Arran with several requests. He needed land bases where sick men could be cared for, pilots in case the fleet was forced by weather to sail further up the Forth or to Dundee, stores of supplies at the waterside and good-sized fishing boats to ferry fresh water and take the sick ashore. He also asked that the barques of Andrew Sands and another skipper called Wytte should be sent from Dundee to chase small vessels bound from Leith to France.

On 29 January, the Queen had her captain, James Cullan, who had stayed at his house on the Shore of Leith, load his ship with supplies for the retreating French force, but on his way to meet them he was captured by Winter, 'whereof the Queen took much displeasure.' Three days later, Winter reported to Norfolk that in spite of the Congregation's efforts to stop them, the French would be back in Leith within 24 hours. (The Congregation had destroyed a bridge at Tullibody in Clackmannanshire, but the retreating French had dismantled the village church and rebuilt the bridge in a night.) The Lords of the Congregation were going home to gather forces for an attack on the port.

In the meantime, Winter was becoming concerned about the state of his men, who were short of clothing and suffering from the cold. He had enough supplies for a fortnight at the most. The French had wasted the coast of Fife from Stirling bridge to within 10 miles of St Andrews, so there were no supplies there, but he could buy from Dundee, Perth and St Andrews, if Norfolk would send him £700.

Winter's next dispatch, on 12 February, contained the welcome news that two victual ships, *Primrose* and *Robert* of Ipswich, had reached him. However, his men were in desperate want of warm stockings and hose, for which he needed £1000. (We tend to think of 'hose' in terms of flimsy modern tights, but they were in fact substantial garments, often made of a coarse woollen fabric called kerseymere.) He was preventing supplies reaching Leith and Inchkeith, and had landed 300 men on the Inch, where there had been a skirmish. He had received a great deal of help from Fife 'a country of much victuals', and merchants from Aberdeen and Dundee were gathering at Burntisland with wine, salt, salmon, herring and cod, in anticipation of the arrival of the English army.

The merchants had a long wait as the army did not arrive at Leith until 6 April. The reasons for the holdup were the familiar ones of delays in the arrival of ships and supplies. An added factor was the need to convince Queen Elizabeth of the need for the expedition, as she held the purse strings and had inherited her grandfather's attitude to spending money on wars. She would have much preferred to have the matter settled 'by diplomatic means'. Even after the army had finally arrived beside Leith, Lord Grey, the commander, received contradictory orders from the Queen and the Council. This was the last thing he needed at that point. He had encountered great supply problems on the march north. The Scots had hidden their stores from the French, and were equally reluctant to part with any of them to their new allies. When they could be persuaded to do so they charged so much that the soldiers had to pay two or three day's wages for one day's food. Apart from the Lords' own men, the Scots numbers were lower than he had anticipated and the troops would only stay for 20 days as they were not being paid wages and had only what they had brought with them to live on. His own troops were suffering from sickness and exposure, which, together with desertions, meant that he was short of 2000 men. There was not nearly enough forage for the horses which were becoming steadily weaker. To cap it all, the ordnance had not yet arrived from London.

Conditions in Leith were not much better. Ten days before the arrival of the English, d'Oysel, the French commander, reported that he was running out of money to give his men for food and prices had increased by a half in the last month. At the end of the month he would have to start issuing rations. Two thirds of their gunpowder was gone and none was available locally. He had lost some men from 'desertion, poverty and fault of heart'. The winter weather which had made the English Admiral so concerned for his men had affected the the French as well. A contemporary report stated; 'The French long after summer. Their misery is such, it is a wonder their lives escape.'

The English fleet was also very short of supplies. On 6 April 1560 there was a report that it had actually left the Forth, but it was still there on the 17th, when 14 supply ships arrived with provisions for 30 days. In spite of its problems, the English army proceeded with its siege arrangements until 'the town of Leith was enclosed in such sort that no man might pass neither in nor out, and the siege was laid to it in three sundry parts with 12 cannons besides 20 shot of small pieces.' The first large structure to be built, early in April, was Pelham's Fort, covering an area of three acres half way along the present Restalrig Terrace. From here, a ditch was carried westward to a point half way between Broughton Burn and Broughton Road, where another fort of a similar size, Mount Somerset, was placed. The completed siege works extended west of the Water of Leith and stretched for about a mile by the time they were finished early in June 1560.

For a month after its arrival in April the English army lay at Restalrig. There were sorties and skirmishes. On 17 April, 'The English ships came to the pier of Leith and made the French believe that they would land and the ships shot amongst them and slew 40 of them.' The seaward side of the port was especially vulnerable as it was only defended by boards with sand piled against them. On 30 April the army burnt the mills of Leith and captured all the stores that were in them. Four days later they crossed the Water of Leith and entrenched at Bonnington.

Negotiations still continued with Mary of Guise, but the military men were becoming impatient for decisive action. It had been agreed that Queen Elizabeth would pay for the hire of 2000 to 3000 Scots troops, but Grey could not get them 'for love nor money'. Another commander, Randolph, wrote to Secretary Cecil that he could not understand the Scots, who so loathed the French but would not take action against them. 'In no other country were ever seen so many particular quarrels, which daily cause many to keep off who mortally hate the French.'

At last, on Saturday 7 May the long awaited assault on Leith was launched - and failed. Lord Grey blamed the rawness of the troops, the shortness of the assault ladders and the incompetence of Sir James Crofts, who had commanded the troops to the west of Leith, where the main attack had been launched. Norfolk, on hot bricks at Berwick, blamed Grey; 'his wits and memory are failing'. The English army returned to its routine of skirmishes and artillery battery.

Mary of Guise was no longer in Leith. Now very ill, she had been allowed to go to Edinburgh Castle on 1 April, before the English army arrived. On June

11 she died, thus effectively putting an end to the conflict. Six days later a ceasefire was proclaimed at Leith. Elizabeth sent Cecil to Edinburgh to oversee negotiations, and he wrote her several shrewd accounts of the proceedings. He let Norfolk know that his 'army flock' was doing well and that he was keeping an eye on them. Also, that Lord Grey, whatever had been reported, was a 'noble, valiant and careful gentleman'. The real villain of the piece, it seems, was Crofts (who was tried for treason when he returned to England). Norfolk wrote back wistfully that he would like to see Leith for himself, and on the night of 6 July, he paid the town a flying visit. The end result of Cecil's diplomacy was the Treaty of Edinburgh, whose most important clause stated that Mary Queen of Scots would relinquish all claim to the English throne. It was this stipulation which made Mary later refuse to ratify the treaty, and continue to do so until the end of her life.

On 5 July the orders were issued for the demolition of the fortifications of Leith. All the artillery was to be assembled in the market place, and the French were to demolish the bulwarks (bastions) to the east and south of the town, helped by the Scots. Arrangements were also made for the simultaneous withdrawal of troops. The number of French who finally left was 3,613 men, 267 women and 315 children.

The slighting of the bulwarks did not proceed as fast as had been hoped. Even after the French had left, 'Little London which is next the sea on the east, and Logans bulwark stand clean whole'. On 21 August the Edinburgh Council ordered the bailies to organise overseers for the workmen. On 7 September the Lords decided to hire 200 pioneers to hurry on the work, which was substantially completed a fortnight later. The demolition was, however, not total. It was only intended to render the fortifications useless for the purposes of war. A plan of Leith made in 1709 shows the eastern rampart and bastions substantially intact. Much of the southern earthwork also remained at that date. It appears that much of the stone facing was removed, leaving the earthern walls to erode naturally. In fact, they did not finally disappear until Leith grew beyond its Medieval boundaries, in the eighteenth century. Even then, the outlines of both walls and bastions were preserved in many property boundaries. In some cases they can even be traced today.

As well as being of such significance to Leith, the year 1560 was a turning point for the history of Scotland as a whole. In it, Protestantism was established as the official doctrine of the church in Scotland. This in turn fostered the closer links with England which had been forming throughout the previous decade, leading eventually to the Union of the Crowns, when James VI, son of Mary Queen of Scots, succeeded to the English throne. Perhaps even more importantly, it saw the last major incursion of a foreign army onto Scottish soil for nearly a century. Although the land was not to be free of civil conflict for some years to come, the absence of a foreign threat eventually allowed trade to flourish, and our Port with it.

6

A Village... To a Town

> Upon the 19 day of August 1561, Marie, Queen of Scots, our sovereign lady, arrived in the Road of Leith at 6 hours in the morning accompanied only with two galleys...at 10 hours the same day, her Highness landed upon the Shore of Leith and remained in Andrew Lamb's house by the space of 1 hour, and thereafter was convoyed up to her palace of Holyrood.

In the nineteenth century a highly romantic picture was painted of Mary's landing at Leith. It shows her mounting a broad flight of stone steps to a quayside crowded with rejoicing subjects and an official welcoming party with flags, banners and guard of honour. In fact, she arrived a week before she was expected and the hour she spent in Andrew Lamb's house was needed for the hurried assembling of a suitable escort to 'convoy' her to Holyrood. But what did the Queen see, as her galley manoeuvred into the harbour and tied up at the foot of the steps which she would ascend to the Shore?

Leith was still a very small place. The earthworks of the French fortifications still bounded it on the east, west and the south. The shore line of South Leith lay little further north than Bernard Street, and that of North Leith along what is now Commercial Street. Much of even this small area was open ground, especially in North Leith, which still consisted of a single Street with a few wynds running off it.

Along the narrow, filthy streets were crowded houses, granaries, booths, workshops, stables, vaults and cellars - and ruins. Some buildings, notably the King's Wark, had never been repaired after the destruction of the 1540s. During the seige St Mary's and St Anthony's churches had been damaged (church towers were often used by the besieged as vantage points for placing artillery and so came under heavy fire from the besiegers). Many houses at the east of the town had been damaged or destroyed by the main bombardment, which had come from the artillery mounds on the Links. Many in the southwest quarter had suffered in the fire following an explosion in a gunpowder store. It was estimated that as much as a third of the town had been affected in one way or another.

The Queen's first step of her return to her native land was taken onto a flagstone quarried at Granton by Alexander Reid, brought to Leith by Lawrence Tod in his boat and laid by David Graham and his masons. Andrew Lamb, whose house she graced for an hour, was one of the wealthiest men in Leith. His home was not the 'Lamb's House' which can be seen today, but it may have stood on the same site. Andrew never forgot that day, or his Queen. Years later, he called one of his ships the *Mary Grace*.

The Tolbooth

The well-known events of Mary's short personal reign had no recorded effect on Leith, although the startling happenings in Edinburgh must have caused much excitement. She did, however, make lasting changes to the life of the Port. The first marked the royal favour which Leith had enjoyed for most of the century. Since the burning of Restalrig Tolbooth by the English in 1544, there had been no proper courtroom or jail for the town. The people had been making do with a 'tower' belonging to the Logans, which stood at the east end of St Leonard's Lands, and now wanted to build their own Tolbooth. Edinburgh, inevitably, had been doing its best to prevent them. Mary, as superior of Leith, was approached for her help and in 1563, after repeated requests to Edinburgh to cease their inevitable obstructions, she wrote a final letter to the Provost:

The toolbooth of Leith, built in 1565, as it appeared in the early nineteenth century.

> Wherefore we charge you that you permit our said town of Leith to build and edify our said house of justice within our said town of Leith , and make no stop or impediment to them to do the same, for it is our will that the same be built and that you desist from further molesting of them in time to come, as you will answer to us thereupon.

At last the people of Leith were able to get on with the building, and by 1565 the Tolbooth was finished, a two-storied building with a forestair. In that same year, however, Leith's short-lived triumph over Edinburgh came to a devastating end. The Queen, now married to Henry, Lord Darnley (son of Lennox and Lady Margaret Douglas) was in urgent need of money for military operations in the West. She borrowed 10,000 merks from Edinburgh. The security for the loan was the handing over to the burgh of the superiority of Leith. The transaction was completed on 6 October, with the proviso that Edinburgh was not to use its new powers until the following Easter. Perhaps the Queen hoped to repay the money by that time. Four days after the agreement, the Provost, bailies, council, deacons and burgesses went down to Leith and received sasine of the superiority on the stair of new Tolbooth. At first they tried to ignore the clause about Easter, but they were sharply reminded by the Queen of the terms of the agreement. In fact, when Easter came, Mary issued the first of a series of 'continuations' of the prohibition, which delayed the evil day until the end of April 1567.

By the time this date arrived, however, the Queen had other things on her mind! On 10 February 1567, her now hated husband, 'King Henry', was murdered at the Kirk o' Field (on the south side of Edinburgh), and the house in which he was staying blown up. One of the main instigators of the plot was said to be the Earl of Bothwell, also widely rumoured to be Mary's lover. He was acquitted of Darnley's murder at a farcical trial held in Edinburgh on 12 April, and on 15 May he and the Queen were married at Holyrood. Almost immediately a force was raised against them, and on 15 June they were finally confronted at Carberry. The Queen's forces deserted her, and once Bothwell had left the field she surrendered.

Edinburgh Gains Possession of Leith

On 3 July, when the Queen was safely (for the time being) warded in Lochleven Castle, the entire burgess community of Edinburgh mustered in arms on Leith Links, and the Provost, two of the bailies and some of the burgesses held a court on the Tolbooth stair, created bailies, sergeants, clerks and dempstars (officers of the court who pronounced the 'doom' or sentence) and took possession of the town. For the past ten years Leith had enjoyed more freedom than it was to experience for another two and a half centuries or more, now its subjection to Edinburgh was complete. In theory the reversion of the superiority remained with the Crown, which could purchase it back at any time, but this was purely academic and in practice Leith was entirely bound to Edinburgh.

It would be wrong, however, to imagine that all in the burgh enjoyed a life of milk and honey while all in Leith suffered grinding poverty. In fact it was only the top tier of Edinburgh society, the burgesses of the Guild Merchant, who were completely free to act as they wished. They did their best to control the next rank, the Craftsmen - fleshers, wrights, masons, hammermen et al, who had to struggle to maintain their lawful liberties to organise their own work and trade in the burgh. All the inhabitants below this station (the great majority) were not burgesses and therefore unfree. They were subject to all the restrictions on their activities that affected unfreemen wherever they lived and in general their economic standing varied from poor to destitute.

Likewise in Leith, some prospered and some did not. We have already seen that the skippers had opportunities to do very well, as long as they were fortunate enough to escape shipwreck or pirates. The town had its craft Incorporations (periodically prohibited by Edinburgh), those in North Leith being linked with the Incorporations of the Canongate. Maltmen, brewers, skinners, fleshers, smiths, masons, coopers, wrights, shipwrights, carters, porters, weavers, and tailors all plied their trades.

The maltmen and brewers in particular, as their testaments show, were generally well-off. Ale and beer were drunk by all people of all ages and at all times of the day. Considering the polluted state of much of the local water, this fact probably saved many lives, as the alcohol content of ale would have had a mild sterilising effect on the water used in the brewing. As well as the normal demand for ale for the tables of local people, the brewers of Leith had a large extra trade supplying ships with the enormous quantities of drink needed by their crews. Until Edinburgh forbade women to sell ale, later in the century, many wives supplemented the housekeeping by brewing, and for many widows it was a major source of income.

Even among practitioners of the same trade there were inevitably variations in degrees of prosperity, but in general, the maltmen were at the top of the heap in the hierarchy of wealth in Leith, with the more fortunate skippers next in line. The lowlier members of society, however, could do surprisingly well. Thomas Paton, the only polkman (grain porter) whose testament has survived for the late sixteenth century, had amassed savings of over £146 - possibly because he was a bachelor. William Symson, a sawyer, had a wife and child, but even he had managed to accumulate £80.

Quite a number of Leithers were connected by blood or marriage with Edinburgh burgesses, like Robert Udwart whose father, Alexander Udwart, was no less a personage than the Dean of Guild of Edinburgh, second only in importance to the Provost. Some burgesses tried living in the Port, nearer to their business interests. The burgh invariably ordered them to return and bear the duties of 'watch and ward' with the rest of the 'neighbours'. Edinburgh men had always owned a certain amount of property in Leith, and their numbers increased. As time went on, successful Leithers were made burgesses of Edinburgh, a practice that was deeply resented by the other inhabitants of the port.

Moreover, the hand of Edinburgh had not grasped the whole of Leith. After the Reformation, lands such as Yardheads on the southern side of South Leith, which had belonged to St Anthony's, had come under the Superiority of the Kirk Session, which jealously guarded its independence. They were helped in this by the fact that Yardheads housed many of the wealthy brewers. The Superiority of North Leith and St Leonard's Lands remained for many years to come with the Commendators of Holyrood. (Commendators were laymen who had taken over control of monastic lands from the priors and abbots.)

It will be clear from the forgoing that the relationship between Leith and Edinburgh was not a straightforward matter of the total subjection of the one by the other. There were always the means for individuals and groups to beat the system if they were devious enough or lucky enough. However, the burgh achieved its main aims. It ensured that Leith would never rival it in wealth, and it milked the port of substantial profits which it could apply to its own purposes, even the dues which were specifically intended for the upkeep of the harbour facilities. The Guild Merchant of Edinburgh was no more immune from the corruption of absolute power than is any other body of men.

The First of the Regents

On 24 July 1567 Queen Mary was 'persuaded' to abdicate. Five days later the tiny king James VI was crowned at Stirling, little more than a month after his first birthday. On 22 August, James Earl of Moray, the Queen's illegitimate half-brother, whom William Cecil had considered to be the most king-like of the Scottish nobility, was declared Regent. No fewer than four successive Regents ruled Scotland before James VI began his personal reign. Most of them would have done well to heed the warning contained in a ballad of 1571;

> Since thou art in the Prince's place possessed,
> Look to be praised as thou plays thy part,
> And as thou lives so loved be and taught,
> And always dealt with after thy desert.

On 2 September, 71 of the foremost men of Leith gathered in St Mary's Kirk to sign a declaration that they accepted James' coronation and the 'Regentry' which would exist until he came of age. There were some notable names missing from this document. Some men of this seaport would be abroad, and others might be absent on business, but by no means everyone in Scotland, let alone in Leith, accepted the new regime as lawful.

One missing name was that of Andrew Lamb, but he had a good excuse. On the day that Moray was declared Regent, Andrew's ship the *Unicorn* had left Leith to sail in pursuit of Bothwell, who had taken refuge in his Earldom of Orkney. *Unicorn* was one of four vessels of Leith and Dundee sent on this mission by the Lords, under the command of William Murray of Tullibardine (Constable of Dundee) and William Kirkcaldy of Grange. Three days after they set out they came up with Bothwell's ships sailing off Orkney, under the command of 'Adam Blacader and David Witter, pirates'. They gave chase, but *Unicorn*, the foremost ship, struck a rock and was wrecked. Kirkcaldy of Grange, who was in her, was so occupied in saving his men and artillery that Blacader and Witter were able to escape to Shetland, where Bothwell was being entertained by a local ruler, Olaf Sinclair. Warned of the pursuit, Bothwell at once took ship and escaped to Denmark. Here his past caught up with him and he was cast into prison by the family of an aristocratic Danish girl he had once seduced. He died insane some years later. His office of Lord High Admiral was given to the Earl of Morton in 1567.

Four and a half weeks after they set out, the remaining ships of the pursuit of Bothwell returned to Leith and Dundee, 'frustrat of thar pray', although they had captured one of Bothwell's ships, along with David Witter and another skipper, George Fogo. The Regent paid Andrew Lamb £1000 compensation for the loss of the *Unicorn*. Kirkcaldy of Grange was made Keeper of Edinburgh Castle. Moray was not to know at the time that this was a major political error. It did not, in fact, become apparent until after the Regent's assassination at Linlithgow on 23 January 1570 by Hamilton of Bothwellhaugh.

Civil War

During Moray's Regency a pro-Mary party had been gathering ground, in which the Hamiltons played a prominent part. They wanted the Queen returned from England, where she was now held prisoner. The 'King's men', who opposed the return of Mary and recognised James VI as their new sovereign, were supported by England. After the death of Moray they asked Queen Elizabeth to name a new Regent. She chose the Earl of Lennox, Darnley's father, a choice which might almost have been calculated to inflame the Marians. Neither was it very popular with anyone else. Soon after Lennox's appointment in July 1570, a civil war broke out, which was to last for over three years and bring Leith once more into the forefront of political life.

The port did not become directly involved in the conflict until late in 1570, and in the meantime life went on much as usual. The whole area was recovering from yet another visitation of the Plague which had raged throughout 1569 in Leith, Edinburgh and the Canongate. In addition, a general dearth had pushed up the prices of basic foodstuffs to record levels. In April 1570, the Craftsmen of Edinburgh discovered that certain merchants had bought wheat intending to ship it abroad illegally. They suspected the Provost and Bailies, 'either to be participant of the said transporters thereof or else to have overseen the transporting of the same, or [to] have winked thereat'. This was a golden opportunity for the Craftsmen to hit back at the officials who were continually trying to deprive them of their lawful liberties. They descended on Leith to search for the offending grain. Not only did they find what they were looking for, but also quantities of tallow and butter and other forbidden goods. They had the whole lot carted up to the Edinburgh Fleshmarket, where it was stored until the burgh authorities could deal with it. There was actually an official 'searcher' based at

Leith; John Dalmahoy, who acted for both the Crown and the burgh and was also Officer to the Admiral. However diligent or otherwise his efforts may have been, they were obviously ineffectual.

In 1570, the king of France made a gesture of solidarity with Mary Queen of Scots by issuing a proclamation in all French ports that no Scottish ships or merchandise were to be received there unless they carried Mary's cocket. Several Scottish ships were arrested in France, including some from Leith, and Edinburgh sent an envoy to the French court to ask for them to be released. He was unsuccessful, but Mary herself intervened and had the ban lifted. She obviously saw that there was nothing to be gained from antagonising a powerful section of Scottish society.

The state of Leith harbour facilities had been giving concern for some time. In March 1568, the Edinburgh Council had heard that the pier and the western bulwark (on the North Leith side) were ruinous, decayed and about to fall down. It was agreed that the profits of the common mills should be used to pay for repairs, but work was also needed on the road from Edinburgh to Leith and on St Giles, and the money would not stretch that far. Early in December 1570, 'the maist pairt' of the ships masters, skippers and mariners of Leith were persuaded to agree to the imposition of dues to finance the work. These amounted to 2s on every tun of goods imported or exported, 1s per ton burthen on every ship entering or leaving the port, 2s on every chalder of grain and pulses and one piece of timber out of every 100. The initial agreement was for three years, but the period was extended by a succession of prolongations and in 1603 the impost was made permanent in the 'Golden Charter' granted to Edinburgh by James IV. It was conveniently forgotten that the harbour dues granted by James III had been intended for just such a purpose.

Late in December 1570 an incident occurred on the Shore that foreshadowed the happenings of the next two years. By this time, Kirkcaldy of Grange, keeper of Edinburgh Castle, had come out in support of the Queen. One of his men was visiting his sister in Leith when he came to the aid of one of his fellows who was being attacked by followers of the Laird of Dury, a 'king's man'. It was hardly a major event on the stage of history, but it serves as a curtain-raiser on what was to follow.

The Regent Lennox's main headquarters at the time were at Stirling, but the Earl of Morton had been in Leith with a detachment of men since the previous summer. In May 1571, while Morton was away at Dalkeith, a 'little barque of 30 tons' arrived at Leith laden with arms, armour, money and wine. The cargo was unloaded and transported to the Castle unopposed, while the men of the Castle occupied their time in running horse races on Leith Sands. Maybe this episode demonstrated to Lennox that Leith in its current state was a weak spot in his armour. He had already built breastworks in the Canongate, using packs of wool and skins commandeered in Leith, as cover for the gunners who defended the Canongate Tolbooth during a Parliament which the king's men had held there. (These goods were captured by the Marians at the end of May when they also demolished some of the houses in the Canongate.)

Leith Refortified

Some more substantially defended base was obviously needed. By the middle of June 1571, Lennox was in Leith with a large force which met the Marians in the first of many skirmishes on the 16th of the month. A few days later the Regent began to repair and rebuild the ramparts of Leith. New trenches six feet deep were dug on the east and southeast of the town, and a muster was called there for 1 July. Lennox also wrote to William Cecil requesting that England should aid him by sending a ship of 140 or 160 tons with a pinnace of 30 or 40 tons to act as her tender, to prevent French shipping from entering the Forth with supplies for the Marians. His request was granted, but the fact that a vessel of that size was not available at Leith implies a decline in the shipping of the port, although it is possible that most of the ships were away on trading voyages.

On June 29, Leith skipper John Downie's ship, the *Andrew*, arrived in the Leith Roads. On board was John Chisholm, who had been Mary's Master of Artillery. Since 1564 he had held the lease of the Kings Wark, and had built a 'lang stair' at the end of the Pier, which made it possible to unload boats at low tide. His purpose in this instance was to supply the Castle with more munitions and money. Hearing that the Regent was at Leith, Chisholm landed at Wemyss, but the Regent ordered Patrick Lord Lindsay, Sheriff of Fife, to search for him, and within a day he was captured on his way to North Queensferry and taken to Leith, with some of the money he had brought from France. The munitions were taken out of *Andrew* and sent to Stirling in a boat, but they were intercepted at Queensferry by some men from the Castle, and by this roundabout route finally came to their intended destination.

Within a week a pinnace had arrived from France, bearing Virac, the French Ambassador. He sent a man to spy out the situation in Leith while he himself landed at Burntisland. His spy was captured, Virac was seized and his possessions searched. Among them were found papers showing that John Chisholm had brought far more money with him than he had admitted to the Regent. Chisholm was arrested and under questioning revealed that he had left the rest of the money with the Commendator of Inchcolm. A body of horse was immediately dispatched to retrieve it. Chisholm's goods were forfeited at a Parliament held at Leith by Lennox in August.

The English envoy to Scotland at this time was Sir William Drury, the Marshal of Berwick, whose mission was to try to bring peace between the warring factions. He was based at Leith, from where he sent home regular reports to Elizabeth and her Council. On 1 July 1571 he reported that the 'misliking' of Lennox by both parties was increasing and he stood in grave danger of assassination. Morton was particularly annoyed at not being given the Archbishopric of St Andrews, whose revenues would have been especially useful to him in his expenses over 'this action'. By the middle of the month Lennox's unpopularity was increasing, 'the same not being hindered by Morton'. However, the Marians also had plans for the Regent. On 3 September he was murdered in the course of an attack by the Marians on the King's lords who were assembled in Stirling for a Parliament. The two men who were later executed for the murder, revealed that they had express orders from the Earl of Huntly to deal with Lennox and that Morton had also been a target. The Earl of Mar was appointed Regent in place of Lennox.

The Siege of the Castle

Drury was at first rather worried about the attitude of Mar towards England, but he soon found him, 'one of the most constant men of Scotland, of the best nature and wholly given to peace.' Almost as soon as Mar became Regent preparations began for an assault on Edinburgh, which was to be 'softened up' by a battering from artillery placed around Leith. On 4 October 1571, Mar

A nineteenth century drawing of the house in St Leonard's Lands which was used as a council chamber by the Regents in 1570-73. It is unusual in that it has its gable end to the street and is almost certainly the 'thortor house' ('thortor' = athwart/at right angles to) which at the time belonged to Helen Leys.

arrived at Leith with 4,000 men and artillery from Stirling. Once the guns were in place, on 16 October, the seige began. Mar's heart, however, was not in his work. Drury commented, 'The Regent, with some others, could be content that these troubles were ended amongst them, but Morton, who rules all, unless he and his friends might still enjoy all they have gotten of the other party, allows not thereof.' The bombardment brought little result and the Regent's halfheartedness was compounded by the attitude of his party. 'If you knew what packing and practising are on both sides, you would think it very strange, for surely neither on the King's side nor on the Queen's do they trust one another among themselves.' So wrote Drury, who was in a position to know, as he still continued his negotiations with both factions.

In November, Morton sailed to Berwick to urge Lord Hunsdon, who was in charge there, to ask Queen Elizabeth for men, money and guns. The need for men was urgent because even as the seige of Edinburgh began, deserters were already starting to trickle away from Leith. Scottish commanders were always hampered by the fact that they generally could not afford to pay troops. They were mainly dependent on unpaid levies, who were traditionally required to bring with them supplies for only 40 days. This period over, the troops considered that they were entitled to return home.

When Morton returned to Leith, Hunsdon accompanied him in order to relieve Drury. Hunsdon was fully in agreement with Morton over the need for English troops, but once in Scotland he found that others were not so keen, 'they of the King's side as much mislike to have her Majesty send in any other force, as the other side.'

Leith Becomes a Seat of Government

Meanwhile, the population of Leith had been swelled by refugees from the beleaguered burgh. They included the Provost, Bailies and Dean of Guild. The latter was given the task of ensuring that all skippers obeyed the injunction of the Regent not to ship the goods of the 'rebels' in Edinburgh either in or out. He was helped by the Customar and the Clerk of the Cocket, who were ordered not to pass any goods until the clerk of the ship and the merchants had sworn that they were legal. Six individual skippers of Leith, Kinghorn and Kirkcaldy had to swear before the Privy Council that they would not import or export rebels. Among them were John Downie of the *Andrew*, and George Dawson of Leith, skipper of the *Flying Hart*. The reason for singling them out is not given, but it is fair to assume that they were suspected of supporting the wrong side. John Downie, at least, had already been guilty of aiding the 'rebel' Chisholm.

After the evacuation of Edinburgh the Court of Session was held in Leith Tolbooth, and all the officials of the College of Justice, the Exchequer, the Admiral's Court and the Sheriffdom of Edinburgh were ordered to come to the town. A house on the Coalhill was traditionally held to have been the Regent's lodging during this time. Some Edinburgh burgesses had gone into the country, in an attempt to remain neutral, but they were ordered to come to Leith and swear allegiance to the King or be proclaimed rebels.

By December 1571 the incomers were well entrenched. Some of them were even building workshops and booths on waste land in Leith belonging to Helen Mowbray. She registered her formal consent to this before the Privy Council, with the proviso that it should not prejudice her right to the land in future. The Regent, however, was sure that the Marians were being secretly aided. Refugees from Edinburgh were allowed to go to and from the burgh, under official licence, in order to save their goods. Mar suspected that this freedom was being abused, and in mid-December he revoked all licences and issued new ones, presumably only to trusted individuals. A week after the revocation of licences, Thomas Glen of Leith had to become surety that John Tod of Aberdour would not carry 'rebels' over the ferry.

The new year of 1572 opened quietly. Warlike operations were hindered by a period of frost and snow which lasted from Christmas until the second week of March. On 15 January, the Parliament which had been interrupted at Stirling the previous August re-opened in Leith, and continued until the end of March. (The yard behind 'Morton's Council House' was long known as 'Parliament Square'.) Before it ended, Lord Hunsdon had returned to Berwick, being replaced by Drury, who was accompanied by Thomas Randolph. They found 'this country in great calamity and misery. Thefts, murder, spoils unmerciful.' A Scottish commentator gives more details.

> It was a heavy matter to show the oppression done by the party in Leith to the poor commons about Edinburgh, who caused the whole inhabitants of the Canongate to flit and come to Leith. [The Regality court of the Canongate was held in North Leith Tolbooth from August 1571 until the end of July 1572.] And when they came thereto they warded the most right men, because they refused to pay a stent to the Regent. And also all inhabiters within two miles of Edinburgh were constrained to leave their houses and lands, to the effect that Edinburgh should have no furnishing, and condemned poor men and women to death for inbringing of victual to Edinburgh.

Garrisons were placed at Craigmillar, Reidshaw and Corstorphine to prevent supplies coming to Edinburgh, and all the mills within four miles of the burgh, numbering more than 30, were put out of action. Three hundred Highlanders (the word was then synonymous with 'savages') were billeted in villages and cottages around Edinburgh to keep an eye on the occupants and prevent them from supplying the Queen's men in the Castle.

In April 1572 Mar tightened security. Porters were appointed to guard the five gates of Leith and prevent the 'rebels' being supplied from the port. Only enough victual and coal was to leave the town to supply the garrison at Holyrood. Anyone caught disobeying orders was to be branded on the cheek in Leith market place. (This last edict to apply retrospectively.) It seems that the troops had been getting out of hand. They were ordered to obey their own captains and not make private arrests of persons or goods.

Many vagabonds had taken advantage of the unsettled conditions to flock to Leith, where they seized goods from travellers under pretence of being soldiers.

They were ordered to leave. Anyone found in the town without a legitimate purpose was to be branded on the cheek, and if caught a second time, to be hanged. All ships coming into the Forth were to unload at Leith, and not further up the Firth. Blackness Castle was at this time held for the Queen, and the Regent was trying to prevent Edinburgh Castle from being supplied by this route. A ship and a shallop were sent from Leith to 'keep the narrow waters from them of Blackness', but they were blown off station by a storm, and the men from the castle were able to come out in boats and take several crayers and boats laden with supplies for Stirling.

On 11 May 1572, Du Croque, the French Ambassador, arrived at Berwick en route to try what his intervention might do to conclude matters in Scotland. He waited at Berwick only long enough for a safeconduct to reach him from the Regent, and when he left, Drury accompanied him. The French Ambassador lodged in Leith, but Drury, who had become very unpopular on his previous visit, did not want to risk returning to the town. His first dispatch after his return was written from Restalrig on 23 May. Du Croque was angry at being made to stay in Leith rather than lodge in Edinburgh, as he wished to do. He told Drury that he found the state of Scotland much altered in that a French ambassador there should be restrained and an English one have liberty. Drury commented that, 'Sundry Scotsmen also find it strange'. He also noted that six people had recently been executed for supplying Edinburgh with provisions.

Blackness Castle was still harbouring troublesome 'rebels' who attacked shipping going to Stirling. On 19 June the Privy Council ordered the Leith skippers William Downie (son of John) and Alexander Lummisden to rig out as many ships and boats as they thought necessary for the purpose, to keep the Forth safe. The operation was to be financed by a levy on wine, hides, wool, skins, cloth and coal going up or down the Firth.

At the beginning of July 1572, Hunsdon recalled Drury to Berwick for a few days. Whatever new instructions he had received began to bear fruit when he and Du Croque had a meeting with the Regent a fortnight later. They also saw the 'Castilians', as the Queen's party were sometimes called, and Drury considered that they were now very near peace. 'If I miss it while I find the iron hot, I will with my little strength lay on the hammer.' On 30 July a ceasefire was concluded, to last two months. Drury returned thankfully to Berwick, where he heard that Morton had persuaded the Regent to ask Elizabeth to send a more skilled ambassador the next time. He devoutly hoped the request would be granted, 'if it might please the Queen, I had rather serve her in Constantinople or elsewhere than return into Scotland.'

Elizabeth's interest in supporting the king's party in Scotland was, in fact, cooling, but the French massacre of protestant Huguenots, on St Bartholemew's Eve (24 August), put an entirely different complexion on things. Sir Henry Killigrew the new English Ambassador to Scotland, reported that, 'The news of France clean alienates minds here from putting any great trust in that Court.' The departure of Du Croque was not long delayed.

At the end of October 1572 the Regent Mar died, and on 25 November Morton was elected in his place. This scion of the Douglas stock, 'had never wavered from the anglophile and protestant tradition of his house.' He and Killigrew got on very well, in fact the Ambassador was rebuked by Lord Burghley (ex-Cecil) for accepting unreasonable terms from Morton. This probably meant that he had agreed to demands for more money, which was, indeed, urgently needed. Killigrew's subsequent letters hammered this point home at every opportunity. It was probably difficult for the English Council to appreciate the poverty of the Scottish nobility, who were bearing the costs of the war. They also had to deal with the Queen, who held the purse-strings.

Parliament Returns to Edinburgh

On 15 January 1573, Morton presided over a Parliament in the Edinburgh Tolbooth, which was protected by a rampart of turf and faggots. The culverins of the Castle fired on the Parliament, but all they hit was one dog. There were encouraging signs that all was not prospering with the Marians. A rumour that two of the Castle wells had run dry was confirmed when the garrison began drawing water from St Margaret's well, outside the fortifications. Morton had the well poisoned with white arsenic and fresh limestones, and for good measure, filled up with dead beasts.

After the Parliament, plans began for the digging of trenches around the Castle. During February, calculations were made concerning the number of men and pieces of artillery which would be needed and Elizabeth was persuaded to send some ordnance to Leith.

At the beginning of April four captains and the master gunner arrived from Berwick to survey the area of operations. They were followed by the master carpenter and 100 pioneers, who were to dig trenches, helped by 'idle persons' of the town. Drury sent a hoy to Leith laden with timber and tools. A few days later he himself was on his way to Edinburgh with 1500 troops (the Regent had only 700 men left). Drury must have contemplated this visit to Scotland with some satisfaction. In his oft-repeated 'simple opinion', the action was long overdue.

On the evening of 26 April three English hulks arrived in Leith Roads laden with 23 pieces of ordnance and, 'One Scots piece, smaller than a cannon, called one of the Seven Sisters, which had been taken by the English at Flodden.' The hulks were 'convoyed' by the ships of William Downie and John Cockburn of Leith. Three days later all the ordnance, and the quantities of shot and gunpowder which had also been in the hulks were safely landed on the Shore. More was also fetched from Stirling and from Blackness Castle (which had been recovered the previous January).

On the day the hulks arrived at Leith a mine had been begun to tunnel under the Castle defences and undermine a 'blockhouse' which stood within a spur of the Castle fortifications. The artificers were making a platform on which to mount some of the artillery, on a piece of ground which was, in the opinion of the master gunner, 'Of such advantage that there shall not a man within be able to stir for the shot'.

All these preparations were made without a shot being fired from the Castle, where conditions were said to be desperate. A man who managed to get out of the fortress on 13 April revealed that the defenders were very short of gunpowder, had hardly any water and only salted provisions to eat. Later it was rumoured that the garrison was on the point of mutiny. Seventeen women - wives, relatives and servants of the chief men - were sharing the hardships.

On 4 May the cannon began to be hauled up from the Shore to be planted as batteries around the castle. By the 17th all the batteries were in place. All soldiers who had lately served against the king were ordered to leave Edinburgh, as were the wives of the men in the Castle. They were to remain at least four miles away as long as the seige lasted.

The Fall of the Castle

The bombardment began on 17 May. Eleven days later the 'blockhouse' was won by the miners, and the 200 men in the Castle surrendered.

Within a week the artillery was back on the Shore at Leith, being loaded into several English barques, which left a few days later. Drury was still at Leith on 14 June, but he was only awaiting the return of Killigrew from the wedding of the Earl of Angus and the late Regent's daughter, before marching south with the troops.

The people of Edinburgh and the Canongate who had been in Leith returned to Edinburgh to repair and rebuild and begin to restore their fortunes. In many cases they had helplessly watched as their houses were damaged or destroyed by cannon shot from the Castle, and 40 houses in the Cowgate had been deliberately burned by the 'Castilians'. In fact it was even more imperative that they return, as it was a condition of freeman status that a burgess must reside in his burgh. One Edinburgh man had to apply for special permission to remain in Leith until his sick wife was well enough to be moved.

The captains of the 'Castilians', Kirkcaldy of Grange and Maitland of Lethington were condemned to be executed. Kirkcaldy suffered the penalty, but Maitland died before his sentence could be carried out.

The cessation of civil war after the fall of the Castle was by no means the end of the troubles of Leith. The weather during the 1570s was particularly dreadful. A great drought in the summer of 1573 was followed by an unusually wet summer in 1574 and a wet spring in 1575, which caused the loss of much corn and a subsequent dearth. The position was eased somewhat in 1574, when an enormous shoal of herring came into the Forth, providing cheap food for the poor. Added to the dearth was yet another outbreak of the Plague, with all its attendant miseries.

More Piracy

The decade also saw an upsurge in piracy - but this time it was Scottish ships that were on the receiving end of attacks from English privateers. In all, between

1572 and 1579, no fewer than 25 Scottish ships were attacked, eleven of them in 1577 alone. Sometimes the pirates took only the cargo, but as often as not the vessel itself was lost. One third of the ships which were attacked came from Leith. They included Andrew Lamb's *Mary Grace*, and a ship laden with herring and salmon worth £478, whose master was John Dawson of North Leith. It was at this time that Queen Elizabeth began replenishing her coffers with a share of the profits of English privateers, whose most famous exploits were carried out at the expense of Spain. They were not, however, averse to catching smaller fry.

In June 1574, an English pirate ship commanded by one Robert Istead of Hastings was driven by a storm into Montrose with two Scottish 'prizes'. He and his crew were arrested and tried, then executed at Leith in July. Among Istead's crew was a Leith mariner, Peter Fisher, whose deposition at his examination gave details of his roving career.

About ten years previously he had been in Plymouth, where he was hired to serve in a ship going to Rochelle. The vessel was captured on the voyage by a French man of war and the crew, including Fisher, sent to the galleys. There he stayed for six years, until he was redeemed by some men of Rochelle (probably expatriate Scots), and returned to Leith in a ship skippered by Andrew Redpath. For a year he was employed by Mr Archibald Sandilands of Kinghorn, after which he returned to Plymouth in Robert Sands' ship. There he transferred to William Downie's ship and sailed to Dieppe, where he was hired by a French pirate called Pierre Trenchard. He was in Trenchard's company at the taking of a Dutch hulk laden with pitch and tar.

The hulk and its cargo were brought to Scotland to be sold, and Fisher stayed in his homeland until he was taken on by one of Lord Robert of Orkney's skippers to sail in his ship *Andrew* from Burntisland to Orkney. He returned to Burntisland in Mr John Hume's barque, which carried Lord Robert's Orkney wares. Within two months Fisher was re-hired by Mr John Hume to sail with him to Norway. On the way there they took a hoy laden mainly with copper kettles, which they took to Orkney to be sold by Edward Blacader. Once again Fisher returned from Orkney, this time to Wemyss, where he was hired by a Frenchman to go to Rochelle. After a stay of eleven weeks there, he sailed to Ayr.

It was in Ayr, during the previous November, that he had signed up for a voyage to St Malo, where his ship was arrested. He and a few Ayr mariners were in Dartmouth by March 1574, where Fisher left his companions and went on foot to Plymouth. Here he was taken on by 'Mr Hawkins' - a figure second only to Drake in the annals of Elizabethan seafaring. Fisher was one of the crew of Hawkins' new barque when she sailed to Harwich. At Dover he was sent ashore to find a pilot to take the barque into Harwich, and here he either deserted or was left behind. After two weeks in London, he was hired by Mr Hills, the skipper of Isted's ship.

Perhaps in the hope of being shown mercy, Fisher gave details of three other English pirates currently at large. William Winter had been a pirate for seven years, and had a ship of two and a half tops. Captain Caleis had a hulk of 200 tons and two fly boats. John Story of Portsmouth had a fly boat. The giving of this information did not save Fisher from his fate, but it may have been in the hope of daunting the named three, that the Burghs raised a tax in July 1574 to equip warships to go out against pirates, one of the said ships being the *William* of Leith, and another being a barque provided by Edinburgh. It will be inferred from the continuing depredations of the English, that they were not very successful.

In 1580, the Convention of Royal Burghs made an Act that all goods pillaged by pirates from Scottish ships should be recompensed by a tax on the ship and freight, as well as on goods left unpillaged in the ship. The 'skippers and mariners of the realm' protested against this on three counts. In the first place they argued that the Act was not lawful as it had not been endorsed by the king. Second, they should have been consulted before any such change was made. Third (and perhaps most important), in the past, merchants had refused to help mariners to resist when attacked by pirates, exposing to danger not only their own goods, but the vessels and goods of the skippers and mariners. They brought their case before the Privy Council, which did not consider that they could give a judgement in the case, which they remitted to 'competent judges' (the Court of Admiralty, whose records for this period have not survived).

Finally, in 1587, an envoy was sent to Elizabeth with a petition that restitution should be made to all the Scots whose ships and goods had been despoiled since 1564. The list ran to 34 vessels, and the English responded with their own list of eight ships which had been attacked by Scots since 1581. In the end, however, Elizabeth agreed to grant restitution in 16 of the more recent cases. One of these involved a 'little ship' belonging to Andrew Redpath of Leith (presumably he who had employed Peter Fisher) which had been attacked in 1586 on her way home from London with a cargo of slates. In the same year, a 'scout' of Leith had been despoiled of goods worth £1200 pounds. Another Leith ship, (master, John Dummo), had been wrecked in Scouts Bay and illegally seized by an Englishman.

James VI Begins to Rule

Throughout the troubled decade of the 1570s, James VI was growing up. In 1578 he was twelve, legally old enough to head a government. On 17 October 1579, James made his formal entry into Edinburgh as king. In the summer of 1580, when he was nearly fourteen, he made a progress through Fife and Angus. By this time he had fallen under the influence of his French cousin Esme Stewart, a man twice his age. The king had been brought up under a regime of considerable austerity and loneliness, and had been taught to hate his mother. The results of such nurture were apparent in his response to his cousin's charm. In 1580, Esme was made Earl of Lennox, the hereditary holder of the Earldom having been persuaded to resign the title. Other honours followed and the favourite was admitted to the Privy Council in June 1580. It was owing largely to his influence that Morton was arrested in December 1580 on the charge of having been implicated in Darnley's murder, and executed the following June.

Lennox was extravagant, and encouraged the king to further waste the depleted royal resources. A dinner held at Leith in February 1581 is typical of the kind of expenses James incurred under the influence of his cousin. After a sumptuous meal, the king ran at the ring and then watched displays such as a mock assault on a castle built on boats and called the 'Popes Palace'. Once the castle had been taken it was set on fire. Horse races were run on the sands until some of the jockeys were hurt in a fall. Like his great-grandfather James IV, 70 years before, the king also watched jousting in boats. The sport had been kept up in Leith all that time. Who, one wonders, was King of the Sea in 1581?

Lennox was finally overthrown in August 1582 in a coup called the Ruthven Raid, after which he escaped through England to France, where he died not long afterwards. By the end of 1585 James had taken full control of the government. In July 1586, a league was concluded with England, under whose terms each country was to aid the other in the event of an invasion.

The league was unaffected by the execution of Mary Queen of Scots in 1587, after the discovery that she was involved for a third time in a plot to do away with Elizabeth and put herself on the throne of England. James was hardly likely to want to avenge the death of a mother he had been taught from babyhood to despise. He was more concerned that nothing should prejudice his eventual accession to the English throne.

The Spanish Armada

One result of the execution of the Catholic Mary was the sending of the Armada of ships from Spain in 1588, to invade England. It was thought there was a strong possibility that it would also make for Scotland, where many Northern lords, who had remained strongly Roman Catholic, held a conference in June 1588 and agreed to receive the Spaniards if they came. The king, three earls and 200 barons and lairds had resolved a month previously to resist any attempt by the Spaniards to land in Scotland. Ships were made ready at Leith and Dundee, and all papists and Jesuits were ordered to leave the country.

On 8 August, the Lord Admiral, (the office had reverted to the Earls of Bothwell after the death of Morton,) was ordered to sea. By 10 August, news of the defeat of the Armada had reached Scotland. Men of war from Newcastle were lying in wait in the Forth to capture any Spanish stragglers from the remnant of the Armada, which was making for the North. The next day, a solitary Spanish vessel did come into the Forth and was promptly taken. The rest of the Armada were said to be at anchor in the Moray Firth. By 22 August it was in Orkney and Shetland.

Early in the autumn, *La Ballanzara* of the Armada was wrecked off Ireland, and on 13 October 46 of her crew arrived in Edinburgh. The town fed and clothed them and then allowed them to leave in Andrew Lamb's *Mary Grace* and another ship called the *Grace of God*, which were going to France.

A datestone of 1588 (the Armada year) from a house in Newhaven, showing an 18-gun ship and navigational instruments of the period.

A party of Spaniards were wrecked on Fairisle, and on 26 November 1588, 200 of them arrived at Anstruther in a few fishing boats and then came on into the Forth to try and hire a ship to take them to the Low Countries. It soon became known that among their number were many Spanish noblemen. At the king's invitation they stayed at the Court until the middle of February 1589. The rank and file were not so fortunate. The king ordered the Provost of Edinburgh to provide for them, and some were helped by the nobility, but most were reduced to begging in the streets.

During the summer of 1589 arrangements were made to transport the Spaniards still remaining in Scotland to Flanders. Four ships were prepared at Leith and Burntisland for the purpose, and once the word spread, the Spaniards began to make for those ports. By 22 July, 660 men had gathered, 400 of them fit, the rest sick and lame. They left four days later, but some had taken service in noble households and remained behind. In November 100 more Spaniards left Leith, who had been in the service of Mclean of the Isles since their ship was blown up in Mull the previous autumn.

By this time the king was in Denmark, having embarked at Leith on 22 October and married the 14-year-old Anne, second daughter of the king of Denmark on 23 November. In March 1590 the Privy Council ordered that six of the largest ships possible should be rigged to bring home the king and queen. Edinburgh was to provide two and Ayr, Aberdeen, Dundee and St Andrews, one each. A total of 40 burghs were taxed to pay for the fitting out of the ships, which were to be ornamented with flags, red taffeta streamers and red and yellow hangings. Possibly because March was the beginning of the sailing season for merchant ships, no vessels were available in Leith. All Edinburgh could muster was one ship from Kirkcaldy, the *Angel*, which duly set sail with the rest.

Leith Expands

James VI and his Danish bride landed on 1 May 1590. As she stepped ashore the new Queen saw a very different Leith from the one which had greeted her late mother-in-law 29 years before. An Englishman who visited the port in the 1590s reported that after the French had fortified the place 'it began of a bare Village to grow to a Towne.' Two main factors were responsible for this, an increase in population and a boom in trade.

It has been estimated that the population of Edinburgh doubled between 1550 and 1625. No figures are available for Leith, but the evidence of property sasines throughout the sixteenth century shows that it shared in this trend. The properties registered in North Leith by James Young at the beginning of the 1500s were in the main whole buildings occupied by one or perhaps two households. By the end of the century most North Leith sasines detail the subdivision of larger dwellings into fore and backlands, 'heich' and 'laich' (upper and lower) 'houses'. For example, a waterside 'land' in North Leith in 1600 contained five households. Its three laich houses were each occupied by a single tenant. A mariner's widow lived in an upper hall, chamber and gallery, and another mariner's family in a ground floor room and the one above it.

The few details that survive for South Leith follow the same pattern. In 1580 the Edinburgh council took steps to demolish shops which had been built out onto the fronts of buildings in Leith. There were complaints about exterior staircases, built to give access to upper storeys. In places it seems that rooms had even been built to link the first floors of houses which faced each other across a narrow street.

Leith remained essentially within the bounds of its fortifications until the late eighteenth century, so (as in Edinburgh) buildings had to become taller to accommodate the increase in population. Lambs House, the only surviving early seventeenth century domestic building in Leith, is probably typical of the 'lands' built at the end of the sixteenth century by prosperous maltmen, skippers and merchants. It is several stories high, but narrow, confined by the boundaries of the medieval toft on which it was built - one of the short row laid out for David I along the Shore after he had gifted the original royal port to Holyrood Abbey. Lamb built his dwellinghouse at the tail of his property, fronting Rotton Row. The 'foreland', facing onto the Shore, would have been occupied by a warehouse.

The recovery in trade began late in the 1570s. In spite of the dearth which prevailed at the time, settled conditions under the Regent Morton allowed merchants to operate more freely than had previously been possible. The effect of the upturn on Leith is perhaps most graphically illustrated by the rising number of ships freighted in Edinburgh during the last quarter of the century.

By the 1590s goods exported through Leith paid 72% of all Great Custom collected in Scotland. Practically all the wool exports went through Leith and 80% of the hides and woolfells. Fife and the Lothians were the centres of the expanding coalmining and saltmaking industries. At the end of the sixteenth century, 65% of Scottish coal exports left Leith, and increasing amounts of salt. (In 1575, some Flemish towns forbade the import of Scottish salt because the Scots had cornered the market there.)

There were saltpans very close to Leith. In 1567, Edinburgh granted a 50 year tack of piece of land of about 80 by 100 ells on the south side of Newhaven to three Englishmen for saltmaking. In later years a Fleming called Eustace Roche was employed by the Crown to improve the mining of metals. The venture was unsuccessful owing to the obstructive attitudes of landowners, and in 1588, Roche was granted land at Newhaven to construct 10 pans, in which he was to make a superior grade of salt. Coal and salt were largely responsible for the rise in importance of other ports in the Forth, such as Prestonpans, Culross, Kirkcaldy and Dysart. Crail, Anstruther, Wemyss and Pittenweem were important fishing and fish exporting burghs, but Leith also shared significantly in this trade.

Scottish colonisation of foreign ports had been going on since overseas trading contacts began and by the end of the sixteenth century, there were well established colonies of Scots in Northern Prussia (especially in Danzig), France (particularly in Normandy), Scandinavia, and many towns in the Low Countries, all of which had close links with Leith. For instance, in 1589, the three daughters of William Aikman, expatriate Scot and burgess of Dieppe, and their French husbands, inherited a tenement in St Leonards Lands, which they sold to William Cunningham of Edinburgh. The following year William Cunningham stood surety for two Scots of Rouen in a case involving goods they had shipped in the *Papingo* (parrot) of Leith. Some Leith men were living as far afield as Spain, where James Lawmer of Leith was apprenticed to Hans Wansoute in 1593.

Many Scots had gravitated to the area around Danzig in order to make a precarious living in the isolated country districts of Northern Prussia as 'cramers' or pedlars. 'Kramerwarren' appear in lists of Scottish goods imported into Danzig as early as the fifteenth century. In the late sixteenth century some cramer goods began to be liable for export custom, such as the 83 gross of gloves, 6229 pairs of Leith Wynd hose and 284 gross of points (leather laces) which left Leith in 1594-5. Some of the coarse woollen cloth which had been exported throughout the century also ended up in the packs of cramers. In the main, Scottish wool, hides, coal and salt were not needed in Northern Prussia, but the area was rich in wood, grain, linen, flax, pitch, tar and iron, all of which came to Scotland chiefly through Danzig.

As well as exporting Scottish produce, Leith became a staging post for goods bound from France and Flanders to Scandinavia, such as wine, spices, dried friut and other luxury items. Some of these goods were probably exchanged for wood from Norway. We have already seen that Edinburgh paid cash for Norwegian timber to rebuild Newhaven in the 1550s, but it is likely that payment was often in kind. This was definitely the case in the next century, when restrictions on the export of cereals were lifted, allowing them to be exchanged for timber in Norway.

The Timber and Wine Trades

In the mid sixteenth century Norwegian farming was recovering from a slump. Much land was being reclaimed from the forests. The introduction of water-powered sawmills meant that more and cheaper planks could be produced from a single tree trunk than had been possible when the trunk could only be split along the grain with an axe. Timber was one Norwegian commodity which did not have to be sold in a burgh, so a farmer could set up sawmills on his own land and sell directly to customers who sailed their ships into the fjord where his farm lay. He would be happy to receive luxury goods in exchange, rather than cash which he would then have to spend in one of the burghs, which might be some distance away.

Until the mid-seventeenth century, Scottish timber ships visiting Norway were of only 20 to 30 tons. Sometimes fishing boats as small as 8 tons were used, but in a good year it was possible to make as many as three trips. In 1567, 28 Scottish ships transported timber from the Ryfylke area but by 1602, when regular records begin, there were over 100 per annum. It was this area, in southern Norway, that Leith ships chiefly visited, along with vessels from other East Coast ports. Scottish merchants were mainly interested in Norwegian pine boards (deals), beams (baulks), and barrel hoops (girthstings) of hazel. Spaces in the cargo were filled up with cords of birch firewood (burnwood), but this was not an important item as Scotland has always been generously provided with indigenous fuel.

Timber also came into Leith from the Baltic, and storage became a problem. In 1575 Edinburgh, not unnaturally, objected to the actions of John Logan of Sherrifbrae, who had imposed his own impost on timber left on the street between the Bridge and his house. He had been removing one joist from every 'houpe' (pile or stack) left there, in spite of the fact that storage had always been free, to encourage foreigners to bring their timber to Leith. As far as possible, importers and owners stored their timber in their own yards and closes. The fact that the street had to be used points to a shortage of more secure areas. In 1578, the Burgh paid John Dalmahoy the Searcher 100 merks for his title to 'that part of the lands lying in the bulwark, (Ramsay's Bastion) once called the Common Closets, newly called the Bourse', which had been given to him by Mary Queen of Scots. The bastion formed a level platform which was conveniently placed for access from the Shore and Pier. Its low northern wall was lapped by the sea at high tide, so that large timbers could be floated round to it from the harbour and hauled up for storage. This was the ground which became known as the Timber Bush; the official storage place for timber from that time forward.

Various sources contain scattered references to the different types of timber coming into Leith in the late sixteenth century, but a list of harbour dues of 1603 provides the most complete picture. (The dues quoted here are those charged to freemen of Edinburgh, freemen of other burghs paid double, and unfreemen six times the basic rate.) Boards, deals, single roof spars and bowstings all paid 8d per 100. Double roof spars paid 16d per 100; joists, corbels and wainscot panels, 1d each. Knapholt were narrow boards suitable for panelling and barrel staves. From Danzig they paid 4d per 100, from Norway, 2d. Ready made barrel staves (skows) paid 1d per 100, as did girthstings (barrel hoops). Firewood paid 1d per fathom and whicker spars 2d per 100.

The wine trade for which Leith became famous reached considerable proportions by the end of the sixteenth century. Since the days of Queen Margaret, wine had been coming in to the port from France. At first it was the drink of the aristocracy, but during the later sixteenth century the 'lesser sorts' became more prosperous and able to afford this particular luxury, and imports soared. In theory all wine was supposed to be sold in Edinburgh, but as we might expect, Leithers were not going to pass by such a profitable business. Tuns and puncheons found their way into cellars and vaults, and there grew up perhaps not a roaring trade, but certainly a whispering one. In 1596 the King legalised these enterprises by granting the right to set up taverns (wine shops) in Leith. His object was to increase his revenues by taxing the new establishments but the people of Leith must have been delighted with this opportunity to cock a profitable snook at Edinburgh.

During the sixteenth century the fortunes of Leith probably fluctuated more than at any other time in its history. Both good and bad times lay in the future, but never again would the town suffer such physical destruction as in the 1540s. The disruptions of the siege of 1560 and 'occupation' by the Regents in the early 70s interrupted the growth of the town, but by the end of the century Leith was flourishing as never before, and ready for the changes that were still to come.

7

After the Union of the Crowns

On the last day of February 1603, Queen Elizabeth of England fell ill. On 23 March, hardly able to speak, she indicated by signs that James VI of Scotland was to succeed her. In the small hours of the next morning, she died. James was at last King of Scotland and England.

Sir Robert Carey, brought the news to his new Sovereign. He arrived at Holyrood late at night on 26 March. Sir Robert had informed James a week previously that Elizabeth had not long to live, but even before he got this news the king had begun to make preparations for his journey south. He set out overland on 5 April with a large retinue, leaving his wife and family to follow as and when they might. There was need for haste. Although Elizabeth's Council were all in favour of James' succession, popular opinion was not so unanimous, and there were demonstrations in London against the new king. The journey overland was a long one, however. By the time James arrived in his new capital, dissent had been subdued, and the people were ready to welcome him.

One of the king's last acts before leaving Scotland had been to borrow 1000 merks from the burgesses of Edinburgh to help defray the expenses of his journey. The town had also helped the king out financially on a number of occasions in the past, and to show his gratitude, on 15 March 1603, eight days before the death of Elizabeth, James had granted Edinburgh the 'Golden Charter'. This document confirmed all grants and charters to the town, from the days of David I onwards, James adding a few touches of his own. Some of the most valuable rights thus confirmed were, of course, those which Edinburgh had over Leith.

The Effects of the Golden Charter

As might have been expected, the ink was scarcely dry on the Charter before Edinburgh began to exercise her new powers. She soon discovered, however, that the king might be 400 miles away, but he had not abandoned the interests of his Scottish subjects. Leith complained vigorously to James, who informed the Privy council in January 1604 that Edinburgh had, under the pretext of the Charter:

> Invented and raised divers innovations upon the inhabitants of the town of Leith and others our subjects dwelling near unto the same, daily molesting them with new and unaccustomed thraldoms, tending to the utter debarring of them from the use of such mean liberties as they have time out of mind enjoyed.

The king instructed the Privy Council to put a stop to the present abuses and make sure they were not repeated in the future. He protested that he had never intended to grant any new rights to Edinburgh, regarding the charter merely as a confirmation of those which had gone before. Unfortunately he had not allowed for that aspect of human nature which will grab at any opportunity, however slim, to further its own ends. The 'Golden Charter' marked a watershed in the worsening of relations between Edinburgh and Leith.

Whatever action the Privy Council took had little effect on Edinburgh, which went ahead with its plans regardless of distant royal disapproval. It has to be said that in the early years of the new century much work was done on the Shore, pier, bulwarks and beacons, but in the main the story is one of increasing oppression and injustice.

In 1604, for the first time, two Burgesses were appointed Bailies of Leith, and this became the invariable practice. In 1607 the ferries came under regulation. Six lead 'tickets' were obtained by the Council, to be given 'to such passage boats as they think good', which would be the only ones allowed to operate on a Sunday. In 1609, the King granted an impost of £4 on each tun of wine sold, and in both Edinburgh and Leith, special stingmen were appointed, to have the sole right of carrying wine to taverns. They had to give the Bailies an account of the number of barrels carried. This impost did eventually benefit Leith. In 1612, the king ordered that the money collected there was to be employed for the good of the town. Initially it was to be used to repair the steeple of St Mary's church and furnish it with bells, then the Tolbooth was to be repaired. Thereafter, the money went to the building and upkeep of a hospital for 'maintaining the widows and orphans of so many drowned and castaway mariners' (King James' Hospital). The Privy Council were instructed to make quite sure that Edinburgh did not get hold of any of the money. South Leith Kirk Session, which administered the fund, needed no such instructions. Through the centuries that followed they ensured that every penny came to them.

Another innovation, ordered by the king, which affected both Burgh and port in 1610, was the appointment of Constables to oversee each quarter of the respective towns. In Leith, four constables were appointed to the Leys quarter (a cooper and three maltmen), and two each to the Dubrow, Hill and Sands quarters. The constables served for 6 months at a time. Their duties were much like those of the present-day police, except that they were also responsible for the cleanliness of the streets - and the modern police constable is not required to arrest Jesuits, priests and papists!

The Water Bailie, appointed by Edinburgh to oversee maritime affairs in Leith, had always been a burgess. Until he died in 1619, the office was held by James Forman. He was not afraid to give orders even to high ranking officers of the Crown, and was not at all popular with the skippers. He came in for a fair amount of verbal abuse and, on occasion, physical violence. The offenders invariably ended up before Edinburgh Council, where they were sentenced to make a public apology for 'verbals' or fined for 'laying violent hands' on the Bailie.

Seamen, particularly skippers, were always more difficult for Edinburgh to control, except insofar as they might usurp the privileges of freemen. Even here, however, the burgh came up against the customary practices of 'portage' and 'part cargoes'. In 1615, Edinburgh tried to deprive the mariners of their ancient freedoms by invoking the clause in the fourteenth century charter of Robert Logan of Restalrig which forbade 'packing and peeling' (trading) in Leith. The Council suddenly began escheating such seamens' goods as they found in Leith. The skippers took their case to the Privy Council. They explained that portage goods were small quantities of a dozen barrels or less which 'past all memory of man' had been given by merchants to ships' crews as part of the freight and hire charges of a voyage. In addition, skippers often made up a full cargo with their own salt, timber, corn or wine. In many cases the merchants who had chartered the ship could not provide sufficient goods to make up a complete cargo, and skippers, who might well be part-owners of their ships, would fill the space in order to make the voyage profitable. The complainers maintained that they always sold their imported goods wholesale to Edinburgh freemen and paid the high unfreemens custom on them. The Privy Council showed its customary reluctance to intervene between Edinburgh and Leith, deciding that the case was not within its competence to judge. Whatever the outcome, the wills and testaments of seventeenth century skippers and mariners give no impression of any diminution in the disputed practices.

The skipper William Duff probably spoke for the whole of Leith when he was hauled before the Council on 11 October 1626 for an 'undecent' utterance about one of the Bailies. He was sentenced to be imprisoned, but as he was taken from the court he 'misbehaved himself in most unreverent speeches in saying that the sailors of Leith were persecuted persons, as the Israelites were by Pharaoh'. For this piece of rank insubordination, he was ordered to be put in irons during the Council's pleasure. They did not even let him go when he publicly apologised over a week later.

In April 1619, the Council seized on a recent statute of Parliament 'that maltmen should not have deacons nor be a craft anywhere within the realm'. The maltmen of Leith were known to hold meetings daily, elect a deacon each year, admit freemen of the craft on payment of an entry fee and generally 'usurp the liberty of a free craft'. The Council humbly confessed to itself that this disgraceful state of affairs had arisen through its own negligence, and resolved to put the matter right. All the maltmen of Leith were summoned to a court and told that in future none of them were to make malt without licence from the Provost and Bailies. Applicants would be 'examined' by three or four of their peers who would report to the Council on their suitability. All their malt was to be ground at the burgh's mills, paying a 'multure' of 1 firlot for every chalder, and brewing was only to be done with malt made in Leith and ground at these mills (ie, not with imported malt). All disputes among them were to be settled by the Council or the Bailies of Leith. They were expressly forbidden to come before the Sheriff of Edinburgh (thus going over the heads of the Council) although they were allowed to bring cases in the court of the Privy

Council. In August 1619, 36 maltmen were formally 'admitted' on payment of £6 13s 4d.

In September 1619 it was the turn of the coopers. They were to be subjected to the same examination and admission procedures, but in their case the examiner would be the Deacon of the Edinburgh coopers. What is more, they were to buy their barrel staves and girths only through the Council, which would 'yearly take good and sufficient order' for the same. Only 12 coopers were admitted, and they had to pay £20 each. Freemen coopers of Edinburgh were to be allowed to work in Leith as long as they did not reside there.

The selling of wine without a licence from Edinburgh had been forbidden since the late sixteenth century, but in 1620 the ban was extended to ale and beer sellers and to the brewers themselves. As well as needing a licence, ale house keepers had to sell only beer brewed locally, and brewers could only use malt which they had bought from authorised maltmen.

In 1629, Edinburgh finally put the seal on its power over Leith by buying the reversion of the Superiority of the port. As the holder of the reversion was entitled to buy the Superiority at any time, this meant that Edinburgh was now completely secure in its rights. Inevitably the existing constraints on the town were tightened and a few new ones introduced. Feu duties on property were raised, as were the dues payable when a property changed hands. The grain markets which had customarily been held in Leith were abolished, and Leithers were forbidden to store grain in their town. Maltmaking, brewing and baking for sale were forbidden.

Leith at last boiled over. A petition was drawn up and signed by the chief inhabitants of the town, who claimed to represent between 8000 and 9000 fellow indwellers. On 18 July 1629 it was shown to the Privy Council, who were told that an advocate was going to London to present it to the king. As well as complaining of Edinburgh's actions regarding Leith itself, the petition pointed out that over the last 17 years, the Burgh had 'surreptitiously' purchased rights which effectively gave it complete jurisdiction over much of the Lothians, impingeing on the rights of the King, Officers of the Crown and members of the nobility. From the point of view of Leith the worst aspect of this extension of power was that the rights of the Lord High Admiral of Scotland in Leith and its approaches had been taken over by Edinburgh.

The petition also contained accusations of irregularities in the execution of justice, which were expanded on in a later document. Leithers summoned before Edinburgh Council were given only a few hours notice instead of the legally required two days, and they were not allowed procurators. In court they were forced to sign documents which they were not allowed to read and which contained blank spaces to be subsequently filled in by the Council. Sentences meted out for breaking Edinburgh bye-laws were harsher than those for breaking the laws of the land. There was little chance of redress for these abuses as Leithers were forbidden by Edinburgh to take cases to the Sheriff Court. Their only recourse was to apply to the Privy Council, which was reluctant to give judgements in these cases.

The Masters and Mariners sent a short petition of their own. In 1609 their right to collect Prime Gilt and organise their own fraternity had been confirmed by the king. Subsequently, Edinburgh had got hold of the confirmation documents on promise of returning them, a promise which had not been kept. The main petition accused the Burgh of appropriating the Prime Gilt itself. Merchants of Edinburgh freighted foreign ships, so that whereas 30 years before there had been 80 or 100 ships in part ownership of masters and mariners, now there were fewer than 10 'sufficient' merchant ships belonging to Leith. (This was not the only reason for the decline in shipping, and the merchants themselves pointed out that as many of them were part-owners of the ships in question, the accusation itself had little foundation.)

The seamen felt that they should be allowed some trading rights as they were often part-owners of their ships and were allowed to trade freely in England, where the burgh monopolies had effectively died out, and Ireland, where they had hardly existed. Many mariners, they said, had already been forced by poverty to serve on foreign ships, even those of enemies of Scotland and England.

Analysis of the testaments of 63 Leith skippers who died in the first four decades of the seventeenth century suggests that they were in fact doing rather well at the time of the petition, even if the number of large ships had decreased. If there had been a slump, it seems to have been in the decade 1610 -20, but another one was on the way and its first effects may have been beginning to be felt in 1629. If debts are deducted from the total value of goods plus money owed to the deceased, the figures for the average skipper's estate look like this:

1600 - 1609	£153
1610 - 1619	£710
1620 - 1629	£2450
1630 - 1639	£1531

Once Edinburgh heard about the petition, the Council sent off its own letter to London. At this date, the king was Charles I, who had succeeded his father in 1625. The letter he received from Edinburgh was full of complaints about the 'contempts and disorders committed by some of the inhabitants of Leith'. James VI would have known all about the situation between Edinburgh and Leith and been able to make a fair assessment of the problem. Although he had been born in Scotland, Charles had left it at an early age and knew little of his native land. Moreover, his was a weak character, and his instinctive reaction to a challenge to authority was the repression of the challengers. Accordingly he advised Edinburgh; 'if you find that these commotions have proceeded upon any seditious humour without any just cause of offence given them, that you repress the same as is most meet for the reforming thereof and preventing the like hereafter'. The burgh was also to refuse any appeal against sentences already given.

Meanwhile, Leith's representative in London was not having a happy time. He fell ill soon after his arrival and the people he asked to represent him before the king would not take his case seriously. However he persevered, and in the end the king was brought to consider the matter more fully. Some members of the Privy Council were also in London, and they may have been able to help Charles to understand the situation. By February 1630, Edinburgh had been made to renounce all the rights of Regality which it had acquired in 1603, together with all privileges 'not competent to a subject'. The Lord Advocate was investigating the irregularities which concerned the Crown, and the Barons of East Lothian were negotiating with the burgh over the matters which infringed their privileges. The decreet forbidding Leithers to store cereals was overturned as it was prejudicial to the gentry who sold grain directly to Leith merchants.

It is doubtful whether this success brought much benefit to Leith, but at least Edinburgh had been shown that its power was limited and it would not be allowed to get away with flagrant breaches of the law.

Trade

At the last meeting of the Privy Council before James VI left for London in 1603, one of the matters discussed had been the question of the freighting of ships, which in 1629 was to feature among the complaints of the Leith skippers. James wanted to bring Scottish practice in line with that of England and decree that foreign ships might not be hired to carry merchandise while Scottish ships were available. It was objected that other countries might retaliate, especially France, whose trade was important to Scotland. The king argued that the French had to sell their wine each year and so would not refuse to send it to Scotland on Scottish ships. No decision was made, and there the matter rested for the next eleven years. In 1614, however, the king resurrected the idea. The Convention of Royal Burghs discussed it and in January 1615 sent James their: 'Reasons Why They Should Not Be Prevented From Freighting Foreign Ships'. These are worth quoting at some length as they reveal much about overseas Scottish trade at the start of the seventeenth century, threequarters of which went through Leith.

> The greatest number of the best ships of Scotland are continually employed in the service of Frenchmen, not only within the dominions of France, but also within the bounds of Spain, Italy and Barbary, where their trade lies, which is a chief cause of the increase of the number of Scottish ships and of their maintenance. Whereas by the contrary, the half of the number of ships which are presently in Scotland will serve for our own private trade
>
> We are not in such a case here in Scotland as the subjects of other kingdoms, wherein there is continual intercourse and commodity by resort of strangers, by whom their wealth and estate grows; and there are no strangers that repair to this kingdom except such as import timber and other gross merchandise of small worth.

If the policy were to be implemented:

> We will be compelled to leave our trade of herrings which we transport to the East Countries (Baltic), because the best occasion of the transport thereof is offered only in the months of September and October, in the which season we have the commodity of some Dutch (Deutsch = German - Dutchmen were referred to as 'Hollanders') ships here, which have imported timber within this realm and will be content to transport our goods for a third of the freight which Scottish ships may serve for, because if they lack this employment they will return empty. And the owners of Scottish ships cannot undertake these voyages except at great and exorbitant freights, seeing they will be constrained to lie the most part of the winter season in the East Countries by reason of the frosts enclosing them there.

These quotes are worth bearing in mind, although as in most petitions the case is oversimplified and exaggerated. However, the points made here are borne out by some of the incidents of the next 30 years, and in other cases throw light on matters which might otherwise be obscure.

Shipbuilding at Leith

The abovementioned 'increase in the number of Scottish ships' meant that, even though many foreign vessels were bought, shipbuilding was still very much a part of the life of Leith. In 1610 Edward Mcmath, an Edinburgh burgess, had a ship built in the Timber Howff (Bush). Edinburgh Council sent three representatives to the launch in May, to make sure that the fence of the Howff, which had to be taken down to let the vessel out, was properly repaired.

Edward Mcmath's ship must have been too large to be built at the Sherrif Brae, above the Bridge. All the available evidence points to North Leith as the shipbuilding centre from the late sixteenth century onwards. There was space there, especially at the Sandport, to build vessels as large as anyone wanted, so it seems that all the North Leith yards were full when Edward Mcmath needed his ship.

Andrew Davidson, who later emigrated to Norway, had a yard in North Leith near the Bridge at the end of the sixteenth century. In 1609, when the timberman John Younger died, he had a bark on the stocks. His yard lay a couple of hundred yards east of that of Andrew Davidson's. Nearly 170 years later the first dry dock in Scotland was to be built on or very near the same site.

John Younger may have been the builder of the 'ship being built, standing on the stocks' which features in the will of John Gibson, a skipper who died in 1601. He owned an eighth share worth £200. Comparison of the total value of various ships computed from the testaments of their owners, teaches a certain caution in drawing firm conclusions from such sources. Different valuations can vary wildly for what appears to be the same vessel. However, a large barque was later valued at £1300, so John Gibson's ship may have been something similar.

The bark that John Younger was building when he died was valued at only £66, but the testament of another skipper may give a clue to what is going on here. John Lowrie, who died in 1603, seems to have been collecting ships' timbers, maybe with a view to having his own vessel(s) built. He had two keels, 87 ribs - old and new, an assortment of oak and pine deals, a 'new balk for a ship' and two tree trunks. He seems to have obtained his old timber by dismantling wrecks, in the course of which he had collected 1364 nails and 68 old iron bolts weighing 31 stone. It may be that the future owners of John Younger's bark had provided their own materials and the value ascribed to the vessel was the shipbuilder's fee for work already done.

In 1619 Archibald Coustean of North Leith appears on the scene. He came into the Canongate Bailie Court to sue Thomas Porteous who had found his gold ring and would not return it. Archibald died in 1640, the owner of a flourishing shipbuilding yard. He had recently launched the hull of a bark worth £1300. Her master, John Riddoch, had already been appointed, but she was not yet rigged. In his yard stood the frame of 'a little bark newly led upon the stocks to be built'. All the timbers for building her were there, and most of the equipment needed for her rigging. He had more timber in a second yard, and he owned an eighth (250 merks) of another bark of which Alexander Reid was master and which was currently at sea. Another North Leither, James Pitillo, who died at the same time as Archibald Coustean, left 'oak timber for building a ship' worth 200 merks.

It was quite possibly Archibald Coustean who built the bark *Janet*, for the skipper Abraham Turnbull, around 1624. She is the first named Leith vessel built for a private individual of which we have any record. She probably set out on her maiden voyage in the spring of 1625. In June of that year, Abraham Turnbull appears for the first time in the accounts of the collector of Primegilt. He paid 29s, the kind of sum which was paid by small barques bringing timber from Norway. By September the *Janet* was in the Northern Isles with the fishing fleet, where Abraham lent herring barrels and salt to two Fisherrow mariners who were rather tardy about returning them. Usually it was Abraham who was being pursued for payment of debts. In 1626 he owed for 80 ells of sail canvas and the following year for a cable weighing 756 Flemish lb.

In view of the comments in the Masters' petition of 1629 on the decline of Leith shipping, it might seem surprising that shipbuilders should be in such an apparently flourishing state. However, the ships mentioned in the petition would seem to have been comparatively large merchantmen, which were generally bought in the Low Countries. Leith would have produced the barques and boats, large and small, which belonged to the port. It is also easy to forget that the actual building of ships was not the chief source of a timberman's income. More lucrative were the constant repairs and overhauls needed by wooden vessels. Skippers would routinely have their ships 'outred' by a timberman before leaving on a voyage.

Leith also saw ships at the end of their of their lives. In 1607 the wreck of the *Pelican* was lying in the harbour. At least one eighth of her belonged to the skipper Robert Brown, valued at £200. Her master, Andrew Ochiltree, subsequently bought her in partnership with a Frenchman called Simon Hege.

Andrew sold her hull to Hugh Somerville of Leith and a baker called John Anderson for 400 merks. At the time of his death in 1617, Andrew still had her 'anchors, sails, cables, tows, munition and whole apparelling' which he estimated to be worth 1,000 merks.

Wrecked ships were a godsend to the bakers of Leith, 'the whole country being almost naked, and many years ago spoiled of all the timber within the same'. Peat and coal are totally unsuitable for firing 'beehive' bread ovens. They need a fuel which gives a fierce heat while creating as little ash and soot as possible. 'Burnwood' came in on the ships from Norway, but only as stabilising packing for the larger timbers. William Brown, a baker who died in 1590, had in his yard £37-worth of 'old broken ship timber for the oven'. (At this date new ships boards sold at £3 a dozen, so a pile of broken pieces worth £37 must have been of considerable size.)

In 1613 an old wrecked ship in the harbour which belonged to the baker John Flukar was getting in the way, and the Edinburgh Council had to order him to remove it. In 1626, Gilbert Dauling, another baker, paid the skipper John Luikup 250 merks for the hull of the *Charity*, which was lying behind the bulwark on the North Leith side of the harbour. Gilbert broke up the hull, but came into dispute with John Luikup over the 90 stones of ironwork which he recovered but did not hand over to the skipper as agreed.

The Timber Trade

Timber merchants were supposed not to exist in the 'unfree' town of Leith. However, they appear regularly among the 70 Leithers who were fined by Edinburgh for trading, between 1600 and 1636. Where the goods involved are specified, wine and timber figure most often. Wine selling was allowed in Leith under licence, but timber dealing was never officially countenanced. Nevertheless, considering the scale of the operations, the dealers were rarely fined.

The timbermen James Fleming and George Sanderson, who died in 1611 and 1614 respectively, were never penalised, and yet they traded quite openly in large quantities of deals and spars. George in particular kept some of his stock in the Timber Bush and would have had to pay Edinburgh for the privilege. His 38 creditors lived mainly in towns and villages around the Firth, but five of them were Edinburgh burgesses.

Hugh Lyell was fined £30 in 1615 for buying a shipload of timber and selling it in Leith. When he died four years later he had in his yard in Leith: 2000 deals, 600 roof spars, 1000 girthstings, 60 knapholt, 50 corbells and various other pieces estimated to be worth a total of 2000 merks. His daughter Agnes married another timber dealer - William, one of the ubiquitous Downies. He was fined along with two others in 1632, when Edinburgh had one of its periodic purges of trading in Leith.

The most successful of them all, however, was Andrew Rae. He never appeared before the Edinburgh Council in spite of his widespread trade. When his testamentary inventory was taken in 1620 his stock consisted of 1000 deals,

500 whicker spars and 300 roof spars. This was not a lot compared with the contents of Hugh Lyell's yard, but Andrew died in August and Hugh in September. August was at the beginning of the timber-ship season in Leith and the last ships came in November - the sailing pattern mentioned in Petition of the Burghs to the king. The scale of Andrew's operation is revealed by the list of his creditors, which covers two and a half closely written sides of foolscap. Altogether he was owed £2905 by an assortment of customers of all social classes from lords and lairds to boatmen. Like George Sanderson, he drew his clients mainly from around the Firth, although a lot of the villages around Edinburgh are represented, along with several towns of inland Fife.

In his will he stipulated that Alexander, his eldest son by a previous wife, must help Janet Porteous his stepmother 'in the trading with timber' until he married (when she was to give him a bed with its furnishings, a food cupboard, a table and an iron fireplace which had been left him by his mother). Janet was not so fortunate as her late husband and in 1622 she was fined 50 merks for timber trading. The actual charge was that of selling timber in Leith before offering it to Edinburgh. (It seems that the Burgh had at last capitulated to the extent of allowing unfreemen to sell timber in Leith so long as they stuck to the ancient rules governing freemen.) Janet was not deterred from her business. In October 1623 she paid Prime Gilt on a shipload of timber from Norway. A year later she paid the dues for three barks, and in November of the same year, her stepson Alexander paid for a shipload. In 1632 Andrew, her own eldest son, was helping his mother in the business. He was fined £20 and ordered to desist from trading until he was made a freeman. This 'burgessification' of favoured Leithers was a practice deeply resented by the rest of the port's inhabitants.

Janet Porteous died on 21 October 1634. The day before she died she drew up her own inventory. The vigour of mind which this implies had borne fruit in a flourishing business. The timber in the close beside her house was worth £258, she had 3200 merks in ready money and she was owed £2797. This was somewhat offset by debts totalling £3607, but two years after her death her son Andrew seems to have come across an overlooked account book. He registered an addition to her estate of £3336 in debts owed to her.

Perhaps the most surprising timber dealer in Leith was a baker called William Gray, whose bakehouse was in Broad Wynd. The Gray family did, however, number skippers, mariners and at least one cooper among its members. Also, bread was one of the cereal products which Scots exchanged for Norwegian timber. (Malt was another, and in 1608 the skipper John Mowbray took 140 bolls of malt in the *Angel* to Norway for James Douglas of Leith and brought back timber for him.) Like his fellow dealers, William Gray bought timber by the shipload - two in October 1623, three in July/August 1624, and the cargo of a yacht in March 1625. It seems that when the yacht returned to Norway, William was a passenger, because he died in Bergen in May of the same year.

After his death a very sorry state of affairs came to light. He may have started by exchanging bread for timber, but from at least 1619 all his dealings were in cash, and incompetence or bad luck had left him with very little apart from debts. The shiploads of timber had been paid for with borrowed money. Nine loan bonds going back six years and totalling £1242 in principal and £198 in interest, were found among his papers. His assets in Leith consisted only of timber in the Bush worth about £250, some furniture valued at 100 merks, and 120 merks owed to him. His son John set out for Norway in June in the hope of recovering any money or goods that might be in Bergen. He discovered 22 Norwegian creditors, but the sums they owed were small, totalling only £84. In all, the estate was worth only £572 6s 8d, less than half of what was owed.

John learned from his father's mistakes. He seems to have confined himself to the bakery trade, and when he died in 1669, he was the one who was owed money - £952. He himself owed only the rents of his bakehouse, booth and dwelling house and the fees of his servants.

Most of the timber these entrepreneurs were dealing in came from Norway. The port of Birren (Bergen) is mentioned time and again. The Burghs' petition on the question of freighting foreign ships contains a clause which specifically concerns this trade:

> Scottish ships cannot conveniently serve for the importing of wainscot, knapholt, tar and other gross wares within this kingdom, because they are not able to serve upon so easy conditions as Dutch (Baltic) ships, which are served by 3 or 4 mariners at the most. And if great freights were given for such wares, all the wares above written could scarcely be sold for double price.

Like the rest of the petition, this is an exaggeration of the true position. Scottish ships certainly sailed to Norway for timber, just as they went to the Baltic and managed to return without becoming frozen in the ice. (The *William* of Leith, for instance, was at Danzig in September 1625.) However, the point about the need for a small crew if the voyage was to be economic could be one reason why Scottish timber ships at this time were of only 20 to 30 tons, and might even be little 8 ton fishing boats. The small size of ships of the Norway trade is borne out by the Prime Gilt returns for Leith for the years 1623 to 1625. The most paid on a shipload of timber brought from Norway in a Scottish ship is £2 10s, and the dues could be as low as 10s. Baltic skippers, on the other hand, were never charged less than £2 8s for cargoes of timber during that period, and the master of one hulk (the bulk carriers of the day) paid as much as £9 in 1625, for a cargo of knapholt.

Preserved in the minutes of the Leith Bailie Court is a charter party between John Roule of Leith and George Gourlay, skipper and burgess of Kinghorn, master of the *Blessing*, for a voyage to Norway to buy timber. John Roule was a merchant, another of the vocations which was supposed to be closed to Leithers. He had his finger in just about every profitable pie that was going, but he was only fined two or three times during a long career.

The charter party was drawn up on 25 April 1625, the day before the *Blessing* sailed up the Forth to either Torrie or Carriden to take on coal. When they arrived at their destination, George was to sail his ship as far up the beach as he might while still ensuring that she would float at high tide. There they would stay for three tides while John Roule loaded her with coal. When she had taken in as much as she could and still stay afloat, she was to stand off into deeper water while the rest of the coal was loaded. Once she was full, George was to sail her to Burntisland harbour and stay there six days while the merchant saw to the customs formalities.

> And thereafter with all possible diligence, how soon wind and weather may serve, the skipper obliges himself to carry and transport the said ship and coals directly, God willing, to Birren in Norway and there make deliverance of the said coals as becomes. And thereafter to pass to the wood with the forsaid ship and stay at the wood and Birren twenty days only. Within the which space the said John Roule obliges himself to load and input in the forsaid ship her full ladening of timber great and small as he pleases. So much as she may easily stow fore and aft under the over overlap. And thereafter the skipper obliges himself to bring and transport the said ship and timber to the Haven and Port of Leith and make deliverance thereof to the said John Roule or his factors honestly as becomes.

This voyage was by no means John Roule's only venture in the timber trade. In 1626, Robert Wyllie sued him for three years back fees 'for serving him in Norway and Leith'. The following year John Rea, one of the officers of the Water Bailie, took him to court to recover three fathoms of firewood, one for each year, for 'laying and placing of all his ships to the Shore, come from Norway during the said time'.

For a man whose trading activities were so extensive (they encompassed other goods besides timber) John Roule and his wife lived in surprisingly modest accommodation. On the same day that John Rea claimed his 'backhander' from them, Marion Bowman, the widow of the skipper William ('Laird') Downie of North Leith, pursued them for payment of £10 rent of a 'heich hall, chamber and back gallery' which they had rented the previous year in her land in the Sands quarter. They were also ordered to return a 'backit form of wainscot' which they had taken away with them at the end of their term.

Once a timber ship had safely reached Leith and tied up in the harbour, the crew might reasonably suppose that all danger was past for the time being. Skipper John Anderson had 'no mind of evil' at 7.30 one Friday evening in July 1626. His ship was berthed beside the Shore, and he and his crew were sitting peacefully at supper on deck. Suddenly a party of nine apprentice coopers, 'being convenit together in their drunkenness', sprang down into the ship:

> and perforce took up burnwood and skows from the skipper and in most barbarous and cruel manner struck and abused him, and have cruelly hurt and wounded him on the face between his eyes and have almost dung out his left eye. And with their feet thrust down their (the crew's) meat standing upon the overlop and gave the skipper many wounds and bruises with burnwood and stones, committing thereby a great riot.

The ringleader, Alexander Gardener, apprentice to George Mungo, was imprisoned and fined £20, the rest were fined £5 each. Alexander Gardener had never been a satisfactory apprentice. He was the son of James Gardener a gunner and burgess of Stirling, and had been bound to George Mungo in July 1621 for five years. (Perhaps the drunken spree was in celebration of the completion of his indentures.) During the five years he had been absent without leave for a total of 370 days, for which his father and George Logan of Leith, his sureties, owed George Mungo 189 merks. George began court proceedings against his errant apprentice and his sureties in 1625, but it was not until 13 February 1627 that the bailies of Leith ordered them to pay for six months absence in 1625, with £5 6s 8d expenses.

John Roule's charter party mentioned another of the commodities which were becoming increasingly important to the trade of Leith and of the ports of the Forth in general - coal. The coalfields of Lothian and the coast of Fife were expanding rapidly. When James VI visited Scotland in 1617, one of the marvels he was shown, was the coal workings of George Bruce of Culross, which extended far beneath the Forth. The industry was inextricably linked with the production of salt, having originally developed mainly to supply the saltpans which mushroomed around the Forth. Scottish salt was mostly coarse and full of impurities, but much in demand for such purposes as salting hides.

The equally important fishing industry used finer, imported salt to preserve herrings and salmon. In 1630, the tireless entrepreneur Mr Nathaniel Udward of Leith, together with the Master of Requests, obtained from the king a 31-year licence to make salt by a new process which was said to produce a finer product while reducing the amount of fuel needed by fifty percent. Shortly after the granting of the licence, the king caused much consternation by suggesting that the export of Scottish salt to England should be limited. The Privy Council protested that any such measure would affect the coal industry as well as the salt workers, and put at risk the livelihoods of 10,000 people. If pits had to be abandoned as a result, they could not later be recovered, as without the constant working of the pumps they would be flooded within a month.

Shipping Trends

The Prime Gilt accounts which give details of some of the ships which brought timber from Norway also bear out some of the other points made in the burghs' petition. They cannot be regarded as a complete record of ships visiting Leith, as avoiding payment seems to have been something of a local pastime, and the masters of the Trinity Hospital periodically had to remind the collectors to be more diligent. There is no way of knowing how efficient the compiler of these particular accounts was in his task. However, they do provide evidence of trends in the use of the port by different types of shipping in the two years which they cover, ie October 1623 to October 1625.

One striking feature is the comparative lack of foreign vessels, as mentioned in the petition. Only about 60 are accounted for, and this includes 14 English ships in 1624, a figure which may have been atypical as no English ships are included in the accounts for 1625. They probably came in 1624 to relieve the dearth which Scotland had been suffering since 1622, five of them were from corn growing areas, and one carried a cargo of beans. In 1625 the harvest improved and there was no need for further relief.

Of the other foreign ships, the largest number were from the Baltic, twentythree in all. They arrived between July and October. Their cargoes, as one might expect consisted mainly of timber, tar, iron and beer. When the question of the freighting of foreign ships was finally resolved in 1619, the Burghs argued strongly for an exception in the case of Baltic vessels:

> for this Easterling trade consists altogether of such necessary wares as the country cannot lack, especially timber, pitch and tar, which being nearly nine tenths of that whole trade, they are not able to bear such freights as our country ships may serve for. Neither have we ships meet and commodious for that trade. But these wares being imported by strangers at easy and reasonable freights, they are accordingly sold at moderate prices to your Majesty's subjects.

Twelve Flemish ships came, carrying beans, corn, apples and other goods. They had no main sailing season but arrived all the year round. French ships came between April and July, six in the first year, but only two in the second. This vindicates king James in his opinion that the French would not stop using Scottish ships to carry their wine, and other sources show that Leith ships made regular trips to Bordeaux and returned laden with wine.

For Scottish ships other than those belonging to Leith, there are 56 entries in 1623-4 and 27 in 162-5. Of the other major Scottish ports, St Andrews, Aberdeen and Dundee are mentioned, but only a couple or so of ships came from each one. The rest were from towns around the Forth.

One notable visitor from Burntisland was Andrew Watson's ship, which made two visits and paid £9 each time. This ship was probably the *Blessing*, which Andrew Watson captained when she was sent out against rumoured Spanish invaders in 1627. She is mentioned in several sources of this period and seems to have been of substantial size. The low number of local ships in 1624-25 is mainly accounted for by a sharp drop in visits from vessels of South Queensferry and Kirkcaldy.

The Customs

Prime Gilt had been collected at Leith for several hundred years, along with all the other impositions due to the Crown and to Edinburgh. At the beginning and end of each voyage, merchant and skipper would have to do the rounds of all the various officials who were waiting to relieve them of their money. This may not have been quite as arduous as it sounds, as collectors often used a local tavern as an unofficial office. By the start of the seventeenth century, we can see the beginnings of a system which would be more familiar to us today. The collection of the Great Custom, for instance, was now organised by 'Farmers' who employed their own collectors. In 1620, the customar at Leith was George Archibald, who has left us his accounts for November 1620 to November 1621. George Archibald operated from a Custom House in the Kings Wark, a part of Leith which still belonged to the Crown. The building itself was held by Sir Lewis Stewart, who collected £166 13s 4d a year in rent. There was storage for confiscated goods and any others that might need to be held until their owners could collect them. The customar also hired a vault for the purpose. John Mitchell was paid £111 2s 4d a year for carrying merchandise to the custom house. William Murray received £1000 for 'visiting' all the ships which went in and out of Leith, and he was helped by four searchers. The Custom House clerk's fee was £400 and he was reimbursed for all account books, paper and ink which he bought. George Archibald himself was paid £769 6s 8d. Sir Henry Wardlaw, one of the receivers, was given £6367 10s. Altogether, out of receipts of £15,387 6s, only £924 5s remained after all was paid. This does not seem like a very efficient system, but it was presumably found satisfactory at the time.

All the imposts due to Edinburgh were collected by the official who was still known as the Farmer of the Wild Adventures, but who before long would dwindle into a 'Collector of Shore Dues'. The metters of corn, salt and coal came under his control.

In the second decade of the century, brokers begin to be appointed by Edinburgh to serve at Leith. Their function was to assist merchants and skippers both native and foreign in the freighting of ships and any other business they might want to transact. The number of ships freighted in the Edinburgh Tolbooth had dwindled to one a year by the middle of the third decade, the brokers having taken over this function.

Although Leith ships still plied their ancient routes to the Baltic, Flanders and France, since late in the sixteenth century they had been venturing further afield. A number of them regularly visited Spain. It would seem from the comments in the Petition that normally they went on there from France, having been freighted by French merchants. Some Leith seamen died in Spain, but the danger of disease was ever-present in every part of the world. The unique peril of a voyage to Spain was the pirates of North Africa - the Barbary Coast - who issued out into the Atlantic, and sailed as far north as the English Channel.

In the summer of 1615 the *Unicorn* of Leith was pursued and overtaken by Turks 'and after a sharp and bloody conflict between them they were in the end overcome, made captives and carried to the town of Algiers in Barbary, where they were presented in the open market to have been sold as slaves'.

Luckily for the crew, a Scot named James Fraser was living in Algiers at the time, and he persuaded the slave dealer to let them go free for a payment of £140. The eleven mariners involved promised to repay him when they got home. This proved easier said than done, and they had to apply to the Privy Council for help. A letter went out to presbyteries and Kirk sessions throughout the land explaining that the men were 'reduced to that extreme point of misery that they have nothing of their own wherewith to repay the sum', and asking for donations. Edinburgh put in £10. The Privy Council's letter makes it clear that this was not an isolated occurrence and that contributions had been paid in the past for the relief of captives in Barbary. It would seem, however, that this was the first incident involving Scots.

Twenty years later, the crew of the *John* of Leith were not so lucky. Their ship was bound to Rochelle with a cargo of cloth, when she was captured off the coast of France by three Turkish men-of-war and sunk. The master, John Brown, and 10 of his men were sold as slaves. In chains weighing 80lb, they were forced to turn a mill by day. At night they were put in 'foul holes 20 feet underground where they lie miserably, expecting to be eaten by rats and mice'. They were fed on dusty barley bread and water. Somehow, they managed to get a message to the Privy Council asking that a subscription might be raised to pay their ransoms.

One reason why skippers were willing to brave the dangers of the Barbary Coast was that Spain was their source of a new and highly profitable commodity - tobacco. In December 1621, John Auchmowtie, skipper of the *Grace of God* of Leith died at Cadiz. Among his goods on board were 178lb of tobacco worth £543, but he was by no means the first mariner to bring home a consignment of the 'weed'.

James VI's hatred of smoking is probably one of the better known facts of British history. Early in 1616 he was alarmed to hear 'that the use, or rather abuse, of taking of tobacco has lately crept in within his Highness' kingdom of Scotland, a weed so infective that all young and idle persons are in a manner bewitched therewith'. He ordered the Privy Council to forbid merchants, skippers, mariners and all other subjects to import or sell the evil herb. Any that was found was to be escheated, half, as the phrase went, 'to His Majesty's use', and half to the informer.

The Council did its best to carry out the order, but the trade was already so well established and profitable that the battle was really lost from the start. Recognising that large stocks existed, the Council announced an immunity from prosecution for anyone selling tobacco before 31 March 1617. After that date the court cases began. By the end of the year, 27 Edinburgh men and 30 Leithers were caught. The standard charge was the selling of 10st at 16s per ounce. In reality the amount was usually only a few pounds, although in 1618, Gilbert Hunter of Leith admitted to selling 600lb. He said he had an arrangement with Captain Murray of HMS *Charles*, which was stationed in Scotland, who had been granted a 21-year sole licence to import and sell tobacco in 1616. Gilbert had promised his customers that if their purchases were confiscated he would refund their money. Fortunately for him, only three of them were caught, all of whom were highly indignant when he then went back on his word!

Only two other Leithers were prosecuted for trafficking in tobacco in 1618, probably because they were all so experienced in concealing illegal trading activities. Edinburgh burgesses were not so wily - 41 of them were caught. In that year the Council also cast its net wider: Dysart, Kirkcaldy, Dundee, Aberdeen, Arbroath, Montrose and Perth were all involved, as well as Kinghorn, Burntisland, and the Canongate nearer home. Sixtytwo inhabitants of these places were prosecuted, including five Aberdeen men who were charged with being 'tobacconists'.

In 1619 a duty of 20s per pound was imposed on imported tobacco, but the prosecutions continued. So far, only Captain Murray might legally bring in the substance. The price on the black market varied wildly, from as little as 42s per lb to as much as £6, but it is not clear whether the variations reflected the quality of the product or the state of the market. By 1625 tobacco formed part of the normal stock-in-trade of the taverns of Leith.

The Charles

The tobacco monopoly was granted to Captain Murray to supplement his income, which was by no means secure. His ship, HMS *Charles*, had originally been sent to Scotland to protect Scottish shipping from North Sea piracy. (The use of HMS to denote a naval vessel did not become general until the nineteenth century, but it will be used in this book to avoid confusion with merchant ships.) In 1614 king James had sent out a ship and a pinnace against pirates who were attacking Scottish shipping. Two years later, Edinburgh sent three Leith merchantmen to capture a great pirate ship which had taken two Scottish vessels and was currently provisioning in Orkney. She was brought into Leith and her contents auctioned for a total of £13, 094 15s 3d. Twentyseven of her crew were hanged 'within the floodmark'.

In August 1616, a month after the capture of the pirates, the *Charles* was sent to Scotland, to be on permanent station. The expense of maintaining her fell upon the Privy Council, who agreed to pay Captain Murray 10,000 merks per year for normal running expenses, with extra if it was needed for any special duties. The first of these was a voyage to London in March 1617, to bring back a load of tapestries, silver plate and provisions which had been bought there for the King's imminent visit to his native land. As this was the height of the Spring sailing season it proved difficult to get pilots to take the *Charles* out of the Forth. In the end, four Kirkcaldy skippers were 'pressed' into service. The *Charles* was back in the Forth by the end of April, only to be greeted by one of its notorious violent storms. She was forced to cut her anchor cable to avoid being sunk.

By the summer of 1619, the *Charles* had been idle for some time and the Privy Council decided that she should be laid up at St Margaret's Hope with a skeleton crew of three men and a boy, in order to save money. Her ordnance was to be stored in Edinburgh Castle, her sails and rigging at Leith, and Captain Murray was to receive a retainer of 2,000 merks per year. No sooner had this decision been taken than a message arrived from the king that the *Charles* was to sail to Orkney with the Commissioner whose task it was to collect duties and teinds from the Dutch fleet that was fishing there. (The previous year the *Restore* of Leith, under her skipper David Gardin, had made the voyage but had only arrived after the fishing fleet had left.) Nothing further is heard of the *Charles* after this task, and it may be assumed that she rejoined the fleet in England.

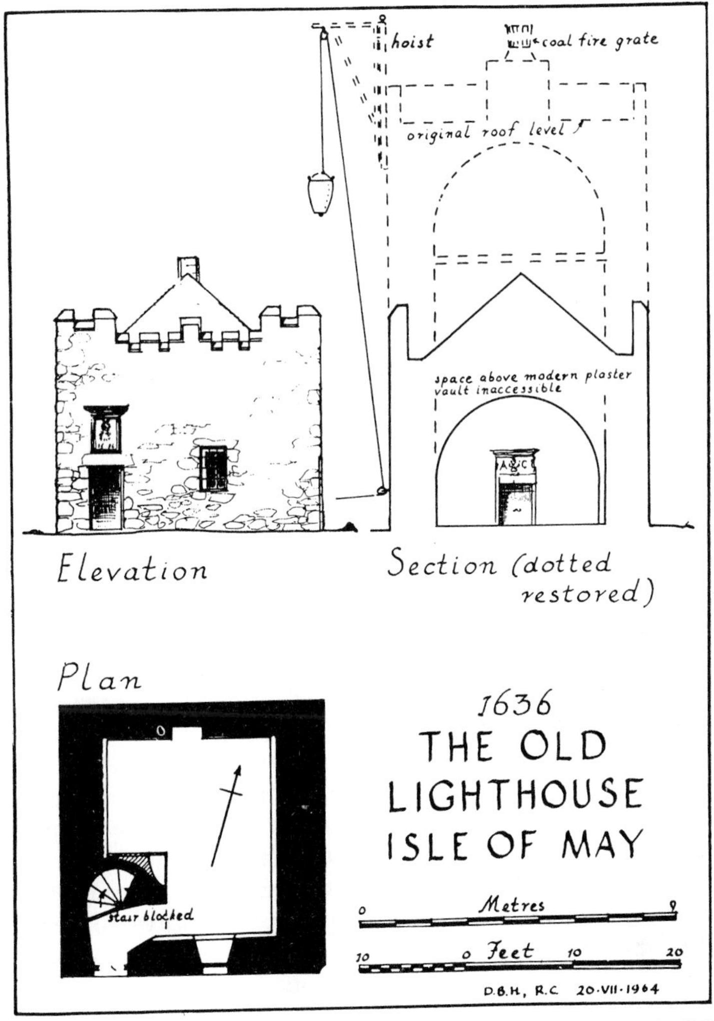

The Old Lighthouse, Isle of May (By courtesy of the Scottish Archaelogical Forum and Mrs D. Hague).

The Dunkirker Incident

Apart from the activities of pirates who occasionally operated near the mouth of the Firth and the inevitable fights and drunken brawls which feature in the life of any seaport, the first half of the seventeenth century was a fairly peaceful time for Leith, except, that is, for an incident which began in 1622. Spain was at this time at war with the Netherlands, the maritime branch of the conflict being conducted from her Low Countries port of Dunkirk. Ships of both sides were cruising off the Scottish coast. At the beginning of June 1622, a Dunkirk ship of war cast anchor in Leith Roads and her master requested permission to provision her there. The Privy Council sent for the King's opinion and he replied that the Dunkirkers were to be received as friends and supplied at reasonable rates. Edinburgh Council and the Water Bailie were instructed to comply with the King's orders and the crew came ashore.

Before long, two Netherland wafters and a pinnace, under the command of the Admiral of Zeeland, discovered the Dunkirker which they attacked. The battle was only interrupted when the tide ebbed and all the vessels went aground. Some of the Dunkirkers on shore hurried up to Edinburgh to tell Lord Melros, Secretary to the Privy Council, what was going on. He instructed the Edinburgh Magistrates (Provost and Bailies) to gather an armed force, and the Constable of the Castle to have cannons ready to be taken down to Leith. The Water Bailie was sent down with a herald and trumpeter to order the combatants to keep the peace, and one officer from each ship to come before the Privy Council.

When the delegates arrived before him, the Earl of Melros told the Netherlanders that great offence was taken at their attacking a friend of Scotland in the very mouth of her principal harbour. They replied that the Dunkirkers had attacked them at sea and taken prisoners, which they now refused to release. As the Earl had no power to force the Dunkirkers to grant the request of their enemies, he had no alternative but to allow all concerned to return to their ships. The most he could do was to place cannon on the Shore, ready to fire if there was any trouble.

It soon transpired that an almost identical situation had arisen at Aberdeen, and for the next eleven months the Privy Council wrestled with intractable commanders on both sides, none of whom wanted to be the first to leave, and all of whom played every delaying tactic in the book. The position was complicated by the fact that it was 'well known that one of our ships that trades in Flanders is worth four of the best Holland ships that come here'. On the other hand, Flanders was in this case represented by its Papist Spanish conquerors. The good Calvinists of Leith and Edinburgh were firmly on the side of the Netherlanders. Two ships of the English fleet were also sent to the Forth, but seem to have had little effect on the situation.

At last, at the beginning of May 1623, the Dunkirkers agreed to leave Leith harbour, where they had been lying. On the first Sunday of the month the Dunkirk ship took on her Leith pilot and eased herself away from the quayside - only to turn east out of the channel and run aground on 'a shoal visible to every man's eye'. She was towed back to the harbour where she stayed for a week before setting out again. This time she left at night, and again ran on the very same shoal. Her commander was thought to be afraid of attack by the Netherlanders. He even had the pilot murdered so that he could pretend that he had been given the wrong bearings. He did not escape, however. The unsympathetic locals would not come to his rescue a second time, and the Netherlanders moved in to attack the disabled Spanish ship, which was within the beacons 'not a pair of butts length outwith the Pier'.

A herald was sent to command the Netherlanders to desist, but the Water Bailie had great difficulty getting a boat to take the herald out to the ships. The journey was wasted in any case as the Netherlanders took not the slightest notice. Even the efforts of some of the most august members of the Privy Council only caused the Admiral of Zeeland to cease firing. The other Netherland vessel kept up her bombardment until the falling tide grounded her. As soon as the Dunkirker also went aground her crew came ashore, only to be attacked by 'a multitude of base fellows, as well of the adjacent country as of Edinburgh and Leith', who stripped them even of their clothes. The ship itself was looted by the Leithers, but once the Netherlanders realised what had happened they boarded her and claimed her for the Prince of Orange.

As quickly as they could, the Privy Council had cannon set up near St Nicholas' chapel (Janet Porteous supplied the timber for the platform) and ordered the Netherlanders to surrender, but they delayed answering until the tide rose sufficiently for them to sail out of range. The Chancellor of Scotland then claimed the Spanish ship for the King and ordered her to be brought in to harbour. He himself helped to man the ropes by which she was towed in, together with many of the other Privy Councillors. The question of who in fact owned the vessel might have kept the lawyers happy for many a long day, but the Netherlanders, mercifully, settled the matter by subsequently setting her on fire. The wreck was left where it was but soon began breaking up, the floating timbers damaging vessels in the harbour at high tides. In October 1625 the Provost of Edinburgh was ordered by the Privy Council to have the remains removed.

The Defence of the Seas

At the outset of the 'Dunkirker' incident, James VI was officially neutral towards the Netherland/Spanish conflict. By the time he died, on 27 March 1625, a force of English volunteers was fighting on the side of the Netherlands. This meant that both English and Scottish shipping was now subject to attack by Spanish vessels. Also, 'the broil which not long since fell out between the Hollanders and Dunkirkers in the very haven of Leith has given us sufficient proof of the necessity of forts to defend the havens and towns therunto adjacent from sudden surprises'. At the same time as they ordered the Spanish wreck to be removed from Leith harbour, the Privy Council appointed the Muster Master of Scotland to visit seaports, decide how they might best be defended and submit an estimate of the cost.

A month later, one of HM ships, the *Assurance* made an inadvertent visit to Leith. The English fleet had been sailing to Holland when it was scattered by a storm. After 20 days battling against the winds, *Assurance* came into the Forth and anchored in Leith Roads. The Privy Council ordered that her exhausted stores were to be replenished, the ship herself repaired and the many sick men on board housed, clothed and fed. By the end of January 1626, she was ready to return to England, but so many of her crew had died that 56 replacements were needed. Thirtytwo Leith skippers were ordered to serve, but in spite of promises of good wages and a free passage home they refused. Not only would it have been a demotion to serve as a crew member, but many of them no doubt were preparing for their own voyages. Fisherrow was tried next, but with the same result. Eventually the skippers were offered the option of providing proxies, and when the *Assurance* left Leith at the start of February, only six of them were serving personally, two as pilots. The rest of the Scottish contingent consisted of Leith mariners, with a few from Kirkcaldy, Musselburgh and Dysart. The ship arrived in the Downs at the beginning of March, having captured two Spanish ships on the way.

Assurance was one of the larger ships in the English fleet. From 1621 to 1624 she was flagship of a small squadron patrolling the English Channel. Her companions bore names famous in British naval history: *Victory*, *Dreadnought* and *Nonsuch*.

In 1626, Charles I began assembling two fleets, one to go to Spain and the other to keep the Channel clear of Spanish ships. He ordered the conscription of all Scottish ships which carried ordnance. In July, the Commissioners of the Royal Burghs wrote to explain why this was impossible. Because of the long peace, most of the best ships had been sold. The ones which remained were all away on voyages, and only small barques without ordnance were left. Most Scottish mariners were fishermen of the Fife coast and were currently fishing in the Isles. They were not expected home until September, when they would be preparing to take their fish to Bordeaux.

The king wisely dropped his original idea, but instead ordered that three ships should be bought and equipped to defend the Scottish coast. One of the three ships which the king intended to buy was at Leith, and three Leith skippers, James Home, George Smalum and Andrew Keir were deputed to inspect her and see if she was suitable. Presumably she passed the inspection because on 23 August she was at Burntisland under the captaincy of David Murray awaiting her crew. Leith and fifteen other local ports were ordered to provide a total of 144 men (a contemporary estimate states that a ship of 300 tons needed a crew of 100). Once again, men were reluctant to come forward and on 20 September the ship was still at Burntisland waiting to leave to collect her two companions from the Thames. The Privy Council ordered the Provost of Edinburgh to produce the required mariners or give a good reason why he could not.

When the tiny flotilla was finally assembled and on station on the Scottish coast, no use was made of it for nearly six months. It was put under the control of the Earl Marischal who never ordered the ships to sea, in spite of the fact that Dunkirkers sank Scottish ships even within sight of the coast, and increasing numbers of mariners were taken prisoner. What defence there was came from the dozen or so 'privateers' who were granted letters of marque, including John Morton, master and owner of the *Blessing of God* of Leith (value £2000) and William Robertson of the *Archangel* (jointly owned by seven Edinburgh burgesses). Two of HM ships were the *Unicorn* and the *Thrissel*, the latter under the captaincy of James Auchmowtie, possibly one of the seafaring Auchmowties of Leith.

In March 1627, the three ships were finally used - to transport Scottish troops to Gluckstadt to fight for Charles I's uncle, the king of Denmark. The troops were assembled and billeted on the people of Leith and Edinburgh, but the captains refused to put to sea until they had received their back pay, due from the previous November, and money to victual their ships. By the end of April the soldiers' involuntary hosts were demanding the money due for feeding their guests. Finally, at the beginning of May, the Collector of Taxes agreed to lend the necessary money out of his own resources, to be recouped from the next lot of taxes collected (this was not the first or the last time he had to do this). By the end of May the transports were at last on their way.

By July the ships had returned, and the king decided to sell them. A wrangle then developed between the Earl Marischal and the Admiral, who wanted to buy them. Before the matter could be resolved, rumours were heard of the enemy off the coast. The ships were hurriedly provisioned and four others hired to accompany them: *Blessing* of Burntisland, *Grace* of Dysart, *Alexander* and a pinnace. The invasion rumour proved false, but when they returned, the ships found themselves once more in service, this time to 'waft' two vessels which had been hired to carry troops to the Isle of Rhe in France. This duty over, the flotilla was at last disbanded. *Thrissel* and a second ship were sent back to England. *Unicorn* stayed at Leith, under the command of the Admiral.

Attacks by Spanish shipping were probably an important factor in the decline in the number of Scottish ships mentioned in the Leith masters' petition of 1629. Only two or three Leith ships are recorded as having been lost, but when Dysart petitioned the Privy Council for aid a few years later, the document mentioned the loss of 36 of her ships by wreck or Spanish attack during this time. It is reasonable to suppose that actual losses by Leith were proportionately higher. The paucity of records is probably due to the fact that ships were only mentioned in court when there was some chance of getting them back.

While the war continued at sea, the question of land defences had not been forgotten. The decision was taken to fortify Leith with a rampart or wall around the town and blockhouses to guard the harbour. Edinburgh was very keen to be responsible for the fortifications, as a means of increasing her control over the port. It was to this end that the Burgh bought the reversion of the Superiority, thereby sparking off the Leith petition to the king. In the end the threat receded and nothing came of the fortification plan.

In November 1630, the Privy Council received a proposal from the King that a light be erected on the Isle of May. The following year he proposed that one be placed on the Skairheads as well. The skippers and shipowners of Leith and all the East Coast Burghs were consulted about the plan, and all reacted with enthusiasm. Some testified that if such a light had existed they would not have lost ships in the past. Crail, Pittenweem and Anstruther commented that the light would be especially welcomed by fishermen. Herring shoals had recently appeared in the mouth of the Forth, and they were fishing there rather than making the voyage to Orkney and Shetland. Once the idea had been fully explored and discussed, in 1635, a patent was granted to John Cunningham and James Maxwell to collect dues of 4s per ton on foreign ships and 2s on Scottish ships for the building and upkeep of the light.

From the portion of the original building which still remains it appears that it was a square three-storied 'tower house' with a turnpike stair in one corner giving access to the upper floors and the roof. John Cunningham's arms, with the initials of his father Alexander, are carved on an overmantel in the ground floor room, where the light keeper and his family lived. The light was provided by a coal fire burning in a brazier on the roof. On windy nights the brazier could consume as much as 3 tons of coal, all of which, at the beginning, had to be carried up the stair by the light keeper and his family. Later a hoist was provided for the purpose. The ash was thrown over the side of the roof parapet onto a heap which can still be seen. For nearly two centuries this first 'Light of May' guided mariners into the Forth from the North Sea.

The herring fishing in the Forth and elsewhere was a trade with centuries of history behind it, but in the early seventeenth century a new kind of fishery was introduced to Leith. In 1626, Mr Nathaniel Udward was granted a licence to fish in Greenland to obtain oil for his soapworks in Leith. He sent out the first Leith whalers, 'two great ships, well furnished and appointed'.

The advent of whaling to Leith perhaps typifies the seeds of change which were being planted there at the beginning of the seventeenth century. The staple exports of wool, hides and skins were dwindling in importance. Other traditional products like coal and salt were becoming more central to the economy. The timber trade was booming. Totally new commodities such as tobacco were coming into the country. Slowly Scotland was beginning to produce for herself articles which she had previously bought from abroad. A Leith smith called John Kyle had begun making anchors in the late sixteenth century, blazing a trail that subsequently became increasingly well-trodden. As well as Nathaniel Udward's soapworks, Leith housed a starchmaker who produced his wares by the ton. The local women had taken up the knitting of worsted stockings which were exported by the thousand. A new bureaucracy was taking shape, and the ships of HM navy were becoming a familiar sight in the port. Inch by inch, Leith and Scotland were creeping into the modern era.

8

The Life and Times of Henry Bell

One day late in the summer of 1636 Henry Bell, skipper of Leith, married Isobel Riddoch, daughter of another skipper, William Riddoch. In 1660 Henry Bell died, his second wife, the redoubtable Susanna Luikup, living on until 1677. The forty or so years between the first marriage of Henry and the death of Susanna spanned all the major upheavals of the mid-seventeenth century. They, their relatives and associates were involved in a variety of ways with the events of the period. Henry's own career was typical of that of a successful Leith skipper, but it was also shaped by the historical events in which he became caught up.

The marriage contract of Henry and Isobel was drawn up at Edinburgh on 17 June 1636. The date of the marriage has been left blank, but it was to take place by the following Martinmas (November 11) when a tocher (bride price) of 1000 merks was due to be paid to Henry by his father-in-law. Henry himself would match the sum, and the whole 2000 merks was to be invested in property or employed in trade, with the advice of William Riddoch. This was standard procedure, and the bulk of the document is taken up with legal rigmaroles designed to ensure that Isobel's rights in the money were watertight and that it would descend to the correct heirs on the death of either of the principals. The contract was witnessed by skipper David Logan husband of Henry's sister Isobel, Florence Martin, skipper of Leith (probably Isobel Riddoch's uncle, her mother's name was Margaret Martin) and the Leith merchant Alexander Riddoch, the brother of Henry's new father-in-law.

William Riddoch was an elder of South Leith Kirk Session at the time of his daughter's marriage. The following year he was appointed Kirk Treasurer, a post which he held until his death. He was in fact an Aberdeen burgess, who had moved to Leith at some time before 1627, when he bought a house in the Kirkgate. At the time of his daughter's marriage he owned a barque, which he sold three years later.

The origins of Henry himself are something of a mystery. There were plenty of Bells in and around Leith, but the only recorded seafaring Bell was David, a skipper who died in 1581. He may have been one of Henry's ancestors, but no connection has yet come to light. There were many Bell skippers and mariners in the other Forth ports, and Henry's origins may lie in one of these.

While Henry and Isobel were settling into life together, Susanna Luikup was well into her first marriage, to the skipper George Hegin. Susanna was a member of a well established North Leith family, whose men had for generations been skippers and mariners. She had a sister called Euphame which might be a help in pinning her down to a specific branch of the family, but the Luikups were very traditional in their approach to naming children and Susanna and Euphame were 'family names'. It seems most likely, however, that this particular pair were the children of the skipper James Luikup, who died in 1616. His children Robert, Susanna and Euphame were named in his testament as minors. Later documents seem to link Susanna with another James Luikup, skipper, who may have been her elder brother. Eldest sons inherited their father's landed property, and are not often mentioned in testaments, which deal with the moveable goods which were divided between a man's other heirs. Susanna Luikup and George Hegin had a son, John, and two daughters, Margaret and Susanna. Margaret was of marriageable age by 1646, so her mother probably married George Hegin in the early 1620s. In law a girl could marry as young as twelve, but in practice, because of the need for her father to provide a tocher, she was more likely to be 20 or older, when he would be well established in his trade.

The Queensferry Connection

The year of Henry Bell's marriage, 1636, was also important in the life of South Queensferry. The connection will become apparent as we trace Henry's life history, but for the moment we need only note that in 1636, South Queensferry renewed its charter as a Royal Burgh, a process which cost the town a lot of money. The repayment of its debts was a constant worry to the burgh council over the next few decades, and one of the means they used to raise funds was the admission as burgesses of 'outlanders', who would pay the burgh for the privilege.

Most were gentry from the surrounding countryside, but in 1639 the Leith skipper William Hegin, Susanna Luikup's brother-in-law, was admitted burgess. He was newly married to Isobel Martin, daughter of Bessie (?Isobel) Bell, and the Leith skipper the late John Martin. Isobel had inherited land in Queensferry and a share in a ferry boat from her father, and was the ward of her uncle Florence Martin, also a Leith skipper, who had also witnessed Henry Bell's marriage contract. She was something of an heiress. Besides the property in Queensferry, she owned two tenements in South Leith, one of them in Rotten Row; and a waterside land in North Leith.

At the same time Florence Martin's mariner son, also Florence, was living in Queensferry. Florence junior was married to Margaret Dawling, the daughter and heiress of a Queensferry burgess. In 1646 he himself was made a burgess by right of his wife, and his agreement with the council at that time reveals why burgesship could be important to a Leith skipper such as William Hegin. In the first half of the seventeenth century, the home port of the Forth fishing fleet was Dunbar. In late autumn, at the end of the 'herring drave', the boats would assemble there, and the burgesses of the towns around the Forth would meet to buy herring which they then salted for sale. (Much of the fine Rochelle salt that was imported into Leith was destined for the 'drave'.) As a burgess, Florence would be entitled to trade at Dunbar. However, he was heir to his parents' tenement in Leith, and the Queensferry council were concerned that once his father died, Florence would go and live in Leith, cease to pay his burgess dues to them, but still use his burgess ticket at Dunbar. After some negotiation, he agreed to give up his ticket if he went to live elsewhere, or pay a £100 fine.

The Covenant

In the year after their marriage, the peace of Henry Bell and Isobel and of all the people of Leith and Edinburgh was disturbed by the events which were ultimately to plunge Scotland into a complicated series of wars. Charles I had crowned a succession of follies by attempting to impose a new prayer book on Scotland. When the new form of service was used for the first time in St Giles Cathedral on 2 July 1637, it provoked a riot which led to the drawing up of the National Covenant in February 1638. Copies were sent throughout the land to be signed by all those who supported it. The complex issues involved here are perhaps best summed up in the simple form in which they eventually crystallised in the public mind. The Scots saw the Covenant as a rejection of the Catholicism which they were sure the King was trying to force on them. To the Covenanters, the main symbols of this supposed papistry were the bishops, and the first round of the Covenanting struggle was known as the Bishops' Wars.

Leith was one of the first places in which the Covenant was signed. However, the two ministers of South Leith Kirk were opposed to it. The senior minister's post was in the patronage of the Laird of Restalrig, who happened at this time to be Lord Balmerino, one of the committee which had drawn up the document, and an implacable opponent of the King (he had in fact been tried for treason in 1633/4). Not surprisingly, the 'first minister' of Leith was removed four months after the drawing up of the Covenant, a fact which was duly noted in England. The other minister fled the country.

Meanwhile, Scots who had been serving in the King of Sweden's wars on the Continent came flocking home to swell the army of the Covenanters. The returners included David Leslie, who was to become the General of the Covenanting army. The King began to assemble a force to march into Scotland.

One of the linchpins of the King's strategy was his castle of Edinburgh. Lord Ruthven, the Governor of the Castle lived in Leith. In December 1637 he had made the Kirk a very handsome present of a gold communion set, in order to procure the best seat for himself and his family on a Sunday. They were given the whole front pew of the tailors' seats, and the right to a burial for himself in the church, if necessary. Early in 1639, however, he was forced to 'steal away from Leith....else to have run the hazard either of his life or liberty.' He took refuge in the Castle.

In the summer of 1638 HM ships had begun to stop and search Scottish vessels for arms and ammunition, but when Henry Bell set out on a voyage to Rochelle in the autumn he made his passage unmolested. His ship, the *St John* of Leith, arrived home early in April 1639, with 600 bolls (about 7½ tons) of salt, on which he paid £14 6s 8d shore dues, £3 15s mettage (measuring) and £1 3s 4d anchorage to Edinburgh. Henry had been promoted to Skipper in the two years since his marriage, at which time he had been designated 'mariner'. The *St John* was probably his first command, and the fact that she sailed to Rochelle, coupled with the high anchorage charge, indicates that she was one of the larger Leith ships of the time.

Hamilton in the Forth

While Henry was away, work had started on the urgent building of fortifications around Leith. Every able bodied man woman and child hurried to help. Even members of the nobility carried baskets of turves to add to the walls. The Marchioness of Hamilton was particularly active, organising gangs of gentlewomen to labour with the rest. Three weeks after Henry's return, on 2 May, an English fleet of 28 ships under her son the Marquis of Hamilton arrived in the Forth, and shipping into Leith virtually halted.

Hamilton was in the Forth until 20 June 1639, and in that time only four ships came into Leith - in the second week of May. *Janet* of Wester Wemyss came from North Berwick with oats, *Charles* of Aberdour, from Dunbar with wheat and oats, *Neptune* of Elsinore with timber, and *Margaret* of Peterhead with bere. During the time he was in the Forth, Hamilton reported the capture of four vessels. The first was on 19 May, when one of his pinnaces chased and took a hoy of Bremen 'although the hoy sailed better'. On board were 20 or so Scottish officers and their families, returning from the Swedish wars to fight for the Covenanters. He allowed the women and children to go ashore, but the men he sent to captivity in England. A few days later he sent home some of his own men, who had smallpox, in a Scottish prize. As most of the men came from Suffolk, the ship was sent to Yarmouth, with orders that she was to be laid up there until further notice. On 25 May, he 'sent to Berwick a pretty Scots ship. If I had had men to have manned her I would have kept her by me, for she goes exceeding well.' At the same time he sent south a caique laden with barley. No more captures were reported after that, so it looks as though all the other ships making for Leith had been warned. Under normal circumstances, at that time of year, around a dozen ships a week could be expected to come in to the port.

Hamilton remained on his flagship the *Rainbow* throughout his visit, possibly because his mother was said to be waiting at Leith with a loaded pistol, ready to put a bullet through him the moment he set foot on land! He suffered all the discomforts which had always beset invasion fleets in the Forth. His men became ill, fresh water was scarce, and his stores were mostly rotten.

The purpose of sending Hamilton's fleet to the Forth was to support the English army, which was supposed to invade Scotland. In the event, it got no further north than Berwick, where, on 18 June, the King and the Covenanters came to an agreement (the Pacification of Berwick) which halted hostilities for the time being. The king's command of 20 June, to disband the fleet and sail home came as a welcome release from a situation which Hamilton had already decided was hopeless. A ship and a 'whelp' were left in the Forth under Richard Feilding as a token presence.

Ruthven in the Castle

One person who probably wished he could have sailed south with Hamilton was Ruthven, still marooned in Edinburgh Castle. A spy had told Hamilton early in 1639 that the only ammunition available for the Castle guns was flintstones. When Ruthven reported to the king in November, the situation was not much better, 'we find the people more ready to cut our throats than to let us have one barrel of powder or match.' He proposed to the king an elaborate stratagem for sending him ammunition hidden in barrels of beer, and nervously outlined a system of communication signals in case he should be completely cut off. He ended his report by begging the king not to upset the Covenanters in case they attacked the unprepared Castle.

The Covenanters for their part were able to get supplies with the greatest of ease. In July, the *Marie* of Leith came in from Amsterdam with 50 tons of muskets, swords, pistols, pikes, gunpowder, cannon balls and match, and 6 brass cannon. Another ship skippered by John Carse of Leith brought arms from Campveere in September. An English skipper who was in Leith in December reported seeing boxes of muskets, bandoliers and pistols being landed.

All that Ruthven could do was recruit as many men as possible and hope their arms would arrive in time. At last, on 22 January 1640, the *Providence* sailed from Tower Wharf laden with arms and ammunition from the Tower of London, and carrying 100 troops. She and her escort, HM pinnace *Expedition*, arrived at Leith on 12 February. Their arrival, not unnaturally, 'engendered a strange suspicion among the common people and....much commotion in Edinburgh and opposition to the landing of the men.' However, the landing proceded (it was rumoured that Hamilton had forewarned the Provost of the ships' arrival) and the men and ammunition were convoyed up to the Castle. By the second week in April the newly-arrived soldiers were under siege by the Covenanters.

During the spring and summer more ships arrived at Leith with supplies for the Covenanters, although a few were taken by the king's ships which were cruising off the east coast. This blockade may not have had much effect on the Covenanters's supplies, but it seriously affected Edinburgh's trade. All Leith ships were laid up during the summer of 1640. What is more, at least 80 Scottish ships in England had been arrested by the king.

The Covenanters may have been superior in numbers of arms, but they were frustrated by the impregnability of the Castle. It was lack of water that finally forced its surrender by Ruthven on 15 September 1640. The surviving 70 men and 32 women in the Castle were badly dehydrated and hardly able to walk. However, they managed to struggle down to a ship at Leith, under a Covenanter escort which guarded them from the crowd of Edinburgh people, many of whom had lost relatives to cannon fire from the Castle.

In the midst of all this, Thomas Gilmor, a merchant burgess of Edinburgh, had been courting Susanna Luikup's sister Euphame. On 5 December 1640, he received 2000 merks, the first instalment of her tocher of 3000 merks, from George Hegin, Susanna's husband.

The English Civil War Begins

After the fall of the Castle, an uneasy peace prevailed in Scotland. The King even made an official visit in the autumn of 1641, but in England his relations with Parliament were going from bad to worse. By August 1642 Parliament was at war with the King.

Two months after the outbreak of the Civil War, Susanna Luikup's husband George Hegin died. He left clothes and household effects worth £171, and one gilt and one silver cup. The debts owing to him totalled £1594. There was £225 for part of the 'outred' of the *Katherine*, of which he had been master, and £575 freight money due from some French merchants. He had been importing salt from Rochelle, and was owed £564 for a consignment, by an Edinburgh burgess. His total moveable estate was worth £1765 scots, as long as his debts could be recovered. There is little doubt that Susanna was quite capable of getting what was due to her. The impression of a strong personality which is conveyed by her firm handwriting, is borne out by the surviving evidence of her business activities.

A 'shrinking violet' would have been no use as a wife to a seventeenth century Leith skipper. He needed a helpmeet who could be relied upon to look after his business affairs while he was at sea. If necessary she might have to appear in court on his behalf, stave off creditors, and sell his goods as advantageously as she could. It was a big help if she could read and write and had some understanding of legal processes.

Susanna fulfilled all the requirements for a skipper's wife and this stood her in good stead when she found herself a widow with three children to support. She was no doubt helped by the fact that she was surrounded by relations. The possession of a brother-in-law who was a merchant burgess of Edinburgh was hardly a disadvantage. Widows commonly carried on the trade of their late husbands, and some were very successful. A glimpse of Susanna's activities can be had in a letter to her from Patrick Bartholomew, dated at Campveere, 10 April 1645. He begins 'Loving aunt' and signs himself 'Your affectionate cousin'.

She had sent him a barrel containing 30lb of yarn, a piece of black cloth and 25 merks. The spinning of linen yarn was a major occupation of Leith women at that time. Most of the lint they used came from the Baltic, and records contain many instances of women buying from skippers and merchants. Providing an indigent widow with lint to spin was one form of charity. Susanna, her daughters and maidservants (of which most people had at least one) had been busy with their 'lint wheels'. The black cloth was presumably to be sold and the money used with the 25 merks to buy sugar or currants. Patrick decided on currants, and sent her 150lb, in the care of one of the sailors on the ship. He told her that yarn was not fetching much, and proposed to buy half of it himself. The best plan for the rest was for him to weave it for her and send the cloth home for her to sell. He asked her to tell him how wide she wanted it to be.

While Susanna was struggling to keep her head above water, political events were moving fast. In England, although the Parliament party was predominantly non-conformist and the King's men were supporters of the established church, the conflict was seen as political rather than sectarian. To the Scots, however, the supremacy of Presbyterianism was the only issue that mattered. The Marquis of Hamilton, as King's Commissioner, tried throughout the autumn of 1642 and the winter of 1643 to get the Scots to support their sovereign in return for a royal guarantee of the continuance of Presbyterianism in Scotland. This might have worked if popular feeling had not already moved on to a further stage. In the spring of 1643, a Scottish delegation visited Charles at Oxford to inform him that unless he agreed to the reform of the Church of England, the Scots would join forces with Parliament.

The Solemn League and Covenant

In August 1643 a joint commission of Parliamentarians and Scots drew up the Solemn League and Covenant in Edinburgh. Under its terms, Presbyterianism would continue in Scotland, the churches in England and Ireland would be reformed (to the Scots this meant that they too would become Presbyterian - the English had other ideas) and political union of the three countries would be assured. The Solemn League was accepted in England in September, and in November it was agreed that 18,000 foot soldiers and 2,000 horse from Scotland would serve in the Parliament army.

A couple of weeks later the Solemn League and Covenant was signed at South Leith Kirk by the inhabitants of Leith and Restalrig. A solemn fast was held on Sunday 22 October. Signing days for Leith were the following Tuesday and Thursday after the sermon and Friday after morning prayers. The people of Restalrig (who were now Leith parishioners) would sign on the afternoon of Sunday 29th, after they had attended the Sabbath worship. Those who could not write were signed for by the Reader.

Leith Links was the traditional place for musters of Edinburgh and Leith militia companies, and a couple of weeks before the signing of the Solemn League, the Kirk Session had been informed that a 'rendezvous of the fourth man' was to be held on the Links at 24 hours notice, sometime in the near future. The levies who mustered at Leith in the autumn of 1643 may well have marched willingly to war, to fight for the Covenant and the Presbyterian cause. By the time a second muster was proclaimed in late February 1644, some of the potential heroes were rather less enthusiastic. This particular story of the search for recruits concerns South Queensferry, but similar scenes were no doubt repeated throughout the land.

Queensferry was a very small town. It consisted of one main street along the waterfront with a few wynds off it, and only had to supply about half a dozen soldiers for the army. Volunteers who would hold themselves in readiness for call-up were few, so the Council were reduced to nominating the men they thought most suitable. They then had the problem of making sure they stayed in the area. In April 1644 they chose William Glen a mariner on John Allan's ship 'as a young man without burden of wife or children and one that may be best spared forth of the burgh to go on this present expedition'. Three councillors were dispatched to Bo'ness, where John Allan's ship was berthed, to bring back the unfortunate William. Four days later he was in the Tolbooth, along with Daniel Haddoway, another sailor, both having refused to join the military. In the end they were forced to sign an agreement to hold themselves available if needed. William probably thought he had finally escaped when his old skipper, John Allan agreed to re-employ him. It was just a pity for him that John was not one of the elite who skippered vessels bound for France or Spain. William got no further than Stirling, whence Samuel Bailie was sent to fetch him in August.

If William had gone for a soldier, he might have participated in what South Leith Kirk Session called, 'the great and glorious victory the Lord gave to our armies in England against Prince Robert (Rupert) beside York'. Sunday 14 July 1644 was kept as a day of thanksgiving for the victory. The battle in question was Marston Moor (2 July), the engagement that decisively turned the tide of Royalist victories. Eight weeks later, Leith was keeping a day of public humiliation for the defeat of the Covenanters by the Royalist James Graham (the Earl of Montrose) at Tippermuir on 1 September.

Montrose headed a force of Scots-Irish recruited in Antrim, which he had joined in Ardnamurchan in August 1644. His army was swelled by highlanders who joined him as he fought his way round the North during the following twelve months. At one time he came as far south as Perth, causing a mild panic in the Edinburgh area, but he swung north again. His final victory came at Kilsyth on 15 August 1645, after which he entered Glasgow. However, he was faced by the perennial problem of generals of Scottish volunteers, who did not consider themselves bound to serve for long periods. His highlanders began to return home, and he was finally defeated at Philpshaugh on 13 September, by David Leslie. Montrose himself escaped to fight again another day.

Plague

Philipshaugh occasioned no rejoicings in Leith, which was recovering from its last major outbreak of Plague. As early as December 1644, Edinburgh Council had forbidden vessels from Newcastle and other 'suspect places' to come in to the port without permission. By the beginning of April, however, three people in Leith were 'steekit up', being provided with food by the Kirk Session during their quarantine. They were the first victims of one of the most virulent outbreaks of the Plague that Leith had ever experienced. The population had been weakened by a dearth in 1644. Added to this were the stresses of being at war and of financial worries brought on by the high taxation needed for the support of the army. The last 'visitation' had been in 1605, when a village of timber 'lodges' sprang up on the Links for the accommodation of the sick. In 1645, the same precautions were taken. The habitations of the dying were distinguishable by little groups of witnesses gathered at their doors, straining to hear the last wills and testaments being feebly dictated within.

James Gray was deputed to make coffins, and when he fell victim to the sickness, George Aldinston took his place, but they could not keep up with demand. From time to time, 'plague pits' have been discovered in Leith. Many of the bodies are simply wrapped in coarse blue-bordered blankets.

Once a victim and his furniture had been removed to a lodge on the Links, his house was fumigated with smoke from smouldering heather, whin or straw. Sometimes the fire got out of hand and the house burned down. On 24 June the Kirk Session ordered that water was to be available whenever a house was being fumigated, but this did not save the home of James Ramsay, a metter who died at the end of September. His testament noted that,'defunct had certain ready money which was burnt within his dwelling house, and being melted and run together was estimated to the sum of £20'.

There was also Plague in Edinburgh, and when Parliament sat that August, it met at Perth. An act was passed there for relief of Leith, which stated that the dead in the port outnumbered the living. On 14 December 1645 the outbreak was officially pronounced to be over and Leith began to take stock of its effects. The Kirk Session had the number of dead counted up. In the Sands Quarter (Broad Wynd area) - 227; in the Hill Quarter (Coalhill area) - 390; in the Tolbooth Quarter - 609; in the Leys Quarter (St Anthony's and Yardheads) - 1195. The sum total was 2421. The figures reflect the distribution of the population in Leith. A contemporary stent roll and muster roll reveal that the Sands Quarter had the lowest number of inhabitants. The Leys Quarter seems to have been a teeming slum.

The effect of the Plague on the seafaring community can be estimated by comparing a list of Leith skippers and mariners compiled by Trinity House in 1643 and the muster roll made five years later in 1648, which listed all males between the ages of 16 and 60. The mariners' list of 1643 contained 176 names, only 64 of which appear on the Muster Roll. Of course, a number of men would have died naturally within five years. Added to this would be men who were over 60 in 1648, but these together would not normally amount to nearly two thirds of the total. The numbers seem to have been quickly made up, however. According to the Muster Roll, about 30% of 'fencible men' were at sea at the time it was drawn up. As the total number involved was 510, this means a seafaring population of around 160 - not far off the 1643 figure. One implication is that for a few years after the Plague, most Leith ships may have been manned by relatively inexperienced crews.

Family Matters

The Plague claimed William Riddoch, Henry Bell's father-in-law in July. In December, William's daughter-in-law, Beatrix Hodge returned to the Kirk

Session, two silver basins, four great silver cups, three communion tablecloths and the charter chest. Her husband, John Riddoch had also died, and it was probably at this time that Henry lost his wife, John's sister Isobel.

Isobel Bell, the widow of the skipper David Logan (her second husband) was another victim. She left their only child, David, to the curatorship of her brother Henry and of her son-in-law William Hegin.

The skipper James Seton of Leith had also lost his wife in July 1645. He wasted little time in finding a new one. On 8 March 1646 a marriage contract was concluded between him and Susanna Luikup for her daughter Margaret Hegin. Susanna herself paid her daughter's tocher of 2500 merks. James Seton contributed 3000 merks. The contract was witnessed by an advocate, a writer, a clerk and Henry Bell. Two years after their marriage, the couple used some of their money to buy a property in North Leith. James Seton was yet another of Henry Bell's associates who was a burgess of Queensferry, having been admitted in 1640 for the payment of 10 merks per year. He may well have been older than his new mother-in-law. His name does not appear on the 1648 muster roll, and unless he had somehow managed to get himself exempted from military service, this means he was over 60 at the time.

A fortnight after his own marriage contract was concluded, James Seton was one of the witnesses of Henry's contract with Susanna Luikup. The other witness was Thomas Gilmor, Euphame Luikup's husband. Susanna provided her own tocher of 1000 merks and Henry agreed to add 3000 merks. Susanna's influence on her new husband may be indicated by the fact that most of his surviving personal papers date from after his second marriage.

Henry had escaped the plague by a voyage to England. In November 1645 he was in Newcastle, where he received £50 sterling from a merchant of the town, to be delivered to John Brown of Prestonpans. John Brown's receipt is dated at Leith, 7 January 1646. In May 1646 Henry obtained a receipt at Leith from a Newcastle shipbuilder, for the expenses of building a new ship (£3516 scots). The vessel was probably the *Hopeweil* of Leith, of which he was master by the autumn of the same year. In November 1646 he bought £833-worth of tackle for her, and soon after that, four guns.

Henry seems to have been at sea in August 1647, when Susanna paid £70 for a year's rent on their house in Leith. This is the last record of payment of rent among his papers. In the Leith stent roll of October 1647 Henry is assessed as a 'heritor' or property owner. He may have been living in the house of his ward, David Logan, in the Sands Quarter, the house being assessed as worth £100 per annum. The highest assessment in the Sands Quarter was £2000 and the lowest was £20 (Florence Martin). Henry's valuation puts him in the lower 50% of heritors there. However, the Sands Quarter contained the highest proportion of valuable properties of all the four quarters of Leith. In terms of overall figures for the town, £100 was very respectable indeed.

Henry was also stented as a trafficker (trader) and here the picture is rather different. His stent was £33, which puts him in the top 15%. (William Hegin was rated at £40 and James Seton at £20). He seems to have set up as a taverner.

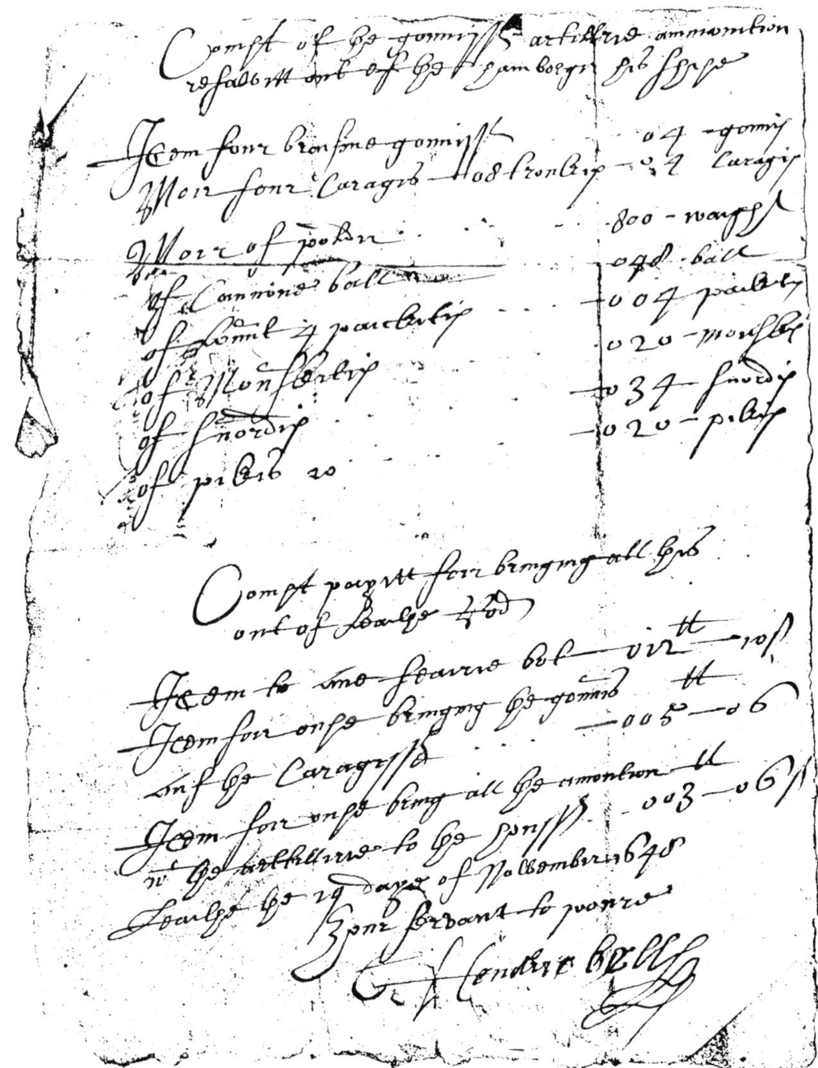

A list of the armaments returned to store from the *Hamburger*, written by Henry Bell (By courtesy of Trinity House, Leith).

In April 1648 he imported 4 tuns of wine, on which he paid duty of £116 13s, and which was probably intended for sale in his own tavern. The following year he paid Edinburgh's collector of impost on wine sold in Leith, £46 18s 8d for 2¾ tuns of french wine and £8 10s 10d for half a tun of Spanish sack (sherry). Since Edinburgh started granting tavern licences to Leithers at the end of the sixteenth century, skippers had taken full advantage of this opportunity to become vintners and legitimise the trade which they had always carried on illicitly. To sell the wine a taverner, usually a woman, would be hired by the year for a fee of about £20 scots. Usually these servants were perfectly trustworthy, but sometimes when the accounts were reckoned up at the end of the year, the taverner was found to owe her employer rather a lot of money. Henry's taverners, operating under the eagle eye of Susanna Luikup, only once gave him that kind of trouble.

In March 1648, while Henry was away on a voyage to Bordeaux in the *Hopeweill*, Susanna paid James Seton 2500 merks, the final instalment of her daughter's tocher. Henry came home in April, and the following month, the *Hopeweill*, was one of six ships chartered by the Committee of Estates to guard Scottish shipping for four months, for a fee of £250 sterling (£3000 scots) per month. The flotilla was to consist of 3 ships of 20 guns and 3 frigates of 16 guns. It seems that the *Hopeweill* was one of the larger vessels - the skipper of another, the *James* of Wemyss, was only paid £120 per month. Once the time was up, the *Hopeweill* seems to have been sold to a Hamburg owner. She was henceforth known as the Hamburger, and was skippered by one Derik Rymsen. Before the new owner took possession of the *Hopeweill* some armaments - four brass guns, along with powder and ball, 20 muskets, 34 swords and 20 pikes - were returned to the ammunition store of the Committee of Estates in Edinburgh.

While Henry was going about his lawful occasions, the political situation had taken yet another turn. To the parties of the Covenanters, Solemn Leaguers and several others - with which we, mercifully, have nothing to do - was now added the Engagers. Many Scots had become disillusioned with the Solemn League when it became apparent that the establishment of Presbyterianism in England by the Parliament was in reality, no more than a pious hope. At the end of 1647, three Scottish Commissioners made an 'Engagement' with the King, promising him Scottish support. In July 1648, an army headed by Hamilton crossed the border into England, where it was defeated by Cromwell at Preston in August.

Once the Engagers were safely defeated, their opponents the 'Protesters' took control. On 12 September an abortive meeting of the two parties was held in South Leith Kirk, to discuss a possible agreement. (A tenant of the Kirk Session was later excused the 1648 ferme of his land, which had been ruined by the Protestors' horses.) Twelve days after the meeting, the Session condemned the Engagement as unlawful. Early in October, Cromwell visited Edinburgh and allied himself with the Protestors.

Sunday 14 December 1648 was a public day of fasting before the renewing of the Solemn League. Seven soldiers were forced to stand up in South Leith kirk and 'made their public satisfaction before the pulpit for being in the unlawful engagement'. Three days later, the Solemn League was sworn there by both men and women holding up their hands. Some sledders who had been pressed into carrying for the Engagement were made to stand up and be publicly rebuked. Just for good measure, in case some malignants had gone undetected, the entire congregation was then subjected to a general rebuke.

Henry was probably castigated along with all the others. He was certainly in Leith on 9 January 1649, when he bought a sixteenth share in his new command, the *Fortune* of Leith. She was a ship of 133 tons - probably the vessel of the same name of which John Riddoch had been master at his death in 1645. Her subsequent master had been David Cairns, from whom Henry bought his share.

On Friday 26 January, Henry witnessed the marriage contract of his second step-daughter, Susanna Hegin. She was to marry Robert Punton, skipper burgess of South Queensferry. Her mother was paying her tocher of 2000 merks, to which her husband would add a similar sum. The other witnesses were Robert Punton's brother George, bailie of Queensferry, and the other bailie, Robert Hill, William Hegin and Thomas Gilmor, Susanna Luikup's brothers-in-law, James Seton her son-in-law, and Samuel Wilson skipper of Queensferry, Robert Punton's brother-in-law. (The house built by Samuel Wilson and his wife Anna Punton can still be seen in South Queensferry.)

Scotland Opposes the Parliament

Even as the witnesses signed Susanna's marriage contract, Charles I was being 'tried' for treason by Parliament in London. Four days later he was beheaded on a scaffold at Whitehall. When the news broke in Scotland her immediate reaction was to proclaim Charles II 'King of Great Britain, France and Ireland'. The Scots were now opposing the Parliament.

In April, the *John* of Kirkcaldy sailed to Breda, with a body of Commissioners who had with them a copy of the Solemn League and Covenant intended for Charles II to sign. The king declined to sign the Covenant at this stage, although events forced him to do so later.

Meanwhile, the Committee of Estates in Scotland had been considering their situation and had decided that one measure which they should take for the defence of the realm against the Parliament, was the re-fortification of Leith.

The Committee passed the organisation of the work to Edinburgh, and on 9 April, the Council considered how they might proceed. The Treasurer was ordered to borrow £20,000 scots and a warrant was to be obtained for digging 'sods, faill and divot' on all common lands within half a mile of Leith. The spur work of the Castle was currently being demolished, and an order was made that all horses that came to Edinburgh with ale and beer were to carry stones from the Spur to Leith.

By the beginning of May 1649 hundreds of shovels, spades, mattocks and barrows had been bought. Two men had ridden to Queensferry to arrange supplies of lime, much of which was provided by Samuel Wilson, Robert Punton's brother-in-law. Folds (enclosures) had been built in which to store the lime, and a shed for the barrows and tools. Toolbags had been made from hardin (coarse linen). A windmill had been constructed, possibly to work the pump which was later used at the sections built near the water. If this was its purpose, it was not a success, as workmen had later to be paid to man the pump - even on the Sabbath.

Work began on 14 May. Two engineers were in overall charge, with two directors of the earthworks and three other assistants. Eleven grieves were employed, each in charge of a gang of workmen. The workforce was gathered by means of a drummer going daily through the town announcing that men were needed; between 60 and 70 a week was the usual complement while the work was at its height. The fortifications were begun simultaneously on the North and South sides of the Water of Leith. It seems that the plan was to work inland, eventually encircling the town.

As well as being brought from the Castle, stone came from the quarry at South Queensferry. It was mainly supplied by Samuel Wilson, James Dawling (son-in-law to Robert Punton's brother, Alexander) and Thomas Simpson. Sand for the mortar was dug from the beach and brought up by William Baillie's two horses, and a load of oyster shells was bought for use in making mortar.

By March 1650, the following materials had been used:

Wallstone,	
large boatloads	33
small boatloads	33
Stones at 6s each	9313
Ashlar stones	326
'Rebats'	760
Turves	123,511
Lime	250 tons

Added to all this was a 'muck midden', which was bought from John Anderson for £10.00. He spent six weeks in September and October carrying it by horseloads to the fortifications.

In the end, all this money and effort were spent in vain. The fortifications were never finished. Even if they had been, it is doubtful whether they would have been effective against a full-scale assault. Several observers commented that the earth of which they were mainly built was too sandy and loose. The walls could not bear the weight of many guns, and constant repairs were needed to keep them standing at all. The details which survive of the building of the earthworks do, however, give some idea of operations a century previously when the more effective French fortifications were built.

While activity on the fortifications was at its height, Henry Bell was away on a voyage to Denmark in the *Fortune*. Before he sailed in June 1649 the ship was 'outred' or refitted. Repairs were undertaken and the ship provisioned at a total cost of over £1600 scots. *Fortune* returned in August with a cargo of grain.

Later in the autumn, Henry set sail again, and by October he was in Bordeaux, where he delivered a parcel of cambric to an Edinburgh merchant. By the beginning of January he had returned from Bordeaux to Leith with a cargo of wine.

1650 was a year of political tension. Scotland's support of Charles II was an annoyance to the Parliament. The Scots themselves had already found that Charles would not reward them with a promise to uphold the Solemn League, pointing out that only the Parliaments of England and Ireland could consent to Presbyterianism being established in their respective realms. The king unofficially encouraged Montrose to pursue another campaign in Scotland. This ended in defeat in May 1650. Montrose was captured and publicly hanged in Edinburgh. After the failure of the campaign, Charles finally signed the treaty of Breda, which committed him to uphold the Solemn League, and set sail for Leith where he landed on 23 June. Cromwell immediately ordered the invasion of Scotland. On Monday 29 July, Charles reviewed his troops at Leith, was feasted in Edinburgh and then returned to Leith to stay in Lord Balmerino's Lodging. His stay was a short one. By now, Cromwell was at Musselburgh and the king was advised to leave.

General Leslie had assembled a force of 40,000 men. For nearly three weeks they successfully defended a fortified line between Leith and Edinburgh (which later became Leith Walk).

Inchgarvie was manned by South Queensferry men, with twenty guns commandeered from the local ships. Robert Punton lost three sakers and two minions out of the *George* his brother's ship, of which he was master. He did not get them back for 12 years.

Work redoubled on the Leith fortifications. Horses were commandeered to carry turves. Soldiers were ordered to work on the walls. At the beginning of August 1650, Parliament ships entered the Forth and stopped the supply of stone from Queensferry. Houses in Edinburgh were being demolished to provide clear sight lines from the City wall. Their stones were carried down to Leith for use on the fortifications. It seems that building now concentrated on the rampart to the east of the town, which formed a northward extension of the 'Leith Walk' rampart. It was this section which was still substantially complete sixty years later.

After Dunbar

Eventually, Cromwell was forced to fall back from Musselburgh having been unable to breach the Scottish line of defence. On 17 August, the Scots army marched in pursuit, leaving a garrison at Leith. On 3 September, they were defeated by Cromwell at Dunbar. The victor immediately made for Edinburgh. In December he received the surrender of the Castle and took up his quarters there. His soldiers were already quartered in Edinburgh, Canongate and Leith. At first the victor kept a tight rein on the vanquished, 'the seas also were closed up by the enemy (Cromwell), whose ships enclosed us on every side, that no man was able to travel by sea....without a pass.' Several Scottish ships were brought into Leith as Parliament prizes in the twelve months which followed the English victory.

A note in South Leith Kirk Session records sums up the local effects of the invasion.

> There was no session held from the 7 July 1650 until the 26 December 1651 by reason of the great troubles and wars between Scotland and England. The Scots army lying in leaguer in Leith and about it, and after the defeat at Dunbar the ministers and most part of all the honest people fled out of the town for fear of the enemy.

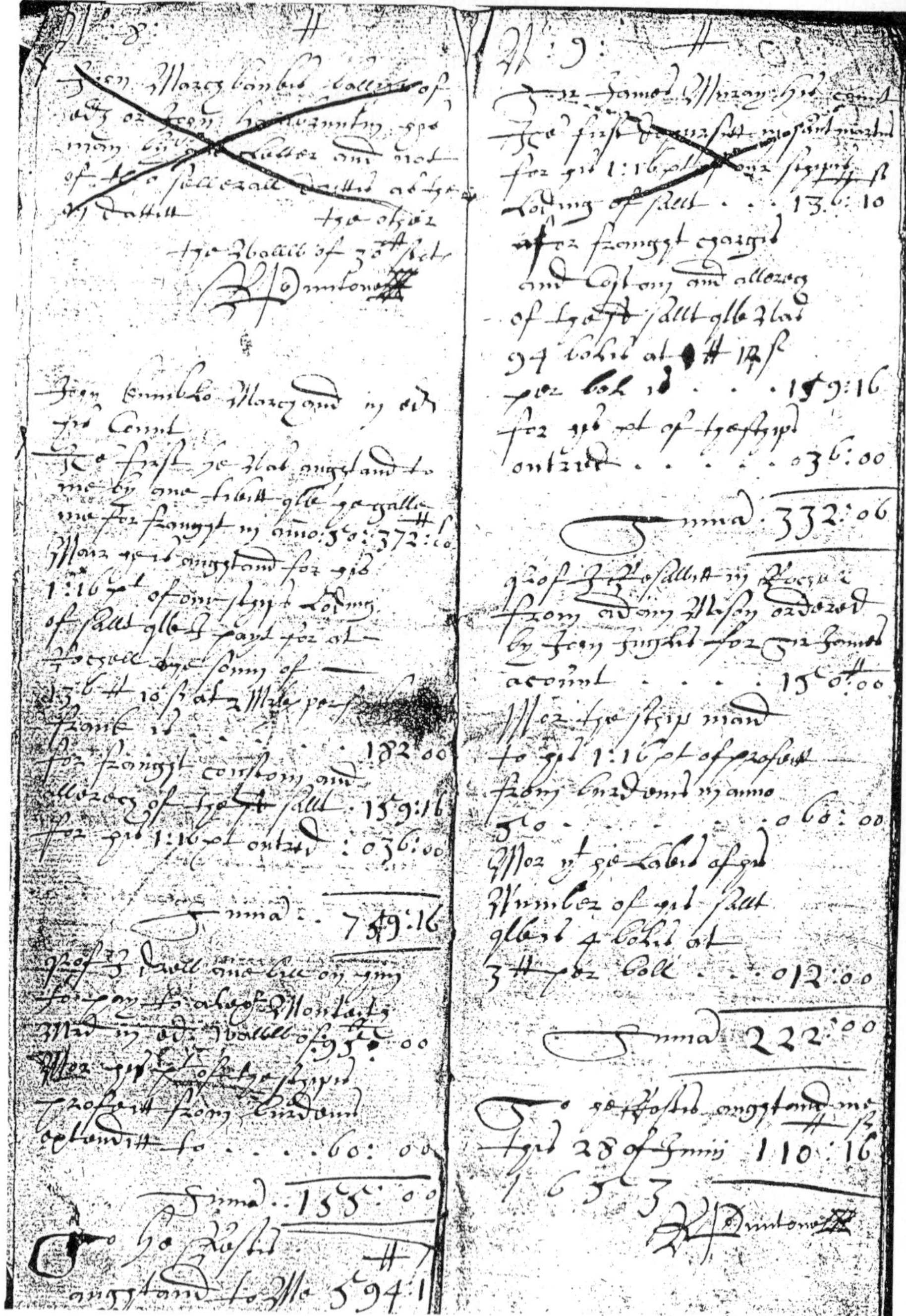

A page from Robert Punton's account book (By courtesy of Trinity House, Leith).

Cromwell returned to London just over a year after Dunbar. The last letter he wrote in Scotland was dated at Leith, 4 August 1651. He left General Monk in charge, and it was he who continued the conquest of Scotland, which was completed when Dunnottar fell to his troops on 26 May 1652.

After Dunbar, Edinburgh also saw an exodus of ministers and prominent people, including the Provost, Bailies, and most of the Council. Henry's brother-in-law, Thomas Gilmor, was made of sterner stuff. He stayed put, and was one of the committee of 30 men elected to take the place of the absent Magistrates. He remained in office until October 1652, when the Parliament's Governor once more allowed Burgh elections.

Henry Bell just missed the coming of Cromwell. In the summer of 1650 he set out on a voyage to Bordeaux. He must have left before the Parliament ships arrived in the Forth in the August. He would have returned in December, by which time Cromwell's troops were firmly established in Leith. Robert Punton, who was living in Leith at that time, and who also made a voyage to Bordeaux in 1650, probably sailed in company with him.

Henry's Family in South Queensferry

The people of Leith scattered to Edinburgh, Canongate, Restalrig and Craigend, where many of them still were a year later. Henry Bell's family went to South Queensferry. When he and Robert Punton returned from Bordeaux they found their wives and families already in their new homes - in Henry's case, a house rented from Alexander Punton, Robert's brother. Henry's stepdaughter Margaret was also living in the town, with her husband James Seton.

In 1651, Robert Punton's brother George died, and immediately a family row broke out over his testament, in which Susanna Luikup was soon embroiled. Her two sons-in-law were very different in character. James Seton was a successful skipper, a pillar of the Kirk Session and prominent in the affairs of the Trinity House, who went on to become a burgess of Edinburgh. Robert Punton seems to have staggered from crisis to crisis, keeping his head above water mainly by borrowing from his family. In 1652 he drew up an account book, probably to see where he stood in the wake of the settling of his brother's affairs. He was owed quite a lot of money by various people, but seems to have done little about recovering these debts. The book records several loans by his mother-in-law. In two instances he seems to have been defeated by his calculations, so that 'I know not if he be owing me or I owing him'.

One debt he was quite sure about was that of 1000 merks to James Seton, who had no compunction about demanding his money. In order to raise it, Robert sold off some land he owned near Peebles, and made over to his brother-in-law all that he might inherit from George. James in his turn owed money to Susanna Luikup, who seems to have acted as the family banker. He made over to her his interest in George Punton's legacy in order to pay off his debt, leaving her with the unenviable task of claiming her rights. The case may never have been resolved. In spite of vigorous efforts by Susanna to bring it to a conclusion, it was still going on nearly 20 years later.

On 19 May 1653, Robert Clephane of Campveere wrote a letter to Henry, from which it appears that he had been there fairly recently:

> Sir, My love to be remembered to you and to your bedfellow and family. This day I have received yours with a bill of 140 guldens and have presented it to Samuel Wallace who has answered it. I thank you heartily for the pains you have taken and if I can serve you at any time you shall find me willing. Your clothes you left here are very well as yet for I have and shall have a care of them. I drew 100 guldens upon James Seton, which I hope he has answered, if it be come to his hand. I pray you commend me to him and to his bedfellow.
>
> This in haste. Your friend to my power
>
> Robert Clephane

This is the only indication that Henry carried on skippering during his first years in Queensferry. The other surviving documents from these years are bills for wine, in quantities which imply that he was still running a tavern.

The English in Leith

In Leith, meanwhile, the problems of having an English garrison quartered on the town were offset by a reduction in interference from Edinburgh. General Monck was in control of the port, but affairs were in fact run by the depute governor, Timothy Wilkes. In December 1651, it was announced by beat of drum that all might trade freely in Leith. This proclamation was closely followed by others regulating the local trade boom. Leith stablers and innkeepers were ordered not to charge more than 8d a day for stabling a horse. Bakers were only to make ½d and 2d loaves, and sell them on Tuesdays and Fridays in 'the usual market place at the Bridge End', but they were also allowed to sell in Edinburgh itself. Butchers had been cashing in on the increased demand by buying up carcases from the surrounding areas. They were restricted to selling only meat they had themselves slaughtered.

Relations between the occupiers and the town became so cordial that in October 1651, the soldiers of the garrison were forbidden to marry Scots women without written permission from Timothy Wilkes or the Major of their regiment. Another edict possibly constituted a crack-down on less regular liaisons. Soldiers were forbidden to keep female servants after February 1652.

Vessels came and went without having to pay dues to the Water Bailie, although the merk per tun, which went to the upkeep of the kirk ministers, was still collected - with difficulty. The Governor-depute also held courts, in place of those which had been held by Edinburgh:

> wherein justice was administered summarily to all parties complaining, without partiality or favour, their carriages and ways in that behalf condemning ours here in Scotland, as was alledged by many who, having actions and complaints given in before them, returned from them with great contentment.

This dispensing of impartial justice was a feature of Cromwell's regime in Scotland which was praised even by his opponents.

In October 1653, however, Parliament re-established Edinburgh's rights in Leith. In 1654, Cromwell was made Protector of the Commonwealth and it seemed to the people of Leith that the Governor and his Depute might well support them if they sent a petition to Cromwell asking to be delivered from Edinburgh's grasp. A lengthy document (which had been drawn up as early as 1652) was sent down to London, detailing all the ways in which Edinburgh oppressed the town.

Meanwhile General Monck was giving some thought to ways of strengthening Leith's defences. The Edinburgh Council was most unhappy about the idea, and in November 1654 they sent a deputation to Monck to discuss some proposals he had made. Negotiations were still going on at the beginning of 1655, when General Monck wrote to Cromwell, urging that any confirmation of Edinburgh's privileges should include some relief to Leith, and that the liberties of English and Scots merchants there should be safeguarded. Cromwell having looked at Leith's petition, sent it back to be dealt with by Monck.

The question of Leith's defences was still unresolved. In February 1655, the building of a Citadel was proposed, but another option was still on the cards. Monck was also considering completely enclosing the entire town. This proposal greatly alarmed Edinburgh, and on 5 May 1656 they offered to give Monck £5,000 sterling if he built a Citadel instead. It may have been this offer or some other bribe which finally persuaded Monck to support the City's claims in Leith. A contemporary diarist certainly thought there was a connection between the matter of the Citadel and the restitution of Edinburgh's claims. He wrote that Edinburgh was threatened with the taking away of her liberties if she did not contribute to the building of the Citadel.

To be fair to Edinburgh, however, it must be remembered that these were desperate times financially. The economy had been shattered by years of war and disruption in trade. Since the late sixteenth century, Scottish commerce had been heavily underpinned by borrowing. The swift and impartial justice of the Commonwealth meant that creditors found it much easier than previously to get redress. Many of even the greatest in the land were ruined at this time. The merchants of Edinburgh were struggling for survival, and could not afford to loose any source of income.

The final cost of the Citadel which was built in North Leith, was £100,000 sterling (£1,200,000 scots). It was built mainly of turf faced with undressed stone, and enclosed an area of between three and four acres, stretching from the seashore to a point near the Water of Leith, at the south end of the present Old Churchyard. It was pentagonal in shape, with a bastion at each of the five angles. A traveller who saw it while it was still entire wrote:

> The works around are faced with freestone towards the ditch, and are almost as high as the highest buildings within, and withal thick and substantial. Below are very pleasant, convenient and well-built houses for the Governor, officers and soldiers, and for magazines and stores. There is also a good, capacious chapel.

The main port (gate) - all that remains of the Citadel built in North Leith by General Monck in 1655. This late nineteenth century engraving shows the house which once stood on top of the port, but which was later demolished.

It was built over the site of St Nicholas' chapel, whose burial ground was still used by the people of North Leith. They were given a new cemetery, the present 'Old Churchyard' next to the Water of Leith, behind the chapel of St Ninian. A number of gravestones were transferred to the new site.

The chief sufferers from the City's renewed dominance of Leith were the English merchants who had established themselves in Leith to supply the garrison. Trade in England had been free for as long as anyone could remember and the English merchants did not take kindly to this return to the Middle Ages. One English incomer told the Speaker of Parliament that he hoped Leith's petition for separation from Edinburgh would be granted. 'That town having been under the greatest slavery that ever I knew, one should be subject to the other no more than Westminster to London.'

The English did, however, gain one small victory over Edinburgh. They made such a fuss about the merk per tun, most of them refusing point blank to pay it, that in November 1654 the Council were forced to free all English goods from payment. However, this was a very minor concession, and in 1655, John Baynes the Receiver General of the Commonwealth's revenues in Scotland, did his best to discourage his brother-in-law, who was thinking of trying his luck in Leith. 'Truly here is no encouragement as yet for any to come hither for trading, for here are already more than do well thrive; and except this town of Leith get the privilege of a free borough within itself, without dependence on Edinburgh, many that are now in it will remove for England again.'

Two of the English merchants who did not remove, died at Leith. Barnaby Darroch came from Yarmouth. His warehouse in Leith contained sugar, copperas, alum, rosin, tobacco, woad, paper, books and wine worth £327 sterling (£3924 scots). He also had his own weighing scales, strictly forbidden from Edinburgh's point of view. He owned shares in two Leith ships and one Yarmouth vessel and had £1000 sterling in ready money. The furnishings of his one chamber in Leith were worth £25 sterling (£300 scots) - this at a time when all the 'household plenishings' of a successful Leith skipper might be worth only £100 or £200 scots. He was owed a total of £46,107 scots.

John Pennington had been a haberdasher. His stock was worth about half of that of Barnaby Darroch. Apart from several sorts of tobacco, he sold typical haberdashery goods - cheap fabrics, sewing materials, ribbons, bodices, combs and paper. These were all goods which had previously been available only in Edinburgh.

Convoys

The locals, though no doubt bitterly resenting Edinburgh's renewed power over them, were used to the situation. They did, however, benefit from the presence of a garrison with money to spend, especially if they happened to be brewers or taverners. Even the nuisance of having soldiers quartered in the town was not so bad if the hosts were paid. There was also the presence of the Parliament ships to bring work to the local timbermen, smiths and sailmakers. Although Monck had secured the mainland, 'Charles Stuart's freebooters' continued to operate off the coast, aided by the French. During almost the whole duration of the Commonwealth and beyond, England was at war with the Dutch and, for a while, with Spain, both of whose fleets menaced her shipping. Commonwealth ships were stationed the full length of the east coasts of Scotland and England, and in the English Channel. There were usually at least four frigates stationed off Scotland. When not cruising on station, they performed various escort duties.

Two fishing fleets left England each year. One was the Iceland fleet, still making its yearly voyage. The other fished around Orkney. Each fleet was escorted by two frigates, those assigned to the Orkney station often calling at Scottish east coast ports, including Leith. Regular convoys sailed from London to Leith and other places with supplies for the garrisons in Scotland and they also needed escorts. Then there were the Scottish merchant vessels. Typically, a frigate would start collecting its merchant convoy in Orkney and work its way down the east coast until it reached Leith. There the ships would divide into two groups, according to whether they were bound for London or the North Sea. A frigate would take the second group to Norway. If any ships were going to the Baltic, they would be escorted as far as Elsinor. On its way back, the frigate would pick up homeward-bound vessels. If these included ships for London as well as for Scotland, their escort had two options. If she could come up with another frigate, then the convoy would split once it was off the Danish coast. If there was no other suitable ship in the area, the whole fleet would make for Leith, the London vessels sailing on from there.

The ships going directly from Leith to London would be initially escorted as far as Tynemouth. Here, others from the area would join the convoy. If the escort was under orders to sail to Yarmouth, where there was a refitting station, she would go on with her little fleet. If not, she would return to Leith and the merchantmen would have to wait for another frigate to pick them up. This convoy would split once more off Tilbury Hope, where yet another frigate would join those bound for Bordeaux and Rochelle. Similar arrangements in reverse applied on the return journey.

In March 1654 HMSs *Primrose, Duchess, Unicorn* and *Sun* were in the Orkneys. At the beginning of April they put in to the Forth and Captain Sparling of the *Primrose* wrote to the Admiral from Leith Roads asking for two more frigates to be sent to keep down some Brest men-of-war, as *Unicorn* and *Sun* had gone on to Newcastle to victual. Even as he wrote, the Admiral was issuing orders to HMS *Gainsborough* to sail to Leith with pay for the soldiers. A day later, on 6 April, HMSs *Raven* and *Providence* arrived in Leith Roads, having convoyed in 15 merchantmen and a ship with ammunition from London. A few days later they sailed for home, *Providence* arriving at Tynemouth on 26 April. Here she found HMS *Weymouth* waiting to escort a convoy to Leith. *Raven* was not so fortunate. She was captured by six Dutchmen and taken to Shetland (where the Dutch had established a foothold). *Weymouth* and HMS *Sparrow*, which had promised to assist her, 'ran away to Leith'. This must have been one of the last actions in the current war between England and Holland, which ended in that same month (but not for long).

Edward Booth, one of the English merchants who had settled in Leith, was the agent of the Navy victualler. He organised the provisioning of the Naval ships which put in to the port, out of the garrison's supplies. Repairs and caulking were done by the local shipwrights, captains often paying them with a promissory note to Edward Booth.

Early in 1656 HMS *Basing* was at Leith. Her captain was later court-martialled for impeding HMS *Paradox* in her pursuit of a Spanish frigate off the Scillies. Her crew accused the captain of being constantly drunk. They said that while in Leith, he had sent ashore several hogsheads of the ship's wine 'to a man residing at the sign of the Three Tuns'. In May 1656 HMS *Nonsuch* lost both her topmasts and had to come into Leith to refit. She then escorted a convoy to Norway and back to Aberdeen and other ports. In August she returned to Leith Roads to clean and revictual. The captain borrowed £28 19s from Edward Booth to pay the carpenters who did the cleaning.

HMS *Greyhound* was blown up off Holy Island in June by four Dunkirkers, with the loss of all but two of her crew. HMS *Bonaventure* arrived at Leith from Ireland in the same month to replace her on the Scottish station. In August HMS *Nicodemus* came in for repairs, having chased two or three Spanish men-of-war away from the Scottish coast. In October the pink *Weymouth*, commanded by Robert Wilkinson, arrived in Leith with a convoy. She was a leaky ship with only one deck, which sailed 'heavy', but she acquitted herself well in the one action in which she was involved. In May 1657, off Tynemouth, she fell in with a Humber collier, whose skipper told Wilkinson that two of his companion vessels had been taken by two Ostend men-of-war. *Weymouth* gave chase, and when she came up with the Ostenders, engaged them in a battle which lasted three hours. The fact that *Weymouth* was low to the water was in her favour. Although the men-of-war were able to fire broadsides at her alternately, only her sails and rigging were damaged. At nightfall the enemy withdrew, leaving the *Weymouth* with the ships she had rescued.

A disadvantage of being low in the water in Scottish seas, was that the ship was always swamped in the frequent storms. Lack of watertight hatches and cabin doors made life uncomfortably wet at such times. By the beginning of 1658 Wilkinson had become heartily sick of his pink, and asked for a transfer. His request was finally granted in 1659, when he was given command of the frigate HMS *Satisfaction*, remaining on station in Scotland. Frigates had two decks and were less vulnerable in a storm, but a complaint in September 1658 from the captain of HMS *Advice* shows that Robert Wilkinson may not have after all escaped the wet. *Advice* had just come in to Leith to victual, having brought a convoy from Elsinor. Her captain, Frances Allan was very concerned about the state of her.

> She is now so open above the water that no oakum will keep in her seams, so there is not a man that has a dry cabin, and the great cabin is as bad as any place in her for wet....but under water she is as firm as any ship in England, and if repaired and cleaned, as stout a ship with a sail as any fourth-rate frigate can be.

A month later she was at Chatham, refitting for service in the Channel. By this time the water had got down to her ballast, and the captain had to have holes cut in the well to let it go down to the pumps.

Henry Falls Foul of the Parliament

There is no record of any Leith ships being lost by enemy action during this time, but the need for convoys and the constant presence of English ships must have had a profound effect on the life of the port. In 1654 Henry Bell, still residing in South Queensferry, was once more on the high seas. He had a new command, the ambiguously named *Loyalty*, which belonged to the Edinburgh merchant Robert Beattie. In January 1654 he sailed her from Leith with a cargo of wine. A month later he reached Newark on the Clyde, where there was a Commonwealth garrison. There he unloaded his wine and took on a cargo of herrings and Irish butter, leaving at some time in March. By 4 April he was back home, where he paid his wine bill.

Before too long he was at sea again, only to have his ship 'taken by the *Sucklie* by virtue of a commission granted to Issac Philips and her commander Clement Smith'. Whether this was a general commission for arresting enemies of the Commonwealth or whether it specifically applied to the *Loyalty* does not appear. The Government may have been suspicious of Henry's voyage from the Forth to the Clyde in the spring. He had, after all, sailed unmolested through the area where the Royalist ships were operating. On 7 June, the Edinburgh Council recorded in its minutes a testimonial to the effect that the voyage had been made solely for trading purposes.

Henry may have had some reason to feel guilty. He was obviously seriously worried because on 24 July he made his will. 'I, Henry Bell, sometime skipper of Leith, now dwelling in Queensferry and at present in the City of London upon my lawful calling. Praised be God in perfect health.' He left all his goods to his 'well-beloved wife Susanna Luikup' and appointed her his sole executor. The will was witnessed by the *Loyalty*'s owner, Robert Beattie and a London merchant called Peter Anderson. It seems that Henry was not personally suspect, however. By the beginning of August he had found a new ship, the *Hope* of Bristol, the *Loyalty* being still under arrestment. Robert Beattie formally discharged him from his old command, and he was free to take up the new one. On 8 September, the Provost of Edinburgh wrote to the Parliamentary Commissioners in London, asking them to assist Robert Beattie in his case, which was due to come before the English Admiralty Court.

December found Henry in Le Croisic, a small port on the west coast of France a few miles north of St Nazaire. Ships which had been to Bordeaux for wine, often took in a cargo of salt on the return journey. Rochelle was the main port for the salt trade, but Le Croisic was one of the alternatives. At Le Croisic Henry met Robert Beattie's brother John, who was living at Nantes. When John returned home he found news waiting, which he lost no time in passing on:

> Sir and loving friend. I have at my arrival from Croisic received two letters from Mr Robert Beattie, the like from Mr Kay and Mr Baugh, who desire to have their love remembered unto you. Mr Beattie hath gained his process as it appeareth by the sentence, copies of which I send you here enclosed (see below), but his adverse party is appealing, which will put him to great charges and am afraid that when all comes to him there will be but little of the same remaining, reckoning the great charges he is at. I pray God send him to have a good issue thereof.
>
> I hope you will be all ready to go to sea before this comes to you and that you will take the opportunity of the first fair wind. In the meantime, I must tell you as a friend that it is thought we shall have open war with England very shortly, from

which God keep us. I pray you keep this very secret and let no man know that you have got news, not so much as your Mate, but see with my brother what papers you both have that may prejudice you in case any stay should come, and seal all together in paper and let my brother deliver the same to M Berand my good friend until such time as you are ready to go away, and when you go to sea, have a special care to see all they papers you have and lie each sort aside and have them all overboard if needs be, for you know papers will many times do more hurt than good. This being what the present offers, with my love remembered to yourself and your Mate and the rest of your company, wishing you a prosperous voyage. I rest your assured friend at command. John Beattie

The 'sentence' referred to in the letter was the judgement given on 11 November in the case between Robert Beattie and the men who were claiming the *Loyalty* as a prize. The judges concluded that the seizure was just, but that as Robert Beattie was a citizen of the Commonwealth he should have his ship and goods back and pay the expenses of the lawsuit. The only exceptions were to be the goods of Renee Meinier of Angers, the ship's surgeon and of another man called William Roger.

It would seem from John Beattie's letter that a third Beattie brother was on the *Hope* with Henry Bell and that all four of them had Royalist leanings, to put it no higher. Their voyage home was unmolested, however, and at the end of December they were safely in Scotland.

The Family Returns to Leith

By this time the family circle in Queensferry had broken up. James Seton had moved to Edinburgh, having acquired a third share in a brewery. On 13 September 1654, he had been made a burgess. In April 1655 his wife, Margaret Hegin, died. Her testament makes no mention of any children of the marriage, but she and her husband had boarded two of Robert Punton's daughters for three years - and had not been paid.

At Whitsunday 1654, Susanna Luikup, with her daughter Susanna and her family, had moved into the house in Leith belonging to Henry's nephew, David Logan. When the army first took over the town, anyone who would not swear allegiance to the Commonwealth had been forced to leave. In 1653, however, all property was restored to its owners, on condition that it was let only to tenants approved by the Governor-depute, presumably including Susanna and her family.

The inventory of David Logan's house, taken in 1645 after the death of his mother Isobel Bell, shows it to have been a two-storeyed building of seven rooms, possibly the 'foreland' of a larger tenement. In 1645, the main downstairs room, the hall, had contained a table, chairs and form, a French dresser and a cupboard and built-in bed. The cooking fire with its spits and pots and pans was in this room as well. A touch of luxury was provided by 11 'painted boards'. Next to the hall was a small chamber with a bed, table and whicker chair. Beyond this room was a larger chamber which seems to have been Isobel's own room. As well as three beds and other furniture, it contained a looking glass and her lint wheel. Three of the upstairs chambers were furnished as bedrooms, the fourth, probably a little 'penteis' over an archway to a back yard, contained only two old tables.

In 1622, David's father had been licensed by Edinburgh to sell ale, beer and wine and keep a hostelry. From the number of beds in the house (ten), it would seem that this was the hostelry itself. Henry seems to have continued in the tavern business there - he had the cellars extensively repaired and altered. He may have continued the other side of the business, although as there must have been about ten people living in the house at first, there would not have been a lot of room for guests.

All too soon, Henry's household was broken up. Early in 1656, Robert Punton borrowed the Trinity House mortcloth (pall) for his wife's funeral. In June he had to ask for it again for one of his daughters, on both occasions he was allowed to have it without payment. In October 1656 Henry and Susanna bought from Robert all the furniture and household goods in their house which had belonged to him and his late wife.

In little over a year, Susanna Luikup had lost both her daughters and a granddaughter. All she had left were her son John Hegin and two granddaughters, Susanna and Margaret Punton, who probably continued to live with their grandparents. There may, however, have been another young relative in the household. An undated letter from Euphame Luikup to her sister concerns a certain John Luikup.

> Loving sister
> I have sent the bearer, John Luikup, to you with my husband's consent, desiring you to have a care of him and to put him to the writing school and to hold him at it until such time as he be called back again. And you shall have contentment for such time as he shall happen to remain with you. As for sarks, I shall have them to him or any(thing) else that (he) shall stand in need of. No more, but my love to you.
> All I rest
> Your loving sister Euphame Luikup'

On 8 May 1657, one John Luikup, made his will at London:

> Be it known unto all men by these presents, me John Luikup private seaman, forasmuch as Henry Bell, skipper in Leith in the nation of Scotland, has sufficiently furnished me for my intended voyage to the East Indies. And now seeing the voyage is very long and dangerous and that in reason he ought and should be repaid, and that I not having any certain means to pay him withall. Therefore (in the case it should please the Lord to call me out of this mortal life before my return)

The will made Henry the young man's sole executor, and another document drawn up at the same time gave him power of attorney. Nothing more is heard of John Luikup. We can only hope that the Lord stayed his hand, and that a suntanned John returned safely to Leith.

In the first few years after his return to Leith, Henry seems to have made his living solely as a vintner - a profitable trade in a garrison town. In 1657 he resumed his seafaring career. The Navy records for this time show that, although ships from Scotland were still being convoyed to the Baltic, voyages to London were now fairly safe. Early in the year Henry sailed as master of the *Elizabeth* of Berwick.

On 1 April 1657 Henry settled his accounts with David Logan and was found to owe him £32. The money was delivered by Susanna Luikup, and at the bottom of David Logan's receipt appears the following rhyme:

> Thus after compting fine and fair,
> Let friendship rest for ever mair.

Unfortunately it did not. As is so often the case, money lay at the root of the problem. David Logan's house needed a lot of repairs (it had probably suffered during the early years of the occupation of Leith). Henry paid for these, and David was too tardy about reimbursing him. During the summer of 1657 the whole roof was mended, a chimney which had fallen down rebuilt, and a new chimney installed in the front cellar. There is also mention of work done on the kitchen. As there had been no kitchen in 1645, it may be that Henry had one built. Henry paid the cess of the house, and David's fines for absence from three head courts. He lent him money and supplied him with 'strong waters'. Added to this was £60 'for his diets this 4 years at several times'. It seems that David was a bachelor skipper, who boarded with Henry and Susanna between voyages. The bill for all this was £344 8s scots, which remained unpaid. For their part, Henry and Susanna never paid David his rent.

The Job

Henry was now master of the *Job* of Leith. On a voyage to London he undertook some commissions for a merchant called Edward Wheatly, who wrote to him in February 1658:

> Kind sir
>
> I have received your letter, but it was soaked in the rain so that I could scarcely read it, but made a shift to understand that you have sold the runlets of wine and have bought tallow. Pray let it be the best, for methinks it is very dear. However, I am content to give as others do, and as for your [timbers,] I have been with Mr Ellis and he tells me the beadle of Dieres Hall he thinks may buy them when the Hall is ready, for now it is abuilding and is not finished, therefore they are not disposed of. Pray do me the favour as to go to Mr Simons and pray him to tell Ensign Nichols that I have sent to him in Thomas White, two pipes of canary and 32 gallons of Alicante. I sent him a letter to that purpose formerly, but have not received any answer. If you would desire Thomas Pullein to write me word how he received the Malagas I sent him in your ship and whether they are disposed of or no, I shall think myself engaged to you, for let me write what I will to him, I can

get no answer from him again, and therefore to write to him I think will be to no purpose. I pray you do this favour for me and you will much engage him who is your loving friend to command.
Edward Wheatly'

This letter says all that needs saying about the relationship between the English garrison at Leith and the skippers of the port.

Late in 1657, Henry set up as a brewer. At the end of January 1658, at the Excise Office in Leith, he paid the collector, John Anderson, £28 15s arrears of duty on malt. Thereafter, regular payments appear for the rest of the year, at a rate which shows he brewed 2¼ bolls (about 3cwt) each week. On 24 May, at Edinburgh, Susanna Luikup also received a brewing licence. She promised to pay 50s scots per boll of malt brewed. She was limited to 5 firlots (1¼ bolls) of malt a week and had to agree ' not to enlarge my brewing vessel nor brew with nor for others'. Her licence lasted only until 10 November, when it would need to be renewed.

Susanna needed her licence because once again Henry was away in 1658. He made a voyage to London in the late spring. While he was there, the *Job* underwent repairs in Billingsgate Dock. The Dockmaster's receipt for groundage is dated 25 June. Henry's presence at Billingsgate suggests that he had carried a cargo of fish.

Job arrived back at Leith at the beginning of July. She was due to be sold in August. In the six weeks preceding the sale, she was put in dock and caulked, and some work was done on her half deck. Henry may have remained her master. He is described as such on the receipt for the May Light dues which he paid in December 1658.

In the summer of 1659, Henry was once again in London. He sailed with a convoy of vessels from East Coast ports which left Leith in August. This was his last voyage. He died in April 1660, just a few weeks before his King came 'to his own again'. Charles II landed at Dover on 29 May.

Widowhood

Susanna Luikup was now a widow for the second time. Widowhood was a serious business in the seventeenth century. Most women lost as little time as they decently could in finding another husband. After the plague of 1645, for instance, South Leith Kirk Session had been so overwhelmed by widows wanting to re-marry, that it decreed that each woman must wait until at least nine months after the death of her husband. Other problems had arisen as a result of the wars, as in the case of a woman who told the Kirk Session that she had a witness who would swear that her husband was killed at the battle of Kilsyth. She was told she would have to find another witness before she could re-marry.

However, it seems that re-marriage was not an option for Susanna. She must have been aged around 60, but this would not have deterred potential suitors if she had been wealthy enough. Her first problem was the settling of Henry's estate. From the 1640s onwards, as the economic climate worsened, increasing numbers of creditors were made testamentary executors by the Scottish Commissary Courts. This meant that they could 'intromet with the goods and gear' of their late debtors in order to recover what was due to them. Thirtyseven testaments of Leith skippers were registered between 1644 and 1690. In sixteen cases, nearly half of the total, the executor was a creditor. Seven of these creditors were widows, making sure of securing the money due to them under their marriage contracts. It was Susanna's sister-in-law, Isobel Martin, who had inaugurated this trend in 1658, and she herself took advantage of it after Henry's death.

The first task was to make an inventory of the late Henry's goods and financial affairs. 'The inside plenishing of my dwelling house and the habilements of my husband's body' amounted to £200. The owners of the *Fortune* still owed £400 for an 'outred to Holland' and the owners of the *Job* £60 for another outred. There were a few other small debts, but the main creditor was David Logan. As well as £244 for repairs to his house and other items, Henry and Susanna had lent him £1020, on which he owed three years interest of £183. In 1661, David reacted to this claim by taking Susanna to the Bailie Court for 7 years' rent of his house and a couple of other small debts. Her counter-claim for £344 probably decided the issue in her favour.

Henry himself had also had debts. He owed Andrew Duff of Edinburgh (husband of Margaret Luikup) 500 merks, and a Kinghorn skipper called John Boswell, 900 merks. Susanna paid both these creditors. When Henry's testament was registered in October 1661, its preamble stated that as well as securing her life interest on 2000 merks, half of her marriage settlement, Susanna became a creditor for the two above sums. This meant that she could claim the money out of Henry's estate.

The exit of the garrison from Leith after the Restoration of the monarchy left Susanna with another problem. In July 1661, the king ordered that the Citadel, which had been built at such enormous cost, was to be demolished - all except for the northern portion which formed a defence against encroachment by the sea. In the Citadel were a number of guns which had been commandeered from ships at various times over the previous ten years. Before demolition began they were removed to the Castle, and between 25 July and 28 November 1661, fifteen individuals presented petitions to the Privy Council for the return of a total of some 130 pieces of ordnance. Most had lost between two and six, but the *Hopeweill* of Kirkcaldy had been carrying 14 and the *Jean* of Queensferry, 13.

Included among the guns were the sakers and minions which had been taken from Robert Punton's *George* for Inchgarvie. Inevitably, Robert owed his mother-in-law money, and in order to clear the debt, in December 1661 he made over to her two of these guns. She was also claiming four minions on her own account. William Hegin's widow, Isobel Martin claimed six, on behalf of herself and the owners of the *John* of Leith. James Seton claimed two.

Susanna Luikup's list of the money owed to her and Henry Bell by David Logan (By courtesy of Trinity House, Leith).

Trade was also becoming more restricted. Once the Occupiers were safely out of the way, Edinburgh pounced on the merchants who had set up shop in Leith. In September 1660, five remaining English merchants were warned that they would only be allowed to continue trading until the end of the year. The following May, the Bailies were given twelve days to close all the merchant shops in Leith. In November 1662, the City decided to restrict the number of vintners in Leith to a dozen, a measure which may have had a more direct effect on Susanna if she had carried on that side of Henry's business.

She certainly continued to brew. In 1661, she is included in a list of the brewers of Leith who lived in the Barony of Broughton, which means that she had either moved to North Leith, or was living in the Coalhill. The latter is the more likely, as there is no other evidence to connect her with North Leith. An agreement that she made with the Collector of Excise in 1662, shows that she was brewing about half as much malt each week as Henry had done.

Her son, John Hegin, was now established as a merchant, and he became increasingly involved with his mother's affairs. She may even have been living with him. Among the many receipts which she carefully kept, there are none for house rent. John stood surety when Susanna borrowed money, as she did from time to time. By 1667 he seems to have gone into partnership with her. From that date, loans were made to them jointly. The merger may have been prompted by Susanna's increasing financial problems. Her brewing output had become insufficient to support a viable ale-house trade and she had bought beer and ale from an Edinburgh brewer, who sued her for payment in Leith Bailie Court in October 1667.

Susanna adopted the traditional expedient of widows and took in a lodger, John Binks a Leith merchant. However, she borrowed so much from him, that when the time came to collect the rent, it was swallowed up in her debts. In spite of her money troubles, she was in fact one of the luckier widows. Florence Martin's widow had to ask Trinity House for money to repair her house, which seems to have been practically falling down. Susanna's sister-in-law, Isobel Martin, was so poor that she also had to ask the Masters for help, to which she was doubly entitled as the daughter and widow of skippers. What had happened to all those properties in Leith which she had inherited from her father? 'Widow Hegin' received her last pension from the House in February 1671.

In 1674, Robert Punton died. He had been lodging with John Stewart of Leith, and it fell to Susanna to make an inventory of his goods. These were few enough. His furniture consisted solely of two old green chairs, a table and two kists. He had a featherbed and bolster, but his landlord must have provided the bedstead and the linen. One of the kists contained Robert's clothes, the other his personal papers (which were given into Susanna's custody). His only other possessions were a candlestick, a brass basin and two tin plates. Robert's daughters, Susanna and Margaret, entered into the curatorship of George Dundas of Duddingston, who no doubt figured somewhere in the web of Punton kinship.

The girls could hardly have stayed with their grandmother, who was by now herself a Trinity House pensioner. On 5 December 1673, she received her first monthly payment, 'to Widow Bell - £4 16s'. In February 1677, for the last time, 'Mistress Bell' was paid £14 8s for one quarter.

In due course, one of her granddaughters became an inmate of the House. In the minutes of a meeting of the Masters, 31 July 1699, appears this entry;

> having found several goods and plenishings be Susanna Punton, one of the pensioners in the house, now deceased, and inventoried the same. Do ordain the same to be rouped and sold for payment of the charge of her funeral, and the rest of the value to be applied for the use of the Poor.

It may have been among Susanna's effects that they found her grandmother's papers. Perhaps they kept them safe for some distant relation who never came to claim them. However they came to be there, they lay in the Kist for the next 150 years, flesh on the bare bones of the history of just one Skipper of Leith.

9

Metamorphoses

The seventeenth century was a time of change for Leith. In 1600 the port was just starting to emerge from a medieval chrysalis. By 1700 it was being administered in a way that was recognisably modern. The change was by no means uniform. Pockets of medievalism persisted up until the nineteenth century, perpetuated by a deeply conservative Edinburgh. But other forces were at work, before which the city was increasingly forced to bow.

Leith men who travelled abroad could see that the stranglehold of the burghal system was breaking down. The burgesses of Edinburgh themselves often challenged the old bye-laws. The statute which required a burgess to reside in his burgh was particularly troublesome to merchants whose businesses were based in Leith. More and more of them defied their Provost and Bailies on this issue, and throughout the century, the number of 'merchants of Leith' increased, especially after the Parliamentary occupation.

Other ports on the Forth, which had previously been of minor importance, grew as the century wore on, and started to take business away from Leith. Edinburgh was forced to make concessions on various dues and charges in order to entice merchants to use the port. Another vexation, about which they could do little, was the rise of Glasgow, which was better placed geographically to exploit the tobacco and sugar trade with the British colonies of the American continent, which expanded during the seventeenth century in spite of English protectionism.

The Royal Navy became heavily involved with Leith during the Dutch Wars. HM ships used it as a victualling and repair station, and convoys became a normal part of maritime affairs during almost the whole of the second half of the century. This naval involvement was to continue for another 100 years and more, and become a major element in Leith life.

Reform of the Customs

One of the reforms which the Commonwealth government attempted in Scotland was the reorganisation of the Customs. The old arrangements had evolved from the medieval system, whereby the Great Custom was collected by the burghs and paid to the King. At the end of the sixteenth century the Customs had been leased out to tacksmen or farmers, and the resulting loose organisation was now in need of an overhaul.

When, in 1655, Thomas Tucker was sent up from London to carry out the reforms, he based himself at Leith. He was one of the Englishmen appointed a

Commissioner of the Scottish Customs Board, some of whose Scottish members were already tacksmen of the Great Custom. The Commissioners were concerned not only with the Customs on imports, but also with the duties paid on salt and the excise on ale, beer, and spirits. Their remit was to lease the Customs anew and to establish a new impost 'the old one having been discontinued in the uncertain times'. In 1656 Tucker reported on what had already been achieved.

One of his main findings was that it was not possible to impose English methods in their entirety on Scotland. Conditions north of the border were very different from those he had been used to. For instance, in England excise on ale and beer was calculated per barrel of the finished product, in Scotland the criterion was the amount of malt used in the brewing. Moreover Scottish barrels, called trees, were not of standard size. After an unsuccessful attempt to standardise the barrel at 11 Scots gallons, it was decided to leave things as they were, for the present.

The Commission had more success with the duty on salt. Tucker's comments on this product are full of insights into the salt trade of the Forth coasts, and the herring fishing. There were salt pans between Stirling and St Andrews on the north side of the Forth, and between Stirling and Berwick on Tweed on the south side. The owners of the pans (the Masters) paid no wages to their workers (the Makers). Instead, they contracted for a fixed amount of salt, according to the quantity of coal with which they supplied the Makers. Any surplus production belonged to the Makers. They sold it to cadgers (itinerant fish dealers) and salt sellers, who travelled the country with their wares in baskets - carried by a pack horse if they were lucky. The Masters stored their salt in girnels until they could send it to England or overseas. The problem here was to find some way of imposing duty on the salt sold by the Makers. The Masters would pay on the contents of their girnels, but;

> to require an account or anything else of the workmen (who, besides their infinite poverty and miserableness are - were it not a breach of charity - to be esteemed rather brutes than rationals) was a thing altogether impossible, nor ever can be reputed so much as probable by any who have seen either the persons or the places.

To appoint an 'accounter' at each saltpan would be uneconomic. The Makers carried out their transactions secretly under cover of night, so there was no way of collecting at point of sale. The problem was solved by constant questioning of cadgers and other buyers, who were required to show a certificate of duty paid on any salt in their possession. 'To get peace for themselves', they made sure that any salt they bought had paid duty.

A different problem arose with fine imported salt, which was used to preserve food, especially fish. Salt bought for fish curing was not dutiable. It was the custom for families to buy fresh fish and salt it for their own use. At the beginning of August, as the herring-fishing season approached, there was a steep rise in the sale of foreign salt, under the pretence that it was all needed for fish preservation. The Commission made regulations to ensure that duty-free salt would only be used for its legal purpose.

Tucker studied the collection of import duty in Leith as a pattern for the rest of the country. Leith was already the 'Head Port' for a district stretching from Berwick on Tweed to Stirling, but since the establishment of this arrangement, trade had expanded at ports further up the Forth. Bo'ness was now the busiest port on the 'Narrow Waters' above Inchgarvie, so a Customs post was opened there, covering the coast from Stirling to Cramond, the river Almond forming the boundary between the two districts covered by Leith and Bo'ness. One other Customs post was established on the Forth, at Burntisland. Dundee, Aberdeen and Inverness covered the rest of the east coast.

The masters of many ships, especially the Dutch (whose vessels were adapted for shallow waters), had been in the habit of bypassing Leith and landing their cargoes on the shore further up the Firth, where there were no Customs officers. Pursuit of these smugglers with boats was not possible 'by reason of the violence and tempestuousness of the course and water of the Firth'. To put a stop to the practice, the Commissioners had half a dozen soldiers stationed on Inchgarvie, where all ships going up the river were stopped. If a ship was found to be carrying goods, a customs official was put on board, where he stayed until the vessel reached its destination and was unloaded.

> which has very much awed the merchants and seamen, prevented much deceit and will, in much measure, restore the trade of Leith, which has been but too much impaired by the ships running up the river and landing goods along the coast.

At each Head Port, there was to be a Collector with a staff of searchers who boarded and searched each ship as she came in to port. The unloading of the cargo was supervised by waiters, who were to spot any contraband which the searcher might have missed. The waiters were paid quarterly 'by results'. Any man who was not deemed to have made sufficient seizures of contraband would not receive the maximum rate. Waiters had previously worked only at the port to which they were assigned, but because of fluctuations in trade, in future they would be employed wherever they were needed. At Leith, there was to be a Head Searcher, who was responsible for organising the waiters and assigning them to their ships.

At Leith also, the Collector had an assistant and a Checker, who was present at all receipts. The Itinerant Surveyor, who had responsibility for visiting and inspecting all Customs posts was based there. Vacancies at other ports were filled from Leith, and new staff were sent there to be trained. There had been a Custom House in the King's Wark since shortly after the letting of the Customs to tacksmen. In 1683, the office was destroyed by a fire in which the Leith Customs ledgers were burnt to ashes. All that has survived is a handful of books which were presumably elsewhere at the time of the fire.

A waiter was stationed at each of Leith's four subsidiary ports, Eyemouth, which had previously been a base for smugglers, Dunbar, Prestonpans and Musselburgh. Dunbar was only busy from mid-August until late September, when salt was imported for the fishing. The waiter stationed there was responsible for the whole coast from Eyemouth to Prestonpans. The many small vessels which came to Prestonpans for salt were considered a smuggling risk, so there was a waiter there, who shared responsibility for the coast as far as east as Dunbar. The fourth post, at Musselburgh, had one waiter in charge. The stretch of flat open sands between Musselburgh and Leith offered no illicit landing places.

Tucker said of Leith itself that it was;

> a pretty small town fortified about, having a convenient dry harbour into which the Firth ebbs and flows every tide; and a convenient quay on the one side thereof, of a good length, for the landing of goods. This place formerly, and so at this time, is indeed a storehouse not only for her own trades, but also for the merchants of the City of Edinburgh, this being the port thereof.

The private storehouses of Leith consisted of vaults for wine, girnels for grain and cellars for a variety of merchandise. The Custom House had its own cellars where goods which had yet to pay custom were housed, often for several months.

In 1643, the Timber Howff (Bush) was enlarged northward and westward, and its eastern end was strengthened against encroachment by the sea. Fifteen years later, in 1658, the Howff was divided into sections to be let out by Edinburgh for profit. At the same time a stone wall was built along its northern boundary, from the head of the pier on the west to the start of the fortifications on the east. The wall fulfilled two functions: it stopped the timber being washed away and prevented theft. The dues charged on timber stored in the Howff are detailed in a list of 1676. They ranged from £3 for 100 wainscot to 1s for an oak board or a great fir timber. Foreigners, who paid double dues, began to unload their timber at Fisherrow and other ports. In 1686, the Council had to reduce foreigners' shoredues and Timber Howff charges to the single rate paid by burgesses, in order to encourage them to unload at Leith.

The Weigh-house

One of Edinburgh's jealously guarded Burgh privileges was that of weighing goods at the Tron. There were several reasons why the burghs had a monopoly of weighing. In the first place it ensured that only standard weights were used - standard for the burgh, that is. Actual weights could vary considerably from place to place. Staple goods such as wool had to be weighed at the Tron, enabling the burgh officials to spot illegal traders more easily.

All dutiable goods had to be weighed at the official place, so that the correct dues could be calculated. From the point of view of the burgh, however, the main advantage of the system was that a charge was made for the service, any profits, once the weigher had been paid, going into the town's coffers. The Edinburgh Tron had long become inadequate for its function and a weigh-house was built in the early sixteenth century.

The people of Leith were supposed to use the Edinburgh weigh-house for all their needs. Not surprisingly, illicit weighbeams were set up in Leith, and from time to time there were prosecutions for illegal weighing there. Some individuals were allowed their own weighbeams, such as smiths, who charged for large orders by the stone of iron used. The agent of the Earl of Hopeton had a beam for weighing the lead ore which was shipped into Leith from the noble lead mines in Lanarkshire. He was prosecuted in 1644 for weighing goods in Leith which should have gone to the weigh-house - the last prosecution in a series stretching back into the late sixteenth century.

In 1649, the Edinburgh Council decided that the situation had got completely out of hand, and resolved to build a weigh-house in Leith. Robert Milne the master mason and John Scott the wright were awarded contracts to convert the Catchpell (tennis court) in the King's Wark for the purpose. The resulting building was of three stories. The weighbeams were housed on the ground floor, which was entered by a wide, high door with a pulley fixed over it. The upper stories were let out as lofts (they were initially used as magazines by the English garrison). The lofts were reached by external flights of wide stairs, one at each end of the building, with a large landing at each storey from which an entrance door opened. Under each stair was an arched passage, giving access to the yard at the back of the building. In the Weighouse itself printed notices were prominently displayed, detailing the weighing charges. The Edinburgh Council promoted this new facility as a benefaction to the inhabitants of Leith. The beneficiaries, however, were unimpressed by the City's generosity. In their petition to Cromwell they complained of the weigh-house as yet another instance of Edinburgh's tyranny.

The Rise of Bureaucracy

One tradition which was permanently changed by the English occupation concerned the duties of the Water Bailie. He or his officer had always been responsible for organising the berthing of ships at the shore, collecting the shoredues and arranging ballasting. In 1653, a Mr Benjamin Huskings was appointed Quaymaster, with responsibility for these functions. The title of subsequent officials was later changed to 'Shoremaster', but the job remained the same, the Shoremaster being appointed and paid by Edinburgh. After the Restoration the Water Bailie made no attempt to reclaim these duties, probably because he had too much else to do. He had to make sure that all incoming ships declared their cargoes for payment of Petty Custom to Edinburgh, and it was he who was responsible for law and order in all Leith maritime matters which did not come within the province of the Admiral of Scotland. He worked in the face of constant hostility from Leithers. On top of all this, he was also a merchant burgess of Edinburgh, with his own business to see to. As the century wore on and trading became more complicated the office of Water Bailie was increasingly seen as an onerous burden, and at least one elected man refused to take office. In 1693 both the Water and the Baron bailies finally gave up the struggle to carry out their duties in Leith. A fourth bailie was elected, who was allowed to live in the port 'for the repressing of vice and disorder'.

A minor source of Edinburgh's income, which was collected by the Shoremaster, was 'cranage'. There had been at least one crane at Leith since the early sixteenth century, but it must have given little trouble as it is hardly ever mentioned in the Council minutes. In 1671, however, the tacksman of the shoredues complained that ships were using their own tackle for unloading, and he was making nothing from the cranes. If cranage had been at all profitable to the City, we can be sure that the Council would have come up with some method of forcing skippers to use their crane. In the following year they did reduce their charge from 4s to 3s per tun. From 1671 dates the only known picture of the Leith crane. It appears on the date stone of a house belonging to the Porters of Leith, which shows that it was worked by an enormous wheel, turned by a man walking round inside it, just like a turnspit dog. In this carving the crane is being used to unload barrels from a single-masted vessel, with lee boards bearing the symbol of a flying horse.

Besides the shoredues and the petty customs, the third main impost charged by Edinburgh at Leith was the Merk per Tun, which went towards the upkeep of the local ministers. The successful English resistance to paying this charge during the Commonwealth seems to have sparked off a general reluctance to pay, which continued after the garrison left Leith in 1660. By 1671, so many Edinburgh merchants were avoiding the impost that the Council was forced to make concessions. A number of merchants were unloading at other ports on the Forth, where the merk per tun was not charged. The rise of the alternative ports was also a problem for Edinburgh in other ways. Ships were being built in them and skilled mariners were deserting Leith in order to live in them. The Council decreed that merk per tun would not be paid on goods carried in ships which had been built in Leith since 1660, or on ships skippered by men living in North or South Leith or the Coalhill. In 1681, all timber imports from Norway were freed from the merk per tun in order to encourage shipbuilding.

An illustration of the kind of dues and payments for which a skipper was liable is given by an entry in the ledger of the Edinburgh merchant, George Clarke, made in 1688. He had a share in a ship which had just returned from Danzig, and the skipper had sent him his bill:

	£	s	d
The May light	19	10	00
Primegilt	13	00	00
Beaconage and Anchorage	7	8	4
Shoremaster	3	18	00
Flag money	1	10	00
A boat to help the ship in	00	14	00
Shore dues	33	11	8
Plank mail (paid to the porters for use of their gangplank)	2	16	00
To the rowers	12	00	00
To the seamen to drink	2	16	00

	£ s d
Custom of lint, knapholt, deals, planks and entry to the Waiters	187 2 6
To the workmen (porters) for carrying the whole lading	80 00 00
Bush mail (timber bush)	18 00 00

We have already seen that the late sixteenth and early seventeenth centuries were prosperous times for Leith and Edinburgh. The boom in trade had brought many foreign merchants to Leith, and in 1613 Edinburgh had started appointing brokers to help them in freighting their ships. In this respect Leith was ahead of London, which did not have brokers until some time later. The last broker to be appointed by Edinburgh was Jacob Van Statten, who took office in 1660. It is hardly likely that the need for brokers disappeared after this date. The assumption must be that private individuals took over the job after this date.

The Shoremaster, Great and Petty Customs Collectors, and Brokers, with their clerks and assistants, constituted an embryonic modern port bureaucracy. In 1600 the port was being run by the Water Bailie and the Tacksmen of the Customs. By 1700 it was firmly in the hands of professional administrators.

Trades Incorporations and Fraternities

However, the story does not end with the penpushers and paper shufflers. Leith also had a small army of workers, without whom business would have ground to a halt - porters, metters, carters and coopers. Each trade was largely self-governing, with interference from Edinburgh when it saw fit. The porters fell into two categories. The stingmen were appointed by Edinburgh to carry wine to taverns and report to the Clerk of Leith on how much each tavern used. The polkmen acted as general porters, with their own trade association. In 1666, they incurred the displeasure of Edinburgh when they began preventing non-members from working in the port. They were summoned to explain themselves to the Council. The meeting resulted in new regulations and a revised organisation. The porters were henceforth to be divided into six companies of twelve men, each with a foreman. The drum was to be beaten twice a week through Leith for the next fortnight, to make up the numbers. Entry money was reduced from £20, to £4 for an unfreeman and £1 6s 8d for an unfreeman's son. A long table of charges was printed, one copy to be displayed in the chamber of the Clerk of Leith, and the other in the weigh-house. By 1671 the porters had their own convening house.

The metters seem to have been associated with the porters for most of the century, but by 1695 they were sufficiently numerous and well-established to be granted the right to have their own Incorporation, headed by a Boxmaster. This method of organisation survived up until 1967, when the last vestiges of ancient port regulations were swept away by Act of Parliament.

The carters and sledders had long been an Incorporation, independent of

Edinburgh insofar as such a thing was possible. The Burgh regulated their charges and complained about the damage to paved roads caused by iron-shod cartwheels, but in the main they were left alone. They grazed over a hundred horses on the Links and owned property in the Kirkgate, where they built a convening house in the eighteenth century.

The coopers were another body which was well established by the seventeenth century. Before the Reformation they had formed the Fraternity of St John. As we have seen, they were allowed to have their own Incorporation under supervision by Edinburgh. Once this was sorted out they operated largely unmolested by the Edinburgh magistrates. Their only appearance in the Edinburgh court in the second half of the century, concerned a dispute between the coopers of North and South Leith over the right to work on the Shore.

The porters, carters and the rest were all attached to one of the large Incorporations of Leith, of which there were four. Two of them, the Traffickers and Trades, each embraced a number of smaller organisations. The Maltmen accepted merchants and doctors. The skippers and mariners stood alone, in their own powerful Fraternity with its headquarters at their 'hospital' in the Kirkgate. During the seventeenth century, the name of the 'Fraternity House' became shortened to 'Ternity House' and by the eighteenth century had been corrupted to 'Trinity House'. The mariners of North Leith ran a seperate but affiliated Fraternity until at least 1690.

The original function of the Fraternity was purely charitable, but in the seventeenth century, the Masters of the House began their involvement with the work for which the Trinity House is generally known - the provision of pilots. The first official pilot was appointed by Edinburgh in 1649. He and his deputies came under the supervision of the Water Bailie. However, during the

The tablet of the Association of Porters of Leith, 1678. It shows barrels of wine being unloaded by a 'treadmill' crane from a two-masted vessel with lee boards. Two 'stingmen' are shown in the top left-hand corner.

Commonwealth occupation the Masters needed the help of the Water Bailie in recovering their papers, which had been confiscated by the occupiers. For the next thirty or so years, the Water Bailie took the chair at the meetings of the Fraternity which thus became involved in the organisation of the pilot service. In 1684 the then Water Bailie, John Johnston, organised the first annual election of a Master, Assistant Master and Treasurer/Boxmaster of the House, who took full charge from that time on. The chief pilot continued to be appointed by Edinburgh, but he was chosen by the Masters in conjunction with the Water Bailie. The Masters also undertook responsibility for the provision of a pilot boat. Linked with the pilot service was a system of signalling with flags to indicate to ships in the Roads when the water was deep enough for them to enter the harbour.

Vessels were charged pilotage according to their draught:

Draught	*Charge per foot (Scots money)*
Up to 7 feet	10s
8 feet	12s
9 feet	13s 4d
10 feet	16s
11 feet	20s
12 feet	24s
13 feet	28s
14 feet	30s

The Masters of the House also acted as arbitrators in some maritime disputes and examined would-be skippers and pilots as to their fitness for command of a vessel.

As well as its more obvious charitable functions, the Trinity House possessed a mortcloth (pall) which it hired out to members and their relatives. The use of a pall was thought to add immeasurably to the dignity of a funeral and in cases where relatives could not afford a coffin, it was of real benefit. The very poorest were not charged for its use. All guilds and incorporations which could afford it had at least one. The wealthier organisations and the kirks owned several, of different sizes and qualities. The importance of the pall may be gauged from the sums which the North Leith skippers were prepared to spend in buying one of their own. The outlay is all the more significant because the North Leith men financed themselves solely by their own contributions (Crown money), and usually had only about £50 Scots in their box.

9 ells of velvet at £16 13s 4d per ell	£150 5s
for lining, and the poke thereto	£ 10 16s
for a fringe weighing 3lb 3½oz	£ 56 13s
for sewing silk and fringes for the poke	£ 1 9s
for the workmanship thereof	£ 6 13s
for extraordinary charges about the business	£ 3 0s
	£279 8s

Shipbuilding

One group of tradesmen which it hard to assign to an Incorporation is the shipbuilders. Were they wrights or were they mariners? Apprentice timbermen were taught 'sea affairs' and some shipwrights were also skippers, so on balance it seems they must have belonged to the latter group. By the end of seventeenth century they had their own organisation, the Society of Carpenters, based in North Leith.

In 1643, four years after Edinburgh acquired the superiority of North Leith, an unspecified number of inhabitants of the town were brought before the Council for digging docks to build and repair ships within the floodmark without a licence from the City. These docks were formed by digging out an area of the river bank and then extending the area by building out walls to enclose part of the river bed. Unrestricted dock building would have considerably narrowed the harbour. Six years later the timbermen and shipwrights of Leith were still digging their docks and refusing to pay docksilver to the collector of the Petty Customs. In 1657 Edinburgh had a major dispute with William Couston, a skipper of North Leith, who was building an illegal dock. He produced an old charter proving his right to do so, but the Council refused to accept it. They dismissed the current Water Bailie Officer for allowing the dock to be built, and ordered William to demolish it. He ignored the order, and it was not until the Council imprisoned him that he finally complied. William was a tenacious character, however, and five years later he had built another dock. His son or brother Archibald, also a skipper, carried on the business. When he died in 1671, he had a half share in 'the new bark', and a boat which was building in his yard.

Edinburgh had its own dock in North Leith. In 1678, the skipper James Simpson and several merchants, his co-owners, applied to build a ship of 300 tons and 40 guns there. They made their application on 12 June, stating that they were collecting together the necessary materials and expected to have them ready by 1 August. The Council ordered that the ship which was currently being broken up in the dock must be finished by that time and the dock left empty for work to begin. (There is no indication of the location of Edinburgh's dock, but the most likely place was at the Sandport. All the yards beside the Water of Leith were in private hands.) The ship the merchants had built was almost certainly the *Albany* of Leith, of which James Simpson was master. (He was also the first elected Assistant Master of Trinity House in 1684) The *Albany* is first recorded in the Customs accounts for April 1681, when she returned from a voyage to Bordeaux. She sailed to Danzig in the autumn of the same year, and thereafter made regular voyages to Bordeaux and Cadiz.

The regulation of shipbuilding was a matter of national importance. In 1646, in order to encourage the craft, imported pine timber was freed from paying merk per tun. In 1681 the Committee of Trade in Scotland reported on the state of the nation's shipping. Their opinion was that Scotland had twice as many ships as her trade could employ. A survey carried out in 1668 had found 215 ships of burden in the ports of the realm, as well as numerous barks and great boats. In the 1681 report the number of ships lately built and bought was estimated to have doubled this total, and many were judged to be overlarge for Scottish trade. The Committee proposed that a list be made of all Scottish ships and a standard size be imposed on all those built in future. Those that were too large were to be sold. In April 1681 Parliament passed a comprehensive Act concerning Scottish trade, in which the question of shipping was addressed. No size restrictions were imposed, but the buying of foreign ships was forbidden. Shipbuilding was further encouraged by the abolition of custom on timber, sails, anchors, cables and ropes.

In August 1685 the Privy Council received its first application for a skipper to buy a foreign ship. In all, three licences were granted in that year, but the Privy Council refused two in the following January. One was from James Dredan, skipper of Fisherrow, who had lost his own ship and wanted to buy a dogger of 50 tons belonging to a Dutchman. In March the would-be vendor presented his own petition. He had brought his dogger to Cockenzie laden with his own goods, but they were spoiled on the voyage and rendered unsaleable. He did not even have enough money to get home and was desperate to sell his ship. In the same month nine other skippers petitioned to buy ships from abroad:

> in regard there is not enough timber in this kingdom fit for building of ships, nor will the carpenters undertake to build ships for them and that thereby trade is much decayed and the supplicants greatly prejudiced in lying idle for want of employment, and which tends very much to the impairing of His Majesty's Customs.

In September 1686 the last petition was presented. After that time, this particular attempt to boost shipbuilding seems to have been abandoned.

The seemingly interminable 'Dutch Wars' which broke out intermittently throughout the time of the Commonwealth and up to 1672, affected Leith in a number of ways. We have already looked at the organisation of the convoys which were necessary to protect shipping in the North Sea and the Channel. Vessels bound for Bordeaux and Spain did, of course, have the option of sailing round the top of Scotland and down the west coast, but the longer route added to freight charges, and the bulk of Leith's trade was with ports on each side of the North Sea.

The Royal Navy and the Privateers

From the time of the Restoration onwards, Scottish seamen were regularly enlisted in the Royal Navy. Lists were drawn up of the numbers to be provided by each port. One roll of 1664 demonstrates the relative size of the ports around the Forth and the East Neuk of Fife:

Lothian Ports - west to east		*Fife Ports - cont*	
Bo'ness	24	Inverkeithing	6
Grange	6	Burntisland	12
N&S Queensferry & Cramond	12	Kinghorn	6
Leith and Newhaven	**20**	Kirkcaldy	20
Prestonpans and Cockenzie	20	Dysart	6
Fisherrow and Musselburgh	10	Wemyss East and West	6
Dunbar and Belhaven	10	Leven	3
		Elie and Earlsferry	6
Fife Ports - west to east		Largo	2
		Pittenweem	6
Culross	6	Anstruther Easter and Wester	12
Torryburn	6	Crail	8

The importance of Bo'ness is particularly striking, bearing out contemporary allusions to its rapid growth.

The might of the Royal Navy was supplemented by privateers, many of which were licensed in Scotland after the Admiral of Scotland was given Royal permission to grant warrants for the purpose in 1665. In 1666 the French and Danes allied with the Dutch, and the applications for privateer licences came thick and fast. Twentyfour were granted by the Privy Council in April,June and July of that year. One of the first was the *Lamb* of Leith, commanded by John Brown. She brought two prizes into Leith on 1 July, one laden with wine and the other with timber. *Lamb* had been in company with HMS *Rothes*, commander Captain William Hamilton, who brought in four vessels laden with wine. Gideon Murray, in HMS *Thistle* was also with them, taking three prizes of his own. John Brown's commission was renewed later in the month. Altogether, during June and July 1666, some 30 or so prizes were brought into Leith.

Early in April 1667, the greatest prize ever seen in Scotland was brought into the Roads, an East Indiaman with a cargo of silk. Three weeks later, the Navy Board's informant in Leith reported that Leith ships had taken a total of 13 prizes off Spain and France. Three days after he dispatched his letter, in the early evening of 30 April, a Dutch fleet sailed into Leith Roads. They were not entirely unexpected, and a chain and boom had been fixed across the harbour mouth. Thirty cannon had been mounted on the remaining walls of the Citadel and twenty elsewhere about Leith.

Three Naval frigates were in the Forth at the time, but they made no move against the Dutch that night. It was said that their Captains were drunk, but as the Dutch had between 30 and 40 ships, it is possible that they were merely being prudent. General Dalziel's regiment, which was stationed in Edinburgh, marched down to Leith, along with the local militia. On their way they met a stream of women and children fleeing to safety in the city. When the soldiers arrived in Leith they manned the cannon and fired on the Dutch ships. The beacon at the harbour mouth was taken down to confuse any ship trying to enter, and in the afternoon of 30 April a prize which had been brought in by Captain Hamilton was sunk at the harbour mouth, foiling an attempt by the Dutch to send in a fireship. To the extreme frustration of the waiting forces, the enemy did not attempt to land. Instead, as the wind was in the south, the fleet sailed over to Fife and bombarded Burntisland. Casualties were light: one sow, one hen and one rat! When evening came, the Dutch sailed out of the Forth once more, and headed north.

A Naval squadron of ships under Sir Jeremy Sands was sent to look for the Dutch fleet, but without success. At the end of May the squadron put into Leith. They arrived in foggy conditions, keeping together by periodically firing their guns. Not unnaturally, the local people assumed that they were the Dutch come back again and a panic ensued. It was not until Sir Jeremy sent messengers ashore that calm once more prevailed.

Sir Jeremy was a thorough man, who had brought his ships in to carry out a muster of the pursers' books. He was not impressed, either with the pursers or with his findings. Many of the ships needed new masts and cables and he frankly informed the Navy Board of his opinion of the standard of refits carried out in the Thames. He was outraged at the local price of cordage; 52s a cwt for rope which sold in Hull for 30s. He complained that there were no provisions for his ships, although the Navy Victualling agent at Leith had three weeks notice of his arrival. In his opinion the agent was 'very dull, negligent and careless' and more interested in working as a factor to the local merchants. Beer was in particularly short supply, but he would have to get it from Newcastle as the Leith brewers were unwilling or unable to brew for him.

The squadron was also short of men, the appalling shipboard conditions which were normal at this time having taken their usual toll. Leith and the other ports nearby were accordingly visited by press gangs. This was much resented as many men would have volunteered if given the chance. Sir Jeremy, however, was a brisk operator. In spite of the lack of supplies, within five days of their arrival at Leith all but two of the squadron were out again on station. Their commander declared that he would 'hasten his ships out as fast as they come in and not let them be idle'. Even he, however, could not have expected the two which remained at Leith to go out on active service. They were the *Milford* and the *Nightingale*, which had been involved with two other frigates in an encounter with 60 Dutch ships off Norway. The four had taken 14 of the enemy vessels, but only at the cost of a great deal of damage to themselves. *Milford* and *Nightingale* had had to give up all their masts and sails to make the other two frigates seaworthy. They were still waiting for this equipment to arrive when Sir Jeremy set sail on 20 June, six prizes having been brought in during his stay.

In July, so much salt was brought in by privateers that the price dropped dramatically. A Leith ship was operating in the North Sea, the *Anthony*, commanded by Captain Wood. She took nine prizes in three weeks. Four of them were sent to Scotland, including an enormous vessel of 900 tons which came in to Leith on 21 July. The flood of prizes continued throughout August, with a further 16 taken by Naval ships and Scottish privateers. The spate was only halted by the signing of the Treaty of Breda on 28 August, bringing peace with Holland, France and Denmark.

In March 1672 the war with the Dutch was on again. Scots once more flocked to get letters of marque, this time from the Duke of York, who had been made Lord High Admiral. One Naval captain spoke with many Dutch and Swedish merchant ships while cruising off Heligoland in the autumn of 1672. 'All in general complained of the cruel usage of the Scotch privateers, which plunder all they meet.' Certainly, some 30 or so prizes had been brought into Leith alone during the preceding summer. The Dutch crews were turned on land to fend for themselves, it being too expensive to maintain them in prison. The final peace with Holland was signed in February 1674.

Transportation

During the Commonwealth, a number of Scottish 'rebels' had been transported to the British colony (Plantation) on Barbados. After the Restoration it seems to have occurred to the Scots that this was a good way of getting rid of undesirable elements in society. The Privy Council began to grant warrants for the transportation of 'strong and idle beggars, Egyptians (gypsies), common and notorious whores, thieves and other dissolute and loose persons, banished or stigmatised for gross crimes'. The first recorded request to the Council was made in 1662 by the Edinburgh magistrates. Thereafter, almost every year, shipowners would apply for a licence to round up transportees and one or two ships would sail from Leith in the autumn, bound for the 'plantations'. Criminals sentenced to banishment would be kept in the Tolbooths of Edinburgh and Leith until the transport ships were ready. Some prisoners actually applied to go to the Americas, like two women in 1667. They had been remanded for a long time, but no-one had appeared to testify against them and they were starving. (At this time, prisoners or their relatives had to supply their own food.) They were ordered to be sent to Barbados or Virginia on the next ship, probably the *Ewe and Lamb* of Leith, which made annual trips between 1666 and 1672, in company with the *Good Intent* or the *Convertine.*

Not all settlers in the New World were involuntary ones, however. In 1666, James Gibson, bound for Virginia in the *Phoenix* of Leith was licensed to transport criminals, but at the same time it was proclaimed by tuck of drum through Edinburgh that anyone wanting to go to Virginia should go to Captain Gibson's house. There 'he shall have good condition of clothes and other furniture and all encouragement to such a profitable voyage'. Three years later the Privy Council recorded that:

> Whereas his Royal Highness the Duke of York, Lord High Admiral of England etc, did Propose to His Majesty in Council That he would be pleased to have liberty that such of His Majesty's Subjects in Scotland as shall be induced to take conditions as planters of New York (which had just been named after him) may be permitted to transport themselves thither in Vessels from Scotland, And to be

> allowed to make their Voyage and return in a way of Trade, Or to remain at New York upon the account of the Fishing Trade, or transporting the Growth and manufacture of New York to the Barbadoes or other His Majesty's plantations in America.

The Duke had authorised the *Hope* of Leith (350 tons) and the *James* of Leith (250 tons):

> To pass from Scotland to New York with such persons of the Scots Nation as shall desire to plant there, and to trade between the said places as they shall have occasion. Or to remain at New York upon the account of the Fishing Trade.

Convicted criminals and blameless settlers were not the only ones to sail from Leith Roads to America. There were also consignments of what we might call political prisoners. Episcopacy had been restored along with the monarchy in 1660, but the Covenanters continued to operate in Scotland. They met in 'conventicles' which were forbidden by law. Anyone caught attending such a meeting might be sentenced to banishment. In 1666 there was an unsuccessful Covenanting uprising which marched on Edinburgh. The prisoners of this rebellion were kept in Greyfriars Churchyard until 1668, when they were sent to Virginia in the *Convertine*. Covenanters were sometimes allowed home on bail to put their affairs in order and provide themselves with clothes and provisions for the voyage. On at least one occasion the unmarried brother of a family man was allowed to go in his place. A farewell letter from a Covenanter banished to Pennsylvania is full of his faith in God to keep him from harm. His main fear was that he and others might be seduced into the wicked ways of the Quakers who inhabited the colony.

In 1679, after the battle of Bothwell Bridge, another 258 Covenanters went on the *Crown* of London. Her master was Thomas Teddico, whom a contemporary diarist described as:

> a profane, cruel wretch (who) used them barbarously, stowing them up between decks, where they could not get up their heads except to sit or lean, and robbing them of many things their friends sent for their relief. They never were in such straits and peril, particularly through drought, as they were allowed little or no drink and pent up together till many of them fainted and were almost suffocated.

This was probably an accurate description of conditions on all the convict transport ships. In this instance the agony of the passengers was shortlived. The *Crown* was wrecked in the Orkneys with the loss of all on board except some of the crew. William Paterson, the Edinburgh merchant who had chartered the ship petitioned the Privy Council for compensation.

For those who survived the voyage, banishment could mean the start of a new and better life. Letters sent home by settlers often contained news of former prisoners who had made good. An applicant for a transportation warrant was of the opinion that successful deportees could enhance Scotland's international reputation:

several other persons so sent away within these nine or ten years have become very active and virtuous persons, their idleness and poverty having formerly corrupted them, whereby not only the reputation but even the interest of the country receives much advantage.

In 1670 we have the first mention of a ship transporting prisoners from Glasgow. By the 1680s, more or less equal numbers were leaving from the Forth and the Clyde, but by the last years of the decade the practice seems to have died out on the east coast. The last recorded convict transport to leave Leith was the *John and Nicholas* - 180 tons, 12 guns, master, Edward Barnes - which sailed on 11 December 1685.

This is not to say that voyages to the Americas ceased, far from it. In 1685 at least four ships sailed from Leith to New Jersey, Jamaica, and Barbados. At least one ship sailed to the New World from Leith in 1690. However, the port was not ideally placed for this trade. By the end of the century, Glasgow was the main Scottish point of departure for the colonies.

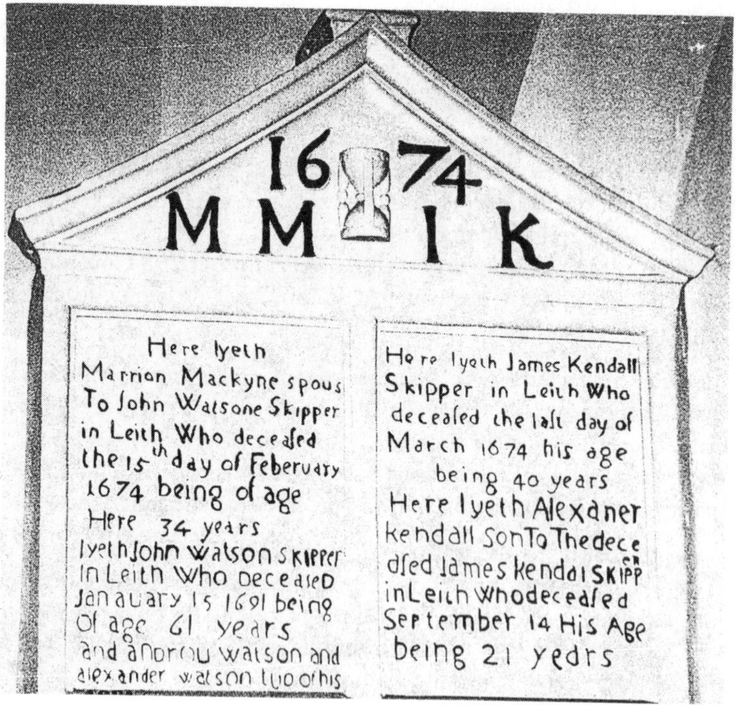

Double memorial in South Leith Kirk to two Leith skippers. James Kendall was one of the more successful skippers of his day (Courtesy of Captain J. Thomson).

Trading Patterns

According to Thomas Tucker, Leith had twelve or fourteen ships belonging to her in the 1650s, two or three of 200 - 300 tons, the rest small vessels for carrying salt to England, 'the chief part of the trade of these parts being driven thence, the rest being from Norway, the East-land (Baltic) Low Countries or France'.

This pattern of a few large ships, plus a little fleet of barks and boats was one which continued throughout the century. The large vessels undertook the long voyages to the Baltic, Southern France and Spain. Barks and boats sailed to Norway, England and the Netherlands. Barks, however, could vary in burthen between about 50 and 100 tons, and the size of some of the cargoes imported from London and the Netherlands shows that the vessels which carried them were not all that small.

Barks may have carried a lot of salt to London from Leith at the time when Tucker was writing, but the existing Customs records make very little mention of this commodity. Admittedly, the sample is small, only seven years between 1666 and 1690, but other goods appear far more frequently. Another surprising omission is that of coal. It only appears in four years out of the seven. There is also no mention of salt herring and salmon after 1672. The main exports were cloth and skins. Linen cloth averaged 35,000 ells per year, and woollens 52,780 ells. Sheepskins averaged 17,000 per year and other skins (of dogs, goats and various wild animals) 7,850. Gloves were exported up to 1648 (the import records mention materials for perfuming them). The numbers of worsted stockings were counted in thousands of dozens, the total increasing as time went on.

Thousands of oysters went out each year, although the quantity steadily diminished from 721,000 in 1666 to only 10,000 in 1690. Fresh oysters could be transported no further than Flanders, but, pickled and packed in small casks, they went as far afield as Danzig. In 1672, 16,000 lobsters went down to London. One unexpected export was eggs, in barrels containing 50 or 100 dozen. Isinglass, which is used for preserving eggs was one of the varied goods imported from Flanders. Presumably associated with egg production were 'feathers for beds', mainly exported to London.

The destination of the goods was usually London or Flanders. Practically all the skins went to Flanders for instance. Small amounts, especially of cloth and stockings went to the Baltic and Bordeaux. Grain was usually destined for Norway.

A list of imports would need several pages. In the main, their sources remained the same. Spain was the new market at the start of the century, and in the 1660s the New World began to be exploited by Scottish merchants. For the rest: wine came mainly from Bordeaux; flax and tow from Danzig; timber from Norway; tar, pitch and metals from the Baltic - the familiar pattern in fact. This is an over-simplification, of course. Bordeaux, for instance, was also the source of chestnuts and walnuts (measured by the English bushel) and weavers' reeds. Towards the end of the period, unexpected goods such as French wine began to be purchased in Danzig.

Life was becoming more luxurious, and the market for new commodities ever growing. Paper, for instance, was needed in ever-increasing quantities now that more people wanted to read printed books. Much of it came from northern France, along with thousands of 'Coudebeck hats', a fashion accessory that was obviously much in demand. Galls were imported from London by the hundredweight, to make ink. In fact, a list of all the varieties of goods which came from London and Flanders would cover several pages. Here is just a sample:

alum
apothecary wares
barrel hoops
baskets
bells
blue paper
candlesticks
candy sugar
childrens' toys
chocolate
cinnamon
clothes brushes
coffee
combs
corks
cosmetics
curtain rings
dates
drinking glasses
drugs
earthenware
fine furniture
fire irons
floor brushes
garden seeds
grey paper
hat brushes
hatbands
hats
hops
hour glasses
indigo
lantern horns
lemons
linseed oil
loaf sugar
madder
mattresses
nutmeg
onions
oranges
pasteboard
perfumes
pins
potash
printing paper
red lead
sassafras
saucepans
shoes
shovels
smoothing irons
sumach
tea
tobacco
trenchers
turmeric
whalebone
whicker cradles
white lead
wire
woad

The one notable omission is that of fine fabrics. Some velvet, silk and satin was imported, but usually in small quantities for the use of a private individual. The implication is that the rich had their best clothes made elsewhere and that everyone else wore Scottish woollens and linens.

We have already seen that tobacco began coming into Leith at the turn of the century. Until the Restoration it was imported from London and Flanders, but when ships began to sail from Leith to the New World, they brought back cargoes of tobacco and sugar. The first recorded Leith ship to sail to the Americas was Henry Bell's old command, the *Job*. She returned to Leith from Virginia in March 1667, under the command of John Gourlay. On board were 20,500lb of leaf tobacco, consigned to two Edinburgh merchants. One of her crew, George Allan, had brought back 150lb of tobacco on his own account. In the following September the *Express* of London arrived with a cargo of ginger, and sugar - white, powdered and unrefined.

In order to ensure that all these goods ended up at the correct destinations, each merchant's consignment on a ship was entered on a bill of lading. Skippers

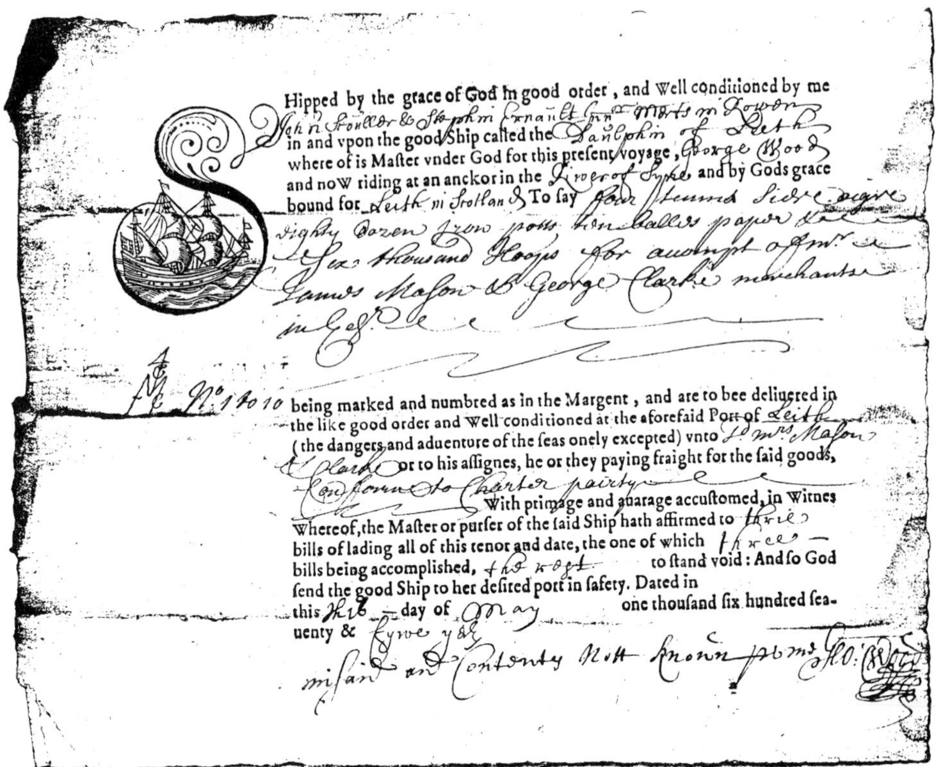

Hipped by the grace of God in good order, and Well conditioned by me John Fowler & Stephen Arnault merts in Rowen in and vpon the good Ship called the Dolphin of Leith whereof is Maſter vnder God for this preſent voyage, George Wood and noW riding at an anckor in the River of Syne and by Gods grace bound for Leith in Scotland To ſay four ... eighty dozen iron potts ten balles paper ... Six thousand hoops for account of mr. James Mason & George Clarke merchants in Edr.

No 1 to 10 being marked and numbred as in the Margent, and are to bee deliuered in the like good order and Well conditioned at the aforeſaid Port of Leith (the dangers and aduenture of the ſeas onely excepted) vnto sd mrs Mason & Clarke or to his aſſignes, he or they paying fraight for the ſaid goods, Conforme to Charter pairty With primage and auarage accuſtomed, in Witnes Whereof, the Maſter or purſer of the ſaid Ship hath affirmed to three bills of lading all of this tenor and date, the one of which three bills being accompliſhed, the rest to ſtand void: And ſo God ſend the good Ship to her deſired port in ſafety. Dated in this 16 day of May one thouſand ſix hundred ſea-uenty & fyve yrs

... Contents Nott known ... Geo: Wood

A bill of lading dated 1675, for goods shipped from Rouen to Leith, in the *Dolphin* of Leith, George Wood master (By courtesy of Edinburgh City Archive).

seem to have carried a supply of these documents, because even those issued at foreign ports are written in English. By the last two decades of the century, bills of lading were printed documents, with spaces left for the relevant details to be filled in. In some cases the initial S was very ornate, with a picture of a ship filling the lower curve of the letter. The wording followed a standard pattern of which the following is an example:

> Shipped by the Grace of God in good order and well conditioned by ***Jan Kembillo merchant in Amsterdam*** in and upon the good ship called the ***Lyon of Leith*** whereof is Master under God for this present voyage ***James Kendall*** now riding at anchor in the ***Road of Rotterdam*** and by God's grace bound for ***Leith in Scotland*** to say ***one matted pack*** being marked and numbered as in the margin [***merchant's mark***] and are to be delivered in good order and well conditioned at the aforsaid Port of ***Leith in Scotland*** (the danger of the seas only excepted) unto ***Alexander Baird Merchant in Edinburgh*** or to ***his*** assigns, he or they paying freight for the said goods ***according as others pay*** with primage and avarage accustomed. In witness whereof the Master or purser of the said Ship hath affirmed to three Bills of Lading, all of this tenor and date, the one of which three

Bills being accomplished the other two to stand void. And so God send the good Ship to her desired port in safety. Dated in ***Rotterdam the 27 [ ] 1690***

The rather meagre surviving records show large fluctuations in the number of ships coming into Leith each year. The figures culled from the Prime Gilt records may be low (between 37 and 63) because of the difficulty of ensuring that every ship paid its dues. On the other hand, the Customs accounts, which are presumably more accurate, give only 55 for 1689 and 60 for 1690, so the Prime Gilt figures may not be so very far from the mark. These figures, however, are only for ships engaging in foreign trade, whose cargoes paid Great Custom. The records of the Shoredues for 1638/9 (and to a lesser extent the Prime Gilt accounts) reveal the extent of coastal shipping coming into Leith.

The bulk of these vessels were bringing cereals, in quantities varying from 10 to 30 chalders (20 to 60 tons). The grain was mostly bere and malt for brewing, and rather less oats or oatmeal. Only a small proportion was wheat. Comparatively little was from southern Scotland: 130 chalders of bere/oats and 20 chalders of wheat from Dunbar; 69 chalders of oats/bere from Eyemouth; 75 chalders of bere/oats and 12 chalders of wheat from North Berwick. The ports of the Forth provided 189 chalders of grain altogether. By far the most came from the northeast. There was even 133 chalders of bere and malt from Orkney. The quantities arriving from just the northern ports are as follows:

	Chalders of Grain
Arbroath	66
Banff	31
Caithness	84
Cromarty	48
Cruden	64
Downe	282
Erroll	123
Findhorn	9
Fraserborough	97
Montrose	272
Gordon	43
Newburgh	156
Peterhead	119
Stonehaven	25
Tain	4
Thurso	27
Aberdeen	31
St Andrews	17
Dundee	122
TOTAL	1619
OVERALL TOTAL	2247 chalders (4494 tons)

The other indigenous goods were fish - both salt and dried - hides, skins and salt beef, but grain, mainly for local consumption, was by far the major item.

Apart from the merchantmen and the grain boats and barks, the other main category of vessels was the boats which brought in coal, peat and slates. They paid anchorages of between 2s and 6d 8d (ships paid anything up to £1 3s 4d). Over the year there were 214 entries for these boats, some of which appear more than once.

During the century, Leith saw a number of enterprises by individuals who set up manufacturies of goods that had formerly only been obtainable abroad. Starch, soap, glass, pins, tobacco, sugar and linen were all made or processed with varying degrees of success. Of more interest to the seafaring community were the ropeworks which were started, first at Newhaven in 1638 and then in Leith itself in 1682 and 1694.

In 1674, Edward Burd, skipper of Leith and burgess of Edinburgh, petitioned the Council for permission to keep a shop in Leith to sell 'necessities for ships'. According to him, ships and men were often in danger on foreign voyages until they could get to a place where they could obtain supplies. A bonus of his scheme was that much of his merchandise could be made in Scotland, thus providing employment. The list of goods that he intended to sell shows that he was hardly intending to be a ships' chandler as we would understand the term: iron guns, bullets, chain shot, stink pots, hand grenades, linstocks, priming irons, powder barrels, gun wheels, cannon powder, blunderbusses, cartridge moulds and diameters for cannon sights. In the following year he was forbidden to sell goods in his shop which could be made by the trades of Edinburgh, Canongate and Leith. The prohibition was passed while he was away at sea. When he returned he explained to the Council that the trouble had been stirred up by two Leith anchor-smiths, and undertook to sell only goods made by local tradesmen. Under these conditions he was allowed to continue.

The Darien Scheme

The growing entrepreneurial spirit of the seventeenth century confined itself to individuals for most of the period, but in the last decade it found a more ambitious outlet. As early as 1681, a memorial to the Committee of Trade in Scotland had recommended the setting up of a colony on Cape Florida, but the idea was not seriously considered until the 1690s. In 1693, the Committee made firm proposals for the establishment of overseas trade. In 1695, King William sanctioned the setting up of the 'Company of Scotland Trading to Africa and the Indies'. The actual intention was to found a colony (to be called New Caledonia) on the Darien Isthmus, through which the Panama Canal would be cut a couple of centuries later. The mention of Africa and the Indies unfortunately attracted the hostility of the powerful East India Company, which threw its financial and political weight into efforts to defeat the designs of the Scots.

In June 1696, however, Scottish hopes were high. Alexander Stevenson, merchant burgess and skipper of Edinburgh, and James Gibson, his counterpart in Glasgow, were commissioned to buy and have built suitable ships for the expedition. Four were built at Hamburg, all of 350 tons and carrying 56 guns. Two of them, the *Caledonia* and the *Installation* were launched in March 1697, their outfitting not being completed until Michaelmas. The other two were launched a month after the first pair, but were destined to remain in Hamburg until the following year. At the same time, two more ships of the same size were being built in Amsterdam, the *Rising Sun* and the *Unicorn.* The two vessels from Hamburg arrived in the Forth in November, when the *Installation* was renamed the *St Andrew.* The *Unicorn* sailed from Amsterdam, but the *Rising Sun* was still there in March 1698, frozen into the ice.

Early in 1698, the Company bought a small ship in England - presumably the pink *Endeavour*, which sailed from Leith Roads with *Caledonia, St Andrew* and *Unicorn* in July 1698. On board the four ships were 1200 settlers. They arrived at 'the great harbour of Caledonia' on 4 November. In September 1699, five more ships left for Darien from the Clyde, one of them being the *Rising Sun.* They were not to know that the first expedition had failed, owing largely to disease and lack of supplies. The latter was blamed on an English policy of refusing to sell the Scottish settlers necessities at her West Indian colonies. The policy had been forced on King William by powerful vested interests such as the East India Company which viewed the Scottish venture as a threat to its trade. The same pressure had prevented English investment in the scheme, which would have put it on a sounder financial basis.

On 11 November 1699, *Caledonia* arrived in the Sound of Isla, with just 200 survivors. *Endeavour* had been lost, *Unicorn* was badly damaged and laid up in New Jersey, *St Andrew* had been left at Darien. The second expedition established itself at Darien, but came under attack by the Spaniards and was forced to capitulate in March 1700. The Company continued to send one or two ships a year to Africa or India, but it was never a commercial success. The loss of Scottish capital through the Darien disaster was a major factor in the economic weakening of the country, which was to lead to political union with England in 1707.

10

The Carpenters

Whether they knew it or not, and they probably did not, Leith shipbuilders at the beginning of the eighteenth century already had hundreds of years of history behind them. John Cornton, who was living in St Leonard's Lands in 1439, is the first *named* shipwright in the port, who probably worked on the barge which James I had built at Leith in 1433. His predecessors have left no record of their activities, so we cannot tell when the craft first came to Leith. It may be that the Flemings who were brought over by David I to help establish his new Royal Burghs, included shipbuilders among their number, who built vessels at his port of Leith. Many of the names of parts of ships used in Old Scots, such as 'rais' (yards) and 'jungfrau' (deadeyes) have their origin in the Low Countries.

Indeed the term 'timbermen' which we have encountered from the fifteenth century onward, was one of these Low Country loan words. By the start of the eighteenth century it had been replaced by the name 'carpenters'. The traditional name had all but died out in Britain, although it persisted in Northern Europe. (When Eric Newby served on a Scandinavian grain ship just before the Second World War, the vessel's carpenter was called the 'tymmerman'.) By the end of the eighteenth century, the modern term 'shipbuilder' was in common use in Leith, but his workplace was called the 'Carpenter's Yard', and his workmen, carpenters.

We have already noted the existence of the Society of Carpenters in North Leith. The very fact that they called themselves 'Carpenters' suggests that the Society was formed near the end of the seventeenth century. The Mariners' Society of North Leith seems to have amalgamated with Trinity House in 1691 or soon after, and it may have been at this time that the Society of Carpenters was formed to take care of its own poor.

Seafaring in Leith tended to be a family tradition. The same surnames recurr repeatedly among the skippers and mariners of the Port, sometimes after a lapse of several generations. Shipbuilders, however, came and went. After the Cornton dynasty died out in the late sixteenth century, the craft seldom persisted for more than a couple of generations in any one family.

As with any other craft, shipbuilders relied on demand for their product, but they were particularly vulnerable to changes in trading patterns. We have already noted various seventeenth century documents which link the state of shipbuilding to the state of trade when they were written. In the eighteenth century the same picture continues. At the end of the 1740s, sources begin to speak of a rapid increase in Scottish trade. The number and size of Leith ships increased dramatically and shipbuilding followed the trend.

During the eighteenth century the Royal Navy continued to provide work for Leith carpenters. In 1707 a French flotilla bearing the Stewart Pretender to the throne of Britain alarmed the Government by visiting the east coast of Scotland. In 1709, in response to threats to shipping from French privateers, the Lord High Admiral conferred the command of HM ships in North Britain on the Provost of Edinburgh. This command continued until the signing of the Treaty of Utrecht in 1713. There was sporadic convoy activity throughout the century, until in 1777 a period began during which British shipping was under threat, at different times, from America, Spain, Holland and France. From this date until the Battle of Waterloo in 1815 brought to an end the Napoleonic Wars, regular convoys sailed from Leith. It was the local carpenters who carried out any repairs and refits of naval vessels which could not wait until they returned to the Naval Dockyards in England. In 1781 a small Naval Yard was established, employing 250 men to supply HM ships calling at the port.

Shipbuilding in the Early Eighteenth Century

In 1710, Edinburgh presented a petition to Queen Anne for permission to raise money to improve the facilities of the harbour. They wanted to attract more shipping to Leith because trade in the City had diminished after the Union of Scotland and England in 1707. The Privy Council was no more, and Scots Members now attended Parliament in London. Consequently, the 'considerable persons' of Scottish society resided mainly in England and Edinburgh was suffering from the loss of their custom. The petition included the suggestion that wet and dry docks should be built; 'for the convenience of building, fitting and careening HM ships of war and trading vessels' - the Provost was taking his new duties as Admiral seriously!

Commissioners for the Navy had surveyed the Forth in 1708 (producing a plan of Leith in the following year) but to Edinburgh's dismay, had concluded that South Queensferry would be a more suitable site for development. The Council asked the Masters of the Trinity House to prepare a report showing that in fact Leith would be preferable to any other place on the Forth. In February 1709, the Council received the report, which included these observations on the current state of shipbuilding in Leith:

> That as for dry docks, there are two or three large and convenient places on the north side of the said harbour which may be formed with as little charge as anywhere in Britian, the ground being only clay and sand, where there is already a great deal of conveniences built, both for carpenters, ships' stores and others. Yea, ships of 30 or 40 guns have been dressed in the said docks as they are now. Also between the west pier and the old middle pier called the Ballast Quay (ie, at the Sandport), there might be a convenient launch made for building, dressing and cleaning of ships at a small charge.

The Council used the Masters' report as the basis of its petition to the Queen. Permission to improve the Harbour was granted, but no money was forthcoming from the Treasury and the scheme languished. In 1717 an Act of Parliament was passed which empowered Edinburgh to raise the money needed to finance the proposed works. Although the Council borrowed heavily, little of the grand design was realised. All that happened was that a stone extension 1200 feet long and 24 feet broad, was built in 1720, onto the existing wooden pier. The historian Maitland, writing 40 years later, commented that the work was so badly done that some parts fell down even before they were finished, it needed constant repair and would probably be completely ruinous within a few years. (Fortunately he was wrong in his speculation.) This was the first of several improvement schemes mooted during the century, none of which came to fruition.

At the time of Edinburgh's petition there are records of three shipbuilders working in North Leith, in the 'two or three large and convenient places' mentioned in the Trinity House report.

Robert Davies

Robert Davies leased a yard on the downriver side of the Abbot's Bridge. He had made a prudent first marriage, to Janet Livingstone, daughter and heiress of the Court of Session Clerk. In April 1709 he was made a Burgess and Guildbrother of Edinburgh, by right of his wife. The next year, Davies renewed a petition to the Edinburgh Council for permission to build a more convenient dock for repairing large ships and to erect mooring posts. (There was already a dock, known as Lyon's Dock and measuring 60ft by 24ft, to the east of Davies' yard, which seems to have been built in the last quarter of the previous century.) Robert Davies had previously approached the Council about this matter, and they had surveyed the site and approved his plans, but had not yet given him the go-ahead. Because of this delay he had already lost contracts to repair several small merchant ships, which had gone to Queensferry instead. The Council granted his request, with the proviso that if their current negotiations for a Royal grant to build a dock came to fruition, the tack would be void. Two years later, Edinburgh granted Davies a 12-year contract to build and maintain their two ballast boats.

Robert Davies dock has caused some confusion among historians of Leith, who have followed an early nineteenth century writer in assuming that it was the dry dock which was built on the same site 64 years later. Robert Davies did make a dock, which was later referred to as 'the waste ground...of old a Dock or harbour'. However, at this date, a dock was a rudimentary affair, consisting, as in the previous century, of a wall or walls built out from the land to enclose an area of the riverbed and make a small private harbour.

A petition presented to the Edinburgh Council in the middle of the eighteenth century reveals the primitive nature of shipbuilding docks at this time. The premises in question, which lay behind the Sherrif Brae and were owned by Mary Cairns, the widow of a tobacco merchant, were purchased by Edinburgh in advance of one of their chimeric improvement schemes. The two docks

The 'Carpenter's Stone' from a house, possibly built by Robert Davies, which stood near St Ninian's chapel. The vessel on the stocks is probably one of the barks or sloops which were the main type of vessel built in Leith at the time.

there lay unused for three years while the City made up its mind what to do with the land. In the end it was sold back to Mary, who petitioned for compensation for the damage done to it by neglect.

> as part of the subjects sold were two docks for building ships, lying upon the Water of Leith, which by reason of spates of the river and high floods, occasions an yearly repair, but being neglected all the time that this affair was depending before the commissioners, it has now cost your petitioner a considerable sum to put these two docks and the other fences of her grounds exposed to the water, in the same condition they were in at the time of the purchase ... The channel of the river near to those docks was almost covered with large stones, which both served as a bulwark to the docks and the other fences of her grounds, and were also a quarry at hand for repairing them. However, immediately after the several purchases were made, with a view to improve the said harbour the whole channel of the river was cleaned and the above large stones were taken away....and applied for the Town's use. By which means the petitioner has not only lost the advantage of the above natural bulwarks, but must unavoidably be put to a constant expense of purchasing and bringing stones from a distance for their repair.

On a map of the area made some 15 years later, there appears a dock of the type which Mary Cairns seems to have been talking about. It consists simply of a wall built out nearly parallel with the bank in the direction of the flow of the river, forming a short narrow funnel of protected water where small vessels could be moored while under repair. There may have been a slip at the head of this constricted dock where boats could be hauled out of the water. Davies himself took advantage of the fact that the river bank below his yard had a right-angled 'kink' in it to form two sides of his proposed dock.

It may have been Robert Davies who built the house whose date stone bore the inscription, 'God bless the Carpenter of North Leith who built this house in 1715'. The house in question, described as a 'mansion' stood near St Ninians' Chapel, facing onto North Leith High Street. The stone was removed at the beginning of the nineteenth century and built into the wall of a house in Coburg Street. It also showed the emblem of the Carpenters' Society - a ship with three strakes, and flags fore and aft - and bore its motto, 'Trahunter siccas machinae carinae'.

In 1718, Davies married for the second time. In the marriage contract he is styled 'HM Shipbuilder in Leith' (probably appointed by the Provost during his Admiral phase). It seems his dock improvements had paid off. Shortly after his marriage he bought the land behind the Sherrif Brae, which later belonged to Mary Cairns. Five years after his marriage, Robert Davies died, leaving his widow with four young children, a boy (who died in childhood) and three daughters. At his death he had a small vessel on the stocks worth £300 scots. The inventory compiled by his widow was very detailed, and the list of the contents of his yard evokes a picture which will be familiar to anyone who has ever visited a traditional boatbuilder:

New oak timber	£25
309 deals at 6d each	£ 9
a new boat	£ 4
All the other timber, with boats, masts, bollack, sheaves and oars	£ 6
The wreck of an old pink	£12
Two anchors, about 13cwt in all	£ 9 15s
Another old anchor	£ 1
An old capstan	5s
Five pitch pots in furnaces	£ 1 5s
Two small pots	4s
A parcel of old blocks	10s
A parcel of old ropes in two lofts	£ 2
Four millstones and two grindstones	£ 1

(All the monetary values are in sterling. This will be the case from now on. Scots money will be indicated where appropriate.)

The contents of Davies' yard did not comprise his entire stock. Shipbuilders in Leith were always short of space in which to store their timber, and used every available close, yard and wasteland they could find. Robert Davies stored quite a lot in his own garden, mainly masts and spars, notably the main, fore and mizzen masts of 'the old pink'. Below his Summer House was a pile of firewood, including 'an old broken boat'. He kept more old timber in the Sherrif Brae and at the back of North Leith Kirk (St Ninian's chapel). There is no mention of tools in his inventory, in fact they are only mentioned in one out of the dozen or so eighteenth century carpenters' inventories. Walter Goalen (1792) had a parcel of work tools worth £1 5s. The implication is that shipbuilding tools were fairly basic and of small value, even by the end of the century.

The Robertsons

A contemporary of Robert Davies was James Robertson. He was the only North Leith shipbuilder at this time who owned his own yard, along with several other properties in the town. He was also a prominent member of St Ninians Kirk Session, being elected treasurer in the early 1690s, in spite of his protests that his business kept him fully occupied. Robertson and his first wife, Helen Law, bought a waterside waste ground, tenement and garden in North Leith in 1697. The waste ground had been given to the Kirk Session by the late David Durie 'for the use of the poor.' Durie was also a carpenter, who had been working in North Leith in the 1680s.

In 1704, James Robertson and his second wife, Margaret Gray, bought from James Law of Hillhousefield, the:

> foreland, backland, stable and houses on both sides of the Close called *Short's Wynd*, with the yard at the head of the said Wynd and the Quay of the Harbour of Leith at the foot of the said foreland, bounding with the said harbour in a straight line.'

To the west of this property lay the land which had once been occupied by the carpenter William Coustean, who had been in such trouble with the Edinburgh Council in the previous century, for trying to build out a dock into the harbour. William was now long dead, and in 1704 his land belonged to the skipper Edward Laing.

James Robertson built a 30-foot ferry boat for the Skippers' Society of North Leith in 1691. He repaired the pilot boat for Trinity House in 1700, and in the same year built the *Margaret* for the skipper Thomas Weir. He also repaired the Ballast boat for Edinburgh in 1710 and the pilot boat again in 1712. In the first half of 1714, James Robertson died, his only heir being a daughter (Isobel) by his second wife. His business seems to have been carried on by Patrick Robertson, possibly his brother. Patrick was later joined by another James Robertson, who was probably his son, as Patrick died in 1747 and James lived for a further 40 years. Two years before his death, Patrick Robertson leased a dwelling house facing the Glasshouse and a building yard to James Warden junior, another carpenter (see below).

There was also a Peter Robertson building ships in South Leith in the 1720s, in a dock behind the Sherrif Brae, an area which had probably been used for shipbuilding since the days of the carpenter John Cornton, whose house was nearby in 1439. The size of vessels built there would always, however, have been limited by the need to get them under the Bridge after launching.

James Beattie

The third shipbuilder known to have been working in North Leith in 1710, was James Beattie. He enters the record in 1703, when he built the bark *John* of Leith. His yard seems to have lain to the south of Broad Wynd and contained Lyon's Dock. James Beattie died in 1733, and it is clear from his testament that he was a man of some affluence. Of all his contemporaries, his is the name which appears most frequently in the Admiralty records, and other sources suggest that in fact he was probably the busiest carpenter in North Leith. His yard was a training ground for the shipbuilders of the future. In a dispute with Robert Davies in 1715 over some timber, one of Beattie's witnesses was his employee James Warden, father of the carpenter of the same name who leased a yard from Patrick Robertson later in the century. Two more of his men bore surnames which will appear again in this account; James Young, David Dryburgh. He also employed a Peter Robertson - possibly the man who has just been mentioned as working in the Sherrif Brae five years later.

Leith Shipbuilding up to 1738

John Young, who died in 1731, was probably the contemporary of the last three. His yard, like Peter Robertson's, was in South Leith, above the Abbot's Bridge. In spite of the handicap of having to get his vessels under the bridge, he built up to 70 tons, and an average of 100 tons per year.

John Young, James Beattie and Peter and Patrick Robertson all appear in the Gold Penny records, which survive for ten of the years between 1726 and 1738. Gold Penny was a duty paid to Edinburgh on all ships built or sold at Leith. During these particular years it was levied at the rate of 3d sterling (3s Scots) per ton burthen.

Peter Robertson and James Beattie both built ships of 100 tons in 1726/7, but this was not repeated. The more usual size built was between 20 and 40 tons, but individual vessels might be as large as 70 tons or as small as 12 tons. James Beattie was the busiest. He never built fewer than three ships in a year, in 1732 he built five. Most of the carpenters built two or three vessels a year, sometimes having two on the stocks at a time. Each ship took four or five months to complete up to the launching stage, after which she would be rigged. In the years before 1733, the average yearly tonnage built was 410. After this date although there was one extra regular shipbuilder in Leith, the average yearly tonnage dropped to 330. The actual yearly figure fluctuated between 200 and 435 tons.

Leith men were capable of building much larger ships, like the 300 ton vessel built at the end of the previous century, but the demand at this time was mainly for small coasters. Some owners came from Forth ports such as Alloa, North Queensferry, Inverkeithing, Burntisland, Carron, Kincardine and Kinghorn. Their vessels were probably coal barks in the main. Some were from further afield: Perth, St Andrews, Arbroath, Fortrose, Peterhead, Portsoy, Banff, even Westray and Stenness in Orkney.

Much of the timber used in the ships was bought from timber merchants. They imported mainly from Norway, although such exotica as mahogany, walnut and redwood were becoming more common. Some shipbuilders also imported direct from Norway, especially the 'crukit timber' used for the ribs of ships. However, more native timber was becoming available, and this the shipbuilders bought direct from the suppliers. In 1727, sixteen tons of oak came into Leith from the Moray Firth and some from Portsoy. Just over three months before his death, in March 1731, John Young contracted with William Law of Erroll to buy 'the old planting growing upon the estate of Erroll' for 4500 merks scots (£60 sterling). A later shipbuilder, Thomas Willison, bought 'crukit' oak timber from the woods of Newbottle in 1752. Quite large amounts of oak and other timber came from ports in Fife and from Bo'ness. Some of this wood originated in Norway, but some may have been grown nearer home.

Repair Work

It is all too easy to forget that the actual building of ships was only a part of the carpenter's trade. Much of his work, probably the bulk of it, involved cleaning and repairing many of the hundreds of vessels which visited Leith each year. The 'outredding' accounts for ships invariably include payments to a carpenter for work done to make the vessels seaworthy. Wooden ships were subject not only to encrustation with barnacles but also to attack by wood-boring organisms. They had to be periodically careened - beached and heeled over so that the hull could be scraped and tarred. Quick, hot fires of whin stalks were used to burn off much of the encrustation of sea creatures and a whin-stack was an important adjunct to a shipyard. Pitch and tar were the universal water-proofing agents, but they could not preserve ropes and timber for ever. Rigging and woodwork needed constant renewal. Storm and collision damage had to be made good.

If just one carpenter's account book had survived, we would have a better picture of this side of the business. As it is, we can get glimpses from the lists of debtors in their testaments. For example, James Warden (1745) was owed money by fifteen ships masters, including £4 11s 3d by the commander of the Custom House Yatch. Robert Davies (1724) was also owed by the commander of the Custom House Yatch, in this case the debt totalled £74. James Beattie (1733) was owed money by ten ships masters for work done on their ships and by eight others to whom he seems to have acted as a banker.

The Next Generation

Until the death of John Young in 1731, he, James Beattie and Peter and Patrick Robertson were the only carpenters actually building ships in Leith. James Jamieson appears in the record after John Young's death. His yard lay next to a piece of wasteland on the north side of the foot of Broad Wynd. His may be the ornate tomb North Leith burial ground, of an unnamed carpenter who died in 1749 aged 59 years. The dates of the deaths of most of his contemporaries are known, and it was in 1749 that John Sime bought the yard which Jamison had occupied. In 1766 Jamison's two sons, both merchants in Leith, inherited some property in Broad Wynd (South Leith). One of them, John Jamison, seems to have become a successful timber merchant.

In 1732, John Tod started in business. By 1738 he had become the Boxmaster of the Society of Carpenters of Leith. At some time between 1710 and 1726 the Society of Carpenters had acquired a tenement on the east side of Broad Wynd, whose rents (£9 10s per year in total) helped to swell their funds.

After James Beattie died in 1733, three new builders started to pay Gold Penny. One of them, John Sime, married James' widow Margaret Gordon only a few months after his death, and presumably took over his yard. In James' will, dated two years before his death, he mentions two sons, James and John. James died before 1747. John was still a minor in that year, but he either died young or took up some trade other than shipbuilding. John Sime had been apprenticed in Leith at some time around 1720, so was probably in his thirties when he took over the yard. It is possible that James Beattie had been his master. John Sime's first marriage had ended by 1748, by which time he was married to Margaret Hogg. She was the mother of his son John, who later became his partner and subsequently took over the business. Margaret Gordon lived until 1797, being described in her testament as the first wife of the late John Sime senior and widow of the late James Beattie. She must have been very young when she married James. No record has been found of any divorce of John Sime and Margaret Gordon. It may be that she had been his wife merely as a result of a 'handfasting'; legal but more easily repudiated.

Patrick Robertson owned two yards, one of them being next to the North Leith Glasshouse (glassworks). When James Warden junior set up in business in 1733 he leased the Glasshouse yard from Patrick. When he died, in 1745, he had only just renewed the lease. He had also had some connection with James Beattie, who left him 500 merks scots in his will. It was James Warden who built the *Edinburgh and Glasgow Concert*, a packet boat of 50 tons, which was launched in August 1736. The year before his death, James Warden leased Patrick Robertson's house and garden which stood at the head of his yard. The house had two stories and contained five rooms, including a dining room with two cellars beneath, overlooking the Glasshouse. When James Warden died his household goods were inventoried and valued by Janet Sutherland, a sailor's widow, and the contents of his yard - some new timber and two wrecks - by John Sime. His books were valued at 15s by Gideon Crawford, a bookseller. Six of them were connected with his business:

Mair's	'Book-keeping'
Wilson's	'Navigation'

Park's	'Art of Sea Fighting'
Bomain's	'Description of the Coast of Guinea'
Cole's	Dictionary
De Chale's	Euclid

Most were theological works:

Ambrose's	'War With Devils'
Taylor's	'Holy Living and Holy Dying'
Patrick's	'The Devout Christian'
Guthrie's	'The Saving Interest'
Marshal's	'The Gospel Mystery' (newly published that year)
Durham's	'The Unsearchable Riches of Christ'
Scougall's	'The Life of God in the Soul of Man'

He also possessed Camden's 'Antiquities'

Patrick Robertson himself died two years after James Warden. In the same year, the North Leith Glasshouse which stood near his yard was burnt down and the Glasshouse Company moved to a site in South Leith to the east of the Timber Bush, which became the centre of a flourishing glass manufactury in Leith.

The Second Half of the Century

Thomas Willison built a vessel of 20 tons in 1733, after which no more is heard of him until 1751, when he and John Willison (probably his son) were building a ship at the Sandport, for the newly formed Edinburgh and London Shipping Company. The Company provided more regular sailings to London than the packet boats which had operated since 1720. The ship which the Willisons were building for them was probably one of their 200 ton brigs. These vessels were uncomfortable and slow and the introduction of fast, commodious smacks later in the century was hailed as a great advance. In 1756, the Willisons occupied the yard on the west side of the foot of Broad Wynd in North Leith; their tenancy at the Sandport was possibly a temporary arrangement for the building of a large vessel. John Willison was still in business in the same yard in 1770, but he does not figure in the Edinburgh and Leith Directory published in 1773, so may have died or gone out of business by that date.

By the middle of the eighteenth century, trade at Leith was on the increase, and the number of shipbuilders began to expand. In 1751 five merchants presented a memorial to the Edinburgh Council, showing:

> That the want of a sufficient number of able ship builders and carpenters in this country has been long the subject of universal complaint, and as the spirit of trade has for some time past prevailed and every day seems to increase, that particular branch must of course increase also and the want of able builders will be the more sensibly felt.

> That Mr James Crawford, shipbuilder and carpenter from London, and who served his apprenticeship at Leith, has lately come down here at the request of the memorialists and other traders, in order to carry on his business. And as your memorialists are humbly of the opinion that he may be accommodated with docks for building and repairing ships at Leith. This memorial is humbly offered to the Honourable Council to entreat that they would cause the North side of the harbour of Leith be carefully inspected and allow to Mr Crawford what shall appear to them most convenient for his purpose upon such terms and conditions as they shall think proper.
>
> The memorialists beg leave to observe that of late some gentlemen who have been several years improving themselves in the art of Shipbuilding and Draughting, both in the King's and merchants' docks at London, have frequently signified their inclinations of settling here, and were always discouraged for want of docks. And the Honourable Council will easily perceive that such discouragement to able tradesmen must be a great loss to the trade of this place. As it must in some measure be a bar to future improvements in that valuable branch of trade and may be a means of carrying it to some other part of the country.

The Committee appointed to look into the question found that all the harbourside yards in North Leith were fully occupied. James Crawford was granted a strip of land 60 feet wide a the Sandport, to the west of the Willisons, for which he was not to be charged rent for the first two years. However, the land in question was the subject of a dispute between Edinburgh and John Sime, so Crawford was not able to get possession of it. He managed to get a lease of a small yard next to John Sime's, but it was not large enough to accommodate ships of any size. In 1753 the Sime dispute had been decided in favour of Edinburgh and the Shipping Company no longer had any use for their ground at the Sandport. Crawford successfully petitioned for the ground which the Company had vacated. By the following year he had also obtained the yard next to the Bridge. The Willisons occupying the yard to the east of him. His name appears in Williamson's first Edinburgh and Leith Directory, in 1773 - the last record of his presence in Leith.

The mention of the 'draughting' of ships in Robert Crawford's petition and James Warden's posession of a volume of Euclid, shows that this new generation of shipbuilders was no longer using the 'rule of thumb' approach which had been the norm in shipbuilding in previous centuries. The spread of literacy and the publication of a number of books on Marine Architecture in the eighteenth century brought more scientific methods within the reach of even the humblest carpenter.

Improvement Schemes

In 1754, Edinburgh came up with another scheme for improving the harbour. The original idea was to cut through or demolish the Abbot's Bridge and make a sluice at the New Quay (a short projection which had been built out from the

Shore just below the Coalhill) to create a basin further upriver. It was at this stage that the unfortunate Mary Cairns sold her land in Sherrif Brae to Edinburgh. Two of her neighbours, whose lands were not acquired by the City, were Hugh Wood, carpenter, and William Taylor, boatbuilder. Hugh Wood died in 1760, but his son, also Hugh, was already in business as a merchant and did not follow his father into the shipbuilding traae. William Taylor built a pilot boat for the City in 1764. When he died in 1774, he had just built a new tender for the Customs Yatch.

According to the City's 1754 plans, the new basin was to contain, 'docks, wharves, quays and other proper conveniences ... for building, repairing, loading, unloading, wintering and laying up of ships and vessels.' The plan would enable 'ships of burthen' to be built upriver, suggesting that facilities in North Leith were now pushed to their limit.

The Adam brothers, John, James and Robert were approached by the Council for their help, but they were busy working on Hopeton House and declined the invitation in a letter to the Lord Provost. It seems that they had also been somewhat put out by their previous treatment at the hands of the City Council.

> My Lord
>
> We had the honour of Your Lordship's letter yesterday. We have been solicited at different times by different members of the Committee for Improving the Harbour of Leith to give our opinions and plans for directing the proper manner of making the alterations there. This, they seemed to imagine, would occasion small avocation from our present business. It might indeed be so were we to do it slightly, but this would be little to our credit or their advantage, and to do it to purpose, your Lordship well knows, could not be the work of a day.
>
> We are so sensible of your Lordship's friendship that a hint alone would prevail with us in this affair if we were not at the same time persuaded that it would not be agreeable to your Lordship to see us engaged in anything so inconvenient and hurtful to ourselves as this would certainly be, by drawing our attention from those other works your Lordship knows we are presently engaged in.
>
> We formerly refused several private works of importance that were offered us at a time when we were made to believe that we were to be employed in the execution of the public buildings in Town, that we might have the more time to direct them to purpose. But when that was over we engaged in other business that now takes up all our time and attention. Nor did we expect from the manner in which this was done, ever to be applied to again by the Town, either to design or undertake for them, when they could find so many people of their own whom they could trust with affairs of consequence, and indeed your Lordship will easily believe we were far from regretting this, when we found it was only in cases of trouble and difficulty that we were to be consulted, but where profit promised to arrive, that must be thrown into other hands. Besides this, those designs we lately gave them have been so altered that we now wish sincerely they may not go under our names.

Thus my Lord, we have laid before you Lordship our reasons for declining this affair and we persuade ourselves they will appear in so strong a light that it will sufficiently excuse our not complying with a request from you Lordship to them who have the honour to be with the greatest gratitude and esteem

My Lord
Your Lordship's
Most Faithful and Most Obedient
humble servants

Jno Robt & Jas Adam

The first plan of the Council was scrapped, to be replaced by another, involving the building of docks on Leith Sands, but this also came to nothing for lack of finance. The Council had hoped to fund the improvements by means of a levy of between 1d and 6d per ton on goods coming into the harbour. The merchants and ships masters felt that there were already too many impositions charged on their goods by the City and their opposition was sufficient to halt the entire scheme.

Robert Dryburgh

Also in 1754, yet another new shipbuilder appeared in Leith. Robert Drybrough was granted a three-year tack of part of the Sandport, which had been recently vacated by James Crawford and the Willisons. In 1760, he asked for a longer lease. Because he had no security of tenure he had not built a 'proper fence' and the sea was encroaching on his workyard. Much of his timber and plank had been stolen. A new lease was granted, to run for 19 years. Three years later, the Earl of Elgin approached him with a view to building a ship to carry lime. The Earl sent to Shiels near Newcastle for details of the kind of vessel he wanted, and in the meantime informed Robert Drybrough that:

> I don't expect hearing anything about the affair until the end of the week, therefore thought it proper to let you know that you might take any other work in hand in the meantime. Let me know by the bearer if you could build a vessel with a deeper hold than five foot and a half under the beam, and to draw but four foot water when load(ed).'

While he was negotiating with the Earl, Drybrough secured a contract to build a ship for HM Excise. She was launched in November 1764, and according to the Edinburgh Evening Courant was 'the most elegant in point of construction and shape ever to be built in Scotland'.

Friction

By 1766, two more shipbuilders had set up in business in North Leith, James Donaldson and Charles Hay. They probably worked on the piece of land between the Ballast Quay and the Glasshouse Quay, where a later Hay had a boatbuilding yard in 1790. This was, indeed, probably the only piece of land available at the time. Together, the six North Leith carpenters petitioned the Council in 1766 for its help in a dispute with one of their neighbours. At the end of the seventeenth century a ropewalk had been set up which extended along the high water mark from the Citadel to the Sandport. After the ropeworks ceased to operate in about 1720, the North Leith carpenters had been allowed to use the old walk as a site for their whin stacks, 'as being the only place of safety, and least hazardous to the town of North Leith.'

One of the properties on the north side of the Street, whose back yard abutted on the ropewalk, had been acquired by a slater, Alexander Ramsay of Edinburgh. Ramsay had set up a tile manufactury in his yard and had been granted permission by the Dean of Guild to make a road for carts to bring sand to his works from the Citadel and part of the Ropewalk. He was now demanding that the carpenters remove some of their whin stacks to make way for his road.

The Council came down on the side of the carpenters, possibly annoyed that Ramsay had gone over their heads to the Dean of Guild. This was, however, the start of a running feud between Ramsay and the carpenters which only ended at the end of the century, when the City repossessed the land in question in preparation for the building of the first Wet Docks.

John Sime and the First Dry Dock

At the time of the carpenters' petition, John Sime, who headed the list of signatures, was the premier shipbuilder in North Leith. He had just taken his son John into partnership. Early in his career, Sime senior had bought and rebuilt a ruinous tenement, which presumably formed his first home. In 1738 he bought a dwelling house, with its waterside yard on which the Glasshouse was later built, and the pier and part of the shore belonging to it. The house was destroyed in the fire which razed the Glasshouse in 1746, but John Sime rebuilt it and added a 'square' of dwelling houses in front of it, possibly to accomodate his workmen. This complex, which was demolished at the turn of the century, was descibed by an eye-witness as an 'imposing tenement'. In 1749 Sime bought four more properties in the same area, including the yard next to the Glasshouse, which had been occupied by James Jamieson. Besides all his own property, he continued to lease the yard he had 'inherited' from James Beattie.

In July 1770, John Sime and son petitioned the Council for permission to build a dry dock in their yard next to the Glasshouse Quay:

> it has often been represented to us by the shipmasters and principal merchants trading to this port, that it was a great loss to the place, the want of a Dry Dock for the repairing and cleaning vessels, more especially those of any burthen, because the men cannot get properly under them and cannot work above three hours in a day for the tides. Secondly it is impossible to get the work near so well done, as it is always wet. Lastly, repairs could be done on easier terms, as a moderate charge for opening the Dock would not come near equal to the expense of wages, when men are paid a days wages for working one tide or three hours. Besides, a ship can be fitted out and dispatched in one third part of the time that it takes at present.
>
> We have been at some pains in procuring a plan of a proper dock and find that a good dock might be built there, but which will amount to a great deal of money... We also are well informed that there is no place in this harbour where such a dock can be built, but in the yard belonging to us, presently used for building vessels upon. And find that it would require to be carried down into the basin at the foot of that said yard, next to the Glasshouse Quay, about 25 feet....We are willing to build a proper dry dock at our own expense. Provided your honours will grant us liberty to carry the same as far into the forsaid basin as will be found necessary and allow the earth to be taken out of the ground to be shipped free from Shoredues....Indeed, without this we should be at a very great loss to get the earth carried off or laid down. We also hope your honours will allow us to carry some stones off the Sands, as there will be some large stones needed.

The Master and managers of Trinity House endorsed the need for a dry dock in a document signed by twenty of their number.

A committee was appointed to consider the petition and survey the proposed site. In March 1771 they presented a favourable report to the Council, which granted its permission, with some provisos intended to prevent the gates of the new dock from obstructing shipping in the harbour when they were open.

(It is John Sime's dock whose outline can still be seen in an open space just to the south of the Cooperage.)

Campbell's 'History of Leith', published in 1827, states that the first dry dock in Leith was built in 1720, as a result of the 'improvements' proposed in 1710, and several later authors have accepted this statement. However Maitland, writing in the mid-eighteenth century, devoted quite a lot of space to the harbour 'improvements' of 1710-20, but made no mention of the building of a dry dock. Several sources of the 1770s and 1780s specifically mention that John Sime's dry dock was the first to be built in Leith, so it seems that Campbell erroneously assumed that Robert Davies' early eighteenth-century dock was a dry dock, and was one of those which were already old when he was writing.

The author of 'The Modern Universal British Traveller' mentions John Sime's dock:

> That part called North Leith is a very poor place, without any public building except an old Gothic church. There is a small dock capable of admitting ships of 150 tons. The harbour is generally crowded with vessels from many different parts.

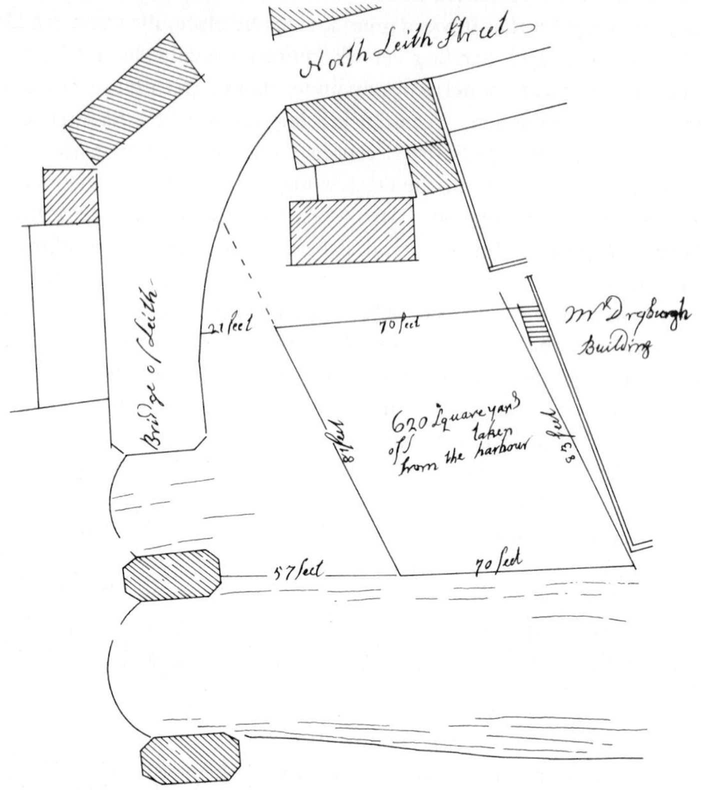

The plan submitted by Robert Dryburgh to Edinburgh Council, of the ground needed to build this dry dock in 1774 (By courtesy of Edinburgh City Archive).

His book was published in 1779, but he must have visited Leith during the early years of the decade, because in 1774, Robert Drybrough followed John Sime's example, by building a smaller dry dock in the yard lying just north of the Bridge, which he had acquired from James Crawford. A few years later Drybrough was 'by the hand of Providence rendered incapable of business'. His dock was advertised for lease, but there were no takers. Eventually John Sime was persuaded to take it over. The 'deplorable malady' from which Robert Drybrough suffered did not prevent him from receiving £130 per year from John Sime for the lease of his dock. He even outlived Sime senior, dying in 1793.

By 1778 John Sime senior had either died or retired. It was his son alone who obtained the tack of the entire Sandport at that date (Robert Drybrough's lease having expired), on condition that he would give up half of it if it was needed by another shipbuilder. He needed extra building land because he had obtained a contract from the Navy to build a sloop of war, HMS *Fury*, the only naval ship to be built at Leith in the eighteenth century. Naval sloops of the time were of between 350 and 400 tons burthen - too big for his yard. He had to construct a platform, at considerable expense, on which to lay out mouldings and build the *Fury*. The launch of this fine vessel in 1780 was marred by the death of one of the carpenters, killed when one of the shoring timbers fell on him. John Sime held the tack of the Sandport until his death in 1796.

By the early 1780s John Sime occupied the two dry docks, his original yard and the whole of the Sandport. These holdings comprised more than half the shipbuilding land in North Leith, and it is not surprising that he was accused by some of being a 'monopolist'. As a later detractor of his put it, 'when we have only one shop to go to, advantage is taken of it and we must pay dearer for commodities'. One of John Sime's supporters retorted that his prices were a great deal lower than those charged at Glasgow, and up to 40% lower than those of Liverpool. What is more, he did not insist on immediate payment of dock dues, with the result that some were never paid. Sime claimed for himself that:

> It is well known all over Great Britain what improvements he has introduced, and how he has enlarged the circle of his operations and increased the number of artificers in all the various branches of trade and manufacture depending on shipbuilding....Nor have (his) operations been confined to the business of the dry docks alone, for....he has not neglected the business of shipbuilding, but has on the contrary employed every foot of ground which he could procure for that purpose. Under his encouragement too, a manufactury of ships' anchors and other iron work for Naval purposes has been brought to a perfection and extended on a scale heretofore unexampled in Scotland.

Whatever may be the truth about John Sime's monopoly, two at least of his fellow tradesmen were not at all happy with the situation and in 1786 they attempted to alter it. Accordingly, the City Council received a petition from James Crawford and his partner Walter Goalen, that they might take over John Sime's lease of the Sandport, which was about to expire. The petitioners explained that they had operated for some years in the port and built a number of sloops, but 'labour under great disadvantages in their business, for want of a dry dock and proper places to build upon.' They pointed out that John Sime was only using the Sandport to store timber, which he could do just as well in his other properties, and asked that they might build a dry dock in it. Their complaint was that Sime had 'monopolised almost the whole trade of building and repairing ships in the port into his own hands' whereby 'the hands of many industrious people have been tied up'.

Sime, however, must have had friends on the Council. The petition was refused, on the flimsy grounds that the proposed dry dock must be entered through a breach in the Ballast Quay, and that the land was needed for the storage of timber. John Sime rubbed salt into the wound by offering the petitioners the lease of Robert Drybrough's dock, which still had six years to run.

Another Improvement Scheme

It was not long, however, before he himself was to suffer at the hands of the City. In 1787 an Act of Parliament empowered Edinburgh to undertake desperately needed improvements to the harbour. The scheme of 1754 had been promoted because of overcrowding caused by an upturn in trade. By 1787 the situation was even worse. Between 1752 and 1787 the tonnage of shipping belonging to Leith alone had increased from 5,703 tons to 17,150 tons, and the average size of its ships from 55 to 100 tons. During the same period the annual amount of shipping using the harbour had increased by over 42,000 tons. The only improvement carried out during that time was the building of a short quay in North Leith, later called the Custom House Quay. A plan of the harbour drawn up in 1787 shows vessels crammed into the narrow river mouth, lying four abreast all along the Shore. Boats are squeezed in wherever they can find a space. Goods from the outermost ships at the Shore had to be unloaded across the decks of the inner vessels, causing much bad temper among crew and porters alike. The overcrowding meant that accidents were frequent, and could be fatal.

A grandiose plan was drawn up by Robert Whitworth which involved two alternative strategies. The first was a variation on the plan of 1754. The Abbot's Bridge would be demolished and replaced by a drawbridge from the New Quay to the foot of the Broad Wynd in North Leith. The river above the bridge would be widened and deepened and a docks complex built above Leith Mills. The other plan was for a somewhat inadequate dock on the site where the first wet docks were later built. Rival plans were submitted by a number of individuals, all of whom poured scorn on the ideas of the rest. Increasingly acrimonious pamphlets were produced on the subject, and a good time was had by all. Finally, the only elements to be rescued from the imbroglio were the demolition of the Abbbot's Bridge and the building of Whitworth's drawbridge, thus providing extra harbour accommodation further upriver.

In order to improve access to the drawbridge, streets were widened on both sides of the river, involving the destruction of a number of properties. The chief victim in South Leith was a rambling tenement at the foot of Tolbooth Wynd, bearing the magnificent name of 'Babylon'. In North Leith the Council were empowered to acquire lands on either side of Broad Wynd 'not exceeding 100 feet in breadth' and properties in North Leith Street on the line of the new road (later called Bridge Street).

John Sime leased a smithy on the west side of the foot of the Wynd and a yard 'at the back of Mrs Macintyre's shop' on the north side of the Street, from William Brough, a Leith merchant. There was a yard on the west side of the Wynd, belonging to Captain John Brown (once in the hands of John Willison), which John Sime also occupied. On the other side of the Wynd, he leased two building yards from a ships master called John Young. One or both of the latter would be the original yard(s), which his father took over from James Beattie. All this was swept away, and its loss lent extra urgency to his (successful) petition to the Council for renewal of his tack of the Sandport, which ran out in 1789.

The owners of John Sime's leased property in Broad Wynd were compensated for their loss, the payments being calculated on the basis of 12 or 14 years-worth loss of rents. He himself owned a house there which was summarily demolished by the Council with no compensation to him. It had housed one of his foremen, who he had to rehouse in South Leith at a cost of £16 per year rent - a sidelight on conditions of employment at the time. Sime did, however, gain at least one benefit from the building of the drawbridge. He supplied two timber platforms for the south end of the bridge, at a charge of £94 4s 8d.

The Society of the Carpenters of North Leith were also losers in this wholesale destruction of property. Their tenement in Broad Wynd housed half a dozen tenants, three of them carpenters, and was worth £9 10s per year in rents. They were compensated by a payment of fourteen times the annual rent, as the money was for charitable purposes. This fact was duly taken up by North Leith Kirk Session who also owned a school and schoolmaster's house in Broad Wynd. The Kirk Session had not received such favourable terms as the Carpenters, and protested to the Council about it. Like the Kirk Session, however, the Carpenters also owned property elsewhere in Leith. 'Back of the Kirk' they had a tenement with eight tenants and a rent roll of £19 10s per year. This was possibly the 'mansion' from which the 1715 date stone was later removed. Their other property, in Anchor Close (Edinburgh), was almost as profitable. Its eleven tenants paid a total of £18 15s per year. In 1800 the Carpenters acquired another house, at the 'Head of the Dock'.

John Sime's monopoly did not wholly exclude other shipbuilders from carrying on in business. The 'Statistical Account' of North Leith, compiled by the minister in 1791, mentions that there were 5 master-builders operating there, employing about 150 carpenters at 1s 10d per day. These men had lately built 'a number of fine vessels from 200 to 300 tons'. Besides John Sime, the principle active builders were James Crawford, Walter Goalen (who died the following year), and Mr Hay, a boatbuilder. The fifth was probably Robert Drybrough who, notwithstanding his 'deplorable malady' appeared in the Edinburgh and Leith directory as a shipbuilder until his death in 1793. His affairs were in the hands of trustees, although the business was carried on under his name.

Robert Menzies

One of Drybrough's trustees was Robert Menzies (whose eldest son was named Robert Dryburgh Menzies), who took over the lease of his dry dock from James Crawford when it expired in 1793. Four years later he bought it outright. From this small beginning, in a dock which could not accommodate ships of more than 100 tons, grew the firm of Menzies and Son. Robert Menzies was the first lessee of the dry dock which was completed in 1806, just to the north of the entrance to the first Wet Dock. In 1841 the firm which he had founded launched the RMS *Forth* of 1940 tons, the largest ship to have been built at Leith up to that date. Four years previously they had built the *Sirius*, the first steamship to cross the Atlantic. Messrs Menzies and Co finally went out of business after the Second World War. Its life of about 160 years made Menzies the longest surviving shipbuilding firm in the history of the port.

The Turn of the Century

In 1796 John Sime died. His will, made in 1789, named four trustees. One of those was John McLaren, master of the North Leith Iron Manufactury, which was probably the anchor smithy which John Sime had referred to in 1789 as one of the benefits he had bestowed on the community. In the will, the trustees were instructed to sell all Sime's properties in North Leith; several houses, a yard and the dry dock. They also took over his shares worth £2,000 (£40,000 scots) in the Bank of Scotland and his cash deposit there of £100. The money was to be used to set up a trust fund in favour of John Kirkpatrick, only son of William Kirkpatrick Esq, who owned property near the Citadel. John's mother was to receive £80 per year for him until he was 21, when he would inherit all that was left.

Two of John Sime's foremen, messrs Strachan and Gavin, leased the dry dock and building yard from the trustees, and in 1798 were granted the lease of the Sandport. By 1807 they had vacated the dry dock in favour of a new yard, still in North Leith, but above the site of the Abbot's Bridge. Robert Menzies took over the dry dock from them.

Morton's Patent Slip

The demolition of the Abbot's Bridge had opened the upper part of the harbour to larger ships and meant that shipbuilding could expand in that part of the river. In the early years of the nineteenth century Thomas Morton went into business in a yard on the north side of the Water of Leith, just south of North Leith burial ground. It was here, in 1818, that he that he built his newly invented patent slip, described by Campbell in his 'History of Leith' published in 1827:

> a contrivance which supplies the place of dry docks in any situation....an inclined plane on which are iron railways. On these a carriage, sufficiently capacious to receive the vessel to be hauled up and furnished with truck wheels is placed....The carriage, being properly adjusted and prepared, is let down the plane....When the ship to be hauled up had been brought directly over the carriage, she is allowed to settle down upon the machine....A strong iron purchase-chain being attached to the carriage and which is connected with and wrought by a wheel and pinion, capstan or other mechanical power at the upper end of the slip, the vessel is hauled up the inclined slip...by six men to every 100 tons.

In Campbell's opinion the Patent Slip had many advantages over a dry dock. In the first place, it cost only a tenth of the price of building a dry dock and could be used in situations where this was not feasible. There was better access to the underside of the ship and the light was better for working, especially in

Leith 31 May 1786

Sir

According to your desire I have mad an estimate for Building a Ballast Boat, to be Twenty four feet long & Eleven feet Broad, and about four & a half feet depth, to be covered on the outside with 2½ & 2 inch firr plank, on the inside to be two inch oak plank on the bottom and the other plank to be two inch firr, with a oak beam a Midships properly kneed & bolted, to finish & compleat such a boat with all Carpenter & Smith work and every thing fit for immediat use will cost Sixty Pounds Sterling I am

Sir your hble Servant

John Sime

7th June 1786

Agreed that Mr Sym build the above Ballast boat at a sum not exceeding Sixty pounds sterling

[illegible]

Estimate by John Sime for building a ballast boat for Edinburgh Council in 1786 (By courtesy of Edinburgh City Archive).

winter. Working conditions were also a lot cleaner, dry docks always containing a certain amount of mud. The whole process was a lot quicker than getting a ship in and out of dry dock, reducing the price of taking a ship of 300-400 tons out of the water and relaunching her to £2 or less. When several ships were being worked on at once they could all be on one slip and it was easy to add a new one to the end of the line. By the time of writing, the slip was in use in all the principal dockyards in the UK, one had been bought by the French government and another had gone to the Imperial Russian Dockyard at Nicolaev.

The year after the publication of Campbell's account of the slip, Morton's yard was taken over by Robert Menzies and Son. The new occupiers immediately became embroiled in a dispute with an Edinburgh coal merchant whose ships unloaded at the Charlestown Wharf, which lay between Menzies' premises and St Ninian's Kirkyard. The coal vessels blocked the access to the patent slip, and, with the co-operation of the Shoremaster, Menzies' men had begun to cast them adrift. The dispute eventually came to court, but the outcome is unknown. After leaving their original yard, Mortons operated in Leith Walk and at Granton. They later returned to Leith and it was Hugh Morton and Co, which built the 1300 ton SS *Leith* in 1862.

Alexander Sime

The name of Sime did not disappear from the scene for long. In September 1807, a carpenter called Alexander Sime left his ship in London. In May of the same year he set up as a shipbuilder in Leith, in partnership with the Robert Liddells senior and junior, and James Brunton, the latter three men providing the capital. They took over the smaller of the two dry docks from Robert Menzies, who had moved to the new dry dock to the north of the first Wet Dock. During the previous year, Liddell senior had become manager of the Edinburgh and Leith Shipping Company. It is probable that part of Alexander Sime's remit was to repair the Company's smacks. John Sime's trustees had not carried out his instructions to sell his docks. The newly-formed Sime and Company leased their dock from Mr John Kirkpatrick, who was now an Edinburgh advocate.

At first the business prospered. When the partnership was dissolved in June 1809, on the retirement of Robert Liddell senior, the books showed a yearly profit of £1,500. As a recipient of a third of the profits, according to the original agreement, Alexander Sime had done very well for himself. After the retirement of Liddell senior, the remaining partners set up two companies; Liddell and Brunton, insurance brokers and general merchants, and Alexander Sime and Company, shipbuilders. In 1812 James Brunton withdrew from both concerns. There was no formal dissolution, but the firm of Liddell and Brunton came to an end, the books showing a loss of £993. Robert Liddell continued in insurance broking and Alexander Sime and Company (also known as Sime and Liddell) carried on building ships.

The following year they built the smack *Lord Melville* for the Old London and Leith Shipping Company. Smacks had replaced brigs on the London run in 1791. They were faster and much more comfortable for the passengers.

In spite of this contract, business was falling off. Although their partnership had shown a profit of £700, Robert Liddell left the shipbuilding concern. Alexander Sime was able to continue, on condition that he paid off their joint bank account. He was enabled to do so by a loan from James Brunton, who once again became his partner. However, Brunton himself was in difficulties. In 1814 he became bankrupt in so far as his personal business affairs were concerned, although he continued in his partnership with Alexander Sime for a further year.

In 1815, the final blow fell. In March of that year, James Brunton left the partnership, Alexander Sime owing him £1,896. Alexander carried on alone, but in the autumn, John Sibbald and Co, merchants of Leith, went bankrupt, owing Alexander Sime nearly £800 for repairs to their vessels. This in itself might not have been too important, but the firm had been one of his main sources of business. He in turn owed large sums, his main pursuer being a wholesale stationer who was due £1471 for timber. On 5 December 1815, Alexander Syme was declared bankrupt. His total debts amounted to just over £6,000.

The report on his affairs compiled by his main creditor, shows that when times were good Alexander Sime had made some shrewd financial moves. He owned a quarter of the property at the head of his dock, but his greatest profit had came from another property deal. In 1811 he had bought property in North Leith for £1600. He subsequently sold half of it to the City of Edinburgh for £2,200 and the other half to a John Beattie for £2,700. (This large rise in value suggests that the land was needed for the building of the new docks.) Most of the money was ploughed into his business, but some of it was spent on buying a piece of land at Laverock Bank in his wife's name and building a house on it. His wife also owned a share in a company connected with Montego Bay, Jamaica. By the terms of her marriage contract she could claim £800 from her husband's estate, but she agreed to waive her rights in the money if she could keep her household goods, valued at £130.

As far as the actual shipbuilding trade was concerned, the contents of his yard were valued at £1,301. For repairs on a total of 24 vessels he was owed sums ranging from 2s 3d to £71 8s 9d. Sime had a brig on the stocks which he was building for a Captain Hay. The contract to build the vessel had stipulated that the Captain would pay £800 when her frame was completed, a further £800 when the frame was clad with timber, and the balance, £1239, when she was launched. As the first two instalments had been paid, the Captain agreed to pay £307 for work already done on the final stage, and take over the ship himself. One of Sibbald and Co's ships, the *Lincoln* was still in Sime's dock. She was arrested for payment of the sum due for her repairs.

The Company's affairs were finally wound up in February 1816. Sime's men and three apprentices had found other work. The creditors had had an offer from the owner of the brig *Southesk* who wanted to put her into the dry dock for repairs. The *Lincoln* was under arrestment and was to stay in the dock while the *Southesk* was repaired. Alexander Sime was to recieve an allowance of 2 guineas a week. On 15 May his goods were rouped.

One might have thought this would be the end of him, but for the next two years he still appears in the Edinburgh and Leith Directory. In 1818, he acquired a partner, the firm being known from that time on as Sime and Ranken. It also moved to new premises, leasing one of the new dry docks opening off the second Wet Dock, which had been finished in 1815. As Robert Menzies had moved to the first dry dock to be built in the new complex, (completed in 1806) it was probably at this time that both the old docks became abandoned, as Campbell relates in his 'History of Leith' (1827):

> Until lately, these ancient docks were wholly deserted and fast falling into decay.... They are now, however, resuscitated, and within their lately desolate precincts may again be heard the cheerful sound of carpenters' mallets.

The 'resuscitator' of one of the docks, was, in fact, Alexander Sime himself. In 1823, while Sime and Ranken continued to operate from its dry dock in the new complex, he set up on his own, back in his old dock near the kirk. The other dry dock was in use by William Butement, one of Leith's more ephemeral shipbuilders (his firm of Butement and Young went into liquidation in 1843). Sime and Ranken ceased business in 1829, and Alexander Sime disappeared from the scene in 1833. It is noteworthy that early nineteenth century shipbuilding partnerships tended to be shortlived. It was the family firm of Menzies which survived into the second half of this century.

New Dry Docks

In all, three dry docks were provided in the new Wet Docks complex. In 1818 a surveyor was employed to report on the progress of the work and he included comments on the dry docks. By this time all three had been completed. The two mentioned in the report opened off the north side of the second dock, being completed in 1817. They were pumped out by means of a steam engine, the first mention of such a covenience at Leith.

> I have great satisfaction in reporting that the construction of the two new dry docks turns out to be most satisfactory, as they are almost perfectly watertight and in all other respects perfectly suitable for the purpose for which they were intended.
>
> I am very sorry to find that the one intended for a public dock (ie, not leased to any one firm, but available for shore-term hire) has been very little occupied. This will, I fear, continue to be the case unless a complete stock of timber and other materials for repairing ships were to be had on the spot, and this I am confident will never be furnished by the committee as it would lead into a world of trouble and probably would produce no advantage to them.

The surveyor recommended finding a contractor to supply materials or else letting out the dock, preferably to Robert Menzies. The second dry dock, as we have seen, was occupied by Sime and Ranken.

Shipbuilding in Leith continued to have its ups and downs, its failures and survivors, but it went on until 1983, when the closure of Henry Robb Ltd brought to an end just over half a millenium of recorded shipbuilding at the port.

Note: The early-eighteenth-century shipbuilder Robert Davies invented one of the first closed diving machines.

11

The Shore and The Bush

The heart of a port is the place where its ships load and unload. This may be a vast complex of docks or a simple wharf or quay. In Leith, up to the end of the eighteenth century, it was the Shore, whose name proclaims its origins, as the beach at the mouth of the Water of Leith, where David I had established his new harbour in the twelfth century. 'The place vulgarly known as *lie shor*' is named in early charters. Maintaining the Shore and the piers which were built as time went on cost Edinburgh a lot of money, though nowhere near as much as was collected in the dues that were meant to pay for their upkeep. The centuries-old system of leasing out the collection of the dues was still in operation at the start of the eighteenth century. The lessee of the dues was known as the 'Tacksman of the Shore Dues'.

At the start of the century, the Shoredues were by no means the goldmine they were to become for Edinburgh as time went on. Uncertain times meant that the Tacksmen, as in the case of other Leith Tacks, were sometimes unable to pay their full tack money. The advent of the Old Pretender to Scotland touched Leith only slightly, but even this brief brush was sufficient to upset the fine balance between profit and loss. As well as stationing men-of-war on the Forth, the Government ordered all boats to be laid up from August to November 1715, so that no trade was done. The three Tacksmen of the Shoredues, lost heavily and were remitted £77 of their tack rent. The Tacksman of the Edinburgh Fishmarket also suffered as the fishing boats had been unable to operate.

In October 1715 the Earl of Mar, in arms in the North for the Pretender, sent Macintosh of Borlam south with 2500 men to reinforce the Earl of Derwentwater in Northumberland. Three men-of-war were stationed off Burntisland to prevent him from crossing the Forth by the recognised route. However, there were other ferries, and on 13 October, Macintosh crossed from Elie instead. In spite of this, forty of his men were captured and incarcerated in Leith Tolbooth. On the next morning, their commander marched west along the coast in order to rescue them. Campbell says, 'The approach of 50,000 cannibals could not have discomposed the heroic Edinburghers more than did this counter-march of old Mcintosh'. Their City was, in fact, quite safe. The Pretender's men intended only to rescue their comrades. They burnt down the Tolbooth door, ransacked the prison, and commandeered all the brandy in the Custom House. Perhaps to tease the people of Edinburgh, for they cannot seriously have expected to hold it, they captured the Citadel, and fortified it with guns from the ships in the Harbour. The local militia refused to volunteer

Leith Harbour about 1700, from a painting in Trinity House. On the extreme right are the ruins of the King's Wark, which was destroyed by fire in 1683. The openings under the farther pier allowed timber to be floated through for storage in the Bush.

to fight them and had to be ordered out by the Magistrates. The Duke of Argyll marched down from the City to challenge Mcintosh, but had to return for scaling ladders. At this point, the 'rebels' withdrew and continued their march south, eventually joining forces with Derwentwater as planned.

The Duties of the Collector of Shoredues

The Shore Dues Tacksmen at that time were John Dickson, John Smith and Robert McKinlay, who held the tack from 1709 until 1730. Subsequently it was taken over by John Parkhill, John Alphen and Alexander Chalmers. In 1734 they employed Thomas Chalmers as their Collector of Shoredues. Inserted in the Shoredues ledger for that year is a list of his duties:

> You are to enter in this Register all vessels which have come into the Harbour of Leith since Martinmas 1734. Excepting such Ferry Boats as belong to Burntisland Kinghorn and Kirkcaldy, coming from these places without goods and having only passengers on board.
>
> You are to take particular care, how soon any vessel arrives to enter the true date, the master's and merchants' names, and place from which it comes. And immediately when livered (or sooner if you can know it with any certainty) you are to note the true qualities and quantities of the cargo, and whether the same is free or unfree. You are to take special care that all Ships Masters and others liable,

> pay their Beaconage and Anchorage before they are quite livered [unloaded], or at least immediately thereafter, for if you allow them to sail without paying, you are hereby certified it shall be charged on you, and stopped out of your salary.
>
> All vessels from London, Newcastle or Holland or from the North Country with fish, oil, butter, skins etc, collected at the plank end, are to be accounted for by you within 8 days after they are fully livered. Therefore you are to allow none, whether factors or others, to carry their goods from off the Shore till you are satisfied. If you do, it shall be on your own account and charged on you as above.
>
> And if any person without paying or consigning to the full extent of the dues (and you'll take care to require no more than the table allows) pretend to carry off their goods, you are to hipotheque [take in pledge] and secure such a quantity thereof as shall be sufficient for our payment. For which goods you are to offer your receipt, mentioning their being hypothecated by you for their refusal of the payment of the Shore Dues etc.
>
> You are also to discharge the Workmen and others from assisting in carrying off said goods, as directed in your printed Table, signed by the Treasurer, precept by the Admiral of Leith [one of the Bailies] etc. You'll also notice the clause in said Table whereby you are authorised to exact the whole merk per tun if the goods imported shall be foreign, and full Shore Dues, whether foreign or inland, from such persons as shall refuse to pay their just dues.
>
> You are [to] make out, sum up and deliver over to us weekly your account of cash received, distinguishing what is proper to last year from this.

In its essentials, this is a fair job-description for the Collectors from that time on. It could be an unpleasant job - merchants and masters regarded the Collector in much the same light as motorists today regard traffic wardens. It became, however, literally a job for life.

Alexander Moodie

Alexander Chalmers was one of the Tacksmen for some 30 years, and it was he who devised the method by which the books were kept during his time. After Thomas Chalmers, Roger Moodie became Collector. In 1740 he took on his nephew Alexander Moodie on a 5-year apprenticeship. Alexander was still at the Shoredues Office in 1758, when the City, unable to find a Tacksman, took over the administration of the Shoredues - permanently, as it turned out.

Alexander Moodie was appointed Collector by the City Treasurer, and the following year he was established in his office by Act of Council. He had been having difficulties with ships masters and others, who were being tardy about paying their dues. The Council felt that an official appointment would give him more authority. He was paid £60 per year, out of which he had to employ a clerk. Two assistant collectors were paid £26 between them.

The new Collector was a conscientious clerk, but he seems to have lacked the force of personality necessary to make a success of pursuing debtors. In 1761 the Council noted that:

> The collection of the Shore Dues is attended with considerable loss to the City by reason that the merchants and others who import or export goods to and from Leith neglect to pay the dues of such goods, and some, when afterwards craved, refuse that they belong to them, or that they only had such a quantity.

In future the Collector was to detain on the Shore all goods intended for export until their dues were paid. If the dues were not paid immediately on imported goods, or a pawn given, the Collector was to impound them and have them stored in Leith Weigh-house until the dues were paid. These measures appear to have worked. The amount collected in 1761 was £100 up on the previous year.

The Bulker

In 1761 also, that rather mysterious official, the Bulker, enters upon the eighteenth century scene. The job probably originated at the time when Leith began to handle any quantity of goods which were not sacks of wool, packs of hides, barrels of fish or tuns of wine - the 'bulks' on which Shoredues were originally calculated. Barrels were a particularly difficult area, as each commodity was packed in a distinctive cask. Fish came in herring or salmon 'trees'. Wine and other beverages came in tuns, butts, hogsheads, half hogsheads, ankers, tierces, quarters et al. Then there were barrels - and barrels! The job of the Bulker was to decide how many tuns (later tons) each commodity represented. Some goods were 'bulked' by the barrel rather than by the ton.

The Bulker's services were normally only required in the case of 'general ships' - vessels carrying goods belonging to seven or more individuals or 'having seven [merchants'] marks on board'. Shoredues were also paid according to the tonnage of the vessel itself, and it was the Bulker's job to decide on a figure in disputed cases. He did this either by reference to the shipbuilder's vendition, or failing that, by measuring the ship itself. He was allowed 10% of all the Shoredues he collected from the ships he bulked, and paid 1s 6d for each ship he measured.

The Bulker in 1761 was William Oliphant. Alexander Moodie tried to make him give up full copies of all cargoes liable to Shoredues. If this had been possible it would have certainly made the Collector's job a lot easier. The Council decided, however, that it was unrealistic to expect the Bulker to comply. Instead, he was instructed to give the Shore Dues Office an abstract of the whole 'barrel bulk' of goods which paid freight, to be taken from the ships master's books. Any master who refused to let William Oliphant see his books was to be brought before the Magistrates.

More Trouble for Alexander Moodie

By 1763, although the amount of Shoredues collected each year was steadily rising, the Council was becoming alarmed about the amount of arrears of payments. A committee consisting of the two Bailies, the Treasurer and the ex-Treasurer was appointed to look into the method of collection, the arrears outstanding and how the yearly accounts were checked. Six months after the committee was appointed, Alexander Moodie was required to find two cautioners for his intromissions as Collector.

Not surprisingly, Moodie found all this thoroughly alarming, and in May 1764 he asked that if the Shoredues were ever again leased, a clause be inserted into the articles of roup that the present collector be retained by the new Tacksman. (Such was the case when the dues of the Edinburgh and Leith Weigh-houses were rouped.) He hoped that if his appointment were permanent he might have more authority over the ships masters. The committee which was appointed to consider the petition reported that in spite of the extreme difficulty of collecting the dues, Moodie had been very faithful in collecting and handing them over:

> It is a fact well known that the more zeal Mr Moodie has shown in collecting and ingathering the Shoredues from the several persons liable in payment thereof, he has so much more incurred their odium and ill will, which has appeared on many occasions.

The Council adopted the committee's recommendation, that Moodie be appointed 'during his good behaviour, of which behaviour the Magistrates and Council are to be sole and final judges'. If they were not satisfied with him he was to be given six month's notice of dismissal. He was to account with the Treasurer once a month, and give a quarterly account of arrears. His salary remained at £60 but he no longer had to pay a clerk out of it. In fact, two clerks were now to be employed by the City at a total salary of £60. The allowance for two assistant collectors was still £26 per annum. It seems that there was currently no Bulker; William Laurie, land surveyor of Leith, was to be paid 5gn a year to measure ships for the Collector.

The Inspection and its Aftermath

After this token of the City's confidence in him, Alexander Moodie may have felt that he could breathe easy again. However, in 1765 the amount of Dues collected, which had been steadily rising, suddenly fell by about £500. The Chamberlain decided to inspect the Shoredues books and in 1766 presented a severe criticism of them to the Council. Three books were kept; a general Register of ships coming in, and Dues paid on unloading; a Ledger containing the accounts of persons not paying Dues immediately; and a Cash book, in which money received was entered.

The Chamberlain had found that there was no way of telling from the books how much was owing in arrears. The Registers had not been totalled at all, and there was no record of sums paid to the Treasurer. Moodie was ordered to total each page in each Register from 1758, when he took over as Collector (a backlog of eight years), and to make an abstract of the totals at the end of each book, differentiating between inwards and outwards dues. Each account in the Ledger was to be abstracted under the following headings:

1 The number of the page in the Ledger from which the account was taken.
2 The name of the person to whom the account belonged.
3 The full amount due, as shown in the Ledger.
4 The amount of the account that he had actually received.
5 He was also to make a list of all arrears outstanding at 11 November 1765.

He was given the totally unrealistic period of four months in which to achieve all this, while at the same time carrying on with his daily business at the same pace as before. Although he hired an additional clerk at his own expense and worked early and late, by 18 February 1767 only the first four years had been completed. The Treasurer reported to the Council that Moodie was doing the best he could, and they allowed him another six weeks, on pain of dismissal if the work was not finished. He hired another two clerks, and by dint of allowing himself only three or four hours sleep a night, was able to finally hand over the books in August. The work had been hindered by the lack of some excerpts from the Customs books which he needed and had been unable to obtain, in spite of repeated requests.

Once the amounts of arrears had been ascertained, the next step was to recover them. Alexander Moodie now found himself burdened with court case after court case before the Leith Magistrates as he pursued debtors. The merchants themselves hit back by taking him to court over such matters as his right to insist on a pledge for the payment of Shoredues. Some who owed debts of as much as 20 years standing insisted on inspecting his books, ostensibly on suspicion that he had pocketed the money himself.

Having put the unfortunate Collector through all this financial constraint and emotional turmoil, the Chamberlain did not bother to report to Council until the end of June 1770. It transpired that the arrears for the eight years totalled £2675 11s and that Moodie appeared to owe the City £121, although it was difficult to be sure about this as the books were so complex. Part of the debt consisted of £49 embezzled by a clerk named Wright, before 1766. The extracts needed from the Custom House were still not forthcoming.

The Council generously decided not to pursue Moodie for the £121 he might or might not owe them, as long as he paid the embezzled £49 (85% of one year's salary). He was to make up the accounts for 1766 to 1769 in the same way as the ones he had adjusted, and a new way for keeping them would be decided later.

The Shore Dues Committee

Moving at its usual lethargic pace, in 1772 the Council decided that as the Shoredues were now 'the most considerable branch of its revenue' the First Bailie's Committee would audit them annually. The following year a special

Committee was appointed to oversee the keeping of the books, pursue debtors in court for payment of arrears and decide which arrears were 'absolutely desperate' and could be struck off the books - in the event there were not many of the latter. This body was the first Shore Dues Committee, elected annually from this time onwards. Its original remit to decide on matters to do with the Shoredues was gradually widened to include any matters concerning Leith which were not already the province of an existing Committee. It always included one or two Bailies, the present and past Treasurers, a representative of the Edinburgh Trades and another from the Merchants. If necessary, the Provost was also elected.

The next major report on the Shoredues was presented to the Council in September 1775. It had been decided that although they had no reason to suspect Alexander Moodie's honesty, the confusion of his books and his 'supine negligence' in collecting the arrears justified them in altering his condition of employment from 'during his good behaviour' to 'during the pleasure of the Council', as was the case with all their other employees. The number of books he was to keep yearly was reduced to two, with arrears to be clearly evident. (Decreets had been obtained in the Leith court against most of the existing debtors.) A clerk in the Custom House was being paid £15 per annum to give the Collector the excerpts he needed from the Customs books. There was once again no Bulker and it was proving difficult to find a suitable person for the post. (Shipmasters who collected their own Shoredues of general ships were allowed the 10% fee which would have been paid to the Bulker.)

The Council voted the Chamberlain a 'gratification' of £25 for his trouble over the Shoredues. Poor Alexander Moodie got nothing, even though he presented a humble petition the following year, detailing the sums he had spent on hiring extra clerks, and lighting and heating two rooms in his own house for them to work in. Together with an allowance for his own trouble, the sum amounted to £70.

The Start of the Sandeman Era

For the next eight years, business at the Shoredues office proceeded smoothly enough. In 1784 it was decided that another clerk should be appointed, bringing the number up to four. The appointee was Patrick Sandeman, who turned out to be about as unlike Alexander Moodie as possible, as we will see. The old Collector was still plagued by the hostilities of the debtors who the City was pursuing through the courts. These pressures, together with his conscientious application to his work 'broke his heart' and in February 1785 he died, leaving a widow and six children, five of them under 14 years of age. He had spent most of the 45 years of his working life in the impossible position of trying to enforce payment of a tax for which there was less and less justification. The ships masters and the merchants could all do arithmetic, and they could see that the City was not using the dues for the upkeep of the Harbour. As they had no way of venting their anger at this injustice on the Edinburgh Council, they unloaded the whole burden onto the defenceless Collector.

When Alexander Moodie's widow later petitioned the City for an annuity in 1788, she said that when her husband died, 'it was by his enemies said he had died rich, in order to asperse his memory, but when his affairs were looked into, your petitioner found to her sad experience that he had scarcely left the patrimony she brought him, which was employed in building the house at the head of the Broad Wynd' It transpired from the same petition that not only had Alexander Moodie repaid the £49 embezzled by Wright, but also £176 abstracted by another clerk, William Allan. The City had treated its loyal employee extremely shabbily, and it did not do much better by his widow. She was granted only an annuity of £25 per annum for the next four years.

Patrick Sandeman, the new clerk, had been appointed at a higher salary than the three already at the Office. When Alexander Moodie died it was Sandeman whom the Provost appointed as interim Collector. In spite of the Council's efforts to make Moodie keep his books more efficiently, they were several years behind and Sandeman took on the task of bringing them up to date.

Office Procedures Reviewed

In the summer of 1785 a new Collector was appointed. He was Adam Thomson, brother of a member of the Council, who had been living in Ireland. If Alexander Moodie had been diligent but ineffectual, Adam Thomson was thoroughly untrustworthy. Without Patrick Sandeman, who was made Deputy Collector at the same time, the affairs of the Shoredues Office would speedily have collapsed into complete confusion.

At the appointment of the new Collector the Council reviewed the Office staff and their salaries. Thomson was to have £100 for salary, plus £50 for office rent (£15) coal, candle and stationary. Patrick Sandeman's salary was rising by leaps and bounds. He had been appointed at £35 per annum. At the review another £10 was added to this, and as a result of a private petition two months later, he was granted a further £15, bringing the total to £60 - an increase of nearly 100% within three years of his appointment. At the time of Moodie's death he had been training an apprentice, Mr Veitch, who was now appointed a clerk at a salary of £20. It is not clear whether he was an addition to the strength or whether one of the other three clerks had resigned.

The review reveals that the Office employed a runner for 7s per week, and a Collector at the Ferry Boat Stairs at the same wage. Both were said to be 'very proper for their present station'. The sub-Collector was very necessary as there was considerable controversy over paying dues for goods carried by Ferry Boats. The boatmen maintained that they were not liable to pay; the City maintained that they were - and might was right in this instance.

In 1787 also, the Council decided to overhaul the current procedures in dealing with 'general ships', and a report was presented to them detailing 'the present mode of conducting that business'.

> When a vessel is ready to take in general goods, the shipmaster calls at the Office for a ticket or warrant to ship the same. This ticket permits him to ship goods from a number of different merchants, whose names are noted on the back thereof (these merchants previous thereto having granted obligations to draw out an account of the goods shipped by them and to pay the same every half year or oftener if required) and also the goods for which they pay the dues. Goods shipped by merchants or others not specified on the back of the ticket, the shipmaster for the most part either got payment at shipping, or another ticket which is presented upon the merchant giving security for the same at the Office.
>
> Upon the vessel being loaded or cleared at the Custom House, the shipmaster gives an account of the cargo from the Custom House Papers or his intake book, from which the dues are made up, by charging the different merchants who have granted the forementioned obligations with the goods shipped by them, striking off those who have paid the dues at the Office, and charging the shipmaster with the rest.

General ships presented problems in collection of dues as it was much easier for their masters to circumvent the system, as the Report goes on to explain and attempt to remedy:

> The most of the London shipmasters and several of those in the foreign trade not conforming to the above is the reason of wishing to consult what would be the most proper method of obliging them to observe the regulations.
>
> A plan was proposed by Mr Gray of arresting the vessel and to oblige the shipmaster either to pay the dues or re-land those goods for which no security is given. This was done and two vessels arrested. Though it had not the desired effect, yet it made them more careful afterwards in observing that security was given before shipping, but with regard to others, we found it difficult to pitch upon one for a proper example, as they afterwards sailed to the Roads before giving an account of their cargoes, and some has given no account whatsoever. I understand we cannot arrest without specifying the particular goods and marks, which would be a very difficult matter.
>
> Upon the regulations being made out from the late Act of Parliament, the Council has appointed a person to attend particularly to the goods and shipping outward, and since that time the dues have been much more exactly collected.
>
> Still some of the shipmasters will not, as hinted above, conform to the regulations by giving an account of their cargoes at the Office, and others, though they do give an account, yet will not pay the dues on the goods they have taken in, without security being given, although the goods thus taken in are, in general, but very few, owing principally to the vigilance of the person on the Shore. The Dues on a whole cargo unaccounted for being only for the most part from sixpence to six or seven shillings, yet to prevent others following their example it will be proper that some active measures be taken.
>
> The only plan which might prove effectual, if proper to be adopted, is that the shipmasters before they begin to load their vessels, to be desired to consign money

> or grant an obligation to pay the dues upon the goods for which no security is given, and to settle the same before sailing, and upon their not agreeing to this, that a person should be stationed at their vessel for to send to the Weigh-house all goods the dues of which are not paid at the Office, or upon any goods being shipped for which no security is given, to prosecute the shipmaster and crew for taking in said goods without a ticket.

Adam Thomson

As it debated the weighty problem of how to abstract the last shilling of Shoredues from reluctant ships Masters, the Council was unaware that it were steadily being relieved of many pounds by its very own Collector. Adam Thomson kept his guilty secret until the accidental breaking of his kneecap brought his spirits so low that he could no longer bear the weight of his guilt. In a letter to the Provost of 4 December 1788, he confessed that as well as owing the Council £50 which they had advanced him on his appointment, he had embezzled £150 to pay off debts which he had left behind in Ireland. 'I am sorry to add that I still owe several debts to a considerable amount, which I have not the strength to inform your Lordship of at this time, as I write in a degree of agony I cannot express' - as well he might! The sum involved may seem small enough to us, but it represented one and a half times the salary of a man who today would be earning perhaps £15000 to £20000 a year.

If Thomson had not been related to a Council member, he would probably have been dismissed out of hand. (Considering all the precautions surrounding his appointment, he might well have not been employed in the first place.) As it was, the invaluable Patrick Sandeman once more came to the rescue. He had in effect being carrying the work of the Office ever since Thomson's appointment, and he was now made Joint Collector, with sole charge of the cash. He himself paid off the £150 debt and was to be repaid by retaining £50 a year out of Thomson's salary for three years. At the end of that time, the salaries of the two Collectors would be amalgamated (£160) and then shared equally between them. To the £50 advance which Thomson owed was added £14 for stationary. He was to grant the City a bond for the £64, so that it could be recovered if he were ever in a position to pay it.

These arrangements dealt with the money owing to the City. There was also the question of Thomson's private debts, which totalled £170. Patrick Sandeman dealt with these too. He agreed with the creditors to retain £42 a year out of Thomson's salary and pay them by instalments. If he had also insisted on the £50 due to him, it would have left Thomson (a married man) with £8 a year to live on. In fact, he concentrated on paying the private creditors and allowed his partner to keep most of the £50. By 1792 he was still owed £89, and Adam Thomson was in trouble again. This time 'family distress' was the ostensible cause of his problems, especially the expenses of the illness and death of his wife. Including the £89 he still owed Sandeman, he was in debt to the tune of £175. He petitioned the Council for permission to continue the arrangement by which Sandeman retained £50 per year until all was paid. The Council agreed, subject to various safeguards in case of the death of either party before everything was paid off.

At some time in the winter of 1794, Thomson died, the City paying £10 towards his funeral expenses. His daughter Margaret, left in distressed circumstances, petitioned the Council for aid and was refused. If the widow of a diligent servant could get little from them, the daughter of a heedless one could expect nothing, even though she was hardly to blame for her father's improvidence. However, William Thomson, first clerk in the Shoredues Office received a pay rise of £10 per annum, so perhaps Margaret was provided for after all.

Patrick Sandeman, Collector

Patrick Sandeman was now officially sole Collector of Shoredues. He lost no time in reminding the Council of what a valuable employee he was. No only had he kept the books in an exemplary fashion by working many hours overtime, he had collected nearly all the arrears due preceding 1785 - some £4000. This claim is borne out by a petition in the previous year from William Strachan WS, the City's Procurator at Leith court for the last 13 years. He had dealt with many cases arising 'from the multiplicity of business carried on at the Shoredues Office'. Most of these had been settled out of court, which meant that Strachan received no fee, although he had spent trouble and time over them. With the petition came a certificate from Patrick Sandeman that he had 'given the above a great deal of trouble by taking advice etc, for which he had made no charge.' The Procurator was given just 10 guineas to compensate him for all his extra work over 13 years. When Sandeman petitioned for compensation for his trouble over the arrears he was granted £80. He continued in office until his retirement early in the next century; efficient, reliable and fearless in his pursuit of defaulters.

With the appointment of Patrick Sandeman the office of Collector of Shore Dues became not only lifelong, but almost hereditary. When Patrick retired, his place was taken by WB Sandeman who served until a few years before his death in 1878.

The Porters

The history of the Shore is not merely a matter of the upkeep of stones and mortar, it is also the history of the landsmen for whom it provided a livelihood: coopers, porters, metters, carters, Customs officials and collectors of the Prime Gilt, Shoredues, Merk per ton and all the other dues with which ships and cargoes were burdened. Now it is a quiet place by day, a convenient car park, a place to have lunch or a drink at one of its restaurants and bars. In the eighteenth century it teemed with life, becoming more and more crowded as the number of ships using the harbour doubled and doubled again and again.

The most numerous of the Shore workers were the Porters. By the start of the eighteenth century they were known as 'Workmen' The old distinction

A cartoon of 1736, the year in which excise duty was first imposed on whisky. It shows a sailor, carter and porter discussing the news on the Shore.

between the stingmen who carried wine and other barrelled goods, and the polkmen who mostly dealt with grain, wool and other goods which came in sacks or packs had disappeared.

In 1695, the 'Workmen in Leith' were erected into a Society, by an Act of the Council of Edinburgh. This was the date at which they were first organised into Companies, a system which survived for over 250 years. Each Company consisted of twelve 'lusty, able men', who would elect an 'oversman' - with the help of the Bailies. Any shortfall in numbers was to be made up by 'tuck of drum' through the streets of Leith, but only with the permission of the Bailies. If the men of a merchant's chosen Company were not available, the work was to go to another Company. If theft or damage occurred in one Company, all the others were to be equally liable for restitution. On top of their normal work, the Companies were to keep the Shore clean from the end of the Abbot's Bridge to the windmill (now the tower at the west end of Tower Street, originally built as a mill for crushing lead ore). By virtue of the Act, the Workmen were now a Corporation, charging an entry fee which went towards the upkeep of their sick members and the widows of the deceased. The rate was £4 Scots for an unfreeman and 2 merks (£1 6s 8d) for the son of a freeman.

The Act of Council allowed for between four and six Companies. In the event, four were formed, each of whose members was allotted a numbered badge. The Companies became known as Telfer's (badge nos 1-12), Graham's (13-24), Crawfurd's (25-36) and Hodge's (37-48).

'Unentered Porters'

In 1749 the Council considered a petition from the Workmen, complaining that about a dozen 'unentered' men were working as porters on the Shore. The matter had come to a head when Sylvester Stewart, one of their members, had tangled with one of these illicit workers. The man in question was Thomas Fife, ' a person of very indifferent character', who was seen to be carrying goods to a ship. Stewart 'desired him to set down his lift, and not take the entered Workmen's employment or bread from them, when they were standing idle upon the Shore'. As a result of the ensuing disturbance, the magistrates fined Stewart 10s. The petition requested that the Council forbid the employment of men who were not members of the Society.

The Council moved at its normal speed and it was not until the following year that a list was made of 'Unentered Porters Who Work on the Shore of Leith'. It shows that the estimate of a dozen or so was far too low. There were in fact 29 men, mostly in their 30s and 40s, although the youngest was 17 and the oldest 58 (there were later complaints that many of the Leith porters were too old for their job). Most of them were family men, having a wife and two or three children - the largest family contained six children but some men had only one. One of the illicit workers, Alexander Lawson, gave the excuse that he was a discharged soldier, a status which seems to have given men the right to work at trades to which they would not otherwise have been entitled. (Another old soldier later set up as a Metter.)

Seven years later a dispute arose over non-payment by a merchant of porters' dues for sacking his meal. The amount involved was only 10s, but the Porters' petition makes it clear why they could not let even this small sum go unpaid.

> We...are all of us poor men and have nothing to support our families but what we labour hard for by the sweat of our brows...Yea for the planks we go upon, we pay for them lying upon the Shore when they are not using...We hope that your Lordships will not allow our wages to be demitted for any man's private interest, for the sacking meal upon the Shore requires more care and attention than any grain.'

The New Companies

In 1763, because of the rapid increase in trade at Leith in the middle of the century, Edinburgh decided that three new Companies of Porters were needed. At the end of 1770, the men were finally elected and sworn in. Before long two of the new Companies had acquired names - Stevenson's (badge nos 61-72) and Gibson's (73-84). James Stevenson (no 62) and James Gibson (no 74) were among the men appointed in 1770, and presumably the first 'oversmen' of their respective Companies. The other company (49-60) seems never to have been given a name, being known as 'The First New Company'. In the 1780s, the Companies ceased to be named in official records, being known as the 1st, 2nd, 3rd or 4th Old Companies, and the 1st to 3rd New Companies. Their names appear, however, in later records, so it would seem that they continued in use unofficially. In 1787, two Companies of Corn Porters were formed, the men being given the numbers 1 to 24. The two new companies brought the total number at the end of the century to nine - employing 108 men.

A Porter appointed to a vacancy was given the number of his predecessor. Most vacancies occurred through death, but a few lived long enough to be 'superannuated' and others resigned to take up other employment, usually in the Army. A few men transferred to other Companies. It is not clear whether this was for personal or financial reasons.

The Metters

One very specialised branch of the Porters was the Metters. Originally, as we have seen, their function was to measure the grain and salt imported into Leith so that the petty customs and other dues to be paid on it could be calculated. It was important to Edinburgh that the men who did this job were working in the City's best interests. This was why, in 1551, the Council began appointing and swearing in the Metters who worked at Leith. By the end of the seventeenth century the original three men had increased to twenty in number and, in the same year as the Porters, the Metters were erected into a separate Incorporation.

During the eighteenth century the fortunes of the Metters fluctuated much more than those of the Porters. They dealt with a restricted range of commodities, which meant that they were more vulnerable to alterations in the volume of imports of those goods. At the start of the century they handled mainly grain and coal. Salt had provided an important part of their work, but the industry in Scotland was considerably reduced by this time. By 1800 most of the measuring of coal was done privately, but the Metters had acquired other commodities such as bark and kelp. Grain, however, continued to provide most of their work and this class of goods was particularly susceptible to fluctuations in quantities arriving at Leith.

Regulation of the Metters

The original act of Incorporation allowed the Bailies of Leith to appoint Metters, but by 1716 this had led to problems. Too many men had been allowed in and there was not enough work to provide a living for all of them. The position was complicated by the Metters' method of providing for the widows of deceased members, which in turn depended upon their method of working. A list was kept of members of the Incorporation in order of seniority. When a member died, those below him in the list moved up. The names of new members were added at the bottom of the list. As each ship came in a metter would be allotted to measure her grain or coal, these 'Turns' being taken in strict rotation according to the list of names. If trade was bad, or not in full season, this could result in each man having a Turn only every month or six weeks. Even in good times, the amount of each cargo could vary widely. In order to ensure that everyone had a fair share, the takings for each week were pooled and then divided among all the Metters. The widow of a Metter could continue to work his Turn, in person if she were strong enough, or by employing another man to work for her, in which case they would each get half the pay. In practice, most widows employed a man to work for them, and these 'widow's Turns' provided a kind of apprenticeship for new members.

In 1703 there were 31 Metters and seven widows, and the number of men was reduced to 20. In 1715 the Council once again limited the number of men to 20 and forbade any more women to be allowed to mett. In the event, two widows were allowed to continue with their Turn, but six more were to be allowed half dues for life, after which no more were to be admitted. This was by no means the end of the matter, however. The question of the support of widows remained a problem for the Metters. It was, of course, even more of a problem for the widows themselves, but few people were too concerned about that. Periodically the Council forbade women to mett and the men concurred in the prohibitions, but it was one thing for a comfortable burgess to sit in the Council Chamber and pass edicts, it was quite another to watch the widow and family of one's erstwhile colleague starve. Women continued to take up their Turns until the beginning of the nineteenth century, when the Metters set up a barely adequate pension payments scheme for them.

After 1716 it was the City Council that decided how many Metters should be employed. In 1735 there were eleven, and the Council received a petition asking that no more be appointed for the time being, 'the trade in Leith being very much failed...May it therefore please you Lordships and Honourable Council to consider the petitioners' poverty, and thereupon to refuse any application from others...that we be not rendered the more miserable here.' This was by no means the last petition the Council received from the Metters on this subject. The subservient tone they adopted may strike us as somewhat distasteful, but it was the normal mode of address for any supplicant at the time.

The Weighing of Coal

The 1735 petition contained a footnote, 'if coals were weighed as in other places it would please and be an advantage both to buyer and seller'. The Metters were not to know what trouble this simple request was to cause them. At that time, coal and peat were measured in 'deals', great rectangular wooden boxes, 7 feet by 4 feet by 18 inches deep. It took the Council two years to make up its mind to replace the deals with weighbeams, but in the autumn of 1737, two Bailies, a Deacon and the Committee for Public Works had a day out in Leith superintending experiments with coal of different qualities to find the average weight of a deal. (For some reason known only to themselves, the Council had decided that the Metters should continue charging dues per deal, in spite of the fact that the coal was weighed by the hundredweight). The experimenters spent 13s on a coach to take them there and back and £2 5s 3d on their refreshment at McDougall's in Leith.

The Committee concluded that a deal should be deemed to weigh 'twentythree hundred English weight' - just over one ton. The dues should be 1d sterling from the seller and a halfpenny from the buyer, whether free or unfree. 'And the weigher or metter to be bound to put the coal into carts carefully, without any further fee. And for that end, every metter or weigher to provide themselves with three backets (shallow wooden containers normally used as scoops for lime and salt) at least, for gathering and loading the small coal.' Peat continued to be measured in the deals. Two weighbeams belonging to the City were taken out of store and set up on the Coalhill, the Metters being responsible for their upkeep. Then there was an unwelcome development. In January 1738, John Inglis, an Edinburgh baker, was appointed Overseer of the Metters by the Council. He had charge of the weights and measures, and responsibility for seeing that the Metters obeyed all the Council's regulations. The eleven Metters had to pay him a twelfth of their income and accept Inglis as their Boxmaster. The Council was obviously aware how unpopular this would be, as they appointed him a Constable, so that he could enforce his authority.

The new system had teething problems. The Council had to pass a new Act in March forbidding the measuring of coal or the weighing of peat, and ordering the Metters to have tables of their charges printed and publicly displayed in Leith. In April, their Overseer decided that his allowance was insufficient, and the Metters were ordered to give him an extra 6d each per month. They must have wished they had never mentioned weighing to the Council!

The order for the Overseer's extra allowance was rescinded in 1741. Two years later the Boxmaster was John Haddaway, one of the Metters. In 1744 the Metters made an agreement with three labourers to 'tak kar of the brods (weighing pans) and wayts as far as Lyes in owr powr and to Lock them Evry Night and open them Evry Morning'. It would seem that after the initial experiment the Council admitted defeat in the matter of Overseers: they were certainly never mentioned again.

The Scales

One result of the change which was permanently with the Metters, was the cost of upkeep of the scales, which was mainly carried out by a smith. The support for each weighbeam consisted of a pair of 'triangles' - two wooden legs joined at an acute angle at the top and linked by an iron bar at the base. The two triangles were linked at the top by a short beam (baulk) and by iron bars at the base. Under the baulk was fixed a 'pair of shears', a flat piece of metal with a hole at each end, bent to the shape of three sides of a rectangle. Into this the weigh-beam was fixed with a swivel bar, which passed through the holes in the shears. At least one of the scales had a pointer fixed to the shears, which hung vertical when the correct weight was reached. The scale-pans or 'brods' were wooden platforms or shallow boxes hung on chains, which were removed each night and kept under lock and key, with the weights. As well as quite frequent repairs to the scales, the Metters had to pay for upkeep of the weights. Their handles had a tendency to fall off, and from time to time the weights had to be adjusted.

The Metters did their own upkeep as far as possible. They kept a supply of nails, tar and grease for use on the scales, and offset the cost of repairs by supplying old iron for the smith to use. At the end of the century, one Metter each year was elected to take charge of the scales - an officer who became known as the Toolmaster.

New Metters

Judging by the lack of petitions from the Metters to the Council in mid-century, they seem to have benefitted by the upturn in trade at the time. In fact in 1753, their numbers were increased from 17 to 20, with usual proviso that the widows (five at this time) be forbidden to work. Two of the men appointed had a farming background and the other had been a brewer. James Comb had been tenant of a farm at Cramond, but his landlord had sold the farm and the new owner intended to work it himself. As a farmer he had had considerable experience of measuring grain and the Council approved his application. Walter Auld was from Dedrig in Mid-Calder. He had been in farming all his working life, working for the Earl of Buchan and Lord Torphichen. He was now in straitened circumstances and unable to support his family of five children. His application was accompanied by a testimonial stating that he was of honest character.

Walter Meicklejohn was appointed in 1754. He had lived in Leith for the past 19 years, during eight of which he had run his own brewery. Bad debts and other misfortunes had forced him into bankruptcy. His testimonial, which bore ten signatures, said that 'notwithstanding of these misfortunes, he is looked upon to be a very honest man, and has always retained a fair character...he is a man of sober life and conversation and well affected to His Majesty, his person and Government'. The Jacobite Rebellion of 1745 was obviously still very fresh in everybodys' memories.

Hard Times

By 1772 the Metters were once again in a bad way. There were 29 of them, when half the number would have been sufficient for the work which came their way. Their petition on the subject was prompted by problems with non-members who were doing work which should have come to them. An ex-army sergeant called George Thomson had started measuring small coal at Leith. He had persuaded the skippers of the coal brigs to employ him rather than the Metters and had even obtained an injunction against them in the Bailie Court forbidding them to measure small coal. The Metters explained that, 'the small coal is the best branch of our work, is one with very little expense as nothing is needed but a half barrel to measure them with, whereas the great coal needs long attendance and great expense in keeping up the standard and beams and scales and weights for weighing the coal.' What is more, one of the chief coal merchants of Leith was doing his own weighing, and an importer of oak bark had taken over its weighing from the Metters.

For their part, the merchants complained about malpractice by the Metters, who were not above increasing their receipts by foul means if fair ones did not make them a living. During one bad patch, the Metters were making only two shillings a week each, so it is not surprising that they sometimes succumbed to temptation. It is worth remembering that the Metters could do other work if it was available, especially at times when they only got one Turn in a month. The problem here is that alternative employment probably dried up just at the times when the Metters needed it most.

Their petition of 1775 graphically illustrates some of their problems. Their rates had not been raised since 1738. The increase in the amount of grain imported since then had benefitted them little as it mostly belonged to freemen who only paid them a farthing a boll. In 1738 most of the grain importers had been unfreemen, paying a halfpenny per boll (the Metters called the ships carrying unfreemens' grain 'halfpennyworths'). Food prices had also risen during that time. Working practices had changed, with the recent introduction of bushel measures to replace firlots. As the bushel was a smaller measure, they now had six measurements to make per boll instead of four as formerly. The problem of private individuals weighing coal and bark continued.

> The Metters are above half of the year idle, and their business when throng is the most severe for the time than can well be figured, particularly in a ship with grain heated, and it has always been remarked that their lives are short, and them who are able to work much oppressed with widows and disabled members [currently 8 widows and 3 old men], and are not able, on the whole, to get a living as a Metter.

The Council seems to have ignored this plea, because things were no better at the end of the century. In 1799 the Metters presented yet another petition, having some time before had various requests remitted to the Shore Dues Committee with no result. They again pointed out that their fees had not been raised for 50 years, during which time the cost of living had risen considerably. There were still 20 Metters and it needed 7500 bolls of grain to give each one a Turn, and even then it would provide less than one Turn per month. At present they only got one Turn in three months, providing 6s 3d to support themselves and their families. The upkeep of the weighing scales was costing them £6 - £7 per year, and they had also to keep up the funds of their Incorporation in order to pay sick benefit and widows' pensions. They could not increase their income by measuring grain in the merchants' lofts, because the merchants used their own men to do the work. They and/or their wives and families must, however, have been supplementing their Metting income; they could not otherwise have survived, if it was as low as they said it was. Merchants had previously complained that most of the Metters were too old for their work. If the trade did not provide a living wage, it is not surprising if young, fit, family men were not engaging in it.

The Metters asked for a rise in fees according to an amended table enclosed with the petition (see below) and to have the sole measuring of corn and weighing of bark, kelp, salt, coal, stucco, chalk, peat etc. The weighing had formerly been their privilege, but the merchants were now employing old soldiers and other men to weigh their goods.

Table of Metters' Dues 1799

	Present		Proposed	
	Free	Unfree	Free	Unfree
Measuring grain from ship - per boll	¼d	½d	½d	¾d
Measuring grain from loft - per boll	½d	½d	½d	¾d
Measuring meal from ship/loft - per boll	½d	½d	¾	1½d
Weighing bark - per ton	5d	8d	8d	1s
salt - per ton	5d	8d	8d	1s
kelp - per ton	2d	4d	4d	8d
stucco - per ton	2d	4d	4d	8d
chalk - per ton	2d	4d	4s	8d
coal - per deal	1d	1d	2d	4d
small coal - per barrel	⅓d	½d	½d	¾d
peat - per boll	1d	2d	2d	4d

The result of this petition fell far short of the Metters' hopes. The rate for measuring grain was raised to ⅓d for freemen and ½d for unfree. The council refused to consider banning merchants from using their own men to weigh goods. The Porters presented a petition at the same time as the Metters, which gives a similar picture of hardship.

The Call-House

The nineteenth century was only seven days old when the Council made a decision which stirred the Metters to outright rebellion. They proposed to set up an office at Leith for the hiring of Porters, Carters and Metters. From the point of view of the merchants this was a very good idea. The Council also would welcome the chance to get a tighter grip on the harbour workers.

For the workers involved it meant a complete loss of independence. They would be entirely under the control of the Office Keeper, who would assign them their work and regulate their numbers. None would be allowed to work unless he had signed on at the office and if anyone had a complaint against them, it would be dealt with by the Office Keeper, an appointee of the Council. On top of this, each man was to contribute 1s per quarter for the Office Keeper's pay.

The Council held its fire for a year, then on 28 January 1801 it appointed the Office Keeper, David Baveridge. Three months later he complained that, while he had had many applications from merchants for workers, the men themselves completely boycotted the Office, utterly refusing to sign on. The Council ordered that the Porters and Carters must do so under pain of stiff penalties, culminating in dismissal. A fortnight later the Metters contributed £2 'for the defence against a callhouse, in company with the Porters and Carters'. They must have been successful. Five years later new regulations were drawn up for the Porters, and there is no mention of a 'callhouse' or anything like it.

The Metters Revived

The first quarter of the nineteenth century was a bad time for the Metters. Their numbers dwindled until in 1812 there were only a dozen of them. The victory at Waterloo in 1815 finally removed the threat of French privateers which had dogged Scottish shipping for the past 45 years. This might have been good for trade in general, but it meant that merchant convoys no longer gathered at Leith to wait for their Naval escorts, and much business was lost to the Port. The Metters were even reduced to borrowing money in order to carry out the charitable obligations of their Incorporation. By 1822 there were only seven of them left and they applied to the Council for a new constitution. The resulting 'Society of Sworn Meters and Weighers of Leith' revitalised their trade. By 1828 their numbers had almost doubled, and they never seriously declined again until the Second World War in 1939.

The Timber Bush

One of the many bones of contention between the ships masters and the Shoredues office during the eighteenth century was the question of dues on timber. It was of relatively small value in itself, so the imposition of even modest dues could disproportionately affect the merchant's profit margin. Besides Shoredues, they also had to pay the City for storage of their wood in the its official repository, the Timber Bush. Edinburgh considered the Timber Bush to be one of its sources of income from the port. The actual history of the Bush throughout the period suggests that it may at times have been more of a liability than a benefit to the City. Most of the Tacksmen of the Bush Dues had great difficulty in covering their expenses, and by the end of the century, much of the ground had been feued to individuals.

In 1700 the Bush stood alone on a jutting piece of land between the Sands to the north and what is now Bernard Street to the south. The buildings lining the Shore bounded it on the west, and on its eastern side the Links ran down to the beach. Its northward boundary still retained the angular outline of the sixteenth century Ramsay's Fort in which it had been established. It was enclosed by walls, in which were two official entrances, the one from the Shore, and the 'back gate' in the eastern wall. Just inside the Shore entrance was a shed where the ropes for the crane were kept. Near the back gate was a house, known as the 'Bush House' which, during the early years of the century, was occupied by either the Tacksman or the Collector of the Bush Dues.

At the start of the century the Bush seems to have been underused. In 1692, merk per tun dues were reimposed on timber, resulting in a sharp drop in imports. The impost was removed the following year, but the Tacksman for the 1692 only managed to recover half his tack rent. He was also brought to a 'low condition' by the capture of some of his goods by the French. In 1695 the Edinburgh Council remitted some of his tack rent. A plan of Leith published in the same year shows the Bush sparsely dotted with a few stacks of timber.

The Tacksmen

At the turn of the century the Tacksman was William Wilson. His attitude to the Tack can only be described as the triumph of hope over experience! In 1699 he took a three-year lease at a rent of £680 per year for the first two years and £880 for the final year. His receipts were as follows:

1699 - 1700	160,000	(pieces?) timber at 5 merks per ton	£533 6s 8d
1700 - 1701	102,000	~	£340 0s 0d
1701 - 1702	104,000	~	£406 13s 4d

Over the three years Wilson paid the Council £2240 in tack rent and received only £1280 in dues, a shortfall of £960, of which the Council graciously remitted him just £100. At Martinmas 1702 he did not renew his tack, but the Council appointed him to collect the dues for the ensuing year. They amounted to only 380 merks. For one more year he collected the dues, after which we lose sight of him for a while. He appears in the record again in 1707, by which time he had taken on the Tack again for three years - at a rent of 1320 merks per year! One wonders what on earth he thought he was doing.

In the year 1706-1707 only 97,185 (pieces?) of timber came into Leith, the dues amounting to just 500 merks. As Wilson himself explained in his subsequent petition to the Edinburgh Council:

> which is a demonstration beyond all exception that the petitioner is involved in a Tack that threatens his utter ruin unless your Lordships and Honours have sympathy with him and commiserate his misfortune and grant him an ease. Which the petitoner's honest heart would not, if he were in any way in a condition to support the burden. And to evidence the truth thereof he has borrowed money as far as his credit could go and paid the Chamberlain 800 merks for the last year, which is 300 merks more than the duty of the timber imported did yield.'

Perhaps the import of timber was rising, which encouraged William Wilson to take on such a ridiculous Tack, but as the dues for 1702 to 1703 only amounted to 300 merks, the quantity of timber would have had to have increased at least five-fold for him to have made a profit. An unlikely scenario, to say the least.

The Timber Bush seems to have attracted the incompetent. William Richardson, the Clerk of the Weigh-house, took the Tack for two years at the Public Roup in 1716 and had to borrow to cover the first year's tack rent. His takings for the second year did not cover the rent and he had to carry over the first year's deficiency as well. In July 1719 he still had not paid his arrears and the City Treasurer had him imprisoned 'in the Tolbooth of Edinburgh, where he had lain a fortnight past in a most destitute condition, being entirely forsaken by his parents and friends, who will by no means concern themselves with him.' The committee appointed by the Council to look into the case was of the same opinion as Richardson's family - that the shortfall was his own fault. Moreover his cautioner, William Livingston, was in bad circumstances, and only able to offer 500 of the 800 merks demanded by the City. The Council decided to accept the reduced sum, rather than lose the whole.

Richardson had also been something of a disaster as Clerk of the Weigh-house. His Tacksman, John Bruce, brought a complaint against him in 1719. Many of the notes of lyage (storage) and weighage had not been entered in his books, and he had 'intromitted with' dues worth more than £700 scots, which he could not repay. Bruce asked the Council to get the books put in order and recover the money, because without it he could not pay his tack rent.

The Timber Bush Dues

During the second year of Richardson's tack of the Bush, a new table of dues was published, perhaps in an attempt to increase the takings. The dues were modest enough, considering that they were in the devalued Scots currency, and covered storage for up to a year:

120 deals or single trees		6s	8d
120 double trees		13s	4d
120 x 14-ell trees	£1		
120 x 16-ell trees	£2		
120 x 3 foot oak or beech knapholt		10s	
120 x 4-5 foot knapholt	£1		
120 x 6 foot knapholt	£1	10s	
120 x 9 foot wainscot logs	£3		
120 x 12 foot wainscot logs	£4		
each oak/beech plank of 10-18 feet		1s	
each fir plank of 14 feet or more			6d
each piece fir timber larger than a 16-ell tree		1s	
each 100 square feet oak timber other than knapholt and wainscot		10s	
each last of goods commonly sold by the last (pitch and tar)	£1		
each 1200 slates or 1000 pan tiles		6s	8d

All dues had to be paid for the year, in advance, timber being sometimes left in the Bush for two years or more. Unfreemen paid double dues and were obliged to store their imported timber, tar and pitch in the Bush or in the Town's Yard behind the Weigh-house. If they failed to pay, the Tacksman was empowered to seize goods worth twice the amount owed. If they were not redeemed within 30 days, he might sell them.

Timber unloaded at the Shore was brought in through the western gate, but logs destined for the sawmill which stood on the Links, were thrown into the harbour and floated round. Logs and large 'crukit' timbers for shipbuilding were floated to the Sandport, where the carpenters had their own sawpits. While goods remained in the Bush, the Tacksman was responsible for their security. He gave the owner a receipt when his timber was brought in and had to deliver up the correct amount when required. When owners and their men intended to remove goods they had to inform the Tacksman, who then had no further responsibility for them. Unless the timber was to be shipped at the Shore, it had to be removed via the eastern gate.

In order to prevent the Tacksman from charging too highly, one table of Dues had to be fixed on the gate of the Bush and another in the Weigh-house. The penalty for failure to do this was £40. If the tables were not posted, the first man to inform the Council would be excused all harbour dues on the next cargo he imported. The fine for overcharging by the Tacksman was 50 merks (£33 6s 8d scots).

The paucity of references (two) to the Bush in the Council Minutes for the 1720s suggests that the amount collected in dues increased during that time. From 1725 to 1735 the City was able to realise a yearly average of 724 merks (£40 10s) in tack rent. However, an Act of Council of 1733, in answer to a petition by the Tacksman, stated that the Bush was by no means crowded with timber.

There had been a certain amount of pilfering, and the 1733 Tacksmen suspected the sawyers who worked in the Bush. The men were ordered to find caution for their honesty, and to work only during the daylight hours. There had been some quibbling over what size of timber constituted a fir plank (much used in shipbuilding). The Council decreed that it must be at least 3 inches thick and 11 to 14 inches wide. The charge for it would then be ½d. Unfreemen had been attempting to evade charges by storing their goods elsewhere. The Tacksman was empowered to levy dues from them wherever their goods might be lodged, and impound the goods if necessary.

The Demise of the Tacksmen

By 1736 the Bush had once again become unprofitable, and it was impossible to find anyone to take the tack of the Dues. The Tacksmen of the Impost on Wine agreed to be responsible for their collection. In 1738, there was still no Tacksman, and the City appointed its own Collector of Bush and Weigh-house dues, at a salary of £35 pa. Resistance to payment was high, however, and the

Leith court officers had to be ordered to assist the Collector in his duties. In spite of this, he still owed the City for two years' dues in 1741. In the following year, the tacks of the Bush and Weigh-house Dues were revived on a joint basis, shared among three Tacksmen. No-one was prepared to take an individual risk on such a doubtful venture. However, even this expedient did not answer. The tack was intended to last for six years, but by November 1744 the Tacksmen had ceased to collect any of the dues, which became the responsibility of the Clerk of the Weigh-house. One of them had died insolvent without paying his Tack rent, one had previously withdrawn from his Tack and the remaining man resigned his share in April 1745. The City managed to recover the Tack rent for the period before November 1744, but had to be content with whatever the Clerk of the Weigh-house could manage to collect for the current year.

Development in and near the Bush

Leith had hitherto been largely confined to the limits of the sixteenth century fortifications, but in the eighteenth century the town at last began to expand outwith these ancient boundaries. One obvious area for development was the unused sandy ground to the east of the timber bush. The first occupant of this land was the architect William Adam, father of the more famous Robert and his two brothers, all of whom followed their father's profession. The Adams imported considerable quantities of building materials through Leith, and in 1735 William petitioned the City Council for a feu of 1¼ acres of the Links 'sometimes flooded by the stream tides' on the east side of the Bush and the Stage Coach yard, which lay to the south of it. The land ran down to the beach, and was bounded on the east by the road from Leith to the Sands. William enclosed the plot to make a repository for his materials. A year later he bought from the Council a plot of similar size on the further side of the road to the Sands. After William died, in 1748, these yards were inherited by John, his eldest son. By this date the second piece of land was smaller by a 30 foot strip, which William had given up to the proprietor of the Glasshouse which was built to the north of his yard in 1747, after the burning of the original premises in North Leith.

The Bush itself began to be seriously divided up at the end of the 1740s, probably as a result of the City's difficulties over the collection of Dues. Another factor was the upturn in trade and consequent investment in industry, which began at about this time. Two pieces of the Bush had already been feued, one in 1716 to Samuel Mclellan, and another on the south side, to James Syme, an Edinburgh slater, in 1727. In 1725 John Wilson of Edinburgh had been granted a lease of ground at the east end for a marble polishing works, and since at least 1733, one James Sutherland had leased a small yard.

William Mitchell, owner of the Sawmill on the Links, also held the lease of a yard in the Bush, which expired in 1748. He had built a stable and hayloft there, and when he petitioned for the grant of a new lease, the Council would only entertain his request on condition that the new lease would allow them to demolish the buildings if it should become necessary. He was granted a 19-year lease, to be finalised once he had paid up his arrears of rent.

William Mitchell presented his petition in March 1748, and it sparked off a succession of similar requests. On the same day, the owners of the Glasshouse asked for more land in order to extend their premises, and a Leith merchant attempted to solve a pressing problem. His name was David Oliphant, and he owned a house opposite the Weigh-house, whose back premises overlooked the Bush. Stacks of timber were built right up against his ground-floor windows, cutting out the light. Moreover, the stacks were so high, that a potential burglar could easily reach his second-floor windows simply by climbing up them. The boys of Leith used the Bush as a playground - among other things they were accused of taking away pieces of timber. David Oliphant complained that they climbed up the stacks and broke his windows. He asked for a feu of a strip of land 20 feet wide, and the length of the back of his house (60 feet), which he intended to enclose with a wall. However, William Mitchell's stable must have rankled with the Council. David Oliphant's very reasonable request was refused, on the grounds that land in the Bush was intended only for the storage of timber. A month later, however, he successfully petitioned for a lease of the same strip of land, to last for three periods of nineteen years.

Colin Campbell, with John Campbell, cashier to the Royal Bank of Scotland, had begun to quarry marble at Nether Lorn. In April 1748 they petitioned the Council for space in the Bush to set up a marble polishing works and to store slate, which they intended to import. There was an area on the south side which was too rough and uneven for the storage of timber. They proposed to level the ground, enclose it with a wall, and build 'shades' (open-sided sheds or loggias) to shelter their workmen. The Council granted them a 57-year lease of a plot 174 feet long by 38 feet broad. They were allowed one gate in their new wall. The Company spent nearly £400 on their new buildings, but unfortunately the Marble Works were not a success and in the late 1750s John and Colin Campbell were forced to buy out the rest of their partners. In 1760 the Council granted them permission to sublet their premises in the Bush. Seven years later, these were taken over by Christopher Wood, an Edinburgh coal merchant. John Wilson's marble works, for which he had obtained the lease in 1725, was more successful. His son was still in possession of 'The Marble Yard' in 1777.

The Boiling House

The year 1750 saw the beginning of regular whaling from Leith, when the newly-formed Edinburgh Whale Fishing Company sent its first ship, the 330-ton *Trial* to Greenland in April (see Chapter 12). She was still away in July, when the Company petitioned the Council for land on which to build a house for boiling blubber. The area in question was a part of the Sands, immediately outside the north wall of the Bush. Because the Bush had been enclosed by the northeast 'starwork' corner of the Leith fortifications, it projected northward for 38 feet at that point, forming a 'nitch'. (In the shelter of this projection, riders in the Races held on the Sands were weighed.) The measurement from the 'nitch' to a Lead Mill at the north end of the Shore was 300 feet, and it was part of this area that the Whale Company wanted.

The Council agreed that;

> this is a detached spot and the nearest void place to the Harbour for such a building and therefore, in their opinion, the fittest for rolling of such weighty casks as the blubber is put up in before it is boiled, by a passage that might be made from the Quay to this stretch of Sands, round the house next to the Lead Mill (the present Tower), which by laying part of it with timber would be exceeding convenient for this purpose.

The Company was granted a 57-year tack of a stretch measuring 80 feet westward from the 'nitch' and equal to its width. They were exempted from paying rent for the first 19 years of the lease because of the expense of setting up the business.

The inhabitants of Leith, especially those living near the Bush, were less than happy about their prospective neighbour, and sent a strong protest to the Council. It was signed by, among others, David Oliphant and Alexander Skirving (tenant of the Bush House). They objected to the smell, which must have been dreadful indeed if it was worse than the normal reek of middens and cesspits, which pervaded the town. There had been a suggestion that the works should be sited in North Leith, but this was rejected. The reasoning was similar to that put forward in a similar dispute in the seventeenth century. As the prevailing wind is from the southwest, '...it must be less ground of complaint of smoke and stink if the house is placed here than if it is placed in any part of North Leith.'

The other worry concerned the risk of a fire being started in the stored timber in the Bush by sparks from the chimneys of the Boiling House. The protestors pointed out that a petition to build the Glasshouse on the same site had been refused on these grounds. They considered for some reason that the Boiling House would be far more hazardous.

The Council took this complaint more seriously. By the terms of their lease, the Company had to raise the north wall of the Bush by at least three feet above the eventual height of their Boiling House. Any chimney stacks were to be made in their own north wall and not on the wall of the Bush. At first they stipulated that the roof must take the form of a lean-too rather than a set-on or pavilion type. However, when the Company obtained plans of the latest thing in Boiling House architecture from London in 1751, it was found that a pavilion roof was essential. Moreover, they would need a plot 90 feet long. The cost was estimated at £500, too much to spend on buildings on land that was only leased. They requested a feu, but the Council was reluctant to grant this, and compromised with a 99 year lease.

In the end, the Company obtained a strip 91 feet long, tapering from 38 feet at the 'nitch' to 28 feet at the western end. The reason for the odd shape was that their north wall had to be in line with the north wall of the 'nitch'. They built a Boiling House 43 feet long, with a loft over it, in the western half. A shade 48 feet long filled the rest of the plot, entered by a gate on the seaward side.

Overcrowding

Another industry which was gaining ground in Leith was the importing and processing of tobacco. In 1751, Alexander Brown, a tobacco merchant requested a plot of land in the Bush to build a warehouse. The Council granted him the Town's Yard, another timber repository, situated behind the Weigh-house. The City established a new yard of 100 feet by 55 feet, within the 'nitch' in the Bush. Along the length of the north wall they built a shade, using materials from the old shade in their former yard.

In 1752, the Council began to be alarmed at how little public space was now left in the Bush;

> of late the trade of their Port of Leith is greatly increased, and that although in some former years grants have been made to private persons of part of the Bush of Leith, which for the future ought not to be done, as it very much straitens the trades who were formerly accommodated with proper conveniences therein.'

They tried, unsuccessfully, to reclaim some of the ground feued to John Adam outwith the east end of the Bush.

A New Tacksman and Reorganisation

One consequence of the upturn in trade was that at last a Tacksman was found for the Weigh-house and Bush dues - David Oliphant, whose house backed on to the Bush. Now that this problem was solved, the Council decided on a thorough overhaul of the organisation of the Bush. To bring some order to the place it was to be divided up by two east/west roads, intersected by three others running north/south. All roads were to be kept clear of timber to allow carts to pass each other, and the timber was to be restowed in proper order. The Tacksman would tell porters where to stow their loads and was authorised to move any quantity of timber up to 120 deals if the space was needed by a larger cargo. Sawpits were to be confined to the space near the west wall. Tar and pitch was to be lodged only in the shade. The practice which had recently arisen of storing lead in the Bush was to cease, as it was destroying the roads.

The review also attempted to maximise profits. The table of dues, which had not altered since 1717, was to be revised, (in fact it was merely reissued) and the stipulation about double charges for unfreemen was reiterated. Porters bringing in timber without the knowledge of the Tacksman would be dismissed. Security was to be tightened. The main gates and their locks would be repaired and the keys given to the Tacksmen. They would be opened at 6.00am in summer (8.00am in winter) and closed at 8.00pm in summer (4.00pm in winter). The door in the north wall made for the Whale Fishing Company was to be blocked up and the entrances to their boiling house locked, the key to be held by the Tacksman. Ten other individuals and companies had private entrances into the Bush which 'rendered (it) almost useless as a safe repository...no Tacksman for many years past has received any dues for goods lodged there, the people always losing, or pretending to have lost, a greater value of their timber than all the dues amounted to.' Until these private gates were dealt with the Tacksman could not issue receipts which made him responsible for security.

Boys caught removing deals by the porters would be held by the Tacksman until a 1s fine had been paid. The Tacksman would keep an account of the timber lodged in the Bush by each owner, but would not be responsible if the owners' men moved it or removed it without his permission.

Hygiene was also considered. Workmen were forbidden to use the Bush as a 'house of office'. Anyone living in the neighbouring houses who was caught throwing 'nastiness' out of their windows was liable to prosecution by the Tacksman.

How much, if any, of this programme was carried out is not clear. Certainly, by 1762, the tack of the Bush dues was once more such an unattractive proposition that no-one could be found to take it on, and until 1767 the Bush was in the hands of the City. During that time no dues were charged, as no-one was appointed to collect them. James Ballet was asked by one of the Bailies to keep the gates repaired and pay the men who opened and closed them morning and evening. He tried to keep an account of the timber stored there from the Customs accounts. These, of course, showed only the amount imported, which did not necessarily all find its way into the Bush. Ballet himself, in the report he submitted to the Council in January 1766, commented that most of the planking was carried directly to North Leith, presumably for the use of the shipbuilders. He also pointed out that 'the kind of timber now imported differs much from what it was formerly. Few of these are to be found in the printed Table of Dues'. His opinion was that a new Table should be drawn up, with the help of the Wood Measurer.

Ballet's list of all timber imported in the years 1762 to 1765 shows that that there was indeed a much wider variety than the categories covered by the official Table. This in itself must have contributed greatly to the difficulty of calculating and collecting the dues.

The City's inertia was such, however, that the Council did not get around to seriously considering the position of the Bush and Weigh-house until 1768, when they instituted yet another inquiry. The appointed committee reported that no Bush Dues had been collected since 1762, although the Clerk of the Weigh-house had collected the dues payable there. They accepted that the timber now imported was very different from that brought into Leith at the time when the table of dues was drawn up. It was uncertain whether it was legal to change the table, but after consulting the original grant of the 'common closets', now the Bush, in the Golden Charter of 1603, they decided that the City had the right to do so. This was to be put in hand immediately. Arrears on the payments as per the present table were to be recovered, and the practice of allowing credit for Weigh-house Dues to be stopped. It was another two years before the new table of Bush Dues was approved and a new Tacksman found -John Jamieson, a merchant of Leith and possibly a descendant of James Jamieson the shipbuilder, who held the lease of the Town's Yard in the Bush.

John Jamieson faced enormous difficulties in his task of making the Bush pay. It was at least eight years and probably longer, since anyone had payed dues there. His first battle was with William Mitchell and his partner John Tod. They leased the land which had originally been granted on the strength of William's ownership of the Sawmill. Their lease stated that they were excused from dues, but Jamieson pointed out that as the Sawmill no longer existed, they should no longer be exempted. By 1774 so many people had refused to pay, that Jamieson had a long list of prosecutions pending in the Court of Session, the sums involved amounting to £213 5s 8d. Edinburgh decided to prosecute offenders as well, because until all the actions were settled, Jamieson's tack, which had run out, could not be renewed.

The Weigh-House

At the same time that John Jamieson took over the tack of the Bush, one of his fellow-merchants, Thomas Walker, did the same for the Weigh-house. He also was faced with the consequences of years of neglect. The building had not been repaired since 1751, when the whole of one end had been practically rebuilt. Now the main gates and the inner doors needed attention, and all the locks were totally inadequate, exposing the goods stored within to the danger of theft. The paving was so broken up that water was lying permanently in the cracks, damaging stored goods. Many windows lacked glass, letting in rain and snow. The Clerk's office was 'so low and damp that it is hazardous to the Clerk's health to work in it.' It needed to be lined with boards. It was so poorly lighted (no candle was allowed for it) that no business could be done there after 3.00pm in winter.

The smaller of the two weighbeams was unfit for use, so that small amounts of goods had to be weighed on the large beam. The weights had not been adjusted for years, and now weighed light. What is more, there were not enough of them to weigh anything heavier than 14½cwt, whereas casks of ashes and yarn might weigh as much as 20-25cwt. 'The want of those weights are supplied by the porters getting into the scale, which is not only improper and hurtful to the beam, but dangerous to all concerned.'

Over the year, the Council had allowed increasing numbers of private individuals to use their own scales and weights. Now two thirds of all imported iron, all tallow from beasts slaughtered in Leith and all butter in lumps of more than six pounds were lost to the Weigh-house. Walker thought it 'hard to pay such a heavy rent for the Weigh-house and be deprived of what is the common dues, which will ultimately land on the Town, as though (he) must at first be the loser, no other will give such a rent again if the present practice is allowed.'

The inadequate response of the Committee sent to investigate the complaints was to have the doors repaired and secured, three new windows put in and the weights adjusted. The last item was particularly shortsighted as the City had spare weights and a small weighbeam in its own store, which would have cost it nothing to supply to the Tacksman.

The Bush Feued and Extended

The tack of the Timber Bush was never renewed, although John Jamieson continued to be called the Tacksman. He and his two partners collected the dues until 1780. After paying the fees of the Collector and the man who opened and closed the gates, and for various repairs, they were worth only about £15 a year to the City. In 1780, most of the ground was feued out. Plots were bought by William Robertson and George Henderson. John Learmonth bought a large area in the northwest corner, which he extended by taking in about a quarter of an acre of the Sands. By the end of the year, only about half an acre was left for public use.

In 1781, a small Naval Yard was established on the western half of the land to the east of the Bush which had belonged to the Adam brothers.

Most of the feued land was built on, mainly warehouses. Jamieson himself built a large warehouse on a plot he had leased to the south of the Town's Yard. He later obtained a feu of the plot and of the Yard itself, on which he built another warehouse.

In 1792 the Whale Fishing Company applied for an extension to their premises in order to help their 'languishing' trade. To the south of their Boiling House was a small area with a well which they had always used for cleaning bones and storing casks. Although this ground was not included in their lease; 'even when the Bush was a general repository of deals for all the merchants in that trade, this area was always reserved by the Good Town for the use of the Whale Fishing Company.'

The company also beached its boats on the Sands to the north of the Boiling House, where they were so damaged by 'idle boys' that the cost of making them seaworthy when they were needed added considerably to the expense of fitting out their ships for the sea. They were granted a lease of the ground in front of their Boiling House and of the part of the Sands in line with John Learmonth's extension and another made by a Mr Martin at the east end of the Bush.

Most of the leaseholders and feuars of land in the Bush were timber merchants who established private timber yards there, but in 1806 they were among the signatories of a petition to the Council for some public storage space. Some cargoes of timber were being sent to other ports for lack of space in Leith, and they proposed that an area of the Sands should be set aside for the purpose. Although the petitioners were told to produce plans and estimates for the new yard, nothing seems to have been done about it. Within a few years, however, timber yards were established on the seaward side of the new Wet Docks.

Only four years after the above petition, the Leith Directory lists only one timber merchant among the tenants of the Timber Bush. There may well have been others who did not appear in the Directory, but it is likely that most had begun to use the timber yards which formed part of the new Docks complex. The tenants of the Bush listed in the Directory for 1810-11 are as follows:

Beck, Kerr and Co	wholesale merchants
Brodie Alexander	corn merchant
Brown Robert	merchant
Calvert F	porter storehouse
Coldstream/Carstairs	merchants
Davidson and Gray	stone warehouse
Dryden John	blockmaker
Duncan James	insurance broker
Hutchison T	wood merchant
Jamieson J & R	merchants
Panton George	merchant and agent
Scott John	merchant
Short William	vintner
Smith James and Co	wholesale merchants, ship owners and agents
Williamson and Gavin	rope and sail makers
Wishart James	ship broker and wharfinger

Trinity House

No history of the port of Leith in the eighteenth century would be complete without a mention of the Trinity House. The Masters of the House continued their charitable work, supporting the widows of their members both in the Hospital and as out-pensioners. Less frequently the children of members were helped. A few of the members themselves became recipients of pensions, but this was rare at a time when men worked well into old age and in a profession where a large proportion of them died comparatively young. The pensions were still financed by the Crown Money (Prime Gilt went to the upkeep of the Hospital), and they rose 'in line with inflation'. In 1747 there were about a dozen pensioners, receiving an average of 3s per quarter. By 1771 there were twenty, and the average pension was 8s per quarter. Within the lifetime of an individual widow, her pension would be adjusted according to her circumstances. For a younger woman it was regarded as a supplement to low earnings, the elderly and infirm received more help. Captains' widows were also better provided by the House, as Masters paid higher dues to the Crown Money fund. They might get as much as £5 per year - a sum which can be compared with the £5 - £8 paid to a sailor for a voyage to the New World.

The House was consulted by the Edinburgh Council about any proposed improvements to the Harbour, and the Masters supported the many petitions to the Council from Captains whose vessels had been damaged by 'sitting down' on rocks in the various berths. They had close links with the Shoredues office, whose Collector also gathered in the Prime Gilt. The Shoremaster too had connections with the House. He, among other things, was Chief Pilot Master, and (unofficially) consulted the Masters in the provision and licensing of pilots and the use of the flags which signalled when the tide had risen enough to let ships get over the bar. For at least the last quarter of the century, the Shoremaster was a member of the House.

12

Jolly Tars - Hearts of Oak

At the time of the Parliamentary Union of Scotland and England in January 1707, the Scottish navy consisted of three men-of-war which had been commissioned by the Scottish Parliament in 1696 to guard the coasts against French privateers. *Royal William* and *Royal Mary* (named after the King and Queen) patrolled the east and the *Dumbarton Castle* the west coast. The threat from the French was intermittent, and in quiet periods the vessels were chartered by merchants - the pattern which had prevailed in Scotland since time immemorial. After the Union, the three frigates were absorbed into the English Navy, as fifth and sixth rates, the *Royal William* and the *Royal Mary* being renamed HMS *Edinburgh* and HMS *Glasgow*, as their original names were duplicated by other Naval ships.

France was engaged in so many land wars at this time, that she was forced to reduce the size of her navy. However, the French Government encouraged its mariners to become privateers, and these individuals presented a considerable threat to Scottish shipping. Although Scotland was still trading, as she always had, to ports of the North Sea and the Baltic, the bulk of her shipping in the early eighteenth century was coastal. Even these little coasting barques were threatened, however, as they carried grain, coal, salt and other goods from port to port. French privateers did not confine themselves to the rich pickings of the English Channel and North Sea. The barques and fishing boats of the Scottish coast presented an easy target. A clutch of them could as yield as much profit in total as one large but well-armed merchantman.

Convoys - The Theory

In July 1708 the Convention of Royal Burghs sent a petition to Queen Anne's consort, Prince George of Denmark, who was also Lord High Admiral. They requested that the naval vessels which were already convoying Scottish merchant shipping overseas might also call at the ports from the Forth to the Orkneys on the east and the Isle of Man to the Clyde on the west coast. 'We entreat your Royal Highness in your great wisdom would be pleased to consider that seeing a great part of our trade is only from one harbour here to another, that therefore some ships of a small force would be of great use to protect us...'

Early in 1709 the Admiral granted the Convention's request and ordered a small squadron of Naval ships up to the northern coasts. Command of HM ships in Scottish waters was conferred on the Provost of Edinburgh. For the next four years all HM captains stationed off Scotland received their instructions for escorting convoys from the Provost, and all the merchants and ships masters of the East Coast Burghs sent their requests for convoys to him. It was during the Provost's period as 'admiral' that Edinburgh first began to consider major improvements to Leith.

As in the seventeenth century the organisation of the convoys centred on Leith. A victualling agent was based there, although this arrangement broke down in 1710 when his contract ran out. Two ships, HMS *Mermaid* and HMS *Greyhound* were in the Roads at the time in need of provisions before they could leave. The agent was finally persuaded to supply them with stores for two weeks, but this was not enough for the *Greyhound* to convoy a group of merchantmen to Gottenburg as planned. They had to set sail without an escort, and as a result two or three of them were captured.

Altogether, five of HM ships were employed in Scotland during the years 1709 to 1713, usually three at a time. They were organised in a similar fashion to that of the escort ships of the Commonwealth 60 years earlier. One or two vessels would cruise down the coast from Orkney, collecting their 'flock' on the way. A system of signal flags and gunshots was worked out so that the escorts would not have to waste time coming into harbour for each group of ships. At Leith, the fleet would rendezvous with the local merchantmen, and others which had made the port by themselves. In the Roads the shipping would be sorted out into destination groups and escorted to the ports for which they were bound. On the return journey the system worked in reverse.

Convoys in Practice

This, at least, was how it was supposed to work. In practice a combination of weather, enemy action and changes of plan ensured that the operation was often far from smooth.

Scottish recruits for the army in Flanders were due to leave Leith on 1 April 1710 and the Admiralty ordered all three of its ships to convoy them. The Provost had to ask them to leave one behind to escort 40 sail which needed to go to the north, and to bring back the victual barques which were waiting to come south. Some thirty vessels had been waiting for nearly a month in the Cromarty Firth and the grain they carried had heated up in their damp holds. By the time their escort sailed from Leith, 2000 bolls had been put ashore to dry out, and the rest was about to be unloaded. Furthermore there were two Frenchmen in the mouth of the Cromarty Firth, which had already captured two Dutch fishing boats. More victual ships were waiting in the Moray Firth, and at Fraserburgh and Peterhead.

When the transports sailed, under the escort of *Mermaid* and *Greyhound*, they took with them the merchantmen which were also bound for the Low Countries. More were waiting for them at Dunbar, where they were pinned into harbour by a 'swarm' of privateers.

When *Greyhound* returned to the Forth she went into Queensferry to refit (she was possibly the ship to which Edinburgh Council was referring when it complained of losing work to Queensferry for want of a suitable dock at Leith).

The work was only half completed when her Captain was put out to receive instructions from the Provost to convoy some merchants to Gottenburg. He pointed out that the refit was long overdue. Once it was finished, however, he set out as instructed, arriving back in the Forth by 22 June.

In August *Greyhound* was away once more, this time to the Orkneys, where merchantmen from Virginia, New England and the West Indies, who had come 'north about', were waiting for her escort to Leith. In order to pick up these vessels as quickly as possible, *Greyhound* had to abandon the original plan of collecting ships from Dundee, Montrose, Aberdeen and Fraserburgh. However, HMS *Glasgow* and HMS *Sheerness*, which had been sent to the Forth to convoy the New World ships south, were sent to Montrose to bring down the vessels waiting there and deal with the privateers which had recently taken seven barques in the area.

The presence of the Naval ships may have afforded some protection to convoys, but it did little to discourage the privateers, who cruised about in small companies, and effectively blockaded most shipping into its home ports for much of the time. In 1711, the navy sent only two vessels, and in April of that year the Convention of Royal Burghs complained to the Admiralty that their ships had lain for many months in Leith Roads 'so far within land that small privateers have come up the Firth almost in their view and made prizes, insulting at the same time the shore and calling for supplies, both of provisions and even pilots, on pain of military execution'.

The Pressgang

The Convention's petition mentions another matter which was becoming almost as great a problem as the privateers - the pressing of seamen. Before the Union, Scottish seamen had been strongly encouraged to join the Navy, and individual commanders of ships off her coasts were not above sending their own raiding parties ashore. However, it had never been Naval policy to officially impress Scots. It had even been, on occasions, expressly forbidden. All this was now at an end.

The unbelievably appalling conditions which prevailed on board Naval ships, meant that the Service was continually losing men from disease and desertion, quite apart from the hazards of war and weather. The Navy represented a bottomless pit of manpower requirements. In times of war, which meant in practice for much of the eighteenth century, the Pressgang became a familiar sight in Leith and the surrounding area.

The operation was efficiently organised. In the spring (war at sea, as on land, tended to cease during the winter) a Naval ship would appear in Leith Roads. On board would be the Regulating Sea Officer, who was in charge of the exercise. Under him were Lieutenants who led the Pressgangs in the actual gathering up of recruits. Among the Regulating Officer's papers was a bundle of Press Warrants, which he handed to the Provost of Edinburgh. These documents were for distribution among the Constables of Edinburgh and Leith, who assisted the Gangs in rounding up their victims. The Warrants were usually valid until the end of the year, after which local seafarers were relatively safe until the following spring. The unfortunates who were caught often found themselves in the West Indies or some equally distant location, sometimes for years on end, during which time their families were forced to fend for themselves.

As upholders of Law and Order in the days before the Police Force came into being, the Constables were not popular with some sections of the community. The office was not voluntary. Constables were chosen yearly by Edinburgh Council, and there were instances of men refusing to serve. Quite apart from

By the Commiſſioners for Executing the Office of Lord High Admiral of Great Britain *and* Ireland, *&c. and of all His Majeſty's Plantations,* &c.

IN purſuance of His Majeſty's Order in Council, dated the Seventh Day of May, 1790, We do hereby empower and direct you to impreſs as many Seamen, of ſtrong bodies and good health, as you poſſibly can procure, giving to each man ſo impreſſed One Shilling for Preſt Money. And, in the execution hereof, you are to take care not to demand or receive any Money, Gratuity, Reward, or other Conſideration whatſoever, for the ſparing, exchanging or diſcharging any perſon or perſons impreſſed or to be impreſſed, as you will anſwer it at your peril. This Warrant to continue in force 'till the *Thirty first* Day of *December* 1790: And, in the due execution of this Warrant, and every part of the ſame, all Mayors, Sheriffs, Juſtices of the Peace, Bailiffs, Conſtables, Headboroughs, and all others His Majeſty's Officers and Subjects whom it may concern, are hereby required to be aiding and aſſiſting to you, as they tender His Majeſty's Service, and will anſwer the contrary at their peril. Given under our Hands, and the Seal of the Office of Admiralty, the *twenty first* Day of *May* , 1790.

P. Hopkins.

Hood

A. Gardner

By Command of their Lordſhips,

Jn. Ibbetson

An eighteenth century press warrant, as issued to constables in Leith and Edinburgh (By courtesy of Edinburgh City Archive).

the discomfort of having to carry out socially unpopular duties, there was the nuisance of being permanently on call while following one's everyday occupation. Assisting the Pressgangs was one of the less attractive duties of a Constable, and James Donaldson of North Leith must have felt doubly aggrieved at the fate which befell him in July 1757.

A 'Pressed' Carpenter

Donaldson was a ships carpenter who was appointed Constable by the Bailies of the Canongate in November 1756. He was a reputable family man, and a member of the Kirk Session. During the summer of 1757 there was a Press of landsmen for soldiers (the army was another bottomless pit), and Donaldson not only assisted with it in the daytime, but by night as well, after a hard day's work in the shipyard. On 26 July, Captain Ferguson, the naval Regulating Officer, sent a party ashore in North Leith. One of the men they apprehended was Donaldson. In vain he showed them his Constable's baton and protested that he was exempt from impressment. The Lieutenant put him on board HMS *Princess of Wales*, which was lying in the Roads.

All the other Constables immediately formed a deputation to the Canongate Magistrates, who sent a strong protest to Captain Ferguson along with a letter from the Provost. Ferguson replied that as Donaldson was a ships' carpenter and had been to sea, he was liable to be pressed, no matter what his official status. The Provost sent another letter, as did the Lord Justice Clerk and the Lord Advocate, but to no avail. On Monday 1 August, when HMS *Arcturus* set sail from Leith to escort a convoy to London, Donaldson was aboard her.

The Canongate constables resigned their batons in a body, 'and refuse to act any longer under a law which has proved insufficient to protect them'. Not only were the Magistrates thus deprived of their law-enforcers, but the quartering arrangements for the soldiers billeted in their area were thrown into confusion. Quartering was part of the Constables' responsibilities both in Edinburgh and Leith, where troops continually came and went, necessitating constant re-arrangement of billets.

In the end the Provost wrote to the Admiralty, requesting them to instruct Captain Ferguson to release his 'recruit'. Here the record ends, and we do not know what was the carpenter's eventual fate. It does not, however, seem likely that the Lords of the Admiralty would be too concerned about the problems of the Canongate Magistrates or of one obscure ships' carpenter.

James Donaldson's story happened during a shortlived war which started in 1755 and had finished by the end of the decade. The bulk of the evidence for Pressgang activity in Leith comes from the years after 1770, and onwards into the nineteenth century, the period of Nelson's victories and later, the Napoleonic Wars.

Volunteers and Pressgang in Edinburgh

The Government began fitting out a Fleet in the autumn of 1770, and on 12 October, the Privy Council informed the Provost that seamen were required. He would be receiving Press Warrants giving his Constables authority to take up 'such seafaring men as shall lurk about the City, Port and Liberties of Edinburgh' and deliver them to the Regulating Captains. The Provost, however, was not entirely sure what might be the legal implications of the execution of the Warrants. He consulted the opinion of Counsel.

1 Were Constables to assist any Gang not actually headed by a Lieutenant?
 - No
2 Could men be taken from the City without examination by the City Council?
 - Yes
3 What must the Magistrates do if they received a complaint?
 - There is no general rule. Each case must be taken on its merits.
4 If the Magistrates perceived abuses, what could they do?
 - They might check any activities which disturbed the peace.

A fortnight after the Privy Council sent its letter to the Provost, Captain Napier, the Regulating Officer, sailed from London with several Lieutenants and a letter of introduction from the Admiralty. At the end of October, the Provost wrote to all seacoast towns warning them of the impending impressment. On 1 November Warrants were issued to all Edinburgh and Leith Constables. They included the instruction to give each pressed man a shilling (the 'King's Shilling') for 'pressed money' and a warning against accepting bribes to release conscripts.

At the end of November, a Royal Proclamation was promulgated, offering a bounty of 20s to any man who volunteered for service. The practice of serving seamen leaving their ship and signing on in another in order to claim bounty would be severely punished. Edinburgh offered an additional bounty of a guinea (£1 1s) for an ordinary seaman and two guineas for an able seaman. The ships waiting at Leith to receive them were HMS *Rendezvous*, on which served Lt Walsh, the organiser of the Press gangs, HMS *Portland* and the sloop *Hazard.*

Volunteers had to report to *Rendezvous* where Lt Walsh assessed each man's rating and then sent a list up to the Council Chamber bearing the names and rates of the men. The men themselves were also sent up to appear before the Council, but the bounty was not paid until they were on board ship. By 19 November, six able seamen had volunteered for service on *Portland.* Lt Walsh duly sent them up to the Council, with a note:

> All that is mentioned in the annexed list will appear before you, except James Rennie, who I thought necessary to ship off, being a fine fellow. After examination, if you find them entitled...please to send the Bounty per bearer, taking his receipt.

At the end of December he had to write to the Council again:

> Peter Mcdougal, an Edinburgh man and ordinary seaman, is actually on board the tender by some means. He is not marked down for the Bounty of a guinea which the Town allows. His wife is constantly plaguing me....I cannot give it to her without your approbation.

By the beginning of January 1771, 54 men had volunteered, most of them able rates.

After his arrival at Leith in October 1770, Captain Napier had compiled a list of all the seamen now working in and around Edinburgh, who had served in the previous war (this in spite of the fact that the King had granted an indulgence to serving seamen at the end of that war). On 3 December, he informed the Provost that these men had had long enough to volunteer, and he intended to send his Pressgang to the City to flush them out. He hoped for the Provost's co-operation, 'which will make this service go smoothly and without disturbing the peace of the City.'

Informers

The Regulating Officer was helped in making his list by various informers, who were paid for their information. Some were just troublemakers, like the individual who stated that one Adam Neil, who worked at Mr Fleming's printing works in the Old Fish Market Close, had once been at sea. Mr Neil lodged a complaint with the Provost, who subsequently received a letter of apology from Lt Walsh. The Pressgang seems to have caused some disturbance at the printing works and Lt Walsh explained to the Provost that their orders were 'not to offend man, woman or child' or to damage the houses or furniture of any they visit. Offenders were put on board a tender and subjected to military discipline - which presumably meant flogging.

Printers seem for some reason to have favoured ex-seamen as employees. In 1805 information was given against William Bell, working for Lawrie and Co, printers. 'He is a middling sized man, dark complexion and thin.'

In the same year, the Town Clerk received a letter about another print worker:

> Sir
>
> I am extremely sorry for so doing, but for the preservation of myself and others, I am forced to inform you that William Ferguson (son to Mr Ferguson, Painter, Grassmarket) at present working with Mundell and Son, Printers, has been at the sea for the space of three years and upwards, and with all the ferocity of a seaman threatens my destruction, and will no doubt accomplish his design, without you in your goodness prevent it, by sending him thither again. Therefore I trust that you, considering the immediate need for seamen, and the great danger I am in from such a fellow, will use your endeavours to secure him and preserve me. I am Sir, with due respect,
>
> Yours etc. (unsigned)

By this date, the Gangs were not only after discharged seamen, but also deserters, although one would have thought that if these had any sense they would have got as far away from the coast as possible. The Press Service Lieutenant, Lt Meheuse proposed a search in the Edinburgh public houses on the night of Monday 1 April 1805 and asked the Provost for a Constable to assist him. His request was refused, although the Provost promised his co-operation in any search for named individuals. Lt Meheuse duly came up with some names and three Constables were ordered to be at the Council Chamber that evening, but not to go with the Pressgang unless they had seen the information which the Lieutenant claimed to possess.

Other Victims

Social undesirables were likely to find themselves involuntarily on board one of HM ships. In November 1770, the Provost offered Lt Walsh some of the current inhabitants of the Tolbooth. The Lieutenant replied that he could not spare an escort to bring down 'any man you would wish to get quit of', but if they could be taken down to the *Rendezvous* by the Town Guard, he would keep any that were fit for service.

In December, one Banks complained to the Provost that he had been unlawfully pressed into the Navy. Lt Walsh could not attend the hearing at the Council Chamber, but:

> One Mackenzie, a Grenadier of the 22nd, will appear at the Chamber, who will inform you of the circumstances of his being pressed, and I think prove his character to be such, as the Town would be eased by his absence.

The Provost also offered Captain Napier some Boys, presumably orphans maintained by the Town. However, the Marine Society and Sir John Feilding were apparently supplying plenty of Boys, and none were needed from Edinburgh.

Protest

It is easy to imagine the fear and anger which the Impress Service aroused, especially among the poor, who were the most likely to suffer from its operations. On the night of 11 July 1779, a handwritten notice was posted on the east gate of St Giles Churchyard, where it was found in the morning by one of the gravediggers. It seems to refer rather to the pressing of men for the Army than for the Navy, but is probably a fair representation of the feelings of many who suffered at the hands of either Service.

> To The Publick
>
> In order to put a speedy end to the present alarming incrochments on the liberty of the Inhabitants of Scotland by Impressing etc. Who can say but the life and liberty of the Meanest Mechanick is Equally dear to him as that of the Richest or

> Most powereful. There is no alternative. We must Distroy or be Distro[yed]. Let us take the first opertunity [to] put to Death privily those in [the] highest offices viz Lord Adv[ocate] Aire and General Skeem General Aughton both Civil and Military without distinction as they eithe[r] are themselves Villains or their Servants. There will be less loss t[o] the Publick or their own Famely tho a Thousand of them be pu[t] to Death ____ then if one hun[dred] Plowghmen or Mecanicks Loss Liberty. Avail yourselves like men.

The perpetrator of this 'outrage' remained anonymous, and his intended targets remained alive. So, unfortunately, did the Impress Service at Leith, for at least another 27 years.

The Voyage of the Christian

In theory at least, sailors on merchant vessels were exempt from impressment, and the fact that they were employed on trading voyages during the summer probably kept most of them safe from the attentions of the Pressgang. Leith merchant ships, as we have seen, still sailed mainly to their traditional destinations, but they now also visited Spanish ports in the western Mediterranean. Between two and four vessels sailed to the New World each year, mainly to Charleston, New York, Boston, Jamaica and Grenada.

In 1726 a group of Edinburgh merchants decided to try and break into the market for Newfoundland cured cod, which Bristol merchants were successfully exploiting. One of their number, Edward Burd junior, was sent as 'supercargo' (the merchant who travelled on a ship and acted as factor for those with goods on board) on a fact-finding trial run to St Johns in Newfoundland. The ship was the 70-ton *Christian* of Leith, jointly owned by the merchants. Her master was Alexander Hutton, the son of one of the partners.

The *Christian*'s main cargo was 32 barrels of biscuit, intended for sale to the English ships which visited Newfoundland each year to fish or to buy fish from the local boat owners. The Captain and his wife, Edward Burd and another merchant also loaded some trading goods of their own: woollen and linen cloth, shoes, stockings, hats, capes, buttons, buckles, boot strapping, gartering, tape, thimbles, needles, pins, thimbles and spoons. With the proceeds of the sale of the biscuit and goods, plus notes of credit on a London merchant, Edward was to buy a ship-load of cured cod, sail to the Cadiz or Barcelona and sell it there.

Haven on Orkney

The *Christian* sailed from Leith Roads at 4.00 pm on Friday 3 June 1726 and by noon on 8 June, according to Edward's journal, they were:

> abreast of Duncansby Head, and so entered into Pentland Firth with a design to have proceeded directly through between Dunnet Head in Caithness and the Hoy Head, which is the highest land in Orkney, but there coming on a terrible storm

of wind at SSW and SW, we were obliged to bear away down to Kirston Harbour, where we came to an anchor at 5.00 pm

Thurs 9 June - This morning there came into this harbour two very fine galleys (belonging to the Hudsons Bay Company in London) bound for Fort Albany in Hudsons Bay. There are no other ships employed by the Company but these two. Their loadings homeward consist of beaver and other fine furs.

(The Hudson's Bay Company regularly recruited many of its crews in Orkney)

The weather was no better so Edward and Captain Hutton spent the day in Kirkwall, where they visited St Magnus' Cathedral and the ruins of the Bishop's Palace. Our journalist noted that the Mainland was covered in moor and moss, except in the valleys, where there was very good pasture and arable land. He noted that this land was 'very capable of improvement'. Like all visitors to Orkney he was struck by the lack of trees, except for a dozen or so ashes in a yard in Kirkwall. His opinion was that the lack was due solely to the inertia of the inhabitants, as 'roots and greens' grew very well.

The two men returned to Kirston Bay the following morning, but the weather kept them there for a further four days. Other vessels were forced into the Bay by the storm, and when the *Christian* finally sailed on 14 June, she was in company with half a dozen others bound for the Clyde. One or two had come from the Baltic, but most were from Caithness with cargoes of grain. Edward took the opportunity to write to William Hutton and his own father, via John Muir of Bo'ness, master of one of the grain ships. On 16 June they had their last view of Scotland, as St Kilda dropped away behind them.

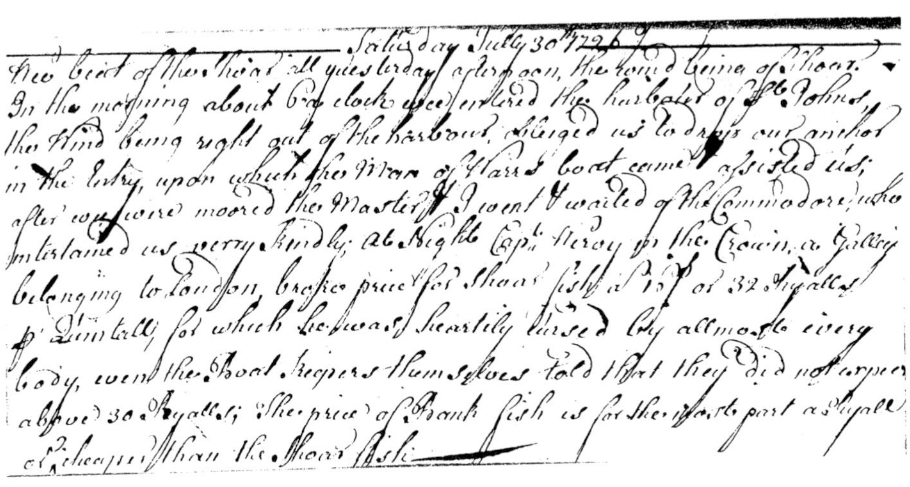

Saturday July 30th 1726

New beat of the Shoar all yesterday afternoon, the wind being of Shoar.
In the morning about 6 a clock wee entered the harbour of St Johns,
the Wind being right out of the harbour, obliged us to draw our anchor
in the Entry, upon which the Man of Warrs boat came & assisted us;
after wee were moored the Master & I went & waited of the Commodore, who
entertained us very kindly; at Night Capt. Percy of the Crown a Galley
belonging to London, broke price for Shoar fish at 18 or 32 Ryalls
p Quintall, for which he was heartily cursed by allmost every
body, even the Boat keepers themselves told that they did not expect
above 30 Ryalls; the price of Bank fish is for the most part a Ryall
or cheaper than the Shoar fish

A page from Edward Burd's journal, describing the arrival of the *Christian* at Newfoundland (By courtesy of the Scottish Record Office).

Crossing the North Atlantic

For the next month, the Journal consists of details of the weather - mainly wet, hazy and drizzly. On 15 July:

> at half past nine we saw a sloop bearing WSW bound for the eastward, which we at first imagined might be a Pirate, but by good luck he happened to be as much afraid of us as we were of him, for upon our bearing down upon him, he run away and left us.
>
> *21 July* - We this morning saw a great many whales about our ship, which made us think we had been upon the [Newfoundland] Banks, but we were mistaken.
>
> *23 July* - at five pm we saw an island of ice...We bore towards it to make it plain...it appeared about the height of Caltoun Crags and very near as broad above water. We had a great many fowls flying about the ship which certainly belonged to this island, having seen none of them before, nor yet after we lost sight of it. There were other two small islands of ice near to the big one. At 10 oclock at night we brought to and lay under a foresail, with thick weather...being afraid of falling in amongst those islands of ice in a dark night.
>
> *26 July* - Spoke with a brigantine bound from the Banks to shore, which he said was 25 miles away.
>
> *29 July* - About 5.00 pm we made the land, to the great joy of us all ...distance 9 leagues. We run the whole night into the shore. In the morning we were within a league of it.
>
> *30 July* - We beat off shore all yesterday afternoon, the wind being off shore. In the morning, about 6 o'clock, we entered the Harbour of St Johns. The wind being right out of the Harbour obliged us to drop our anchor in the entry, upon which the man-of-war's boat came out and assisted us. After we were moored the Master and I went and waited on the Commodore who entertained us very kindly.
>
> *31 July* (Sunday) - We went to Church this day, where we heard a very good discourse from one Jago, an Englishman and parson here. He makes about £150 sterling a year of it, which he collects from the inhabitants of the place and Masters of the ships that come here, either upon the fishing accounts or to buy. This might make a very handsome living for him if he could drink less Punch and Black Strap [a mixture of rum and molasses].
>
> *1 August* - We this day took a wharf for heaving down the ship, for which we had to pay a guinea [she was leaking and they had to heave her down to search her bottom]. Likewise a storehouse at 50s per month...In the evening we drunk King George his health, this being the anniversary of his accession to the throne. Upon this occasion the *Argyll* man-of-war, who lay Commodore in this harbour, was finely illuminated. Bonfires and firing of guns etc.
>
> *2 August* - We this morning haled our ship to Captain Weston's wharf in order to heave down. I this evening drunk a glass with Captain Richard Newman, Admiral of the Harbour, about purchasing of our [return] cargo.

Newfoundland

The Admiral of the Harbour was the Captain of the first to arrive of the fishing ships which came from England each season to fish on the Banks. He organised the fishing and arbitrated in disputes, guided by an Act of Parliament which regulated the fishing. He advised Edward to buy his fish from the local fishermen in Torbay, about 3 miles distant, where he would get it cheaper. This turned out to be poor advice, and Edward decided to sail south to Ferryland where he was told he could get Bank fish, which was just as good as Shore fish for the Spanish market. Bank fish were held to be inferior because they were smaller. Also, the initial stage in the curing process was to lay the fish in salt until the fishing vessel returned to the shore, where it was dried. Because of the distance of the Banks from the shore, Bank fish was in salt for up to six weeks.

The *Christian* was still being repaired. While he waited for her to be ready to sail to Ferryland, Edward visited the Bay of Bulls, about seven leagues away, to see if he could find a seller there, but without success. They set sail for the south on 11 August and arrived in Ferryland on the same day. The next morning Edward found a supplier of fish, who also bought a large proportion of their biscuit. They had to return to St Johns to get the biscuit, which was in the storehouse.

When they arrived back at Ferryland they found the weather was too bad for them to load the fish. Edward used the spare time to try and recover some debts owing to James Blair and Company - a fruitless exercise. Three of the debtors were dead and another had gone to live in Leghorn. The only one he was able to track down was a 'toping merchant in this place'. He spun James a complicated rigmarole, at the end of which it transpired that any money which might have been recovered was with some people in London.

On Sunday 21 August:

> We were at Church this day (which is held in The Doctor's, a public house) where we heard a sermon from Mr Milns, chaplain to the *Argyll* man-of-war, who came here to advance the interest of the Gospel, and at the same time to add a little to his own, for he made about 40 guineas by staying here about four or five weeks.

The following Saturday the weather at last improved sufficiently for the loading of the fish to begin. The operation took three weeks, during which time Edward sold some of the goods he had brought with him to trade. He also sold the rest of the biscuit, but was disappointed in the price he got for it. Apparently, so many ships came to Newfoundland, all of which brought biscuit for sale, that the price was kept low. His main preoccupation, apart from the prices of fish and biscuit, was the threat of war with Spain, which would affect his trading in the Mediterranean. He was reassured to find that no-one he spoke to seemed to anticipate war, all leaving for their markets as soon as they were loaded. Even better, no-one else seemed to be making for Cadiz or Barcelona, so there was a good chance that the *Christian* would be the first to arrive there with a load of fish.

Edward's last act in Newfoundland was to write letters to William Hutton, his father, and the London merchant who had supplied him with a letter of credit. The originals he sent by a ship bound for Plymouth. Copies went by another, bound for Dartmouth.

At last, on Thursday 22 September:

> We sailed this forenoon about 11 of the clock, bidding adieu to Ferryland and all the rogues in it...As to the character of the Ship masters here, all that I have to say of the best of them is that they are not such great Rogues as some of their neighbours...it is impossible for one that deals with them to be too much upon his guard.

However:

> I don't see but that our people might pursue this trade with as good success as the West Country Englishmen do. I'm sure we might always get our servants cheaper than they do. It might perhaps be some time before we fell into the method of catching and curing the fish as well as they.

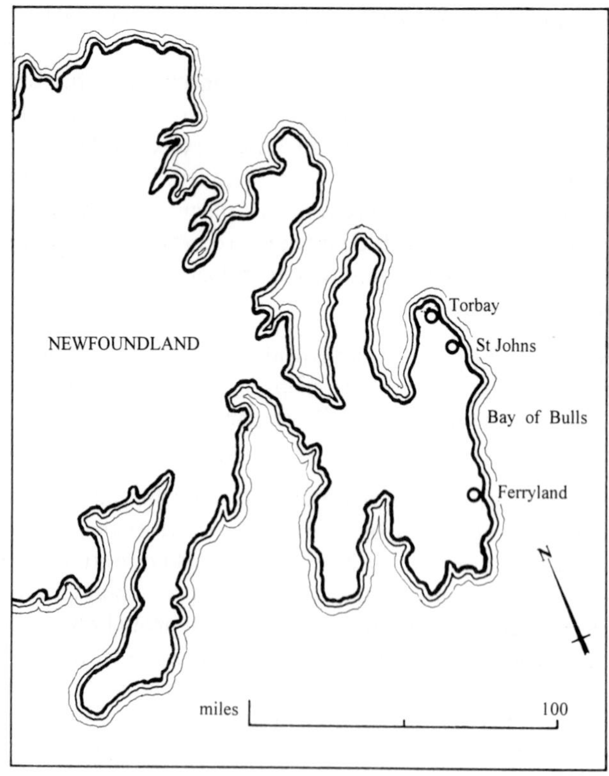

Map showing the places visited by the *Christian* in Newfoundland.

In the Mediterranean

It was on the 'intolerably tedious passage' to Spain that the first potential impediment to the trade became apparent. The ships involved would have to be a lot faster than the *Christian.* Many other vessels passed them as they made their stately progress across the Atlantic, and it was not until Sunday 13 November that they finally sighted the Spanish shore. Two days later the *Christian* anchored in the Bay of Cadiz, and Edward went ashore to visit the houses of the merchants where letters were usually kept. He was expecting to find instructions from a factor called Mark Pringle, who was to act for him in the selling of the fish and the buying of a cargo of wine and cork. No letter awaited him anywhere, and it was he who wrote to the factor to inform him of the *Christian*'s arrival. He also wrote to William Hutton and his father, but the letters were not posted until 6 December, when his ship finally arrived at Barcelona, where there was an established postal service.

At Barcelona Edward found a buyer for his fish with no difficulty, although the price was lower than he had hoped, owing to the *Christian* having arrived after other fish vessels. The unloading, however, was continually held up by what he considered to be a superfluity of 'holly days'. His efforts to buy cork came to nothing as the season had been bad. He obtained a contract to carry 120 pipes of wine from Villosa to Gibraltar, but once again the Popish practices of the locals, together with the elements, slowed up the loading; 'Sunday 8 January - Friday was a holly day, therefore they would not work, and yesterday was bad weather'.

On 14 February they finally arrived at Gibraltar, only to find that the threatened war had at last broken out and it was being besieged by the Spaniards. 'This rupture is a very great disappointment to us, and the more so in that the former part of the voyage being unlucky, we had the greater dependence upon what was to come'. However the seige, which was being conducted from the landward side of the rock, did not prevent the *Christian* from tying up beside the mole and discharging her cargo. Presumably there were fewer 'holly days' in Gibraltar, as the unloading only took eight days. Edward and the Captain entertained themselves by observing the progress of the seige, often from the batteries on the ramparts. Edward also bought some 'Barbary skins and mats'.

His instructions in case of war had been to sail to Bordeaux for a cargo of wine, and on Thursday 16 March the *Christian* finally sailed north with 30 other ships, under the convoy of HMS *Dursley.* We must leave her at anchor off Blois on 5 April, the date of the last entry in the Journal.

The Whalers

Whether or not a Scottish fishery was attempted in Newfoundland, Scots had been whaling off Greenland for more than a century when the *Christian* made her voyage. Whaling from Leith began in 1616 when James VI granted a patent to Sir George Hay and Mr Thomas Murray to fish whales for 35 years. Some years later Nathaniel Udwart sent ships to Greenland in order to obtain oil for use in his soapworks. At the turn of the century the Greenland Fishing Company had a boiling house in the Timber Bush, but it is uncertain how often it was used at that time. The *Concord* of Leith went to the Davis Straits in 1736. Over the next fourteen years there are sporadic sailings to the same destination. One or two Leith men sailed to Greenland in 1747, 1748 and 1749, and duly paid their 'Crown Money' (poors fund) to Trinity House.

However, in the late 1740s Scottish whaling was given a shot in the arm when the Government instituted a bounty of £2 per ton on all whalers. In 1750 the Edinburgh Whaling Company was set up, but it was not the only concern to take advantage of these new funds. Dunbar became a whaling port at the same time, and there was another partnership, known as the Merse Company. A short-lived enterprise was set up in Aberdeen in 1754, its two ships being the *St Anne* and the *City of Aberdeen*. Corruption or incompetence on the part of the Company's first Clerk coupled with insurance problems caused by the outbreak of war in the middle of the decade, caused its demise in 1763.

The Trial

The Edinburgh Whaling Company, however, flourished. Its first ship was the *Trial*, brought up from London in the winter of 1750. She was a 333 ton merchant ship with her bow strengthened to withstand the pressure of the ice. She set sail on her first voyage from Leith on 17 April under the command of William Allan. Her crew of over 40 men came mostly from Leith, Newhaven and Edinburgh. A few were from other ports in the Forth, such as Bo'ness. This implies that many local seamen had recent experience of whaling. The Company would hardly have employed complete novices on such a potentially hazardous venture.

On 22 September 1750 the *Trial* returned from a voyage, which had been successful, but not without its difficult moments. Her ships' surgeon was Dr Gregory Grant who:

> not only behaved with the utmost care and attention in his way, performed several cures and operations with success, and brought home all the crew in perfect health, but also made many curious observations in the country, with which the learned were highly pleased.
>
> In a case of the greatest difficulty and hazard, he took the command of the ship upon him for some time, and was, in the hands of a kind Providence, the sole instrument of saving the ship and crew.

The Company were so grateful to him that in December 1750 they presented him with 'a large case of chirugical instruments, the neatest that could be made, with an inscription and device on a silver plate, signifying the intent of the gift.' Dr Grant, however, had decided that he had had enough of seafaring and declined, though offered unlimited wages, to sign on for a further voyage.

The *Trial* sailed to Greenland again in 1751, this time in company with the *Royal Bounty*, which the Company had bought in London. Once again they left in April and returned in September, the pattern which was to become familiar over the coming years, although the ships could return as early as July. In 1753, the *Prince of Wales* (master, Matthew King), the *Campbeltown* (master, George Steel) and the *Edinburgh* joined the other two vessels. In later years when the two Aberdeen ships and the ones from Berwick and the Merse joined them, the fleet which sailed from Leith in April must have been an impressive sight. It would seem that throughout the 1750s at least four Leith ships went to Greenland each year. In 1754 the *Royal Bounty* brought back no fewer than 10 whales, which was considered a great feat. The average catch was five or six carcasses per vessel.

A Whaling Fleet

By 1757, Leith Roads had become the habitual mustering point for the vessels of the Edinburgh, Aberdeen, Dunbar and Merse Whaling Companies. They sailed in company not only for their mutual protection against loss of life at sea, but against the enemies of Britain in her latest war (1755-60). There was much concern about the best method of insuring the whalers, and a letter from Thomas Hogg, who was concerned in the Edinburgh Company, gives a glimpse into the state of whaling at that time. It is not entirely clear from his letter whether he is writing about Edinburgh vessels alone, or about the fleet as a whole but he talks of insuring four ships in the current year for £1200. One whaling ship had been lost 'by sea hazard' in 1756, and in 1757 another had had to be left behind in the ice. One of those lost may have been from Leith, as only four ships of the Edinburgh Company made the trip in 1759.

As for protection against the enemy, convoys had been promised by the Government, but none had so far materialised. There was talk of a mutual insurance scheme among the Companies, but Hogg considered that in wartime this was too big a risk to take. From one port alone, 19 out of 20 merchant ships and fishing boats had been taken by the enemy.

During the 1760s and into the next decade, only the *Royal Bounty* and the *Campbeltown* sailed from Leith to Greenland. The *Trial* and the *Edinburgh* seem to have resumed life as merchantmen.

In 1771, the Company had 221 shareholders, holding in all 366 shares worth £25 each. Most of them were Edinburgh men, a few were from England and elsewhere in Scotland. Nineteen were Leithers, mostly merchants with one or two brewers, coopers and butchers. The shipbuilders John Sime and John Tod each held one share.

Capture by the French

During the Napoleonic wars the Company's fears of loss by enemy action were realised. In 1794 the Leith Greenlandman the *Raith* was captured by the French on 21 July, three days after leaving Shetland. The story is told in a letter from the clerk of HMS *Brilliant* to a friend of the Captain's, James Pirie WS, whose only son was one of the crew:

> The treatment of the crew on board the [French] squadron was humane and lenient as the rigours of war would admit, not aggravated in any measure from national or hostile antipathy. Their treatment after being landed and imprisoned at Dunkirk was conformable to the decree of the Convention, acted up to in France universally, Captain Young and your son being considered and treated upon an equality with the rest of the unfortunate crew and deprived of their clothes etc etc, except that wherein they stood. When marched to St Omer they were (as at Dunkirk) indiscriminately confined and your son, not having any money, was restricted to the established allowance of the prison, viz 1lb bread, and of aqua pura 2 litres per diem - a small portion of beef, which was affected them at Dunkirk, being here curtailed from their subsistence.
>
> Tanner [the writer's informant] being obliged to remain some time at Dunkirk after escaping from St Omer, before an opportunity offered from his escape from thence, was then joined by one of the crew of the *Dundee* Greenlandman of Dundee, captured at the same time as the *Raith*. From this man he learned that your son, Captain Young and others of the prisoners at St Omer were removed about 150 miles further in the Country, the day before he effected his escape, where, no doubt, if confined their treatment would be the same, but as their situation was hereby removed so far from the sea as to render their escape less practicable, a stronger probability exists of your son and Captain Young obtaining their parole, in which case their circumstances would be (and I hope are) considerably ameliorated.

In a letter of his own, James Pirie describes:

> the distress of the wives of that unfortunate crew, and in particular Mrs Young, who has a family of six helpless children and separated from one of the best of husbands. They wish if possible that their husbands should be exchanged. The French prisoners in the Castle here [Edinburgh] earnestly wish for the same thing and one of them, whose father is a man of consequence in Dunkirk has sent a letter of credit in favour of Captain Young and my son.

Here the correspondence ends and we are left to hope that Mrs Young and her children were reunited with their husband and father, and James Pirie with his son - not to mention the prisoner in the Castle and his father, the 'man of consequence' in Dunkirk.

Nineteenth Century Whaling

By the end of the century the Edinburgh Whaling Company was said to be 'languishing', but whaling from Leith continued until 1842, when the number of ships lost in the ice finally outstripped the owners' ability to replace them. The vessels were a little larger by now, 300 to 400 tons (some of the earlier ones had been only 250 tons), and carried a crew of 40 or 50 men, mostly from Prestonpans, Cockenzie and other fishing villages in the Forth. More men could be picked up at Lerwick if they were needed. Each whaler always carried a young surgeon. The ships left in March, to the accompaniment of cheers from crowds lining the Shore and piers. If they sailed as far as the Davis Straits they would return in October or November. Greenland trips were a few weeks shorter. Apart from the ships of the Company, there were several other whalers belonging to Leith, but they discharged at Bo'ness, where their blubber was boiled and where the vessels themselves were laid up for the winter.

When the new wet docks were built, the whalers unloaded there. The heavy iron-bound casks of blubber were hoisted from the holds and rowed to the Shore. At the start of the nineteenth century the Boiling House still backed onto the Sands, but as time wore on this area was built over. A wide passage, Tower Street, was left between the back of the Boiling House and the new buildings, and it was by way of this street that the casks were brought to the House. The proprietors of the Company were Peter and Christopher Wood, and the 'strong, pungent, oily smell' that pervaded the town during the blubber boiling was known as 'Woods' scent bottle'. After sailings of the Woods' ships ceased in 1842, there was no more whaling from Leith until Salveson and Son began running ships from the Port to the Antarctic in 1908.

The men-of-war of the Royal Navy, the traders plying traditional routes, the little *Christian* braving the vast Atlantic to try out a new venture, the merchantmen importing rum and tobacco from the New World, the coasters bringing grain from Caithness, the fishing boats and the whaling ships. These vessels and the Leith men who sailed in them epitomised the spirit of eighteenth century Scotland, in which the bedrock of tradition furnished a foundation for the adventure of the new.

13

Miscellanea Chronologica — Nineteenth Century

1801

The Old East Dock Foundation Stone was laid on 14 May by Robert Dundas of Melville. This was the first of the Leith docks designed by the civil engineer, Charles Rennie.

1806

The Old East Dock was opened on 20 May, by the Lord Provost of Edinburgh. Artillery fire from Leith Fort and from HM warships in the Roads, signalled the opening. This, the first dock of its kind in Northern Britain, was five acres in extent. A graving dock lay on its north east side, opening into the Harbour, whose first tenant was Robert Menzies. The new Dock was entered by a lock, so that vessels could lie afloat at all states of the tide. The smack *Buccleuch* (of the Edinburgh and Leith Shipping Company) and the *Fifeshire* Packet were the first vessels to enter the new Dock.

1809

A 'Martello Tower' was erected on Mussel Cape Rocks at a cost of £17000, as part of a scheme to defend the new docks and the City of Edinburgh against possible attack by the French during the Napoleonic Wars (which ended in 1815). The Tower was about 10 metres high, and was built of solid masonry of brick and stone about 2 metres thick. The invasion never came, and the tower was left to decay until 1850, when it was renovated by the Royal Engineers and occupied by artillerymen from Leith until 1869. It was then abandoned and never again used. The Tower is now land-locked, and a key remains in the possession of Forth Ports plc.

1810

The Old West Dock was begun. This was the second dock of Rennie's scheme, and lay to the west of the first dock.

1812

The Custom House was built at the Sandport. The old Custom House had stood on the east side of the Tolbooth in Tolbooth Wynd. In 1819, a market was built on its site.

1813

The first viable steamship to enter Leith came to the port in this year. It belonged to Henry Bell, a Bo'ness ships' carpenter, who began running excursion steamers on the Clyde in 1812. He brought his steamer the *Comet* to his old yard (Shaw and Hart) at Bo'ness for an overhaul, and on 21 May she paid her first visit to Leith Harbour. Henry Bell started an excursion run between Leith and Bo'ness, for a single fare of 7s 6d (35½p) (An experimental steam-powered vessel had been tried out at Leith in the eighteenth century, but the design was not successful.)

Leith Commercial List was published for the first time.

1817

The **Old West Dock** was completed. It was the same size as the earlier Dock and was entered from it by a passageway crossed by an iron swing bridge. Together the Docks could accommodate over 100 of the type of ships operating at the time, which were usually around 150 to 200 tons. Two graving docks

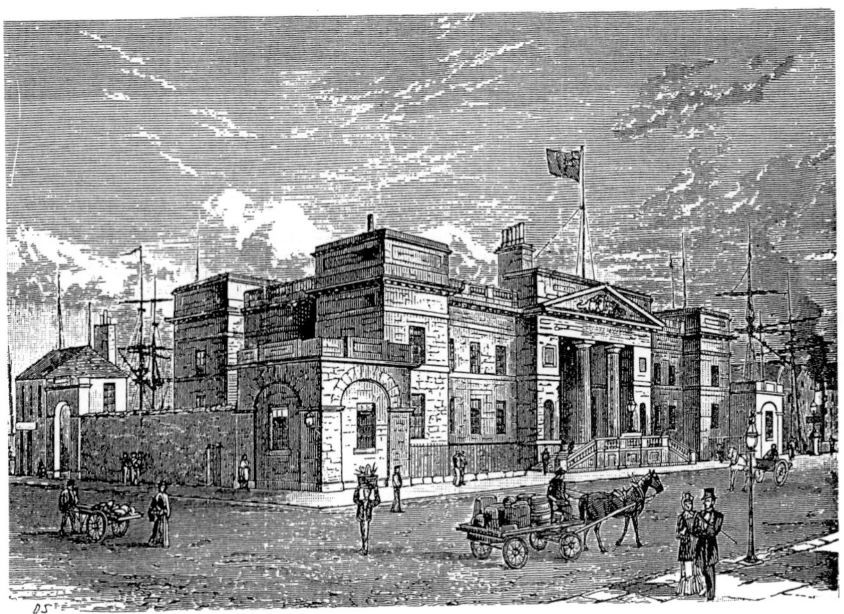

The New Custom House, built in 1812.

opened off its north side, one of which was for public use and the other for lease, its first tenant being Alexander Syme. Together with the surrounding warehouses, timber yards and buildings the Docks now covered an area of 15 acres. The total cost of both Docks was in the region of £300,000.

The Trinity House present building was erected on the site in the Kirkgate which the Fraternity had occupied since the sixteenth century

1818

The Junction Bridge was built to carry the new Great Junction Street between the foot of Leith Walk and the western end of the new Docks. The Bridge marked the southern extremity of the Harbour of Leith.

1820

The Edinburgh and Leith Seamen's Friendly Society was instituted.

1821

The Trinity Chain Pier was opened. It afforded a deep water berth for steamers plying in the Forth. Steamships were generally larger than sailing vessels, and were being built longer and deeper every year. The Docks at Leith were too small and shallow to accommodate the larger ones.

1822

George IV landed at Leith on 15 August, to begin the first visit of a British monarch to Scotland since the days of Charles II. Libidinous and gluttonous, bibulous and treacherous; the former Prince Regent was probably one of the least worthy monarchs to sit on the throne of Great Britain. Only his immense charm rendered him tolerable to his associates, and only traditional respect for the Monarchy reconciled his more sober subjects to his outrageous behaviour. His visit to Scotland, however, was greeted with almost hysterical fervour by the populace in general. In Leith, civic pride at the honour of having first sight of the King knew no bounds.

> Leith was crowded beyond all description on the day of the landing; every window was filled with faces, if a view could be commanded; the ships' yards were manned, their rigging swarmed with human figures; and the very roofs of the houses were covered. Guarded by the Royal Archers and Scots Greys, a floating platform was at the foot of Bernard Street, covered with cloth and strewn with flowers; and when a single gun from the *Royal George* [anchored in the Roads] announced that the King had stepped into his barge, the acclamations of the enthusiastic people, all unused to the presence of royalty, then seemed to rend the heaven....The cannon of the ships and battery pealed forth their salutes, and the combined cheers of the

> mighty multitude filled up the pauses. An immense fleet of private boats followed the royal barge, forming an aquatic procession such as Leith had never seen before, and a band of pipers on the pier struck up as it rounded the head of the latter. As the King approached the landing stage three distinct and well-timed cheers came from the manned yards of the shipping, while the magistrates, deacons, and trades advanced, the latter with their standards lowered. So hearty and prolonged were the glad shouts of the people that even George IV - the most heartless king that ever wore a crown - was visibly affected....Considering the character of the man who was the object of all these joyful demonstrations, they may be taken as interesting evidence of the lengths which loyalty to a sovereign will carry people.

When the King landed at Leith he was wearing the uniform of an admiral, but as a compliment to his hosts, he assumed the kilt at his formal Levee. In view of his gross corpulence (the portrait painted in honour of his visit is flattering in the extreme) there were those who wondered if this step was altogether wise. When one of the doubters ventured to express his reservations, Lady Saltoun reassured him, 'Nay' she said 'we should take it very kind of him. Since his stay will be so short, the more we see of him the better.'

The spot where the King first set foot on Scottish soil was marked by a massive inscribed plate bearing a representation of the scene. It became known as the King's Landing, which in recent years has been adopted as the name of a housing development sited on the opposite side of the Old Harbour.

The last execution for Piracy 'within the flood mark' at Leith took place on the Sands, the gibbet being erected nearly opposite the foot of Constitution Street. The hanged men were Peter Heaman and Francis Gautier, who had seized the brig *Jane* of Gibraltar, for the sake of the large amount of money she was carrying, and sunk her off Ross-shire. They had subsequently been arrested in Lewis.

1825

The Naval Yard, which had been situated between the Timber Bush and the Glasshouses, was moved to a site at the far end of the West Dock. The area of water at that end of the Dock was later known as the Queens Dock. The naval yard was never heavily used although it remained Government property for many years, finally becoming absorbed into the Docks complex in the 1860s, when railway lines were built over it, to carry Caledonian Railway Company rolling stock.

1826

The East and West Pier extensions were begun. The first piles were driven in, with great ceremony, on 15 August - the fourth anniversary of the visit of George IV. The final length of the East Pier was more than half a mile, and of the West Pier, 1500 feet. The two piers terminated within 200 feet of each other.

Leith Roads, 1824. Part of the Martello Tower can be seen on the left of the picture.

They were intended to give added protection to the approaches to the Harbour and the Docks. An infamous sand bar had always tended to form at the already shallow entrance to the channel. As vessels of ever deeper draught needed to get into the Harbour, the bar became increasingly troublesome. The breakwater extensions carried the mouth of the Harbour, and with it the bar, out into deeper water, and the channel was kept constantly dredged.

1828

The first Docks Commission was set up. In 1825, the City of Edinburgh had proposed to set up a joint stock company to run the Docks. As this would have kept it permanently in the control of Edinburgh, the move was successfully opposed by the most powerful men in Leith. The Docks Commission of 1828 was an improvement on the joint stock scheme as it allowed for some representation by Leith, although the majority of the Commissioners were still from Edinburgh.

1829

Mons Meg, the huge seventeenth century cannon, which had been captured by the English, was returned from the Tower of London to Edinburgh. It landed at Leith and was drawn by eight strong horses along Bernard St and up Constitution St on its way to the Edinburgh Castle, where it may still be seen.

The launch of the *Forth* (1,940 tons) from Menzies' yard on 22 May 1841. She was built for the Royal Mail Steam Packet Company and was the first mail vessel in service.

1833

Leith gained Independence from Edinburgh. The City was declared insolvent in this year, and after the passing of Burgh Reform Bill, Leith became a separate burgh. The first Provost of Leith was Adam White. Powers were conferred on him as admiral, and on the bailies as admirals-depute.

1835

Granton Pier was begun by the Duke of Buccleuch. The first part was opened on the day of Queen Victoria's coronation, 28 June 1838, and named the Victoria Jetty.

1837

Menzies and Co launched the SS 'Sirius' from their yard near the East Old Dock Gates. She was the first steamship to cross the Atlantic Ocean. The voyage lasted 18 days, during which she ran out of coal. The crew were forced to burn timber and resin in order to keep steam on her boilers.

The sailors' home on the Shore, built in 1883, under conversion into an hotel, 1994.

1838

The Docks Commission in its final form was instituted by Act of Parliament. The care of the Docks and Harbour was vested in eleven Commissioners. Three of them were to be appointed by Leith and three by Edinburgh. The remaining five were to be chosen by the Lords of the Treasury, to whom the Commissioners had to apply for permission to raise money for improvements to their facilities. It was specifically enacted that no member of either Edinburgh or Leith Councils might be a Commissioner. Later in the century the number of Commissioners was increased to 15.

The Petty Customs of Leith were transferred by Act of Parliament from Edinburgh to Leith. The Merk per Ton was abolished. (The merk was at that time worth 1s 1½d, 5½p.)

1839

The Mariners Church and School were built at the Citadel. The church still stands on the corner of Commercial St and Citadel St. The school is now Leith Nautical College.

1840

Leith Sailors Home was opened in premises in Dock St.

Leith Chamber of Commerce was instituted.

1846

A Report on the Docks and harbour was submitted to the Treasury. Its main submissions were that:

1. Vessels had to lie four or five abreast at the quays as there was insufficient space in the Docks.

2. There was no patent slip or graving dock large enough to accommodate steamers, which had to be repaired at Dundee or London.

3. There was no low-water jetty for landing passengers and light goods. For twelve years past, the need had been seen for a low-water landing place for large London to Edinburgh passenger steamers. Instead the East Pier, too narrow and weak for the traffic or to take a railway, had taken 16 years to build and had just reached the low-water mark. Most steam traffic now used a neighbouring pier, with an estimated loss to Leith of £5000 per year. The

steamers of the Edinburgh, Hull and Leith Company, which still used Leith, had to lie aground, with the consequent risk to their hulls and machinery.

4. At low tide the entrance to the Harbour was all but dry.

5. The Shore Dues had not been revised for the past 60 years. Some charges were still levied in Scots money and the dues were full of other anomalies. Dock dues were being charged to vessels which were too large to get through the Dock gates.

6. Rubbish was being thrown into the Water of Leith and carried down into the Harbour.

1847

The Victoria Dock was begun. It was designed by the engineer James Rendel and built by Mr Barrie.

1848

A Parliamentary Bill was passed to revise the schedule of rates. The Commissioners had, as a result of the above report, appointed James Rendel to produce a scheme of improvements for the Docks. His proposals were as follows:

1. To extend the East Pier by 1000 feet.

2. To convert the West Breakwater into a pier and extend it by 1750 feet.

3. To strengthen the West Pier thus formed so that it could bear a railway.

4. To form a low-water landing place at the end of the new West Pier, to have no less than 9 feet of water around it, even at the lowest tides.

5. To deepen the channel so that it would have 20 feet of water at high neap tides and 25 feet at high spring tides.

1852

The Victoria Dock, one of the results of the 1846 Report, was opened in July. The first ship to enter the new Dock was the SS *Royal Victoria*, of the London, Leith, Edinburgh and Glasgow Company, carrying the royal standard of Scotland at her masthead. The Dock measured 230 metres long by 92 metres wide and the depth over the entrance sill was over two metres lower than that of the Old Docks. It cost £200,000 to build and enabled the port to take the large steamships which were now well established in the Forth. The engineer of the project was James Rendel. At about the same time, the East and West Breakwater/Pier extensions were finished.

At Granton, a patent slip was built. The first ship was launched from it in the following year.

1853

Report by James Rendel to the Docks Commissioners on the state of the Docks:

> 8 Great George Street, Westminster, Oct. 15th, 1853
>
> Gentlemen, As requested at your meeting on the 27th ult. I now beg to lay before you in writing , the substance of the verbal Report I then made on the state of the works of the Dock and Port generally, but more particularly of the new works as executed and proposed, the progress making with the repairs of the Old East Breakwater, and the deepening of the Harbour by dredging - and
>
> First - as regards the New Hydraulic Swing Bridge over the passage between the two Old Docks - This Bridge on a new construction has now been sufficiently long in use to prove its great strength and adaptation to the passage of bearing Railway trains, at the same time that it can be opened and closed in four minutes by two men only; whilst its simplicity is such as to make its maintenance very economical.
>
> Second - The Low Water Pier and Railway leading to the same from Leith Railway Station are now complete with the exception of the metalling of the Horse Track. At the Pier there is now a depth of from 8 to 9 feet at Low Water Spring Tides, a greater depth than was calculated upon when the work was undertaken. Its arrangements are also found to afford all the anticipated facilities for embarking and disembarking passengers and goods, and though at present it seems but little used owing, as it is said, to the greatly improved state of the Harbour Channel up to the Town (Leith) Quays, yet I feel quite sure that, as its advantages become known through the influence of the mercantile members of your Board, and through the exertions of your Officers, this work will prove, as your predecessors anticipated, a great public convenience as well as a source of considerable revenue. As regards the completion of the Horse Track for the Railway, I explained to the Superintendent of the Works the best mode of forming it, and he has, I presume, by this time carried my instructions into effect.
>
> Third - The New West Breakwater and Timber Arching are quite finished. They are in excellent condition, and answer most completely all the objects for which they were executed. All the exposed portions of the Timber work should be well coated every Summer or Autumn with hot coal tar, having a small admixture of pitch, and the Roadway planking, as this composition is laid on it, should be well sanded.

Fourth - The Old part of the West Breakwater will require some repairs during the next Summer, but the extent of these will be best determined after the Winter gales are passed.

Fifth - As regards the New East Breakwater - All the piling and other timber work stands excellently, and the Stone paving which was disturbed by the gales of last year is now nearly all repaved. The cost of this operation will not exceed the sum allowed by the late Contractor for the same; and as the rubble hearting will now be more consolidated there is reason to expect that the whole will now be permanently secure. All the Wood work of this Breakwater should be coated over once a year as before recommended for the West Pier; and in both cases the whole of the piles and wales should be well examined at the lowest ebbs of the Tide in the year, to see that the Timber is not exposed to the ravages of the worm.

Sixth - As to the repairs of the Old East Breakwater - The inner portion of this Breakwater repaired and heightened in 1850 and 1851, extending to two thirds of its whole length, is in a most satisfactory state. It is also found to admit of the safe deepening of the Harbour Channel without risk to the old works of the Breakwater, and as expected it had the effect of preventing a large quantity of sand from being washed over it into the Harbour Channel. The works now in course of execution for the remaining portion of this Breakwater are making good progress, and will, I doubt not, be completed by the end of this year. It is probable that the whole of the Stone flagging of the repaired parts of this Breakwater may have to be taken up and relaid in the course of a few years; for as the filling on which it is laid is new, it must be expected to consolidate and leave the flagging uneven. The cost of relaying it, however, will be but trifling and need not be attended with any inconvenience to the Public.

Seventh - As regards the Old East Stone Breakwater - It is to be apprehended that the Harbour face of this old work will have to be sheetpiled for its whole length before the Harbour Channel can be completely dredged out. Since this Breakwater was founded, the Channel has been much deepened, and with the deepening now in progress may undermine it. By the early Spring the dredging below or northward of this Breakwater will be so far executed as to enable me to form a more conclusive opinion of the extent to which these repairs will be needed, and I will take care to give you the earliest possible intimation of the extent and cost of the work.
If the Commissioners should be able to obtain funds for the execution of the proposed Dry Dock [Prince of Wales graving dock] and Building Slip on the site of this Breakwater, all outlay on its repair would be rendered unnecessary; but in such case these new works would have to be actively commenced in the Spring of next year.

Eighth - As to the new Dock [Victoria] - The whole of its works and its entrance are in a most satisfactory state. The Gates, the Entrance and the Guiding Dolphins are as perfect as such works can be for all purposes of trade. It is however much to be regretted that the heads of the Entrance Piers are not yet properly lighted so as to mark beyond all question when the gates are open. For the want of such lights it was reported to me that a vessel ran foul of the gates before they were opened, and from the account given me of the accident, it is clear that nothing but the great strength of the gates saved them from very serious damage, and the Dock from being run dry; the consequences of which to the shipping in it as well as to the Dock itself, would have been most disastrous.

This is a subject on which the Commissioners should immediately consult with the Superintendent and Dock Master, and by acting on their advice, make them responsible for the safety of the gates. The sooner also that the Diver's Dress now ordered is procured, and a competent man appointed to use it once a fortnight, in order to examine and clear the sills and platforms of the gates, the better; for as the dredging must be continued during the Winter, the flood tide will carry large quantities of the disturbed silt up to the Gate entrance where it will settle, and want clearing by means of a Diver.

Finally on this head I would observe that as soon as the repairs of the Old East Breakwater are completed; it may be desirable to plank up the Gates of the New Dock in such a manner as to shut in high tides and use the Water at Low Water to scour the entrance. This however must be done with caution and at first when a competent person is present to direct the operation.

Ninth - The works of the Old Docks do not call for remark further than that there appears to be some dredging necessary in them which should be done in the course of the next summer, and that the rights exercised by the Admiralty over a large portion of the West Dock [Queens Dock], appear less than useless to that department of the Public Service, and occasion an increasing sacrifice of commercial accommodation, which seems apparently due to the facts not being clearly understood by their Lordships.

The old iron Swing Bridge removed from the Junction passage, has now been altered and effectually repaired. It is placed across the Lock and combined with alterations in the line of Roadway has greatly improved the entrance to the Northern Quays.

Tenth - As to the Dredging - The new Dredging Vessel is an excellent one and is now working most satisfactorily. The Old Dredger is as usual frequently under repair, and otherwise comparatively costly. The new Mud Punts are efficient, but the old ones are now so old that their incidental repairs require a sum far exceeding the interest on the cost of new and more capacious one. Your failure however in obtaining new Iron Boats on account of the high price demanded, makes me recommend your resorting to wood as the material for their construction; building them upon the works, providing the timber and ironwork and letting their construction to competent Ship Carpenters at piece work.

It is satisfactory to me to be able to report that whereas the cost of dredging used to be upwards of 8d per cubic yard, the cost has been reduced to about 5½d per yard, and that this great reduction has been effected by improved management under Mr Andrew's direction.

As to the progress of the dredging - I find that about 1000 feet of the Harbour Channel have been nearly completed, and that the remainder of it has progressed so far that it is within three feet of its intended depth.

Eleventh - As to the Harbour Lights - It is absolutely necessary that the new Breakwater Heads should be permanently lighted before the winter sets in. The proper course to determine what is best in regard to this important question would be for the Commissioners, as in the case of the lighting of the Gates, to refer it to their Superintendent and Harbour Master. At the same time these Gentlemen should report on the best arrangement for Signal balls etc to be established at the West Breakwater Head; so that in the next year's nautical almanacs (the Admiralty and others) the new Lights and Signals should be made public.

Twelfth - As to the Groins on the East Sands - The Western Groin was damaged by the late Gales. It should be repaired, raised at its inner end and strengthened. It would then I am quite sure, rapidly form the beach in front of it, and thus add to the extent and usefulness of the timber yards there. The most easterly groins act quite as well as could be expected from their size and position.

Finally - I have to call the attention of the Commissioners to the injury which the Harbour is now sustaining from the Sewage matter sent into it from Edinburgh and Leith. This injury has become so serious as to demand their immediate attention. Not only is the quantity of solid matter become so considerable as to cause growing expense in dredging to maintain the proper navigable Channel up to the new Dock, but its less solid products are deposited in such increased quantities in the higher part of the River and opposite to the Old Dock as to have become an intolerable nuisance, which is actually increased by the disturbance necessarily caused by its removal.

That at a time when public attention is so properly called to evils of this most unjustifiable, because easily remediable, kind, something for their suppression will be speedily decided on, cannot I think be doubted, particularly where a City so important and influential as an example as Edinburgh is Concerned.
Now it is from this conviction as much as from its present pressing necessity that I have deemed this the proper time to ask your attention to this subject. Your interest demands it, and it must be regarded as fortunate for your Trust that some of its Members are the Representatives of the Corporations of Edinburgh and Leith, the two local public bodies who will, I doubt not, initiate the proper proceedings for the abatement of such a crying nuisance when fairly represented to them.

But the manner in which such a nuisance is abated is no less a subject of interest to you as Conservators of the Port, than the abatement itself, and it will be requisite for you to see that the Sewers which will be necessary to remove this filth from the Water of Leith are so laid out and carried into the Sea, as to be unattended with injury to the Docks and adjoining property or the Harbour Channel. This I am quite satisfied may be done in an expeditious and comparatively inexpensive manner.

I am, Gentlemen, Your most obed Servant

Jas M Rendel

1860

The debt of the Dock Commission to the Treasury was cancelled by the Harbour and Docks Bill, which passed the House of Lords on 19 July. The debt amounted to £230,000, and the Treasury accepted £50,000 in cancellation of it. So important was this measure to the commerce of Leith, that it was celebrated in the town by fireworks displays and the ringing of church bells.

1862

Prime Gilt was abolished and Trinity House became dependent for pension payments on the income from property which it held in Leith. This was said to amount to some £2000 per year. Apart from the payment of pensions, the chief function of the House by this time was the licensing of pilots.

1863

The Prince of Wales Graving Dock was completed at a cost of £60,000. It was 116 metres long and 18 metres broad, and could accommodate the largest steamers afloat at the time with the exception of the SS *Great Britain*. James Rendel was once again the engineer. The Dock was closed by a caisson and emptied using a centrifugal pump, both of which were novel features in Leith. The first ship to use the Dock was the *Czar* which belonged to one of the Docks Commissioners. However, this was before the Dock was officially in use. The first ship to officially use the Prince of Wales Dock was the *Volunteer*. She was repaired during March and no dock dues were charged. In January the Graving Dock accommodated the 280ft *Germania*, of General Steam Navigation Company, trading between Hamburg and New York. She was the largest steamer yet to visit Leith, and there was some difficulty getting her in and out of the Dock, but her owners indicated their intention of using the facilities on future occasions.

1869

The Albert Dock was opened on 21 August by Provost Watt, with the arrival of the SS *Florence* of the Leith, Hull and Hamburg Steam Packet Company. The opening of the Victoria Dock had been a quiet affair, but the Albert Dock was a different matter. There were 200 gentlemen on board the *Florence*, including all the Commissioners together with representatives of Edinburgh and Leith. After steaming round Inchkeith, the vessel proceeded into the Dock, breaking a ribbon on her way, while the band played 'Rule Britannia' and a salute was fired by a battery of the Royal Artillery. After the official party had disembarked, it proceeded to a lunch at the Assembly Rooms.

The Dock cost almost £300,000 to build, and its dimensions are 335 metres in length by 137 metres in width. Part of the East Breakwater was removed in order to construct an approach area to the new lock. This area, named the Albert

Basin, allowed vessels to clear the effects of the current in the Water of Leith before entering the lock. The lock gates were operated by hydraulic machinery, the first of its kind to be installed in Scotland. It was at this dock that hydraulic cranes from the workshops of Sir William Armstrong of Newcastle were seen at Leith for the first time. The engineers were Alexander Rendel, son of the late James, and Mr Robertson of Leith.

1874

The Victoria Swing Bridge was completed, alleviating the communication problems which had arisen since the opening of the Albert Dock. Constructed of main braced girders, it carried a double rail and road track with a footpath along each side. When open to shipping, the large clear span allowed easy access for vessels navigating into the East and West Old Docks. At the time it was built it was the largest swing bridge in the UK.

1876

Dock Commission membership was increased to fifteen as a result of the Leith Harbour and Docks Act. Six were elected by Port users paying more than £4 per year in dues. Three were elected by owners of ships registered at Leith, three by Edinburgh City Council and one each by Leith Chamber of Commerce and the Edinburgh Merchant Company. This arrangement lasted almost unchanged until the docks came under the management of the Forth Ports Authority in 1968.

1877

The Reclamation Bulwark of the next phase of Dock building was finished. It stretched from the east end of the Albert Dock to a point near Seafield Toll, enclosing an area of 108 acres. There were several severe storms in the Forth during the time it was building, but only once was the work breached. Repairs on this occasion cost £500. The design for the bulwark included a promenade and drive along its top, with a fine view of the Forth.

The Scottish Shipmasters Association (The Shipmasters and Officers Protection Association) was founded. Its objects were: to promote good maritime legislation, to render navigation safer by lighting and marking the Scottish coast, and to provide for the widows of members.

1881

The Edinburgh Dock was opened on 26 July by HRH the Duke of Edinburgh, who arrived on board the SS *Berlin*, a vessel of the Leith, Hull and Hamburg Steam Packet Company, whose ships bell is now in the boardroom of Forth Ports plc headquarters. The ceremony was watched by more than 80,000 people.

The Duke was in the Forth as Commander of the reserve squadron of the ironclad fleet. On the day of the opening, the squadron was drawn up in two lines in the Roads, clearly visible from the shore. The *Hercules*, with the Duke's flag flying from her mizzen, was the last of the line, nearest to the shore. Ahead of her were *Warrior*, *Defence* and *Valiant*. In the port line were *Lord Warden*, *Hector* and *Penelope*. The naval ships were surrounded by a fleet of yachts, pleasure-boats and other vessels, including the 370ft steamer *Garth Castle* of Donald Currie and Company, forerunner of the Union Castle Line.

The proceedings began when the Provost, Magistrates and Council of Leith, together with the Commissioners and other dignitaries, were taken by steamer to the *Hercules*, where they presented the Duke with a loyal address, in a silver casket. At noon the whole party, along with Prince Henry of Prussia, General Macdonald and the staff at head-quarters in Scotland, with many other officers, went on board the *Berlin* and proceeded towards the new dock. The hydraulic swing bridge over the dock entrance had been opened at twelve oclock by the four-year-old son of the Resident Engineer. As the *Berlin* steamed in, she broke the ceremonial silk ribbon stretched across the entrance, and the Duke declared the dock open, naming it the Edinburgh Dock. A cannon salute was fired from the seawall, and the spectators in the stands, on the quays, and on the manned yards of the surrounding shipping, cheered.

After performing the ceremony, the Duke attended a banquet given by the Dock Commissioners. In the afternoon, he drove up to Edinburgh, where another silver casket awaited him, containing an address of welcome from the City Council. He also visited the Botanical Gardens, where he planted a Hungarian oak tree in front of the botany classroom. He finally arrived back at Leith at six oclock, embarked at the Victoria Dock, and returned to the *Hercules*.

The dock cost £350,000, measures 475 metres by 198 metres, and included a dry dock cut into the west end of the centre jetty. It lies to the east of the Albert Dock and is connected to it by a passageway.

1883

Leith Sailors Home. The foundation stone of a new building was laid. It is in the Scottish Baronial style and stands on the corner of Tower St on a site granted by the Docks Commission. The Home had accommodation for 56 seamen and 9 officers. Fifty shipwrecked seamen could be accommodated in dormitories in the attics. There was a restaurant, dining room, recreation room, reading room, officers' sitting room, bath rooms and lavatories.

1896

The Alexandra Dry Dock was completed this year. Measuring 100.58 metres by 14.48 metres, this facility helped to further enhance the rapidly expanding ship building and repair trade within the port.

The Czar and Empress of Russia landed at Leith on 22 September.

14

Sail Gives Way To Steam

The trade between Leith and London played a significant part in the life of the port from its earliest days. Regular records only begin in the seventeenth century, but with a combination of fragmentary survivals and imagination we can build up at least a partial picture of the dealings between the two ports.

In the days of the Normanised David I, who had spent his childhood at the English court, ships sailed regularly from Leith to London. They mostly carried salt and dried fish for the London markets and brought back luxury good for the king and the Norman nobles who had settled in Scotland. The first serious disruption of the trade was caused by the advent of Henry I in the early fourteenth century.

For the next three centuries the political situation governed the state of trade with London more than with any other of Leith's traditional ports of call. At times when the English were in the ascendant in Scotland, most of the traffic would be from the south, as English ships arrived with stores for the occupying garrisons. At other times, Leith vessels would sail down the coast, usually with fish for the London market. The other main Scottish exports; wool, cloth and hides, were not much in demand in England, but fish was always needed, especially during the six-week fast of Lent. The importance of this trade to Scottish merchants is shown by the fact that the frequent existence of a 'state of tension' between the two countries did little to discourage it. Only an outright ban by one or other nation would put a temporary stop to the sailings.

Once James VI was installed in London in 1603 there was every incentive for an increase in the volume of English goods being imported into Leith, which was now by far the largest port in Scotland. In the seventeenth century an enormous range of commodities were shipped from London, and the number of vessels engaged in this trade steadily rose throughout the period. There was also an increase in the carrying of passengers, as Scottish courtiers travelled back and forth, although the discomforts of the sea voyage meant that many still went overland. The Parliamentary Union of 1707 accelerated the trend, as the circle of regular travellers to London widened to include a variety of legal and government personnel, their families and friends. Almost continuous Continental warfare necessitated the constant movement of troops, most of whom were transported by sea, and often debarked at the mouth of the Thames where they were transhipped to sail to the area where they were needed.

Regular Sailings to London

By the early years of the eighteenth century so many ships were sailing regularly to London, that the 'London skippers' formed a distinct group among the masters of Leith ships. Around 1720, packet boats began London voyages, but their sailings were irregular, and so infrequent that they could be advertised in the local press well in advance. Such were *Bon Accord* (1720) and the *Unity* (1722) whose masters could be contacted via the local Coffee Houses.

In 1750 the Edinburgh and London Shipping Company was set up to provide more regular sailings. The following may be one of their advertisements (Edinburgh Chronicle, 2 June 1759):

> For London, the ship *Reward*, Old England built, William Marshal master, now lying at the Birth at Barnes Nook, Leith Harbour, taking in goods, and will sail with the first convoy.
>
> The said master to be spoken with at the 'Caledonia' or 'Forrest's Coffee House' Edinburgh, or at his house in Broad Wynd, Leith.
>
> NB - This ship is an exceeding fast sailor, has good accommodation for passengers, and good usage may be depended upon.

The ships used at this time were 'clumsy and bluff bowed brigs' of 160 to 200 tons. They were primarily cargo vessels, with one small and inconvenient cabin for passengers. In order for a voyage to be profitable, the ship had to carry as much cargo as possible, and would wait to sail until she was full. This meant that there were no regular sailing times. Moreover, being almost entirely square-rigged, the brigs were not particularly good sailors, and were often delayed in transit by bad weather. In general, only those who could not afford the cost of an overland journey travelled by sea.

About 1770, the salmon shippers of Berwick began to use smacks to carry their fish to London. The graceful lines and large spread of fore-and-aft canvas of these vessels ensured a faster trip, especially when sailing before the wind. They could also sail much closer to the wind than most other craft, so could remain at sea in light airs, when most other ships were forced to lay at anchor. The practice grew up of travellers taking the coach to Berwick and embarking there. In this way they avoided a long, uncomfortable and expensive journey by road.

The Leith Smacks

It did not take the Berwick owners long to realise that if they started their smacks from Leith, they could be sure of picking up a good number of passengers. In 1777, for instance, the 'Caledonian Mercury' announced that the smack *Edinburgh* would sail from Leith on a fixed date. Finally, in 1791, the Union Shipping Company of Berwick established a headquarters at Leith and began regular sailings from the port, calling at Berwick for salmon en route. In 1797 the Berwick Old Shipping Company also began sending its smacks to Leith.

In 1802 a group of Leith merchants set up the Edinburgh and Leith Shipping Company, the first of the Leith Smack shipping lines. Their six vessels were built at Bridport in Devon, one of the chief centres for smack building. Their crews were exempt from being pressed for the Navy. In common with all ships at the time, the smacks were armed, and several of them actually made contact with the French. On 23 October 1804, the *Britannia* (of the Edinburgh and Leith Company, and the *Sprightly* (of the Berwick Union company) encountered a large French privateer off Cromer. They came under heavy fire, which they returned to such effect that the privateer's sails and rigging were badly damaged and she had to retire. The smack's sails were holed by bullets, but none of her crew were injured. The following year, the *Swallow* (Berwick Old

A model of the London and Edinburgh Shipping Company's smack, *Comet*, of 160 tons. She was built at Bridport in Devon in 1809/10 by William Good, at a cost of around £2,000.

Company) was attacked off Flamborough Head by a ship carrying 14 guns. She replied with her carronades and the privateer was beaten off. Such encounters were common at that time.

In 1809 the London and Edinburgh Shipping Company was formed. (It was to last for 150 years, finally ceasing to trade in 1959.) The new Company took over the six smacks of the Berwick Union Company: *Eliza, Sprightly, Fifeshire, Coldstream Packet, Edinburgh Packet* and *Leith Packet.* They ordered five more to be built by William Good of Bridport, all of 160 tons and costing 12-13gn per ton. *Trusty, Prompt, Pilot* and *Comet* were delivered in 1810. *Eclipse* followed in 1811. Three more smacks were later built for them by Robert Menzies: *Favourite* (1819), *Robert Bruce* (1823 - she was not named after royalty, but after the Company's current manager) and *Royal Sovereign* (1826).

In 1812 the other Berwick Company (now known as the Berwick Old Shipping Company) also decided to stop operating from Leith. Another new company, the London and Leith Old Shipping Company was set up with six vessels, three purchased from the Berwick Company, two built at Bridport and one at Leith by Alexander Sime. In 1814, the last Leith smack company came into being, the Edinburgh, Glasgow and Leith, with four vessels. The formation of this company brought the number of London smacks sailing from Leith to 27, the maximum number which ever frequented the port.

In 1819 for the first time, the Edinburgh and Leith Post Office Directory gave details of the Companys' ships and sailings.

Conditions on a Smack

William Reid, a Leith bookseller, owned shops at no 40 Shore and at the west end of the Custom House. He sold, among other things, telescopes, board games and packs of cards for the use of passengers on the smacks. In 1819 he published a small directory giving details of smack sailings (as in the PO Directory) the accommodation on board, fares and short notices of places to be seen on the voyage. Passengers were very keen on keeping a personal log giving distances sailed each day and details of the weather. William Reid's directory contained a printed table which its owner could fill in for this purpose.

> The table and notices will prevent many inquiries at the Captain at very improper times, when his attention ought not to be taken from his duty in the management of the vessel.

From Reid's Directory (and from the update published in 1824) we learn that the smacks varied from 130 to nearly 200 tons burden. Each had a ladies and a gentlemen's cabin, the latter being the larger of the two and used as a general saloon and dining room during the day. The ladies cabin was in the nature of a retreat for the gentler sex, especially when the gentlemen got down to some serious drinking in the evenings. Both cabins were handsomely decorated, with shining brasswork and gilding, and furnished in the latest style, 'even Piano Fortes have lately been introduced.' Each was surrounded by bunk sleeping-berths, and the latest smacks even had staterooms, lighted from above and with space for a writing desk. Large families would take over one or both of the cabins, together with the surrounding berths.

Steerage passengers lived on deck, no doubt hoping that they would have fine weather and a record passage of two days. If they were really unlucky the voyage could take as long as ten days - the average was five. The Directory hastened to reassure the genteel that social distinctions would be decently observed:

> As the steerage passage is, on account of its cheapness, that commonly taken by persons whom want of money would render unwelcome to many, or want of manners render intolerable to all; the company in both cabins is, usually, what persons not over fastidious or over full of aristocratic feelings and prejudices would scarcely hesitate to describe as 'tolerably select'. Where exceptions occur, the individuals who form them are, for the most part, kept sufficiently in check by a majority of the well-educated and the well-bred.

The crew consisted of a Master, Mate, Steward and 10 or 11 sailors. This large number of men was needed to handle the enormous mainsail.

> The Master is generally one who has been brought up in the trade and, and will almost without exception be found intelligent, good tempered and obliging. The Steward's business is to wait on the passengers, and it will seldom be found either neglected or performed without due respect and civility.

A passage under these conditions sounds delightful - if only one could avoid seasickness. Reid had some thoughts to offer on this as well. The sufferer was advised to stay on deck as much as possible and bathe the face frequently with cold salt water. Animal food was to be eaten sparingly and spirits restricted to a little brandy and water - which had been known to effect a cure in itself. The prudent, however, would purchase some 'Effervescing Powders' from Mr Milner, druggist, No 78 Shore, 'which have proved of remarkable efficacy in curing this distressing complaint.' If even Mr Milners Powders failed, the sufferer could take comfort in the thought that vomiting 'is in the highest degree wholesome' cleansing the stomach of 'bad humours, which, if retained, might vitiate the chyle and render the blood impure and disordered'. So however rough the voyage, one way or another the passengers would step onto the wharf at Wapping in the pink of health, having paid £3 13s 6d for the cure if they were 'cabin', or £1 5s steerage.

A Voyage to London

In 1830, another bookseller, RW Hume of no 57 Shore, published a humorous log book of a return voyage to London on a smack. Half of each page was left blank for the owner to keep his or her own log. The book is full of rather heavy-handed humour and some terrible verse, but it gives a lively flavour of what a typical passage may have been like.

The volume is dedicated to the managers of the Smack Companies, messrs Gourlay, Crichton, Ogilvy and Bruce. The dedicatory poem is typical of the author's offerings throughout the book:

> To you the managers for these sweet craft,
> Those trim-built, handy seaboats y'clept Smacks.
> Name sui generis, not that borne 'Abaft
> The binnacle' upon the stern. Your *Hawks*
> And *Scotts* and *Wellingtons* and *Czars* won't waft
> These vessels one knot faster through their tracks.
> 'Tis their intrinsic value, not a name.
> A smack though named the *Snail* would sail the same.'

(The second verse is worse than the first.)

> There is a considerable bustle - and very interesting that same bustle is - on the days on which the Smacks leave Leith for London. The loading and unloading of so many vessels forms a point of *loud* and *deep* interest to many of the good people of Leith, and to those of Edinburgh to boot. Merchants are superintending the transit of their goods. Friends the embark- and debark-ation of their relations. Seamen and porters 'stowing away' or 'shoving ashore' packages, and carters, with horrid din, delivering or lifting their hires.
>
> Many a lovely face is seen on the quarter deck, clothed in smiles, or after the manner of the April shower, 'Tears and smiles together'; and full many a travelling cloak and fur cap are moving about in rapid whirls, with their owners within and beneath them, busy in the ignoble, though quite necessary avocation of looking after trunks and other luggage.

Manager	Are all your passengers on board, Captain Trip?
Captain	All aboard sir
Manager	Then haul away - mind your helm and keep her clear of that vessel on your starboard bow.
Captain	Hulloa, you there, get your cork fender, d'ye hear.
Sailor	Aye aye sir
Captain	We'll be aboard of that schooner in an instant.
Sailor	All clear sir. All clear.
Captain	Where the devil is this coal box going? Haul away for'ard there. Clap the line to the winch and heave away I say.

> The vessel has started from her berth and is moving down the harbour. Drawbridge hove up - vessel through Bridge - passing Custom House on the left, an elegant building - Royal Landing Place on the right - here George IV first stepped on Scottish ground. A cast metal inscription to commemorate that happy event, 'O FELICEM DIEM'. A good representation of the 'Royal Landing' is painted on a sign board hard by.

O cam ye east or cam ye west
Or bring ye news to me man
Or were ye at the Pier o' Leith
And did the landing see, man?

> Immediately on passing the Custom House the extensive range of Wet Docks 'with their forests of masts' falls on the eye. On the right again is the Tower, whence are descried ships from every land and clime, and from whence is communicated to the merchants the arrival of each respective vessel, not by word but by sign, such communication being telegraphic.

Once the ship has cleared the Harbour we are introduced to the passengers. There are six ladies. Mrs Martingale, a skipper's wife, is going to meet her husband with her two daughters Anna Maria and Madelina, who have had a good education and can 'play the piano and sing and a' that'. Miss Antique, an elderly spinster from Edinburgh, is accompanied by her lap-dog Chloe. Miss Antic is a theatrical lady and Miss Traverse is a pretty girl from Fife who is travelling with her father, the 'old seadog' Captain Traverse. The three gentlemen are a chandler from Holborn called Mr Brown, the author and one other who remains anonymous.

The 'Log' devotes much space to details of the entertainment to be had on board. On the first evening, Mr Brown and the author flirt with the Misses Martingale on deck after supper. On the second night the company retire to bed at 10.00pm, all except Captain Traverse who gets together with Captain Trip in the Gentlemens' Cabin for several glasses of grog and a 'yarn'.

Fishing was a popular pastime among the gentlemen. The author fished for two hours on the third day, but 'caught nothing except a few haddock with a silver hook from a fisherman alongside'. (A sportsman who kept a short journal of a voyage on the smack 'Buccleuch', not only fished a lot but took pot shots at just about every living thing the ship encountered.)

After tea on the fourth day the passengers organise a regular concert. Mr Brown recites Collins' 'Ode on the Passions'. Miss Antic dances a minuet with Chloe around the cabin table. Anna Maria reads a Highland ballad and Miss Traverse and Madelina sing a duet. The author sings a Jacobite ballad, and Captain Traverse a catch, purported to have been learnt in Leith:

Let London be the Cockney's pride
Her commerce, wealth and a' that.
Prosperity's full flowing tide
May gar them crousely craw that.
But I'll sing o' the Port o' Leith
While I have breath to draw that.
Her auld black wa's, her neuks and raws,
The Reach, Coalhill and a' that.

On the seventh day after leaving Leith, the smack enters the Thames:

> Not less than 400 sail, size varying from a 74-gun ship to a wherry, needled their way up the river in company. Such a number of vessels, from all quarters of the globe, pushing on to the 'world's market town', making all possible exertion to gain their port and at the same time to avoid collision with each other and to keep clear of the thickly-planted sandbanks. The many-toned voices of the leadsmen (one in each vessel) as they ever and anon 'sing out' the depth of the water. Add to this the beautiful scenery of both sides of the river, intermingled with fields of flowing corn, among which, to the distant eye (such are the windings of the river) the vessels seem to glide.

In London

According to the log of the smack *Queen Charlotte* the crew would spend their time in London working on board. In July 1813 for instance, she lay at the wharf from the 7th to the 18th of the month. After discharging goods, the crew painted her hull and cabin, checked over the rigging and replaced worn ropes. Her mainsail was unbent, sent ashore for repair and replaced. The couple of days before departure were spent taking in ballast and loading goods and luggage.

A very different picture is painted, however, in a letter to the *Queen Charlotte*'s owners, the London and Leith Old Company. The most popular embarkation day for the return journey from London was Sunday. In 1813 it was proposed by the Edinburgh and Leith Company that this should be changed to a weekday. There were various commercial reasons for the proposal, but these cannot have been very pressing as the scheme came to nothing in the end. However, the question of Sabbath observance inevitably arose, and the comments of the LLOC's Wapping wharfinger on the matter show a different side of the behaviour of the smacks' crews when let loose in London:

> As an unworthy member of the Established Kirk of Scotland I deplore, in common with many others, the little attention paid to the strict observance of the Lord's Day in London, but in my humble opinion it would not be amended by keeping the smacks' sailors at the Wharf on that day. On the contrary, not one of them, from the Mate to the Cabin Boy would ever think to be persuaded of going to a Place of Worship, but being idle, spend the day in drunkenness and insolent merriment. The Boys and Protected [from impressment] men are about the streets drinking and quarrelling with the Girls of the Town, or insulting every respectable man or woman that passes, insomuch as to become a complete nuisance to the neighbourhood, and frequently calls for the interference of the Police. Those that dare not go on shore have their friends and doxies come to see them on board, and if any unnecessary waste of provisions takes place, it is then. I speak feeling, and find a kind of relief on a Sunday morning or afternoon when by the sailing of the two smacks from our wharf the neighbourhood gets rid of 20 or 30 ungovernable fellows, and three times that number from the other wharfs in the vicinity. The simple question seems to be whether the observance of the Lord's Day is

> better attended to by these men being engaged in useful employment and pulling ropes, or by idleness and debauchery.

The behaviour of the Scottish crews must have been fearsome indeed if it could lower the tone of Wapping - not an area of London noted for its refinement!

The Comet

It was in the same year that this letter was written that the first infinitesimal cloud appeared on the horizon of the Smack Companies. Henry Bell, an ex-shipwright from Bo'ness, began running the *Comet*, excursion steamer, on the Clyde. When she needed repair he brought her to his old yard, Shaw and Hart. Before returning her to the Clyde, he used her to run trips between Bo'ness and Leith. Her presence in Leith Harbour on 21 May was noted by the *Edinburgh Courant* as being the first sighting of a steam boat in the area. From being noteworthy as curiosities, steam vessels soon became a familiar sight at Leith. Finally, in 1821, the Edinburgh Steam Packet Company began running three regular steamships between Leith and London. Ten years later the London, Leith, Edinburgh and Glasgow Company replaced their smacks with three steamers; *Royal William, Royal Adelaide* and *Royal Victoria.* In 1836, the London and Edinburgh Steam Packet Company merged with the General Steam Navigation Company, which operated out of Granton. Two companies retained their smacks for the time being, but in 1844 replaced them with schooners and clippers which were cheaper to build and could be sailed with smaller crews as their sails were smaller and less unwieldy. After a reign of just over 50 years, the celebrated Leith Smacks had been deposed.

The London and Leith Old Shipping Company

The story of the London and Leith Old Shipping Company (the only one which would have nothing to do with steamers) illustrates very well the decline and eventual eclipse of the Leith Smacks. This was the third Smack Line to be set up at Leith, in 1812. The first minute in its earliest minute book is dated 10 August:

> At a meeting held this day in the Exchange Coffee House to consider the offer made by the Old Shipping Company of Berwick for three of the vessels belonging to it viz: the *King George, Queen Charlotte* and *Caledonia*. The following gentlemen were present -

John Crawford	(Leith merchant, first Chairman)
Patrick Hodge	(Leith merchant, first Deputy Chairman)
John Black	(first Manager)
William Thorburn	
George Dunlop	(Leith merchant)
Alexander Sime	(shipbuilder)

John Gavin	(shipbuilder - of Strachan and Gavin)
Thomas Hill	(fish curer of Burntisland)
James Harper	
George Carstairs	
Thomas Thomson	(Leith merchant)

It seems that the initial offer of ships had been made by Robert Gladstone, the Chairman of the Berwick Old Shipping Company, on 2 July. The first item of business on the agenda was to consider his letter of 4 August, in which he asked £3,700 for each of the three ships, the *Caledonia* having recently undergone a thorough repair.

> Should the above meet your approbation, the Committee still being wishful that your Company should slip into their shoes in the Leith trade, they will give you every assistance in its power as to accommodation etc.

The 'gentlemen present' thought the price rather high. A committee was appointed to examine each vessel as she came into Leith from London. Some of them would then to go to Berwick to negotiate a better price. The other question to be settled with the Berwick Company was a share of the lease of the Leith and Berwick Wharf at Wapping in London, of which they currently held half. The wharf belonged to a Mr Briant, a quarter was held by the Tay Company of Dundee and the other quarter by the wharfinger, Andrew Lawrie, who also acted as shipping agent for the Smack Company. Mr Lawrie had also written to offer his services, his first step being to distribute any publicity material the new Company might have printed.

> I shall most readily agree to load and unload no other vessels at the Wharf for Leith etc, but what belongs to the intended new Company, and I flatter myself with a little exertion and proper management it will yet be the most prosperous from your Port.

The Wharfinger followed his letter up to Leith and was present at the next meeting, held on 21 August to elect a committee to go to Berwick for the negotiations. A week later, Patrick Hodge, Alexander Sime, Thomas Hill and William Christie (Leith merchant) set out on their mission. They had been carefully instructed as to how they were to proceed:

1. To get half the lease of the wharf, or else an undertaking that no other shipping company be allowed to unload there, from Leith or any other port in the Forth.
2. To pay not more than a total of £10,000 for the three smacks.
3. To get a monthly charter of two other vessels of the Berwick Company until the new Company could build its own.
4. To get an agreement that the two Companies would not interfere with each others trade.
5. To use their own judgement on any matters not covered by the above.

FOR LEITH,

To Sail on 29th June at [illegible]

The London and Leith Old Shipping Company's Smack

WALTER SCOTT,

WILLIAM DICK, Com.

Elegantly fitted up with every possible Convenience for the Accommodation and Comfort of Passengers;

IS NOW TAKING IN GOODS AT THE

LEITH & BERWICK WHARF,

NEAR THE TOWER,

FOR

EDINBURGH	Dunblane	Hamilton	Dumbarton	Wigton	Musselburgh	Ayr	Campbleton	Wemyss
Haddington	LEITH	Anstruther	Kirkcudbright	Port Glasgow	Linton	Kinross	Kilmarnock	Kincardine
Dunbar	Inverkeithing	GLASGOW	GREENOCK	Bo-ness	Stranraer	Burntisland	Prestonpans	and
Hawick	Dumfries	Stirling	Dunfermline	Lanark	Peebles	Bathgate	Paisley	All Places
Selkirk	Alloa	Kirkaldy	North Berwick	Dalkeith	Linlithgow	Falkirk	Kilsyth	adjacent.

Goods insured to Leith, on Moderate Terms.

The Captain to be spoke with, on the Wharf, or on Board; and Information to be had as to the time of Sailing, &c. on the Royal Exchange, and of

Mr. EMANS, Edinbro' Castle, opposite Somerset House, Strand.
Mr. JOSEPH SMITH, Bookseller, 193, High Holborn.
Mr. SIMPSON, Fishmonger, Catherine-street, Strand.
Mr. CARTER, Butcher, Minories.
Mr. INGLIS, Bread & Biscuit Baker, 75, St. Paul's Church Yard.
Mr. DUDGEON, 18, Bedford-street, Strand.
Mr. ALEX. FORTUNE, Fancy Bread and Biscuit Baker, 12, Bridge-street, Westminster.
Mr. Wm. IRVING, Bread and Biscuit Baker, 114, Strand.
Mr. REID, Bread & Biscuit Baker, 10, Leadenhall-street.
Mr. T. DUTTON, Boot & Shoe Maker, 25, St. Martin's-court.
Mr. BARBER, Bread and Biscuit Baker, 121, Oxford-street.
Mr. G. GREGORY, John o' Groat's Hotel, 61, Rupert-street, Haymarket.
Messrs. CHRISTIAN BROTHERS, & Co. Wholesale Coffee Dealers, 27, Skinner-street, Snow-hill.
OLD WHITE HORSE CELLAR, Piccadilly.
Mr. W. PRICE, Boot and Shoe Maker, 101, Minories.

Malcom Macnaughtan, *Agent.*

Not accountable for Accidents by Fire at the Wharf.

N. B. A SMACK sails from the above Wharf, every SUNDAY and THURSDAY direct for LEITH.

Teape & Son, Printers, Tower-hill.

An advertisement for the Old Shipping Company's Wharf in London.

By 4 September the deal had been struck. The Company had paid £9000 for the three smacks and was to take possession of each one as she arrived at Leith. *Queen Charlotte* had been built at Berwick by Joseph Todd and Co in 1802, and was registered as a 136 ton sloop. *King George* was the same size, class and age, having also been built at Berwick, by Robert Gowans. Their masters were William Nesbit and William Halliburton respectively. William Nesbit had been master of his ship since her launch. *Caledonia* (master Robert Nisbet) was older and smaller than the other two. All the masters were kept on by the new Company.

The *Swallow* and the *Commercial* were chartered from the Berwick Company for six months at £180 per month each, plus 1gn per cabin passenger and ½gn per steerage passenger.

The Company also took over a quarter of the lease of: 'The Hoy and Helmet public house and the wharf at the back of it, once called Burr Wharf, then Beal's Wharf, then Briant's Wharf, now the Leith and Berwick Wharf.'

The accommodation included three warehouses, two counting houses and two stables with haylofts. The wharf lay on the south side of Lower East

Smithfield, with the Thames to the south, Millers Wharf to the east (the berth of the London and Edinburgh Company) and the Glasgow Wharf to the west (berth of the Edinburgh and Leith Company). In other words it was in the Pool of London, just downstream of Tower Bridge. Andrew Lawrie was sole manager, at a salary of £250 per annum plus 4% of all freights he collected and a free house at the wharf. He paid his clerks and other employees out of the wharfage dues.

On 12 September the Company held its first shareholders meeting at the Exchange Buildings in Leith. There were 23 subscribers from Leith, 12 from Edinburgh, one from Musselburgh, and Andrew Lawrie. The four negotiators who had been to Berwick were thanked for obtaining a good bargain, the contract of co-partnery was read and directors for the coming year elected, along with trustees to hold and convey property. John Crawford and Patrick Hodge were thanked 'for their unwearied exertions in forwarding the business and promoting the interests of the new Company'.

Open For Business

The new directors lost no time in getting down to business. Within a fortnight they had appointed John Black manager (salary £200 plus 2½% of profits), and his staff of cashier (£100), collecting clerk, landing and shipping clerk and book-keeper (£90). An account was opened for the Company at the Commercial Bank and for the manager with the British Linen Company. Mr Veitch, writer, was to be the Secretary and keep the minutes. One of the manager's four cautioners was William Reid the bookseller. The cashier's cautioner was Robert Menzies the shipbuilder, holder of two shares, who was at that time a Leith Bailie.

The ships masters were to be paid at the same rate as those of the other two Companies: 7gn per voyage, 10% of the passage money, and an allowance for carrying troops. This last item, together with the carriage of war supplies formed a significant proportion of the income of the Smack Companies at that time.

Fares were also fixed at the same rates as those of the other Companies:

Cabin	half bed	£3 13s 6d
	whole bed	£5 5s
	children under 6yrs	£1 1s
	~ 6 - 10 yrs	£2 2s
	~ 10 - 15 yrs	£3 3s
Steerage	sailors/soldiers/landsmen	£1 11s 6d
	troops (each)	£1 5s

Messrs Black and Sime were sent to Glasgow to appoint an agent and carrier there and publicise the new Company. The manager was instructed to get a horse and covered wagon in Leith for the conveyance of goods. By the first week of October Robert Grieve had been appointed agent in Glasgow at £80 per annum, plus 1gn per week for the warehouse men and £10 per quarter for a horse and cart. James Atkin and Son, the Glasgow Carrier were to carry the Company's goods to and from that place.

New Smacks

After some negotiation, it had been decided to award the contract for building two new smacks to William Good of Bridport, who had recently built for the London and Edinburgh Shipping Company. His price of £14 a ton was initially felt to be too high, but he refused to drop it as he only used English oak, which was daily increasing in price. Baltic timber for the decking had also kept up its high price, in spite of the reopening of trade to the area after the defeat of the French before Moscow.

Alexander Sime was to build one smack for 14 gn a ton, to be the same as those from Bridport (one difference was that the English builders use copper nails in the decking instead of iron). The contract to supply sails went to John and William Dickson and for ropes to Scales and Son and the Leith and Edinburgh Ropery. English shipbuilders were usually cheaper than the Leith firms and built most of the Leith smacks. Contracts for sails, ropes, blocks, furnishings, painting and other ancillary services were awarded locally, however.

At the beginning of December, William Nisbet, master of the *Queen Charlotte* went to London in the *King George*, on his way to Bridport to superintend the building of the smacks. His son, William junior, took over his command. Andrew Lawrie had heard rumours that the shipbuilder was in financial difficulties, and Captain Nisbet was instructed to transfer the contract to another firm if this proved to be true. Happily, all was well, and the *Ocean* and the *Lord Wellington* duly arrived in Leith to be outfitted for sea, in the following autumn. In the interim, as well as the two ships from Berwick, the Company hired the *Mary Ann* of Bridport, and the *Friendsbury* from the Edinburgh, Leith and Hull Company.

At the beginning of February 1813 the contract for joinery in the cabins of the new smacks was awarded. A month later, mattresses, stools and tables were contracted for. The carronades were to be made at Carron, and 16 guns were bought for the two Bridport smacks. Robert Paterson of Leith was to paint the *Lord Melville*. Adam Anderson was to supply stoves for all three ships. Contracts for upholstery went to three Edinburgh firms.

On 16 April 1813, the *Lord Melville* was launched from Alexander Sime's yard. The following day the Company wrote to her namesake, The First Lord of The Admiralty, to inform him of the event. He replied that he was flattered to be thus honoured, and asked for details of the dimensions and tonnage of the Company's best smacks. In July of the same year, the Company bought the houses at the foot of Queen Street, just by the berth where its vessels tied up. Here the office was established, at no 77 Shore.

A Good Start

At the AGM in October 1813, the Company had not begun to show a profit, but the following year the profits stood at £7,200, and a dividend of 10% was declared. In January 1815 it was proposed that a new ship should be built to replace the *Caledonia.* She was old, small, and unpopular with the passengers. The final decision was postponed until the following autumn, when the Company's financial state would be clearer. When this time came, however, the victory at Waterloo had brought the Napoleonic Wars to an end. Lucrative government contracts to carry troops and stores were severely curtailed, and the Smack companies began to feel the pinch along with many other shipping concerns throughout the country. In Leith the problem had been compounded by the establishment of a fourth Smack Company, the Edinburgh, Glasgow and Leith. The full effects were not felt immediately, however, and at the AGM the Company's books again showed a healthy profit of £7985 and the dividend remained at 10%.

The price of grain had fallen and other provisions were cheaper because of the peace, now that ships no longer had to wait for convoys or run the hazards of an unprotected voyage. Seamens' and other wage were reduced as a result. In response to pressure from shippers, some of the Companies had already lowered their freight charges. The Old Shipping Company decided not to follow suit.

Collision and Loss

At the beginning of December 1815 the Company suffered its first major setback. The *Lord Melville* collided with and sank the collier brig *Williamson* of Sunderland, at a point between Yarmouth and Hull. She managed to rescue three of the brig's crew, but herself began to take in water, and had to put in to Hull. Her repairs cost £120, and the owners of the *Williamson* sued for compensation.

One remarkable feature of the Company's proceedings was the lack of insurance for its vessels. Under the terms of the original contract of co-partnery, a sinking fund was established to cover the cost of replacing any vessel that might be lost. In the first year of its existence the Company had insured each of its vessel against fire, but once the policies lapsed they were not renewed. The premiums were high and this must have influenced the decision not to continue. Some insurance cover was continued for minor items, but losses, repairs and claims for salvage and damages were paid out of Company funds.

By March 1816 things were bad enough for the Company to have to begin to make economies. The Masters' commission was reduced by half. In June, advertisements in the Edinburgh papers were reduced to one a month. Also the Company applied to Trinity House for permission for its Masters to pilot their own vessels. In July, the lack of passengers was becoming so acute that a reduction in fares of half a guinea was contemplated, but as the other

Companies were not reducing their fares, any decision had to be postponed until they could be consulted. In August came the news that the Wharf had made a loss of £375. In September, the Tay Company, which held a quarter of the lease, went out of business.

The AGM in October was a gloomy affair. Loss of the carriage of troops had resulted in a shortfall of £2150 in passage money over the previous year, and freight money was down by £900. The Company had spent £3494 on repairs, including £435 on a thorough renovation of the cabin of the *Queen Charlotte*. The result of the case of the loss of the brig was still unknown and there was the added threat of a claim for £2200 by a firm whose seed had been damaged when the *Lord Melville* was arrested in London after the collision. In the circumstances the year's profit of only £1146 was added to the sinking fund, which consequently stood at £5,085. There was, of course, no dividend that year.

Captain David Gourlay, who had lately become a Director, represented the Company at the *Williamson* trial in November. He had gone to much trouble in collecting evidence and having models made, but in spite of his best efforts the decision went against the Company, which was faced with £3000 (later reduced to £2500) in compensation and costs. In February the shareholders were warned that they might have to contribute £5 per share to the bill if the pending appeal was unsuccessful.

In March 1817 the wages of Masters, mates and men were reduced and it was further suggested that they should be paid a yearly salary rather than per voyage. The following month the masters' percentage of passage money was replaced by 2½% of the profits of their respective vessels, to encourage each one to take care of his ship and prevent waste.

Andrew Lawrie also suffered. He had for some time been suspected of not pursuing the Company's interests with sufficient vigour. He was in his late forties, elderly by the standards of the time, and had been suffering from cataracts for the past four years, although an operation in the previous year had been successful. Ever since the formation of the Company, representatives had been regularly sent down to London to check up on the Wharfinger. Now he was informed that his percentage on freight money was to be reduced in order to pay for 'an active person', who would pay more regular visits to the Merchant Houses and the Exchange in order to drum up custom. In spite of Mr Lawrie's protests, Mr Hay was sent down to London to act as a 'walking clerk to pick up goods' as he had been doing in Edinburgh.

In April the Company was forced to borrow £1000. Throughout the summer the monthly profits were anxiously monitored and found to be depressingly low. The amount of goods carried had not diminished, but the fall in freights had had catastrophic consequences.

In June Captain Gourlay came up with a proposal to combine with the two other old Companies to run smacks from Dundee, which now lacked any such service, owing to the demise of the Tay Company. The Edinburgh and Leith Company were said to be willing to combine with the Old Company to run two ships a week from Leith and one from Dundee. Nothing came of this scheme, but Captain Gourlay's zeal was duly noted, and later bore fruit both for him and for the Company.

Malpractice and a New Manager

In August the Company considered selling some of its ships to the other Companies. At the end of September, with the AGM looming, the Committee who were balancing the books reported a loss for the year of £2000. Another result of their investigations was the resignation of Mr Black, the manager, early in October. The indefatigable Captain David Gourlay was promptly appointed in his place.

The year 1818 opened with little prospect of improvement. Lost property which had been accumulating in the office for several years was sold early in January, but realised only a very small sum. In March the Directors heard that they had finally lost their appeal in the *Williamson* case. They were faced with a bill for £2500. Rather than appeal to their increasingly hostile shareholders, they borrowed the money from the British Linen Company.

Low returns on freights were being compounded by private competition among the managers of the shipping companies, who were offering discounts in order to attract custom. The Directors resolved to put and end to 'this pernicious system'. Tables of freights and fares were to be printed and circulated to the public and to agents and wharfingers. After 1 April these rates were to be strictly adhered to, with a fine of £25 (a quarter of a senior clerk's salary) for anyone found breaking this rule. The fine would form a reward to the informer, and the miscreant would be dismissed. A practice had grown up of bulking weighable goods and weighing bulkable goods in order to manipulate freight charges. This was to cease forthwith.

In July the investigation into Mr Black's books finally revealed that he owed the Company £1359. At the same time, Andrew Lawrie was found to owe £1090. Then the cashier died, owing the Company £824. The pursuit of the manager's and cashier's cautioners extended over several years, and in the end very little of the money was recovered.

However, perhaps owing to the rigorous new rules concerning freight charges and to the vigour of the new manager, business was improving. In September 1818 a contract was concluded for the building of a 180-ton smack. Once again the builder was William Good of Bridport, whose tender was 40s per ton lower than any Leith firm could offer. The water closets on the three newest smacks were moved from their decks to their cabins. At the AGM, the Directors were able to report a prosperous year, although profits were not sufficient to merit the payment of a dividend.

Recovery

The next year was very much the same. At the AGM on 30 September 1819, the Shareholders were told that the former heavy damage to ships and goods had been reduced to nearly nil. All expenses were much reduced. Only £250 had been recovered from Robert Menzies, the cautioner of the late cashier, who had stood surety for a maximum of £500. The Directors did not think the expense of a lawsuit to recover the rest was warranted. The affair of the former manager was not yet settled, but the Directors did not hesitate to attribute their late problems to his mismanagement. The profit on the year amounted to only £1207, still not sufficient for a dividend to be paid. However, there seemed to be every hope of a good year to come.

A fortnight before the AGM, the new smack had been launched at Bridport and named the *Walter Scott*. She went to sea for the first time the following April. In November 1819 a joint committee of the four Shipping Companies considered a proposal from none other than Mr James Watt, for operating steam packets, but the Old Company declined to be concerned in such a venture.

The calm of the year 1820 was only ruffled by the conduct of the Berwick Company in 'poaching' one of the Old Company's best Masters to be its manager. At the AGM a dividend of 12½% was announced. Captain Gourlay was voted a gift of £150 for his efforts on behalf of the Company, and his salary was raised to £350. This improvement in fortunes was sustained for several years, but the Company was never again even to approach the profits of over £7000 which it had made in its early days.

An Amalgamation

In 1820 the number of Smack companies was reduced to three by the amalgamation of the Edinburgh and Leith and the Edinburgh, Glasgow and Leith Companies into one concern, to be known as the London, Leith, Edinburgh and Glasgow Company (LLEGC). The shipbuilders Alexander Sime and Thomas Morton valued their ships. Those of the EGLC were the largest, most valuable and most numerous. As well as its five smacks, all around 200 tons, the Company owned 12 sloops of 50 to 80 tons which operated between Leith and Glasgow via the Union Canal. It also had a 94 ton steam tug, valued at £1095 for her hull plus £1550 for her engine. The Company owned three horses, a black waggon horse, and two other blacks named Jamie and Tom.

The Edinburgh and Leith Company had only two horses, and its seven smacks were smaller and in worse repair than those of the other Company. However, its holdings of property in North Leith were much more valuable. They consisted in the main of all the buildings on both sides of Shorts Wynd, a yard at the head of it and a quay at its foot. This had all belonged to the Carpenter James Robertson, who had bought them in 1704. His only child, Isobel, had married a ships master called Frederick Symons, and it was from their daughter that the Company had bought the property.

The Company's other main block of property comprised a wharf on the west side of the Drawbridge, with some new offices and houses at the back of it, fronting on Bridge St. A dwelling house, presumably for the Manager, fronted on Sandport Street. The new merged Company was based at the North Leith wharf, away from the crowded berths on the South side of the Harbour. It may also have been more convenient for the steamships which the Company soon began to acquire.

Competition from the First Steam Packets

A year after the merger, the new Company began sailing three of its smacks between Belfast and Glasgow. The future looked bright, but a cloud was looming on the horizon of the Smack Companies, and it was one which would eventually extinguish some of them for ever. In the spring of 1821 the newly formed London and Edinburgh Steam Packet Company began sailings of its first steam vessel the 420 ton *City of Edinburgh*. She was powered by two engines, each of 40hp and her saloon could accommodate 95 diners. In the following two years, she was joined by the *James Watt* (449 tons, two 50hp engines) and the *Soho*, (510 tons, 60hp engines). The final vessel, the *Tourist* which joined them in 1824 was only 200 tons, but each of her engines generated 100hp, which made her very fast. The average steamer passage to London was only two days. The saloons were 'commodious and superb' and the Ladies Cabins 'lofty, airy and elegant'. The Aberdeen and Leith Shipping Company was already running the steam yacht *Velocity* to Aberdeen and two other steam boats, *Tourist* and *Brilliant* were plying to Aberdeen and Inverness.

Many passengers were understandably keen to try this new rapid and luxurious mode of travel. What is more, the new Company charged cabin passengers only 2gn. Set against these factors were the noise and dirt which inevitably attended steam travel, and the fact that many people regarded steam engines as dangerous monsters, which were more than likely to explode, as had happened with a number of early steam rail locomotives. Nevertheless, the new development was sufficiently threatening to cause considerable consternation to the Directors of the Smack Companies.

The Old Company decided to start letting half beds as they had done when they first set up in business. The Directors felt that the size of the bedrooms in the steamers was such that they too would be let as double rooms. Captain Gourlay was instructed to admonish the Masters, who were not making enough efforts to get business in the Merchant Houses of either London or Edinburgh. They had also failed to treat the 'friends of the Company' sailing on their ships with due distinction. If there were complaints in future they would lose pay.

At the 1821 AGM the Directors voiced their apprehensions concerning the steamships:

> The competition from vessels navigated by steam in that branch of the Company's business for which the vessels may be said to be chiefly adapted, has been such

> during the past season, though in its infancy, as to inspire considerable apprehension as to the coming year.

Nevertheless, the past year had been successful, and the dividend was set at 12%.

Consolidation

The next year was a quiet one. Captain Crichton of the *Walter Scott* was brought before the Admiralty Court for flying the Blue Ensign at sea. *Lord Melville* damaged the *Nimrod* of Sunderland, whose owners had to be compensated. *Lord Melville*'s mate was lost overboard, and the Company granted his widow a pension of 3s per week.

In June 1822, Captain Crichton was dismissed for 'outrageous conduct'. No details are given, but he had used improper language to Captain Gourlay - and not for the first time. Perhaps he was protesting about the prospective wage cuts, which came into force on 1 July:

Mates were reduced from	£5 5s	to £4 4s	per voyage
Seamen	£3 3s	to £2 10s	
Cooks	£2 12s 6d	to £2 2s	
Stewards	£2 2s	to £1 11s 6d	
Carpenters	£3 13s 6d	to £3	

Labour relations at this time were such as present-day managers can only dream about. The workforce meekly accepted the most iniquitous treatment and managers could hire and fire at will, with little danger of any kind of comeback. It has to be said, however, that the Company seemed to have treated its 'servants' reasonably well by the standards of its day. Very few men were dismissed, and then only for repeated misdemeanours. Stewards were the most at risk, usually for surly behaviour towards the passengers. The occasional clerk was discovered to have dipped into the Company's funds, and one or two crew members were caught smuggling - whisky and silk handkerchiefs on one occasion. Drunkenness was always a problem in this hard-drinking age and profession. Drinking at sea by a Master was held to be the most serious because of its potential consequences. However, it was the new steam companies who were most concerned about the alcohol intake of their Masters.

Because of their long practice and high level of skill in handling sailing ships, most skippers could bring them into harbour and berth them almost with their eyes shut, and the fact that the Master may have taken a wee dram or two made not much difference. However, a man given command of a steamship was in a very different position. These vessels handled very differently from sailing ships in confined spaces, taking much longer to slow down and stop for instance. Steamship owners insisted on strict sobriety in the Masters who were to 'drive' these unfamiliar and highly expensive vessels.

In spite of the competition from steamers during the 1820s, the Old Company's business held up fairly well, with profits usually in the region of

£3500 to £4750. In November 1823, a contract was signed with Messrs Bayley and Co of Ipswich to build a new smack (*Sir William Wallace*, which came into service in April 1825). In December the hull and boat of the *Caledonia* were sold to Henry and Jemima Gamble and Robert Liddel junior (once the partner of Alexander Sime) for £300.

During 1824 the new steam company completed its full complement of four steamships. The other two Smack Companies lowered their cabin fares in June, to 2gn. At first, the Old Company refused to follow suit, but the passengers forced it to change, by threatening to transfer to other ships. By the end of the year, the three Companies had brought their charges into line with each other.

The time was now approaching for renewal of the lease of the London wharf, but negotiations had scarcely begun, when Andrew Lawrie, whose affairs had been in question for some time, finally went bankrupt, owing money to both the Leith and the Berwick Companies. The owner of the wharf died at the same time, and his sons decided to sell, giving the two Companies first refusal. Initially they gave the idea serious consideration, as the value of the property had been considerably reduced owing to the building of St Catherine's Dock just downriver. It seems, however, that the asking price was not low enough. The Companies did, however, take over the whole lease; one third to the Leith and two thirds to the Berwick Company.

Sir William Wallace was such a success that the Company had another smack begun by Bayley in 1825. She was the *Earl of Wemyss*, the largest yet, at 202 tons. She made her maiden voyage in the spring of 1827. Incredible as it may seem, another sailing ship Company, the Forth and Thames was set up in 1826. It did not last long, however. The existing companies bought its four smacks, even before they had finished building, in order to prevent undue competition.

In August 1827, in an attempt to reduce passage times to a minimum, the Company instituted a competition amongst its Masters. A register was to be kept of the times of arrivals at Leith and London, and the Master who made the shortest passages at the end of the year was to be rewarded. In the event, Captain Crabbe of the *Earl of Wemyss* put up the best performance. He received 10gn and his mate 2gn. Captain Brown of the *Lord Melville* was almost as good, but it was felt that his ship had incurred too many repairs as a result of minor collisions. In consequence he got only 2gn and his mate 1gn. The same was awarded to Captains Johnson and Nesbit and their respective mates. Captain Tulloch and his mate got 1gn and ½gn. The results reflected the fact that the better vessels were sailed by the most experienced Captains.

These awards were made in September 1828, and the minute that records them also mentions the change that had been made in wharf arrangements in London. Both the Leith and the Berwick Companies had moved from Lower Thames Street to Irongate, the new wharf being now known as the 'Leith and Berwick Wharf, Irongate'. It was in a far better position, just downriver of the newly-built St Catherine's Dock, and the rent was very little more than that of the old wharf.

Shipwreck

At about the same time, on 26 September, the *Queen Charlotte* was run down and sunk eight miles off Lowestoft, by the collier brig *Sylvan*. The 'Queen' was now an old lady (25 years), and her value had dropped to £1000. Moreover the *Sylvan* was clearly in the wrong and her owners had to compensate the Company. The loss of the *Lord Melville* in March 1829 was far more serious. In this case there was no question of compensation, as the loss was the result of a collision with the *Lord Wellington*. All were agreed that this was a complete accident, in which no-one was to blame.

The two smacks had been on their way home, sailing in company on a dark and squally night. They had reached Berwick Bay, *Lord Melville* being ahead of *Lord Wellington*. She started to go about to tack but would not answer her helm and went rapidly astern. *Lord Wellington* immediately put up her helm, but she did not wear as fast as *Lord Melville* went astern, and the two collided. After making sure that she was not taking in water, *Lord Wellington* went back to see if she could find any survivors. In fact all but two on board were safe, but they were in a small boat and she missed them in the dark. They endured an uncomfortable eight hours before the boat finally came ashore.

Not long before the loss of the *Lord Melville*, a new ship, the *Duke of Buccleuch* was ready for sea. She was built at Leith, by Robert Menzies and was said to be 'the finest vessel of her class ever to have left the Port'.

Steam Gains a Hold

In January 1830 the LLEG lowered its fares and the other companies had to follow suit or lose business. The London and Edinburgh Company decided to reduce the wages and victual allowance of their crews, and the catering for the passengers, but the Old Company declined to take such measures. In March the Directors of all three companies met in order to discuss the possible acquisition of steam vessels. Once again the Old Company decided against the measure. The following year, however, the LLEG began to replace its smacks with steamships leaving only the Old Company and the London and Edinburgh Company still running solely Smacks. From 27 Leith smacks in the heyday of the Companies, within ten years the number had been reduced to about a dozen. The Old Company, however, decided to defy progress. As the Directors reported at the 1830 AGM, 'The Company is a Sailing Company, with no need to wish nor to fear a change'.

It is easy, with hindsight, to dismiss this attitude as one of blinkered ignorance, but at that time steam engines were very unreliable. It is unlikely they would have been allowed to operate at all if modern safety standards had been in force at that time. However, the Company might have been content to overlook this fact if they could have raised the enormous sums of money (in the region of £10,000 per vessel) necessary to buy steam vessels. As it was, they could only cut costs and hope that the dash for steam would be just a passing fashion. There was still a certain amount of troop transport work available, and the salaries of the Company's agents at the Custom House and in the New Town and High Street were cut.

Smuggling

June 1831 saw one of the occasional discoveries of smuggling by servants of the Company. The steward of the *Walter Scott* had taken 17 gallons of whisky to London, when he only had a permit for six gallons. The mate had taken six gallons without any permit at all! His consignment was by way of an order from one of the clerks at the wharf. It emerged that he had known that a former steward had habitually taken whisky to London for sale, but had not informed the Captain 'as was his duty'. Both steward and mate were dismissed. The Captain appeared to have no knowledge of what had been going on, but was warned to be more vigilant in future. There can be little doubt that this incident was only the tip of a very large iceberg. Wages were so low, opportunities for smuggling so obvious, and places for concealment so varied that the practice must have been endemic in all branches of the Trade.

The Schooner

The year 1831 was a good one, with profits up by about £1300. The next year, the Directors' report to the AGM could confidently state that steam navigation for the past few months had been as fully operational as it was likely to be for some considerable time. 'It seems not likely to inflict any injury that may not be conquered by the usual weapons of this Company - exertion and economy.' Steam was better for the carriage of light goods which needed to be moved quickly, but it could not carry general goods any more cheaply than sail if the Steam Companies were to make a profit.

Nevertheless, the Directors had been considering bringing its fleet up to date. The latest thing in merchant ships was the schooner; a two-masted vessel with a capacious hold. During the 1830s the London and Edinburgh Company had five schooners built. In March 1833 the Old Shipping Company contracted with Robert Menzies to build one of 200 tons, which would have twice the cargo capacity of a smack. The hold was made larger by sacrificing cabin space, which was becoming less important as passenger traffic declined. Troops were still being transported, but they had always travelled steerage in any case.

The Case of the Earl of Wemyss

In September 1833 the *Earl of Wemyss* was stranded on a Norfolk beach in a storm. This in itself was bad enough, but her passengers discovered that the although the Company would return their fares it would not compensate them for their lost luggage, which they said had been stolen by the local inhabitants. Some had also lost relatives and friends in the disaster, and they began to make public accusations of negligence. These were so damaging that at the AGM the Directors were compelled to issue their own version of events. The accident had occurred off Brancaster:

> During one of the most dreadful hurricanes that ever has been experienced upon that coast within the memory of the oldest man living at the time. The ravages of which, both upon sea and land, will never be forgotten. Its effects were appalling and heartrending. Dead bodies driving ashore the whole of Saturday night from the suffering vessels, from one end of the Norfolk coast to the other. And within the precincts of the small town of Cromer, 84 bodies were picked up and buried in the church yard of that place upon the Sunday. The morning of which day the ever-to-be-lamented catastrophe occurred to the Smack 'Earl of Wemyss' by which eleven lives were lost, from circumstances which were not within the power of man to control or prevent
>
> Notwithstanding the severe beating of the *Earl of Wemyss* upon the sands for two whole tides, in a most tremendous sea, not a floor or a foothook has been broken, while the wrecks of the other unfortunate vessels were strewed over the beach in pieces. She lost a great part of her keel and gabbard strakes, and all the oakum worked out of her seams, so that the tide flowed into her as though she had no bottom, until they dug the sand away and got a quantity of bullocks hides, which she had on board as freight, nailed over the bottom, and four extra pumps on board, with 50 men. They were then enabled to move her by keeping the extra pumps and her own four pumps....constantly going, until they with great difficulty got her into Brancaster creek, about two miles from where she was stranded.

It was in the creek that the passengers' luggage was seized by the son-in-law of the local Lord of Manor, invoking an obsolete Medieval law whereby a third of the goods on a wrecked ship belonged to the Lord of the Manor on whose lands she was stranded.

Her master, Captain Nesbit, was suspended. The following August he applied to be reinstated, but at an Extraordinary Meeting of the Directors, the Dean of Guild spoke out strongly against his re-employment. The memory of the previous September was obviously still raw in the minds of some influential people. Captain Nesbit was sacrificed to public opinion, although he was granted £5 a month for a year, while he looked for other employment.

More Problems

By this time, the new schooner was launched - the *Camilla*. For a few years she was quite successful. In particular she relieved the other vessels of bringing empty casks back from London so that they could carry more profitable cargoes. However, when the competition for freights once again increased, it was found that she was too large to be often filled with a cargo to London. In 1843 the experiment was tried of chartering her for a transatlantic voyage, but for this traffic she proved too small to be profitable. In 1844 she was sold for £1100.

The price points up the relative cheapness of schooners over smacks, when contrasted with the £3300 paid by the Company for smacks of a similar age in 1813.

In 1836, the fine balance which had been achieved with the steam Companies was once more tipped in their favour. They had begun carrying some heavy goods, and in order to remain competitive the sailing Companies had been forced to reduce their freight charges yet again. The Old Company's profit in this year was only £864, as against £2161 in the previous year and £2580 in 1834. The London and Edinburgh Company made a loss on the year, and seriously considered dissolution.

In 1837 the *Ocean* was sold for £1000, and the staff of the Leith office took yet more salary cuts. David Gourlay, the manager, led the way with a voluntary reduction of £150, nearly a third of his salary. The Captains' allowance for beer money was stopped, and the wages of the porters and carters were cut by an average of 1s 3d per week. For the first time the sail and steam Companies met to come to an agreement about freights. The sail companies were allowed to undercut the steam freights on some goods by as much as 25%. This actually represented an increase in their freight charges and they were forced to cut some of them again when shippers complained. One reason for this new spirit of co-operation may have been the advent of the 'transient vessels' (tramps) complained of in the Directors' report for that year. These casual carriers could afford to undercut even the steam Companies, who were threatened in their trade for the first time. Passenger carriage had by this time almost ceased in sailing vessels, and most of the stewards had been dispensed with. In spite of all efforts, however, in 1837 the Company made a loss of £233.

In 1838 the *Lord Wellington* was sold for £800, and part of the London wharf was let to the Belfast and Dublin Steam Packet Company for £500 per annum. The Norwich Smack Company had also been allowed facilities there, which brought in another £150 to £200 per year. However, as steamships grew in size, the practice was growing of vessels discharging goods in mid-stream into Thames lighters, which diminished the incomes of the wharves by as much as 50%. Passenger traffic completely ceased, all the remaining stewards were dismissed, and the Company started converting their vessels into schooners. They began with the *Sir William Wallace* the last ship to be worked on by the Leith shipbuilders Butement and Young, who went bankrupt while she was still in their dock.

Better Days Again

The dismal year of 1837 proved to be a turning point in the fortunes of the Company. From then on it began once more to make a profit, albeit only in the region of £1000 per year. In 1841 the *Duke of Buccleuch* was converted into a schooner, the last of the Company's smacks to suffer this fate. The *Earl of Wemyss* and the *Sir William Wallace* had their cabin space further reduced, and their holds strengthened to allow them to carry extra loads.

At about the same time that work began on the *Duke of Buccleuch*, David Gourlay resigned. He had suffered for some time from a respiritory complaint, and since 1835 had been granted an annual holiday in the country for his health. During the previous year he had been allowed two assistants, who were appointed joint managers on his retirement. Captain Gourlay was voted a pension of £100 a year, but he did not live to collect even the first payment. He died in September 1842.

Clippers

The threat from the steamships had affected sailing ship owners in other parts of Scotland, and in the late 1830s the Aberdeen shipbuilder William Hall had been commissioned to build a fast sailing vessel which could compete with steam. He took as his model the 'Baltimore clippers' which had been developed in America in the early years of the century. Their hull design was long and low, the bow sharp with an angled stem post, and the stern inclined. The area of hull offering resistance to the water was thus greatly reduced. William Hall experimented with models in a tank, and came up with a version of the clipper in which the bows acted like a plough. He built his first ship, the *Scottish Maid* in 1839. (She subsequently made the voyage from Leith to London in 33 hours.) William Hall's first vessels were not the classic three-masted, square rigged clippers of the mid-nineteenth century, although he did go on to build the first small tea clippers, the *Stornoway* and the *Chrysolite.* The early Hall clippers had a two-masted, fore and aft schooner rig and are sometimes referred to as 'schooner clippers'.

Another of Hall's early schooner clippers was the *Lightning*, and the Old Company initially considered buying her, but this idea was dropped. Instead they compromised and the *Walter Scott* was given a clipper bow by Lachlan Rose and Son of Leith. However, the sale of the *Camilla* in 1842 brought in some spare cash, and it was decided to have an iron clipper built at Aberdeen. Iron vessels were able to carry heavier loads than wooden ones, and needed less expensive repair and upkeep. William Simpson and Co of Aberdeen got the contract for the new ship. Her cost was higher than that of a schooner, at £3080, ready for sea, but Simpson was willing to take the *Duke of Buccleuch* in part exchange. The clipper, the *Prince of Wales*, came into service in the spring of 1845. The benefits of the change were seen immediately. From the first, the two clippers consistently made higher profits than the schooners.

The London and Edinburgh Company had three clippers built by Hall himself; the *Nonsuch* and *Rapid* in 1840 and the *Swift* in 1842. In 1848 Robert Menzies built them the clipper *Dart*

A New Threat

By 1842 the steam Companies were themselves in competition with the railways, which gradually took away practically all the passenger traffic and a substantial amount of light freight. Early in 1849 they threatened to end the mutual freight agreement unless the sail Companies reduced their freight undercut from 25% to 10%. The two sail Companies compromised at 15%. By this time the Old Company was effectively running only three vessels, the *Walter Scott* being used only as a spare ship. Another iron clipper was commissioned, this time from Alexander Hall of Aberdeen. In 1850 she was named the *Princess Royal.* Profits for this year and the next were in the region of £2000, but the remorseless competition from the railways continued, and in 1852 the profits halved. In the same year the London and Edinburgh Company bought its first steamship, the 350 ton *Prompt II*, at a cost of £9068. The Old Company was now the only one left using only sailing vessels.

Sail had declined in other areas too. In Leith, by 1855 only the two London Companies and the Carron Company (which sailed a ship to Liverpool each week) were using sailing ships outside Scotland. Individual owners may well have done so, but they were becoming very much a minority.

The Old Company managed to keep its head above water in spite of an increase in wages which was forced on it in 1853, but in November 1856 the steam Companies again reduced their freights. The reduction thus forced on the sail Companies cut the profit per voyage from the already narrow margin of £45 to the impossible figure of £15. A Special Committee of the Old Company met on 4 December to consider what might be done to improve business and cut costs yet again. Initially they recommended increasing advertising, hoping to attract full cargoes, which would restore the profits to £45 per voyage. Then they looked at wages. It was felt that crews and porters could take a cut early in the following summer, the Accountant could be dispensed with and also the Managers' Clerk. The Directors' allowance of £72 pa could be halved. The salaries of the Managers were protected until the autumn of 1857, but could be reconsidered then.

In February 1857, three of the Directors who lived in Leith were deputed to look into the state of trade and of competition with the steam Companies. In March an agent was appointed to canvas for new customers on a commission basis. By autumn it was obvious that none of these measures had had any effect, and the Directors considered approaching the London and Edinburgh Company to see if they would buy the four ships. However, the Company's London Manager suggested reducing the number of vessels by one and carrying on. Instead of introducing a motion for dissolution at the AGM as they had intended, the Directors reported that although they had made a loss of £674 on the year, they intended to carry on with only three ships and hope that the saving on crews' wages would improve matters.

The End of the Company

July 1858 saw the meeting of yet another Special Expenditure Committee, which recommended further wholesale reductions in wages and salaries, cuts in provisions allowances for crews, and various other measures. The Directors, however, decided that there was no point in carrying on, and the 1858 AGM was the last:

> After upwards of 40 years of great general prosperity, the Old Shipping Company has, during the last two years, been doomed to experience an unfortunate reverse.
>
> During these two years, and particularly during the last, business has been considerable, and at former rates of freight would have been satisfactory, but owing to the ruinous competition between the three companies [sail and steam], a considerable loss has been incurred, in spite of all the reductions of expense the Directors considered practicable.

A motion to dissolve the Company was carried. Over the first four months of 1859 the company's property - office, warehouse, cellar and Manager's house were sold. They fetched rather less than had been hoped. The ships were auctioned on Friday 11 March. The reserve put on the *Walter Scott* was £650, on the *Sir William Wallace* it was £950. The *Prince of Wales* had a £1450 reserve, and the *Princess Royal*, £1350.

At the beginning of April advertisements were sent to the Press for the benefit of those having claims against the Company, and shippers with freights still

The entrance to Leith Harbour, 1826. The vessel with a large mainsail in the centre of the picture is a smack. The Pier is on the left and on the right can be seen Menzies' shipyard.

outstanding were contacted. In May an interim payment of £10 per share was made to all shareholders. The Company's charitable fund was kept on in order to continue payments to its six pensioners. (Some years previously all Masters and crew members had been instructed to make their own pension arrangements.) The Manager was given a gratuity of £50, the apprentice Clerk £10 and the office Cleaning Woman £2.

In January 1860, all debts not yet collected were written off and a final payment of £1 8s 6d per share made to shareholders. The final minute, dated 4 August 1860, records a decision to sell all books and papers except the ledgers (which were needed for a final audit) for waste paper. Much did in fact eventually disappear down the sewers of Leith, but all the Minute Books and some other books and papers survived, most of which are now in Edinburgh City Archive.

The Supremacy of Steam

The London and Edinburgh Company continued to build and buy steam vessels (35 by 1903) and went on to become the oldest steamship company in the world. It was finally dissolved in 1959.

The LLEG continued to acquire steamships, but it disappeared from the picture at some time between 1857 and 1860, whether through dissolution or merger is not clear.

By 1860, apart from the Carron Company's sailings to Liverpool, what regular sail traffic there was from Leith was local, or bound for East Coast ports or the Northern Isles. Steamers for the same destinations left mainly from Granton where there was a new pier offering deep water accommodation to these large ships. Most of the steamers for London, Hull and Newcastle operated from Leith, and foreign steam trade was expanding. Ships of the Leith, Hull and Hamburg Steam Packet Company sailed regularly to Hamburg, Stettin, Copenhagen and Konigsberg. The Rotterdam and Leith Company plied to Rotterdam and the Leith and St Petersburg Company to St Petersburg.

Of course, it would be many years before the last commercial sailing ship came into Leith. For some bulky cargoes which did not need fast transit, such as grain, sail continued to be a viable proposition up until the Second World War. Photographs of Leith Docks taken in the early years of this century still show a 'forest of masts'. However, the age of steam was long and successful, and however imperceptible the process, sail at last gave way before it.

15

Coal and Rail

In the Great Customs accounts for 1492 we find the first record of the export of coal from Leith. In that year, 17 chalders (about 34 tons) was shipped from the port, paying custom of £1 2s 8d. At the time, and for nearly two centuries thereafter, Fife and Lothian coal was mined primarily as fuel for the salt pans of the Forth. For other uses, wood and peat were the universal fuels. Little coal was exported, as there was only a small market for it. The limited amount which was shipped at Leith seems to have been 'small coal' for use in the smithies of the Low Countries.

During the sixteenth century there was a steady increase in the amount of coal exported from Leith. In 1551, when Edinburgh began to appoint the 'metters of coal, salt and grain' at Leith, some 360 tons of coal paid Custom at the port. By the last decade of the century the yearly average was in the region of 700 tons. The surviving evidence suggests that Scandinavia was one of the outlets for Scottish coal in the sixteenth century. Leith coal exports may have financed some of the Norwegian timber trade into the port.

Seventeenth century Shore Dues and Prime Gilt books record increasing numbers of 'coal barks and boats' coming into Leith. Very little coal, however, was exported. Recorded quantities ranged from 376 tons in 1673 (over half of which went to English ports) to as little as 28 tons in 1686. In some years there were no exports of coal at all. With the exception of the year of 1673, all recorded coal exports from Leith in the seventeenth century were bound for the Low Countries. Fife ports, such as Kirkcaldy, Burntisland and Dysart seem to have been more important than Leith as coal exporting harbours for Fife coal, and smaller ports such as Prestonpans played a large role in the Lothian export trade at this time.

The decline in Forth salt production during the eighteenth century by no means diminished the demand for coal. Urban centres such as Edinburgh were increasing in size, and although the poor continued to use peat (much of which was shipped through Leith), anyone who could afford it burned coal. Industry was also on the increase. Smithy coal had always been an important commodity, but brewing, soap boiling, sugar boiling, whale oil extraction, and glass making were all Leith/Edinburgh-based coal-using industries which expanded throughout the century.

By the start of the nineteenth century we are well into the Steam Age. In 1813, the works of the Glass House Company at Leith were advertised for sale, among its assets being a 16hp steam engine. The first steamship to ply on the Forth appeared in the same year. The dry docks opening off the West Wet Dock (completed in 1817) were pumped out by a steam engine, the first of many in the Docks. From the 1820s onwards, steamships became increasingly familiar at Leith. The demand for steam boilers and, from the 1840s, iron ships, brought heavy engineering to Leith, notably at Hawthorn's engineering works in Sherrif Brae, Morton's in the Docks complex, and other smaller concerns, all of which needed fuel for their forges and steam-powered machinery. The advent of gasworks early in the century also provided a voracious market for coal.

Early Coal Transport

For the Lothian coal owners, the transporting of all this 'black diamond' to the point of consumption became an increasing problem. As early as 1606 a wooden tramway had been planned at Inveresk, in this case to carry coal to the saltpans. The wagonway that was built at Stacks (near Bo'ness) in 1646, served a similar purpose. In 1715, the Earl of Winton made the mistake of backing the Old Pretender. His estates, which were sequestered by the Crown, included coal pits near Tranent. These pits came under the administration of the York Buildings Company, which built a wagonway in 1722 from Tranent to Cockenzie harbour, whose course can still be traced. In 1779 the pits and track were acquired by John Caddell of the Carron Company. At about the same time John Wauchope of Edmondston and two others built an inland wagonway from Newton pit at Edmondston to Little France. There may well have been other Lothian wagonways, but as the tracks were of wood and not very extensive, traces of them would be easily obliterated once they became disused.

By 1800 yearly consumption of coal in Edinburgh alone was running at some 200,000 tons, a figure which was to almost double during the next 30 years. The entire tonnage was transported by cart and the price was high, £1 per ton compared with a maximum of 11s per ton at Glasgow. The pits which supplied Glasgow were nearer to the city and the owners had organised an efficient system of 24cwt carts hauled by strong horses, each making three trips a day. The carts of the Midlothian owners held only 12 cwt, made one trip a day each, and were drawn by inferior animals. Glasgow had the further advantage of the Monklands Canal, which provided cheap transport for coal from the pits east of the city.

The Edinburgh and Dalkeith Railway

During the first decade of the nineteenth century, Henry Seton Stewart made plans for a railway to bring coal from the Midlothian pits to Edinburgh. In 1812, Sir John Hope, who already had a wagonway from his pit at Pinkiehill to Fisherrow harbour, joined with John Clerk of Eldin in another scheme. The Duke of Buccleuch had possible railway routes surveyed by John Farey in 1816 and Robert Stevenson in 1818. All these schemes foundered for lack of financial backing, but in 1822 the Edinburgh and Glasgow Union Canal was opened. It ran from the Forth and Clyde Canal to a terminal basin at Port Hopetoun, just

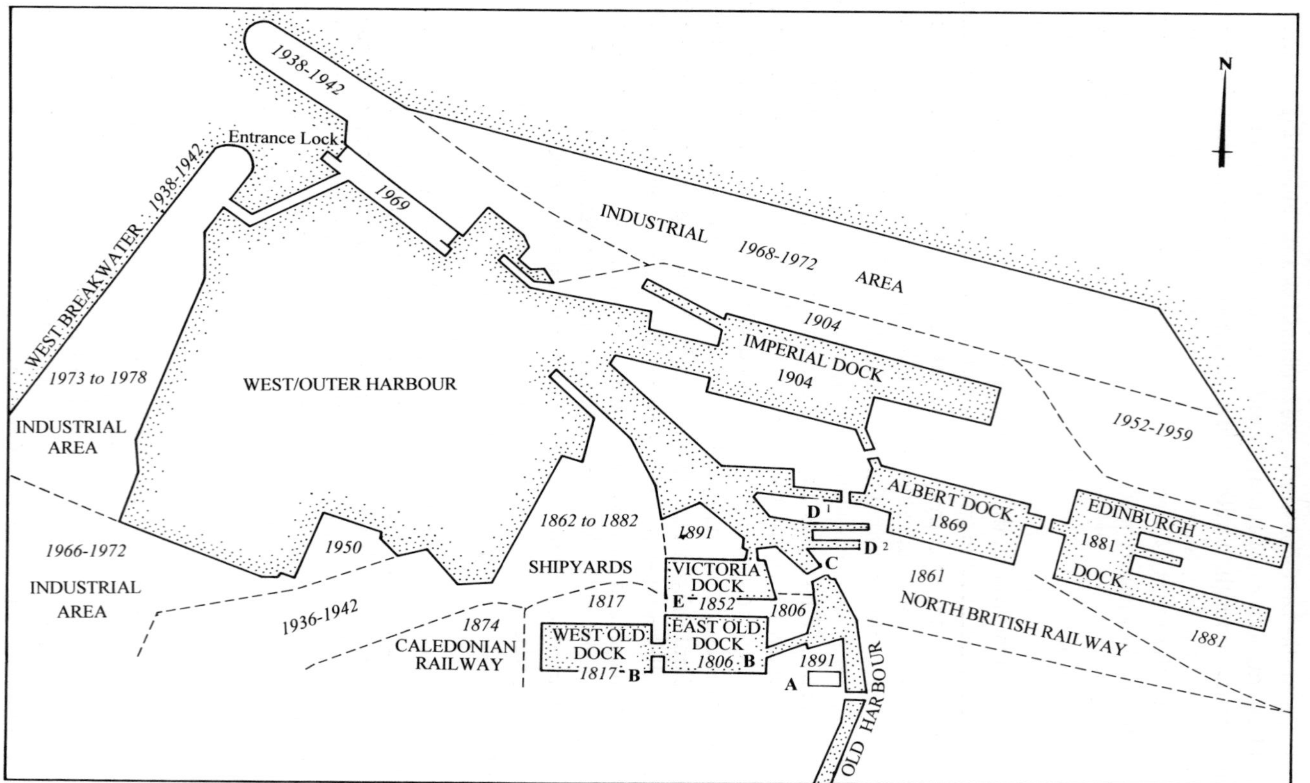

Plan of the nineteenth and twentieth century development of the Docks' complex.

south of Edinburgh, threatening to bring cheap Glasgow coal right into this main market of the Midlothian owners. The threat was heightened by plans to open a railway linking the Monklands pit near Glasgow, with the Forth and Clyde Canal, which ran eastwards from the Clyde and opened into the Forth at Grangemouth.

In 1824, the Duke of Buccleuch's factor John Grieve (who had built Sir John Hope's Pinkiehill wagonway) produced a plan to build a railway from the Duke's Lothian pits to St Leonards on the south side of Edinburgh, with a branch to Fisherrow Harbour for exports. A number of other Midlothian coal owners were also interested, and at a meeting in the Royal Exchange Coffee House Edinburgh, in September 1824, the Edinburgh and Dalkeith Railway Company was born. An Act of Parliament was needed to authorise the building of a railway and this the Company obtained in 1826. Five years later its main line was complete. It snaked from Craighall to the St Leonard's Depot, touching at the pits of the coal-owning Company partners. (The St Leonard's area of Edinburgh included the site of the 'hospital' of Holyrood Abbey which had St Leonard's Lands, Leith, as one of its original endowments.) In 1832 the branch to Fisherrow was completed. Sir John Hope and the Marquis of Lothian provided threequarters of the coal traffic, and the latter built a private extension from Dalhousie Mains to his pits at Arniston. The Duke of Buccleuch's share of the traffic was only about five percent, but it was enough for it to be worth his while building his own extension to his Smeaton and Cowden pits in 1838. Two other owners, Stenhouse and Robert Dundas of Arniston, accounted for the balance of the traffic. The rest of the shareholders included Edinburgh lawyers and bankers who went on to finance other railway projects.

'Railway Coal'

Robert Dundas's experience graphically illustrates the effect of the new railway on coal production in the area. By cart, he had transported 200 tons to Edinburgh in a year. By rail this amount rapidly increased to over 7000 tons. Altogether the Edinburgh and Dalkeith Railway was soon carrying some 300 tons a day for its coal-owning shareholders. The cost of rail transport was just over half that of carting, but there were benefits to the domestic customer which went beyond the question of price.

Before the coming of the railway, the Edinburgh coal market was completely unregulated. Coal merchants and carters were notorious for their dishonesty, giving short weight and selling inferior quality at inflated prices. The railway Company installed one of the recently-invented weighbridges at St Leonards, worked by an official weigher. Each cartful of coal weighed there was given a certificate which stated the weight and quality of the coal, and the time of departure of the cart. Inspectors watched the carts through the streets to make sure there was no shady dealing. 'Railway coal' became a guarantee of quality, much promoted in the Company's advertisements.

The First Passenger Service

The various coal owners employed agents, whose offices were near the St Leonard's depot. It was one of the Marquis of Lothian's agents, Michael Fox, who started a passenger service in 1832 by running an old stagecoach on the line. (All the Company's traffic was horse drawn, each train having a guard with a bugle to warn pedestrians of its approach in built-up areas). The new service proved such a success that within a few years the Company took over the passenger business. They never issued tickets, however, for the simple reason that many of their clientele had no idea where they wanted to get off! The rest regarded questions about their destination as an intrusion on their privacy, describing the enquirer as, 'Yon speirin' loon'. In spite of this apparent handicap, passenger traffic was extremely profitable to the Company.

The Leith Branch

As soon as the Edinburgh and Dalkeith commenced in business in 1828, Bailie Hardy of Leith proposed a branch from the new railway to the port, and at a meeting of interested shareholders held shortly afterwards, Leith representatives were asked to provide figures showing the amount of business to be expected. The total yearly amount of coal used in Leith, according to these figures, was 50,000 tons. Half of this was for domestic consumption, 10,000 tons for public works and 15,000 tons for the use of steamships and for export. In 1832 plans were finalised to bring a branch of the Edinburgh and Dalkeith Railway from Niddrie round the coast to Leith, in order to supply the town with coal and to provide cargoes for export at cheaper rates of freight. The branch was floated as a separate company (initially called the Forth Railway Company), but the shareholders were much the same as those of the main line, with the addition of Leith Town Council.

In 1830 the branch was opened, with a passenger station on the east side of the foot of Constitution Street. Westward from the station, the Company was granted a strip 36 feet wide and 30 feet from the buildings to the south of the line (to the northernmost boundary of the Timber Bush), to run a line along the Sands to the foot of the Shore. This 66-foot-wide strip eventually became Tower Street, which is still unusually spacious. As well as the station, at the foot of Constitution Street were the coal depots of the Marquis of Lothian, Sir John Hope and Robert Dundas of Arniston, all of whom employed agents in Leith. The Company had also installed a weighbridge, supervised by Mr Alexander Robertson. (This first railway line to Leith, after many vicissitudes and changes of ownership, is now the last remaining line at the port, terminating at a goods depot about a mile to the east of the site of the original station.)

The Railway and the Docks Commission

The Sands to the north of the Timber Bush and the Glassworks came within the ambit of the Leith Dock commission, and in 1839, Sir John Hope applied to it for ground for an additional coal depot. The existing joint depot lay on the seaward side of the line, extending about 60 feet northwards, to the limit of normal high tides. Each proprietor had a storage area of 680 square yards within the depot, but Sir John wanted a further 300 square yards to accommodate his expanding trade. When the Commissioners visited the site they found that the Marquis of Lothian had laid a private siding between the line and his depot, which was obstructing access to the east of the foot of Constitution Street. He was ordered to remove it.

Not long afterwards, the Leith Police Commissioners requested an area of the Sands at the foot of Assembly St, to use for a Dung Depot (the police were responsible for cleaning the streets and emptying public 'necessaries'). Street scrapings and sewage were much in demand as fertiliser by market gardeners, who would cart it from the Depot. Other rubbish was placed where it would be washed away at Spring tides. The stench and the accompanying clouds of flies were much complained of by the proprietors of the nearby Glasshouse - they cannot have been too pleasant for passengers alighting at the Railway station! Once again an unauthorised siding was found to have encroached on the proposed site, this time belonging to Robert Dundas. He too was ordered to remove.

In 1840 the Commission built a road (Tower St) from the foot of Constitution St to the Shore. It was to have a footpath 6 feet wide, a 20 foot width of causeway (cobbles) and at least four feet was to be left between it and the railway. A new eastern pier was also being built out northwards from the foot of the Shore. In 1841 the Edinburgh and Dalkeith Company applied to the Commission for permission to extend its rails onto the quay at the head of the new pier in order to get its wagons closer to the ships. The Commission delayed its decision for various reasons and the lines on the pier were still quite new when the Edinburgh and Dalkeith was sold to the North British Railway Company in 1845.

Railway Fact and Fantasy

By this time, railway fever had well and truly gripped Scotland. An Edinburgh, Leith and Glasgow line had been proposed in 1831, but it posed too much of a threat to the traffic of the Forth and Clyde Canal. The new Company had to restrict its operations and finally received its Parliamentary Act in 1838 as the Edinburgh and Glasgow Railway, terminating at what is now Edinburgh's Haymarket Station. The proposed extension to Leith never materialised. However, in 1845 the Dock Commission was considering proposals from four Railway Companies for lines to Leith, which could be extended into the Docks. The Caledonian Railway Company wanted to run a line to the west end of the wet docks, to the portion of the West Dock belonging to the Admiralty, known as the Queen's Dock. A Junction Railway was proposed from Granton, which would run along the north side of Commercial St, next to the warehouses. The Edinburgh, Leith and Granton Railway intended to run a branch line to North Leith.

The most ambitious scheme was for an Atmospheric Railway, to be run on pneumatic lines, such as Mr Brunel was (ultimately unsuccessfully) experimenting with on the South Devon coast. In 1845 there were two competing Companies; the Edinburgh and Leith Atmospheric Railway, and the Edinburgh and Leith Atmospheric Direct Railway. Rivalry between them was fierce and bitter, but by the start of 1846, the former had prevailed. In February of that year, the Commission learned that the Direct line had been abandoned, and the plan was now based on Mr Robert Stevenson's report for the ELAR. The line would run from the new North British Company station under North Bridge in Edinburgh, then via a tunnel under Calton Hill to Nottingham Place. From this point it would run south to Leith, where a viaduct would carry it over the houses as far as Constitution St. Here the Atmospheric section of the railway would end, and after a perpendicular drop of 20 ft (!) the track would continue as a conventional railway. After crossing the Edinburgh and Dalkeith track it would continue on to the harbour where it would divide. One branch was to run out along the East Pier, the other to continue up the Shore to the Lower Drawbridge, cross the harbour, and terminate just to the west of the Custom House.

In the event, only the Edinburgh, Leith and Granton branch line materialised. It came into North Leith from the south, by way of a bridge under Great Junction St, just to the west of the bridge which carried the road over the Water of Leith. Shortly after this point it entered a tunnel, emerging about half way along Citadel St. From the end of the tunnel it ran due north, entering the Docks just to the left of the main gate in Commercial St.

The First Dock Railway

In the course of its initial deliberations in 1846, the Dock commission decided that all rails within the Docks should be laid by its own contractors, in order that it might maintain control over railway operations on its premises. The Commission was also determined to prevent any one Rail Company getting a monopoly of the use of Docks rails in the future.

The first set of tracks was laid on the South Quay of the Wet Docks in the spring of 1847 by Alexander Kinghorn, who was currently building an extension to the East Pier. The original intention had been to use flat-soled rails laid on longitudinal wooden sleepers, but a report made by the engineer, Mr Leslie, in October 1846, recommended ordinary rails laid on stone blocks. This system would initially be more expensive, as the causeway would have to be lifted, but there would be no problems of decay and replacement of sleepers. The rails also could be lighter than normal as horses were to be used in the docks instead

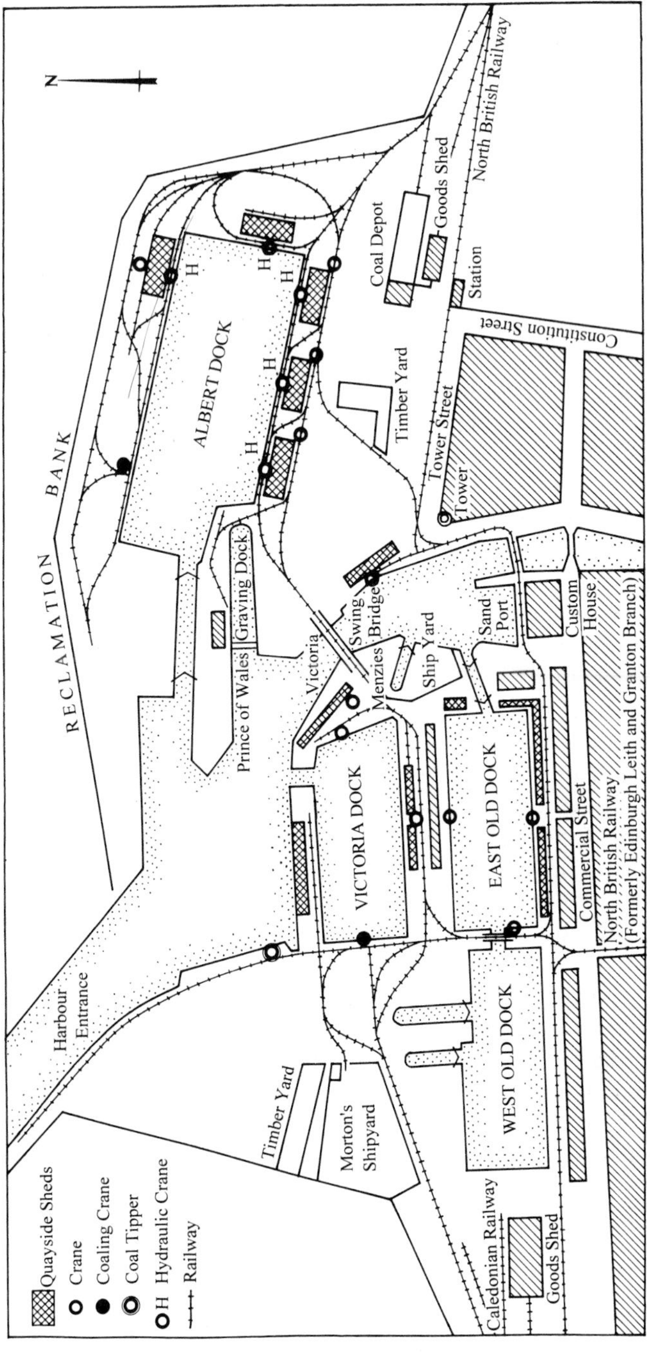

Plan of the Docks in 1872, showing the extent of the railway network.

of locomotives. Mr Leslie suggested the use of extra-deep cast iron chairs, such as he had made for Dundee docks. The existing rubble (irregular) cobbled causeway was not suitable for laying rails in. Squared blocks would be needed, or asphalt with a two foot wide strip of causeway between the rails for the horses' feet.

A certain amount of haggling went on between the Railway Company and the Commission over compensation for the ground of the Public Works Yard at the Docks entrance, where the Company's rails entered the premises. The Company also objected to the Commission's insistence that it pay rent for the Dock rails, pointing out the projected gain to the Commission in the form of increased Harbour dues. However, it finally agreed to pay the demanded 7½% per year of the cost of the rails. The Commission in its turn agreed to make no charge for the ground it had to give up at the Public Works Yard.

The system of Railway Companies paying rent for the Dock rails always caused a great deal of trouble. Arrears would build up for years until they totalled thousands of pounds. The Shore Dues office, which handled all dues charged within the Docks and the Old Harbour, would then have to produce calculations based on the amount of rail-laying done since the last settling up. The resulting bill would be presented to the Company concerned, which would inevitably contest it. Finally, after much time-wasting and haggling, the Commission would accept a settlement which was much lower than the original demand. Set against the losses on this particular branch of income, however, was the enormous gain in Shore Dues on ships and goods which would have been lost to Leith if the railways had not been there. It was also much to the advantage of the Commission to have complete control over the running of trains on its premises. The system persisted until the 1880s, when the Commission agreed to lay rails for the Railway Companies at the new Edinburgh Dock, the Companies to pay the cost. This was the plan adopted for all subsequent rail-laying operations.

Alexander Kinghorn finished work on the first set of Dock rails at the end of May 1847. The original plan had been for a single line, at a cost of around £13,000. In the end a double line was laid, costing nearer £25,000. The guard plate, guard rails, switch boxes and covers were obtained from James Millar and Co, spikes and chairs from William and Robert Musket, rails from Dundyvan Iron Works of Glasgow and stone blocks from George Johnston and Co of Craigleith Quarry.

The North British Railway Brings Steam to South Leith

Concurrently with their negotiations with the ELG Company, the Commissioners were also dealing with the plans of the North British for its newly acquired line in South Leith. The Company was relaying all its former Edinburgh and Dalkeith track (which it had acquired in 1845) to conform to the Standard Gauge, and by January 1847 it had applied to Parliament for a Bill for relaying the Leith branch. The Commission was concerned with the stretch which ran on its property on South Leith Sands. The Company intended to build a new station, for which it needed more ground on the Sands, and it also intended to relay the track westwards to the Shore, as well as that on the East Pier. As the North British used steam locomotives the question of safe public access to the Sands was of prime importance. The Commission also firmly stipulated that although locomotives might be used as far west as the Shore, they were to come no further onto its property. This concession was mainly for the benefit of steamship passengers, who would otherwise have been held up at the Constitution St station.

Although the Commission was willing to grant a concession for the section of track from the station to the Shore, the Commissioners were still concerned about the question of access to the Sands to the east of the railway station. Together with the Town Council and the Police Commissioners, in March 1847, they petitioned the Lords of the Admiralty, objecting to the Bill for the North British branch to Leith. Their Lordships were involved in the dispute because the area of the Sands required by the North British was technically within the flood mark. In January 1848, the Company made the necessary adjustments to its original plans, and the Commission gave it permission to go ahead with its track-laying, according to their previous agreements. However, the mills of government grind exceeding slow, and it was not until the end of 1848 that the North British obtained an Act for its Leith branch. The Company applied to Parliament for permission to run locomotives on the branch at the end of 1850 and again in 1856. In 1857, the Dock commission finally formally approved the extension of the North British line to the Harbour, and the use of locomotives thereon.

Trouble in the Docks

In the meantime the railway at the Docks was having teething troubles. In March 1849 a horse belonging to the Edinburgh and Glasgow Railway (which was using the ELG line to send goods to Leith) had its hoof torn and sustained other injuries when its foot became caught in the rails. The EGR demanded compensation from the Commission for the injury to the horse and the cost of its treatment by 'Mr Dick, Vetinary Surgeon'. There had been other similar accidents at the same spot at the Docks entrance, and the Commission's engineer was instructed to fill up the offending rail slots with wood.

A few months later, the Commissioners in their turn complained to the Edinburgh and Northern Railway. (This, at least, is how the Company is designated in the relevant Commission Minutes, but it must be a slip of the pen, as two years previously the ENR had amalgamated with the ELG to form the Edinburgh, Perth and Dundee Railway Company). The complaint concerned 'the reckless manner in which Trucks are driven along the Quays of the Docks'. A Customs Land Waiter had been weighing cheese in his box on the quay, when the box was struck by the first railway truck to enter the Docks on the morning in question. The Railway Company maintained that the horse was going no faster than a quick walk, and that trucks had safely passed the same box for the whole of the previous day - implying that the box must have been moved. It also made a counter-claim that much time was lost by railway employees, who frequently had to clear the rails of goods unloaded from ships, and that the Docks men did not keep the tracks free of rubbish, which could take up to two hours to clear away. There was, in fact, a fair degree of antipathy between Dock employees and Railway men in these early days. The railway drivers disliked taking orders from Docks officials, and the carters and porters resented the loss of much of their work to the railways. Accusations of mutual insolence and abusive language were an inevitable accompaniment to complaints made by either side.

Early in 1852, the Custom House complained to the Edinburgh, Perth and Dundee about

> two cases of extreme recklessness of driving of Railway trucks by their servants on the lines of railway which are laid down along and under the sheds on the south sides of the Docks, much to the inconvenience of parties engaged in landing goods from ships, and in both instances at the imminent risk of personally injuring our Landing Waiters, who at that time were in official Boxes, taking accounts of cargoes.

The problem was passed over to the Commission to deal with, and one practical step was taken to relieve congestion on the wharf. The Custom House scales had been hung from large wooden pyramid frames (similar to those used by the Metters) which took up a lot of space in the quayside sheds. These frames were replace by travelling hooks slung from a beam fixed along the length of each shed.

It might have been anticipated that these complaints would be the first in a long succession stretching down the years, but in fact the operation seems to have worked fairly smoothly on the whole. The usual day-to-day disputes, annoyances, and minor accidents inevitably occurred, but there was very little that was sufficiently serious to merit formal complaints. However, a slight injury to a dock worker in 1855 led to a Commission ruling that railway horses must be led rather than driven, while in the Docks.

Extending the Dock Railway

So successful indeed was the Docks railway, that plans were soon being made to extend it to the new dock (Victoria Dock) which was begun late in 1850, and to the West Pier which was also being built. Trucks on the West Pier line were man-hauled. A Superintendent's report of 1859 reveals why:

> I have carefully examined the Roadway on the West Pier, and am decidedly of the opinion that the best thing to be done is not to meddle with it [ie not to lay a proposed wooden horse track between the rails], but if Horses are permitted down, to repair it from time to time as may be required. This morning....I granted leave

> for some of the Artillary Horses to take down a Russian Gun. I went down the pier at the same time, and I assure you that both then and in returning, I feared a serious accident would occur from the plunging of the Horses. The Roadway was in good order, but the Horses could not walk upon it. They slipped about in an alarming manner, and at last the experiment was given up and they proceded down and up on the planking. When a steamer passed there was more plunging, and I felt relieved when they were fairly off the pier. I do not think anything has been said to the Commissioners about the Mess that the Pier will necessarily be in from Horse traffic, nor has the danger from a Horse taking fright and running away been pointed out.

In order to carry the railway line further north, to the new dock, a more suitable swing bridge was needed over the passage between the East and West Old Docks. It was decided to obtain one which was operated by hydraulic power, from Elswick Engine Works of Newcastle. The new bridge arrived at Leith by rail early in 1853, and came into use in June of the same year, the old manually-operated bridge being repaired, altered, and re-located over the entrance lock to the Old Docks. Four months after it came into use the hydraulic bridge was reported as being a great success. It took just four minutes to open, and required only two men to operate it. At the same time as the bridge was installed, the Commission briefly considered having a hydraulic crane erected at the Docks. The proposal was quickly dropped, but if it had gone ahead, Leith would have had the distinction of owning one of the early cranes made by the celebrated Mr, later Sir William, Armstrong of Newcastle.

In the meantime the railway network had been extended to include lines along the south and west quays of the new dock, laid by Thomas Hutchings and Co of London, who also contracted to lay paving on the south quay. The line on the south quay was to have branches running into the sheds that were being built there, and it was suggested by the Surveyor that rather than having points to connect the lines, a 'traversing frame' (traverser) should be used.

> The traversing frame travels at right angles to the rails, the frame running on a flat plate. It is drawn across the line in which the wagon is moving, and when the wagon has run on the frame, the whole is moved sideways until on the line of the rails the wagon is wanted to be brought on, when it is taken off direct to its destination....In a quay, the [points] switches are continually getting out of order. The wide space obliged to be left for the tongue is dangerous, and it gets filled up with dust and rubbish. Also in shunting, the wagon must be first drawn ahead, then back, then ahead again. With the traversing frame, the horse need never be taken off, but helps to pull the wagon across the lines.

After some deliberation the Commissioners decided to install one traversing frame as an experiment, at a cost of £91. Their caution was justified. While rail traffic consisted of single trucks drawn by individual horses, the frame was adequate for its purpose. However, the number of trucks in a train quickly multiplied as trade expanded, and the frame soon became obsolete. It was finally dismantled and sold for scrap less than ten years after it was first installed.

New Docks

The new Victoria Dock was opened on 17 August, 1852. Mrs Grant, confectioner, provided the Official Party with fruit and cake at one shilling per head, and Messrs Bell, Rannie and Co supplied six dozen of champagne and four dozen of sherry. A hogshead of ale was broached for the men. The new dock soon became heavily used by steamers, which were being built larger with every year that passed. Sailing ships were also increasing in size as they bid to compete with steamships - those bringing cargoes of guano were of 1200 to 1500 tons, larger even than the steamers. As early as 1855, only three years after the opening of the new dock, when the London Leith Edinburgh and Glasgow Shipping Line transferred its steamers to Leith from Granton, some Commissioners considered 'that the time is near when the Victoria Dock will be found insufficiently large for its purpose'. In its early years the dock was adequate for the shipping which frequented Leith, but as vessels of larger dimensions began to appear, the new harbour at Granton, which had far better deep-water facilities, began to take trade away from Leith. However, in 1854 the Victoria Dock was in such demand that railway lines were extended to the north wharf, which eventually became the berth of the Hull and Hamburg Line.

The building of the Prince of Wales graving (dry) dock, which opened in 1864 did not in itself affect the railway network in the Docks, but it was the first major building operation for which materials were brought in by rail. The bulk of the sandstone used in its construction came from the Craigmillar Quarry, and the contractor, Alexander Millar of Granton, leased part of the quarry and

The West Pier with its railway tracks, circa 1880.

laid a branch to it from the North British line. He also ran a line from South Leith station across the Sands to the site of the graving dock.

Coal Handling

We have already seen that the initial reason for the presence of railways at the Docks was to facilitate the coal trade. In this it was extremely successful. From a total of 50,000 tons handled in 1828, the estimated figure for coal shipped at Leith in 1855 was 170,000 tons. Apart from a rather inadequate chute installed on the Shore in the late 1840s, there was no mechanical coal handling equipment, almost the whole tonnage being loaded and unloaded by hand. This situation could not long continue, and in 1856 the Edinburgh, Perth and Dundee Railway Company petitioned the Dock commission for a steam or hydraulic crane or shipping staith to be installed at the Victoria Dock. The manager pointed out that at the Company's harbour at Tayport, 200-250 tons a day were shipped by a single staith.

A new Docks Superintendent, John Balbirnie, had recently been appointed who knew a lot about coal handling, having previously been manager of a large coal works in England. He was sent to Glasgow to examine the coal-shipping methods in use there and report on the best, with an estimate of the cost. Balbirnie recommended a 20-ton steam crane, which could handle one ton per minute:

> The wagon runs onto a cradle attached to the slings of the crane chain. Steam is let on. The wagon in its cradle is raised. The traversing motion of the crane is then communicated and the wagon gradually brought over the hold or barge placed for the reception of the coal. The cradle with the wagon is now tipped by a very simple contrivance. The door spring or fastening released and the contents dropped.

In the autumn of the same year, the North British petitioned for a Coal Shipping machine on the east side of the harbour. They did not get it, but subsequent similar petitions reveal that small ships (30-250 tons) were visiting the railway berth at the foot of the Shore. In fact, the Old Harbour was by no means made redundant as a result of the building of the new Docks. Small vessels which could lie aground at low tide continued to use it in large numbers.

The Steam Crane

John Balbirnie's plan for a steam crane at the Victoria Dock was approved, and permission was given for it to be erected at the centre of the West Quay. (A 30-ton manually operated goods crane was being built on the East Quay.) The railway lines at the steam crane site were altered to provide a siding beside the crane's engine house, connected by a turntable with the line along the quayside. The contract to build the crane was awarded to Messrs Glen and Ross of Glasgow, the cradle being made by Morton of Granton (ex Leith). Fresh water for the boiler was laid on from the mains, rather than using the very dirty supply from the Dock. Work began in March 1858 and by early January 1859 it was finished. Almost immediately, having been refused a coal tipper at the foot of the Shore, the North British successfully petitioned the Commission for permission to build a drawbridge, to carry its line on the Shore across the harbour to the area behind the Custom House. From there it would cross Dock Place, enter the Old Docks via the eastern gate, and join onto the rails of the South Quay, thus giving the Company access to the steam crane.

Once it was erected, the steam crane needed thorough testing before it could be brought into use. In April 1859 the Superintendent took over responsibility for it from the contractors. His test run revealed that it took far too long (3-4 hours) to get up steam, and that 6-7 cwt of coal were needed for the operation. A taller chimney (55 feet) was built to improve the draught. The cost of getting up steam was offset by a rule that the crane would not handle a train of fewer than 20 wagons. On 12 September 1859 the Superintendent reported that the alterations to the railway lines at the crane were finished, and that three vessels had so far been loaded there:

> to the satisfaction of all the parties concerned. The first vessel, the SS *Emmeline* [charged only half dues - 2d per ton] received part of her cargo at the rate of 2 tons per minute, but that was under very favourable circumstances and could not be maintained, because in the first place the coals were not ready, and in the next they could not be trimmed so fast as they could be put on board.
>
> The success, however, of the Crane has in my opinion been complete, and it may be reckoned that vessels of average capacity may be loaded at the rate of 400 tons per day. Under the old process of hand loading, this operation would have occupied a week.

As do many technological advances, the new crane brought unemployment in its wake. The army of dock labourers which had been needed to load coal was now largely redundant. The full effects may not have been felt at first, as smaller ships and those which did not want to queue for the crane were still hand-loaded, but once coal cranes were erected at Granton in 1861, many larger vessels went to load there, leaving Leith men with less work. The trade of 'coal trimmer' expanded - gangs of men armed with rakes and shovels levelling the coal in the ship's hold as it was tipped in by the steam crane - but this could not wholly offset the loss of employment for the dock labourers.

The Drawbridge

In the meantime the North British pressed on with its drawbridge over the Harbour and its new line of rails. At first the bridge was only planned to have an opening span of 40 feet. The engineering firm of Hawthorns protested to the Dock Commission that this was only the same width as the bridges further up the Harbour, which were already causing a lot of problems for steamships trying to get up to their Sherrif Brae works for repairs. (Paddle steamers in particular needed extra width to accommodate the paddle wheels mounted on their sides.) The narrow span of the old drawbridges had already affected the shipbuilding which had begun to expand in the Upper Harbour earlier in the century. Mortons had abandoned their patent slip in the early 1830s, and Menzies, who took it over, had long returned to more convenient premises in the Docks.

Initially the Commission were disposed to dismiss Hawthorns' appeal, but after further petitioning it gave way, and the final span of the bridge was 50 feet. The new drawbridge was opened for use by the North British on 14 May 1860. In its first six months of use, the new railway line carried 15,000 tons of coal and 6,238 tons of other goods. (These figures were almost equalled by the Edinburgh, Perth and Dundee in the same period.) Shortly after the opening of the bridge, the Docks Superintendent was given permission to lay an extra line of rails on the South Quay of the Old Docks to carry the increased traffic.

While work continued on its link with North Leith, the North British at last brought the first steam locomotive to its South Leith station, on 12 July 1859. Immediately disputes arose over the level-crossing gates on the line. The prevailing system was that all gates were kept closed and locked across the access roads, and keys given to those who might need to use them. Would-be sea bathers found that the two existing 'underpasses' beneath the railway embankment were choked with rubbish, unpaved, and unusable at high tide. They took to climbing the walls of the railway and crossing the rails on the surface. The Dock commission took exception to its employees having to use a key, and after much negotiation the North British at last agreed to employ a keeper at the crossing east of Seafield Baths, if the Commission would grant the land for his lodge. However, the gates were still kept closed across the road rather than across the railway, in spite of the fact that the opposite arrangement was in use at the Constitution St level crossing.

The Caledonian Railway

In 1861, the great rival of the North British, the Caledonian Railway, applied to Parliament for a Bill to construct a branch to Leith. It was to run from a point near Crewe Toll on the railway to Granton, to the west end of the Old Docks. The Bill went through with unusual speed, and in April 1862, the Commission signed and sealed an agreement with the Caledonian granting the Company the land it needed for the new line to the Docks.

Further Expansion

Late in 1861 the Superintendent reported that the dock facilities were already insufficient for requirements. In April 1862, with the new Prince of Wales graving dock nearly finished, the Commissioners requested Alexander Rendel, the son of the late James Rendel, engineer of the Victoria Dock, to submit designs for a further new dock. The resulting plan was for two docks, running

View of the Shore from the North British Railway drawbridge over the harbour, circa 1880. The bridge was demolished at some time between 1901 and 1911.

east/west, on land to be reclaimed to the north of the Prince of Wales Dock. It was decided to begin with the westernmost of the two, and in February 1863, a report was presented to the Public Works Loans Committee, in advance of the usual petition to the Treasury for permission to borrow the necessary funds.

The 1863 report stated that the Old Docks could only take ships of up to 400 tons. The Victoria Dock was capable of handling even the 1200-1500 ton guano ships, but their deep draught of around 20ft meant that they had to be lightened of some of their cargo in the Roads, in order to get over the sill of the Dock entrance. In the ten years since it was opened, steamships had much increased in length and the very largest could not get into the Dock. Many passenger steamers were forced to use Granton. The problems caused by the length of the ships were aggravated by the fact that the entrance to the Dock was in one of its long sides. If there was a vessel in the berth opposite the entrance, there was not enough room for some steamers, most of which were now at least 230 feet in length, to turn once they were through the gates. A list was given in the report, of some of the largest ships using Leith:

Sailing

Constantine	183ft x 35ft	1262 tons	22ft draught
Frenchman	195ft x 35ft	1155 tons	20ft draught
Lorenza	177ft x 35ft	1061 tons	20ft draught

Steam

Leith	245ft x 30ft	1311 tons	21ft draught
Czar	216ft x 29ft	895 tons	17ft draught
Stirling	198ft x 28ft	762 tons	18ft draught
Cronstadt	245ft x 31ft	1200 tons	20ft draught

(The SS *Leith* had in fact been lost in 1862, and the SS *Cronstadt* was still building.)

In spite of these disadvantages, many steamers were using the Victoria Dock in 1863, but the lack of space there slowed down loading and unloading times. Steamers needed to be in port as short a time as possible in order to make best return on their heavy capital cost. The lack of a lock at the Dock entrance meant that ships could only get in at high tide, further slowing the traffic turnover through the Dock. Sometimes ships could not get in at all, as the Docks were full. Groups of vessels tended to arrive together. Sometimes there was a glut of shipping, sometimes there was none at all, and space was needed for all to be accommodated at one time. The report emphasised the importance of the Railway facilities at the Docks:

> A good deal of the success of Leith is....to be attributed to its connection with Railways, for it is not at all probable that with the Docks and Harbour as they existed up to 1852, and *without* Railways, there would have been any great increase of Trade.

Before the Edinburgh and Glasgow Railway Company gained access to the North Leith branch line, Grangemouth, which was linked with Glasgow by the Forth and Clyde Canal, had been a serious rival to Leith. The new Caledonian branch to Leith would greatly promote the shipment of pig-iron from Glasgow, exports of which from Leith were already running at 74,000 tons per year, having increased more than threefold over the previous eight years. They were expected to increase even more as a result of a recent French treaty, under which there would be direct steamer trade between Leith and Dunkirk. The North British was already well situated to exploit the opportunities afforded by the proposed new Dock, and a bridge over the Harbour would open it up to the Caledonian.

While the Public Works Committee considered this report, the Dock commission tackled the question of material for the new Dock. Once again, the North British was to be approached over bringing stone from Craigmillar, and also over continuing to transport clay from Craigintinnie Meadows, as it had for the Prince of Wales Dock. It was estimated that a total of 150,000 tons of stone and clay would be brought by rail. A further 50,000 tons would be obtained from elsewhere. The Commission thought that as a public body it was more likely than a private contractor to get a reduction in dues, from the 3d per ton per mile which the North British had charged Alexander Wilson when he was building the graving dock. (It was wrong.) The North British agreed to carry the stones and clay, stipulating that the contractor was to provide the wagons, or rent them from itself. Trains were not to be less than 17 wagons long, and on arrival of a loaded train, a string of empty wagons was to be ready for the return journey to the quarry or meadows.

Problems at the Graving Dock

The contract to build the new Dock was awarded to William Scott of Kilmarnock, engineer for the Peebles and Broughton Railway, in July 1863. By December he had arranged with the North British for the transport of stone and clay, but he was having trouble with Alexander Wilson, who, in turn, was in dispute with the Dock commission. The new graving dock engine house (now part of the Leith Port Office) had caused the Commission much trouble and expense. This was not really the fault of the contractor. The engine house was built on reclaimed land, the clay sub-soil being 29 feet down. To sink piles at the engine house site would have cost an extra £200, so Alexander Rendel had not stipulated that this should be done. Consequently, soon after the building was handed over to the Commission the walls round the water tanks and the coal store began to give way because of subsidence, and the whole had to be rebuilt. More seriously, the mountings of the three boilers also began to subside, and their feed and steam pipes were in imminent danger of cracking. In order to remedy this fault, the boilers were slung on stout malleable iron beams, fixed into the engine house walls at their extremities. 'So that' remarked the Docks Superintendent, 'if the walls on which the Beams rest do not give way, there need not be any fear for the Boilers.'

The Commission still owed Alexander Wilson some £7000, which it refused to pay until he agreed to an abatement of the sum, in view of their extra expenditure on the engine house. Wilson, in his turn, took the line that the faults had occurred after the Commission took over the building, and that he was therefore not responsible, especially as he had built according to the engineer's specification. The dispute rumbled on and was not finally settled until after Wilson's death a few years later. In the meantime, William Scott had to negotiate with him for the use of his line to Craigmillar Quarry (part of which Wilson leased) and for possession of the line he had made from South Leith station to the graving dock. As Scott wrote to the Commission in December 1863:

> I am now fully satisfied that he is determined to throw every obstacle in the way so as to prevent the works being properly gone on with, and as I have no control over him, I will feel obliged by your using such means as will cause him to move without further delay all his materials from the Ground allotted to me at Leith, so that I may get full possession.

By May 1863 all was resolved. Alexander Wilson had removed his materials from the ground and William Scott had taken up Wilson's rails to the storage area and replaced them with his own. He was using a locomotive to haul stone to the land reclamation bulwark, the first stage of the new works.

The Caledonian Access to the Docks

On the other side of the Docks, the Caledonian Railway Company was also building an embankment, between Newhaven and Leith, in order to reclaim the land at the west end of the Old Docks which it required for its goods depot. At the end of March 1864 the Company's contractor needed to get a locomotive from Pilton to the Leith end of the embankment. He was given special permission by the Dock commission to run the engine over the lines at the Old Dock and onto a temporary extension he had built westward from the rails at northwest corner of the Victoria Dock. This was the first locomotive ever to enter the Docks.

By May 1864 the Caledonian goods station was nearly finished and the Docks Superintendent began plans for the rails which would link the station with the Docks. A double line formed a direct connection with the rails on the south quay of the Old Docks, but the Caledonian wagons were not allowed to cross the hydraulic bridge between the Docks, which was to be for the exclusive use of the North British (which had by this time taken over the Edinburgh, Perth and Dundee, and thus owned the line to North Leith Citadel Station). A line was taken directly to the steam crane from the Caledonian station, running to the north of the old dry docks and south of the shipyard behind them, which had been for several years in the occupation of S&H Morton. A siding was built into Morton's yard itself, first touching at a sawmill which stood at the northwest corner of the Victoria Dock.

Granton Harbour and Pier, circa 1880.

Work on the rail-laying began in August 1864, when a gate was built in the wall between the Docks and the station. Caledonian trains began to run in the Docks on 1 September 1864, but work on the rails continued, lines and sidings being laid on the north side of the Old Docks. At the request of three Steamship Companies, rails were also laid to continue the double line round the southeast corner of the Victoria Dock, with a siding by the wall of Menzies yard (the dry dock and yard built as part of the East Old Dock development, and opening into the mouth of the Harbour).

The Coal Trade Expands

During the summer of 1864, the Caledonian put in a request to the Dock Commission for another steam crane, in order to avoid competition with the North British for the existing crane. However, the Commissioners were curiously reluctant to improve their coal-shipping facilities at this time. This reluctance is all the more incomprehensible in view of the very strong competition from Granton, where coaling cranes had now been in use for three years and there were better deep-water berthing facilities. Steam cranes were, of course, expensive, but the Commission had only the previous year turned down yet another request from the North British for a coal tipper costing not much more than a hundred pounds.

The application for the coal tipper made three main points. In the first place, small vessels of 30 to 200 tons could load at the tipper without paying the expense of getting up steam at the crane. Secondly, vessels lying near the crane would not be turned out of their berths for small shipments. Finally, steamers loaded and discharged at the same time, and there was no room on the quay beside them for trucks of coal. Lighters or barges could load with coal at the tipper, and ship it over the side of the steamer furthest from the quay. However, the Docks Superintendent was not happy with the scheme, and it was dropped.

At the time of its request for a tipper (March 1863) the North British had also asked the Commission to support its application for a Bill for a rail network in Fife. The Company already owned the Thornton and Dunfermline line, on which much coal was brought to Leith from the Cuttlehill, Townhill and other collieries. They had also acquired lines from collieries in West Fife, and were planning to bring a railway down to the Queensferry crossing of the Forth, which was much shorter than the Granton Ferry. The proposed route would also reduce the distance between Leith and the collieries by as much as 12 miles. In the event, the Company was denied its line to Queensferry, but its other plans materialised, with a consequent rise in business at Leith.

The problem of coal-shipping did not go away. In his report at the time of the Caledonian's request for a second steam crane, in 1864, the Superintendent had stated that the existing one was not used to even a quarter of its capacity. However, in September 1865 the Commission received a letter from James Currie and Co (managers of the Leith, Hull and Hamburg Steam Packet Co, which accounted for nearly half the steam tonnage using the port) complaining about long queues for use of the crane. On 17 occasions during that summer, steamers of their Company had been forced to load coal at Granton, because they could not get a turn at the crane in reasonable time. One ship had had to wait five days for its turn at Leith. A month later the question of a tipper was reopened, as the North British had taken over the Edinburgh and Glasgow and Monklands Railway Companies and increased coal traffic was anticipated. At the same time, Currie and Co requested that a steam crane be erected on the West Pier, with an engine shed on adjacent reclaimed ground. The Commission once more promised to consider the proposals - with no result.

The Railway Overseer

In the meantime, the presence of two rival Railway Companies in the Docks was leading to complaints of chaos in the system. In January 1866, James Fairgrieve, an employee of the North British, was appointed Overseer of the Railway Traffic of the Docks and Harbour, at a salary of 30s per week. A year later he was succeeded by Adam Sandilands. The duties of the Railway Overseer cannot have been too arduous, as within a few years the office of Inspector of the Water of Leith was added to them. This sluggish stream was, in effect, an open sewer carrying domestic and industrial waste, which it deposited in the Harbour. Detection of throwers of especially noxious rubbish into the river was part of the duties of the Dock commission.

A New Fuel

It was in January 1866 that petroleum was shipped into Leith for the first time. The *Eva* of Dundee berthed on the north side of the Old Dock with 2000 barrels on board. The Docks Superintendent was understandably nervous about having this highly volatile substance on his patch. The captain of the ship assured him that it was crude oil and non-flammable. An experiment involving setting light to a small amount, heavily diluted with water, proved that the resulting blaze could only be extinguished by the exclusion of air.

The Superintendent forbade any lights or fires on the *Eva* while she was in harbour, and allowed her to land only as much each day as could be removed during working hours. This was a slow process as a cart could only carry one barrel at a time. In spite of all precautions, the barrels leaked into the cinder surface of the quay, rendering it inflammable. As petroleum was regularly handled at London, Liverpool and Glasgow, the Superintendent wrote to those ports to ask them about their regulations. In essence they amounted to a ban on fires on the ships and restrictions or prohibitions on storage at the docks. At Glasgow, petroleum was only allowed to be unloaded at a berth well away from the rest of the docks.

The Coal Trimmers

Having dealt with the question of this new kind of fuel, the Dock commission turned its attention once again to the old question of coal shipment. In February 1866 it began to explore the possibility of directly employing the coal trimmers at the steam crane, who had hitherto worked as independent gangs. The Superintendent consulted the four largest coal exporters; Mr D R Macgregor, Turnbull Salveson and Co, Mr Latour, and Mr Watson, who all opined that the Commission should trim coal at the rate currently paid by merchants, ie 3d per ton. In March he wrote to the same firms, and to Colin Duncan and Son, Cuthbertson and Son, and Thomson, Stoltz and Zoff, inviting their comments. They were rather lukewarm about the scheme. Thomson, Stoltz and Zoff, in fact, were against it, pointing out that there were plenty of trimmers available, and that they preferred to choose their own men. Turnbull and Salveson were in favour, but thought that the combined crane dues (2d per ton) and trimming dues (3d per ton) should be reduced to a joint payment of 4d per ton. Colin Duncan said that it was the ships masters rather than the merchants who paid the trimming dues and this system should continue.

In May the Superintendent contacted 'the most respectable coal trimmer in the port', with a view to his employment by the Dock commission. He would not require any tools to be provided by the Commission, as he had plenty of his own shovels and trimming plates. His charge would be 3d per ton for single decked ships and 4½d for two-deckers, for which trimmers had always been paid an extra allowance, over and above the official rate of 3d per ton. There the matter rested until November 1867, when the Superintendent was instructed to take on trimmers, who would provide their own tools and charge 3d per ton for single and 4d for two-decked ships. The Shoredues office was to levy the charge along with the crane dues and then pay the coal trimming element weekly to the man the Superintendent had put in charge of the trimmers.

Railway Rivalry

During 1866, complaints continued about the coal shipping facilities at Leith. The North British was especially concerned about the deficiencies, as it had no access to the cranes at Granton, and more and more ships were loading coal there because of long waits for the crane at Leith. The only comfort offered them by the Dock Commission was that there would be ample facilities at the new dock - still three years from completion. The Caledonian did have cranage at Granton, but the Company's preference for the rival port rebounded on it when it asked the Commission to support its Parliamentary application for branch lines in Lanarkshire. The North British had a similar application pending at the time, and the Commission decided to support it in preference to that of the Caledonian.

The rival Railway Companies were also concerned about equality of access to the new dock, when it should be opened. This matter was of especial interest

Views in Leith Docks, circa 1880.

to the Caledonian, marooned on the far side of the Water of Leith with, as yet, no means of crossing it, unless the Company could come to some arrangement with the North British for the use of their drawbridge. The Dock Commission asked Alexander Rendel to produce a report, which he did in August 1866.

Rendel thought that because of the current rapid expansion of trade, it was best to decide the general Railway scheme as soon as possible, so that it could be carried out piece by piece when appropriate. The present North British line on the Sands and at the foot of the Shore blocked access to the Sands in a manner that would cause an impossible situation once the new dock was opened, as Constitution Street was to be continued northwards to give access to the dock. All North British lines westward of that road extension should be removed and the rails to the east diverted to run eastward of the new road. They would then run westward along the south quay of the new dock and cross the Harbour by means of a swing bridge upstream of the entrances to the Victoria and Prince of Wales Docks. From the swing bridge they would pass between Menzies yard and the entrance to the Victoria Dock, then along the quay between the Old and Victoria Docks to the Caledonian Station, with branches to the existing lines. This arrangement would also give the Caledonian direct access to the new dock.

The present railway bridge would be retained for occasional use by trains, but it would be of most use to carts, which would be bound to increase in number once the new dock was opened. (It was, in fact, not demolished until early in the next century.) A future drawbridge over the entrance lock to the new dock would give the Caledonian the shortest access to its north quay, but this would not be needed yet awhile.

Included with the report was a plan, which was sent to the Railway Companies for their comments. The Caledonian made no recorded reply, but the North British made several observations. They wanted a line from the proposed swing bridge to the west end of Tower Street, and extra land to be feued to them at their station in order to put Rendel's plan into practice. They also offered to sell their drawbridge to the Commission.

Locomotives Come to the Docks

In February 1867 the Caledonian requested permission to use a locomotive to push wagons up to the steam crane siding. It was granted, during the pleasure of the Dock commission, on condition that only lightweight engines were used, as the Docks rails would not bear the weight of main line locomotives. The Superintendent was instructed to frame regulations to ensure the safety of shipping and of the traffic on the quays. For four years this was the only locomotive in use at the Docks, but in July 1871, the North British began using a 14cwt engine. The new Albert Dock had by this time been open for two years, and the Caledonian were still using six horses there, which they continued to do into the 1880s. The system which evolved used locomotives to bring trains of wagons to the crane or tipper. Individual wagons would then be positioned by horses to be picked up by the loading apparatus. This procedure continued until World War I (1914-18), when hydraulic capstans started to take over from horse-power at the coal hoists and cranes.

More Coal-Shipping Problems

The situation with regard to the steam crane was still deteriorating. In 1867 the Dock commission asked the Superintendent to revise the regulations for its use and to try shipping coal on the north as well as the south side of the crane, in order to speed up its operation. Shortly after the Albert Dock opened in 1869, one of the three hydraulic cranes installed there was given over to the coal trade, but the problem now was to get the Railway Companies to organise a quicker system for the haulage of wagons. The Superintendent had a spare capstan which he proposed to install at the side of the crane to turn the wagons as they arrived, ready for lifting. A letter from the coal shipper Albert Stoltz, written in 1871, reveals some of the reasons for the delays. He complained that the crane at the Albert Dock was only loading an average of 300 tons per day, when it was capable of 100 tons per hour!

> The reason that such a small quantity is shipped is that the coals are not brought forward quickly enough by the Caledonian Railway Company. It is a known fact to all shippers that thousands of tons of coal are standing at the Caledonian Station for shipment by crane in the Docks, and they cannot be brought over with anything

> like dispatch. We had lately the SS *Aberdeen* to load with about 1200 tons. We had all her cargo ordered from the pits for Thursday last and they were all forwarded in good time. The steamer got into the Crane berth on Thursday night and should have been loaded by Saturday night. Owing, however, to the coals not being in the Albert Dock for shipment, the ship had to wait Sunday, Monday and Tuesday, and the Caledonian Railway Company took two days to bring about 300 tons over from the Caledonian Station to the Albert Dock.

Mr Stoltz attributed this leisurely manner of proceeding to the fact that the Caledonian used horses, of which they had only a few, to bring the coal to the Dock. (It was probably not so much the actual speed of the horses that was the problem, but the limitation on the weight of coal that could be moved by each animal.) He asked the Commission to get the Company to use a locomotive instead. The opening of the Victoria Swing Bridge in 1874 solved much of this particular problem. A year after it opened, two hydraulic cranes were in use at the Albert Dock for loading coal, and an extra line of rails had to be laid from the Bridge to the Dock to carry the increased traffic. In 1878 a telegraph wire was set up between the Caledonian station and the Docks for the better regulation of coal shipping.

In 1871, the Dock commission finally agreed to install a coal tipper for loading small vessels. In the November, the Superintendent informed them that as the coal trade had increased over the past year, and was continuing to increase, there was an urgent need for more coal handling equipment. He recommended a hand-operated tipper for lighters and small craft, to relieve the pressure on the coaling cranes, 'as the pressure on this branch of the trade of the Port is very great, I would most respectfully urge the Commissioners to consider this question at as early a date as may be convenient.'

By the following January it had been decided that the tipper should stand on the West Pier, the rails there being extended so that coal wagons could get to it. By the end of July 1872 it was ready for use and was an immediate success, especially with the lighters used by the Steamship and Tug companies to coal their vessels. (Fuel used in steam ship engines was known as 'bunker' coal.) By 1875 a second tipper had been installed on the West Pier. By the end of 1876 two hydraulic tippers for loading large vessels for export, were in use on the north side of the Albert Basin, the area just before the lock into the Albert Dock.

A comment in the 1876 Winter Circular of the coal shippers James Waldie of Leith, sums up the Dock commission's slow reaction to trading realities:

> Since the completion of Railway Communication to the West about ten years ago, the trade in Coal has rapidly utilized the facilities slowly afforded by the Dock Commissioners. Up till 1869 only One Crane for shipment of Coal was at work. In November of that year another was put to work, while not until June 1875 was a third erected. Although there are now at work Three Cranes and Two Tipping Machines, of total possible working power of 12000 Tons a week, there is sufficient expansion in the Trade to induce prompt measures by the Commissioners for increasing the facilities still more.

The Expansion of the Coal Trade

In the early years of the next decade, there was in fact a falling off in the Leith coal trade, but this was merely a temporary dip in a steadily rising graph. From the start of the 1880s the story of coal and rail at Leith was one of accelerated growth and expansion. The era of nineteenth century Railway Company takeovers and mergers in the area was at an end. Until the Nationalisation of the Railways in 1948, just two separate Companies continued to own track and run trains in the Docks. The changeover from horse to locomotive power in the Docks, which had begun in the 1860s, continued in response to the rapid rise in volume of traffic and the need for increased speed of loading goods into ships. Coal loading machinery also steadily expanded in the docks.

By the mid 1890s the figure of half a million tons of coal shipped in one year had been reached (helped by the opening of the Forth Bridge in 1890), although there were complaints that the Railway Companies were charging high carriage rates to bring coal from the mines. Thereafter, the amount shipped every year rose steeply, to a peak of 2,230,000 tons in 1913. The First World War caused a decline in many branches of Leith trade, coal shipping among them, although the worst effects were not felt until 1921, when exports of coal slumped to 423,980 tons. Two years later, they actually reached the all-time record figure of 2,270,355 tons, but the average figure for the inter-war years was around 1,500,000 tons. The outbreak of the Second World War brought another sharp drop - to 613,428 tons in 1940. The coal trade never recovered. Over the next 26 years the highest figure achieved was 391,854 tons in 1957. In 1962 it fell as low as 26,000 tons.

Once the reclamation of the land to the east of the Edinburgh Dock was completed in the 1880s, it rapidly became covered with rail track of the Caledonian and North British Companies. The tracks were carefully segregated so that the Caledonian lines were on the northeastern and the North British on the southwestern side of the area, of which each company possessed half. By 1898 there was a total of 18 miles of railway within the Docks precincts, and over half the goods handled there travelled to and from the ships by rail. The opening of the Imperial Dock in 1904 added still more rails to the network. More track was being added east of the Edinburgh Dock, and by the mid 1930s the Docks railway had expanded to a total length of 30 miles.

Coal and Rail - each is the subject of nostalgia and passionate debate. Each is the victim of political ideology, both of the right and of the left. Without both, Leith would not have become the thriving port it is today.

16

'A Difficult Period'

At the turn of the century, everyone connected with the port might have been forgiven for feeling that all was more than well, and destined to get even better. Trade was booming to such an extent that amenities could hardly be improved fast enough to keep up with demand for dock accommodation, quay space, goods handling plant and storage facilities. Tonnage of shipping and cargoes was soaring, and the largest, deepest dock yet in the complex was building. Coal exports in particular went on rising, reaching nearly two and a quarter million tons in 1913. Grain imports did likewise. If the nineteenth century had been the 'coal age' at Leith, the twentieth was 'grain age'. Beginning with the building of the first bulk storage warehouse and elevator by Patmore and Co at the Edinburgh Dock in 1903, (subsequently taken over by the Dock commission) improvements in grain storage and handling facilities proceeded steadily, and still continue.

It was, in fact, the new grain elevator which was at the centre of the first major twentieth century disturbance at the Docks. In July 1911, the Union of Dock Labourers objected to the way work at the elevator was organised, and Union members at the Docks came out on strike. Strikes were nothing new at Leith. In the nineteenth century small disputes had arisen from time to time among mariners and dock workers over pay and conditions. They had been easily resolved by the relevant employers.

The advent of Trades Unions, however, brought a new dimension to industrial conflict. Working class solidarity, and strike pay, gave labourers the confidence to hold out longer for more radical demands. In the 1911 strike the railwaymen came out in support of the dock workers. The Dock commission brought in extra police to support those they already employed at the docks in protecting the men who continued to work. The dock gates were closed in order to keep out the strikers, but the police were powerless to prevent them breaking down the paling between the foot of Constitution St and Seafield Promenade. After the strike was over, the Commissioners had the paling replaced with a wall, thus enclosing the entire docks complex with masonry. This stretch of stones and mortar was much resented by the dockers, excluding them, as it did, from unauthorised access to 'blacklegs' in any future conflict.

The 1913 Dock Strike

The 1911 strike was short-lived, but two years later another dispute arose which was far more serious. This time it was wage rates that were at issue. The rates were set by the local Dock Labourers Employers Association (dominated by representatives of the various Shipping Lines), with whom the Union had made an agreement in 1912 for a wage increase of 1d - to 7d per hour. The men at Grangemouth, Bo'ness and Glasgow got 8d per hour, and when the Leith agreement ran out in February 1913, the Union put in for a similar rate. The Employers Association delayed negotiations, saying that the Leith men got more regular work than other dockers and in any case could not expect an increase so soon after the last one. A fully employed man could earn as much as 35s a week at 7d per hour. For the time, this was good pay, but as was frequently pointed out during the strike, not every man worked full hours each week. Even the best men were dependent on work being available, and the flow of shipping into the docks was by no means uniform. A representative of Leith Shipping Federation, giving evidence in court shortly before the strike, distinguished four grades of dock labourer. Weekly men were employed regularly by shipping companies and averaged 30s per week. Other strong, steady workers were divided into first and second class casual workers. The former could expect to earn about 28s and the second about 20s. Last of all were the men who were used only when there was a rush of work, and averaged about 10s to 12s per week. Some in the last category may well have been poor workers, but given the wretched state of working class health discovered when men were called up for war a year later, many would, through no fault of their own, have been unfit for heavy work.

The strike began on the morning of 26 June, when around 3000 men turned up at the docks at the usual time (6.00 am) but, as the 'Edinburgh Evening News' for that day reported 'not one took up his customary duties'. The 'Leith Observer' commented:

> The stoppage came as a great surprise to the public, as it has also evidently done to the responsible officials of the National Union of Dock Labourers. On Tuesday, Mr O'Conner Kessack [Union negotiator] intimated to the men that he was going to call a meeting of the Executive to place the position at Leith before them, and had taken steps to inform kindred associations *so that nothing unexpected should be forced upon them.* The unexpected has apparently been forced on the mens' leaders...On Thursday morning in the twinkling of an eye, with instructions from nowhere, as far as can be made out, three thousand men ceased work.

The action brought a virtual halt to the loading and unloading of ships. Initially perishables such as butter, fruit and vegetables were discharged by the checkers and clerks of the Companies to which the ships belonged. However, as soon as they could arrange it, Company managers diverted ships with perishable cargoes to other ports. The fruit trade in particular had suffered badly in the 1911 strike, and merchants were concerned for the consequences of the new dispute. In 1911, the shipowners had made strenuous efforts to find alternative labour and keep trade going as far as possible. This time they were prepared to sit it out, and several of them decided to lay up their ships until the strike was over.

Councillor Kibble

On the afternoon of 26 June the strikers were addressed by the local Secretary of the Dockers' Union, Councillor G Kibble. Two meetings were held, one in Dock Place and the other at the Dock Gates at foot of Constitution St, an area known as the 'Logs'. Mr Kibble reminded the men of their other demands; an increase in 'dirty money', Saturday work to finish at 1.00pm, and restrictions on the employment of non-union labour. On the question of wage rates he commented:

> The employers...told them that their average wage was a good one, but when they met with an accident, applied for compensation and told the employers that they were entitled to half of their average wage, they were told that their wage was a poor one. (Great laughter).

The meeting at the Logs was also addressed by John Thomson, the President of the Leith Branch of the Dockers' Union. He warned the porters employed by the Shipping Companies that if they worked while the dockers were out, the latter would not later work with Company porters.

The 130 coal trimmers at the Docks were Union members and came out with the rest, although the Union allowed the coaling of steam trawlers to continue throughout the strike. The metters and some other workers at the grain warehouse were not members, and continued to work, after an initial short stoppage while they adjusted to the new situation. At first, the railwaymen continued working, but once 'blackleg' labour began operating at the docks, they refused to take goods in, although their action was not sanctioned by the National Union of Railwaymen. The one exception they made was to take in trainloads of coal to supply the trawlers. Local carters were not Union members and did not join the strike, but it was estimated that 200 of them were rendered idle by it.

Almost immediately the stoppage began, the colliery managers in the Musselburgh area closed their pits, as they could not get their coal loaded at Leith. One thousand men were laid off at Niddrie and Benhar, and three thousand at Edinburgh Collieries. Wallyford, Preston Links and Elphinstone all stopped work, and by the third day of the strike, Carberry had joined them.

The Dock Commission Reacts

On 27 June, the day after the strike started, the Dock Commissioners held a special meeting. Extra police had been diverted from the Leith force and were now on duty in the docks. Mr Roberts, the Docks Superintendent (who had only taken up his post the previous April) was instructed to act with the Chief Constable in protecting anyone loading or unloading ships, from the unofficial pickets which were 'scouting' about the docks. The pickets were, however, allowed to exercise their lawful right of 'peaceful persuasion'. Those at the gates were giving persons entering the docks the usual challenge of 'What ship?'. So far all was peaceful, but if there were to be any disturbance, the dock gates would be shut and only the holders of passes would be admitted. The novelty of picket duty among the strikers soon began to wear off. As early as 28 June, Mr O'Conner Kessack warned them that any man who did not take his turn at it would get none of the strike pay to which all were entitled after seven days.

Extra Police

There seemed no doubt that the strike would last that long. Both sides were reported to have settled down for a considerable stoppage. Leith Council drafted in extra police, accommodating some of them in the Old Ship Inn and the Commercial Hotel. Gibson's and Currie's Shipping Lines found lodgings for the rest. The total police force in Leith now amounted to 300 men. At a Council meeting on 1 July Cllr Kibble, seconded by TG Edgar, brought a motion, 'that this Council reprobates the action of the Police Authority in bringing in extra police at the cost of the ratepayers'. It was pointed out by other Council members that during the previous strike, the Dock Commissioners had footed the bill for extra police and it was confidently expected that they would do so again. The motion was defeated by ten votes to two. A local shipowner was reported to have referred to his elected representative as, 'that ragtime, ranting Kibble', and it is plain from the tone of the debate that most of his fellow Councillors were of the same opinion. Addressing a subsequent mass meeting of the strikers, Mr Kibble made the time-honoured claim that the presence of the police was 'an incitement to riot'.

The First Strikebreakers Arrive

On Wednesday 2 July, eight days into the strike, 150 strikebreakers who had been recruited by the Shipping Federation to work for 35s per week, arrived by train at the Citadel Station, and were escorted by the police to the Imperial Dock. At the same time a similar number sailed in on the ss *Paris* from London. Others were reported to have been smuggled in from Cardiff, Berwick and English ports in two trucks labelled 'Fish - Urgent'. All the workers were to sleep and eat on board the *Paris*. The Dock Gates were shut, and pickets in the docks were restricted to groups of six men, to be escorted at all times by police officers.

> The strikers' pickets, watching the imported men at work, seemed to derive no little amusement from the manner in which the cargo was discharged....They endeavoured to persuade the imported men to give up work, and in some cases they were successful. About a score of men who had come from Berwick decided to return home, and the Dockers' Union provided them with a meal and 2s each, the men already having their return railway tickets.

Thus the 'Leith Burgh's Pilot' for Saturday 5 July. The paper also carried the information that Mr O'Conner Kessack had been badly injured in a motor cycle accident at the Cramond Brig, while on his way to Grangemouth. He had been taken to Edinburgh Royal Infirmary, and it was expected to be some weeks before he was even convalescent. This was bad news, as Mr Kessack was a skilled negotiator. Although, in the event, he recovered more rapidly than had been expected, it is very possible that had he not been put out of action the strike would have been a lot shorter.

The legality of the shutting of the Dock Gates was questioned at the time by the Union Representatives, although they seem not to have challenged the action as they initially threatened to do. The Commissioners themselves were warned, when engaged in a lawsuit against a solicitor who accused police of assaulting him on their premises, to make sure that the matter of the legality of their action over the Gates did not come up, as they were on shaky legal ground. The strikers may have ultimately accepted the shutting of the Gates, but they were incensed when, a fortnight into the strike, the Commission barred their pickets from the dock quays and sheds, and put up tarpaulins so that they could not even see the strikebreakers, let alone talk to them.

Strike Pay and Child Welfare

On Thursday 3 July, the first issue of strike pay was made. Each man received 10s, a total of £1500. Strikers' children, numbering 156, were being fed under the School Board holiday scheme. On the following day the Dock Commissioners elected a seven-strong Strike Committee, whose members included Provost Smith, 'to act with the Superintendent in all matters arising out of the strike of workers at the Docks'. This meant chiefly the arrangements for protecting the strikebreakers and others, such as carters, who continued to work at the Docks, and ensuring that as much work as possible was able to continue, in order to safeguard the Docks' revenue. The strikers' dispute was not with the Dock commission, but with the Employers Association, so the Committee was not called upon to negotiate with them in any way.

'The Scotsman' for Monday 7 July reported that 26 ships were laid up at Leith and there were 34 steamers there waiting to be unloaded. A further 40 vessels had been diverted to other ports since the start of the strike. Many consignments of goods had never left their Continental ports, the merchants having telegraphed their agents at the start of the strike with instructions not to send them on. Union officials had suggested that the depot ship *Paris* had become a health hazard. A Sanitary Inspector who visited it, however, reported that the ship was in very good order. On the day of the 'Scotsman' report, the *Paris* was joined by the *Lady Jocelyn*, a three-masted ship which had been towed up from London. She was needed to house the 300 men who arrived at the Citadel Railway Station the next day.

At the Station

This influx of 'blacklegs' sparked off the first real trouble of the strike. The strikers had advance warning of their arrival, and from the early hours of the morning, groups were stationed at various places along the Bonnington to Leith road, from which the railway line was visible. A 'bicycle corps' was sent up the line to check as each train whistle was heard, to see if this was the one the men were waiting for. At 4.00 am, around 80 police assembled at the Station, and it was obvious that the train must soon arrive. When it at last came in view, the groups along the road hurled stones at it as it passed. None of the strikers were allowed into the Station precincts, but a large number were positioned in windows overlooking it. When the train came out of the approach tunnel and pulled up to the platform, it was greeted by a hail of stones, bricks and other missiles, which broke 40 of its windows and sent the occupants diving for cover. With some difficulty the police retrieved their charges from under the seats, under the train itself and inside the tunnel, and formed them up to cross Commercial St to the Dock Gates. The way was guarded by a double line of police, but they could not keep the mob at a distance from its quarry. The hours of waiting for the train had been employed in prising up piles of cobble stones from the roads, and the crowd, of about 1000 men and women, launched these missiles at the strikebreakers as they dashed across the road to the safety of the Docks.

Councillor Kibble, of course, appealed to the men for non-violence, but that particular genie is not easily returned to its bottle. On the next day two Dock Commission employees, Cornish and Simpson, who had been working coal cranes were assaulted by strikers, Cornish being struck in the face 'to the effusion of his blood'. Harding and Armstrong, who had also been helping with the coaling, were told that the strikers were 'looking out for them'. A Dock Commission contractor was assaulted on a tram. Three days later, at Edinburgh Sherrif Court, William Ferguson, labourer, was fined £3 for the assault on Cornish and Simpson. Francis Foley, also a labourer, was fined £1 for the assault on the contractor. After these incidents, the Commissioners allowed some of its workers to be housed within the Docks complex for the duration of the strike. There was also increased tension between the strikers and the carters, who still refused to come out in their support.

The Riot

On the afternoon of Wednesday 18 July, ten days after the trouble at the railway station, a mass meeting was held on the Links, addressed by a Mr Houghton, who made what the 'Pilot' considered to be an inflammatory speech. At about ten oclock that evening 'For a brief space of time....Hell was let loose in Leith'. The riot, for such it was, was blamed by everyone on 'unemployable hooligans, of whom there are far too many in the burgh'. Plate glass shop windows were smashed in Shore, Tolbooth Wynd, Henderson St, Kirkgate and Great Junction

St. The targets were mainly licensed grocers and provision shops, whose windows were emptied of bottles of whisky and beer, tinned goods, hams and other valuable items. The disturbances went on until after midnight, and the police made twenty arrests, but very few strikers were found to be involved.

The day after the riot, the Provost approached the Army and the Navy for assistance if it should be needed. The Admiral at Rosyth sent six gunboats, which anchored off Leith for two days and then sailed away. Soldiers at the Castle, Piershall Barracks and Leith Fort were confined to quarters, so as to be available at short notice. The Provost reported on his actions to the Commissioners' Strike Committee. Councillor Kibble protested about them at a mass meeting - adding that the police were the direct cause of all that had happened.

Whether because of the threat of action by the military, or because the violence had worn itself out, there were no further disturbances. The smashing of Bailie Dresner's shop window a few days later was held to be 'an indication of dissatisfaction with the Bailie in his magisterial capacity'. The number of police patrolling the streets, however, was greatly increased. However innocent the strikers may have been concerning the riot, it seems that the population of Leith were becoming weary of the strain the month-old strike was placing on the community. On reporting that the Union had guaranteed the strikers pay for a month, the 'Pilot' commented, 'If the strikers and the employers are not tired of the dispute, the general public are, and there is an intense desire to see an early settlement.'

Parliamentary Involvement

At the end of July 1913, in the House of Commons, the Labour MP for Barrow on Furness asked the President of the Board of Trade if he was aware that strikebreakers for Leith were being illegally recruited on the premises of Gravesend Labour Exchange. The President replied that this was untrue, although it appears that even if recruiters were not actually on the Labour Exchange premises, they were operating not far away. Having brought the situation at Leith to the notice of the House, various Labour Party members ensured that it stayed in view, by asking questions at intervals in the future.

In Leith itself, Cllr Kibble informed a strikers meeting that the Union had received a request from men on the *Lady Jocelyn* for help to get home. They alleged that the Shipping Federation would not pay them their wages and asked the Union to put pressure on the employers to give them what was due to them. There was talk by the meeting of a demonstration to get the men out of the docks. The demonstration, however, did not materialise, and none of the strikebreakers appear to have got away at that time.

Feeding the Children

The School Board had decided not to continue feeding strikers' children, as they did not want to seem to be taking sides in the dispute. A Miss McNab, with the help of the strike organisers, got up a fund to feed them herself. For £10 a week it was calculated that she could feed 250 children a day. By the end of the strike the number was nearer 700. A three-day menu was followed:

First day	- Pies and pudding
Second day	- Soup, plain and currant bread
Third day	- Puddings and boiled rice

The Benefit Match

Strike funds were swelled by 'benefit' football matches. On Saturday 2 August the Coal Trimmers played the Dockers for a silver cup which had been donated by a anonymous well-wisher. Each side had assembled an impressive array of footballing talent:

Dockers

G Robertson	Leith Athletic	J Dick	Cameron Highlanders
J Robertson	Everton	J Devlin	Scots Guards
P Brannigan	Hibs	P Riley	Scots Guards
M Ward	Liverpool	G Purves	Royal Scots
L Laurie	Hearts		
C Dick	Leith Athletic		
W Martin	Musselburgh		

Trimmers

M McKenzie	Chelsea	A Steadman	Cameron Highlanders
J Hughes	Fulham	J Veitch	Scots Guards
J Wood	Sheffield United		
Ja Veitch	Everton		
P Brown	Leith Athletic		
A Walls	St Bernards		
W Walls	Granton Vale		
D Rutherford	Ashfield		

The referee was James Oswald, late of Leith Athletic. The result is not recorded, although if the Trimmers did actually play one man short, it should not be hard to guess!

Negotiations

While preparations were going on for this piece of light relief, the Dock Labour Employers Association had a meeting with Sir George Askwith of the Board of

Trade, on Wednesday 30 July at the North British Station Hotel. Part of the meeting was also attended by the General Secretary of the National Union of Dock Labourers, and another conference was held the same evening, which included Union representatives from Leith. Although these were primarily 'talks about talks' some demands were discussed. The results of the discussion were reported to 2000 of the men at a meeting held the following day in the Gaiety Theatre. They did not amount to much. The employers would not concede the 1d per hour, or even the ½d on which the men were prepared to compromise. The only concession was an offer to give four hours per week minimum employment instead of the current two hours.

The strikebreakers now numbered 800, the *Lady Jocelyn* having recently returned from a recruiting trip with an extra 200 men. Their work seems to have improved over the past weeks, and the 'Leith Observer' for Saturday 2 August reported that the docks were now busier than they had been, with many ships being discharged, lorries passing to and fro and even some railway traffic moving. The railwaymen may have been encouraged to return by the suspension of some of their North British colleagues for refusing to handle Leith goods. According to the 'Observer', since the start of the strike, 67 coastwise and 34 Continental vessels had used the port, some for more than one voyage. Continental passenger sailings had resumed some time before. The employers were obviously not by any means at their last gasp, and the 'Pilot' commented, 'Both sides are more determined than ever to fight, and it will now be a fight to the finish'. Some of the strikebreakers found that this was literally true when they were foolhardy enough to leave the safety of the docks for an evening out in Edinburgh. They were attacked by a mob of dockers.

Solidarity

Late on the night of Saturday 8 August an attempt was made to blow up the hated wall which had been built by the Dock Commissioners after the 1911 strike. The large explosive charge, which could have caused considerable damage, was hastily and clumsily fixed and it was the sidewalk paving which suffered rather than the wall itself. In fact the deed was discovered when a policeman investigating the noise of the explosion, fell into the crater in the dark. No-one had any idea who the perpetrators might be, although there was speculation that the explosive might have been supplied by miners. They may well have been willing to try to bring the strike to an end, as they had been on half pay (£1 per week) since it began.

The dockers were receiving messages of support from a number of their fellow workers, including the Edinburgh Trades, the National Sailors and Firemans Union and the Amalgamated Society of Engineers. Some Unions were donating funds, and Cllr Kibble expressed the view that the men could hold out for a further six weeks.

The End of the Strike

That in the event they did not, was due to the unexpected early recovery of Mr O'Conner Kessack, who addressed a strikers meeting on Thursday 7 August. His tone was markedly different from that of speakers at former meetings. He pointed out that if the coal trimmers were allowed back to work there would be 200 fewer men drawing strike pay. His plea for no more violence was sincere, and he said the time had come for negotiation.

Perhaps Mr Kessack's involuntary retiral from the fray had allowed him to take a more dispassionate view of the situation, but he certainly saw clearly that the dockers stood no chance of holding out against the powerful Shipping Federation. He put this fact to the men at a private mass meeting held in the Gaiety Theatre on Thursday 14 August, and persuaded them that the way forward was a return to work coupled with a modified offer to the employers. Almost unanimously they voted to return the following Monday, having gained almost nothing by their seven and a half week strike.

The strikebreakers worked until the Saturday, when they were returned home. Thanks to the fact that the grain warehouse and elevator staff and the metters had continued to work, grain imports were actually higher than for the same period the previous year, but all other imports were very much reduced. Exports had dwindled to almost nothing, and it was later estimated that the strike lost the Dock Commission £1500. Overall tonnage handled in 1913, however, was higher than in both the previous and the subsequent year. The 'Pilot' detailed some comparative tonnage figures for part of the strike period:

	July 1912	*July 1913*
Coal	175,723	1,911
Pig iron	1,629	9
Malleable iron	252	7
Oil (shale)	2,298	146
Ale/beer	7,105	343
Sulphate of ammonia	3,088	nil

After the Strike

Once the men were back at work, the Dock Commission Strike Committee began the job of dealing with the aftermath of the stoppage. They were chiefly concerned with negotiations with the Town Council over paying for the extra police. Although they had borne the whole cost in 1911, this time the dispute had lasted much longer, and some of the extra men had been used by the Council to quell the unrest in the town. After much sending to and fro of letters on the subject, it was decided that the Commissioners would pay £3120 9s 10d and the Council £1365 2s 8d.

More easily dealt with was the matter of suitable rewards to the twenty Commission employees who had remained on duty throughout the strike, mainly supervising the elevator while ships' crews discharged grain. Mr Jones, until lately the Commission's Grain Warehouse Manager, had even been released by his new employers, the Clyde Navigation Trust, to work with the elevator staff. A sum of £150 was set aside to be distributed amongst these employees. Although the Metters were among the men who had continued at the Grain Warehouse, they were self-employed and therefore not eligible for the Commissioners' reward. Rebates were given to grain and coal shippers whose cargoes had not been handled.

The Committee wanted to offer a monetary reward to the soldiers who had been confined to barracks, in compensation for the inconvenience they had suffered. Service regulations, however, made this impossible. The last act of the committee, in December, was to send a letter of thanks to the men, apologising that they could not give them 'tangible proof of their appreciation'.

The Strike Special Committee was not officially discharged until 20 November 1914. Its outstanding business was passed to the remit of another special committee - the War Committee, which had been set up on 3 September, three weeks and three days after Great Britain and Germany declared war on each other, The War To End All Wars had begun. It dealt the economic life of the country a blow from which it took years to recover, and Leith shared fully in its effects.

The Outbreak of the First World War

On Saturday 1 August 1914, the 'Leith Observer' carried a small article tucked away at the bottom of an inside page; *Effect of War Scare at Leith.* 'The war scare is making itself felt in local shipping and commercial circles'. A steamer due to leave for the Continent the previous night had been stopped, and it was expected that all other sailings would be suspended. During the past two days there had been constant interruptions of telegraph communications with Russia, and the freight market was completely demoralised. The paper also reported the first of the price rises which were to become such a feature of daily life - Russian butter had gone up from 6s to 8s a hundredweight.

A week later, a whole page article reporting on *Principle Events of the Week* was entirely devoted to news of the outbreak of war. The next page announced, *The Great War - How It Affects Leith*; 'in many ways the stern reality of war has been brought home to the people'. The most immediate effect had been a rapid rise in the prices of foodstuffs, many items were already unobtainable locally. The Co-operative and Leith Provident Association stores had been very busy as working people stocked up on food. Sugar had run out at the latter, and small shops had raised its price to 4d a pound.

Continental sailings had almost ceased and no ships were being chartered for goods. Sailings to British ports, however, were continuing. The ss *Breslau*, belonging to Leith, Hull and Hamburg Steam Packet Company, had arrived home the previous Tuesday, having been detained for a day in the Elbe by German Naval restrictions. She left Leith the following day to take home a large party of German tourists. Other Germans in Leith were not so lucky and had gone to England to try and find a ship to take them home. German passengers who had arrived on the *Ceres* were not allowed to land, and preparations were being made in Edinburgh for the registration of aliens. (By the end of the following week, 400 aliens had registered at Leith Police Station. They included 150 Germans and 30 Austrians, who were obliged to report to the Police every Tuesday and Friday thereafter.)

Two other Currie ships, the *Vienna* and the *Corsica* were at Hamburg, and no word had come from them. The *Coburg* was at Danzig, unable to get her cargo of sugar unloaded as all the dock workers there had already been called up. (The Company suspended its Continental sailings the following week.) All the George Gibson Company's ships were at Leith, except the *Moorfoot*, which was at Oran. The Forth pleasure steamers had stopped running, causing problems for many Leith and Edinburgh businessmen whose families were holidaying in Fife, and who had relied on the steamers to get home to them each evening.

Many dockers had been made idle by the cessation of sailings, but as 700 of them were in the Army Reserve that situation would soon be eased. The Territorials had in fact been mobilised at the Drill Hall in Dalmeny St the previous Wednesday. Many of its members were away at sea and had written home for orders. Fifty Naval Reservists had left Leith the previous Sunday. They changed into uniform at the Mercantile Marine Office, and were seen off by the Provost and a large crowd of well-wishers. Two brakes took them to the Waverley Station where they entrained for Chatham.

Two small German steamers, *Otto* and *Adolf* which were in Leith to unload cargo and load coal, had been seized as prizes, and were berthed in the West Old Dock. With them was the ss *Mowe*, which had been bound for Nordeny and had put into the Forth to take on bunker coal. She was seized off Inchkeith and towed in by the tug *Jumbo* of Grangemouth, which had been requisitioned by the Navy. A fourth prize, the *Naute* of Flensburg, laden with timber, had been captured by a British war vessel and brought in to Leith on the previous day.

In order that there should be no confusion over the identity of ships in the Forth, the Admiral at Rosyth issued a code of practice for merchantmen:

1. No ship was to leave or enter the Forth during 'official night' (which began before sunset and ended after the following sunrise) or in fog.
2. Armed examination steamers were stationed on the east and west sides of Inchkeith and all vessels coming up the Forth had to report to one of them.
3. The examination steamers were distinguished by a blue ensign at the ensign staff and a pilot flag at the foremast head, which would be white and red with a blue border.
4. When the Forth was 'closed', ie no ships to proceed upriver, three red balls vertical would be hoisted.
5. No wireless messages were to be taken or sent in the Forth.

6. Outward bound ships must be clear of the Forth by the start of 'official night'.
7. Pilotage was compulsory for all but small craft.
8. Any ships ignoring the regulations would be fired on.

Since the time of the Romans, and probably before, socks have been regarded as essential items of military equipment, of which the Authorities seem incapable of providing sufficient. During the Crimean War, even Queen Victoria had done her bit with the knitting needles. On 15 August 1914, the 'Observer' carried two prominent advertisements on its front page. The North British Hosiery Co. offered 'Special Value in Knitting Wools for Soldiers' Socks etc.' William Tait's Wool Shop announced that 'The Comfort of our Soldiers can be Assured by Supplying Them with Good Hand-Knitted Socks, Helmets etc.' Doctor WD Blaikie of Leith was of the same opinion and set up a committee to organise a supply for the Territorials, which produced some 3000 pairs by the end of September. The 'Observer' printed letters from the organisers of several charities which provided for servicemen and their families. It reported the setting up of the Leith Distress Committee, and itself instituted a 'Shilling Fund' for the poor dependants of Servicemen. (As the war progressed, charities sprang up to provide every imaginable comfort to the troops, notably the 'Wounded Soldiers Egg Fund' and the 'Daily News and Daily Telegraph Fund for Supplying Christmas Puddings to the Soldiers'.)

Another advertisement in the 15 August edition of the 'Observer' insisted that 'Carlsberg Lager is NOT German, as someone with malicious intent is circulating....Carlsberg is brewed by the world-renowned Carlsberg Breweries at Copenhagen, DENMARK....' There were articles on 'The Cost of War', 'Burial at Sea', 'War Stories' 'Experiences of Leith Tourists' (in Germany) and 'Some Old Scottish Sea Dogs' (Sir Andrew Wood and Robert Barton featuring prominently). Suitable items of fiction were not lacking. 'Published by special arrangement...' was a story by H de Vere Stacpoole entitled 'The Hero' and there were two anonymous poems; 'May God Defend the Right' and 'War'.

News from the Docks was that the gates had been closed to the public, most of the horses in Leith had been requisitioned by the army leaving 100 carters idle, and a fifth German prize had been brought in - the schooner *Fidro*. Thirteen ships bound for Newcastle, Hull and Harwich with eggs, butter and bacon had been diverted to Leith because of danger from mines. Two had arrived the previous Friday; the first consignment of food to enter the port for a fortnight. Most of it was to proceed by rail to its original destinations.

Volunteers

Price rises caused by shortages of food and raw materials and the consequent need for rises in pay was to be one of the problems facing the Special War Committee over the next four years. On the occasion of its initial meeting on 3 September, however, it was more concerned with the rapid depletion in numbers of Dock Commission employees, and the question of paying both those who left and those who stayed. Some twenty men had already gone to the army and navy. The wives of married men were given half their husbands' pay. The dependents of single men, presumably aged parents or orphaned siblings, received one quarter. One single man who had been supporting his five brothers and sisters was awarded half pay. None of the enlisted men were replaced, and all were guaranteed their jobs back after the war. Other ports continued their employees on full pay, but deducted their military allowances. The remaining Dock Commission employees were warned that their hours might be cut to reduce the wages bill. Overtime had already been discontinued, except when it was unavoidable.

The Superintendent reported that he had allocated part of no. 8 shed, Victoria Dock, as a Red Cross hospital for wounded landed at Leith from HM ships. He had also had erected a number of temporary latrines for the use of officers and men and the Red Cross nurses.

Wartime Routine

The war was already playing havoc with shipping patterns, although a new routine did emerge after a while. In the meantime, the Committee had to deal with the question of arrangements and layage charges for the 26 ships which had been laid up at Leith during July and August. A similar number of tugs, lighters and other small vessels had been commandeered by the Navy. The question of adjustment of rates, especially for shed storage was one which occupied much of the Committee's time during the war. Firms were continually having to leave goods in store for unusually long periods, owing to delays in loading, non-arrival of convoys, loss of ships and other reasons peculiar to wartime conditions. The loss of carters' horses to the Government caused so many delays in the removal of goods from sheds that the Commission began to allow motor lorries into the docks. Applications for permits to use lorries flooded in for a while, many of them from provision merchants, and quite a few from laundries, which were presumably serving the Red Cross hospital and the military hut encampments which sprang up in the Docks. Railway wagons had been commandeered by the Ministry of Transport, causing more problems for the Commissioners.

The shipping lines shared in the initial chaos, although they too settled down fairly soon to new patterns. After their initial suspension of sailings, George Gibson's steamers resumed voyages to Rotterdam, Harlingen and Dunkirk. Because of the German occupation of Belgium, however, Antwerp and Ghent were closed to them until after the war. The Ben Line had carried on extensive trading in the Baltic, but the war and the Russian Revolution which followed it put an end to this operation. Salveson's was the first Leith shipping company to lose a ship by enemy action. On 30 October the *Glitra*, bound from Grangemouth to Stavanger with coal, coke, iron plates and oil, was stopped by a German U-boat. The crew were ordered into lifeboats, then the Germans opened the ship's sluices and shelled her until she sank. This gentlemanly manner of dealing with enemy vessels was standard procedure at sea until 1916, when the Germans began sinking ships on sight and without warning.

On 21 January 1915, a similar fate befell the Gibson Company's *Durward*, but the three other ships which they lost that year; *Traquair, Astrologer* and *Mascotte* were all mined off the English coast. Almost as bad as loss from enemy action, from a financial point of view, was requisition by the Government. The compensation rate was low and difficult to recover. There was no consistent requisitioning policy which might have spread the burden equally among shipping companies. Those which managed to keep its ships out of the clutches of officialdom did very well, as freight rates rose repeatedly throughout the war. The Government did, however, introduce one plus factor into the system. In 1916, when German U-boats abandoned their former more civilised procedures in favour of 'shoot to kill', the War Risks Insurance scheme was introduced, with premiums far lower than those of private insurance companies. This enabled shipping companies to keep their freights at a more reasonable level. It also encouraged them to sail their ships without a convoy, a move which may not have been popular with the crews, but which released more RN vessels into active service.

On 22 September 1914 James Dickson, the first Dock commission employee to lose his life in the war, went down with HMS *Aboukir*. His widow, who was living at Aberdeen, did not hear of her loss until the beginning of October. She informed the Commission of the death of her husband when she wrote to acknowledge receipt of his half pay.

A selection of items dealt with at meetings of the Commission and the Special War Committee during the first few months of the war gives an idea of the changes which had to be made in the running of the Docks.

October	Special Cases - rates adjustments:
	A Currie ship had to use a 25-ton crane instead of a 10-ton, because of congestion. London steamers taking goods down for Belgian refugees. Ships taking herring to Stettin and Hamburg have had to return to port. North of Scotland Co steamers which have put in to Leith are carrying goods for soldiers and Belgian refugees. Gibson's *Ronan* and *Quentin* have 267 packages on board for Belgian refugees. HMS *Mallard* is in the Alexandra dry dock.
2 October	Commissioners attend a meeting of representatives of Leith, Liverpool, Bristol, Newcastle, Glasgow, Dublin and Cork Docks to consider an Admiralty proposal that the Government be charged only ¾ dues on Transport vessels.

19 October — The Commission Clerk writes to the Secretary of the War Office to acknowledge receipt of his secret communication of the 16 inst. He assures the Secretary that all Commission Employees will be warned to exercise great circumspection in conversation.

20 October — Lieut FRS Bircham RN, of HMS *Vulcan* requests the use of a 120-ton crane for Admiralty work. Granted, at £25 per week. (*Vulcan* was the ship of the Senior Naval Officer at Leith, Captain V Haggard, berthed in the Imperial Dock.)

21 October — The Grain Elevator Warehouse is to be insured against War Risks for one year. By December the Commission's War Risks Insurances were as follows:

Five policies with Lloyds - total cover	£153000
One additional cover note with Lloyds	£ 20000
British Dominions Genl Insurance Co Ltd	£ 5000
~ ~ ~ ~ ~ ~	£ 2000

The Commission approaches the Board of Trade for compensation for loss of trade owing to the dislocation of traffic.
The Superintendent is haggling with Wm Sugg Ltd of Westminster over the increase in price of the firm's gas mantles, from 34s to 48s 6d per gross. Wm Sugg replies that manufacturing materials which previously came from Germany now have to be obtained in England at a far higher price.

November — Special cases - adjustment of rates:

Booking fee of ss *Lancing* for Prince of Wales Dock returned to Menzies, as the dock was used by a mine sweeper. *Lancing* is rebooked for the Imperial Dock.
Thomas Ovens and Son could not remove their cargo from a shed within the time limit owing to a shortage of men. Fixed penalty remitted.
The Navy has blocked a crane. Ramage and Ferguson apply for reduction of crane dues.
Four applications for reduction of shed and quay charges.
Carron Company apply for permission to use their own men to work cranes, with a consequent reduction in dues.
British and neutral ships which put in to Leith by reason of the war are to be exempted from dues.
Remission of dues on *Faun* which took 34 tons of stores to the hospital ship *Rohilla* at Queensferry.
Same to Gibson's steamers *Ronan, Quentin* and *Mascotte* which took 549 packages of clothes and provisions to Rotterdam for Belgian refugees.

27 November Dock Police are to be compensated for loss of annual leave due to the outbreak of war. They are also to be paid a War Bonus in line with that received by the Leith Police from the Corporation.

In December, Alfred Roberts, the Docks Superintendent, put forward some suggestions for making life more comfortable for the crews of HM destroyers and cruisers which were put into dry dock for repairs to shell damage. He proposed to build them four latrines (which were later the subject of much correspondence with the War Office, over who should pay for them), and suggested that the Commission offer Captain Haggard the use of sitting rooms in one of its buildings for the officers and men of the damaged ships.

Manpower Shortages and Rising Prices

By January 1915, 42 men out of the Commission staff of 300 had enlisted, and the Superintendent was starting to refuse to release workers. The men were told that if they insisted on joining up their jobs would not be automatically available to them at the end of the war. This threat slowed the exodus, but did not halt it. In the next six months the Commission lost ten more men.

At the end of February the Commission was forced to look at its pay scales, as the cost of living had risen alarmingly, and the Railway Companies, other public bodies and many private firms had already increased wages. The War Committee put forward a revised list of pay and conditions, which was adopted by the Commission:

1. A War Bonus was to be paid;
   2s 6d per week for men earning under 30s
   2s per week for those earning over 30s
2. The hours of all workmen, except those governed by tides etc, to be 54 per week
3. For those dependent on daylight, weekly hours to be 45½ in winter
4. Only the actual hours worked to be paid for, but in view of the customary payment of full wages all year (ie, even on short winter days) the hourly rates to be adjusted.
5. Overtime at present rates; to be paid after 6.00pm (1.00pm on Saturday) to correspond with the present hours of the Dock Labourers.
6. The old practice of paying higher overtime rates to crane drivers was to cease, but there would be a compensating adjustment in the basic rate.
7. After one year's service, eight days holiday per annum to be granted. After fifteen years, an extra two days.
8. For men who have served over five years, the Superintendent might give a sick allowance of up to half pay for four weeks.
9. Certain men, whose present wages were low, to be given an actual increase.

In April 1915 staff salaries were raised by between £9 and £25 per year. Weekly paid staff received an increase of 2s to 3s. The biggest rise, of 5s, went to the Commissioners' housekeeper.

Other Wartime Problems

By this time various Government Departments owed the Commissioners considerable sums of money in Shore dues of various kinds. Mr Currie, MP for Leith, was approached and asked to put pressure on the defaulters to pay by 15 May, the end of the Commissioners' fiscal year. On his return to London he pursued the matter 'with great energy', as a result of which many outstanding accounts were settled. There still remained a claim for the Navy's use of the wet docks, sheds and various pieces of ground. The Commissioners were willing to accept £1000 in settlement of its claim, but the Admiralty decided to hold a proper investigation into the actual sums due. Captain Haggard was ordered to produce a report, and the Admiral at Rosyth authorised the Commission to request from HM ships details of tonnages, and of stores loaded and unloaded.

During the summer of 1915, the war touched the personal lives of some of the Commissioners. In June news came of the deaths of Lieut Cdr Mungo Campbell Gibson (3 May in the Dardanelles) and Lieut Harry McIntosh, sons of two of their number. Another Commissioner, JW Thomson, was an officer in the 52nd Division. His unit was ordered overseas in the same month. Lieut Cdr Gibson's father was Campbell Gibson, head of the George Gibson shipping line. He survived his son only until the following December.

Buildings were still being commandeered by the Military Authorities. The Customs Officers found a temporary home in a warehouse at the Old Docks. The Old Police Office in Constitution Place was taken over by the Army. The Dock Workers Shelter Hall was given up to a committee which had recently been formed 'for the moral and spiritual welfare of the troops stationed at the Docks', at a nominal rent of 1s a year. As well as recreational facilities the troops needed living quarters. The hutments built for the purpose in the Docks were finished in November.

By June 1915, 52 men out of the Commission staff of 300 had enlisted, and it was becoming difficult to maintain services. The wages of the three men at the Electrical Station were raised in order to persuade them to stay. In July the Superintendent reported that the shortage of Dock Labourers was now acute. In November the Commissioners became worried about the position at the Grain Elevator Warehouse, where they were becoming short of warehouse staff and Metters. After losing a dozen of their members to the forces, the Metters themselves decided not to admit any more members of military age to their Society.

As well as reducing the income of the Docks, the shortage of labour to load and unload ships caused long delays in turnround times. This, coupled with shortages of rail and road transport to remove goods from the quays caused congestion which at times became wellnigh intolerable. The problem was nationwide, and in January 1916, the Board of Trade introduced a list of 'Reserved Occupations', which included Dock workers. The Commission lost no time in providing the local Recruiting Officer with a list of all its men. At the same time, negotiations began with the War Office for soldiers to be allowed to drive motors and lorries at the Docks.

Office workers were also becoming hard to come by. Two young clerks in the Shoredues office who had joined up at the start of the war had been killed by November 1915. It was decided that Lady Clerks and Typists would be appointed in place of enlisted men, a step which was finally taken in April 1916.

Although the Docks were having problems, its shipbuilder tenants were enjoying a boom. Only two new ships were built for the Navy at Leith during the war, but the shipbuilders were kept very busy with a never-ending stream of repairs to war-damaged ships. Menzies requested a 'grid' in the harbour for inspections and light repairs to small vessels, and permission to erect a small furnace in their yard to melt white metal for use in repairing HM ships. This request was authorised but they never got their grid in spite of 'reminders' to the Commission. Much of the Government work going on at the Docks was top secret and in July security was tightened. The Dock gates had been closed to the general public on the outbreak of the war, now all those with official business there had to be issued with passes.

Threat From the Air

In the autumn of 1915 the war ceased to be solely a question of opposing armies slogging it out in a foreign field. The threat of death and destruction was now right over the heads of the folks at home. The Commissioners altered their Fire and War Risk Insurance policies to cover Aircraft and Bombardment Risk.

At the start of 1916 came the death of Mr Peter Whyte, who had been a much-respected Docks Superintendent from 1883 to 1913. At a Commissioners meeting on 14 January the Chairman's tribute to the ex-Superintendent ended with a resumé of the past few years:

> Turning now to look forward from the time when Mr Whyte handed over his executive duties [to his deputy Mr Roberts in April 1913], we have the period through which he has been constantly with us as Consultant. That has been one of the most disturbed periods in the history of the Undertaking. What then appeared to be a great crisis arose as soon as Mr Roberts took up his duties. Labour unrest on a scale never before experienced, at least during the lives of the present generation, seriously interfered with the life of the Port, and resulted in a very serious retardation of the progress of that increase in revenue to which we had become accustomed. No sooner had trade resumed its normal course, and its volume again began rapidly to increase, than the world wide disturbance in which we are now involved overtook us. For a time our anxieties were intense, but with wonderful rapidity we began to feel the effect of the security afforded by the protection of the Navies of Britain and her allies, and, at the moment we enter

> upon the New Year in a financial position immensely stronger than we had any reason to anticipate seventeen months ago.

The winter of 1916 passed uneventfully at home, but in the spring the Commissioners had reason to be glad they had altered their insurance policies. On the night of Sunday 2 April, there was a Zeppelin raid on Edinburgh and Leith, in the course of which some of their property was damaged. Repairs took over a month to complete, and in the meantime the gates, cranes and coal hoists were brought under the insurance scheme. In July 1916, because of the increase in the cost of building materials and labour, all the Docks insurances were increased by 25%. The Commission raised its own labourers' wage rates in November, by up to 1d per hour. Its rates on goods and tonnage had been put up in the previous spring.

Reductions in Manpower and Trade

Labour shortages continued to increase. In spite of the Reserved Occupation scheme, six men were called up in June, five of whom should have been exempt under the new legislation. In December the Superintendent had to give an undertaking to the Board of Trade, not to employ men of military age. The shipyards were also suffering from manpower problems. In the autumn of 1916 they started to employ women. Marr and Son applied to the Commission for 'suitable accommodation' for female workers. Menzies made a similar request and were allowed to convert the Dock Labourers' Shelter near the Custom House for the purpose.

The year 1917 started quietly. Wartime routines were well established. The Commission was rather concerned that the Admiralty were now putting ammunition ships into the dry docks. The Superintendent was allowed to employ a temporary assistant because he was so overworked. The coal trimmers were awarded a war bonus of 20%. Various rates and dues were raised yet again, some by 5%, others by five times that amount. (There was a second rise in July 1917.) Negotiations continued with the Treasury over payment of sums due for Naval use of facilities.

The main reason for this comparative calm was that trade was dropping off, owing to the escalation of the war in the North Sea, and the loss of many merchant vessels through enemy action and requisition by the Government. In January the Admiralty Port and Transit Committee wrote to the Superintendent urging him to dispatch ships more quickly so that each could carry a greater tonnage in a year. He replied that the shortage of land transport would need to be addressed before the desired speed of turn round could be achieved.

In March 1917 the coal-weighing machines at the Edinburgh Dock were allowed to go out of use, and at the same time the Commissioners began to get requests from the War Department for the use of its now considerable spare shed accommodation as repositories for stores. They drew the line at storing large amounts of explosives, but agreed to take mines in sheds nos 1 to 6 on the south side of the Victoria Dock, requisitioned by the Rosyth Admiral in July. Wheat was perfectly acceptable, and the Commission offered to store 50,000 quarters. In May they released no 5 shed, Imperial Dock, for the storage of cargoes of Army flax destined for the Dundee weaving mills. Objection to the storage of explosives was over-ruled by an Order under the Defence of the Realm Regulations, instructing them to place their cranes and quays at the disposal of the Services, when required by a responsible Officer. They had no alternative but to acquiesce, making it clear that they expected the 'responsible Officer' to be held accountable in case of an accident.

Ship repair work continued to expand. In May 1917, Mr John Cran was granted a lease of ground at the Old Docks and part of the foreshore for a Shipbuilding Yard. The total area of ground amounted to 5838 square yards. Not long after the lease was granted the business was incorporated into a Limited Liability Company - John Cran and Somerville Ltd, Mr RA Somerville of the George Gibson Company having become one of the directors. In July, Ramage and Ferguson and Hawthorns both started to extend their premises. The former also asked for permission to build a brick Rest House for female workers. The Ministry of Munitions would not allow a brick building, so a wooden hut was erected, with a drain to the sea. In October, Graham Smart and Annan applied for shipbuilding ground between Newhaven and Leith harbours.

In May 1917, the National Service Scheme came into operation, under which men could volunteer for the Services. Dock Commission employees were instructed to take no action under this new provision, but in spite of this, some did volunteer. In September, in an attempt to stem the flow, the Superintendent was empowered to withhold the dependents allowances which had hitherto been paid to Servicemen and once more to rescind the promise of automatic re-employment.

The End in Sight

1918 opened with a request from the coal trimmers for an increase of 60%. However, food prices were at last levelling off, and they were granted 40%. This first indication that the situation might finally be improving was reinforced by a letter from the Ministry of Shipping concerning, 'the demands the Ports will have to meet when peace is restored'.

> Overseas transport was an all-important factor in the mobilisation for war, and it is obvious that it must play an equally important part in getting the nation back to manufacturing industry and commerce. It must, indeed, be one of the main factors determining the speed with which the men in the Army can be returned to their civilian occupations.

The letter went on to point out that the greatly reduced stocks of food and raw materials must be replaced. There would also be a world demand for replacement of war wastage, and the replenishment of stocks of manufactured goods and coal. It was important to Britain that she should be the first nation to be able to meet demand. The Commission was asked to report on the steps it could take to bring the Port to the point of greatest efficiency, especially:

1. Additional accommodation which could be built now without interfering with war work.
2. What could be provided in the way of extra storage accommodation, extra loading/discharging plant, and improved Railway facilities.
3. Ways of improving turn round in order to deal with the anticipated rush of imports and exports
4. If the Commission thought extra storage would be needed:
   a) Of what kind?
   b) Would it be temporary or permanent?
   c) What would be the best sites?
   d) How could it best be controlled?
   e) Did they need any additional powers in order to provide it?

The report produced by the Superintendent revealed that the cost of even the most pressing requirements would exceed the statutory borrowing powers of the Commission. The surplus revenue for several years to come would be swallowed up by repairs and maintenance postponed because of the war, which included:

1. A 200 acre reclamation embankment on the west side of the Harbour.
2. New cranes at no 5 shed Imperial Dock.
3. Railway lines for through traffic.
4. Obsolete cranes at Albert Dock to be removed.
5. Capstans to be provided for wagon haulage throughout the Docks, which was now almost beyond the capacity of horses.
6. Fitting of hopper bottoms to the bins in the Grain Warehouse to be completed.
7. Extensions and improvements needed to the Hydraulic Pipe system.
8. A new Grain Warehouse and silos needed at Imperial Dock.
9. A new two-storey shed needed at Imperial Dock with associated cranes and Railway sidings.
10. The quays at Albert Dock to be widened for more crane and Railway accommodation.

It was felt that if everything on this list could be done, the Port would be able to handle all the extra traffic envisaged by the Ministry. However, the necessary improvements would be much more expensive than at pre-war prices, requiring large borrowings. Money would be hard to get privately, and if it was only available at a high rate of interest, port charges would have to remain high in order to pay for it. In the opinion of the Commissioners there was a need for Government loans to Ports at a low interest rate.

Apart from this glimmer of light at the end of the tunnel, life at the Docks went on in the old wartime routine. The Dock Labourers were given an extra penny an hour, engineers a 1¼d and other workers between 4s 9d and 6s 9d per week. Rates were raised to cover the increase in wages. More sheds were allocated to the Services. The Admiralty fitted extra lines of keel blocks in the Imperial Dry Dock, so that three destroyers could be repaired there at one time. The OIC Anti-Aircraft Defence requested the use of the Shelter Hall in Constitution Place as an instruction school for men stationed at the Docks.

At the end of July 1918, two more letters arrived from the Ministry of Shipping, and at the start of October a Committee on Trade After the War was set up to consider them. The Superintendent was deputed to attend a meeting of Dock and Harbour Authorities which was to be held in London on Tuesday 5 November, to consider ways of obtaining supplies for Dock and Harbour improvements which would be necessary after the war. He was still in London on Armistice Day, Monday 11 November 1918 - which he spent attending a conference of Port Labour Committee Chairmen and Labour Representatives at Whitehall.

After the War

Although hostilities were at an end, it took nearly a year for the Port to get back to normal. On 19 November, censorship restrictions were lifted on the publication of sailing dates and merchants' itineraries. At a meeting on 6 December, the Commission began to consider how best to resettle its workers. In the second week in December, a number of surrendered German submarines were in the Port on view to the public.

In January 1919 the Chairman, Secretary and one other representative of the Government's Dock and Harbour Dues Claims Committee had a meeting with the Commissioners in their board room to discuss various outstanding accounts. The Commissioners felt they had had a sympathetic hearing, but even so, the question of payment dragged on for months to come. In mid-February the winding up of Government occupation of sheds was put in motion, although it was not until late July 1919 that the last shed was handed back to the Commission. In August, the Navy handed back its wartime accommodation. They had occupied an enclosure at the Imperial Dock since 1 November 1914, Submarine Quarters since 1 October 1915, and another enclosure for the 8th Flotilla from 1 September to 1 November 1916. All the ground was left in good order, so the Dock commission had no need to make any claims against the Admiralty. The Special War Committee was finally discharged on 12 November 1920.

17

More Troubles

After the war, the chief concern of the Dock Commission was the question of improvements in grain handling, cereals now forming by far the most important part of the business of the Port. Until 1914, only 20% of grain shipments was unloaded mechanically. The rest was handled by a highly skilled manual workforce. This body of experienced men had effectively disappeared during the war, and during the years that followed it, mechanisation of grain handling proceeded steadily.

The Depression

At first it seemed as if things were getting back to normal, but within four years came the start of the Depression, which was to cast its shadow over the 20s and early 30s. The effects of the Depression on the Docks workers is exemplified by the experience of the Metters, who were largely dependent for their living on the grain trade. They weighed all the grain unloaded at the docks, paying themselves and the Dock labourers whom they employed, out of the dues which they charged for the weighing. In 1918 and 1920 they were granted rises in their rates by the Dock commission, but in 1922 and 1923, these rates were cut. The Society of Metters held monthly meetings and in June 1925:

> The Boxmaster then addressed the meeting on the exceptional long quiet spell through which we are passing and gave it as his opinion that we should make a bid for other work if possible, and mentioned the porter work at the [Grain] Elevator Warehouse. With this end in view he had approached the Manager there, and he seemed to be rather in favour of the idea.

The Committee was instructed to interview the Secretary of the Dock Commission about the proposal. 'Also to put before him the real state of affairs, as to us being required by the Dock Commission to keep up a big staff here [33] and not having work to be fully employed.'

It was the opinion of the meeting that the Dock commission should compel merchants to give the Metters the weighing of non-grain cargoes. (This had formerly been done by Porters, as there had not been enough Metters to do the work.) The negotiations proceeded slowly, but in April 1926 the Warehouse work was obtained, together with a reduction in the rents of the Metters' Office and their tool howffs. The matter of weighing extra cargoes was not so easy, and was to lead to a great deal of friction with the Porters, who were also affected by the shortage of work.

No sooner had the extra work started than the General Strike began. The Metters were not Union members and had never joined in previous disputes, apart from a partial stoppage in 1913. On the morning of 5 May 1926 they held a meeting to decide whether to join the men who were withdrawing their labour from the Warehouse. All the other non-Union men there would be continuing to work, but the Metters voted to come out from mid-day that day. A week later, however, they had to reconsider, the Boxmaster having been told by the Manager of the Elevator that if they stayed out they could lose their work there. The Dockers and Transport Workers Union had promised its support if the Metters were adversely affected by their action, but there was not much it could do in this situation. Although much concerned about the reaction of the Union men, with whom there had been bad feeling after former strikes, they had no option but to return to work.

The Situation Worsens

In 1927 the Metters tried for extra work loading bone sinews, but they drew the line at coal-bagging, which they were offered. In June of that year, work was so slack that they began to have a day off each, in rotation. On 6 July 1928 they held a special meeting to discuss the situation:

> Mr George Nichol, addressing the Company, mentioned in the course of his remarks that we were gradually losing work such a Geo Gibson and Co's flax and various other odd jobs. These jobs, though possibly not much individually were

The Imperial Dock grain elevator and warehouse.

> on aggregate quite useful to us. He also said that now was the time to look for other work and as a means to this end he, seconded by John Russell, proposed that we along with our weighing take up portering and suggested that we approach the various merchants and offer a combined rate for the same.

The idea was adopted by a large majority. The Boxmaster was empowered to negotiate this with merchants, also to approach former employers to try to regain work, and to try to regain flax weighing from merchants in Kirkcaldy, Leven and Port Glasgow. He was also asked to 'press hard' for casual work at the Elevator. James Watson was deputed to help him and at the next meeting reported that he had visited a dozen firms and been favourably received. George Nichol had been twice to the British Oil and Cake Mills, and had been told that the Metters would be considered if the Company ever wished to change its Porters.

Dispute With the Porters

In January 1929 the Metters began casual work at the Elevator. This was a quiet year. The shortage of work was mentioned at meetings, but as a matter of course rather than of urgency. In March 1930 it was decided to take any portering from quays which they could get. In June, a proposal to amalgamate with the Porters was mooted, but it was voted out at a meeting in August. The fact that it was even suggested, however is a measure of the desperation of the men. The Metters were proud of their centuries-long history of independence and it would be a drastic measure indeed to give it up. A year later, however, things were still no better, and the suggestion was raised once more. This time negotiations got as far as a joint meeting with the Porters in October 1931 to discuss the proposal, which also had the support of the Dock Commission. The Metters took a week to consider and then held their own meeting. Once again the proposal was defeated, by 11 votes to 7.

Shortly after this the Metters applied to the Leith Corn Trades Association for an increase in rates to cover a recent rise in their National Insurance contributions. The Association not only refused, they reduced the rate they already paid. This was the beginning of a four-year period of steady voluntary reductions in rates as the Metters sought to avoid losing yet more work. Relations with the Porters deteriorated, with accusations and counter-accusations flying back and forth of Porters weighing and Metters portering. In June 1932 the Metters were horrified to learn that the Dock commission intended to issue Porters with weighing licences for goods other than grain. The following November they sent a circular to all merchants, reminding them that it was illegal for anyone other than a Sworn Metter to weigh grain. This had the unforseen result that the Dock commission was swamped with a flood of applications for Metters' licences from the employees of merchants. In alarm the Metters sent a strong plea to the Commission for their position to be upheld. The Commission ignored the Metters' licence applications, but they went

The Imperial dry dock, with the harbour entrance and Western Harbour behind it, 1922.

ahead with their plans to allow porters to do weighing work. Their first licences were issued in 1934.

Recovery

In June of that year the Metters' Boxmaster remarked that 'things looked none too bright', but this proved to be the hour before the dawn. In December 1935 the Metters minutes speak of a rush of work and the need to look for some new 'young men' (the society had dwindled to 23 members with an average age of 50 years). The energetic George Nichol, who stood down as Boxmaster that year having been re-elected annually since 1930, was thanked by his successor 'for his services to the Society during a difficult period in its history'. Later that year rates for work began to rise again. Prosperity had returned.

In 1935 the tonnage of imports and exports handled at the Docks was 3,198,625. For the next three years the figure remained over at 3,000,000. In 1939 it dropped by over 250,000 tons. World War Two had begun.

War and ARP

This time the outbreak of war caught no-one by surprise. As early as November 1937 the Dock commission had been discussing Air Raid Precautions (ARP). At that time, and for some years into the war, it was expected that the chief danger would be from poison gas attacks. Early in 1938 (its Centenary year) the Dock commission set up an Anti-gas School, and by December 459 of their employees had been trained in anti-gas measures. Sixty more were undergoing decontamination training, and 174 had volunteered for First Aid classes, when these should be started. At the start of the New Year the Commission opened its classes to non-employees. By the middle of February 1939, 69 employees of shipping lines and other local firms had finished the preliminary course in ARP, and First Aid courses were well under way. By July 231 men had undergone decontamination training, 163 held First Aid certificates, and 132 were familiar with Fire Drill.

Around New Year of 1939 an ARP subcommittee of the Commission had been set up. The Ministry of Transport had asked the Commission to store gas masks for the crews of ships which it might commandeer in the future, and the Minister had begun to arrange Government finance for ARP in Docks and Harbours. The Ministry had also selected Leith to co-ordinate the control of merchant shipping in the Forth. Captain Elvin, the Assistant Dockmaster, was appointed to visit other ports in the area and make himself familiar with local conditions. At the beginning of May he attended an exercise in the Shipping Diversion Room at Whitehall.

In April the Commission came to an agreement with Edinburgh Corporation for extra fire fighting services to be provided in the Docks. The Superintendent (Mr JD Easton) began to make arrangements for Military hutments to be erected at the north-west corner of Imperial Dock, adjoining the military underground power station there. The ground was to include space for an anti-aircraft searchlight. The Superintendent also had to re-arrange berthing facilities in the West Old Dock, to accommodate the 312-foot destroyer that the Admiralty sent to Leith as an additional RNVR training ship.

The Commission had a statutory duty under the Civil Defence Bill to provide training and protection for their employees and to take measures to ensure the continued operation of the Docks for as long as possible during an air-raid alert and for any necessary repairs to be done as quickly as possible. They were also required to provide facilities to increase the working capacity of the Docks (for which Government grants were available) and shelters for people other than their employees who might be in the Dock area during an air raid. In April the ARP committee instructed the Commission Clerk to submit estimates for the cost of both ARP and of schemes to ensure the free flow of traffic during an alert. In May they met to consider his report. The Commission was already carrying out most of the duties laid down in the Bill, and the main concern of the meeting was that work should continue on the Western Harbour Extension Scheme which had begun in 1936. It was felt that almost the whole available grant would be needed for this purpose.

As a start on fulfilling the obligation to provide protection for employees and the general public, the Superintendent was authorised to buy and erect the first air raid shelter, to hold 50 people. Progress in Fire Drill training was discussed and it was noted that the Edinburgh Fire Brigade would be holding a fire-fighting demonstration at the Docks on 29 May. The question of insurance for employees doing voluntary ARP after hours had also to be considered. Some Commission employees had already been called up for a forthcoming Territorial Army training camp. The Commission would make up the difference between Army pay and normal wages.

During the summer of 1939, work progressed steadily on protecting Docks property and personnel. To supplement the purpose-built air raid shelters, part of the ground floors of the Edinburgh and Imperial Grain Warehouses were fitted out to provide shelter for several hundred persons. Electricity station windows were fitted with steel shutters and the machinery given steel covers. Swing bridge gear was given similar treatment. Offices and buildings all over the complex were sandbagged, the bags being filled with sand excavated as part of the Western Extension works. In anticipation of the blackout a start was made on applying white paint to mark bollards and the corners of buildings. The Superintendent went down to Portsmouth to attend a trial of wartime Docks lighting.

At their first meeting after the declaration of war on 3 September 1939, the Commissioners took stock of the situation. The various protection measures were progressing satisfactorily, although they were very expensive, and rates had to be raised by 10% to cover the cost. There was a hitch in the provision of air raid shelters. One steel shelter had been erected, but materials for the rest had not arrived. Steel helmets had arrived for certain workmen and staff, but they were still waiting for respirators. The Commission's original Civil Defence scheme had to be modified, as the Government money available to them would not cover the full cost. Captain Elvin had been on duty in the Whitehall Shipping Diversion Room since the end of August, and Captain Anderson, one of the Assistant Dockmasters, was to be trained as his relief.

By the second week in October, the pace of preparations had stepped up a gear. Four steel shelters were finished and another was building. Seven vaults at the Old Docks, which would hold 800 people, were to be used as additional shelters. Three 'pill box' shelters had been built for bridge and gate keepers and another was under construction (the eventual total was eight). One Fire Station had been built for the City Auxiliary Fire Service and another was on its way. Most of the more important buildings were now protected by steel plates or sandbags and work was in progress on the rest. Experiments were being carried out with blackout lighting on the quays, and white paint markings were being laid down to guide traffic in the dark. The War Office had declared the Port a Protected Place under defence regulations, and authorised the Superintendent to take charge of security. Accordingly, he was issuing Dock Permits and drafting defence regulation Port Bye-laws.

Air Raid

On 9 November 1939 Leith suffered its first air raid in the course of a German attack on the Forth. No damage was done to the Port, but it was found that the existing shelters were somewhat overcrowded. As two more large ones were still under construction and more planned, it was felt that this problem should not recur. Sandbagging and painting continued, with the new addition of Gas Detecting paint for use on prominent objects. The wartime lighting system was still incomplete, owing to supply difficulties, but the combined effects of the blackout and shipping convoys had greatly increased turn round times. Sand boxes and buckets for dealing with fires were now in place in all sheds, and a First Aid Post was being built. Edinburgh was also in the process of providing public shelters and the Commission gave the City permission to build one of brick in the centre of Dock Place, and one at Newhaven.

By the start of December all of the 100,000 sandbags were in place. (Within eight months these revetments were starting to crumble and work began on replacing them with brickwork.) Twelve steel and two concrete 50-man underground shelters were complete and two more were building. (The shelters were finally completed the following February - 15 steel and 2 concrete.) Notices were being put in place to direct people to the shelters. There were now eight ARP posts in the Docks, the windows and rooflights of the Grain Warehouses had been covered with blue translucent paint and orange lighting installed. Gas lighting in sheds had been replaced by electricity which could quickly be shut off after an air raid warning. Dock entry permits were introduced on 11 December.

A Royal Visit

On 26 February 1940 the King George VI and Queen Elizabeth made the first of their wartime visits to the Docks. Their main purpose was to meet representatives of the Merchant Seamen and the Fishermen of the Scottish east coast. Among others, the Commission Clerk and Deputy Chairman were presented to their Majesties at a ceremony attended by the rest of the Commissioners and their ladies. (The Chairman was too ill to attend.) Eight days before the Royal visit, prisoners of war who had been rescued from the *Altmark* were landed at Leith from HMS *Cossack*. The First Lord of the Admiralty, Sir Winston

The visit of King George VI and Queen Elizabeth to Henry Robb's shipyard during World War II.

Churchill, wrote to thank the Commissioners for their assistance on this occasion.

ARP Exercises

By March an Ambulance station had been set up. The ambulances were garaged in a corner of a shed at the Albert Dock, where the fire engines were also housed. Sleeping accommodation for the drivers was found in a vacant office near the Edinburgh Dock. Arrangements were made with the Coasting Shipping Companies for their motor lorries to be used by the ARP in an emergency. To date, the cost of the ARP precautions amounted to £19000.

On the afternoon of Sunday 10 March an ARP exercise was held by Edinburgh, to see how well this expensive provision worked. The scenario included an air raid on the Docks, with damage from high explosive, incendiary and gas bombs. Fifty soldiers and forty Commission employees acted as 'casualties', posted at pre-arranged sites and labelled with descriptions of their injuries. Serious cases were taken by ambulance to hospitals in the City. Thirty walking cases were dealt with by the Commission's First Aid parties and then treated at the First Aid post inside the Constitution Place dock gate. The Docks report centre, ARP wardens, first aiders and decontamination squads were all involved in the exercise. The City's fire fighting arrangements were also found to be satisfactory. There was as yet no gas De-contamination Centre in the Docks, but by the middle of May it was being built and a month later it was complete.

The Western Breakwater

All the while that wartime preparations were being carried out in the Docks, work had continued on the Western Harbour Extension. The breakwaters being built there were modelled on the Great Dyke by which the Dutch had enclosed the Zuyder Zee, it being the first time this type of construction had been used in Britain. When designing the breakwaters, the Superintendent had visited Holland to consult the Dutch Engineer-in-Chief of Waterways and had carried out wave action experiments at the Hydraulic Laboratory at Delft. The contractors for the project, Kalis and Sons of London, were using specialised equipment from Holland, operated by Dutch engineers. In late May 1940, the Naval Officer in Chief at Leith, without warning, arrested these Dutch workers. Presumably as aliens they counted as a security risk, in view of the secret military works which were going on in the Docks. Work on the western breakwater, which was as yet some way from completion, was abruptly halted, as only the Dutch knew how to operate the specialised plant.

On 2 June, the Admiralty officially prohibited any further work on the Western Breakwater. The Commissioners paid Kalis the £12,000 instalment which fell due to them at this time, but there was great concern about the fate of the unfinished and unprotected work: 'The condition of the work is at such a stage that stoppage now will have the effect of exposing the unfinished Breakwater to serious deterioration in the future, and thus destroy work already completed.'

At the end of July 1940 the Admiralty conceded that work on the Breakwater might recommence, but only under any restrictions which the Admiral at Rosyth thought necessary. As these restrictions included non-use of the Dutch workers, and the Navy had also commandeered all the tugs and barges which had been serving the works, the Admiralty permission was effectively useless. Kalis terminated its contract with the Commission, leaving them in serious financial difficulties. They promptly lodged a claim with the Admiralty to cover their losses. Eventually they negotiated a new contract with Kalis for completion of the Breakwater, but because it had to be based on wartime prices its final cost was more than twice the original quote. Because of winter weather conditions, work could not begin again until May 1941, those same winter conditions having meanwhile caused considerable damage, as the Commission had anticipated.

More ARP

While negotiations were going on over the Breakwater, ARP in the Docks continued. Some services began to be manned at weekends, and all wardens were issued with badges. Another ARP practice was held on Sunday 30 June 1940, but it was not long before the Docks once more experienced the real thing. Air raids on the 18 and 22 July caused damage to the quay, roads, railway, hydraulic pipes, electric and gas mains and sheds at the Albert Dock and the Victoria Dock, which cost nearly £10,000 to repair. As in the previous raid, there were no casualties at the Docks.

Ways were now being sought to limit the working time lost as a result of air raid warnings, which caused the men to be in the shelters for long periods during which there was no enemy action. In October a system was instituted whereby two trained members of the Imperial Dock Warehouse staff would take up their station on the roof when an air raid alert sounded, the warehouse being the most conspicuous landmark in the Docks. When the two men considered that danger was imminent, they were to hoist a black ball up a mast, to be specially constructed for the purpose. Each gang working in the Docks was to appoint one member to watch for the black ball, and blow a whistle when he saw it. The whistle would be the signal to make for the shelters. In December the 'spotters' on the Warehouse roof were instructed to telephone firms who did not employ their own spotters with news of the imminent danger.

Firewatching

At the start of 1941 the Government brought in the Fire Prevention (Business Premises) Order. The Superintendent began fixing access ladders to the roofs of Docks buildings, where bins of sand and buckets were placed. In March sleeping accommodation and equipment for firewatchers in the Docks was organised and arrangements made for subsistence allowances during the watch period. Officially the Commission was responsible for ensuring that all their tenants made their own fire watching and prevention arrangements, but the Dock Labour Employers Association agreed to let the Commission organise this for them and recover the cost by a rise in their rents.

A number of firms set up their own Home Guard units at this time. The Commission granted drill facilities to Menzies, Henry Robb, Laidlaw Drew and Co, and the North British Cold Storage and Ice Co Ltd.

Summer and Autumn 1941

Work restarted on the West Breakwater at the beginning of May 1941. A dredger and a floating crane which had been removed to Charleston were floated back to Leith, and two dismantled floating cranes were refitted. The Admiralty agreed to move their barges, which were moored in the bay, when necessary and to give up quay space needed by the contractors. The Dutch key workers were re-employed and permission was given for all Kalis' employees with official passes to go onto the Breakwater. The cost of this final phase of the work which had originally been estimated at £67,000, had now risen to £130,000.

During the summer several berths in the Edinburgh and Imperial Docks were given over to the Navy for ship repairing. Extra railway lines and cranes were erected at these berths, at Government expense. Earlier in the year the Commission had dredged a de-gousing berth at the Imperial Dock for the Navy.

In July 1941 the Dock commission Clerk began to look for alternative office accommodation in Edinburgh, to be used in the event of the Commission HQ being damaged. He also made arrangements for all important documents and some 1000 plans to be photographed and the negatives stored in fireproof boxes in a safe place. The documents were finished by December, when a start was made on the plans.

Blackout lighting restrictions had led to an increase in drowning accidents in the Docks, and as autumn drew on a start was made on providing extra lighting, fencing and white guard rails. Wartime lighting was also installed at four public dry docks. The extra work of supervising firewatching and prevention arrangements was becoming too much for the Superintendent, and in December a Port Fire Guard Officer was appointed, with two assistants to work under him. One of his first tasks at the beginning of 1942 was to collect information for the Ministry of War Transport on the firewatching schemes operated by the Commission and all its tenants. In the Docks, at least, firewatching was having a serious effect on ARP provision as many of the men had to carry out both sets of duties.

The Second Royal Visit

On 5 June 1942, the King and Queen paid their second visit to the Docks, to meet representatives of the Merchant Seamen, Fishermen and Dock Workers (the Boxmaster of the Metters was among the latter). Before starting their tour of the Docks the Royal couple visited the Commissioners' Board Room, where the Chairman, Committee Conveners and Clerk were presented to them.

The Docks had escaped air raid damage for over a year, but in June the road on the south side of the Albert Dock sustained damage which took a month to repair.

The Canteen

In June also, plans began to provide a canteen for Dock workers in the Shelter Hall in Tower St. A mobile canteen selling tea and refreshments had been operating in the Docks since March, a somewhat belated response to a Docks (Provision of Canteens) Order of 1941. A recent visit by the Inspectorate of Factories had, not surprisingly, found this provision inadequate. The Commission was ordered to provide a canteen near the Albert Dock, the Inspector considering the Tower St site satisfactory. The Commission was very reluctant to take responsibility for the canteen, and tried to get it set up as a British Restaurant. However, the Ministry of Food (which would be providing the rations for it) rejected this scheme, and in November 1942 the order was given to go ahead with the building of a kitchen and other necessary alterations. The contract for running the canteen was awarded to the Bar and Canteen Supply Co Ltd, which ran other similar establishments in the district. It opened for business on 3 May 1943.

The Breakwater is Finished

At the end of July 1942 the work on the Western Breakwater was finally completed. On Monday 16 November a commemoration stone, donated by Kalis and erected by them at the end of the new work, was unveiled by the Secretary of State for Scotland, the Rt Hon Thomas Johnston. The following day the contractors entertained the Commissioners to lunch. Unknown to the Commissioners, Mr LE Nobel of Kalis had made a film about the Western Breakwater. After the War, in 1946, he presented it to the Commission.

1942 also saw the start of the National Dock Labour Scheme under which Dock Labour was de-casualised. All Leith Dock workers now became employees of the Commission, although semi-independent bodies such as the Metters continued to operate as they had always done.

Shipbuilding and Repair Expands

The main new feature of life in the Docks in 1943 was the growth in shipbuilding and repairing. Menzies (whose business was entirely devoted to ship repairs) were ordered by the Government to take on female workers, and once more were allowed to use the Dock Place Shelter as a rest room for them. So healthy was the business that it was even worth setting up new concerns. In the following year Marr's dry dock and yard (ex John Sime) was taken over by Mr John Lyall of the Sandport Engineering and Ship Repairing Co Ltd.

The only firm actually building ships in Leith at this time was Henry Robb at the Victoria Yard. Since its foundation in 1918, the firm had taken over three Leith shipbuilding businesses, and was destined to swallow up the rest after the War. During the conflict, Robbs built 42 Naval and 14 merchant ships and repaired or refitted a total of 3000 vessels of all kinds. These figures represent an average of one new ship every six weeks and one repaired every day. At the start of the War, the yard was ordered by the Admiralty to build Flower Class Corvettes. *Delphinium, Dianthus, Petunia* and *Polyanthus* were launched in 1940, and *Lotus* and *Pink* two years later. In 1943-4 came the Castle Class Corvettes *Flint Castle, Hespeler* and *Orangeville.* The year 1942 saw the launch of the first of twelve frigates built at the yard; *Ness* and *Nith,* In the meantime, Robbs had built the minesweepers *Sidmouth* and *Stornaway,* two trawlers, three minesweeper training ships for the New Zealand Government; *Kiwi, Moa* and *Tui,* and the first of a number of Rescue Tugs.

The Flower class corvette HMS *Petunia,* built by Henry Robb, rescuing the passengers of a torpedoed liner during World War II.

Petunia was in the South Atlantic in November 1942 when she was attacked by a U-boat which fired four torpedoes, all of which missed. The Italians later claimed that they had sunk a US battleship at the spot! In the same voyage, *Petunia* herself attacked a U-boat. As the crew manned the depth-charge thrower, up to their waists in water in a howling gale, the depth-charge strop parted. Leading Cook Robert Scott knelt on the deck while his mates heaved the charges onto his shoulder. Then he slowly pulled himself up far enough to tip the charges into the thrower-stalk, from which they were fired. For this he was later mentioned in despatches. Four months later, *Petunia* was in the Tropics where she rescued the passengers of the sunken liner *Empress of Canada*. Leading Cook Scott once more proved his heroism by producing in 24 hours; 900 sausage rolls, 600 bread rolls, stew, soup and hot vegetables for more than 400 people. All this in the steaming heat of a galley designed to feed only the ship's crew.

Dianthus, launched just ten weeks before *Petunia*, was involved in one of the fiercest battles of the Atlantic, lasting five days and nights, in August 1942. The first Lord of the Admiralty told her story in a speech given a few weeks later:

> For nearly three hours one of our corvettes hunted the U-boat in the Atlantic. It was first sighted on the surface. There were violent rain squalls and complete darkness. Accurate gunnery forced the U-boat to dive, but depth charges forced her to the surface again. Four times the little corvette fired everything she could muster, and rammed the U-boat. Clouds of sparks made a fantastic firework display each time she hit her. After the fourth attack the U-boat reared up above the ship's deck and crashed down hard on the fo'clsle. Then the U-boat sank. The fight had lasted nineteen minutes, during which there was great exitement.
>
> Her crew worked through the night to repair the damage she had sustained and make her seaworthy, and she rejoined her convoy the following morning. However, she had lost oil in the conflict, and was left with just 26 tons to get her the 600 miles to home. The men scoured the empty tanks for oil pools which might have been left near the feed pipes. Lubricating oil, gunnery oil and two drums of caster oil from the sick bay were brought into use. Altogether, half a ton of extra fuel was collected - just enough to bring *Dianthus* safely into harbour.

Many more stories could be told about the ships which left Robb's yard for Navel service during the War. Some of the bravest were the tugs, which were used to tow home damaged ships, over long distances and often under attack. *Bustler*, the first to be launched in 1941, safely towed home the badly damaged 14,000 ton merchant ship *Durham* from Gibralter, in spite of constant attacks by U-boats, from which she was protected only by a corvette and a trawler. *Samsonia* towed a 7000 ton vessel 1400 miles while beating off frequent attacks by aircraft. *Hesperia* salvaged 15 damaged ships in the sixteen months she was in service, steaming 38,237 miles in her first 203 days at sea. *Mediator*'s maiden voyage in 1944 comprised 14,000 miles of continuous steaming, during which she did a 3,700 mile heavy tow at an average speed of seven knots.

Henry Robb's was honoured with a visit from the King and Queen when they were once more in Leith on 29 July 1943. Four months later, as many men as the yard could spare were hard at work on a project so secret that not even a hint of it appears in the Dock Commission Minutes.

The Mulberry Harbour

For over a year secret preparations had been going on for the D-Day Landings on the northwest coast of occupied France, which were to take place on 5 June 1944. Every port and harbour in the area was heavily defended by the Germans, and it would not be possible to land armaments and other heavy military equipment from small boats onto the beaches. Furthermore, Britain had no reliable charts of French coastal waters, where the tide could rise and fall as much as 20 feet.

In 1942, in spite of the difficulties, it was decided to build a floating harbour, code-named Mulberry, in sections which could be towed across the English Channel and assembled in situ. The Navy began to make nightly excursions into French waters to take soundings from which charts could be compiled. The engineers began to design the harbour. It basically consisted of a long curved breakwater protecting a basin of water and connected with the land by pontoons. The large breakwater sections had to be built in the south of England in order to minimise towing distances. Most of the pontoons, and 18 pierheads, which were also needed, were produced in Scotland in an operation involving over 100 firms and co-ordinated by Alexander Findlay and Co of Motherwell.

Work began at Leith in December 1943. First a fully equipped shipyard had to be established on the ground newly reclaimed by the Western Extension. Power plant, cranes, launching slips, stores, workshops, offices, roads and railways - by dint of non-stop work by night and day all was ready by the middle of January. On the 26th of the month the first of 13 pierheads was launched. It was towed round to Newhaven fish quay to be finished, as were its successors. The third pierhead was launched on 11 March, after which the already fast pace of work had to be speeded up even more, to produce one pierhead a week. This is even more remarkable when one considers that the yard also built 16 pontoons. To achieve this impossible task 600 men worked day and night. Firms of welders, plumbers, joiners and electricians sent all the men they could spare. The work was completed on time.

The Beginning of the End

After D-Day, 5 June 1944, Britain and her allies knew that the end was in sight. The War Effort at home began to wind down. In August Captain Elvin was awarded the MBE for his work in the Direction of Shipping. The Commission paid the expenses for him to go to London with his wife to collect the award. Civil Defence measures were progressively relaxed. By November, firewatching at the Docks had ceased. The First Aid post was closed down. Although it had never been needed for the treatment of casualties it had been very much appreciated by Dock workers for treating minor injuries sustained at their work.

It was not long before it reopened as a permanent feature of the Docks Welfare provision, run by Leith Hospital.

On 12 January 1945 the Auxiliary Fire Station at the Edinburgh Dock was closed, although the Principal Station at the Victoria Dock continued for the time being. In May the lighting at the docks was returned to pre war brightness. Lights on buoys, which had been dimmed for the duration of the war, were returned to full power. Restrictions were lifted on press reporting and the Commission considered publishing an account of the war work carried out by the Docks.

In June it turned its attention to the disposal of ARP equipment. The Superintendent was to keep anything that was useful for his department. The rest was valued by Jenners and put up for sale, after the Matron of Leith Hospital had taken first pick and ARP members had been given an option to buy. The sale of the equipment was completed early the following year, raising £706.

On 1 October the system of permits for entry to the Docks officially ceased. Since their introduction in September 1939, 28,211 permanent passes had been issued by Head Office, 132,050 temporary passes by the permit office, and 40,000 seamens' permits by the security police. Casual labourers had been issued with thousands of daily permits, of a different colour for each day of the week. November saw the beginning of the dismantling of the air raid shelters, which was completed in June 1946. In December the ARP Committee was discharged.

Life was getting back to normal, but two world wars, coupled with the Depression, had dealt the Port some damaging blows. The immediate post-war years saw Leith at its lowest ebb, and recovery was affected by changes in shipping practices and in the demand for basic commodities. However, in the eight centuries of its history, the Port had weathered many storms. The next half century was to be no exception to the rule.

18

Post War

Britain took some time to recover after the Second World War. The austerity years dragged on, and rationing was still in force. The electorate signalled its disapproval by electing a Labour Government - which repaid its supporters by rationing bread. By the beginning of the fifties, however, recovery could be seen to be on its way, and the Coronation of the young Queen Elizabeth II was hailed as the dawning of the New Elizabethan Age.

The Proclamation of Her Majesty the Queen was made in the immemorial fashion at the 'Pier and Shore of Leith', with full military honours. The Leith Docks Commission marked the occasion by issuing its first Official Handbook. In his foreword the Chairman, Mr EW Burness, looked back over the past years:

> Fifteen years ago, when a Handbook was published by Leith Chamber of Commerce, the new Western Harbour....was in its initial stages. Today the Harbour is an accomplished fact and the inner development is already well under way, with the completion of the two deep water quays and a large reclaimed area ready for industrial development.
>
> The Western Harbour, along with the existing dock facilities which in the last few years have been extensively modernised by the installation of new cranes, enables the Commissioners to offer facilities for the rapid and efficient handling of goods and turn-round of shipping.
>
> Leith, in common with many other ports in the country, has suffered from some post-war depression of trade, but the Commissioners are confident that the Port will gradually regain its former prosperity.

The confidence of the Commissioners was not entirely misplaced, but it is perhaps as well that they could not forsee quite how gradual the process was going to be.

The State of the Docks

The new entrance to the port provided by the construction of the East and West Breakwaters gave ships a dredged channel 400 feet wide, and 18 feet deep at Mean Low Water Spring Tides. A new system of port locating lights, signals and leading lights had been installed. A series of coloured plates on a tide signal tower at the seaward end of the West Breakwater informed shipmasters of the depth of water at the entrance to the docks.

The total water area of the docks was 220 acres and the complex now comprised the six enclosed docks built in the nineteenth and early twentieth century, an inner (Shore) and outer harbour used by coasting vessels, and the new Western Harbour. The gates of the enclosed docks were opened about three hours before high water to allow vessels to enter and leave, and closed at high water. The three larger ones had entrance locks which would accommodate ships up to 300 feet long. According to their handbook, the Commissioners anticipated that the future of the docks lay in the new Western Harbour, which would accommodate deeper, beamier vessels than the enclosed docks, and they had plans to extend the deep water quays which they had recently completed there. They also envisaged industrial use for the 30 acres of reclaimed land to the south of the Harbour.

Of the six inner docks, the four older ones - East and West Old Docks, Victoria and Albert Docks - were comparatively little used. In 1950 the 20-ton hydraulic coaling crane on the north side of the Albert dock, with its associated railway sidings and turntable, was removed to make the berth available for ship repairs. Some work had been done on the Imperial Dock since the war, mainly comprising repairs to its lock gates and the reroofing of sheds. The main effort had been concentrated on the Edinburgh Dock, where sheds had been rebuilt and supplied with electricity from a new sub-station, and 3 and 6 ton travelling electric cranes with capstans installed on the quayside. Altogether there were now in the docks, 47 electric cranes of 1½ to 120 tons, 22 hydraulic cranes of 1½ to 10 tons, 8 mobile, 10 locomotive and 21 hand cranes. There was even a 45 ton steam crane, which was to remain for a further 25 years.

The eight dry docks in the complex were still busy. Six of them, the two Commercial docks in the West Old Dock, the Prince of Wales, Alexandra, Edinburgh and Imperial docks, were in the hands of the Docks Commission. The first dry dock which had been built to the east of the East Old Dock was still leased to Menzies ship repairing firm, as it had been for nearly a century. John Sime's eighteenth century dock was still occupied by Scotts engineering and ship repair company. (This dry dock was not filled in until 1961, by which time it had been in use for 190 years.) The railway network was still extensive, with power-driven capstans to move wagons around the sheds and quays, and there was 80,000 sq yards of shed space.

Leith was the only port on the east coast of Scotland with grain handling facilities, which were consequently fully utilised. There were two grain warehouses, one at the Imperial and one at the Edinburgh Dock, which held a total of 36,000 tons of grain. Each was served by discharging plant, some of it dating from the 1920s, which sucked the grain from the hold of the ship and carried it to the warehouse by conveyor belt. The silos were equipped with apparatus to detect overheating in the grain, and the warehouses had dust-extracting plant. In the Western Harbour, new deep water quays had been built in conjunction with Rank the flour millers, who were in the process of erecting a new mill on the site.

As well as the modernisation of some cranes, other changes were in progress. Most machinery had been converted to electric power, although the coal hoists, dock gates, swing bridges and some older cranes were still hydraulic. Fuel oil was carried to ships by barges, but there were plans to install a pipeline at one of the berths.

There were regular passenger services to Orkney and Shetland, and some to Montreal, Copenhagen, Aalborg, Aarhus, Odense, Reykjavik, Rotterdam, Amsterdam, Bremen, Hamburg and the Faroes. Leith was also a port of call for cruise liners. Some would come in to a deep water berth, but the larger ones would anchor in the Roads and put their passengers ashore to visit Edinburgh. Customs and Immigration facilities, and a waiting room were provided for passenger use.

Principle Imports and Exports for the Year ended 15 May 1952

Imports	*Tons*	*Exports*	*Tons*
Flour, Grain and Meal	319,606	Flour and Meal	7,553
Oilcake	11,726	Ale, Beer, Wine, Spirits	23,546
Bacon, Butter and Eggs	48,396	Coal	136,038
Fish, fresh and cured	15,232	Bunker Coal	76,869
Fruit and Vegetables	31,702	Iron/Steel Manufactures	17,030
Fertilisers	76,609	Paper, Cardboard etc	38,231
Cement	84,715	Animal Feedstuffs	23,666
Iron Ore and Scrap	21,065	Fertilisers	6,725
Iron and Steel	14,869	Linoleum	3,083
Timber	116,265	Fuel Oil	8,592
Wood Pulp	25,071		

In the years prior to 1947, six pilotage authorities had covered the Firth of Forth. By the Forth Pilotage Order of that year they had been amalgamated into a single Pilotage Authority, whose headquarters were now at the Dock Commission's offices in Tower Place. At the Pilot Watch House at the Imperial Basin, a constant watch was kept for ships displaying the signal requesting a pilot. All vessels carrying passengers were required to take a pilot on board from the pilot boats which cruised between Fidra Island and Elieness and eastward of Inchkeith. Towage was available from the Commission's own fleet of tugs based at Leith. The Leith and Granton Boatmen's Association operated four motor boats to assist ships in mooring in the Forth and to service vessels in the Roads.

Henry Robb was now the only shipbuilder in the port, but Menzies and Co Ltd still carried on a repair business. George Brown and Sons, Engineers, had started as a blacksmith's shop in 1820 and at the turn of the century had produced Mascot motorcycles. In 1912 the firm opened a boatyard for building yachts, and in 1953 was still carrying on ship repairing, along with general engineering and pump manufacture. It specialised in converting ships from coal to oil burning engines. This firm was not to be confused with Brown Bros and Co Ltd, established in 1867 and specialising in hydraulic machinery. (Among its more up-to-date manufactures was wave-making machinery for swimming pools.)

Ships which had come to the end of their days might find themselves in the breakers' yard of Malcom Brechin of West Harbour, Granton, which had been in business since 1920.

The timber trade, of all traditional Leith imports perhaps the least affected by fluctuations in demand, still flourished. Wartime restrictions on sources of supply were now at an end, but building regulations still in force were hampering full recovery for the time being. Of the six largest firms, most had been founded in the nineteenth century, but the firm of Park, Dobson and Co Ltd traced its beginnings to a business set up by Andrew Park in 1790. Garland and Roger Ltd, established in 1876, occupied a prime site adjacent to the Docks, and offered a wide variety of timbers: mahogany, iroko, obeche, abura, oak, redwood, whitewood, Douglas fir, hemlock, Columbian pine and a selection of decorative timbers.

Leith Airport

In December 1949 the Docks Commissioners had received a letter from Messrs Christian Salvesen and Co on behalf of Aquila Airways of London, who had been approached by South Cornwall Airways to arrange a scheduled seaplane service between Leith and Falmouth. Salveson's letter contained a request for Leith to be licensed as an airport. As it was only five months since a flying boat had landed at Leith, bringing a Norwegian crew to join their new ship which had been built at Burntisland, the Commissioners were willing to explore the idea, and in February 1950 the Docks General Manager reported on meetings he had held with Aquila Airways and the Ministry of Civil Aviation. The intention was to run a service during daylight each Friday from May to October. The Docks Commission was to provide mooring buoys. They would also arrange for a fire-fighting launch to be available, although this would be paid for by the operators, who would also provide a tender to take passengers ashore. The Commission undertook to provide wind directors, which were available free of charge from the petrol companies which used the port. The Ministry of Civil Aviation stipulated that the landing area had to be at least 6,000 ft in two directions. The cost of the licence was £1 5s for the first year and £1 1s per annum thereafter.

By mid-March, one of docks' mooring buoys has been suitably protected and was in position in the Western Harbour. The firefighting equipment and launch had been tried out and found satisfactory, and meteorological data had been obtained from the Air Ministry. The licence application was forwarded to the Ministry, whose officials inspected and approved the arrangements. On 1 June, the airport was opened by the Chairman of the Commission, the Lord Provost of Edinburgh, Vice Admiral Sir Earnest Archer, Air Vice Marshal Carnegie, the directors of Aquila Airways, and a party of Commissioners.

It must have been something of an anti-climax when on 29 June a letter arrived from Aquila Airways explaining that owing to an almost total lack of bookings, they would have to postpone their service from Southampton to Leith

A horse and cart and lorries loading at the Imperial Dock grain warehouse in 1953.

and Greenock. An increase of tax on fuel and the high cost of the firefighting facilities demanded by the Ministry of Civil Aviation meant that they could not keep fares low enough to attract customers. They could only hold out a faint hope of charter flights in future.

The Commission renewed its licence application each year, and in 1952, four American Mariner flying boats did land at Leith, but they were to be the only users of the airport. In June 1959, on receiving the usual application from the Docks Commission for renewal of their airport licence, the Ministry of Transport sent them a letter pointing out that there were now no civil flying boat operators in UK, and asking if they wanted to reconsider. At a subsequent meeting with Ministry officials it transpired that Leith was the only port in UK to retain an airport licence, which was, in any case, no longer needed for charter use. Moreover, flying boats were now largely confined to the US, with little prospect of transatlantic flights. At this point, the Commissioners decided to discontinue its applications

Civil Defence

A major preoccupation of the Docks Commission throughout the fifties was the question of Civil Defence measures against possible nuclear attack. As the Cold War with the Eastern Bloc countries grew ever frostier, it seemed increasingly likely to many people that such an attack was a real possibility. Britain had been a party to the dropping of the only nuclear bombs ever to be used in warfare, and she had no reason to suppose that other powers might show more restraint.

In December 1949 the Ministry of Transport set up a Port Emergency Planning Committee, and the Commission was invited to nominate an official to liaise with it. Mr JR Proudfoot, the Docks General Manager, was nominated.

The Committee agreed that ports should take Civil Defence measures, but the Ministry declined to issue any concrete guidelines. It was left to the Dock and Harbour Authorities Association (DHAA) to set up its own Civil Defence sub-committee, and Mr A Balfour Kinnear, the Assistant Manager, attended its first meeting in London in May 1951. The main decision taken at this meeting was that ports should set up their own Civil Defence organisation, the sub-committee being responsible for advising individual ports and co-ordinating their arrangements. (Local Authorities were answerable to the Home Office for their Civil Defence measures and received directives on the form these should take.)

It was not yet clear whether Leith Docks would set up its own separate Civil Defence organisation, or act in co-operation with Edinburgh, but it was felt that training of personnel should begin as soon as possible. Edinburgh was already holding courses, and the first of the Docks staff to be trained, Mr CD Boyle and Mr G Watt, attended one of these. In January 1952 they successfully completed the 'green certificate' course, thus qualifying as part time Civil Defence instructors. (Mr Watt later went on to qualify as a Temporary General Instructor.) In the meantime the DHAA sub-committee had agreed and circulated a blue-print for Civil Defence measures to be taken by ports, which the Leith Commission decided to follow. The Ministry of Transport made grants available for any necessary expenditure, and on 5 June 1952, the Commission's civil defence scheme was inaugurated, by the first lecture in a ten-day course for Docks employees. The lecture was given by Edinburgh's Civil Defence Officer, but the rest of the course was taken by the Docks' own recently-qualified instructors. By the beginning of September they had trained 23 Commission employees. In these early days, civil defence at Leith was organised on very much the same lines as ARP had been, during the War. The emphasis was on training in fire fighting, debris clearance, demolition and repairs. In April 1953, First Aid was added to the curriculum and by June, 95 staff had been trained.

Once Leith's own scheme was established, Mr Kinnear remained very much a part of the national Civil Defence organisation. In May 1952, he became one of the two Regional Liaison Officers in Scotland. He was responsible for east coast ports, his opposite number having the west coast under his wing. In June he was once more at a sub-committee meeting in London, helping to organise a two-day Conference to be held at Liverpool in September. In July he attended a six-day course at the Civil Defence College at Sunningdale in Berkshire. Over the next few years he was a regular attender at DHAA Civil Defence meetings in London, and at various courses held at Sunningdale and elsewhere.

In October 1953, Mr Kinnear attended an exercise in London which postulated the explosion of an atomic bomb equivalent to 20,000 tons of TNT, bursting 700 feet above the Thames. This was expected to cause severe to slight damage over a radius of two miles, with 4,000 killed or injured. The risks were escalating - and they continued to grow, until it began to be obvious that the situation in ports after an attack would be immensely more difficult to deal with than had at first been supposed. In 1954, the DHAA sub-committee submitted a memo to the Ministry of Transport suggesting that ports' Civil Defence organisations should be merged with those of local authorities, 'because of the wider area of destruction and devastation which would be created by atomic warfare'. In September 1956, Aberdeen Docks came to an arrangement with its local authority. The rest of the Scottish ports decided to do the same, and a meeting was held to formulate another memo to the Ministry of Transport. A month later, a short course was held at the Civil Defence Central Training School at Taymouth because; 'the organisation and administration of Civil Defence has changed materially in the light of the much more powerful nuclear weapons that have been developed'.

The Ministry took no action as a result of the DHAA memo, so in October 1957, Mr Kinnear was once more in London for a sub-committee meeting. Earlier in the year he had attended a course for high level officials at Sunningdale, at which new nuclear developments and their implications had been explained. These developments and their probable effects formed the main topic of discussion at the committee meeting. It was agreed that no port could now operate a viable independent Civil Defence scheme and they should all be linked with their local organisations, either directly or through membership of an Industrial Civil Defence Association. Finally, in 1958, the Leith Docks organisation was completely revised and merged with the Edinburgh Corps, industrial installations in and around the Docks estate being invited to join in the new set-up.

Royal Visits

On a happier note, the 1950s saw two Royal Visits to the Docks. The first took place on 19 August 1956, when the Queen and the Duke of Edinburgh arrived on the Royal Yacht *Britannia* at the start of a three-day visit to Edinburgh. The Docks Commissioners were notified of the visit in early May and immediately appointed a committee to deal with the necessary arrangements. It was decided that the 22-foot berth in the Western Harbour, beside Rank's flour mill, was the most suitable for *Britannia*, and arrangements were made to have it dredged. Gangways were borrowed from Menzies and Co and Rosyth Naval Base, and the Commission's launch *Figgate* was lent to the police so that they could patrol around *Britannia* while she was in harbour. Shipping was warned that there would be no access to the harbour at the time of *Britannia*'s arrival.

These aquatic arrangements were simple enough. The planning of the dry-land organisation was a different matter. A stand had to be built and suitably decorated with Shipping Company flags, bunting and flowers. Eight hundred guests were invited to fill it. Car parks were organised with the help of the AA and RAC, barriers erected to stop members of the public falling in the water, and First Aid and lavatory facilities provided. The Docks Commission offices were repainted and a lunch organised for the refreshment of Commissioners, senior Docks officials and their wives, after the ceremony. The daughter of the

Commission Chairman was chosen to present a bouquet to the Queen when she disembarked. The Guard of Honour was provided by the 7th/9th (Highlanders) Battalion of the Royal Scots, and the Bodyguard by the Leith High Constabulary. Positions had to be found for the Royal Naval Reserve, the RAF, various youth organisations and the Press.

The rehearsal on 18 August was held in pouring rain, but on The Day the sun shone and 'the ceremony presented a pleasing and colourful spectacle which will long remain in the memory of those present'. As well as a bouquet, the Queen received a presentation copy of the Leith Docks handbook and a framed photograph of Alexander Carse's painting of the landing of George IV. The Rank Organisation made a Technicolour film of the event, and Lord Rank was later presented with one of the three commemorative booklets which the Docks Commission had printed. (Of the other two, one was for the Chairman and the other was placed in the Commission's archives.) The 7th/9th Highlanders were given a copy of the film.

Two years later a scaled-down version of these arrangements was used when the Queen arrived by sea to go into residence at Holyrood in the summer of 1958. On this occasion the Lord Provost of Edinburgh was present to hand the Queen the keys of the City, as he would have done if she had arrived by train, as she usually did.

The Port of Leith stand at the Copenhagen Trade Fair in 1955.

The Pigeon Problem

Throughout the fifties the grain trade into Leith increased by leaps and bounds. The inevitable spillages made the Docks a favoured home for ever-increasing numbers of pigeons. By 1958 the birds had become such a nuisance that the Commission employed the firm of Edwards and Co of London to diminish their numbers. Two operators were at work between May and July, shooting in sheds and netting out of doors. Their final bag was 5,529 birds.

When Messrs Edwards submitted their bill for £1225 they suggested that the Commission grant them a contract to visit Leith every six months to prevent a build-up of numbers. The Commissioners decided to wait and see how the situation developed before making any final decision, in the meantime increasing efforts to minimise grain spillage.

Within eighteen months the population had again reached nuisance proportions. Leith was not the only port affected. The problem had been discussed at a recent DHAA meeting, and a variety of solutions put forward. The Commissioners felt that Avonmouth's method, of allowing one of its employees to use his airgun, was the most attractive. It must work out cheaper than Edwards' cost of 4s 5d per bird. At a meeting on 9 February 1960 it was decided to see if any Commission employee was a marksman. The work of Edwards' men had apparently been hampered by the interference of pigeon-loving members of the public. This time the police would be asked to intervene if necessary, and sanction was sought from the SSPCA. Very soon, some of the grain warehouse staff began netting pigeons in their own time for an agreed sum per corpse. An 'Allan' mechanical sweeper was ordered at a cost of £13 10s to deal with spillages.

By 13 September 1,393 birds had been trapped, but the enthusiasm of the staff was waning, and in order to maintain it, a suitable weapon was ordered for use in the sheds. A no 3 garden gun firing 9mm long shot cartridges was found to be most effective as it would not crack glass or asbestos sheeting.

Payment for shooting was increased to 1s per bird, the employee to provide the cartridges. Shooting did not destroy as many pigeons as trapping, but it was effective in preventing nesting. By October 1961, after 18 months of clearance, the total destroyed was 4,285. The problem was by no means conquered, and starlings were also beginning to be a nuisance. At this point the Commission began to consider using an ultrasonic alarm.

The Early 1960s

In 1962 the Docks Commission published the first of a new series of Handbooks, which were produced annually until the Commission was wound up in 1967. The operation of the Docks had moved on in the past decade. The updating of the cranes in particular had continued and of the eightyfive owned by the Commission, fifty were now powered by electricity, although there was still one steam crane. Six were hydraulic and thirteen worked by hand. The number of coal hoists had been reduced to a solitary appliance, although coal was still the chief export from Leith:

Principle Exports

	Tons		Tons
Flour/meal	3,307	Paper	3,810
Ale/beer/spirits	22,884	Bricks	7,413
Coal - cargo	40,823	Oil-bunker	6,904
bunker	7,094	other	93,778
Iron/steel	14,956		

Principle Imports

Flour/grain/meal	Cement
Butter/bacon/eggs	China clay
Fish - fresh/cured	Iron/steel
Fruit and vegetables	Timber
Fertilisers	Paper
Sulphur	Wood pulp
Oil	

Coal

The pre-war coal trade left the post-war docks with five coal hoists and a coal crane. The Commission's hope that 'Leith will again take its proper place among the major coal loading ports' was not, however, to be realised. The Lothian coalfield was becoming uneconomic, and the Coal Board faced competition from cheap foreign coal. Leith itself was in competition with Methil, the chief exporting harbour for the Fife coalfield. For more than a decade after the war little was done to adjust coal loading facilities. In 1950 the coaling crane at the Albert Dock was dismantled. In the following year, number 5 hoist was taken out of service rather than spend £3,500 on repairing it, but little further work was done until a sudden drop in coal exports in 1958 necessitated a thorough reorganisation.

Since 1931, coal loading (shorework) had been contracted out. In 1958 the contractors were Messrs McLachlan Mackay and Partners, who employed four gangs of six men, working shifts from early morning to late at night. In September a new company was formed, registered as McLachlan Mackay Ltd, which proposed to take over the shorework contract, with a reduced workforce. The Commission consulted the Coal Board, which held out little hope of any upturn in exports, and decided to accept the company's offer. After negotiation with the TGWU, McLachlan Macksy's workforce was reduced by six men. Three of them retired owing to ill health, one aged 73 also retired on age grounds, but a man of 70 was re-employed as a night watchman. The remaining worker, who was only 35 and had worked for just a few months, was offered a

The Outer Harbour deep-water berth, where the Royal Yacht *Britannia* berthed during her visits.

job in the Commission's construction squad. Only one Commission employee was affected by the new arrangements; the Coal Traffic Inspector, who was retired on a pension.

The eighteen shoreworkers who remained were divided into three squads of six, each headed by a foreman. Each week, two of the squads worked the morning (6.00am - 2.00pm) or the evening (2.00pm - 10.00pm) shift and one 'floating squad' worked a normal 44-hour week doing general duties, but was available to man an extra coal hoist if necessary. The shifts were rotated so that each gang became the floating squad once every three weeks. The new agreement included provision for the shoreworkers to be employed on such general duties as would not take work from existing Docks employees. These included such tasks as weeding the railway sidings, digging drains, cleaning out the turntable pits and painting the coal hoists. The facilities in the Edinburgh Dock were abandoned, and just two hoists at the Imperial Dock remained in use.

The new arrangement did not last long. By May 1959 the number of shoreworkers had dwindled to 15 men, who were re-organised into two gangs. The Commission also had reluctantly to abandon shift working for a 44-hour week with overtime as needed. By January 1960 the position had deteriorated even further, and the number of shoreworkers was reduced to one gang of eight men. Coal loading moved back to the Edinburgh Dock, but only one hoist was used, no. 3, which was refurbished at a cost of £10,000.

New Industries

Since the building of Rank's flour mill, other industries had installed themselves at the Docks by 1962. On the reclaimed area to the north of the Edinburgh Dock, Scottish Agricultural Industries had erected a fertiliser factory, Esso had a petrol depot and Tunnel Portland Cement had built a silo. Six acres had also been leased to Fisons, who intended to use it for a bagging plant. Reclamation of 50 acres had begun beside the Western Harbour in 1959, and some of the area had been leased to three haulage contractors for the building of warehousing. Eight timber merchants were now regular users of the Port. Grain imports were still increasing. The storage capacity of the Edinburgh and Imperial Docks warehouses and Rank's Caledonia Mills combined had become insufficient, and more storage was in the pipeline. Problems in grain handling were compounded by the increased size of ships, which led to delays in unloading.

The 1962 handbook listed 22 firms of ship owners and agents based in Leith, offering regular sailings to 22 North Sea ports and the Orkneys, Shetland and Lewis. There were occasional sailings to seven other destination, including Canada, the Faroes, Lisbon and Oporto.

The last Commission Handbook, that of 1967, detailed yet more developments. The industrial concerns on the north side of the Imperial Dock had been joined by Calmix Cement and Gulf Oil. A new flour mill was under construction in the Western Harbour for the Scottish Co-operative Wholesale Society and WI Brine of Edinburgh had established a timber yard there. The Commission had built an extension to their Imperial Dock warehouse which brought their total capacity up to 91,000 tons. The new SCWS flour mill would accommodate 33,000 tons, offering total grain storage at the port of 124,000 tons.

The Vanishing Rail Network

Developments to keep up with new trends went hand in hand with the abandonment of facilities which had served their purpose. One of the most noticeable of these was the gradual disappearance of the rail network in the Docks. Plans of the Port made as late as the 60s show most of the available space covered with railway sidings, and the quaysides lined with track. Nowadays all that remains are short stretches of abandoned rails and traces of the old lines in the cobbles of the roadways. Although lagging many years behind, the decline in rail provision followed the diminution in coal exports, which eventually dropped to a level which could be supplied by road transport. The process began when the coal crane at the Albert Dock was dismantled in 1950 and its associated railway track was lifted. In 1952, North Leith goods station (ex Caledonian) was closed. As the coal hoists were abandoned in 1959/60 their wagon rails also went out of use. In 1965 the dry docks in the West Old dock were filled in, in advance of the filling of the Dock itself. (The infilling of the Old Docks was completed in 1968) At the same time the railway line from the Citadel station was abandoned, along with the rails on the south and west sides of the Dock whose advent had been such an advance a century earlier. In the following year British Rail gave up its rails in Tower Street and up the Shore. At the same time, the Commission were contemplating replacing the coal hoist, which was now very old, and the Chief Engineer reported that BR could not keep up with its 300-tons-per hour capacity. The Commission decided to investigate the possibility of bringing in coal by lorry. In 1967, all track, apart from one line, had disappeared from the Western Harbour, and BR applied for permission to use its ground at Salamander St, at the other end of the Docks, for purposes other than rail traffic.

Improvements

In 1964, the conversion of the Docks to a deep water port had been approved, and in 1967 work was well under way on the construction of a new entrance lock which would ensure an adequate depth of water at all states of the tide. The lock was being built within a coffer dam, and the first stage of the work had been to dredge a channel around the site of the dam so that shipping could continue to get in and out of the port. The bringing of special plant for the dredging work from Holland was held up by bad weather, and although a start was made with local equipment, the dredging was not in full swing until the spring of 1965. In early summer the contractors, Edmund Nuttall and Sons and Co of London, were able to begin work on the dam.

The entrance to the Imperial Dock, where the big grain ships were berthed, was being deepened and widened. The news that the Clyde Navigation Trust

The Macvan container terminal in 1983.

was extending its grain storage, galvanised the Commission into similar plans. A new grain-intake tower was constructed at no 6 berth, with an associated discharge plant. The need for an extra 20,000 tons of grain storage was also met by the extension of the Imperial Grain Warehouse in 1968.

Containers

The demolition of the last relic of a vanished age, the steam crane, coincided with the beginning of a revolution in merchant shipping - Containerisation.

> *From the 1967 Handbook* - Leith, like other ports, has not been slow to face up to this new problem, and already plans are finalised to establish container facilities within the port. New equipment will be installed within the next three months, and a first service between Leith and Rotterdam introduced. Other services will follow.

Containers had first been seen in Britain before the First World War, when early versions were carried on the railways and ferried to Ireland. In 1933 the International Container Bureau was set up in Paris to promote their use, and after the Second World War, British railways provided a lift-van service to the Northern Continent. It was, however, the Americans who were in the forefront of post-war developments and supplies to the US forces during the Korean War (1950-53) were carried in 'Dravo-boxes'. In 1956 the Sea-Land company were the first to load truck trailer bodies on the deck of a modified tanker. Improvements to ship conversions followed, which allowed containers to be stacked in the hold as well as on deck, and in 1964 the world's first purpose-built, fully cellular container ship came into service, sailing weekly between Fremantle and Melbourne.

In September 1965, the Overseas Containers Limited (OCL) international consortium was launched. Competition from America was not the only concern of shipowners at the time. Dock labour, especially in the UK, Australia and the USA was becoming increasingly expensive and, from the point of view of shipowners, unreliable. Pilferage from easily-broached packaging was a world-wide problem.

In 1966 Sea-Land came to the Forth, when it began a transatlantic service calling at Rotterdam, Bremen and Grangemouth. The containers were unloaded by the ship's own gear and distributed inland by Sea-Land's own road transport. Shipping lines based at Leith did not, at first, feel threatened by this new development, as they were not directly involved in the transatlantic trade. A more important factor was the existence of OCL, and in January 1966, a rival consortium was set up; Associated Container Transportation Ltd (ACT). All the major deep-sea lines which had not been included in OCL were represented in this new concern. One such company was Ben Line of Leith, which took delivery of its first container ship, *Bencruachan*, in 1968.

The year 1966 also saw the start of work on the Docks' own container facilities, following numerous enquiries by shipping companies. The 22 foot berth at the Western Harbour was deepened and extended in order to make it suitable for large deep sea container traffic. At the same time, the Gibson shipping line decided to establish its own short-sea container terminal at Leith in conjunction with Scheepvaart en Steenkolen Maats of Rotterdam, under the name of Macvan. The Commission agreed to establish Gibsons' terminal on the north side of the Albert Dock, where the 96-year-old heavy-lift steam crane, which Gibsons still used, was removed to make way for a a 20-ton Derrick Crane to handle the containers. This was to be a temporary measure while further preparations were made for the erection of an Anderson Clyde 'Giant Colossus' gantry-type crane, which would work to both ship and vehicle. The 'Giant Colossus' finally came into use in January 1969.

The End of the Dock Commission

The new entrance lock was officially opened on 28 May 1969 by HRH Prince Philip, Duke of Edinburgh. In the years between its inception and completion, great changes had taken place at Leith, which culminated in the winding up of the Docks Commission at the end of 1967.

Early in 1961, the Labour Government had set up a committee under the chairmanship of Lord Rochdale to enquire into the future of the major UK ports. In August, members of the committee visited Leith in the course of their investigation into the running of ports nationwide. At the end of 1962 the Rochdale Committee recommended the setting up of a National Ports Authority, within which local ports would maintain their autonomy, with a right of appeal to the Ministry of Transport. The DHAA favoured the setting up of an Advisory Council instead, but Leith Docks Commission supported the Rochdale scheme, as the lack of a central government body with a knowledge of ports and harbours had hindered its own negotiations with the Ministry of Transport over the major improvements it wanted to make at the Port. The Commissioners especially welcomed the Rochdale recommendation that an estuarial authority should be set up in the Firth of Forth. It was felt that such a body would eliminate existing anomalies.

The National Ports Council was set up in the autumn of 1963, and almost immediately negotiations began to set up a Trust to administer the ports of the Firth of Forth as a group. In March 1965 the Commissioners approved a draft scheme for a Forth Ports Authority. In the autumn of that year a meeting was held of representatives of the ports which would be affected and the National Ports Council considered the comments which the Commissioners had submitted in relation to the draft plan. In February the scheme was sent to the Ministry of Transport for approval, and by the end of the summer, having been delayed by a General Election, approval was granted. In April 1967 a committee of the Commission was set up to deal with any problems which might arise in the course of setting up the Forth Ports Authority. A banquet was arranged, to take place at the Merchants Hall in Edinburgh on 18 December, to mark the termination of the Dock Commission after 130 years. The final meeting of the Commission was held on 24 November 1967, in order to ratify the election of Commission members which had to be held as a statutory obligation. All the existing members were solemnly returned to office and a Winding-up committee appointed, then; '....the Chairman (Mr A Dick Wood) stated that, apart from the duties to be carried out by the Winding-up Committee till 31st December, this meeting terminated the work of the Leith Dock Commission. He thanked the Press for their interest throughout the years and the Commissioners for their support to him and to his predecessors.'

The Forth Harbour Reorganisation Scheme became law on 6 December, and the Board of Directors of the Forth Ports Authority met for the first time nine days later. The Board had been appointed by the Ministry of Transport from the nominees of:

The National Ports Council
The Chamber of Shipping of the United Kingdom
The Firth of Forth Shipowners Association
The British Shippers' Council
The Forth Ports Estuary Committee
Edinburgh Corporation
Buckhaven, Methil, Burntisland and Kirkcaldy Town Councils
Representatives of the Organised Labour
Two Principal Officers of the Authority Management Group

The Winding-up Committee of the Dock Commission, consisting of the Chairman, Mr Fergus Harris, Mr Mcgill, Mr Crichton, Mr Angus, and Mr Weatherstone, met on 21 December. They discussed several routine matters to do with premises and staff. The Treasurer reported on the accounts paid and submitted up to 22 December, eight certificates were signed for instalments of payments on contracts, and rates were increased by 12½%. The last item on the agenda concerned the disposal of some of the Commission's silverware; 'In accordance with the previous decision of the Board, it was agreed that the Chairman's Chain of Office, the Mace and Rose Bowl would remain within the Dock Offices during the lifetime of the Forth Ports Authority.'

From 1 January 1968, the new Authority began administration of the ports of Alloa, Bo'ness, Burntisland, Grangemouth, Granton, Kirkcaldy, Leith and Methil as a single unit.

Dock Labour

The other change which had been taking place during the Forth Ports reorganisation was an alteration to the conditions under which dock labourers were employed. Since shortly after World War Two, their employment had been administered by the National Dock Labour Board which was set up in 1947 under the Dock Workers (Regulation of Employment) Act, to replace the National Dock Labour Corporation. Under the Act, both employers and workers had to register with the NDLB, which employed staff at Leith to collect money from the employers, which was then paid out in wages and benefits. The Board also maintained a medical centre at the Docks, and contributed towards the running of the canteen in Tower St until it closed in 1954. The passing of the Docks and Harbours Bill in 1966 decasualised dock labour, and charged the NDLB with the administration of a welfare and amenities scheme for all ports. Labour could now only be employed by licencees, and the Commissioners (who were the licensing authority for Leith) had to deal with applications for licences from a number of concerns. The stevedoring in the port was confined to two firms, Forth Stevedores (Leith) Ltd, and Leslie and Saddler Ltd, causing many redundancies among port workers. After much negotiation these two firms were granted licences, and the porters, metters, and coal trimmers were distributed amongst them. When all the arrangements were complete, Leslie and Saddler had 266 men, Forth Stevedores had 281. Apart from the employees of the Commission itself - mainly office staff and departmental heads - these 547 men comprised the entire stevedoring workforce at the Docks.

North Sea Oil

The new Forth Ports Authority was organised into three groups, covering Grangemouth and Alloa (which was closed in 1979); Burntisland, Methil and Kirkcaldy; Leith, Newhaven and Granton. Its formation almost coincided with the advent of a new source of income at Leith - pipes to carry North Sea oil and gas.

Before steel pipes can be laid under sea or land, they have to be coated with a material that will resist corrosion. This material may be fusion bonded epoxy, enamel or iron ore concrete. The firm of Bredero-Price had established a pipe coating plant at the Imperial Dock in 1972. In 1974 it doubled its capacity, and a new 10-ton grab crane was installed on the north side of the Dock to handle iron ore imported for the coating process. In 1978 British Pipe Coaters Ltd was formed by a joint venture between Bredero-Price and British Gas, with the latter holding 51% of the shares in the new company. In the following year a pipe welding bay was constructed by the firm of Santa Fe UK Ltd, on reclaimed land in the Western Harbour for their new pipe spooling vessel *Apache*. Once the piping (which may be up to 16 inches in diameter) is welded, it is wound onto an 80 foot diameter drum on the main deck of the ship. The pipe is then laid at sea by an unwinding process through a straightening plant built close to the stern.

The pipes coated at Leith which are destined for undersea use are coated with a concrete mixture, which increases their weight and helps to stabilise them on the sea bed. The pipes which are manufactured in Britain arrive at the plant by road or rail. Large shipments also arrive by sea from Germany, France, Italy and Japan. Iron ore for the concrete is brought mainly from Scandinavia, although Greek ore is sometimes used. British Pipe Coaters also treated much

The Apache pipe-spooling vessel in Leith docks.

of the piping for the UK natural gas network. By 1989, the firm had facilities in six continents and had coated over 90% of the North Sea pipelines and 3,500 miles of transmission and product lines for mainland Britain.

In recent years, a further joint venture has been established under the title of British Norwegian Coaters to coat pipes destined for the Norwegian sector of the North Sea. A third market has recently opened up in the provision of thermally insulated pipes for flow lines and link lines to marginal and satellite fields in the North Sea. The parent company has now established coating plants all over the world, including mainland China and Siberia. On 1 March 1993, ownership passed to Dresser Industries Inc, but the partnership agreements still operate. A major reconstruction of the plant in Leith has recently been carried out in preparation for the future in what has become a very competitive industry.

Outwith Leith, Forth Ports are involved in the oil industry at the Grangemouth refinery, the Hound Point tanker terminal for the export of crude oil and in the Braefoot Bay terminal for the shipment of LPG and ethylene gas from the Mossmorran petrochemical plant.

Although the oil industry had a major impact on the life of the port, traditional commodities continued to be equally important. Grain figures continued to rise, but owing to improvements in equipment, in 1981 facilities were concentrated at the Imperial Dock and the installation at the Edinburgh Dock was closed down and later demolished. The three suction discharge towers at the Imperial Dock could each handle 220 tonnes per hour. Improvements were made in the grain silos to reduce the risk of a dust explosion, and a dust-free weigher was installed over the lorry loading bay at the rear of the Warehouse in 1981.

Trade

Total tonnage handled each year continued to fluctuate as usual, although the underlying trend was upwards. In 1981 the port handled 2.2 million tonnes, the first time the figure had topped the 2 million mark since 1940. The main reason for this encouraging figure was an upsurge in coal exports. Coal tonnage had been increasing: 1974 - 31,000 tonnes, 1979 - 393,000 tonnes 1980 - 103,000 tonnes (the decrease was due to a falling off of trade at the end of the year) In 1981 the figure was 500,000 tonnes, the increase being due to the Solidarity strike which began with the dock workers in Gdansk (Danzig) in Poland. The strike put a stop to coal exports, and the NCB began exporting quantities of coal to Poland's former customers. The coal from Leith went mainly to Denmark. This upturn at Leith was all the more welcome, as in 1980 Forth Ports had begun to lay off workers because of the economic recession which began at that time. In the same year grain imports at Leith dropped, as the recession hit the Scottish whisky industry.

In the following year coal exports from Leith took a downturn, but barley exports increased. Most of the grain was malting barley, bound for the Continent, but some feed barley went to Poland. Leith is a 'designated intervention port', and 80,000 tons of the barley exported in 1982 went to swell the EEC grain mountain. The rise in grain exports may also have been partly due to the £500,000 publicity campaign launched by the Scotch Whisky Association. So important did barley exports become that in 1983, work started on demolition of redundant sheds to improve facilities at the Harbour, to be used primarily by grain ships of up to 20,000dwt. The work was completed by the following year, and two mobile conveyors, each with a capacity of 600 tonnes per hour, were installed on the quay.

Two years later, work started on the modernisation of the south side of the Imperial Dock, 'to create the best deep water berths available within the Forth'. All original cranes and transit sheds were replaced. In 1986, no 1 transit shed with the quay and storage areas was opened by Lord Brabazon of Tara, Parliamentary Under-Secretary of State for Transport. Four cranes were transferred to the quay, with an additional 10 tonne general cargo/grab crane, purchased second hand to further improve the facilities.

Coal exports had recovered in the meantime, bringing the total tonnage for the 1983 to 2.08 million. By 1985, the grain market had also improved. This factor, together with yet another rise in coal shipments, once more brought the total tonnage over the 2 million mark, where it stayed for a further year. At this time, all coal for export was still brought to the docks by rail, to a fully automatic loading installation on the north side of the Edinburgh Dock, which is rated at 3,000 tons per hour.

The underlying trend of increasing tonnage has continued through the 1980s and 90s with most recent peak being in 1990 when over 3 million tonnes were handled, the highest figure for over 50 years.

In the past the principal commodities handled were coal and grain and although these still remain significant, particularly grain, the pattern of trade has changed. Nowadays the largest tonnages comprise steel pipes, iron ore, cement, petroleum products, sewage sludge, grain, animal feeds with others such as coal, potatoes, salt, fruit and timber, being less significant than previously. One significant recent newcomer is the importation of cars, particularly Fords, from Ghent.

No doubt the changes in the USSR and the re-emergence of the Eastern European countries will see an increase in traffic between Leith and some of its traditional trading partners such as the Baltic States.

More Improvements

Since the nineteenth century, Leith has been a major importer of chemicals. Until recently one of its main clients was Scottish Agricultural Industries, which established a plant to the north of the Imperial Dock in 1959. In 1980 a totally enclosed, Swedish-made Siwertell archimedean screw unloader was erected on the north side of the Imperial Dock, for the dust free discharge of sulphur, phosphate and potash for SAI. The installation was the only one of its kind in the UK, and consists of a series of screw conveyors on a flexible elbow joint, which can get into all the corners of a ship's hold to unload bulk materials. Problems arose with the discharge of sulphur, and a number of modifications were carried out, including the fitting of explosion doors, before this commodity could be safely handled. The unloader was in use for 12 years, until the SAI plant was closed down in 1992 and then was modified for the discharge of cement to a new shed built to meet all of the environmental standards required in the handling of dust-laden material.

Periodically alterations have been made at dock installations to accommodate new developments in shipping. A quay at the Albert Dock was altered in 1979, to accommodate the P&O Ro/Ro ferry which sailed weekly to Sullom Voe in Shetland. Improvements continued at the container terminal. In 1979 the road at the Albert Dock was diverted to allow the terminal to be enlarged. The following year, a telescopic spreader beam was purchased and the concrete compound extended. Work on extending the area available for containers, as well as timber and other goods, was still going on in 1982. The main user of the terminal was Macvan, who were operating a 2,500dwt vessel to Rotterdam every four days in 1982. The following year this was increased to twice a week.

In the period since 1985 a major investment programme has been undertaken at Leith to ensure its progression through the last decade of the 20th century and into the 21st century as one of Scotland's premier ports. The programme got underway with the planning of a modern workshop building for maintenance staff who for years past had worked at various locations dotted around the dock estate. The building was finished in 1987, and contained areas for different sections of the maintenance work, central computerised stores, a comfortable staff room, showers and a changing room.

The port manager and his staff had been accommodated in a series of Portacabins near the Forth Ports Headquarters building, which were becoming dilapidated. The handsome nineteenth century hydraulic station and pumping house beside the Prince of Wales Dry Dock had been redundant since the Albert Dock swing bridge was converted to electricity. However, as a listed building it could not be demolished, so it was extended and rebuilt internally to provide an attractive new office building. Adjacent to the office a new medical centre, shower and changing facilities, and a staff room were built for the labour force. The official opening was performed on 10 May 1990 by the Right Honorable Cecil Parkinson MP, the Secretary of State for Transport.

The programme continued with the building of multi-purpose sheds for timber, grain, animal feed and other bulk products which has resulted in new shed facilities in excess of 15,000 square metres. In addition hard standing of approximately 7 acres has been created to complement the new shed facilities. Further new facilities for cruise liners have been constructed at the Western Harbour giving 240 metres of additional quay together with a secure surfaced back up area. A new tug base has been developed at the lock entrance which then enabled a 300,000 square foot office development to take place overlooking Victoria Dock.

In addition there has been considerable investment in new equipment with three new high capacity grabbing/general cargo cranes on the north side of Imperial Dock, new forklift trucks and bulk loaders and various other types of modern cargo handling equipment. This programme is ongoing and at the end of 1993 the capital investment programme for 1994 was higher than ever at around £4 million.

These investments will ensure that Leith's glories of the past will be matched with an equally successful future.

Land for a new Bernard Street relief road has been set aside with the result that approximately 5% of the dock area incorporating the original enclosed docks has become available for property development. It is in this area that the new 300,000 square foot office is being built and any revenue arising from such developments will assist in funding the dock investment programme.

Manpower Reductions

As a result of increasing containerisation and automation of dock equipment, the staffing strength at Leith had been reduced over the years to a fraction of its original size. In 1973 there was a total of almost 600 staff including dockworkers, operations and maintenance men with 44 administrative, technical and 'miscellaneous'. Throughout the seventies, the numbers remained relatively stable, but the eighties saw a steady reduction. Some of this was a result of natural wastage, but in 1980, the recession started to bite, and registered dock workers began to be made redundant. Between 1980 and 1989, the total number of Forth Ports workers fell by nearly 40%, from 1,314 to 776. The figure first fell below the 1,000 mark in 1984, a year when the miners' strike overshadowed the fact that there were also two dock strikes. In his report that year, the Forth Ports chairman echoed the sentiments of many employers when he commented:

> It is a sad fact that the traditions and working practices of the port industry make it difficult to respond positively to changes and new opportunities. If we are to prosper in the future it is important that all levels throughout the Organisation recognise the need to put behind us outmoded management techniques and restrictive labour practices.

In 1989 the Government abolished the National Dock Labour Scheme, which, in its various guises had protected the pay, employment terms and conditions of dock labourers since 1940. Once again, the Chairman commented on the situation in his report:

> After abolition the former Registered Dock Workers came under the same employment legislation as all the other employees of the Authority, apart from special severance terms. The severance terms provided for compensation of up to £35,000 for the first 18 months after abolition and up to £20,000 for the second 18 months, funded jointly by the Authority and the Government.

The abolition brought about a National Dock Strike which was supported by Registered Dock Workers in all the Authority's ports. At this time, the Authority introduced standard terms and conditions for all its employees which were given to the former Registered Dock Workers on their return to work. In addition, a flexible, interchangeable and mobile labour force was created to enable the Authority to provide a more efficient and cost-effective service to the customer.

At Leith, all the Registered Dock Workers, whose average age was 55, were made redundant over a period of six months. Among the men who walked out of the dock gates for the last time were the remaining three Metters. With them went nearly four and a half centuries of history, the port's last living link with its Medieval past. It should, however, be recorded that it was the historical interest of one of the Metters, Mr Bob Shepherd, which set in motion the sequence of events that culminated in the writing of this book.

The Decline of Rail Transport

Another link with the more recent past which has virtually disappeared from the Docks is the railways. In 1987 the BR freight yard at the eastern end of the Docks estate was handling pipes, fertiliser, chemicals, grain, coal and oil for industries in the docks, as well as goods for other outlets. In that year, Storage Services (Leith) Ltd, which are based at the Western Harbour, opened a distribution centre at the marshalling yard in order to get more of its traffic onto rail. Most goods destined for dock installations arrived at the depot by rail and were then loaded onto lorries for distribution to their various destinations, but chemicals and similar goods were still brought in by railway wagon, over the track which remained around Imperial Dock. The closure of SAI in 1992 meant that most of the significant rail traffic into the docks ceased. At the present day the port remains rail connected and is used intermittently for coal and oil products.

Privatisation

In 1992 Leith Docks as a part of Forth Ports PLC was privatised by means of a flotation on the Stock Exchange. The existing management remained and the programme of investment and the development of Leith as a modern, efficient port has continued. Leith itself, after suffering a long period of decline, is undergoing a revitalisation. One of the visible signs of the new trend is the growth of private housing accommodation, notably the Kings Landing waterside development. Upstream on the Water of Leith, the Cooperage, a nineteenth century industrial building which stands next to the site of John Sime's dry dock has been converted into appartments. Likewise, the Docks estate is undergoing a change of face, as its land assets to the south of the new Bernard Street Relief Road are realised. In October 1993 work began on the first project, a large new building to house the Scottish Office, on the south side of the Victoria Dock.

Leith has come a long way since David 1 established his first haven at the Coalhill over eight and a half centuries ago. Since his time the seaward spread of the harbour which he began has added hundreds of acres to the extent of the town. The little settlement of 1128 could have been engulfed in even the smallest of the 19th century docks. The largest of the vessels which lay in its haven would easily disappear into a hold of one of the modern ships of today which tie up in the Imperial Dock. The differences are obvious. And yet, what is even more striking is the continuity.

Ships arrive at Leith now from countries which were completely unknown to Europeans in the twelfth century, but they also come from ports which have known Leith ships for centuries; Danzig, Hamburgh, Copenhagen, Rotterdam. John Pettendriech, the thirteenth century skipper of the *Thomas*, would not recognise Leith, but he would instantly know where he was by the triple landmarks of the Castle Rock, the Calton Hill and Arthur's Seat. The navigational hazards which James V's sixteenth century pilot had learned to recognise in the Forth are still there, although now they are marked by buoys and lights. A seventeenth century master might have difficulty in finding his Fraternity House and he might not recognise it when he saw it, but he would know St Mary's church just opposite, and if he had fallen on hard times the House could still help him out. John Sime would know his dry dock, and Robert Menzies would be able to point out 'Menzies Corner'.

The Docks today are deceptively quiet. Technology has replaced muscle power and tons of goods are handled at the touch of a switch. Computers have replaced cohorts of ledger-filling clerks. Huge lorries carry loads which would once have filled a hundred carts.

What the future holds, no-one can tell. The only certainty is that Leith will continue to change to meet whatever developments lie ahead, just as she has in the past.

Appendix I

Leith Shipowners and Shipbuilders in the Nineteenth and Twentieth Centuries

by

Captain John Landels

It would be vain to attempt to trace the history of the many Leith Shipowners over the entire period covered by this book, but the numbers involved calls for recognition as they form an integral part of the development and operation of the Port. In the following pages will be found short histories of some of the main shipowning companies whose headquarters were in Leith or Edinburgh, arranged in date order of their foundation. The period covered is mainly that from the advent of steam navigation up to the present day. Some of the older Companies originated in the eighteenth century at the same time as the sailing smack Companies, which have been chronicled in Chapter 14. Some are well-known names, while others may be long forgotten. Some of the smaller and older Companies have been omitted as their records are lost or are too limited to form a coherent narrative.

Gothland, built by Henry Robb in 1932 for Leith, Hull & Hamburg Steam Packet Company.

Many other shipping lines based elsewhere also played a very important role in the port's operations. Names such as *Dundee, Perth and London Shipping Co Ltd, Coast Lines Ltd, North of Scotland, Orkney and Shetland Shipping Co Ltd, Furness Withy and Co Ltd, Antrim Iron Ore Co Ltd, General Steam Navigation Co Ltd* were but a few of the many regular callers into Leith over the years. Nor must we forget the numerous Northern European shipping companies who operated regular services to Leith.

London and Edinburgh Shipping Co Ltd: 1809-1959

The London and Edinburgh Shipping Company was formed in 1809 by a number of the leading merchants in Edinburgh and Leith for the purpose of establishing a regular and superior means of communication for passengers and goods. Previous to its formation the trade with London was chiefly carried via Berwick upon Tweed - goods

Matchless, an Aberdeen clipper built by Alexander Hall in 1846 to trade between Leith and Lerwick. Sailing vessels competed with steam on this route until 1882.

and passengers being conveyed by land between Berwick and Edinburgh, Glasgow and other places.

In 1803 the Union Company, which had for over fifty years traded through Berwick, move to Leith and in 1809 was absorbed by the new Company. The vessels first used were the famous Leith smacks. These smacks were later converted to schooners, which were quickly superseded by the celebrated Aberdeen clippers, until the advancing power of steam finally took over in the middle of the nineteenth century. L&ESC ordered their first steamer in 1852, the iron screw vessel *Prompt*, completed by Barclay & Curle of Glasgow the following year, and with her arrival the day of the clippers were numbered. So rapid was the change that the Company's last clipper was sold in 1857.

No clearly defined form of nomenclature was used, but names such as *Fiona, Fingal, Royal Scot* and *Royal Archer* are well remembered. Both World Wars took heavy toll and by 1941 the fleet had been wiped out, although in the same year the interests of AF Henry & MacGregor Ltd of Leith had been acquired.

The passenger service was never resumed but three cargo vessels were bought and given names with the prefix *Bel*. These vessels re-opened the London route in 1946 but competition was fierce and as the volume of trade declined these vessels were sold off, until in 1958 the *Belvina* went to the breakers' yard. The shipping interest continued in a subsidiary company, London Scottish Lines, for another year before their ships were also sold, and the doors of the London and Edinburgh Shipping Company Ltd closed on 150 years of shipping.

George Gibson and Co: 1820 - 1972

George Gibson, who had started in business as an Agent and Shipbroker in 1797, became manager of the Leith Hamburgh and Rotterdam Shipping Co in 1816. He became a shipowner in his own right four years later, when he acquired the galliot *Isabella*. The

Meteor, built by J. & G. Thomson of Glasgow in 1887 for the London & Edinburgh Shipping Company.

LHRS Company was dissolved in 1844, but George Gibson, joined by his son Mungo, continued in business, using mainly schooners until 1850, when they ordered their first steamer. The new vessel was named *Balmoral* after one of the royal residences, a trend which was to continue over the next two decades. As competition increased on the North Sea and Far East trades, working arrangements were entered into with other Companies. One such arrangement, with James Rankine, a Glasgow shipowner, was to result in a merger in 1920, into the Gibson Rankine line, a name which was to become well known in Northern European waters.

The Company's system of using royal residences as a form of nomenclature changed in 1870 when the name *Abbotsford* was introduced. Sir Walter Scott's novels provided many of the names used thereafter, some on numerous occasions.

The years of the First World War saw many changes and the Gibson connection ceased when Mungo Campbell Gibson was killed in the Dardanelles. Control of the Company passed to the Somerville family, but the name George Gibson and Co was retained.

Containerisation in the 1960s resulted in surplus tonnage, and a move was made into the transporting of liquified gas products. Some of the dry cargo ships were converted for this purpose, with the *Quentin* being the first to take up this new role. When the *Lanrick* was withdrawn from service in July 1969 for conversion, the cargo era of the Company was closed, with all future sailings being maintained by chartered tonnage.

Eventually the Company was taken over in 1972 by the Anchor Line Ltd, Glasgow. Again the name of George Gibson and Co was retained, to manage and operate the gas tanker fleet still using such names as *Traquair* and *Teviot,* from those of Scott's writings which were set in the Borders of Scotland.

Currie Line: 1836 - 1969

In 1836 a small wooden paddle steamer named *Pegasus* commenced trading between Leith and Hull. This new venture, the Hull and Leith Steam Packet Co, developed

Edina. This iron screw steamer was built by Barclay Carle of Glasgow in 1854 for the Leith, Hull & Hamburg Steam Packet Company.

steadily and other small vessels were added to the fleet. In 1852 the Company changed its name to Leith Hull and Hamburgh Steam Packet Co, to reflect the expansion in their trading area.

James Currie joined the Company in 1862, and immediately set about a rapid expansion of the fleet, with the intention of opening up further new trade routes. His brother Donald, of Castle Line fame, often chartered vessels from the LHHSP Co to supplement the mail steamers to South Africa. In the meantime, coastal trade between Leith, Newcastle and Hull was increasing, as was trade to Hamburg and the Baltic. The brothers operated a joint service from 1877, with their Liverpool and Hamburg Line, and it was on these ships that the suffix *Land* came into regular use for naming purposes. Many of the other ships were named after prominent cities, rivers and regions of Central Europe. The coastal ships used names such as *Britannia* and *Edina.* The name *Britannia* was used on no fewer than six occasions during the lifetime of the Company.

So successful did the LHHSP Co become, that in 1890 it contributed no less than 15% of the year's tonnage dues, 21% of goods dues and a corresponding amount in Dry Dock and other charges to the income of the Leith Dock Commission.

At the beginning of the First World War the fleet numbered 37 ships. Three of these were seized by the Germans at the outbreak of war, and five more were caught up in the Baltic. Losses were heavy, and by the time the war ended in 1918, only 17 vessels remained.

In 1919 the Liverpool and Hamburg Line was absorbed into the fleet. From that time onwards the suffix 'Land' was used almost exclusively by the LHHSP Co. The business of M Isaacs and Son of London was acquired in 1933, bringing about a further expansion in trade down the Portuguese coast and into the Western and Central Mediterranean ports. More vessels were either purchase second hand or built, and by 1939 a total of 27 vessels were operating on the various trade routes. Once more war took a heavy toll, with the fleet almost halved by 1945.

During the conflict, in 1940, the company name was changed to Currie Line Ltd. Recovery after the war was slow. The Mediterranean trade gained in importance, but the Baltic traffic was never to return to its previous heights. In 1957, Currie Line entered the bulk traffic trade with a ship named *Roland*. Other bulk carriers followed. Containerisation in the 1960s resulted in further reductions in the conventional fleet, and in 1969 Currie Line was acquired by the Runciman Group and came under the wing of Anchor Line Ltd. Another Leith shipping company had disappeared, although the name still continues as that of a firm of Agents and Forwarders.

Ben Line: 1839 - 1993

William and Alexander Thomson acquired their first ship in 1839, when the wooden barque *Carrara* was built to carry Italian marble from Leghorn to Leith. When Alexander withdrew from the business in 1847, William set up the style 'William Thomson and Co', which was to continue as the managing company until the end of the shipowning interests in 1993.

The trading interests of the new Company widened rapidly and more sailing ships were either bought or built before the first steamship arrived in 1871. The prefix *Ben*, which was to become synonymous with the company, first appeared in 1853 in naming a new barque *Bencleuch*, but the practice of naming ships after Scottish mountains did not become general until near the end of the century. The Baltic trade which had been built up over the years, continued to use names from the locality, but the First World War virtually ended the Company's interest in the area. A reorganisation at the end of hostilities became necessary, and in 1919 'The Ben Line Steamers Ltd (William Thomson and Co Managers)' was formed to merge the many interests into one company.

Fifteen ships were lost during the Second World War, but the Company continued to flourish. Although the head office remained in Edinburgh, the centre of operations for the Far East trade was in London, and the ships made only occasional visits to their home port. Containerisation resulted in a reduction in the fleet numbers, but the Ben Line remained one of the leading shipping companies in Britain until a decision was made to withdraw from shipping, early in 1993.

James Cormack and Co: 1872 - 1936

James Cormack, a former Leith shipping clerk, realised the vast opportunities that existed in the Baltic trades and became a shipowner in 1872, when he purchased the small two-year-old steamer *Ella*. He concentrated his activities in the Eastern Baltic, around the Latvian port of Riga, and as business increased, acquired new and second-hand tonnage, building up to seven ships by 1900. The vessels were mainly employed carrying manufactured goods and coal from eastern Scottish ports to Riga, Libau and Windau. In return large quantities of timber were shipped to Scotland, where demand far exceeded the home supply.

The First World War caused serious disruptions to the Baltic operations, and ships were switched to alternative trades. Nine vessels were lost between September 1916 and the end of the war in November 1918. Undaunted, Cormacks started to replace the losses with the purchase of an ex-German steamer in 1920, renamed *Arniston*. This form of nomenclature, using the names of districts around Edinburgh with the suffix *ton* was continued for the remainder of the Company's existence.

James Cormack died in 1922, followed closely by his two sons in 1929 and 1934. This left his grandson Alistair, only 24 years old, to run the business. Trading difficulties in the 1930s, and shortage of finance, took its toll, and the blue, white and black funnel was seen for the last time in early 1936, when the Cormack houseflag was finally lowered.

John Warrack and Co: 1874 - 1919

John Warrack started in business in 1845 as a Shipbroker and Agent, and soon became known for his ability in dealing with Marine Insurance and Average. In March 1863 he purchased a share in a small wooden snow named *Lady Alicia*. This was not his first venture into shipping as he had been involved with his brother James in Montrose before moving to Leith, where he saw the advantages of a developing port.

Warrack was quick to seize on opportunity, and ordered his first steamer in 1864. The *Argyll* was launched from the yard of Barclay Curle and Co of Glasgow in August of that year, closely followed by the *Moray*. These names were to set the style of nomenclature for the rest of the Company's period of existence.

The *Lady Alicia* had been dispatched to the Australian coast and a new schooner *Glenesk* was trading to the Baltic. Construction of the Suez Canal was under way and Warrack could see the benefits for the future trade, so a trade route to Egypt was set up with the new steamers. As the Canal neared completion further new ships, suitable for the passage were ordered from a number of Glasgow shipbuilders. Trade routes to the Far East were opened up after the *Breadalbane* made her first canal transit in January 1870.

On 3 July 1907 John Warrack died, leaving his son John and nephew James Howard Warrack as his successors. John's interests tended to be elsewhere, and the business was left to be run by James. No more ships were added to the fleet until *Lovat* was delivered by Russell and Co, Port Glasgow in 1911. The older ships were becoming too small for the trade, but the new vessel, at over 6000 grt was much better suited. Unfortunately she was sunk by the armed merchant cruiser *Emden* on 10 September 1914, causing further problems for the Company. As was the case with many other shipowners, the First World War took a heavy toll. The last ship was sold on 24 June 1919, so after a span of fourtyfive years, these vessels bearing the names of many beautiful parts of Scotland disappeared from the seas.

Christian Salvesen: 1879 - 1989

Christian Salvesen had been involved as a shareholder in a number of marine enterprises before acquiring his first ship in 1879. The *Marna* was purchased while under construction at the yard of Austin and Hunter in Sunderland, after the Company who had ordered her was unable to raise the money. The early ships in the Salvesen fleet were mainly employed on the Mediterranean and other Deep Sea trades, but in 1886 a service between Norway and Scotland was inaugurated. This was to be so successful that it continued until 1971.

The Salvesen organisation which was to become synonymous with whaling took a major step in 1907 when an expedition was sent to Antarctica. Indications there were so good that a whaling station was set up in South Georgia in 1909 and given the name 'Leith Harbour'. Vessels were purchased and converted or built to meet the requirements of the trade, which continued until 1963, when Salvesens finally withdrew. Over the fifty-six years in this particular trade, the Company owned and operated over 150 vessels which were directly involved with some aspect of whaling. Many were easily recognised by their names. Perhaps the best example of all was the Company's last factory ship *Southern Harvester*, whose name typified the Company style and whose crews were drawn from the length and breadth of the United Kingdom, as well as from Scandinavia.

After the Second World War, Salvesens entered the coasting trade, and in 1963 acquired the well known Leith company of AF Henry and MacGregor Ltd. The fleet of coastal bulk carriers were employed mainly in the carriage of coal, grain, stone and cement. This business continued until the shipping interests finally ended in 1989.

Throughout their shipping life, Salvesens were involved in almost all aspects of shipping; whalers, tankers, cargo liners, bulk carriers, coasters, trawlers and oil-related vessels. The red, white and blue funnel - which had originally been red, white and black and too similar to the German flag - was known world-wide. The ships' names were varied, but many ended in the letter *a* or started with the prefix *Sal*, while the whaling fleet as already mentioned, used the word *Southern*. It is unfortunate that the Company no longer has a shipping interest, but the name of Salvesen continues in many other enterprises controlled from the Head Office in Edinburgh.

Richard Mackie and Co: 1882 - 1923

Richard Mackie was already a successful businessman when in 1882 he founded the firm of Richard Mackie and Co. He had been active in the coal exporting and shipbroking business of Mackie Koth and Co since 1873, and saw the opportunity to expand into shipowning as a result of increasing demand for coal in the Baltic. His first ship was delivered by the yard of Workman, Clark and Co, Belfast, and named *Newhaven*. The prefix *New* was used on many of the Company's vessels, although second-hand tonnage often retained the name under which they had been previously trading. On 6 March 1898 the Company was incorporated as Newline Steamship Co Ltd with Richard Mackie and Co as managers.

Mackie became Provost of Leith in 1899, a position which he held until 1908. He was knighted during his time in office for his public endeavours and services to the Port.

Like many other companies trading to Northern Europe, Mackie's business was seriously disrupted by the First World War. Some of the vessels were sold as operations to the Baltic virtually ceased. The *Roumainie*, which had been acquired earlier in the year, was torpedoed off St Kilda on 2 September 1915, while the *Waterville* was stranded near Lerwick. The oldest vessel in the fleet, *Newhailes*, which had been acquired back in 1888, survived a torpedo attack on 14 December 1917 in the North Sea, and went on to be the last ship to be sold in June 1923. Sir Richard Mackie died at the end of the same month, and the colours of the New Line were hauled down for the last time.

Russell Huskie and Co: 1892 - 1917

In 1892, David Russell, David Huskie and Alfred Miller formed a partnership to manage and operate two ships called *Tregena* and *Carisbrook*. The ships were operated under single ship companies, namely The Steamship Tregenna Co and The Steamship Carisbrook Co, a situation which was to last for five years until both were sold for further trading. Various other agreements were entered into with London owners and in 1893 management of the Scottish Oceanic Steamship Co Ltd was taken on board, with Russell Huskie and Co as managers. The first ship, *Sunshine,* was purchased from a West Hartlepool company in 1894, to be followed in 1896 by the *Camperdown.* The second ship was immediately renamed *Craigallan* and this set the style for most of the ships that followed. Alfred Miller left the group in 1897 to take up a partnership in Glasgow and at this time the Craigline Steamship Co Ltd was formed with Russell Huskie and Co as managers. The arrangements were to ensure 'the continuation of the business of shipowners, general traders, shippers, charterers, freight contractors, merchants, underwriters, warehousemen, wherry owners, ship chandlers and dock owners in all their respective branches'.

The flag of the new Company was white, with the Leith coat of arms above the word 'Perseverance' in red. It funnel colours were an unusual combination of a red base with a broad green top.

David Huskie died in 1905, leaving David Russell as sole partner in what was now to become David Russell and Co. The Company was operating six ships at this time and David Russell took out a mortgage for £60,000, to be redeemed by 1915. The share issue was also extended to 1500. The following year another mortgage was taken out for £33,000 to be redeemed by 1918. This was to pay for the construction of the *Craigisla* and *Craigforth* but finances may have been stretched by more than they could bear, as *Craigmore* was sold in 1908, when only three years old. In 1909 a further change was to take place when a four-year-old vessel was purchased from Glasgow owners and registered under the Craigmhor Steamship Co Ltd, with David Russell as manager. From thereon fleet numbers gradually diminished and when the *Craigforth* was captured by the Turks at Constantinople in 1914, only the *Craigard* remained in operation. She was lost off Ushant in July 1915 and claims against the War Risk Association to cover the loss of the *Craigforth* were unsuccessful.

An Extraordinary General Meeting was called on 27 December 1916, and in spite of protests from some of the shareholders, it was decided to wind up the interests of the shipping company.

A.F. Henry & Macgregor: 1907 - 1941

Alexander Fraser Henry set up in business in 1893 as a Stevedore and Shipping Agent and was joined in 1904 by John MacGregor to form the Company of AF Henry and MacGregor. They became shipowners in 1907, when they purchased a small steam 'puffer' named *Mayflower* and commenced trading along the East Coast of Scotland and England.

Other small vessels were added to the fleet and in 1910 the name *Kinnaird Head* was introduced. From then onwards the term 'Head Boats' was regularly used in referring to the company of Henry and MacGregor. In 1913, a limited liability company was formed, and larger vessels were acquired as the old 'puffers' were sold. By the mid-1930s the fleet numbered thirteen, with the trade mainly in coal, stone and cement.

Losses in the 1914-1918 war had been minimal, but the Company was not so fortunate during the Second World War, when almost half the fleet was lost through enemy action.

In 1941 the company was taken over by the London and Edinburgh Shipping Co Ltd, but continued to operate independently. Replacements were purchased to cover wartime losses, and in 1952 a programme of new buildings was started, some of the older vessels being sold off as the larger and more modern tonnage appeared.

The founder, Alexander Henry, died in 1952 and control of the company was taken over by Christian Salveson Ltd in 1964. The Henry and MacGregor colours of two white bands on a black funnel finally disappeared in the 1970s, but Salvesons continued to use the 'Head Boat' names until they too terminated their shipping interests in 1989.

W.N. Lindsay. 1932 - 1979

William Lindsay, like many other ship owners had been in business as a stevedore before purchasing his first ship, the steamer *Castlerock* in 1932. The family were also involved in the grain trade and this was the principal cargo carried during the difficult years of the 1930s. It was only after the cessation of hostilities in 1945 that the fleet began to expand, always through the purchase of second-hand tonnage. The Company throughout its existence never built a new ship, and many of the names used by previous owners were retained, with such extremes as *Greenisland* and *Blacksod* as examples. In 1955 a small Dutch coaster was acquired and renamed *Roselyne.* The prefix *Rose* was then used regularly until 1979 when the last vessel was sold.

In 1958, WN Lindsay and Son Ltd had taken over management of Hay and Co (Lerwick) Ltd, a Shetland company who had returned to the shipowning business in 1954 after a break of 40 years with the main purpose of serving their own interests in the Shetland Islands. This association continued until 1985, when the activities of the Lindsay shipping interests which had been solely in management since 1979, finally to come to an end.

The Northern Lighthouse Board. 1800 to date

The Commissioners of Northern Lighthouses came into being through an Act of Parliament in 1786. The main function of the body was to authorise and supervise the construction of a number of lighthouses on prominent headlands around the Scottish Coast. Access was often difficult, and as the need for lights increased a tender was purchased in 1800 to move the necessary commodities by sea. The first ship was named Pharos and this name has been repeated on no fewer than nine occasions, the latest vessel, built by Fergusons of Port Glasgow, being launched on 11 December 1992.

Vessels were occasionally built to serve a particular site. Such was the case with *Skerryvore,* built by Robert Menzies and Sons of Leith in 1839. This was the first steamer owned by the Board, and she was sold in 1843, on completion of the lighthouse on the isolated rock of the same name.

The first lightship arrived in 1807, when a Prussian fishing vessel was purchased, converted at Leith, and renamed *Pharos,* for use near the Bell Rock, a dangerous reef ten miles east of the entrance to the River Tay.

The more general use of tenders to serve the remote sites started in 1846 and has continued ever since. These tenders, registered in Leith, were stationed at Oban, Stromness, and either Leith or Granton. Today, as more lights have become automated and unmanned, the need for tenders has been reduced. Two vessels now cover the entire coastline of Scotland and the Isle of Man. These vessels are also highly automated and accommodation on the flagship is of an extremely high standard, suited to the carriage of the Commissioners and, occasionally, Royalty.

Scottish Fishery Protection. 1882 to date

The origins of the Department of Agriculture and Fisheries for Scotland, which comes under the Secretary of State's Scottish Office, dates back to 1882, when the former Commissioners of the British White Herring Fishery were reconstituted as the Fishery Board for Scotland. The purpose of the Board was to enforce Byelaws and Regulations in an expanding industry, where the numbers of steam trawlers and drifters was increasing rapidly. In addition they were required to investigate new methods of fishing and to monitor fish stocks on both inshore and offshore fishing grounds.

In 1882 the Board acquired its first vessel, the naval cutter *Vigilant,* to carry out protection duties. It was assisted in this task by various Royal Navy gunboats. The Board received special permission for the *Vigilant* to fly a blue ensign with their crest imposed upon it and this flag can still be seen on present-day vessels.

Trawling conflicted with the more traditional methods of fishing off the Scottish coast, and it soon became evident that the old *Vigilant* was inadequate for its task. She was replaced in 1894 by a steam yacht, also renamed *Vigilant*, which was followed by other vessels built specifically for protection duties on the fishing grounds.

In 1886 a steam trawler named *Garland* was purchased to carry out research work, a task which the Department vessels still undertake today.

The derivation of the ships' names is very interesting. *Vigilant* has no particular relevance, but has been repeated on four occasions. Many of the patrol vessels have been named after small islands around the coast, while occasionally a bird or fish species has been used in naming the research vessels. Three names which have been used on more than one occasion are *Brenda, Norna,* and *Minna*, taken from Scott's novel 'The Pirate'.

The vessels, all registered in Leith, patrol from the Border three miles north of Berwick upon Tweed, all the way round the Scottish coast to the Solway Firth, and are still assisted on the offshore grounds by the Royal Navy. They are also assisted from time to time by Nimrod surveillance aircraft, ensuring full coverage of the areas, but still providing a high standard of service to fishermen.

Ship Builders and Repairers

The move from sail to steam during the nineteenth century brought about many changes in the shipbuilding industry. The rapid expansion in ship size and the move from timber to iron and eventually to steel, were predominant factors in these changes. Yards in the Water of Leith were limited in capacity, owing to the narrowness of the river and its meandering course. Once vessels began to be routinely built larger than about 200 gross registered tons, actual building operations moved to new sites with access to open water. The repairing of small craft, however, continued at the eighteenth century dry docks until well after the Second World War.

Mortons, as we have seen earlier, had a yard on the western side of the Water of Leith, just below the Junction Bridge, until the 1830s, when they moved to more convenient premises. Robert Menzies took over Morton's yard for a while, as an adjunct to his other yard in the Docks, but his occupation was short, and once he left the yard ceased to function.

Hawthorn & Co occupied a site in the Sherrif Brae and built quite large iron ships there until well into the nineteenth century. They solved the problem of lack of launch

The steamer *Horseguards*, built in 1872 for Leith shipowners, Wl Laing & Co., entering the Bay of Naples (*Painting by S. Roberts, dated 1887*).

space by setting their slips at an angle, launching down the length of the river. The Company also had a substantial engine works at the same site.

Menzies main site throughout the nineteenth century was at the dry dock at the corner of the East Old Dock, but when the Company built the 245 ft Royal Mail Paddle Steamer *Forth*, for the West India Steam Packet Co, one of the two yards on the north side of the West Old Dock was used. When she was launched in 1840, an opening had to be made at the north end of the yard, so that she had the whole length of the Harbour in which to run.

The building of the Victoria Dock, which was begun soon after, effectively put an end to this option, and all future development for the building of large vessels took place to the west of the new dock, where ships could be launched straight into the Forth. Menzies, however, was content to concentrate on smaller vessels and ship repairs. As larger and larger ships needed repair, Menzies used the big graving docks built by the Docks Commission in the course of the port's expansion. However, the firm still occupied the old Dry Dock and its adjacent yard until its dissolution in the 1960s.

Mortons were one of the first firms to use what became known as the Victoria Shipyards, but in 1877, after a number of objections, Ramage and Ferguson established a yard at the north end of the area, near the West Pier. Their first ship, named *Shamrock*, was launched on 19 February 1878 for Crawford and Co, and they went on to build 296 vessels of various descriptions during the next 56 years. The firm eventually owned three slips, the largest of which could accommodate ships up to 420 feet long, and contracts were fulfilled for companies such as Ben Line, British India Line and Ellerman Line. Perhaps one of the most remarkable vessels produced by Ramage and Fergusson was the full rigged ship, *Kobenhaven*, for East Asiatic Co of Denmark in 1921. Unfortunately

Kobenhaven. Full rigged ship built by Ramage & Ferguson for the East Asiatic Company of Denmark in 1921.

she disappeared without trace off South West Africa in December 1928. The last ship to be built by the Company, in 1933, was an auxiliary barquentine called the *Mercator*, for the Belgian Government.

In the early 1880s Ramage and Fergusson acquired two new neighbours; Cran and Co (later Cran and Somerville) and Hawthorn and Co. Hawthorns already had yards at Sherrif Brae and Granton and were much better known as engine builders and boiler makers, but they built a total of 189 ships at their yards. They specialised in fishing trawlers, but also constructed steam yachts and coastal craft. Hawthorns' engine shop was claimed to be the most modern of its type, and served coal mines, breweries, distilleries and factories, as well as the requirements of many other shipyards on the East Coast of Scotland. The last vessel they built at the Victoria Yard was completed in April 1924, for the Leith Dock Commission.

Two and a half years after Hawthorns ceased shipbuilding, Cran and Somerville launched their last vessel, a 1000hp tug named *Wellington*, for Alexandra Towing Co of Liverpool. Tugs had been their speciality, but among the 136 ships the Company had built during its lifetime were a number of small cargo vessels and other specialised craft. They were constrained by the fact that their slipways were only 260 feet in length.

Henry Robb arrived in Leith in 1913 as yard manager for Ramage and Ferguson. In 1918 he decided to go into business on his own account as a ship repairer and rapidly built up a reputation for his workmanship. When the sites occupied by Hawthorn became available in 1924 he negotiated a lease and commenced building ships. When Cran and Somerville, and his old employer Ramage and Ferguson ceased trading, Robb took over their premises, thus gaining total control of the Victoria Shipyards in 1933.

Robbs became well known as designers and fabricators of passenger and cargo vessels of quality. The yard was also to gain a reputation for the production of tugs of all types and power. The *Wolraad Woltemade*, built for the South African Marine Corporation, measuring 310 ft and with engines developing 26,000 hp, providing a bollard pull in excess of 200 tons, is still one of the largest and most powerful tugs ever built. During World War Two the Company obtained many Government contracts for naval salvage

S.A. Woolrad Woltemade. Built at the Leith yard of Robb Caledon, 1976, for the South African Marine Corporation, and still one of the most powerful tugs ever constructed.

tugs, designed to tow home large merchant and naval vessels which had been damaged by enemy action, often over very long distances.

The yard also produced other kinds of warships between 1939 and 1945. Altogether, Robbs fulfilled over 40 Government orders during the conflict. They also carried out countless repairs to naval and merchant ships. After the war the yard was partly reorganised, and many companies such as Currie Line, Ellerman Lines and Union Steamship Company of New Zealand gave the firm repeat orders.

In 1968 the company merged with a Dundee yard to form Robb Caledon Ltd, ships being built in both ports. Further changes took place in July 1977, after the yards were incorporated in British Shipbuilders. Finally, in 1982, the yard returned to its old style of Henry Robb Ltd, but unfortunately this was not to last. When the Sealink ferry *St Helen* entered the water on 15 September 1983 the order book was empty. By the next summer the yard had closed, and shipbuilding had come to an end at Leith, after some five and a half centuries.

Ship repair continues, with George Brown and Sons Ltd still to the fore. Forth Estuary Engineering Ltd operate from a base beside the Edinburgh Dry Dock. This and the Alexandra and Imperial Dry Docks are used regularly by the two ship repairers and occasionally by outside contractors, but there is no longer the bustle of activity seen around the many shipyards and dry docks of the past.

Appendix II : Maps

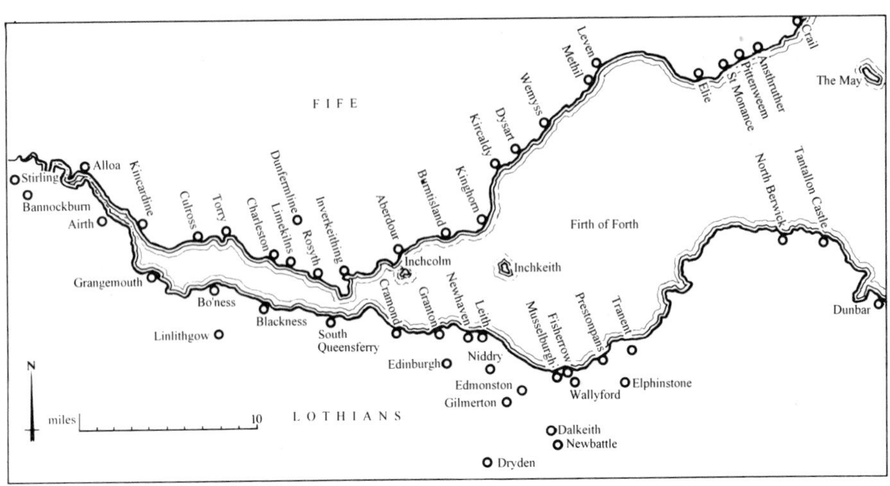

1. The Firth of Forth.

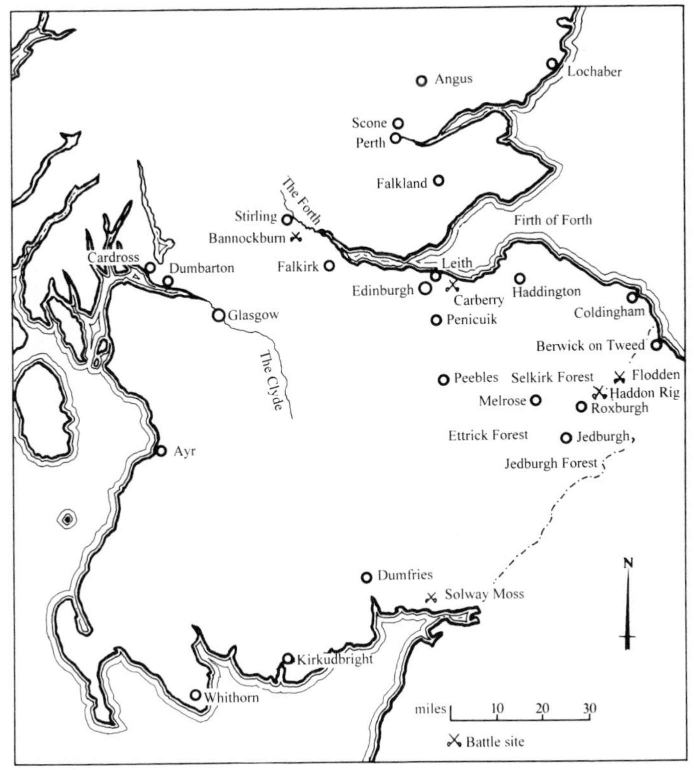

2. Southern Scotland.

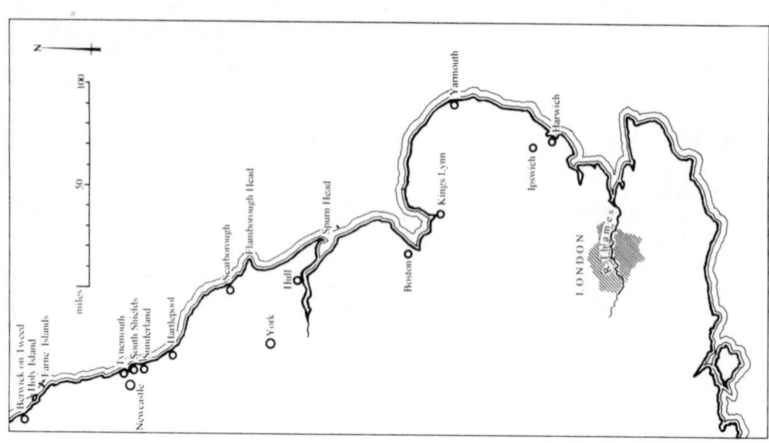

4. The east cost of England.

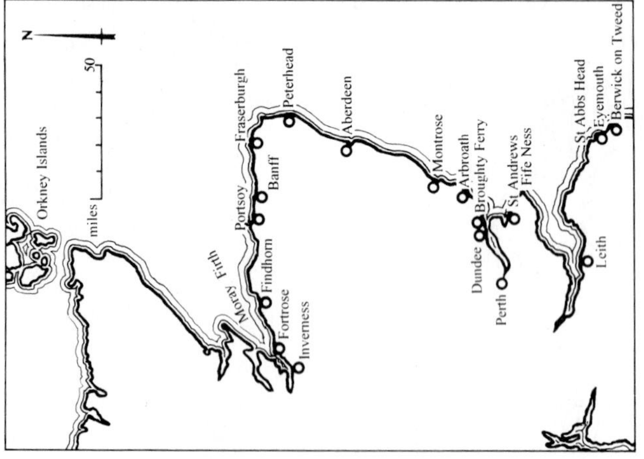

3. The east cost of Scotland.

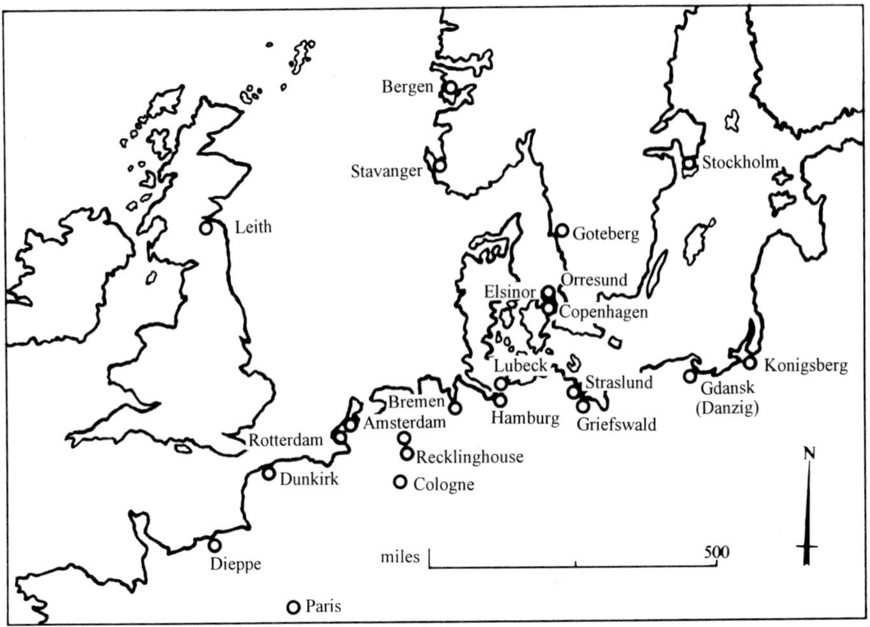

5. North-Western Europe and the Baltic.

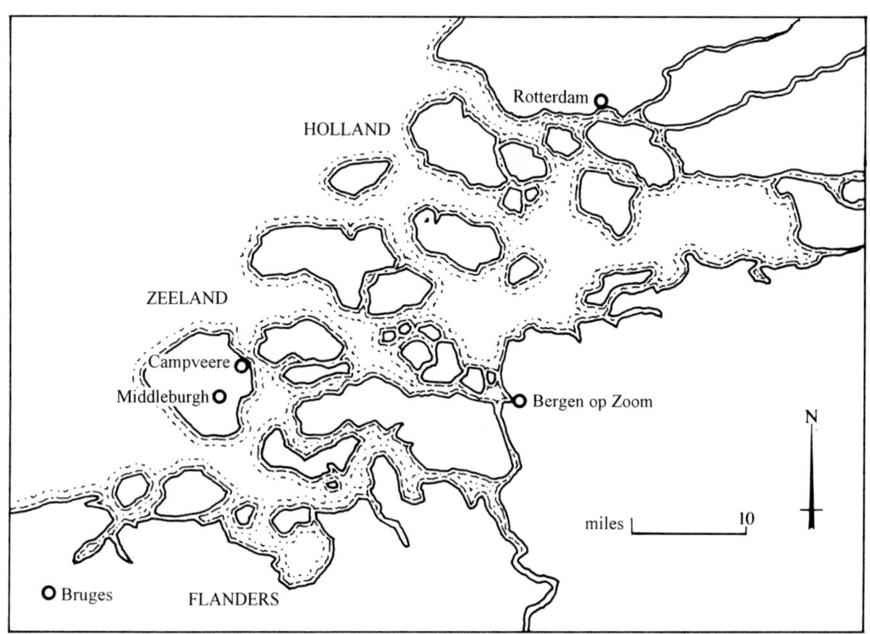

6. The Low Countries.

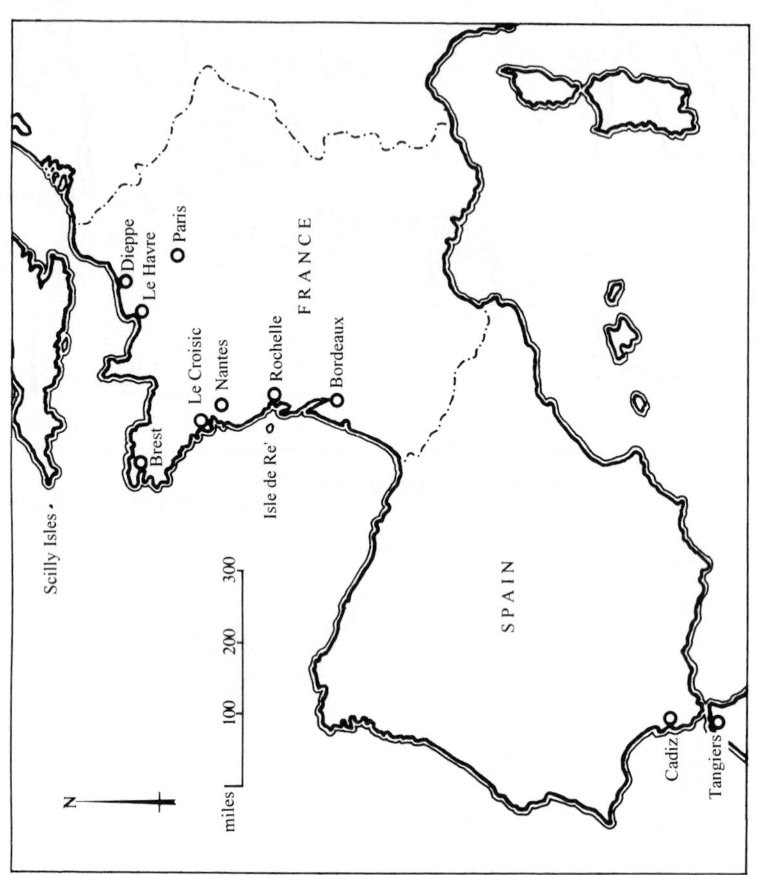

7. France and Spain.

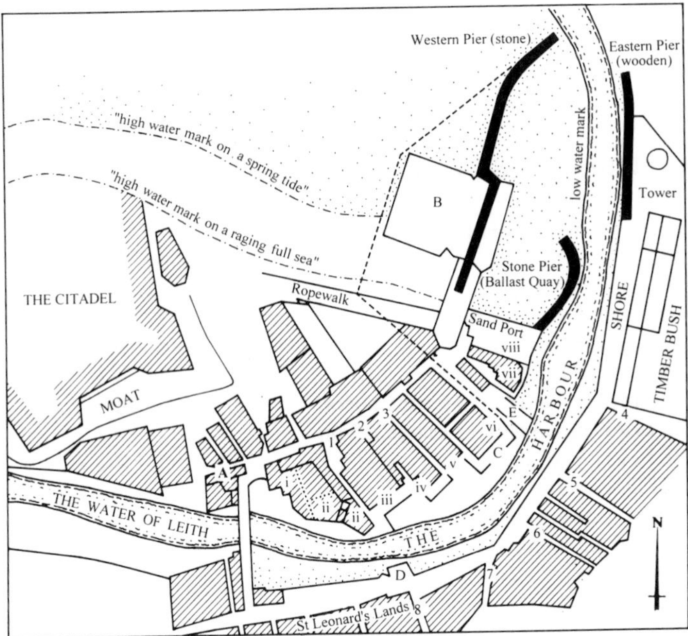

8. Plan based on the survey of 1709, showing the eighteenth-century shipyards of North Leith.

I.	Robert Davies	pre 1709–1723
	John Tod	1723–1753
	James Crawfurd	1753–1772
	Robert Drybrough	1771–1777
	(Built Dry Dock)	1774
	John Sime	1777–1787
	James Crawfurd/ Walter Goalen	1787–1793
	Robert Menzies	1793–1807
	Alexander Sime	1807–1817
	Alexander Sime	1823–1833
II.	[?James Jamison	1731–1747]
	John Willison	1753–1770
	John Sime	1770–1796
III.	James Beattie	pre 1706–1733]
	John Sime	1733–1796
IV.	[?James Beattie	pre 1706–1733]
	[?John Sime	1733–1754]
	James Crawfurd	1754–1787
V.	Patrick Robertson	pre 1728–1747
	James Warden (lease)	?–1746
	James Jamison	1746–1749
	John Sime	1749–1796
	(Built Dry Dock)	1771
	Strachan & Gavin	1798–1807
VI.	Glasshouse Quay & Slip	
	John Sime	1738–1796
VII.	Boatbuilders	
	Charles Hay	pre 1766–1777
	John Hay	1777–post 1787
	Charles Hay	?–post 1798
VIII.	Sandport	
	John & Thomas Willison	1750–1753
	James Crawfurd	1751–1754
	Robert Drybrough	1754–1777
	John Sime	1777–1796

A – St Ninian's Church
B – area of proposed Naval Yard
C – Glasshouse Quay
D – New Quay
E – Building slip

1 – Broad Wynd (North Leith)
2 – Short's Wynd
3 – Sea Wynd
4 – Bernard Street
5 – Broad Wynd (South Leith)
6 – Burgess Wynd
7 – Paunch Market
8 – Tolbooth Wynd

Bibliography

*National Library of Scotland – open shelves

The Accounts of the Lord High Treasurer of Scotland	1493–1574
The Exchequer Rolls	1264–1594
The Register of the Great Seal	1499–1612
The Register of the Privy Seal	1488–1584
The Register of the Privy Council	1567–1691
Acts of the Lords of Council in Civil Causes	1496–1500
Acts of the Lords of Council in Public Affairs	1501–1554
Acts of the Lords Auditors	1466–1494
Calendar of Documents Relating to Scotland	1108–1516
Rotuli Scotiae: Edward I – Henry VIII	
Regesta Regum Scottorum	

*Bannatyne Club

Pitcairn's Criminal Trials – 3 vol	1488–1624
Memorials of Transactions in Scotland	1569–1573
Nichol's Diary	1650–1667
History of Scotland – John Lesley	1436–1561
Diurnal of Occurants in Scotland	1513–1575
Sir James Melville's Memoirs	1549–1593
Spalding's History of the Troubles	1624–1641

Letters From Roundhead Officers in Scotland
Thomas Tucker's Report on the Revenue of Excise – 1656
Expedition en Ecosse
Darien Papers
Miscellany II – Extracts from the Rental Book of St Anthony
Registrum Cartarum Ecclesiam de St Egidii in Edinburgh
Charters of the Collegiate Churches of Midlothian
Cartulary of Newbottle Abbey
Registrum de Dunfermline
Charters of Holyrood
Liber de Melrose II

*Grampian Club

no 14 – St Anthony's Chapel

*Stair Society

Admiralty Court Book	1556–1562

***Abbotsford Club**

Melros Papers I & II
Letters and State Papers of James VI

***Scottish Burgh Record Society**

Extracts From the Court Book of Edinburgh
Edinburgh Treasurer's Accounts

***Scottish History Society**

Charters of the Abbey of Inchcolme
Rentale Dunkeldense
The Book of the Privileges of the Canongate
The Letters of James IV
The Letters of James V
The Scottish Correspondence of Mary of Lorraine/Guise
Darien Shipping Papers
The Balcarres Papers

***Scottish Record Society**

The Protocol Book of James Young 1485–1515
The Protocol Book of John Fowler 1503–1528

***Scottish Text Society**

The History and Chronicles of Scotland – Robert Lindsay of Pitscottie
Leslie's History of Scotland

***English State Papers**

The Letters of Henry VIII
Calendar of Scottish Papers 1523–1588
Calendar of State Papers (Foreign) 1547–1571
State Papers (Domestic) 1637–1666

Edinburgh Central Library (Edinburgh Room)

Maps and plans
Pamphlets and Plans re Harbour Improvements 18th cent
Edinburgh and Leith Directories (beginning in 1773)
Leith and London Smack/Steam Yacht Directories
Journal of a Voyage from Leith to London – 1830
Leith Observer – newspaper

Books

James I	Balfour Melville
James V, King of Scots	Bingham C
Scottish Society in the 15th Century	ed Brown J
Early Travellers in Scotland	Brown PH
Leith and Its Antiquities (2 vol)	Campbell Irons
The History of Leith	Campbell
Who's Who in Scottish History	Donaldson G and Morpeth R
The Edinburgh Histories (4 vol)	ed Donaldson G
The Making of the Kingdom	Duncan AAM
The Later Middle Ages	Nicholson R
James V to James VII	Donaldson G
1689 to the Present	Ferguson W
The Isle of May	Eggeling WJ
The Scots in Germany	Fischer TA
The Scots in East and West Prussia	Fischer TA
Early Travellers in Scotland	Hume Brown
Old and New Edinburgh	Grant J
The Scottish Medieval Town	Lynch, Spearman and Stell
James III	Mcdougal N
Scotland and War	Mcdougal N
King James IV of Scotland	Mackie RL
The History of Edinburgh	Maitland
The Life and Times of Leith	Marshall J
The History of Trinity House of Leith	Mason J
The Metters of Leith	Mowat S
Extracts from South Leith Session Records	Robertson
Sculptured Stones of Leith	Robertson
The Bailies of Leith	Robertson
The Story of Leith	Russell J
Scotland and Europe 1200–1850	ed Smout TC
Ben Line – History and Fleet List	Somner G
George Gibson and Company	Somner G
From 70 North to 70 South – The Christian Salveson Fleet	Somner G
Skipper From Leith	Stanford Reid W
The Statistical Account of Scotland 1791	
The Ordnance Gazeteer of Scotland 1882	

Transport

Classic Sailing Ships	Giggal K
Archaeology of the Boat	Greenhill B
Sailing Ships in Words and Pictures	Landstrom B
Square Rigged Sailing Ships	McGregor DR
The Age of Sailing Ships	Naish GPB
British Sail	Simper R
The Oxford Companion to Ships and the Sea	

Rail Centres – Edinburgh — Mullay AJ
Origins of the Scottish Railway System — Robertson CJA
Regional History of the Railways of Great Britain – vol 6 — Thomas J

Periodicals

The Book of the Old Edinburgh Club
The Proceedings of the Society of Antiquaries of Scotland
The Scottish Historical Review
The Accountants Magazine – Feb 1966

Typescripts etc

Excavation Report – Ronaldson's Wharf, Leith — Simpson, Stevenson & Holms
Address to Edinburgh Institution of Civil Engineers – JD Easton, 1944 — (typescript)
The Port of Leith, Its History and Development – (typescript)
The History of Leith – (private ms)
The Canongate and Leith: Archeological Implications of Development — (Scottish Burgh Survey 1981)

Manuscripts

Edinburgh City Archive

Leith Bailie Court Book, 1625–1628
Leith Court Enactment Book
Leith Cartulary
Leith Shore Dues Books
Records of the Old Shipping Company
Records of the Society of Metters of Leith
Porters Bond Book
Rental of the Carpenters Lands in North Leith
Canongate Court Books
Holyrood Charters
Minute Book of the Commissioners for Enlargement of the Harbour 1754–56
Edinburgh Council Minutes
Edinburgh Treasurer's Accounts
Dean of Guild Accounts
Burgh Register of Vassals
Mcleod and Moses Bundles (material ancilliary to the Council Minutes)
Maps and plans

Scottish Record Office

Trinity House Records
Customs Records
Testaments

Register of Deeds
Hamilton Correspondence
Edinburgh Register of Sasines
Journal of a Voyage from Leith to Newfoundland
Journal of a Voyage on the Smack Buccleuch

Scottish Record Office – West Register House

Leith Docks Commission Records
Admiralty Court Records
Commissary Court Records
Shipping Company Records
Railway Records
Maps and plans

Printouts Available From the Author

(0383-724960)

Fifteenth Century Leith Ships
(compiled from safeconducts, 1409–1490 – giving name of ship, master and merchants, tonnage, cargo and miscellaneous details)
Leith Ships Mentioned in Andrew Haliburton's Ledger, 1496–1499
(name of ship/master, cargoes, dates of arrival and departure)
The Formation of James IV's Navy, 1500–1513
(names of ships, where bought or built and from/by whom, sources of timber. Final composition of navy – ships, masters, no of crew)
Sixteenth Century Navigation – Leith and the East Coast
(from information given by Alexander Lindsay, 1540. Tides, landmarks, soundings, dangers)
Contrasting Lifestyles of Two Sixteenth Century Leith Mariners
(household inventories of Patrick Brown, 1574, and James Lightman jnr, 1575)
Ships Into Leith: 1624–1690
(no of ships arriving from different foreign ports in 14 individual years during the period. Ships from the Low Countries, France, England, Germany, the Baltic, Norway and America)
Leith Ships and Shipbuilders: 1726–1738
(list of all ships built at Leith during that time; names, tonnages, owners, builders, date of launch)
Timber Stored in the Timber Bush: 1762–1766
(over 50 different items of timber and the amounts stored)
Shore Dues Figures: 1758–1784
(amount collected and expenses for each year)
Crew, Equipment and Provisions of the Trial: 1750
(the first whaling ship of the Edinburgh Whaling Company – complete list)
Leith Smack Company Sailings: 1819
(office address, name of manager, names of ships and masters, sailing dates, London wharves; of the four smack companies)
Tonnages Handled at Leith: 1910–1993

Subject Index

Ships' Index

See also Appendix I.